# Ventures
# in
# Social
# Interpretation

## Henry Winthrop
UNIVERSITY OF SOUTH FLORIDA

APPLETON-CENTURY-CROFTS/New York
DIVISION OF MEREDITH CORPORATION

*301.24*

*W73v*

*65,321*

*March, 1969*

## ACKNOWLEDGMENTS

I am grateful to the following journals for permitting me to reproduce previously published papers of mine in this volume and for consenting to any adaptations, modifications or revisions which I might choose to make in them for the purposes of the present study. In some cases revisions include changes in the title, itself. Items accompanied by an asterisk had not as yet been published during the period the present volume was in press.

THE AMERICAN JOURNAL OF ECONOMICS AND SOCIOLOGY:

1. "Some Psychological And Economic Assumptions Underlying Automation," *American Journal of Economics and Sociology*, Part 1, Vol. 17, 1958, pp. 399–412. Copyright 1958 by the *American Journal of Economics and Sociology* and used with their permission.

2. "Some Psychological And Economic Assumptions Underlying Automation," *American Journal of Economics and Sociology*, Part 2, Vol. 18, 1958, pp. 69–82. Copyright 1958 by the *American Journal of Economics and Sociology* and used with their permission.

3. "Some Sociological and Ideological Assumptions Underlying Cybernation," *American Journal of Economics and Sociology*, Vol. 25, 1966, pp. 113–26. Copyright 1966 by the *American Journal of Economics and Sociology* and used with their permission.

iv

4. "Some Roadblocks on the Way to a Cybernated World," *American Journal of Economics and Sociology*, Vol. 25, 1966, pp. 405–14. Copyright 1966 by the *American Journal of Economics and Sociology* and used with their permission.

5. "The Meaning of Decentralization for Twentieth Century Man," *American Journal of Economics and Sociology*. Copyright will be held by the *American Journal of Economics and Sociology* and this paper is used here with advance permission.*

THE DALHOUSIE REVIEW:

6. "Space Colonization and the Quest for Community," *The Dalhousie Review*, Vol. 46, 1966, pp. 233–48. Copyright 1966 by *The Dalhousie Review* and used with their permission.

DARSHANA:

7. "Towards A Philosophy Of Culture," *Darshana*, Vol. 2, No. 4, 1962, pp. 24–40. Copyright 1962 by *Darshana* (Moradabad, India) and used with their permission.

DARSHANA INTERNATIONAL:

8. "Education, Science and Social Complexity," *Darshana International*, Vol. 3, No. 4, 1963, 53–75. Copyright, 1963 by *Darshana International* (Moradabad, India) and used with their permission.

9. "Some Proposals Towards Experiments in Peaceful and Non-Competitive Living," *Darshana International*, Vol. 4, No. 2, 1964, 74–97. Copyright 1964 by *Darshana International* (Moradabad, India) and used with their permission.

10. "The Intellectuals, the Educated and the Trained," *Darshana International*, Vol. 5, No. 3, 1965, 32–42. Copyright 1965 by *Darshana International* (Moradabad, India) and used with their permission.

11. "Science, Technology and Social Order," *Darshana International*, Vol. 6, No. 3, 1966, 13–24. Copyright 1966 by *Darshana International* (Moradabad, India) and used with their permission.

12. "The Inconsistencies Of Community Expectations," *Darshana International*, Vol. 6, No. 4, 1966, 32–41. Copyright 1966 by *Darshana International* (Moradabad, India) and used with their permission.

THE EDUCATIONAL FORUM:

13. "Education and the Problems of Community," *The Educational Forum*, Vol. 29, No. 2, 1965, 171–77. Copyright 1965 by *The Educational Forum*. This material was used by permission of Kappa Delta Pi, an Honor Society in Education, owners of the copyright.

JOURNAL OF EXISTENTIAL PSYCHIATRY:

14. "Social Zombieism—The Anti-Existential In Modern Life." Reprinted by permission from *Journal of Existential Psychiatry*, 3:343–60, Spring 1963. © 1963 by Libra Publishers, Inc.

EDUCATIONAL THEORY:

15. "Methodological And Hermeneutic Functions In Interdisciplinary Education," *Educational Theory*, Vol. 14, 1964, 118–27. Copyright 1964 by *Educational Theory* and used with their permission.

JOURNAL OF EXISTENTIALISM:

16. "Culture, Mass Society and the American Metropolis. High Culture and Middlebrow Culture: An Existentialist View," *Journal of Existentialism*. Copyright will be held by the *Journal of Existentialism* and this paper is used here with advance permission.*

17. "Culture, Mass Society and the American Metropolis. Mass Culture, Lowbrow Culture and Folk Culture: An Existentialist View," *Journal of Existentialism*. Copyright will be held by the *Journal of Existentialism* and this paper is used here with advance permission.*

JOURNAL OF HUMAN RELATIONS:

18. "The Disappearing Art Of Being Serious," *Journal of Human Relations*, Vol. 10, 1961, 84–95. Copyright 1961 by *Journal of Human Relations* and used with their permission.

19. "The Meaning Of Culture: Culture As Human Relations," *Journal of Human Relations*, Vol. 11, 1962, 105–21. Copyright 1962 by *Journal of Human Relations* and used with their permission.

20. "The Dilemma of Modern Man," *Journal of Human Relations*, Vol. 11, 1963, 276–88. Copyright 1963 by *Journal of Human Relations* and used with their permission.

21. "The Space Sciences And Social Change," *Journal of Human Relations*, Vol. 12, 1964, 127–41. Copyright 1964 by *Journal of Human Relations* and used with their permission.

22. "Leisure And Mass Culture In A Cybernating Society," *Journal of Human Relations*, Vol. 13, 1965, 93–109. Copyright 1965 by *Journal of Human Relations* and used with their permission.

23. "In Quest Of Community," *Journal of Human Relations*, Vol. 14, 1966, 457–72. Copyright 1966 by *Journal of Human Relations* and used with their permission.

24. "Some Social Pathologies Of Political Overcentralization," *Journal of Human Relations*, Vol. 14, 1966, 605–19. Copyright 1966 by *Journal of Human Relations* and used with their permission.

LAND ECONOMICS:

25. "Modern Proposals for the Physical Decentralization of Community," *Land Economics*, Vol. 43, 1967, 10–24. Copyright 1967 by *Land Economics* and used with their permission.

IL POLITICO:

26. "Political Overcentralization In A Complex Society: Three Types Of Resulting Pathology," *Il Politico*, Vol. 31, 1966, 239–60. Copyright 1966 by *Il Politico* (Italy) and used with their permission.

SCIENCE EDUCATION:

27. "Professional Projections Of Future Science And Technology And Their Bearing On Social Change," *Science Education*, Vol. 50, 1966, 471–81. Copyright 1966 by *Science Education* and used with their permission.

# Acknowledgments

SOCIOLOGICAL INQUIRY:

28. "Political Innovation And Social Complexity," *Sociological Inquiry*, Vol. 33, 1963, 78–96. Copyright 1963 by *Sociological Inquiry* and used with their permission.

29. "The Meaning Of Structure And Coordination In Social Planning," *Sociological Inquiry*, Vol. 33, 1963, 144–56. Copyright 1963 by *Sociological Inquiry* and used with their permission.

SYSTEMATICS:

30. "The Archetypes Of Human Concern," *Systematics* (Great Britain), Vol. 3, 1966, 334–60. Copyright 1966 by *Systematics* and used with their permission.

TEACHERS COLLEGE RECORD:

31. "What Can We Expect From The Unprogramed Teacher?," *Teachers College Record*, Vol. 67, 1966, 315–29. Copyright 1966 by *Teachers College Record* and used with their permission.

WESTERN HUMANITIES REVIEW:

32. The Psychological Costs Of Urban Life," *Western Humanities Review*, Vol. 21, 1967, 155–62. Copyright 1967 by *Western Humanities Review* and used with their permission.

I am grateful to the following publishers for permitting me to use quotations or reproduce material from works published by them as indicated below:

AD HOC COMMITTEE FOR THE TRIPLE REVOLUTION

33. *Triple Revolution. Cybernation. Weaponry. Human Rights.* Prepared in 1964 by the Ad Hoc Committee for the Triple Revolution and used with their permission.

CAMBRIDGE UNIVERSITY PRESS

34. *The Two Cultures And The Scientific Revolution* by Sir Charles P. Snow. Copyright 1959 by the Cambridge University Press and used with their permission.

CENTER FOR THE STUDY OF DEMOCRATIC INSTITUTIONS

35. *Cybernation: The Silent Conquest* by Donald N. Michael. Copyright 1962 by the Center for the Study of Democratic Institutions and used with their permission.

HARPER & ROW PUBLISHERS

36. *Profiles of the Future* by Arthur C. Clarke. Copyright 1958 by Harper & Row and used with their permission and with the joint permission of Victor Gollancz, Ltd., London, England.

## HARCOURT, BRACE & WORLD

37. *The Autobiography Of Lincoln Steffens* by Lincoln Steffens. Copyright 1931 by Harcourt, Brace & World and used with their permission.

## HOLT, RINEHART AND WINSTON, INC.

38. *The Sane Society* by Erich Fromm. Copyright 1955 by Holt, Rinehart and Winston and reprinted with the joint permission of Routledge & Kegan Paul Ltd.

## MANAGEMENT SCIENCE

39. "General Systems Theory—The Skeleton of Science," *Management Science*, Vol. 2, 1956, pp. 197–208, by Kenneth Boulding. Copyright 1956 by *Management Science* and used with their permission and with the joint permission of the author and The Society for General Systems Research under whose auspices the paper was republished in its Yearbook.

## THE PUBLIC INTEREST

40. "The Study of the Future," *The Public Interest*, Vol. 1, 1965, pp. 119–30, by Daniel Bell. Copyright Basic Books, 1965 and used with their permission and that of the author.

## RANDOM HOUSE

41. *Growing Up Absurd* by Paul Goodman. Copyright 1960 by Random House and used with their permission.

42. *People Or Personnel* by Paul Goodman. Copyright 1965 by Random House and used with their permission.

43. *Culture Against Man* by Jules Henry. Copyright 1965 by Vintage Books, Inc. (Random House) and used with their permission.

## SIMON & SCHUSTER, INC.

44. *After The Seventh Day* by Ritchie Calder. Copyright © 1961 by Ritchie Calder by permission of Simon & Schuster, Inc.

## SOCIAL SCIENCE INSTITUTE

45. *USA Today* by Helen & Scott Nearing. Copyright 1955 by Social Science Institute, Harborside, Maine and used with their permission.

## THE SOCIETY FOR GENERAL SYSTEMS RESEARCH

46. "General System Theory," in *General Systems, Yearbook of the Society for the Advancement of General Systems Theory*, Vol. 1, 1956, pp. 1–10, by Ludwig von Bertalanffy. Copyright by the Society for General Systems Research, 1956, and used with their permission and that of the author.

# Acknowledgments

UNIVERSITY OF CALIFORNIA PRESS

47. *Organization, Automation And Society* by Robert A. Brady. Copyright 1961 by the University of California Press and used with their permission.

JOHN WILEY & SONS, INC.

48. *Science And Economic Development* by Richard L. Meier. Copyright 1956 by John Wiley & Sons and used with their permission.

To my wife

GUSSIE

whose unflagging help, devotion, and
encouragement can never be adequately
acknowledged

# Preface

This volume explores some of the impacts which science and technology have, or may have, on our lives. In the course of such an exploration, however, other themes take on considerable importance. Since science and technology also tend to introduce routine into our lives and because they tend to push us toward ends which the community never bargained for originally and which exist in striking contrast to those notions of the good life which have been part our Western heritage, other matters must be given our attention. We shall therefore find ourselves re-examining the meaning of culture, the purposes and uses of leisure, and the nature of a genuine education that maketh the whole man. These latter concerns serve as a guidepost against which to assess the value and importance of the ends toward which science and technology are driving us and enable us to note the directions science and technology are forcing us to take—directions which may lead away from the traditional and still meaningful values of the humanistic ideals of the West.

The volume has been divided into five parts. Part I, *Technology and Some of Its Social Consequences,* is a critical examination of *some* of the social consequences of such technological developments as automation, cybernation, and space technology. Part II, *Culture, Leisure, and Education,* restates the great Greek educational ideals of paideia for an age of science and technology. Part III, *The Burden of Social Complexity,* deals with the effects on our lives of the increasing social complexity created by modern society. Part IV, *The Pathologies of Overurbanization,* considers *some* of the social costs of contemporary urbanization and centralization. Part V, *Technology, Decentralization, and the Restoration of Community,* explores the implications of the decentralist credo in connection with the quest for community. The *Epilogue* suggests some of the tasks that must be faced by a social philosophy fit for an age of science and technology.

# Acknowledgments

The interest in the interdisciplinary aspects of the social sciences which have been reflected in this volume has been shown in different ways by others. I wish to take note here of their recognition of the value and importance of interdisciplinary social science.

I wish to express my thanks to Russell M. Cooper, Dean of the College Of Liberal Arts, University of South Florida, for his steady encouragement of interdisciplinary social science and for his willingness to engage in curricular experiments along these lines. His recognition of the importance of interdisciplinary teaching and research has been a major inspiration to me. Appreciation is also due Sidney J. French and Edwin P. Martin, Deans of the College Of Basic Studies, University of South Florida, for their long-continued support of general education, an area so clearly related to growing developments in interdisciplinary social science. I have learned much educationally from the ideas of both these men. In particular, thanks are due Dean Edwin P. Martin for the educational support he has given the themes of Chapter 6 through a version of that chapter used in sections of the Senior Seminar required of all students at the University of South Florida. I likewise wish to acknowledge the educational debt I owe to President John S. Allen of the University of South Florida for supporting the establishment of a Department of Interdisciplinary Social Sciences at that university. Although I cannot mention them all by name, I also wish to express my gratitude to the hundreds of students over the last few years, who made manifest their enthusiasm for the courses in interdisciplinary social science at the University of South Florida and who spent long hours critically discussing their reactions to the materials presented in the classroom.

I owe an immeasurable debt to the many colleagues on the various professional journals with which I am actively and editorially affiliated. Thanks are due them for their support and encouragement of those concerns which have been reflected in the published papers I have drawn upon for some of the chapters in this volume. In particular, I wish to thank the following persons: Ralph T. Templin, *Journal Of Human Relations;* J. P. Atreya, *Darshana International;* and Robert Meister, *Journal Of Existentialism.* Gratitude is hereby expressed to certain editors for their support and understanding of the interdisciplinary emphasis which I have sought in my published work. In particular, the expression of such gratitude is due Will Lissner, editor of *The American Journal Of Economics and Sociology* and Maxine Greene, editor of the *Teachers College Record.*

I would be derelict in my duty if I failed to record my thanks to those colleagues elsewhere whose appreciation and encouragement of my published work has reinforced my conviction of the importance of inter-disciplinary effort in the social sciences. From among them I can only single out the following: Abraham H. Maslow, Brandeis University; Clark Moustakas of the Merrill Palmer Institute Of Human Development And Family Life in Detroit; Jordan Scher, editor of *Existential Psychiatry* and an active member of the American Ontoanalytic Association; Joseph S. Roucek of Queensborough Community College and an active editor on mumerous professional journals; Professor Oliver L. Reiser of the Department of Philosophy, University of Pittsburgh, whose lifelong support of interdisciplinary endeavor is well-known; Ralph Ross, of Scripps College and formerly at the University of Minnesota, for his unflagging recognition of the intellectual value of the interdisciplinary posture in education; and Stuart C. Dodd, Director of the Washington Public Opinion Laboratory of the University of Washington. Limitations of space make it impossible for me to acknowledge those many colleagues, journal editors, government economists, and friends with whom I entered into an important dialogue respecting those matters which have been the concern of my volume and from whom I borrowed so much.

Most important of all is the help and work of my wife in connection with the preparation of this volume. Only its author will ever know the enormous and back-breaking labors which she sustained in typing draft after draft, in checking bibliographical citations, in proofing, in locating relevant references, in suggesting improvements in format, and in many other chores too numerous to mention here. Without her near-slavery the work involved could never have been completed. An acknowledgements section provides a demanding author with a major opportunity to expiate his guilt for the inordinately heavy duties imposed upon a long-suffering wife. I only hope this confession of sin meets with the approval of my Maker.

H. W.

# Contents

xv

*Part III. The Burden of Social Complexity*

*Part IV. The Pathologies of Overurbanization*

*Part V. Technology, Decentralization, and the Restoration of Community*

# INTRODUCTION *

Much of this volume represents an effort to extrapolate present trends into a probable, social future. Such extrapolations should properly be christened "ventures in social interpretation." One of the strongest reasons for treating extrapolations as ventures in social interpretation has been given by Boulding.[1] The forecaster must recognize that the social system for which he hopes to describe a possible future condition in terms of current trends, is not ahistorical. As a result every system is subject to "system breaks," that is, a change in the system over time so that features of it which have been assumed all along to be constant, prove in the end to be highly variable. Such "system breaks" repudiate a past-based description of the ongoing system, which those who are trying to study it believe will continue to hold for it. A system which has had a "break" is one which has *really* changed. If the would-be prognosticator, however, does not know this, his forecasts will most likely be wide of the mark. For this reason caution dictates that future-glimpsing at a time when social change is producing "system breaks" fairly frequently, be handled with care. Those who are studying the social organism are often unaware of these systems breaks. That is why future-glimpsing should be treated as ventures in social interpretation concerning the *possible* direction of trends rather than as sentential predictions in the social sciences.

*The Reader as Participant–Observer.* The general reader who wishes to obtain information about the more significant concerns of the social sciences is likely to demand something different from what he finds in the standard text in the field. The standard textbook writer imposes on

---

* The Introduction, with adaptations and modifications, has been taken from the following source: Henry Winthrop, "Methodological and Hermeneutic Functions in Interdisciplinary Education." *Educational Theory*. Vol. XIV, No. 2, April 1964, 118–124.

[1] Kenneth E. Boulding. "Looking Ahead to the Year 2000." *Fellowship*. Special Consultation Issue, May, 1965, 26–9.

himself constriction in scope and treatment, in order to satisfy the requirements of professional conservatism—attention to methodological nicety, staying within his field, making use of abundant documentations, etc. One unfortunate result is that the standard text often fails to capture the interest and attention which its subject matter deserves. What is even worse, however, is that some of the matters taken up seem frequently to have little relevance to the life with which the reader is, himself, familiar. He finds it difficult to believe that the abstractions and highly structured exposition of the text are significantly related to the pulsating, throbbing, disorganized, rampant, and apparently aimless activities of the community around him as that community is reflected in his own life and in the mass media to which he is daily exposed—newspapers, popular magazines, movies, radio, and television.

These media of communication sin in one way while the typical social science textbook sins in another. Our mass media provide drama often with little factual basis, an unconcern for accuracy, and no intellectual organization to speak of, when dealing with complex events. The social science text does provide factual accuracy and conceptual organization, but often at the price of draining away the life-blood of the subject matter and its dramatic import. What is needed is an approach which is a halfway house between the style of the textbook and the genre of responsible journalism, in which subject matter is given a deserved, broad-scale treatment which tries to be accurate both conceptually and factually but which executes this treatment so as to sustain the reader's interest. In some such fashion one can keep his learning from being alienated from his life.

*The Need for Interdisciplinary Interpretation.* This objective is the most difficult of all, namely, that of achieving "interdisciplinary" scholarship. There are two main uses of the term, "interdisciplinary." The more esoteric use has reference to some newly emerging fields of scientific research, theory construction, and practising scholarship in which important, new problems and methods of analysis are of major concern. These include such fields as administrative and organizational theory, bionics, cybernetics, decision theory, game theory, general systems theory, information theory, input-output analysis, linear programming, operations research, queueing theory, and simulation theory. The subject matter of the present volume *is not,* in any sense, directly concerned with the results of professional research in these areas.

The second and major meaning of the term, "interdisciplinary," also refers to relatively new types of study, which are not yet standard in our traditional academic curricula, but these types of study have somewhat different characteristics from technical, interdisciplinary fields. These areas of study are generally distinguished by at least one of the following conditions: (1) Some of the studies involved are concerned with problems, processes, and phenomena—referred to hereafter as "the three foci"—which require *information from* two or more traditional fields. (2) Others are concerned with types of problems, processes, and phenomena which are of relatively *recent interest,* though of major social and intellectual importance. (3) Many of the new "interdisciplinary" types of study profoundly involve elements of interpretation and judgment, modes of intellectual organization and patterning, and techniques of evaluation and meaningful correlation [2] which are deliberately excluded from the stricter demands of the older logico–empirical tradition. Probably very few interdisciplinary studies in our second category can be said to exhibit all three of these features, although most probably involve two of them. The three foci, however, can be adequately treated only when certain requirements are satisfied.

In my judgment there are several requirements which have to be met before a study may be regarded as "interdisciplinary" in the second meaning of this term. Therefore, I turn to a full discussion of these requirements at this point.

*The Need for the Synoptic Vision.* The *sources* of information which are germane to the three foci are found scattered throughout various traditional specialties. Sometimes the relevant information is in the possession of individual scholars who are sufficiently broad-gauge to recognize the need and to learn where to find the necessary information regarding problems which require cross-fertilization. Sometimes the needed data can be brought together by a figure accustomed to crossing class lines, educationally speaking, and who is thus in a good position to "pick the brains" of varied experts. This he can do because he can see the problem in larger perspective and is flexible enough to be able to collate the contributions of individual experts. His concern is with the more synoptic vision and he thereby achieves a sense of *that which is factually relevant,* a view which is not likely to be of major interest to any one of the experts or specialists whose erudition is part of the substructure of the task undertaken by the collator. In addition the broad-gauge scholar tries to *fit the pieces* into place, so that they achieve that pattern of mutual relatedness and relevancy to the over-all problem, which will result in a possible solution of it or, at least, in a reasonable interpretation of it which will sometimes enable others to provide a *proposed solution* which, perhaps, may be confirmed or disconfirmed by standard, experimental techniques.

*The Essential Distinction Between the Terms "Generalist" and "Specialist."* The type of collator mentioned above is frequently referred to as a "generalist" but the sense of this word must be made clear. An interdisciplinary scholar does not claim expertness in all of the traditional areas which contribute substantively or methodologically to the three

---

[2] Henry Winthrop. "Meaningful Correlation as a Form of Intellectual Inquiry." *University of Wichita Bulletin.* University Studies, Vol. 32, No. 38, October, 1957. 3–28.

foci. In fact, he frequently does not claim expertness *in any of them* if, by expertness, we mean any or all of the following: (a) that he possesses the range of information in depth which characterizes the specialist; (b) that he possesses the expert's sophistication with respect to method in the expert's own field; (c) that he keeps up with the literature in each of the fields involved in his studies, or (d) that he has himself worked on problems which are strictly berthed in one or more of the traditional specialties with which he is forced to conduct diplomatic relations.

Does this then mean that the *working* generalist (as distinguished from those who merely talk about the need for cultural breadth and holistic understanding) is a dilettante? [3] The question is, of course, largely a rhetorical one. First, the working generalist is likely to be as familiar with the *fundamental concepts* in two or more of the traditional subject matter fields as the specialist, himself, but without claiming equal familiarity with the complex and subtle superstructure of these fields. Second, having concentrated upon one or more of the three foci, he makes it his business to acquire those concepts and that information which are relevant to his concern. Thus, given a relatively new problem to work upon, which demands more information and conceptual familiarity than he currently has, he will acquire such relevant information and the needed analytical skills, even if this involves an intense program. Depending upon the nature of the task he has undertaken, the generalist will have to enter intellectual territory which is relatively uncharted *for him* and he may have to stay there for a long time before he knows his way around. The length of the sojourn, however, is not the point. What is to the point is that he must acquire whatever information and skills he needs in order to deal adequately with his problem.

Finally, he has the function of *patterning and relating* such information and skills so that they are merged into one or more intellectual devices which may prove to be successful in dealing with the task he has undertaken. The necessity of this last function, of establishing the adequacy, relevancy, and adaptability of the materials he has acquired to one or more of the three foci, flows from the fact that one of the special skills cultivated by the generalist more than by the specialist, is that of

---

[3] In his *Old Wine, New Bottles: A Humanist Teacher at Work*, New York: Simon & Schuster, 1962, 137 pp., Moses Hadas points out the strange transmogrification which the word "dilettante" has undergone. The Society of Dilettanti, established in England in 1733, included nonprofessional, that is, nonacademic scholars who were greatly respected for their distinguished labors. Grote, who wrote the best history of Greece was a banker. The best translators of the classics—Andrew Lang, the Earl of Derby, B. B. Rogers, and many others—were not professional scholars. The British still have a respected tradition of amateur scholarship. Similar examples could be furnished for the continent. The point, however, is that today the "generalist" as *amateur* is suspect, precisely because he is not a *professional specialist*. Lost sight of is the essential question "How well has the task been handled?" and not "What kind of training did he get and where did he get it?"

"learning how to learn," that is to say, the generalist tries to sharpen his professional ability at what the psychologist calls *deutero-learning*.[4] This comes automatically from the cross-disciplinary problems which are the generalist's main concern.

There are some nimble minds, accustomed to avoiding genuine intellectual exertion by hiding behind words, who seize upon such descriptions of the generalist, as we have given, and shout gleefully that the generalist is only "another form of specialist." By such semantic legerdemain these critics ignore the activity and objectives needed for a more integrative type of task and thereby make an intellectual temple out of their specialties which, in fact, they may use as caves for social and intellectual retreat.

This brand of playing with words contributes little, if anything. It is of course quite true that much interdisciplinary work is *specialized work* in the sense that it involves information, activities and postures which are unlike those involved in some different kind of work. This is so by definition. However, the nature of the problems, processes and phenomena studied by generalists are frequently such that they cannot be berthed for examination within our traditional specialties, they do not crop up within these specialties, and finally the typical specialist does not try to acquire the intellectual wherewithal to deal with them, even where he notes their existence. That which therefore differentiates the generalist from the specialist, academically speaking, is the substantive latitude and complexity of the problems chosen by or forced upon the former and the greater number of variables which he may have to hinge together in order to achieve an effective discussion or solution. This is not to deny that frequently even greater complexity than that with which the generalist is wont to meet, may be found within problems of a professional or specialized nature. What should be emphasized here is that the closed or open system of the generalist's problem is much more likely to involve a larger number of variables than that of the specialist's and much more likely to involve more diverse segments of specialized information. It is for reasons such as these that we are forced to say that playing with the word "specialization" in such a way as to stress *selectivity of interest* while neglecting the crucial differences in the contexts of the problems with which generalists and specialists preoccupy themselves, contributes nothing to the understanding of the polar antinomy, generalist–specialist, and in addition only succeeds in sowing semantic confusion.

---

[4] The subject of "deutero-learning" is discussed in a nontechnical fashion in chapter 8 of the following volume: Jurgen Ruesch and Gregory Bateson, *Communication: The Social Matrix of Psychiatry*, New York: Norton, 1951, 314 pp. The remarks in the text are not to be misunderstood. The specialist also acquires deutero-learning just as readily as the generalist. However, he tends to employ it in narrower, professional studies pursued in depth rather than in studies of integrative scope. As a result the generalist will tend to be *somewhat more efficient* in studies of the more synoptic variety.

*The Importance of the Hermeneutical Function.* Interdisciplinary collators are likely to be especially gifted in the exercise of what has been called the *hermeneutical function.* In the language of philosophy this phrase refers to the function of *interpretation.* For instance, a good many of the social problems of concern to interdisciplinary scholars do not lend themselves readily to the neat experimental designs of the formal, social scientist. Instead, they must be approached by methods of *intellectual correlation* to which I have already referred. Among such methods, we find, for example, the approaches emphasized by Sorokin,[5] and which he subsumes under the rubric of "meaningful–causal analysis," the methods of philosophical anthropology such as are exercised by Northrop,[6] the methods of phenomenological analysis described by Strasser[7] and the broad, synthetic approaches discussed by Reiser[8] and exemplified by Chardin.[9] There are, of course, dozens of other methods of social or philosophical interpretation which have been found intellectually fruitful, and this is not the place to describe them in detail or to examine them critically. This is the place, however, to emphasize that there are few activities exercised by a good generalist, which are more important or more creative than the hermeneutical function.

In the interpretation of human history, the interpretation of the human condition, and in the interpretation of the meaning of science for problems of human value and the quest for the good life, *hermeneusis is likely to be central.* In holistic philosophical interpretation, in the evaluation of cultural trends and in the assessment of the delicate balance among cultural forces—an assessment which requires what C. Wright Mills[10] has called "the sociological imagination"—*hermeneusis is indispensable.* In the effort to understand human conflict, seen from its subjective side and in terms of the more reasonable theses of philosophic existentialism, in the effort to exhibit the tragic sense of life through analysis in depth and in the attempt to deal with the relation of the general and the abstract to the individual and the concrete in human life—so characteristically a concern of existentialism—hermeneusis is the *sine qua non* for the tasks involved. Wherever a work is dedicated to showing how our Western, humanistic ideals can be applied to our modern contexts of community living,

[5] Pitirim A. Sorokin. *Fads and Foibles in Modern Sociology and Related Sciences.* Chicago: Henry Regnery, 1956. 357 pp. See Chapter 11, p. 272 et seq.

[6] F. S. C. Northrop. *Philosophical Anthropology & Practical Politics: A Prelude to War or to Just Law.* New York: Macmillan, 1960. 384 pp.

[7] Stephan Strasser. *Phenomenology and the Human Sciences: A Contribution to a New Scientific Ideal.* Pittsburgh: Duquesne University Press, 1963. 339 pp.

[8] Oliver L. Reiser. *The Integration of Human Knowledge.* Boston: Porter Sargent, 1958. 478 pp.

[9] Pierre Teilhard de Chardin. *The Phenomenon of Man.* With an introduction by Sir Julian Huxley. New York: Harper, 1961. Harper Torchbooks. 318 pp.

[10] C. Wright Mills. *The Sociological Imagination.* New York: Oxford University Press, 1959. 234 pp.

hermeneusis has to be the central creative activity of the writer. Wherever the presuppositions, the methods or the evaluation of the relevancy of the findings of modern science for social life, are to be examined phenomenologically, the hermeneutic function has to come into play, as Polanyi [11] has shown. In all of these areas, then, the interdisciplinary scholar must sharpen the hermeneutic function, so that the perspectives he presents are meaningful and relevant to the reader and can be used as a basis for action—a basis which is not as strictly scientific as we might ideally desire, but which represents a reasonable estimate and assessment of a highly complex situation.

*The Interdisciplinary Function as the Quest for Wisdom.* There is a type of interdisciplinary endeavor which is motivated by a love of wisdom —a phrase unfortunately rendered "hackneyed" by the degree to which it is used in an alienated fashion—but which we might translate as an attitude that blends two Greek characteristics of the human spirit— characteristics which Bell [12] has emphasized, namely, "sophrosyne" (sweet reasonableness) and "spondaiotis" (appropriate seriousness). Interdisciplinary endeavors motivated by these concerns concentrate on a synoptic view of man's concerns and creativity. These motivations are likely to be expressed in dealing with such concerns as the following: the problems in the quest for value and the conflicts among existing human notions of personal and social welfare; the assessment of the human condition and the prediction of the direction which human history is taking; the possibilities for changing human goals, human nature, and the central activities of men (a concern which, when not infused with the spirit of humanism, technical barbarism refers to as "social engineering"); the effort to determine what should be the proper relations among men, where we know the constraining circumstances under which they live and where we are desperately trying to prescribe what constitutes a good society; and finally the appropriate methods for determining for oneself such matters as the answer to the question "What is the good life?" the means for achieving what Maslow [13] calls self-actualization, and the means for avoiding all the current forms of alienation—alienation from oneself, one's fellow man, the opposite sex, society, work, Nature, and God—as well as emergent future forms of alienation.

Reiser speaks of this type of interdisciplinary venture as the quest for wisdom, social guidance, and social planning, that is, the level of World Philosophy. Such interdisciplinary endeavor is usually forced to range pretty much over the whole of human knowledge and concern. The

[11] Michael Polanyi. *Personal Knowledge: Towards a Post-Critical Philosophy.* Chicago: The University of Chicago Press, 1958. 428 pp.
[12] Clive Bell. *Civilization: An Essay.* West Drayton, Middlesex: Penguin Books, 1947. 157 pp.
[13] Abraham H. Maslow. *Motivation and Personality.* New York: Harper, 1954. 411 pp.

interdisciplinary scholar who works in such areas is possibly a *presumptuous tyro,* if we adopt the viewpoint of the narrow specialist and perhaps a *madman,* if we adopt the conscientious position of the establishment specialist. But, since the objective is to screen all the disciplines and winnow out those synoptic considerations which are germane to an overall viewpoint—a winnowing out which will *frequently be carried out in consultation with specialists*—the generalist is really asking a series of questions which reflect concerns clearly different from those of the specialist. He is asking such questions as the following. What knowledge is most worthwhile? How can man best fulfill his own potentialities? What is such and such knowledge good *for?* What are the *social, spiritual* (value-seeking) and *intellectual* implications of this or that discovery, this or that activity, this or that decision? What are the ideal forms of human community? If man is a flicker between eternities, how can he best pour meaning into his life? What is the state of the human condition at any time? Whither is man drifting? How best can we employ what we now know and have, so as to approximate a Wellsian vision of men like gods? Clearly these are not the concerns of specialists, and the methods for dealing with them as well as the range of information they entail, are almost utterly different from those which preoccupy the specialist.

There is a whole congeries of important problems of a scientific, cultural, social, intellectual, or philosophical nature, which today cannot be dealt with educationally except in an interdisciplinary sense. While it continues to remain largely true that interdisciplinary studies are cold-shouldered by most academic specialists or given grudging attention by many in higher education, the growing number of competent generalists may be forcing a new look. If we expect to capture the imagination and the interest of the reader who is both perceptive and intelligent—and in sufficient numbers to contribute to the forward areas of research represented by many of these interdisciplinary studies—we must drastically revise the present curriculum in higher education so as to provide more offerings of an interdisciplinary nature. Many educators have already recognized the educational obsolescence which is so characteristic of some of the traditional specialties in the natural and social sciences. Much of the traditional curriculum is now definitely obsolescent in relation to our current needs in applied natural and social science technology.

Obsolescence is present to a considerable extent in the course offerings in the social sciences. It is, oddly, even present in a number of subjects in the curriculum which are generally held to be integrative, synoptic, or holistic in nature. Survey courses which tend to be *potpourris* of factual findings with neither pattern nor direction, are the major sinners in this respect. Integrative, synoptic, and holistic educational and intellectual functions can no longer be performed by either the traditional specialties in the humanities and the social sciences, by the overarching abstractions of philosophy courses whose content is alien to the cultural, technical, and social realities of the twentieth century, or by the stumbling and disoriented survey course which mistakes a series of pasting operations for intellectual and cultural perspective. These functions are now the proper province of the well-founded, well-designed, well-stocked, and well-taught interdisciplinary studies. It is only in these that we shall find that the wealth of relevant detail needed for pouring meaning into our lives has been knit together into organic and stimulating syntheses. It is only in these that the *hermeneutical functions* can be exercised in a manner which creates excitement and the enlarging of human horizons—an enlargement which is, after all, the basic function of education both in its etymological and its figurative senses. It is for reasons such as these that a philosophy of curriculum-formation will have to seek renewal and make a fairly complete break in part with what were necessities a few decades ago but which are outdated now.[14]

*Some Important Considerations Surrounding Interdisciplinary Work.* Inasmuch as interdisciplinary work in the social sciences may be either of the interpretive or hermeneutical variety or of the strictly methodological kind, it becomes imperative to say something about the relationship of "hard" methodology (the mathematical model, statistical analysis, the logical model) to "soft" methodology, that is, to various types of interpretive and hermeneutic studies, if we may be permitted to characterize the interpretive variety of interdisciplinary work in the social sciences pejoratively, by calling it "soft" methodology.

There can be no question of the essential importance for the social sciences of hard methodology—statistics, mathematics, logic, various types of model-building, and all those methods of rigorous analysis which we find dealt with extensively in such volumes as those by Coleman [15] or McGinnis.[16] The author can say this even though he is not a mathematician, since he has, himself, employed elementary, mathematical methods

[14] In connection with the value of synoptic or interdisciplinary courses in undergraduate education, the reader is urged to familiarize himself with the following volume: Daniel Bell, *The Reforming Of General Education*, New York and London: Columbia University Press, 1966, 320 pp. Bell has suggested, for use in the senior year of college, courses of a synoptic nature which are interdisciplinary in some of the senses discussed above. These courses are part of what Bell calls "The Third Tier," that is, that group of courses in the senior year which follow the first year's background courses (the first tier) and the second and third year's specialized courses (the second tier). The themes and content of the present volume are, to some extent, in line with the third-tier proposals made by Bell.

[15] James S. Coleman. *Introduction to Mathematical Sociology*. New York: The Free Press of Glencoe (Macmillan), 1964. 554 pp.

[16] Robert McGinnis. *Mathematical Foundations For Social Analysis*. New York and Indianapolis: Bobbs-Merrill, 1965. 408 pp.

for the analysis of problems in behavioral diffusion theory [17] and constitutional typologies.[18] Further than this he has had the opportunity to do input–output analysis and linear programming in governmental research in economics. These mathematical modes of analysis represent types of activity which immediately impress their practitioners with the *practical value* of hard methodology. Nevertheless, interpretive analysis should, perhaps, begin where mathematical and statistical methods of analysis end, so as to relate the firm workmanship of a hard methodology to the more global treatment of important problems, which is demanded by the sociological imagination. Much of hard methodology tends to be ahistorical in nature, so that our findings tend to be cross-sectional and may often be causally misleading when we fail to look at our problems, processes, events, and relationships, from the standpoint of their change with time. When it comes to doing justice to events through the dimension of time, perhaps we should regard the studies which are cushioned by hard methodology as the tail of the dog and the studies which have here been called interpretive in nature, as the dog, itself. Hence, the familiar admonition concerning the dangers of having the tail wag the dog!

There are, of course, many reasons why respect for hard methodology is riding high in academic circles today and soft methodology is viewed with suspicion. First, is the fact that the ability to deal with a problem—usually a small-scale one—that demands rigorous methods of analysis, is something that confers a sense of intellectual and professional confidence which cannot be obtained from interpretive effort expended on large-scale subject matter. It can, perhaps, be argued that interpretation is a necessary and central ingredient in the analysis of what Sorokin calls the "complex, multidimensional, sociocultural matrix," an admittedly jaw-breaking phrase for the act of taking society as a whole as the object of analysis. It is much easier to earn one's professional spurs in the social sciences by the "standard operating procedures" of hard methodology, rather than by being intellectually deviant and working with what C. Wright Mills [19] has called "macroscopic" subject matter. By virtue of Zipf's [20] *Principle Of*

[17] Papers by the present writer, employing mathematical models in the social sciences, will be found in such journals as *Mathematics Magazine, School Science And Mathematics, The Fibonacci Quarterly, Sociometry and the Journal Of Social Psychology* His doctoral dissertation, *A Theory Of Behavioral Diffusion. A Contribution To The Mathematical Biology Of Social Phenomena,* dealt exclusively with mathematical models for use in sociology and social psychology.

[18] Papers by the present writer, published from 1940 to 1950, dealing with the mathematical and methodological bases of constitutional psychology and constitutional medicine, will be found in such journals as *Philosophy Of Science* and the *Journal Of General Psychology.*

[19] C. Wright Mills. "Two Styles Of Social Science Research." 553–67. In *Power, Politics And People. The Collected Essays Of C. Wright Mills* (Irving L. Horowitz, editor), New York: Ballantine Books, 1963. 657 pp.

[20] George Kingsley Zipf. *Human Behavior and the Principle of Least Effort.* Cambridge, Massachusetts: Addison-Wesley Press, 1949. 573 pp.

*Least Effort* we can expect that younger men will try to prove themselves professionally through standard operating procedures and seek to avoid the left-field of soft methodology like the plague. One has only to remember that one form of Zipf's principle states that human beings strive to minimize the energy they expend in order to attain their goals. Clearly the energy output needed for the study of a limited problem will often be less than that needed for the study of one's total society.

A second reason for the prominence of hard methodology in the social sciences is a result of the influence of logical positivism and philosophical analysis for almost four decades. One consequence of this is that methods of research which most closely resemble those used in the natural sciences, are the preferred ones. This has led in many cases to an external aping of the rigor of the physical sciences by an uncritical worship of methodology—often, unfortunately, at the sacrifice of social significance. Rigor for rigor's sake has come to be known as "scientism" and the metaphysical assumptions which shore up this posture have begun to be questioned in some quarters. So too, has the conviction that in the social sciences hard methodology is always preferable to soft methodology and hard methodology is always *relevant* to the task at hand. What is an *uncritical* "scientism," if not a species of methodological razzle-dazzle, meant to impress rather than to inform? One does not need to know that a *t*-score is significant at the 5 percent level in differentiating the characteristics of two groups, in order to know that boys are different from girls. Nor would some *measure of association* be needed, which correlates the color of infant panties (pink or blue) with the sex of the wearer.

A third reason why hard methodology cuts more ice than soft methodology in the social sciences, is the ease with which one can prosecute studies employing standard, statistical designs and repress the questionability of some of the assumptions from probability theory which underly statistical procedure. When probability theory assumes that many aspects of social change can be viewed as an expression of the "urn of nature," we tend to play down the fact that, unlike the color attributes of balls in an urn, the characteristics of men and of social processes change over time. This is what Boulding would call a "system break." It is easy for the social scientist to make use of a routine and cookbook employment of statistical procedures, since to do so tends to sanctify the neglect of the time dimension in social research and seems to confer scientific solidity on our results.

The ahistoricity of the average social scientist can be seen in still another way. The economist, the engineer, the production man and the management specialist, will welcome the flow-diagram as an aid in their studies. A flow-diagram, *in part,* is one device for paying one's respects to the importance of time in the study of continuous processes.

How often, then, will one find a flow-diagram in the work of sociologists? It would not be difficult to find modern sociologists and political scientists who are writing, let us say, about exploitation of Negro labor in the Portuguese colony of Angola. But try to find among them a political scientist or a sociologist who makes frequent *use of detailed flow-diagrams,* such as, for instance, one which begins with the early exploitation of black labor in Angola, then represents the specific effects of such exploitation on Portuguese trade and development and terminates by pictorially representing the ramifications which the impact of such trade and development have on Portugal's current international relations. To be sure, one can always find *some* political scientists, historians, economists, and sociologists, all of whom will be definitely historical in their approach to Portuguese colonialism in Angola. What I am trying to say is that there are far too many social scientists in these same categories, *who will prefer to make only current cross-sectional studies of* colonialism or other phenomena of equal importance. This is, of *course,* tantamount to making a methodological virtue out of ahistoricity.[21]

Routine statistical design is also appealing in the social sciences because of the claims which the investigator can make in terms of the "accidental" samples which he so often blithely assumes are "representative" samples of the population of people or events which he is avowedly studying. An "accidental" sample is the one we find at hand—the students in one's classes, the factories in one's community, the Catholics among our senior students, the PTA in our neighborhood—while a representative sample should possess the features which would be found to belong in general to all members of the category or class under study (the parent population). If the investigator generalizes his results from his accidental sample to the total class which he is presumably studying, his conclusions may be impressive. They may appear even more impressive because they are shored up by careful statistical procedures. But they will not always provide a picture which will prove useful for the interpretation of possible future trends. Time and sample unrepresentativeness both have a way of playing havoc with the predictions which have been made.

*The Place Of Value In A World Of Fact.* A last consideration that has moved me to write the present volume is the hope that, perhaps, a working partnership can be created between facts and theories, on the one hand, and questions of personal and social value, on the other. The typical reader who is without any of the ambitions which would surround the

---

[21] This point about the greater relevance of the historical viewpoint, in attempting to understand social relations, over the methodological one, has been made by Barrington Moore, Jr. in "Strategy In Social Science," 111–59. He has emphasized this viewpoint particularly in relation to economic structure and technology. See Chapter 4 of this author's *Political Power And Social Theory,* New York, Harper & Row, 1965, 243 pp.

reading habits of the specialist, wishes to see social phenomena and social events, social processes and the quality of social relationships, related to his own life, both now and in the future. To treat these matters in the usual abstract way found in the standard textbook which eschews value considerations and to substitute methodological neatness for the reader's expectations, is to fail to provide those concerns which will arouse his interest. There is no substitute for the personal touch, for the amplification of the human focus, or for the feeling—if successfully conveyed—that somehow all this has a bearing on the hopes, ambitions, and energies of various groups with which one has identified. No reader comes to a new book to which he intends to bring a serious concern, in a way which would suggest he is a value vacuum. Every reader has a value center of some sort. It may be an intelligently fashioned value bastion or a thoughtless one which has been adopted from others uncritically. It may be relevant to the crisis atmosphere of our time or as dysfunctional as a team of horses would be on a modern, four-lane, superhighway. But there can be no denying that he possesses such a value center and that what he reads must either reinforce that center or rub it the wrong way, thereby forcing some value reconstruction upon him. One does not have to support morally the outlook of the reader. One does have to support it educationally, however, in the sense that the reader's outlook cannot be ignored and put aside.

The present volume deliberately attempts to show the relationship of the facts and theories with which it deals to some of our widespread human concerns. We hope that we have not failed to *distinguish* between fact and value but, even more importantly, we hope we have not failed to show their bearing upon one another. Our excuse for insisting that in some way they be related for the reader, is that much is gained educationally and nothing is lost intellectually. Furthermore something may be gained spiritually, using this latter term in the sense of the quest for value, which is everybody's concern. If the partnership thus effected prompts the average reader to see the importance of a systematic and consistent social philosophy, this will be all to the good.

The reader should realize in advance that a fraction of the present volume tries to look ahead and envision some of the possible impacts of science, technology, invention, and industrial innovation on society. The occasions for such projections have occurred chiefly in some of the chapters of Parts I, II, and V. Today there is quite a respectable contingent of both natural and social scientists who recognize that looking ahead is now a necessity in our complex world and that such looking ahead can increasingly be done on a fairly acceptable, respectable, and scientific basis. Members of this contingent are referred to throughout the volume.

Some conservative writers, like Villard,[22] shy clear of activity of this sort, recognizing that there is more of an immediate payoff and professional prestige in sticking strictly to the traditional factual, theoretical, experimental, statistical, and field-survey concerns of the social sciences. Other social scientists like Zetterberg [23] or the thousands of professional, social scientists and economists in government, prefer to orient social science to the problems of modern industry or the even more important social problems of the American community. A considerable part of the material in this volume—perhaps, most of it—is along traditional lines and describes current, social difficulties. I have, however, not hesitated to look ahead, as some of our social scientists are doing, who seriously feel that we must now try to make a reasonable stab at looking ahead with respect to some of the possible future consequences of recent developments in science and technology.

In addition to trying to guess at some of the alternative shapes which the future might take socially, as a result of emerging science and technology, I have also tried to deal critically with some *contemporary* social, cultural, educational, political, and urban trends, particularly as these appear to be significantly related to excessive urbanization and over-industrialization. Such trends are important in themselves, of course, but in terms of the fact that expanding urbanization and industrialization are being centrally serviced by developments in modern science and technology, our concern with such trends is closely linked to our concern with some of the possible, coming impacts of recent scientific and technological advances. The material concerned with such trends forms the bulk of Parts II, IV, and V. Finally, in many parts of the volume I have tried to suggest new ways of looking at some of the complex issues and problems of our time and to indicate new alternatives in human ecology which may become available in the future.

It is these three basic activities, then, which constitute the concerns of the present volumes, namely, (1) an effort to view critically some current social trends which appear to be heavily associated with increasing urbanization and industrialization; (2) an effort to suggest some fresh ways to view a number of our modern concerns; and (3) an effort to foresee some of the future social impacts of science and technology.

[22] Henry H. Villard. "The Need for Technological Change." 155–83. In *Technological Innovation And Society* (Dean Morse and Aaron W. Warner, editors). New York: Columbia University Press, 1966. 214 pp. In spite of this author's negativism about social forecasting, he has not hesitated to make projections to the year 2000, not only in the paper just mentioned but also in various parts of his volume, *Economic Development*, New York: Holt, Rinehart and Winston, 1963, 238 pp.

[23] For a viewpoint with respect to the possible practical applications of accumulated social science, see Hans L. Zetterburg, *Social Theory and Social Practice*, New York: The Bedminster Press, 1962, 190 pp.

Errors and omissions of treatment are bound to occur in so wide-ranging a task as I have undertaken here. For these I must apologize in advance. The basic concern must be the question of whether the volume —in spite of any errors or omissions—has provided some perspective on the matters which we have taken up. That judgment, naturally, must be left to the reader.

# I

# Technology and Some of
## Its Social Consequences

## ORIENTATION TO PART I

In this section the overwhelming importance of science and technology in the lives of the ordinary citizen living in the technologically advanced countries of the world today is discussed. We shall take the United States as our model of such a country for two reasons. First, since this is our own country, we are naturally more interested in the impact which science and technology have had and can have here. Second, the drama involved is more acute in our own country than elsewhere, precisely because science and technology are in a more advanced stage here than in other countries. Naturally the ways in which science and technology affect our lives are so numerous and complex that it would take volumes to do full justice to this sociological concern. We have, therefore, chosen some examples of *recent* scientific and technological advances which, although few in number, reflect such significant potentialities for social change that they are the concerns of some of the major thinkers of the present age.

In trying to deal with the current and coming impacts of science and technology on the human condition—or, if the purist prefers, the *American* condition—we cannot get far if we adopt a specialized, one-discipline, perspective. The reasons for this lie in the rise of what has been called "mission-oriented research" about current problems. The phrase, "mission-oriented research," refers to the fact that an increasing amount of contemporary research, in both the social as well as the natural sciences, is devoted to trying to understand the nature of a given social problem and to proposing solutions for dealing with it within the compass of certain values presumably held by the American community. That our preview needs to be "interdisciplinary," reflects the fact that we are increasingly recognizing that, in our socially complex and technologically advanced society, there are few, if any, problems which belong strictly within the confines of any single academic specialty. Social problems no longer come to us packaged, bearing a legend announcing that they are strictly sociological, economic, psychological, political, or legal in nature. Most of the significant social problems of our time produce effects of concern to *all* traditional academic fields. What is even more important, efforts to solve these problems require information from many areas of specialization and necessitate the borrowing and lending of a host of academic, analytical, and research skills which have been developed by the several specialties.

For reasons such as these the following chapters interpreting the impact of science and technology on the American condition, not only gather together relevant information from several specialties, but also weave together bits of specialized information so as to bring out more clearly the dimensions of the problem under discussion. The gain, hopefully, is that this will enable us not only to see how the problem would look to different kinds of specialists but, even more importantly, an interdisciplinary treatment is, in a sense, an *operational definition* of the problem. Furthermore, an interdisciplinary treatment of a social problem brings out the nature of *interdisciplinary modes of analysis* as these have been discussed in the Introduction to this volume. In this way one puts flesh and blood upon the skeleton of social analysis.

We shall first take a long and hard look at some of the social effects being created by the problem of automation and at some of the myths and errors which are hardening in connection with this problem. But the impact of automation in our time has been amplified by the rise of computer technology, giving rise to what has come to be known as "cybernation." This term refers to our modern ability to *link up* automated equipment in industry with computers which regulate and control the output of such equipment, so that increasingly fewer people are needed *directly* in the production process. Cybernation carries the promise of a historical breakthrough in the direction of coming closer to some of man's Utopian visions with respect to what a human community can be. But this possible breakthrough to a more socially desirable and more humane type of community, is fraught with pitfalls. It is the discussion of these pitfalls which constitutes the subject matter of Chapters 3 and 4.

Not all the social changes which are over the horizon for American society will spring from automation and cybernation. Space technology has a number of achievements to its credit, which—once they are applied to social life and civilian needs—will transform a great many of our values, both social and economic and, in addition, will suggest reformations in the concept of community, of which future generations are bound to be the beneficiaries. These possible transformations of social value and of community living are the themes of Chapter 5.

# 1

# Some Psychological and Economic Assumptions Underlying Automation*

Public interest in the subject of automation is increasing daily.[1] With the emphasis on the fact that machines will now replace brain power where formerly they substituted for muscular power, the average person feels more directly involved than ever before. A flood of literature on automation has appeared in various quarters: popular magazines, scholarly and technical journals, trade publications and books and newspapers. Most of this literature is optimistic concerning automation's future. Many of the forward glances have been imaginative, however insufficiently critical. Most predictions concerning its expected impact assume the continued existence of those value patterns and social habits which are current.

The promise of material abundance and increased leisure which automation brings has produced a hazy attitude towards some of its unpleasant possibilities and a noticeable lack of enthusiasm for any uninspired discussion of what may be some of its less desirable fruits. Several of the possible unpleasant social, economic and psychological sequelae have been either passed over in silence or touched upon rather skimpily. A failure to do these justice has made for the facile birth of a variety of beliefs which promise to harden into social myths whose dissipation will become increasingly difficult.

The tendency for such myths, once their acceptance is widespread, to take on doctrinal and even canonical status, became abundantly clear at the 1956 meeting of the American Psychological Association in Chi-

* Chapter 1, with adaptations and modifications has been taken from the following source: Henry Winthrop. "Some Psychological and Economic Assumptions Underlying Automation." *American Journal of Economics and Sociology.* (Part I) Vol. 17, No. 4, July 1958, 399–412.

[1] The author has had a continuing interest in the social impact of automation since his service as an economist with the Division of Productivity and Technological Studies of the U.S. Department of Labor.

cago in the symposium entitled "The Social Meaning of Automation." I mention this symposium for several reasons. First, the myths about automation which were put forward at that meeting are not only still with us but now, a decade later, they are being given wide currency. Second, the ideas presented were academically representative of the output of scholarly sources, other than engineers and economists, on the subject of automation. Also, the convictions which were so glibly advanced at this symposium are precisely those beliefs the reexamination of which is reported in the substance of the present chapter. It will then be my purpose to discuss those self-deceptions by which current enthusiasts for automation refuse to deal adequately with the debit side of the ledger and neglect to consider the possible shape of an industrially automated future, straitjacketed by our present value context from which it can hardly be separated.

I.

First, and perhaps the most potent of the current beliefs used to allay the fears of industrial workers that automation threatens their job security and future, is the emphasis on the opportunity for upgrading. At the Chicago symposium a common conviction of the panel speakers was that when automation replaces relatively routine and not too highly skilled labor functions, opportunities to climb the industrial ladder immediately open up. Displaced workers, it was stated, may be retrained and upgraded for more complicated work-functions, such as reading and interpreting control instruments, attending complex machinery and repairing and maintaining such equipment. Also, it was said that these retrained workers report more job satisfaction after automation than before, since their upgraded functions make more of an intellectual demand upon them than did their former more routine duties. That upgraded functions will make more of an intellectual demand than those previously held is also affirmed by outstanding writers on the subject of automation. One writer expresses this as follows:

> Automation will mean that human labor in the advanced technological societies will be used less and less for the routine, repetitive functions involved in feeding workpieces through machines and assembling them into finished products. Labor will be more and more "up-graded" into the kinds of functions performed by the engineer, the designer, the production planner, the skilled maintenance and repair man, the organizer and manager . . .[2] (p. 164)

[2] John Diebold. *Automation: The Advent of the Automation Factory*. New York: Van Nostrand, 1952. 181 pp. This quotation is borrowed by John Diebold from a manuscript by Eugene Staley, entitled *Technology and Human Values*.

The promise of upgrading, I believe, neglects certain psychological considerations. One of these is that each work function and each machine tending operation, requires a *minimum critical range in IQ* (Intelligence Quotient) which is sometimes substantial, sometimes quite narrow, depending upon the occupation. For instance in using the Otis Self-administering Test of Mental Ability, one psychologist has found it desirable to use 36 as a critical minimum raw score for clerical workers, which is equivalent to an IQ of 104. Another psychologist using the Otis Test has found in studying supervisors and skilled workers, such as toolmaker learners and job setters, that the critical minimum score for foremen is an IQ of 88–91 while for inspectors it would have been 109.

Some industrial psychologists are, I believe, prepared to recognize the existence of such ranges, particularly if they are in the human engineering field where research aimed at determining both the type and degree of skill required for operating new equipment of complex design, is their routine function. The ability to attend and service these may require a mean order of intelligence which in many cases will not be found in the pre-automation working crew.

Automated equipment frequently creates a demand for complex skills which are currently in short supply. Such a demand may be seen in the shortage of programmers for computing machines. There are also other complex skills demanded by automated equipment, training for which will be demanding, and there will frequently be some question as to whether displaced workers have the requisite intellectual capacities. The threat which the need for new skills offers a working group about to be affected by the introduction of automation can be measured by the difference between the mean critical intelligence levels required for the old manual functions and the new class of functions bound up with automation equipment. The number of displaced workers whose capacity and aptitudes fall well below these new critical levels may increase as time goes on and equipment becomes more complicated in design, employing new types of mechanization, new principles of automation and new types of instrumentation and controls. The proper handling and use of these will certainly tend to become more difficult.

Argyle [3] believes that

. . . automation will change national labor requirements in three ways: (a) there will be a greater demand for graduates in science and technology, (b) there will be a greater need for all grades of skilled electronic and mechanical engineers, and (c) there will be a smaller demand for semi-skilled men (previously employed on repetition jobs). . . . The second group . . . will be required for

[3] Michael Argyle. "Social Aspects of Automation." 109–22. In *The Push-Button World* (E. M. Hugh-Jones, editor). Norman, Oklahoma: University of Oklahoma Press, 1956. 158 pp.

maintenance work on the elaborate automatic equipment—one of the main jobs in an automatic factory. The more highly skilled men will also play a part in development work, as well as in line management. Several investigations suggest that these men are above average in intelligence and we may roughly place them between 110 and 125 IQ, including about 20 per cent of the population. (p. 116)

If workers from group (c) are displaced from their repetitive tasks by automation, the upgrading they are generally promised is a shift from group (c) to group (b), shortages being pronounced in this latter area. Even if we assumed that the level of ability in group (c) was sufficient to make upgrading easy, the fact that able group (c) workers have been willing to work below par for years, suggests a level of aspiration which will in all probability be accompanied by inertia at the prospect of undergoing retraining for group (b) tasks. These latter will involve a good deal of theoretical knowledge and abstract ability in addition to the manipulative skills involved. But do we have any right to assume that group (c) workers possess the capacities for being refunneled into group (b)? What are the facts which the industrial psychologist is prepared to argue are relevant to the promise of upgrading? Bear in mind that Argyle, himself, argues that "if more skilled men are needed, this means that semi- or unskilled men must be upgraded, or that more youths must have the opportunity of becoming skilled."

Various studies undertaken by psychologists tend to confirm the fact that *mean* IQ varies with occupational level. Super [4] reports the following findings: professional, 115; managerial, 108; clerical, 104; skilled, 99; and semiskilled, 97. Clearly those workers traditionally classified as skilled and semiskilled who fall roughly into Argyle's group (c) do not possess the mean IQ of those who will roughly fall into his group (b) workers whose mean IQ is apparently 115 or more.

A less sanguine set of data is given by Eysenck.[5] He reports average IQ by occupational category as follows: higher professional and administrative classes, 150; lower professional and technical executive groups, 130; highly skilled and clerical groups, 118; skilled workers, 108; semiskilled workers, 97; and unskilled laborers, 86. There is clearly a substantial deviation here from the preceding figure for the skilled group but complete agreement on the average intellectual status of the semiskilled. The difference between the group (b) and (c) means is 18 or 33 IQ points, depending upon which distribution may be the more accurate one. A safer judgment might be to take the IQ *approximately* midway between the two values namely, 123, and think of the IQ difference between the two groups as equal to roughly 26 IQ points (123–97).

4 Donald E. Super. *Appraising Vocational Fitness by Means of Psychological Tests.* New York: Harper, 1949. 727 pp. The data given are from p. 98.

5 H. J. Eysenck. *Uses and Abuses of Psychology.* Harmondsworth, Middlesex: Penguin Books, 1953. 313 pp. The data given are from pp. 87–8.

Results of the Army General Classification Test, likewise reported by Super, show that the *average* AGCT scores of those workers who would be classifiable in group (c), doing repetitive jobs, are 25–30 points less than those of the engineering groups.

Finally let us note that in a more detailed study Lorge and Blau [6] estimated the intellectual demands of the major occupational groups listed in the Dictionary of Occupational Titles. This study was intended to refine the methods and the findings of several previous investigators. The results obtained by Lorge and Blau in terms of *approximate* MA (Mental Age) and *approximate* IQ, were reported as follows: professional, MA 18 up: IQ, 120 up; managerial and official, MA, 17: IQ, 113; semiprofessional, MA, 16: IQ, 107; clerical and kindred, MA, 15: IQ, 100; sales and kindred, MA, 15: IQ, 100; protective service, MA, 14: IQ, 93; skilled, MA, 14: IQ, 93; personal service, MA, 13.5: IQ, 90; agricultural, MA, 13.5: IQ, 90; semiskilled, MA, 13: IQ, 87; unskilled, MA, 11; IQ, 73; domestic service, MA, 10; IQ, 67; and fishery, MA, 9.5: IQ, 63. These findings tend to reenforce the conviction that there are substantial differences in the occupational hierarchy, particularly between the three aggregate groups employed by Argyle. It would be easy enough to marshall additional evidence from psychological research that there is a substantial difference in IQ between groups (b) and (c).

The significance of the difference, however, is that insofar as training for group (b) work calls into play intellectual abilities only sparsely distributed among the semiskilled and unskilled, all talk of extensive upgrading is so much poppycock. Some displaced group (c) workers will, to be sure, possess sufficient talent and ambition. For the overwhelming majority, however, upgrading is not a realistic possibility if the functions to be performed are going to possess the attributes emphasized by Staley, and this for the reason that the levels of abilities and aptitudes called into play for group (b) functions are simply not present in the large majority of semiskilled and unskilled workers. The same is probably likewise true for a good many skilled workers. Ironically enough even if all displaced workers had the wherewithal for retraining, few of them would be called, for, says Woolard, "automation provides an economy in the labor force which, in engineering production, may be in the ratio of 2- to 10–1, but more generally will average at between 5 and 7–1." [7]

What about the second half of Argyle's point that group (b) workers will also have to be recruited from youth? Jobs that many young people would have ordinarily been given if they entered industry are now wiped out by changeovers to automation. Bendiner reports that in one year's

[6] I. Lorge and R. D. Blau. "Broad Occupational Groupings by Estimated Abilities." *Occupations.* Vol. 21, 1942. 289–95.

[7] Frank G. Woolard. "Automation in Engineering Production." 36–56. In *The Push-Button World. Op. cit.*

negotiations "with a leading packer, more rates were 'bargained out' as a result of new machinery than in the last fifteen years put together." [8] Bargained out rates generally indicate imminent occupational obsolescence. In this creeping type of unemployment the person most seriously affected is the one not hired.

What about youth sufficiently gifted to take training for group (b) jobs? There is some question, I believe, as to whether the prospect of performing those functions which would then still be routine, even if sophisticated, will appeal enough to the gifted to prompt them to invest five years of training for them. The same five years invested in many other professional areas, both scientific and managerial, may give freer play to the possession of talent for decision-making and at the same time possibly confer more status. Should such changes in attitude occur, recruitment will be bound to suffer.

II.

Another point emphasized at the Chicago symposium maintained that workers who have been upgraded through a retraining program reported increased job satisfaction. The standard anecdote which is repeated *ad nauseam* in this connection is the story of the upgraded Ford worker who told a newspaper man that he used to go home every evening jittery with exhaustion. After upgrading, everything was different. "Now," he said, "I run a whole battery of machines by pushing buttons and reading dials and go home feeling like talking to my family and reading." Clearly this is not the type of upgrading to which Argyle and Staley are referring. Actually the existing literature furnishes little in the way of reactions to upgrading from group (c) to group (b). However, some psychological studies have been made of changes in job satisfaction following upgrading of a different type. These are worth considering.

Super points out that "it has long been assumed that, even though a person might be able to do the work required by a job in which most of the workers are more able than he, the strain involved in keeping up with the competition would be such as to produce dissatisfaction in the worker." This would lead us to believe that a shift from group (c) to group (b) would be accompanied by dissatisfaction or at least tension for those upgraded employees who would be marginal for their new occupation, that is, who fall within the minimum critical range of intelligence required for it.

8 Robert Bendiner. "The Age of the Thinking Robot, And What It Will Mean to Us." 99–115. In *The Reporter Reader* (Max Ascoli, editor). New York: Doubleday, 1956. 314 pp.

However, it is important to note that upgraded workers in *some* industrial situations report more job satisfaction because of more *extensive* skill demands made upon them and greater interdependency in the work situation. This was ascertained through a study made under the auspices of the Institute for Social Research. This was an exploration of job satisfaction among upgraded workers in a power plant which had changed over to automation. Essentially this upgrading involved only the *addition* of skills to those already possessed by these workers. Each upgraded worker simply had to become multiskilled, assuming work functions which were *combinations* of pre-existing skills. The new skills which had to be acquired were *not of a higher intellectual order* than the old ones. The occupational distinction we are making here is similar to the psychological distinction introduced by Thorndike between area and altitude of intelligence.

The men who were A and B Operators at the time this study was conducted had transferred from operating jobs in the older plants, where they had performed specialized jobs in one of the three production rooms—boiler, turbine and condenser, or electrical. Each of these men had to learn new parts of the production process to a degree almost equal to the skill they already had in their own specialty. Former electrical switchboard operators now had to learn the steam side of the plant; former boiler fireman, the turbine and electrical; former turbine operator, the boiler and electrical.

As part of the on-the-job training for this job enlargement, job rotation was instituted. The men were rotated weekly between the unit control stations, the electrical control station, and other duties in the plant. Rotation has been continued even after the formal training was completed, so that, at the time of the study, the attitudes of the men towards their jobs were affected both by the fact that the job requirements had been vastly expanded over their previous jobs, but also by the fact that they changed the particular job they were doing for another one every week. . . .[9] (p. 60)

This type of upgrading may yield an initial job satisfaction only because of the sense of increased power that comes from the *variety* of functions performed, although, it is to be noted that even with this variety, not all upgraded employees reported increased job satisfaction. Furthermore we do not know to what extent a changeover which was reported to have involved a substantial number of displacements is conducive to an honest reporting of dissatisfaction, where the fear may be present that such honesty may affect one's job in any necessary future displacements.

[9] Floyd C. Mann and L. Richard Hoffman. "Case History in Two Power Plants." 53–65. In *Man and Automation*. Report of the Proceedings of a Conference sponsored by the Society for Applied Anthropology at Yale University, December 27–28, 1955. New Haven: The Technology Project. Yale University, 1956. 117 pp.

Overlooked in the compensation presumably provided by upgrading is the increase in psychological tension which retraining may bring in its wake. The modern psychologist and psychiatrist knows that tension is part of the price we pay for being civilized and in achieving personal growth. His job is to reduce *unnecessary tensions* rather than those which promote personal growth. As mechanization takes over we are witnessing the beginning of something which, for want of a better name, we might as well call "automation tension." Hugh-Jones mentions two examples in this connection. An operator in charge of a control room in an oil-refinery is constantly aware of the enormous value of the equipment for which he is responsible and, considering that a cat-cracker may cost $15 million dollars, he can hardly be at ease. A signal man in charge of a fully electrified railway signal box no longer walks about pulling heavy levers, but instead sits intently in a chair watching flashing lights in a tracking panel and pressing electric switches. His total responsibility is greater than ever since traffic volume has increased over the years.[10] In both these cases physical fatigue may have been lessened but mental strain may be considerably increased.

But does upgrading of the type described by Mann and Hoffman also bring tension in its wake? These authors report the following:

> *Tension and Interdependence.* More men in the new plant than in the old plant report they feel jumpy or nervous about their work. This tension reflects both the enlargement and the feeling of inadequate training. More than a third of the operators report that their training for these new enlarged jobs was too fast, and that it took more than a year for them to feel at ease on their jobs.
>
> Another factor related to the men's feelings of tension on the job is the degree to which they depend on each other for information about the system. Because they found they learned most about the jobs while actually doing the operations —rather than from the formal class-room parts of the training program—the former steam men relied on the former electrical men, and vice versa. The greater the tension level, the more the men report relying on the other men for suggestions and advice about the particular work problems they face on the job. There seems to be some optimal level of interdependence for the men in these plants. Too much or too little leads to some dissatisfaction with the job itself. . . .[11] (p. 61)

Does it not seem reasonable to expect that tension would even be greater when the upgrading is from group (c) to group (b)? The greater kinship feeling reported among operators after upgrading is really the expression of an interdependency needed to lessen *neovocational insecurity* rather than a genuine revamping and improvement of interpersonal relations.

---

[10] E. M. Hugh-Jones. "A Summing Up." 123–49. In *The Push-Button World. Op. cit.*

[11] Floyd C. Mann and L. Richard Hoffman. *Man and Automation. Op. cit.*

III.

A frequent claim made with respect to employees of the group (c) variety, displaced by automation, is that they wind up in service occupations. This claim was not neglected at the Chicago symposium. It is true, of course, that employment in service industries has grown faster than in other lines. But I am inclined to believe that this claim neglects some very important considerations.

Chief among these is the fact that many of the service situations are, themselves, being automated, such as retail vending which relies heavily on packaging rather than salesmanship [12] and face-to-face services such as the sales of tickets for airlines. In addition most automation men agree that the electronic displacement of humans will go farthest and fastest in the office.[13] In fact it is frequently remarked now that engineers evaluating new office machinery express its efficiency in terms of a unit not as yet canonized professionally, namely, GPD's, Girl Power Displaced. Positions which might ordinarily have been open to industrially displaced personnel and which are not of the face-to-face variety, such as bookkeeping, billing, comptometry, and simple forms of accounting, are likewise being taken over by automation. In fact white-collar functions are now being investigated with a vengeance for the possibility of displacing many of them by automation in one form or another.

However, even if automation were not rearing its ugly head in the service occupations, we have to remember that labor mobility from the primary and secondary to the tertiary sectors of the economy, cannot be a permanent process. Many economists have noted this one-way flow to the tertiary sector, particularly Colin Clark, who has been optimistic about the capacity of the service sector to absorb disposable labor from the other two.[14] However, a rational society tends to promote methods by which mental health, educational resources, creative activities and the development of personal abilities, may be self-directed.

Guidance, advisory services, counseling and professional services are largely required when individuals are victims of social and psychological anomie, ignorance, limited education and miseducation of the variety so ably described by Borsodi.[15] As the mean level of education rises and

12 For the probable impact of automation on retailing services see the series of three articles by E. B. Weiss in *Advertising Age*, Feb. 4, 11, and 18, 1957, particularly the second article, "Electronic Communications Revolution Will Force Startling Changes in the Operations of Retailers."

13 See, in this connection, Part II, "Automation in the Office," 16–42. In *Man and Automation. Op. cit.*

14 Colin Clark. *The Conditions of Economic Progress.* London: Macmillan, 1940. 504 pp. A more direct discussion of the point is contained in the same author's, *The Economics of 1960,* London: Macmillan, 1942, 118 pp.

15 Ralph Borsodi. *Education and Living.* 2 vols. Melbourne, Florida: Melbourne University Press, 1948. 719 pp.

as we inaugurate policies of preventive medicine and hygiene and as we invent institutions to prevent or minimize social dislocations, mutual interdependence for services should decline to some extent. Wisdom and education in a rational society should promote autarchy in values and increase the desire to depend upon one's own inner resources. Under such a *long-range* prospect it is reasonable to consider lower demand for services thus reducing somewhat the possibility for absorption of mass displacements in the service sector.

Let us assume, however, that neither of the two considerations concerning the possibilities for tertiary absorption will play as big a role as we imagine. There would still be countervailing arguments against the theory that the service sector can cushion the impact of the temporarily displaced worker. It makes little sense to think of a process whose logical culmination is completely depersonalized production in the form of the completely automatic factory, as one which will also eventually result in pretty nearly everybody performing services for one another. This would be equivalent on a national scale to the ridiculous case of people taking in one another's washing, with the minimally tended industrial machine a large cornucopia out of which flows perpetually an increasing stream of goods.

For an economy of this "air-conditioned nightmare" type where saturation for services per capita might soon be reached, leaving a permanently unemployed service reserve, there is the danger of too little purchasing power to absorb all the industrial manna from heaven or there is the counter-danger of a tendency for all goods to approach the status of free goods thus playing havoc with the very *raison d'être* of an industrial economy. If we are thinking in the *short run* and in terms of the traditional and contemporary, economic structure of the free-enterprise system, such a projection is absurd. If, however, we are thinking in terms of the *long run,* then we may move into what is now being called "the cybernated society"—a possible socioeconomic structure that we shall describe in subsequent chapters. In a cybernated society, that is, one in which goods and services are produced by computer-controlled machines, work may be minimal for us, people may be given some sort of credit claim on all goods and services produced, and the most important social problem may be what to do with leisure. In such a projection of economic existence, where raw material supplies are permanently ensured, we presumably will have a population of artists, writers, scientists, and scholars, largely functioning in a world that thinkers of the type represented by William Morris [16] would have created. But the point is that we are not living in such a world now. Competition and free-enterprise are the dominant ideals. All in all, then, it seems most unlikely that in

[16] William Morris. *News From Nowhere;* or an epoch of rest, being some chapters from a utopian romance. New York: Thomas Nelson & Son, 1941. 247 pp.

the world of the present tertiary absorption is the permanent answer to displacement due to automation.

**IV.**

There are thinkers, however, who do not put their faith in *tertiary absorption* but rather in the ability of industry, itself, to reabsorb the displaced. Distinguished policymakers of the stamp of the Earl of Halsbury still have confidence in the power of the manufacturing sector to make the necessary transfers necessitated by the onset of automation. Halsbury [17] revives the traditional argument of industrial labor mobility, clothed, however, this time in full mathematical dress. Halsbury argues as follows.

It is unreasonable to expect that a worker who has lost his job through automation will subsequently be rehired in some position in the same factory. This, of course, may occasionally happen but it will not be the rule. Now, says Halsbury, let us liken the reabsorption of the unemployed into the economy, to a unimolecular reaction similar to the disintegration of radioactive atoms. He assumes that the hypothesis most relevant to this context is that the probability of getting a job tomorrow is the same as that of getting one today. Let us further suppose, says Halsbury, that $N_0$ men have just been technologically displaced by automation. Then at any later time, $t$, the number still out of work will be given by

$$N_t = N_0 2^{-t/\tau}. \tag{1}$$

In this symbolism $\tau$ is called the half-mile period of the reaction. If it should be the case that $t = \tau$, then equation (1) will become

$$N_\tau = N_0 2^{-1} = N_0/2. \tag{2}$$

Translating equation (2) into our industrial context, says Halsbury, we have a statement that declares that the population of the unemployed (atoms in the original context) will be halved during the lapse of a period of time, $\tau$.

Halsbury's argument then continues. Assume that $\tau$ is one week. Then equation (2) must be interpreted as follows. If 1000 men were automated out of their jobs, 500 will find work again after a week has elapsed, 750 will have found work again after the passage of two weeks, 875 will find themselves reemployed three weeks later, and so on. Thus one can see that one arithmetical consequence of equation (2) is that

17 In the Introduction to *The Push-Button World, op. cit.,* pp. 14–6. For an extended exposition of Halsbury's optimism regarding automation see his "Automation —Verbal Fiction, Psychological Reality," *Impact of Science on Society,* Vol. 7, 1956, 179– 201, and "Integrating Social with Technological Change," *ibid.,* Vol. 8, 1957, 3–15.

only one person in a thousand will still be unemployed (unreabsorbed into the economy) at the end of $10\tau$ (10 weeks in the example), only one in a million at the end of $20\tau$ (20 weeks) and so on.

Lord Halsbury regards the one worker in a thousand who is still unemployed as the *unfortunate victim of a statistical law*. He believes that if we are to consider this worker's misfortune sociologically, it would be best to do so in terms of *signal-to-noise ratio*, a concept that is borrowed from the field of communication engineering. Suppose we do regard unemployment as a social signal. Then, asks Halsbury, when should unemployment be taken as a signal? His answer is that it becomes a social signal only when it rises above the background noise. It becomes a social signal only when it can be distinguished as something special and different from other personal misfortunes whose occurrence is statistically certain for other individuals. Leaning upon an interpretation of this sort, Halsbury remarks that the persistent regional unemployment of the Twenties and Thirties was a signal. The short-term unemployment of the Fifties, however, Halsbury felt at the time, should have been regarded as only background noise.

Halsbury sums up his argument by stating that, in his view, unemployment due to automation will never provide more than a statistical fluctuation in a general background of "noise" which constitutes the context of personal misfortune that must be faced by those living on our planet at the present time.

The first objection to Halsbury's formula is the economic fallacy underlying his mathematical reasoning. That reasoning assumes that the reabsorption of labor will take place. This is precisely the question at issue and precisely the expectation we feel may be unwarranted for an economy whose rate of introduction of automated production throughout, is accelerating. The circular reasoning underlying Halsbury's exposition is a clear case of begging the question. If we assume that reabsorption will take place, then clearly its rate per unit of time can be estimated by his approach. The mathematical exposition as such, however, is completely independent of the *factual and economic question* of whether, under the circumstances of increasing automation, reabsorption will take place at all.

However, suppose we assume that it does take place in certain sectors of the economy. If we are industrially realistic we have to recognize that if this occurs, numbers of other men are being thrown out of work elsewhere due to automation. Even if reabsorption takes place on the optimistic basis assumed by Halsbury (and I imagine that reentry rates from British labor statistics at the time will give the lie to this optimism), the absorption of the unemployed as a unimolecular reaction is likely to be countered by continuous additions to $N_0$ as automation tends to become universal. Halsbury's remarks betray something highly unimaginative and lacking in feeling for the plight of human beings who have reached the end of the line, occupationally speaking. The adoption of a control engineering viewpoint and a signal-to-noise ratio which treats unemployment due to automation merely as a statistical fluctuation, fails to recognize, it seems to me, the long-term irreversible features of labor displacements from the *industrial sector* of the economy.

A more realistic picture of the absorption potential of the manufacturing sector is given by Meier.[18] This author is making reference to the building of an industrial-urban center in nations which are beginning their economic development.

. . . Employment is critical because an apparent paradox has been revealed. Industrialization was introduced as a means for providing useful employment for millions of underemployed rural workers, yet a more careful inspection of the strategies for industrialization led to the conclusion that automatic factories, i.e., virtually workerless installations, were to be preferred whenever technically feasible. . . . (p. 195)

The pattern of consumption conforming more or less to the minimum adequate standard of living, . . . offers a clue to the kinds of work that would need to be done. The fraction required to produce food for the market would be only 5 to 10 per cent of the labor force if it was as productive as the urban sector. Because the productivity of rural labor is almost certain to be less than that of urban labor for a very long time to come, the fraction working in agriculture will be larger than 5 to 10 per cent, but it may decline toward that figure in the long run. Jobs in manufacturing will depend upon how much of the heavy capital goods can be imported, because there is a very small volume of manufactured items consumed in the minimum adequate standard of living itself. If the productivity of labor in manufacturing is equalized with labor productivity elsewhere in the city, then 10 to 15 per cent of the labor force would be required, much of it employed in producing the capital goods required for a growing economy. Construction activity could easily reach 20 per cent of the productive effort. The remainder of the work force, which might exceed half of the urban labor available, would be needed to provide education, health, personal services, municipal services, and other social services. A few more might engage in sports, drama, music, scientific research, and other cultural activities on a full-time professional level. (p. 195)

It can probably be assumed that the use of urban labor forces in technologically advanced countries will be subject to even more severe constraints. Both the economist, Kenneth Boulding, and the computer scientist, Ralph Bellman, have assumed in their writings and public statements that no more than two or three percent of the population will be needed to produce all our basic commodities.

18 Richard L. Meier. *Science and Economic Development: New Patterns of Living.* New York: Wiley, 1956. 266 pp.

The preceding considerations suggest that Halsbury's formulae and optimism regarding *industrial* reemployment are unwarranted. A corrective against this optimism is given by Bendiner,[19] who suggests why displacements in one part of industry undergoing automation are not easily absorbed by another part. Raytheon Manufacturing Company installed a chassis-assembly line with a capacity of a thousand radios per day, which required two employees where formerly two hundred were needed. Automatic controls used in a tanning operation in Milwaukee cut staff by two-thirds. A conventional power plant owned by one company employed a hundred men while a second push-button unit owned by the same firm used twenty-eight men and obtained a 50 percent increase in kilowatt-hours of production. Utility workers were reported to be concerned over atom-produced electric power. A pilot plant intended for Pittsburgh was reported to require only six men to furnish power for the entire city. Woodbury,[20] for instance, cites the following.

. . . Everywhere that you look into accounts of automation advances, you read of the fear of workers being displaced. The Commonwealth Edison Company in Chicago is said to be using an IBM computing machine that will replace 200 people. An oil-industry expert has claimed that a refinery that employs 800 without automation could keep up the same production with 12 men under complete automatic operation. In the Ford plant, during the now-obsolete manual-production days, it required 400 men to turn out one finished block in 40 minutes. Now, 48 workers produce one every 18 minutes. Elsewhere, a huge transfer machine does 540 operations under the guidance of one man; the older method involved 35 to 75 men for the same rate of output. It is reported that in Boston in 1949, when long-distance telephone calls became automatic, 450 toll operators were given their termination notices. The list grows every day. . . . (pp. 145-6)

The reader has probably read of many similar examples in the literature now mushrooming on this subject.

It is not only Halsbury's displaced workers who may find no place for themselves. "Creeping unemployment" which refers to young people who would have found a place in industry if certain skills had not become obsolescent, is also with us. The permanent "reserve" of unemployment thus created is expected to increase. Striking evidence of the advance of automation is seen in the Federal Reserve Board index figure for the manufacturing and mining industries. This figure was 129 both in November 1953 and November, 1954. Over the same period these industries lost one million people. These figures certainly do not justify Halsbury's optimism. Perhaps the most reasonable position to take on

19 Robert Bendiner. *The Reporter Reader. Op. cit.*
20 David O. Woodbury. *Let Erma Do It: The Full Story of Automation.* New York: Harcourt, Brace, 1956. 305 pp.

the myth that automation creates more jobs is, I think, that taken by Bendiner, himself, who says

> . . . But if it frees some only to leave as many others stranded, dazed, and for years without the wherewithal to buy what the machines produce, it will hardly have paid its way—at least for a generation that already has all it can stand in the way of large-scale hazards. A measure of coherent planning, a sustained sense of responsibility in industry, labor, government, and education—these are the least we will need to ease us into the second machine age more smoothly than our luckless forebears went into the first.[21] (p. 115)

21 Robert Bendiner. *The Reporter Reader. Op. cit.*

# 2

# Automation in Relation
# to Social and Cultural Life*

V.

Another prominent myth widely believed by the devotees of automation is that continued automation will release the human spirit for the fruitful use of leisure. If one reads Morris Ernst's *Utopia 1976* [1] (which forecasts for the next twenty years), Sir George Thomson's [2] *The Foreseeable Future* (which forecasts for the next 100 years), or Sir Charles Galton Darwin's [3] *The Next Million Years* (which speaks for itself), one notes a common fabric of assumptions underlying the outlook of all these writers.

These social theorists extrapolate current value patterns into the future. This is a characteristic which they share with our science fiction writers but which is expressed on a much more sophisticated level. They inject into a future dominated by automation those current restless consumption patterns which are euphemistically described as "gracious living," and which are nothing more than a passion for gadgets and an alienative pursuit of externalia. There is some justification, I suppose, for this shortsightedness, if the evidence of consumer behavior provided by the fabulous present is any indication of the "daze" to come.

This placid extrapolation of our current bounties into the western world's industrial future, carries with it the genuine belief that in an automated future several generations hence we shall still be living in terms of "bigger and betterism," that we shall still be on an industrial Roman holiday and on a consumer binge, but on an even grander scale

---

* Chapter 2, with adaptations and modifications has been taken from the following source: Henry Winthrop. "Some Psychological and Economic Assumptions Underlying Automation." *American Journal of Economics and Sociology.* (Part 2) Vol. 18, No. 3, October 1958, 69–82.

1 Morris L. Ernst. *Utopia 1976.* New York: Rinehart, 1955. 305 pp.

2 Sir George Thomson. *The Foreseeable Future.* Cambridge: Cambridge University Press, 1955. 166 pp.

3 Charles Galton Darwin. *The Next Million Years.* London: Rupert Hart-Davis, 1952. 210 pp.

than now. In all these previsions of the future there is no awareness of the Old Testament preacher's remarks about human vanity, no concern with the possibility that modern man may have to reformulate his social and industrial objectives, no realization of the varied ways in which man can recover the ability to express his several levels of being, fully and richly, and no recognition of man's psychological need for multiple techniques of self-actualization.[4]

That we are blind to the need for self-actualization a host of current social philosophers, among whom may be counted Mannheim,[5] Fromm,[6] and Seidenberg,[7] now bear witness. Above all, the writers and scientists mentioned above, show no comprehension of the fact that there will have to be a transvaluation of most current values before a leisured society will make the most fruitful use of our coming freedom from the curse of labor. These devotees seem to have no fears that the automated future may spew forth such social monstrosities as Orwell's *1984* or Huxley's *Brave New World* nor do they seem concerned over some of the disturbing portraits which have been painted in recent years, such as those of Mead[8] and Vonnegut,[9] of a world dominated by the spirit of automation.

If we recognize, however, that America has never developed a philosophy of leisure for the average man, that unlimited consumption is the mainspring for the work habits of the average citizen, and that there is an element of truth in the remarks of foreign observers visiting these shores, who declare that the leisure-time objective of the average American may be described as "having fun," then it is difficult to see in what sense an automated America will release the human spirit for a more vital, more fructifying and more serious use of leisure. Automation may release it, to be sure, but only for more frenzied efforts to have a good time and to avoid being introduced to one's own subconscious. The anomic crushing of the human spirit, so feared by prophets of social doom, is obviously a genuine possibility in a world in which a philosophy of meaningless, standardized and limitless consumption, to be serviced by an industrial juggernaut expected to be almost without limitations as to productive capacity, is held unquestioningly by most people.

---

4 For some of the problems surrounding self-actualization, see the following: Abraham H. Maslow. *Toward a Psychology of Being.* Princeton: Van Nostrand, 1962. 214 pp. See especially, "Cognition of Being in the Peak Experiences." 67–96.

5 Karl Mannheim. *Diagnosis of Our Time. Wartime Essays of a Sociologist.* London: Routledge & Kegan Paul, 1943. 180 pp.

6 Erich Fromm. *The Sane Society.* New York: Holt, Rinehart and Winston, Inc., 1955. 370 pp.

7 Roderick Seidenberg. *Post-Historic Man. An Inquiry.* Boston: Beacon Press, 1957. 246 pp.

8 Edward S. Mead. *The Big Ball of Wax.* New York: Simon & Schuster, 1954. 246 pp.

9 Kurt Vonnegut. *Player Piano.* London: Macmillan, 1953. 352 pp.

To cap it all this dream is equated with the "American way of life," thus constituting a living commentary on the distance we have strayed from the dreams and ideals of the Founding Fathers. The Nearings [10] have some very bitter comments to make in this connection.

. . . As we see the picture, the people of the U.S.A. today are devoting an immense proportion of their energy, time and economic means to physical sensations, exposure to them, indulgence in them and attempts to escape from them. The majority of people are living at the level of physical survival—comfort, satisfaction, stimulation, gratification. "Society is preoccupied with physical ease and only incidentally interested in certain minor aspects of inner discipline. . . . The human psyche . . . is intended to perceive the cosmos, adjust to it, struggle in it, and achieve there an individuation of itself. But our materialism has slain man's good opinion of himself, stripped government of philosophy, taught the common people not to desire personal excellence but to barter in droves for the right to mediocrity." People engrossed in the immediate problems of individual survival, comfort and diversion have neither the time, interest or energy for group problems. In Francis Galton's phrase, they are of little civic worth. . . . (p. 9)

The same plenty leaves a coddled younger generation (which has arrived at the top even before it graduates from high school) with nowhere to go but down. Teen-agers thoughtlessly enjoy the comforts and luxuries of Eastern potentates. One hundred or even fifty years ago who, in the Western Hemisphere but royalty and a scattering of millionaires, had the profusion of luxurious belongings that crowd every middle- and upper-class kitchen, living room, bedroom and bathroom in the U.S.A. today? The young people of a century ago had a few simple, prized possessions and as few clothes. The pampered U.S.A. adolescents of today have closets jammed with things to wear and far more possessions than adults in earlier generations even aspired to. A fur-coated girl at the wheel of one of the latest model strawberry-pink or orchid-colored cars, gleaming with chrome metal and glass, would have been a princess in days not too far gone. Today she is a high school girl taking the family car, or in many cases, her own car, to a football game. (p. 11)

10 Helen & Scott Nearing. *USA Today.* Harborside, Maine: Social Science Institute, 1955. 254 pp. The quotation, 'Society . . . mediocrity,' is from Philip Wylie, *Night unto Night*, New York: Harcourt, Brace, 1944, p. 148. In this same connection and within two months after the Russians had begun The Space Age, a host of critics hastened to warn the peoples of the West, and particularly the United States, that the American Dream was in reality the American Nightmare. Suggestions began to come from all sides concerning the manner in which we would have to revamp our way of life in order to preserve freedom and security. Most notable of these critics was Lester Pearson, winner of the Nobel Peace Prize for 1957. However, *Life* (Nov. 18, 1957), gave official sanction to the importance of re-examining our current conceptions of the good life, by featuring an article by Dr. George R. Price, which pulled no punches, whatsoever, in this connection. Most of the prevailing criticism which has been made by various commentators, has been directed at our worship of gadgetry, comfort, conspicuous consumption and externalia. We are mentioning the emergence of this type of social criticism because much of it is essentially in keeping with that made here and elsewhere in this chapter.

The danger inherent in this myth of increased freedom for the human spirit through mechanization and automation has been capably diagnosed by Fromm [11] in terms of the phenomenon of *alienation*. Fromm illustrates in the two paragraphs which we quote, what he means by this term.

By alienation is meant a mode of experience in which the person experiences himself as an alien. He has become, one might say, estranged from himself. He does not experience himself as the center of his world, as the creator of his own acts—but his acts and their consequences have become his masters, whom he obeys, or whom he may even worship. The alienated person is out of touch with himself as he is out of touch with any other person. He, like the others, are experienced as things are experienced; with the senses and with common sense, but at the same time without being related to oneself and to the world outside productively. . . . (pp. 120–1)

Alienation as we find it in modern society is almost total; it pervades the relationship of man to his work, to the things he consumes, to the state, to his fellow man, and to himself. Man has created a world of man-made things as it never existed before. He has constructed a complicated social machine to administer the technical machine he built. Yet this whole creation of his stands over and above him. He does not feel himself as a creator and center, but as the servant of a Golem, which his hands have built. The more powerful and gigantic the forces are which he unleashes, the more powerless he feels himself as a human being. He confronts himself with his own forces embodied in things he has created, alienated from himself. He is owned by his own creation, and has lost ownership of himself. He has built a golden calf, and says "these are your gods who have brought you out of Egypt." (pp. 124–5)

Alienation, then, refers to that psychological state in which we experience ourselves as strangers. The alienated individual does not possess an intimate sense of self. He does not feel the profound truth of the existentialist observation that man makes himself. He does not generate his own activities from wellsprings of authentic thought and feeling. He does not try to anticipate the consequences of his actions and hold himself morally responsible for their effects upon others. His behavioral repertoire—to borrow a phrase from modern psychology—seems to be strictly a bundle of reflexes, environmental conditioning, unexamined habits, and socially generated attitudes, values, biases, ideas, ideals, and levels of aspiration. Little of what he thinks, feels and does appears to have been worked through by himself. He is a slave to this behavioral repertoire which he idolizes with a variety of rationalizations and he finds no difficulty in justifying the consequences of his acts by invoking high-sounding principles. It is in these senses that we may speak of the alienated person as out of touch both with himself and with others. He experiences himself, as he experiences others, as objects. He lives im-

[11] Erich Fromm. *The Sane Society. Op. cit.* Pp. 120–1 and 124–5.

mersed in what the Hebrew philosopher, Buber, has called the I–It attitude. He is the mass-man who is not creatively and productively related to his world, a world that he experiences only with his senses and with common sense.

The alienation that we find in modern society is expressed in numerous forms. Men may be alienated from themselves, from the opposite sex, from each other, from work, from society, from Nature, and from God or—to put this last form of alienation in terms that are, perhaps, more comprehensible—from what has been called *The Mystery of Being*. Men have created a world rich in goods and services and a complex technology to produce these, which is almost unlimited in its scope. Yet they feel themselves to be creatures apart from this technical apparatus, beings that must serve it and adapt to it, since modern technology has its own imperatives. They do not recognize that they, themselves, have created this technological Moloch and that it is an idol they can remold nearer to their hearts' desires. They feel it to be utterly beyond their control when, in fact, they can change it to suit themselves in a variety of ways. Thus they come to think of the technological society as over and above them, a sweeping wave which will carry everything before it.

Accompanying the phenomenon of alienation is what Fromm calls the *marketing orientation*. By this Fromm means that the individual experiences himself as a thing to be employed successfully on the market. His aim is to sell himself. His body, his mind and his soul are his capital, and his task in life is to invest these favorably, to make a profit on himself. If he does not succeed in selling his packaged personality on the market, he is a failure. As an example of what the marketing orientation does to some of the major themes of western culture, consider the question of love. Fromm [12] makes the following comments.

In more popular terms one can discover the marketing connotation of love in discussions on marital love and on the need for children for love and affection. In numerous articles, in counseling, in lectures, marital love is described as a state of mutual fairness and mutual manipulation, called "understanding each other." The wife is supposed to consider the needs and sensibilities of the husband, and vice versa. If he comes home tired and disgruntled, she should not ask him questions—or should ask him questions—according to what the authors think is best for "oiling" him. And he should say appreciative words about her cooking or her new dress—and all this in the name of love. Every day now one can hear that a child must "get affection" in order to feel secure, or that another child "did not get enough love from his parents," and that is why he became a criminal or schizophrenic. Love and affection have assumed the same meaning as that of the formula for the baby, or the college education one should get,

12 Erich Fromm. *The Sane Society. Op. cit.* Pp. 199–200.

or the latest film one should "take in." You feed love, as you feed security, knowledge and everything else—and you have a happy person! (pp. 199–200)

What is the average man's attitude towards the new leisure most likely to be? A 1957 Gallup Poll came up with the following findings. A group of typical American citizens were interviewed in order to ascertain what they thought workers would do with a four-day week. Opinion was divided but in general it was felt that workers would spend their extra time in recreational activities—fishing, hunting, boating, golf and other sports. Workers, themselves, when interviewed, plumped for working around the house, yard or garden. *Reporter Magazine* [13] commenting on findings such as these, raises doubts about how Americans will use their new-found leisure. From the spate of literature on the coming Era of Leisure it is hard to tell whether we are headed for an Elysium of culture that will put the ancient Greeks in the shade or for a hell of mass boredom modified by home carpentry, hi-fi, plus motels, and ping-pong. After reading much of the evidence pro and con, one is forced to conclude that unless our whole educational system soon addresses itself to developing a nation of rounded amateurs, we shall only be creating more and more time for people who have less and less need of it.

Now the point of all this is that if we move into an automated world in the near future, whose basic values are still the pursuit of externalia (and this is what so many imaginative forecasters prevision), we face a very vivid threat of increasing alienation of the human spirit together with an intensification of the marketing orientation. An increase in these two processes is most unlikely to produce the fruits which optimistic social visionaries are expecting. Should that day arrive when automation has provided the fulfillment of the leisure it promises and if that leisure is used for the passive pursuit of "having fun" via soap-operas, daytime serials, motels, bigger and better girlie-shows, gorier who-dun-its and similar examples of idiot's delight, the day of reckoning will be at hand. Sufficient unto the day is the evil thereof.

VI.

Still another widespread myth which shores up the enthusiasts for automation is the underlying economic belief in the infinite insatiety of human wants. This is one of the most macabre beliefs concerning the input–output aspects of the human organism ever bequeathed by classical economics. It is not only a conviction untrue to human nature but it is also a philosophy which unconsciously advocates increasing gluttony. Yet

[13] Robert Bendiner. "Could You Stand a Four-Day Week?" *Reporter Magazine.* Vol. 17, August 8, 1957. 10–14.

without this philosophy there would be no economic *raison d'être* for most Western democracies.

If everyone suddenly developed the taste for a reasonably simple life, one in which creative activity, self-actualization, and self-understanding were the predominant features, production, as everyone must realize, would decelerate rather rapidly. Our hucksters survive by methods of one-way mass communication aimed at convincing the consumer that he both wants and needs goods which he could easily do without. If Western man were to forego these illusory wants on whose satisfaction our annual increases of capital investment are based, our economy, indeed, would be a shambles.

Any scientific research aimed at determining that roster of human needs which will keep man healthy, mentally, morally, spiritually, and physically, which would allow him unlimited variation in his creative activities, whether these be literary, artistic, intellectual or merely a passion for play and sports, would probably come up with a budget of needs in which many of the illusory status "necessities" of our expanding economy would find no place. Katona [14] who has pioneered in the application of psychological findings to consumer wants has gathered together psychological data and interpretations which tend to show that the saturation for goods depends upon many factors but one of the strongest influences towards a purchase are its status-conferring aspects. Where status was once ensured by *owning* a car, any car, it is now ensured only by owning an up-to-date model. Where status motives are insufficient to ensure the nonfunctional, wasteful purchase, the techniques of motivational research must be employed to induce the consumer to part with his money. The possible social immorality of these techniques has been well-documented by Packard,[15] although motivation research has its defenders too.[16]

However, the fool's paradise of economic activity which depends upon a buyers' market motivated chiefly by status-vying activity rather than genuine need, is a game which, we have reason to believe, must

[14] George Katona. *Psychological Analysis of Economic Behavior*, New York: McGraw-Hill, 1951. 347 pp. Other studies of the relationship between consumer behavior and consumer needs, which may be of interest to the reader in this connection are: George Katona and E. Mueller, *Consumer Attitudes and Demand, 1950–1952*, University of Michigan, Survey Research Center, Institute For Social Research, 1953. Lincoln H. Clark (editor), *Consumer Behavior. The Dynamics of Consumer Reaction*, New York: New York University Press, 1955. Lincoln H. Clark (editor), *Consumer Behavior, II, The Life Cycle and Consumer Behavior*, New York: New York University Press, 1955.

[15] Vance Packard. *The Hidden Persuaders*. New York: David McKay, 1957. 275 pp.

[16] For a brief apologia for motivation research, slanted to the outlook of management, see "Advertising Strategy and Theories of Motivation" in *Cost and Profit Outlook*, 9 (December, 1956), published by Alderson and Sessions—Marketing and Management Council. See also Ralph L. Westfall, W. Harper Boyd, Jr., and Donald T. Campbell. "The Use of Structured Techniques in Motivation Research." *Journal of Marketing*. Vol. 22, 1957. 134–9.

sooner or later pall. Furthermore, it is a game which promotes alienation by getting people all hopped up over externalia and a marketing orientation.

If we shift our attention to the question of whether there are real, functional, upper limits to *consumption in use* rather than consumption via acquisition of goods for status reasons, both common sense and available data yield an answer in the affirmative. The short-run limits on consumption were once ably documented by Pitkin.[17] These short-run saturation limits are expressed not only in terms of physiological limits on consumption for the volume of goods and services purchased per capita but also in terms of the fraction of either income or savings not deployed for total consumption. Pitkin has assembled available data for such commodity categories as food, drink, clothing, shelter, heat and light, entertainment (travel, movie, radio, automobiles, cigarettes) and the use of leisure.

Such consumption-in-use saturation points were found for the pattern of consumer interests over thirty-five years ago and considering that many of the items being purchased today are classifiable within the consumption categories established by Pitkin, there is every reason to believe that use-saturation points exist for these also. Considering that Pitkin reports short-run limits on consumption-in-use, *a fortiori* we can expect limits in the long-run to a consumption spree.[18] Unfortunately the promise of automation is intimately tied up with the continuing conviction that the plethora of goods spawned by industry will indefinitely be used (or at least purchased) by the American consumer. Of this there may be some doubt.

Aiding our changing consumption patterns is a relatively new economic phenomenon, namely, a tendency for a budget of true needs to be satisfied easily but to be superseded by a pattern of luxury purchases. These latter in turn, through the operation of the Freudian pleasure principle (which, in this context, might be described as an infantile form of compulsive buying abetted by the technique of motivation research), pass over sooner or later into the category of "necessities." Clearly here the meaning of "necessities" is different from the meaning of the same term referred to a budget of genuine physical, physiological and spiritual needs. In fact students of consumer markets today are frank to admit that what were once luxuries are now really in the class of necessities.

*Time Magazine* (August 20th, 1956) reports the latest commodity entrees exhibiting this changed status: TV sets, automatic laundry serv-

[17] Walter Pitkin. *The Consumer. His Nature and His Changing Habits.* New York: McGraw-Hill, 1932. 421 pp. See, particularly, the section entitled "When All Limits Get Together." 213–44.

[18] The reader may be interested to know that Pitkin credits the irrationality of our consumption mores chiefly to the American Woman. See the section in the volume cited, "Woman, the Economic Imbecile." 279–312.

ice and biscuit mix, all of which are now components of the BLS cost-of-living index. Among other items which, according to *Time*, may soon make the transition from the luxury to the necessity class are air-conditioning, electric blankets, power steering and other amenities. Finally among the glories of the new luxuries just over the horizon, which advertising has already convinced some consumers they cannot do without, are the following: a brush specially designed to clean the lint from one's navel, electric golf carts for farmers, Egyptian camel saddles and 8-foot, cloth-covered, motorized kangaroos that pop 3-foot kangaroos out of their marsupial but motorized interiors.[19]

We must emphasize once more that the myth of the infinite insatiety of human wants is the ground on which the promise of automation is based. The use of the word "wants" in this doctrine really presents a semantic problem. If we mean by "wants" the items which would be included in some scientific budget of basic needs, a budget from which frills and superfluities have been eliminated, then the doctrine will clearly prove to be false. If, however, we mean by "wants" items for which consumer expectations have been created by mass conditioning, which represent the gratification of socially derived and frequently infantile impulses rather than of physiological needs and of services which promote self-actualization, then certainly this is an entirely different matter. Such mass conditioned wants are merely drain-off foci for "discretionary income."

Theoretically, if we multiply these alienatively *ad nauseam* then, of course, the validity of the doctrine of the infinite insatiety of human wants may be established by our own efforts *a fortiori*, for a world of automation. But what if the American consumer several decades hence, tiring of the Golden Age of Gluttony, finds that he is content with one car for several years, one simple, pleasant looking home, and one fairly enduring set of household goods, appliances, silver and china, together with those appurtenances which make modern life comfortable and which when not jerry-built need not be traded in for the latest make of the same? After all commodities were valued for their functional perpetuity in the not too remote past nor was the esteem in which they were then held necessarily bound up with limitations of income.

What if Western man should tire of newer models of television, more eye-filling sailboats, deep freezers which remain unfilled and similar aspects of the conspicuous consumption that Veblen so loved to mock? There is little reason to anticipate such an economic about face *in the immediate future*, I suppose, although another depression, a superior type of consumer and adult education, or similar traumatic factors, might conceivably bring it about sooner than expected. In the long run,

---

19 Needless to say these have not yet made the BLS cost-of-living index.

however, I suspect that consumer fatigue will set in. I suspect this on psychological grounds, based upon man's most deep-seated intellectual and emotional needs. For these reasons automation's epitaph may well be already written in the limited capacity for consumption and for changing preferences which in the last analysis must be true for all of us. It remains to be seen for what consumption categories these limits are already not too far away.

The psychological factors which set these boundaries to consumption are familiar to all economists. With a continuing rise in productivity the volume of goods per capita for the domestic market must continue to rise. The attendant fall in prices means more purchases spread among more consumers. However, what is the picture for the individual consumer when a commodity in question has made the rounds *at least once* for each consumer desiring it? On the basis of marginal analysis the exchange of $x$ units of income for 1 unit of a given commodity, $y$, will occur if the marginal satisfaction of an additional unit of commodity $y$, just exceeds the increment of satisfaction provided by $x$ units of income. We are here clearly talking about the rate of consumption for the same good (food, drink, clothing, travel, etc.) and, as Pitkin has emphasized, there are clearly physiological limits to this type of consumption.

There must then be a point at which marginal satisfaction for $y$ *in use* (not exchange) may become negative. If one had to eat 4 full-course dinners in the same evening, there would be actual displeasure over the third or fourth. On the other hand it should be clear that the last $x$ units of income cannot in any sense be capable of yielding a negative marginal satisfaction for they can always symbolize the possibility of future consumption. In addition there may be some doubt as to whether the marginal satisfaction curve for income is even *negatively* accelerated since Centers and Cantril,[20] on the basis of certain psychological experiments, report, "The more money a person has the more money he wants." However, shunting aside such a finding until such time as further experimental confirmation is forthcoming, and assuming the traditional negatively accelerated marginal satisfaction curve for income, what reason is there, in terms of classical marginal analysis, for an exchange to take place between $x$ units of income and 1 unit of commodity $y$, in the neighborhood of the physiological limit for $y$?

Let us, however, assume that an argument from marginal analysis is irrelevant and let us stick to the facts of economic life, namely, that goods will be indefinitely absorbed for status reasons and because of the artificial stimulation provided by advertising and motivation research. For this to go on indefinitely we must abandon functional reasons for consumption and collude in a social policy of economic waste of goods and raw materials. It is doubtful if a rational and enlightened economy, still im-

---

[20] Richard Centers and Hadley Cantril. "Income Satisfaction and Income Aspiration." *Journal of Abnormal and Social Psychology*. Vol. 41, 1946. pp. 66 ff.

bued with the Protestant ethic, will permit this indefinitely, although the unsaleable commodities piling up in government warehouses, indicates that at least a beginning has been made in this direction.

Quick substitutability in goods still having most of their usefulness unexploited, will be a social cost of automation which no responsible citizenry can long endure, an item which will have to be added to those other social costs of private enterprise, so ably catalogued by Kapp.[21] The raw materials depletion aspect of social waste is, itself, accelerated to the extent that irreplaceable materials are embodied in the commodities we discard prematurely. This, itself, is a threat to the perpetuation or rise of present living standards. If reason and good will are to play a role in our economic future, we may hope that consumer attitudes will undergo some change. The very desire to preserve present living standards may alter consumer attitudes towards premature substitutability. Future consumers may perhaps be willing to try to avoid an equality of consumer dissatisfaction possibly even at the price of universal rationing.

One thing is certain. Underpinning the drive towards automation is a type of unrestricted consumption which represents current social approval, in a peculiarly infantile form, of the Freudian pleasure principle. This irrationality of current consumption is ably described by Fromm.[22]

Man today is fascinated by the possibility of buying more, better, and especially, new things. He is consumption-hungry. The act of buying and consuming has become a compulsive, irrational aim, because it is an end in itself, with little relation to the use of, or pleasure in the things bought and consumed. To buy the latest gadget, the latest model of anything that is on the market, is the dream of everybody, in comparison to which the real pleasure in use is quite secondary. Modern man, if he dared to be articulate about his concept of heaven, would describe a vision which would look like the biggest department store in the world, showing new things and gadgets, and himself having plenty of money with which to buy them. He would wander around open-mouthed in this heaven of gadgets and commodities, provided only that there were ever more and newer things to buy, and perhaps that his neighbors were just a little less privileged than he. (p. 135)

Inroads on this consumption hunger, in order to compete with Soviet Russia by funneling income into research involving large-scale crash programs and heavy material costs, began to be advocated by various public figures after Sputnik appeared. This plea for the temperate life is, of course, a plea made on behalf of the wrong reason. We are here dealing with a cultural phenomenon of a golden age of misdirected values, which, itself, has to be altered on a large social scale, within the minds

21 Karl W. Kapp. *The Social Costs of Private Enterprise.* Cambridge: Harvard University Press, 1950. 287 pp.
22 Erich Fromm. *Op. cit.* P. 135.

and hearts of our citizens. This has been well stated in the words of Canon Bell.[23]

> If we are to rescue America from Americans, we shall have to raise up a new generation which will live less immaturely. This can happen only if Demos recovers from his present self-applauding jamboree, only if once more he comes to know the comparative values of human living as the race has learned them down the millennia. As we stand revealed by candid examination of the indexes, our culture is childish. If we go on as we are, we shall not produce the kind of citizens necessary for America's continued happiness or safety. We shall not bring forth "a type of man who sums up in his character a quality of understanding, of humility, of truth, of humor, of moral stature, of strength and resourcefulness of mind, of pregnant ideas, of universal sympathy and friendship and love." If we and our children must live out our days in the sort of culture that the indexes indicate, can anything be done by us and for us in the circumstances? If nothing can be done to arrest disintegration, then how can those of us live happily who know what it means to be effectively human? (pp. 46-7)

The coupling of automation with infantile consumption desires may lead to the unhappiest of economic consequences. The exploitation of invention and technology to increase the goods of the spirit can lead to a better statement and practise of the good life. It is difficult at present to see which choice Americans will make.

VII.

A direct consideration that will further limit the extrapolation of our present consumption spree into the future, is that, although energy promises to become almost as free as the unmetered air, irreplaceable resources, themselves, are being utilized at so rapid a rate as to threaten the bounty automation promises for posterity. Even if we accept the more sanguine estimates concerning the resource reservoir of the future, as outlined by Harrison Brown,[24] we still have to recognize that sooner or later there must be a limit to the earth's "biotic potential," using this phrase in Vogt's[25] Neo-Malthusian sense.

This limit may be approached at a faster tempo than ever as the maws of an automated economy deplete our resources at an ever increasing rate. Long before this biotic limit is reached, however, an automated industrial structure may be in trouble for there exists a critical rate of

---

[23] Bernard Iddings Bell. *Crowd Culture. An Examination of the American Way of Life.* New York: Harper, 1952. 159 pp.

[24] Harrison Brown. *The Challenge of Man's Future.* New York: Viking Press, 1954. 290 pp. Since publishing this volume Brown has exhibited a more cautious attitude towards resource availability. See his address before the American Society of Newspaper Editors at San Francisco, in 1957.

[25] William Vogt. *The Road to Survival.* New York: William Sloane, 1948. 335 pp.

resource utilization below which the operation of an automated economy would be faced with a growing fraction of idle capital goods. This critical rate can obviously be reached at a time when raw materials will be far from exhausted but still too limited to meet the processing needs of existing industries pacing the overextended consumption which seems so prevalent now.

A sober view of the limitations upon world resources is reflected by Meier [26] who has turned out some of the most scholarly and careful work to date, concerning the impact of science and technology on Western, industrial life. He states in the last paragraph of the first chapter of his distinguished volume:

> There are also limits to what science can achieve in extending the world's resources. The supply of energy from the sun, or materials from the crust of the earth, is not infinite. There are laws of nature governing energy exchanges and combinations of matter which reduce their utility much further. A careful investigation of the practical limits of world development would be valuable since this would make it possible to define some of the alternatives open to man for his continued occupation of the earth. Realization of the alternatives might eventually lead to some settled view of man's place which would obviate the staggering from crisis to crisis so evident in current prospects. (p. 32)

The point which requires most emphasis, with respect to the relation between consumption and resources in an automated economy, is that the greater the rate of automation the greater the rate of raw material depletion. Unless we are willing to stand by and see plants idle, consumption must continuously increase if automation takes over. Thus a day of reckoning must surely come if we make no plans to husband what we already have. The need for substitute resources has been emphasized by Diebold who is an optimist with regard to automation's possibilities. He says:

> Although automation will result in more efficient use of our physical plant— for example, the use of capital equipment twenty-four hours rather than eight hours a day—our need for power and natural resources will continue to increase during the next generation. What steps must we take to replenish what we draw from nature? [27] (p. 174)

There are clearly optimists and pessimists among those who write on the resource question. There is, however, a tendency to shunt aside the unpleasant jeremiads of the pessimists. If taken too soberly they would convert the American dream into an American nightmare. However,

---

26 Richard L. Meier. *Science and Economic Development: New Patterns of Living.* New York: Wiley, 1956. 266 pp.

27 John Diebold. *Automation: The Advent of the Automation Factory.* New York: Van Nostrand, 1952. 181 pp.

Lyons' [28] writings on our increasingly disturbed ecological balance, Osborn's [29] insistence that our resources are dwindling much too rapidly and Ordway's [30] emphasis that there may be limits to industrial growth and the material basis of cultural expansion, deserve to be taken more seriously than ever by those who face the prospect of automation uncritically. There is a relationship connecting automation, consumption, population and resources. Maldirected, this relationship may do the social order irreparable injury.

Perhaps it would be most appropriate to terminate our discussion by relating the role of banking to the prospects of automation. Bank credit, extended as entrepreneurial capital and translated into capital equipment, will in general mean more goods and more employment. The extension of such credit, however, must be related to such variables as the tempo of automation, the degree of consumer saturation for particular goods, and the distribution of purchasing power in periods when technological displacement is substantial. Extension of bank credit makes sense in a period in which consumer demand for goods and services cannot be satisfied without encouraging the expansion of productive facilities. However, uncontrolled capital goods expansion and accumulating commodity inventories may be socially disruptive if (1) psychological saturation for many goods and services has been reached or (2) unsatisfied demand is present without concomitant purchasing power.

We expect some degree of the latter phenomenon as a result of technological displacement by automation uncushioned by tertiary reabsorption. In the first situation an increase in bank credit for capital expansion would aggravate commodity stockpiling. Bank credit can play a role in the second situation only in the form of consumption loans. A device of this sort would be a very impractical social invention for, although it would accelerate the transfer of goods and services, there would be no long-term prospect of borrowers being able to pay back through securing long-term employment. If we are convinced of the indefinite expansibility of human wants, if we are optimists with regard to the possibility of finding substitutes for depleted raw materials, and if we are convinced that automation will preserve purchasing power by transferring labor from one sector to another of the economy, then we can safely conclude that bank credit will continue to play its traditional role in facilitating industrial expansion and full employment. If we are not convinced of any or all of these stated considerations then clearly the role of bank credit in the future is somewhat ambiguous.

[28] Barrow Lyons. *Tomorrow's Birthright: A Political and Economic Interpretation of Our National Resources.* New York: Funk & Wagnalls, 1955. 424 pp.
[29] Fairfield Osborn. *The Limits of the Earth.* Boston: Little, Brown, 1953. 238 pp.
[30] Samuel H. Ordway. *Resources and the American Dream.* New York: Ronald Press, 1953. 55 pp.

In the immediate present bank credit is vital because of the impressive financial outlays usually involved in introducing automation on a large scale. Where labor cost savings do not compensate for this outlay for some time, management is faced with a period of risk during which time a change in consumer demand or tastes could convert the change-over into a heavy loss. On the whole, however, wise management and sound credit investment tend to reduce considerably the probability of such prospects. The overall conclusion to be drawn then is that bank credit will play its vital role in the coming phase of automation but will have to reinterpret substantially its social and industrial roles in the future, because of the considerations we have chosen to emphasize in this chapter.

The reader should remember that the myths described in this chapter were beginning to form in the mid-Fifties. Now, in the late-Sixties, they have hardened considerably in the thinking of the American Establishment. The undesirability of this hardening is the fact that such myths may be even more dangerous in our current era of cybernation. Automated equipment, now increasingly run by computers and other information-processing devices, may aggravate the social and economic effects that were produced by the relatively simpler modes of automation which existed in the mid-Fifties. These myths—or rather, these beliefs—should be constantly reexamined in the light of our changing technology and the many innovations that are being introduced into the American economy. Perhaps, we can convert some of these beliefs into realities, but if we do so it will be only at the cost of taking stock of our present circumstances, rather than by trying to adapt to technological change in terms of images of the American economy, which are now outdated and illusory.

The reader should note that as of 1966, the question of the coming impact of automation is still controversial. Diebold [31] has noted that there are two schools of thought with respect to automation: a pessimistic and an optimistic school. On the other hand Solow [32] feels that the protagonists of both these schools are wrong. He believes that in a modern mixed economy, full employment can be achieved, for *any* plausible rate of technological change, by a proper and active use of various fiscal and monetary policies. Other important considerations, says Solow, center

---

[31] John Diebold. *Congressional Testimony.* 12–76. In *Automation. Implications For the Future* (Morris Philipson, editor). New York: Vintage Books, 1962. 456 pp. See, particularly, pp. 52–60.

[32] Robert M. Solow. "The Great Automation Question." *The Public Interest,* No. 1, Fall 1965. 17–26. Solow is also the author of a famous paper which has precipitated a great deal of research on the economic effects of technological change—research which is still continuing in economics. The paper in question is "Technical Change and the Aggregate Production Function," The *Review of Economics and Statistics,* Vol. 39, No. 3, August 1957, 312–20.

around such matters as *capacity, investment, aggregate demand* and some related economic considerations, in addition to such factors as the quantity and quality of technological change and technological innovation.

I am keenly aware, of course, that the assessments made in this chapter concerning the probable impact of automation on employment, appear to have been given the lie by observation of the prosperity which characterized the decade, 1956–66. We can make at least two important points addressed to this observation. First, the expected reduction in the need for human labor as a result of automation, the information-processing revolution and computer technology in general, is regarded as a *long-run expectation* rather than a *short-run effect*. It is clear that aggregate demand can be expressed in the form of what economists call *capital widening*. This will occur when existing techniques are extended to employ more people, each of whom uses exactly the same amount of capital stock and equipment as each member of the original labor force. This can occur during the same period in which the employment of the newer technologies of automation and cybernation is rising, but while these newer technologies still constitute only a small percentage of new capital investment.

Such a situation can occur when a substantially new injection of aggregate demand comes from such sources as (1) new entrants into the labor force from the young, (2) elimination of large pockets of poverty through governmental measures, job retraining and job creation in the semiskilled and skilled categories, (3) special rather than general labor expansion, such as that occurring in the teaching and welfare professions, (4) the creation of assured demand through the expansion into the Armed Services of large numbers of people who might otherwise be unemployed, and a host of similar considerations. But considerations of this sort cannot be expected to last indefinitely in an economic sense, although the models of *economic growth* currently employed to justify economic optimism do not always take stock sufficiently of the *distribution* of aggregate demand. [33] Too many of these models depend upon limited considerations, such as a strong tendency to forecast economic development in terms of growth per capita—and thereby increased demand—by concentrating upon such factors as the quotient of the savings rate divided by the capi-

---

[33] For a picture of the models used in studying the economics of growth, the reader is referred to the following. For a non-technical discussion see Jan Tinbergen, *The Design of Development*, Baltimore: The Johns Hopkins Press, 1958, 99 pp. For a technical and mathematical discussion see the following two books by the same author: *Mathematical Models of Economic Growth* (with H. C. Boos), New York: McGraw-Hill, 1962, 131 pp. and *Economic Policy: Principles and Design*, Amsterdam: North-Holland Publishing Company, 1956, 276 pp. For a critique *in part* of a strictly quantitative approach to economic growth, see Charles P. Kindleberger, *Economic Development*, New York: McGraw-Hill, 1965, 425 pp.

tal-output ratio, from which the present increase of the population has been subtracted.

Many of these models, particularly the famous Harrod–Domar model, implicitly depend upon the alleged capacity of the human being to expand his demand for goods and services indefinitely. This is a long-run expectation which demands considerable questioning and skepticism. This assumption of constantly rising consumption leads back, of course, to the remarks already made in this chapter concerning the probable existence of saturation limits for the consumption of goods and services. To assume a continued rise in both aggregate and per capita demand is to assume a standard of living in which the sky is the limit and a social policy of consumer collusion in the waste of natural resources, which beggars description.

The same assumption concerning the expected expansibility of consumption in order for economic growth to continue indefinitely, can be seen in yet another way. We know that under automation and the information-processing revolution, there is a strong tendency for labor to become redundant in both the primary sector of the economy (mining, fishing, forestry, agriculture) and the secondary sector (manufacturing). This seems to be inevitable because of rising productivity. Thus, if aggregate demand is to continue to rise it will have to put in its appearance, *in the long run,* in the tertiary or service sector. But automation and computer technology in general, as we have already remarked, are also accelerating in the service sector. In the long run we should expect labor also to be redundant in the service sector if demand in the form of a *rising standard of living,* grows too slowly to accommodate the total labor displacements into the service sector from the primary and secondary sectors.

However, in principle and in theory, consumer demand could rise so steeply that all such displacements could be accommodated *in the long run.* But once more this would imply, in fact, an unrealistic capacity for the consumption of goods and services—a capacity without saturation limits. Furthermore, the *rate of expansibility* of such consumption would, *in the long run,* have to be greater than ever, because we can anticipate that the *rate in the rise in productivity* in the long run, as a result of automation and computer technology, will also be greater than ever. We are, however—for the reasons already mentioned in our discussion of the assumption of the infinite insatiety of human wants—quite skeptical that such an eventuality can come to pass. In short, it is perfectly clear that it can happen *in the short run.* It is more than doubtful that it can happen in the long run.

The optimists with respect to automation far outnumber the pessimists. The optimists may roughly be defined as those thinkers and analysts who believe that automation is only the latest and most dramatic

wrinkle in the extension of modern technology. Thinkers in this category
are by and large convinced that automation promises full employment
and substantial rises in our standard of living and that these desiderata
can and will occur with no basic political, industrial or economic changes
in the American way of life. In addition, they do not anticipate any far-
reaching, social disorganization or the need for future social reconstruction, arising from the impact of automation regulated by computer
technology—at least not in the foreseeable future. Among such noted optimists—to take but a small sample—are Brozen,[34, 35] Buckingham,[36]
Bright,[37, 38] and Silberman.[39]

This last mentioned writer, a member of the Board of Editors of
*Fortune* and a lecturer in economics at Columbia University, produced
a volume in 1966 whose findings go against the grain of most of the convictions of the pessimists. Using sober, statistical analyses of the economic
and business trends of the Sixties, Silberman reports, for instance, that the
need for blue-collar workers is rising, that in the second half of the Sixties a
labor shortage began to appear in many industries, and that the much-
touted claim of the pessimists—to the effect that the future employment
needs created by automation will lie in the direction of highly trained
professional, technical and managerial workers—has been greatly exaggerated. Furthermore, reports Silberman, the ability to automate many
industrial processes, as with the basic oxygen process for making steel or
in paper mill operations, is proving to be much more difficult than expected. He also finds that the *levels of skill* automation demands are not
going to prove to be much different from those in operation in nonauto-
mated production. The available data convince Silberman that the fears
of the minority—that we are in for severe, industrial change in a few
decades—are wide of the mark. Silberman furnishes the following three
major conclusions which run counter to the beliefs of the pessimistic minority. (1) Automation is not a significant cause of unemployment. (2)
New technology is exerting less of an impact on the kinds of work men
do and the education and skill they need for that work, than is com-

[34] Yale Brozen. "The Pace of Automation." 167–172. In *The New Technology and
Human Values* (John G. Burke, editor). Belmont, California: Wadsworth Publishing
Company, 1966. 408 pp.

[35] Yale Brozen. "Automation: A Job Creator Not a Job Destroyer." *U.S. News.* Vol.
58, March 8, 1965. 94–8.

[36] Walter Buckingham. *Automation. Its Impact on Business and People.* New York:
Harper & Brothers, 1961. 196 pp.

[37] James R. Bright. "Opportunity and Threat in Technological Change." *Harvard
Business Review.* Vol. 41, November 1963. 76–86.

[38] James R. Bright. *Automation and Management.* Cambridge, Mass: Harvard University Press, 1958. 270 pp.

[39] Charles E. Silberman. *The Myths of Automation.* New York: Harper & Row,
1966. 148 pp.

monly believed. (3) Man is not in danger of being dominated by the machine.

Silberman points out that factors other than automation are now significantly related to levels of employment. Among these factors are teenage employment, early retirement, the war on poverty, the operating rate of the economy, changes in nonmachine productivity and the growth of GNP. Other writers, like Culbertson,[40] have stressed the tremendous bearing of an increase in *total demand* upon the actual economic and social effects of the introduction of automation and computer technology.

The pessimists on the whole differ from the optimists in some fairly clear-cut ways. They see in automation and computer technology a radical, industrial break with the past. For the pessimists automation and computer technology offer the possibility of a radical new society and one which will increase the fund of freedom, social justice and well-being. This requires, as they see it, more social imagination than is currently being exercised and a greater willingness to concentrate on the *future social and economic potentialities of automation.* They are less concerned with how many, if any, of their dire predictions will be realized or with the accuracy of the timing of these predictions than with a desire to have public attention brought to bear upon the *potentialities* of automation and computer technology. They are anxious to have more social inventiveness applied to the *potentialities* of automation—potentialities which, they believe, can usher in a more perfect social order. It is because they believe that our present, social system and the ideology of free enterprise will be resistant to an honest examination of those potentialities and that little, if anything, will be done to realize them, that they may be called pessimists. Among the representatives of the minority view, we might mention Seligman,[41] Michael,[42, 43] Theobald,[44, 45, 46, 47] Killingsworth,[48]

40 John Matthew Culbertson. *Full Employment or Stagnation.* New York: McGraw-Hill, 1964. 252 pp.

41 Ben B. Seligman. *Most Notorious Victory. Man in an Age of Automation.* New York: Free Press (Macmillan), 1966. 441 pp.

42 Donald N. Michael. *Cybernation: The Silent Conquest.* Santa Barbara: Center For The Study of Democratic Institutions, 1962. 48 pp.

43 Donald N. Michael. *The Next Generation. The Prospects Ahead for the Youth of Today and Tomorrow.* New York: Random House, 1965. 218 pp.

44 Robert Theobald. "Human Rights in a Cybernated Age." *The Educational Record.* Vol. 45, 1964. 113–121.

45 Robert Theobald. *Free Men and Free Markets.* New York: Clarkson and Potter, 1963. 203 pp.

46 Robert Theobald (editor). *The Guaranteed Income. Next Step in Economic Evolution?* New York: Doubleday, 1966. 233 pp.

47 Robert Theobald. "Cybernetics. The Socio-Economic Revolution." *Fellowship.* Special Consultation Issue, May 1965. 6-13.

48 Charles C. Killingsworth. "Automation, Jobs, and Manpower: The Case for Structural Unemployment." 97–117. In *The Manpower Revolution: Its Policy Consequences* (Garth L. Mangum, editor). New York: Doubleday, 1966. 580 pp.

Ferry,[49] Piel,[50] Harrington [51] and Peck.[52] Some illuminating insights are also available from the authors of some of the occasional papers released by the Center for the Study of Democratic Institutions.[53]

Optimists and pessimists differ to a large extent that is quite understandable. The former tend to take a short-range view, the latter a long-range view. In the short range one can stress, as Silberman does, industrial fluctuations that demand labor of every kind—teenagers, married women, retired and older workers, and Negroes as well as members of the regular labor force. One can also stress the new demand that will be created by our rising standard of living, our increasing population, extensive and new family formation, the elimination of poverty and export demand, particularly for producers' goods and for goods and services required for economic development abroad. Then, too, in the short run one can clearly see that the expansion of governmental services will result in jobs. So too will the inefficient overloading of governmental bureaucracies with superfluous personnel—an overloading that makes use of Parkinson's Law for humane reasons which, in the short run, override questions of labor redundancy. This phenomenon has been well described by Gabor.[54] In the short run one does not have to worry about the 7 to 8 million workers in the defense industries and their place in a future peacetime economy. One can also overlook the social cost of supporting a modern army which, everyone hopes, will never have to be used. One does not have to worry about the jobs of workers who may be laid off in the future by cutbacks in the space program. Finally, one tends to play down somewhat, in the short-range point of view, the technologically displaced worker who cannot be reabsorbed into the economy because, for one reason or another, retraining will not represent real relief. Likewise, one does not have to concern oneself with the economic future of the large percentage of those who are intellectually poorly endowed and one does not have to raise questions as to how much of induced demand represents industrial waste and "illth" in consumption. Many similar considerations not men-

[49] W. H. Ferry. *The New Technology and Higher Education.* A publication of the Whitewater Forum Committee. 1966. 3–19.

[50] Gerard Piel. *Science in the Cause of Man.* New York: Alfred A. Knopf, 1962. 338 pp. See particularly Chapter 3 "Our Industrial Cultures," 97–112 and Chapter 9 "The Economics of Abundance," 272–291.

[51] Michael Harrington. *The Accidental Century.* New York: Macmillan, 1965. 322 pp.

[52] H. F. William Peck. "The Great Transformation." *The American Scholar.* Vol. 35, No. 2, Spring, 1966. 358–69.

[53] See the following occasional papers and conversations, published by the Center for the Study of Democratic Institutions, Santa Barbara, California. Walter P. Reuther, *First Things First,* March 1964, 10 pp. Gerard Piel, *Consumers of Abundance,* June 1961 and April 1965, 10 pp. W. H. Ferry, Michael Harrington, and Frank L. Keegar, *Cacotopias and Utopias,* February 1965, 30 pp. Ralph Helstein, Gerard Piel, and Robert Theobald, *Jobs, Machines and People,* February 1964, 24 pp.

[54] Dennis Gabor. *Inventing the Future.* London: Secker & Warburg, 1963. 231 pp. See, particularly, Chapter 8 "Men and Machines," 103–127.

tioned here, make the short-run estimates of the impact of automation and computer technology, seem bright.

Conversely, in the long run, one *does worry* about these factors. In addition, one worries about the effects of possible saturation in the demand for some goods and services—saturation which produced some of the agricultural surpluses America faced in the past. In the long run one must pay attention also to the consequences that may occur to our increasingly productive technology if foreign producers of raw materials cut off supplies to us and thereby create extensive idle capacity in an automated economy. This may conceivably occur in relation to their own national, developmental needs. It has been estimated [55] that by 1980 the U.S. with 9.5 percent of the world's population, will be consuming 83 percent of the world's raw materials, provided we still have free access to all such sources of supply.

The best way to sum up the differences in viewpoint between the majority and minority views on automation and computer technology is to note the following considerations. The predicted effects of automation will become realities or myths, if men make them so. It is difficult to forecast what men will actually do. What they *could do* is something else again. The application of imagination to the *potentialities* of automation should be of great social concern. A relative indifference to these potentialities is what largely separates majority and minority thinking on automation. An awareness of such potentialities can, of course, help us to reshape the future, thereby determining what shall become myth and what shall become reality.

It is for reasons such as those we have chosen to emphasize above, that we do not feel that the rising employment of the decade, 1956–66, puts the quietus on all arguments which assume a pessimistic outlook for employment as a result of automation and computer technology. The pessimistic outlook may prove to be valid in terms of long-run expectations. Only time and the contingencies of the next few decades will remove thinking regarding the impact of automation on employment, from the realm of controversy.

We therefore wish to close this discussion on a note of compromise. We believe many of the current beliefs regarding automation are psychologically unsound and economically lack a sufficient forward-looking view. We believe that many of these open-ended beliefs are congealing into social myths. If these social myths are brought into focus more responsible attitudes may be formed towards the debits as well as the

[55] This statement was part of the remarks attributed to the Reverend Father Stanislas de Lestapis, S.J., generally considered to be the representative of the Vatican. It was made at the 1954 United Nations Population Conference in Rome. It is quoted on p. 51 of William Vogt's *People*, New York: Hillman/Macfadden Books, 1961, 207 pp. Dr. Radhakamal Mukerjee made some similar observations during the Proceedings of the Sixth International Conference of the International Planned Parenthood Federation.

credits of the second industrial revolution. If this increase in responsibility becomes general, the path for automation to make a better world when guided intelligently, will have been somewhat cleared. After all, few are opposed to automation. It is the abuse, not the use, of the seminal aspects of the second industrial revolution, which is most to be feared.

Until now we have been concerned with some of the expected social consequences of automation. But America has now experienced what was referred to in the Introduction, as a "system break." We have moved from automation to cybernation. It is useful to bear in mind Theobald's [56] distinction between these two terms. In the industrial age which we are now rapidly leaving, human skills were combined with machinery to achieve high productivity. Automation is the most advanced state of this partnership in which ingenious machinery displaces many men and renders many skills obsolete. Automation, however, demands that men with high skills act as overseers for ingenious equipment and the production process which such equipment serves. Cybernation is the term we apply when this same ingenious equipment is run by programmed computers, thus not only eliminating men of rarer skills than those required in automation but also moving closer to work installations in which the needed human beings are very few in number. Cybernation then refers to the direct linkage of automated equipment with the computer rather than with man.

The transition from automation to cybernation raises a host of new problems which were either skimpily touched upon in our first two chapters or not touched upon at all. As a result we now have to take a look at the possible consequences of this most recent of "system breaks," based upon some of the current trends which seem to be developing. Because cybernation represents a drastic historical breakthrough which may force upon us some radical changes in our way of life, it has to be given separate attention. Chapters 3 and 4 will therefore be concerned with the vortex of new dangers and new promises held out to Americans by the industrial spread of cybernation.

Words sometimes fail to be as impressive as pictures. In trying to do justice to the meaning of cybernation, the sense of drama permitted by the human eye, can rarely be captured by an intellectual exposition. The reading of Chapters 3 and 4, could profitably be supplemented by viewing the magnificent documentary, *America: On the Edge of Abundance*. This gripping film will make the promise of cybernation, as well as its future social and economic risks, come alive in a way in which no book, article or chapter can ever hope to do. Chapters 3 and 4, however, will reflect a stock-taking without the attendant drama.

[56] Robert Theobald. "Cybernetics: The Socio-Economic Revolution." *Fellowship.* Special Consultation Issue, May 1965. 6–12, 31.

# 3

# The Sociological and
# Ideological Assumptions
# Underlying Cybernation *

I.

The purpose of Chapters 1 and 2 was to point up the reason for hope and the causes for fear with respect to the potentialities of automation. In addition these chapters dealt with a number of myths with respect to automation. Technological advances have now ushered in what has come to be called cybernation—defined as the combination of the computer and the automated self-regulating machine. Enthusiasm for cybernation is likewise giving rise to myths which may harden unless they are given critical attention. The new myths are somewhat reinforced by certain technocratic thinking which is often ill-informed along economic and sociological lines. What many who hold the more sanguine convictions about the promise of cybernation, lack, is direct and practical experience with recent developments, such as is found in the figure who pioneered in the industrial and managerial possibilities of automation, John Diebold.[1] What the enthusiasts over the promise of cybernation, share with Diebold, is his recognition that technology is primarily an agent for social change. As myths, some of the newer convictions which are developing are an outcropping of what has come to be called *The Triple Revolution*.[2]

* Chapter 3, with adaptations and modifications, has been taken from the following source: Henry Winthrop. "Sociological and Ideological Assumptions Underlying Cybernation." *American Journal of Economics and Sociology.* Vol. 25, No. 2, April 1966, 113–126.

1 John Diebold. *Beyond Automation. Managerial Problems of an Exploding Technology.* New York: McGraw-Hill, 1964. 220 pp.

2 "The Triple Revolution" refers to three separate and mutually reinforcing revolutions which are now taking place, namely, the Cybernation Revolution, the Weaponry Revolution, and the Human Rights Revolution. The first refers to the new organization of production in our time, the second to the fact that new weapons cannot win wars but they can obliterate civilization, and the third to the universal demand for the establishment of social and political regimes in which every individual will feel valued and none will feel rejected on account of his race.

The developing myths concerning cybernation are in part a result of science fiction in technical dress, in part a result of some radical conceptual departures in economic and social thinking by a few economists, and in part the result of conferences which have been held devoted to the social consequences of cybernation.[3]

In evaluating the assumptions of cybernation here I am not declaring either that they are in error or that they are beyond the bounds of possibility. What I do wish to maintain is that if these assumptions remain untempered by institutional realities and by some new and necessary conceptual considerations of an economic nature, they will not prove very serviceable for the task of managed social change. Furthermore, if these assumptions remain unguided by an appropriate social philosophy, a cybercultural credo will remain at best programmatic. Unless detailed blueprints for various forms of needed social change can be worked out by devotees of cybernation, the cybercultural revolution will never enter the realm of *Realpolitik*. There is need, therefore, to examine critically the excesses of enthusiasm which characterize those who are now marching under the banner of cybernation and to suggest some critical remedies which are in order. Enthusiasts for cybernation demand managed change. They are right to do so. Unless, however, our present experts in social management are convinced that it is worth while for them to lend their efforts toward the establishment of a cybernated society, little will be accomplished. These experts are not very likely to be sympathetic unless the excesses already mentioned are toned down and the sobering remedies applied. We shall therefore turn to a discussion of the convictions held by those who are heralding an age of cyberculture and follow this later by a critical analysis of the difficulties which stand in the way of realizing some of the goals toward which social cyberneticians hope to move.

## II. CREDO FOR THE COMING CYBERNATED SOCIETY

The general beliefs held by most of those who are convinced that we are moving toward a cybernated society crop up in several places. Two good sources were some of the papers read at the *Conference on the Cybercultural Revolution—Cybernetics and Automation* (hereinafter referred to as "the Conference") and in the *Manifesto of the Ad Hoc Committee on the Triple Revolution*[4] (hereinafter referred to as "the *Manifesto*"). The overlap between these two sources is so substantial as to warrant

---

[3] Cybernation was the chief theme of the *Conference on the Cybercultural Revolution—Cybernetics and Automation,* held in New York City, June 19–21, 1964. Much of the material in the present paper is based upon the author's notes while attending this conference and conversations with knowledgeable members of the audience.

[4] The complete text of the *Manifesto* will be found, together with commentary by Dave Dellinger and Paul Goodman, in *Liberation,* April, 1964, 9–15.

regarding them as major areas of agreement. We shall at this point, list without discussion, what appear to be the common convictions of many partisans of the coming age of cyberculture.

The theses of cybernation run roughly as follows. (1) Cybernation demands the development of radically new methods in the organization of production. (2) Potentially unlimited output can be achieved by systems of machines which will require little co-operation from human beings. (3) Poverty is no longer necessary in advanced societies. (4) The conventional conviction that reabsorption into the economy of industrial workers displaced by cybernation will always take place, is somewhat questionable. (5) Our current industrial production system is no longer viable. (6) Because of cybernation, society no longer needs to impose repetitive, meaningless, and unnecessary labor upon individuals. (7) The link between work and consumption has been broken and men can now take care of their material wants without having to work. (8) Our institution of currency and credit may have to be replaced by other devices for distributing goods and services. (9) Individuals will shortly be free to achieve self-actualization, status, influence, and prestige from a wide range of activities involving value-systems now somewhat marginal to a society which is almost exclusively preoccupied with production, distribution, and consumption. (10) Government is now in a position to guarantee an income to individuals and families, as a human right, and whether or not work is exchanged for that income. (11) In many respects education, learning, and culture must be drastically revised in content, so that they will relate people to people rather than people to things.

The programs proposed by the signers of the *Manifesto* and which appeared to be acceptable to most Conference speakers include the following. (1) An expansion of our educational system so as to provide for the retraining of the chronically undereducated. (2) Massive public-works programs leading to the construction of dams, reservoirs, ports, water-and-air pollution facilities, and community-recreation facilities. (3) A low-cost housing program to provide approximately one million units per year. (4) Development and financing of rapid-transit systems, urban and interurban, to cope with metropolitan problems. (5) A public-power system built on the abundance of coal in distressed areas, designed for low-cost power to heavy industrial and residential sections. (6) Rehabilitation of obsolete military bases for community or educational use. (7) A more equitable revision of our tax structure. (8) An increased role for the trade unions in negotiating on behalf of workers who are technologically displaced, in bargaining for housing and recreational facilities, in the investment of union funds and in the organization of the unemployed. (9) The use of the licensing power of government to regulate the speed and direction of cybernation in order to minimize hardship and the use of other legislative powers to move as swiftly as possible toward the preceding goals. The preceding programs are proposed for the *transition period* in which we presently find ourselves, a period which is between the dying throes of an economy of scarcity and the birth pangs of an economy of abundance.

Signers of the *Manifesto* have called for managed change. They have called for planning agencies which will collect data necessary to study the social consequences of cybernation, recommend ways of stimulating cybernation in both the private and public sectors, and work toward a socially optimal allocation of human and natural resources. In addition, they want such agencies to work out alternatives to defense and related spending which will be socially functional, and to integrate domestic and international planning, since domestic and world problems now tend to have reciprocal effects on one another. Finally, they want such agencies to bear in mind always that our economic life should be consciously and rationally directed by such agencies which are to be democratically controlled.

Responses to the *Manifesto* have been fairly widespread. One major form of response has been the convening of professional meetings whose purposes were closely related to the convictions of the signers. The Conference, for instance, was typically one of these. In more senses than one, several of the themes of the Conference were elaborations of some of the positions, analyses, and programs proposed by the Ad Hoc Committee. At the same time it is to be recognized that a great deal of novel material was introduced—material lying wholly outside the explicit *Manifesto* of that committee. In a later section I shall restrict myself to some critical comments on the theses maintained only at the Conference —by speakers or audience members—whether these are extensions of the Ad Hoc Committee's position or represent wholly new considerations which are not the concern of the *Manifesto*. However, before doing so, let me emphasize that a good many responses to the lines of concern of the Ad Hoc Committee have occurred independently, some earlier and some later than the date of issuance of the *Manifesto*. Some of these have been critical and some have been sympathetic. These responses are found chiefly in what may be called the avant-garde periodical of ideas although, of course, commentary on these matters has appeared both in liberal and conventional journals. Among these formulations perhaps the items in the following sample are representative: papers by Rousseas,[5] Titmuss,[6] and Rosen [7] in *The Correspondent* (March–April, 1964) and

---

[5] Stephen W. Rousseas. "Automation, Employment and Growth." *The Correspondent*. No. 31, March–April, 1964. 31–44.

[6] Richard M. Titmuss. "The Limits of the Welfare State." *The Correspondent*. No. 31, March–April, 1964. 45–52.

[7] Sumner M. Rosen. "Non-Revolutionary Revolutionists." *The Correspondent*. No. 31, March–April, 1964. 53–59.

by Gans [8] in the same journal (January–February, 1964); a paper by Helstein, Piel, and Theobald [9] in *The Minority of One* (May, 1964); a paper by Hilton,[10] sponsored by the *Fellowship of Reconciliation,* and two papers which appeared in the same issue of *New University Thought* (1963), one by Theobald [11] and one by Keyserling.[12] These few papers represent but a small fraction of the response to the potentialities for a cybernated society. Ideas centering about these potentialities are part of the current *Zeitgeist* in which cybernation is seen as leading society toward a most important and critical juncture.

The themes and concerns of the Conference and indirectly of the Ad Hoc Committee statement are worth continued examination. In the section which follows I should like to indicate those themes of the Conference which, it seems to me, may be headed in the right direction. This will then be followed by an evaluation of what I take to be some of the weaknesses in the position of those who stress the present, overriding importance of cybernation—weaknesses which, I feel sure, will be remedied in the near future as the themes and claims of the cyberculturists receive the hearing and the extended, critical revision which they deserve.

## III. TOWARD THE CYBERNATED SOCIETY

Among the proposals made either formally or *informally* at the Conference which seem to be rooted in a presently genuine but unfulfilled need is the demand that Western education be drastically overhauled. There was genuine agreement among the conference attendants that many aspects of modern education are obsolescent and harmful. A variety of reasons, some related and some otherwise, were furnished to maintain this opinion. Thus programs of vocational training were criticized for training people for jobs which do not exist because they have been cybernated out of existence. On the level of higher education, C. P. Snow's [13] views came to the fore, concerning the imbalance between training in the humanities and training in science. The tendency for educa-

8 Herbert J. Gans. "Some Proposals for Government Policy in an Automating Society." *The Correspondent.* No. 30, January–February, 1964. 74–82.

9 Ralph Helstein, Gerard Piel, and Robert Theobald. "Jobs, Machines, and People." *The Minority of One.* Vol. 6, No. 5, May, 1964. 6–9.

10 Alice Mary Hilton. "Cyberculture in the Transition from a War to a Peacetime Economy." *Fellowship.* May, 1964. 3–9. Also available as a Fellowship Reprint from the Fellowship of Reconciliation, Box 271, Nyack, N.Y.

11 Robert Theobald. "Needed: a new definition of work." *New University Thought.* Vol. 3, No. 4, 1963. 9–14.

12 Leon Keyserling. "What we can do now." *New University Thought.* Vol. 3, No. 4, 1963. 14–26.

13 Charles P. Snow. *The Two Cultures and the Scientific Revolution.* New York: Cambridge University Press, 1959. 58 pp.

tion to exhibit unnecessary and dangerous cultural lag was deplored. One example of this which was emphasized was the alleged futility of economics, that is to say, the impropriety of still leaning heavily upon economic theory which is appropriate for an age of scarcity rather than for an economy of abundance.

A second example of rigor mortis in our institutions of higher learning is the worship of political, economic, social, legal, and historical abstractions and a pronounced tendency to view social processes and the pressures of social change through such irrelevant abstractions. A prime example of this habit in operation is Constitution-worship, consisting of the tendency of lawyers and statesmen to view social change as acceptable only if it is constitutional and to try to obstruct certain kinds of social change as unconstitutional even when they are inevitable. Obviously the proper remedy, as some attendants pointed out, is to change the Constitution, revising it drastically in recognition of Lincoln's remarks to the effect that new times demand new measures and new men. To treat the Constitution as a holy of holies tends to prevent us from seeing it as a document which was quite relevant to an eighteenth-century Enlightenment optimism but which may now possess many features which obstruct a cybernated society awaiting freedom of growth.

Even more importantly, Conference enthusiasts stressed the current need to educate all citizens to the social consequences of science and technology. Only in this way could democratic citizenship assert itself intelligently. It was felt, in addition, that the citizen should be taught more science and be given a larger acquaintanceship with its methods and thoughtways. A better understanding of the scientific method and the scientific attitude, it was agreed, would help to undermine the historical tendency to think in terms of legal, political, social, economic, and historical abstractions. Above all, the college graduate should possess some *nontechnical* understanding of those interdisciplinary research methods which are useful for the study of social complexity. The importance of such methods is already clear from the fact that they have helped to usher in some of the features of the cybernated world which we all now face and some of the features of modern large-scale experimentation and organizational control.

Among the interdisciplinary methods to which we have just referred, one would include such newer modes of analysis as the following: cybernetics, operations research, general systems theory, bionics, simulation theory and technique, information theory, decision theory, game theory, input-output analysis, linear programming, activity analysis, and symbolic logic. Other developments of structural value may, of course, come to the fore over the next decade—developments which may prove of even greater social significance than these. The interdisciplinary areas mentioned are, however, representative of powerful ideas currently at play which are responsible for a good portion of the social change which has recently been our lot. Conference attendants did not expect these newer interdisciplinary approaches to be taught to college level undergraduates, in any technical sense. What apparently was desired was an appreciation in a very broad sense of their content and method and the potential they carried for social change. The *functional understanding* of these areas was clearly a requirement only for the scientist, technician, and specialist.

One distinguished newspaper editor who participated in the Conference stressed the degree to which he was impressed by the cybercultural revolution but pointed out to the other participants the hopelessness of their cause unless they could get their message across to the average citizen. The point made was that a cybernated society would not be achieved without popular understanding and consent as well as sympathy from leadership figures in all walks of life. However, at the present time there is little popular understanding of cybernation and of its social import. Its vocabulary sounds technically forbidding, its ways of thinking are alien to popular black-and-white abstractions, and the problems it tackles and the information it deals with are at present outside the range of interests of the average citizen. Unless these difficulties in communication are overcome in some fashion, those who are knowledgeable about cybernation may find themselves so far in front of the procession that the parade of social change they hope to lead may take an entirely different turn and disappear from view altogether. The impact of cybernation may represent one of the most important phenomena of our time, but if cybernation is allowed to degenerate into an expertise to be thrust upon the citizen rather than a phenomenon to be broadly understood by him, particularly its social implications, it may become only a new form of technical totalitarianism which we may all live to regret.

Some speakers at the Conference also indicated a note of disappointment with democracy, not with the pristine ideals of democracy, but with some of its degenerate, ongoing institutional forms. A number of speakers implied that cybernation made democratic socialism imperative, as the form of society most appropriate to its proper exploitation. Many enthusiasts appeared to agree that democracy's current emphases on intellectual egalitarianism contained the seeds of political and social destruction for a complex society. What some of them appeared to be maintaining was that in some sense the notion that in a cybernated world one man's opinion was as good as another's represents an example of a democratic myth which has outlived its usefulness. The unworkability of our political forms was also emphasized, in that a Congress could not move fast enough to deal with the rapidity of social change now created by cybernation. From some on-the-floor discussion one got the impression that some attendants felt that lawyers, as the class which captures most of our congressional seats, by and large do not have the training or the perspective to understand the features of the contemporary social landscape created by cybernation. Enthusiasts felt that these and other drawbacks to contemporary democracy call for a drastic, political over-hauling in order to accommodate socially to cybernation. In a sense the proposals for new types of planning which are called for by the program of the Ad Hoc Committee on the Triple Revolution would be a step in this direction. So too would be the entire range of proposals called for by that committee under its demand that social change must be managed.

It would not be difficult to take up for discussion various other themes pursued at the Conference, which could easily be supported by so-cially conscious readers with a liberal outlook. This, however, would be beside the point. What is needed at the present time is an honest examina-tion of some of the sins of omission with respect to the difficulties ad-vocates of cybernation will have to face, which were either not mentioned at the Conference or, if mentioned, glossed over. In addition, what is needed is a closer look at some of the tasks which advocates of cyber-culture themselves will have to recognize if they hope to see their efforts attended by some degree of success. Finally, any errors which may permeate the thinking of social cyberneticians must be cheerfully faced. To these considerations, then, we now turn.

### IV. HOW CAN THE COMING AGE OF CYBERCULTURE BE EXPEDITED?

There are certain requirements for success which even a well-intentioned program like that proposed both at the Conference and by the Ad Hoc Committee must meet: Even with current history and technological trends on the side of those aware that cybernation demands a new age and a new type of thinking, these requirements will have to be met.

1. *Designs for Living.*    Neither a cybernated world nor cybernated com-munities will come into existence without some form of precommitment to a given way of life. Hopefully a cybernated world will encourage social pluralism, so that in an age of cyberculture many forms of pre-commitment will capture the hearts of men and women. Order is of the essence in communication and cybernation, and it would be a contradic-tion in terms to talk about a cybernated community or a cybernated world without having a clear notion of the purposes, values, and goals which cybernated order is meant to serve. Thus in a cybernated society men will be forced to examine more closely than they have ever done be-fore the question, "What is the good life?" Attempts to answer this peren-nial question will force men to spell out, with full awareness of what they

are doing, the values which they feel are most worth pursuing. Such answers will also force men to establish their own value hierarchies, which is a sophisticated way of saying that they will be forced to arrange their values in the order of importance they judge these values to have. They will, for perhaps the first time in history, come to appreciate the full force and meaning of the phrase "first things first."

Whatever may be the activities men will be forced to engage in, when trying to make the transition to a cybercultural age, these activities can have meaning only if they are geared to a *design for living,* that is to say, a set of purposes which a cybernated community or a cybernated society sets about to achieve. These purposes themselves may change over time, but a cybernated society will have to find a means of educating men to be flexible in the face of shifts in the spectrum of goals. The *major purpose* of a cybernated society will be the goal of learning how to discover *when new purposes are in order,* learning how to adapt to their current relevancy, and then finding ways of implementing them. The greatest invention of thought, said Whitehead, was the invention of invention. We might paraphrase this by saying that the greatest purpose of human life and the expression of the human spirit may yet prove to be the quest for new secular purposes which augment the quality of life, enhance consciousness, and advance us closer to social perfection.

These purposes may prove to be near or remote. They will depend on social plans which will have to be somewhat analogous to the distinction the economist makes in economic planning, between short-term and long-term economic growth. If cyberculturists are thinking of a works program, of new planning agencies for managing social change only a quinquennium or decade ahead, of the alleviation of stress and suffering caused by problems here and now, then their purposes are proximate. If, however, we are thinking ahead by decades or centuries, we will have to encourage what Margaret Mead has called future thinkings and which she has felt should become a standard part of the educational curriculum. As David Riesman [14] once remarked, we need inquiries on both the level of the here and now and on the level of Utopian thinking, concerning the possibilities of the future. This spirit to some degree is still with him, for Riesman [15] has only recently said

. . . but to tackle at once the withered grass roots of democratic style, with its

14 David Riesman. *Individualism Reconsidered and Other Essays.* Glencoe, Illinois: The Free Press, 1954. 529 pp. See Chapter 5, "Some Observations on Community Plans and Utopia," 70–98.

15 David Riesman. "The Price of Change." *The Correspondent.* No. 31, March–April, 1964. 60–3. In this piece Riesman does not explicitly recommend the need for a Utopian tack, in addition to meeting the practical problems of the here and now, as he does in the item mentioned in footnote 14. However, one can see that he still feels the same way when he asserts that our energies should be engaged on the intellectual frontiers beyond abundance.

complex bases in mutual respect and parliamentary, pragmatic experience, while also seeking national remedies for dislocations of the national economy—these are tasks of a long-run sort for whose accomplishment we need a great many experiments and pilot models. And for these to flower, it seems to me that we need a combination of impatience with things as they are and a long-enduring willingness to see people suffer, to bear disappointment, and to start all over again. The hard-hearted Right can of course not abide this. I hope that the young radicals can (p. 63).

Cyberculturists should not shrink before the charge of being called Utopians for, in all frankness, this is what they will increasingly have to be. They will, however, not be armchair Utopians of the kind largely described by Negley and Patrick.[16] They will be of an entirely different breed, for they will be in many cases scientists and technologists with a genuine interest in and commitment to the humanities and to the quest for social perfection. They will be a breed more desirable than even C. P. Snow's ideal man—the individual who, by his training, has achieved a balance between the natural sciences and the humanities. Even C. P. Snow's ideal did not demand sensitivity to the need for training in the social sciences. This the new breed of cyberculturists seems to promise. Nor, for that matter, did C. P. Snow's ideal demand awareness of the need for moral commitment to alleviate the large amount of human social suffering which we see all about us. Here, again, one can expect to see a great deal of existential concern for the human condition on the part of the cyberculturists of tomorrow.

The long and short, then, of the above stricture is this: The objectives of cyberculture can only be achieved when groups of men can agree on a common design for living, which cybernation can be called upon to implement. A proper and popular educational movement aimed at a needed ideology for cyberculture must make crystal clear to men the social, psychological, and cultural goals which are to be served by cybernation. Anything less than this may degenerate into a form of social disorganization masquerading under the mantle of science.

2. *Programs Versus Blueprints.*   Programs for action, such as those which were put forward at the Conference, are necessary, but clearly they are not sufficient. It is quite true that the initial tasks facing those who would usher in a cybercultural age must concentrate on programmatic objectives. This is mandatory because the initial major tasks are educational ones and constitute problems in communication. Furthermore, there is undoubtedly a leaven of sensitivity upon the part of a large number of scientists and technologists who have not yet been heard from concerning their positions on certain moral issues, problems of

16 Glenn Negley and J. Max Patrick. *The Quest for Utopia. An Anthology of Imaginary Societies.* New York: Doubleday, 1962. 592 pp.

social value and the tasks involved in achieving social justice. Those scientists and technologists who are sensitive must have that sensitivity aroused and crystallized for them in order to enlist their support. A programmatic approach has its greatest value in relation to this task. In devising a proselytizing program we must remember that no voice is wholly lost. The task of communicating awareness concerning the social possibilities of cybernation must be differently handled for a public of scientists and technicians than for responsible laymen.

Once, however, there is strong numerical support from professional quarters, it becomes imperative that social cybernetics proceed from programs for cybernation to blueprints of cybernation. Such blueprints must consist of detailed alternative plans for shifting control of industrial society from a plurality of management corps to a sophisticated, administratively competent and morally sensitive group of planners who can be counted upon to guide the cybernation revolution and to manage change so as to achieve a cybercultural society. Furthermore, such plans must have built-in safety measures to preserve those democratic ideals which are still relevant to our time and, even more, must contain safeguards against all forms of socially and morally undesirable totalitarianism. A detailed blueprint for social change which removed the shackles of control by a plurality of independently acting industrial management bodies only to fetter us to the control of power-loving and socially manipulative technocrats would then become a comic opera for the gods.

The blueprints to which I refer involve many matters. They will call for innovations in institutions of government which are adapted to the mode of production and the relations of production created by cybernation. They will entail the redesigning and replanning of communities, but only after the concept of community itself has been redefined for an age of cyberculture. The most radical proposals which have been made thus far for community and regional planning, such as those of the Goodmans[17] or Gutkind,[18] could prove to be irrelevant for a cybernated society. A cybernated society is likely to encourage community life on a small scale in order to avoid much of the social pathology and alienation which stem from urban sprawl, overemphasis on the cash nexus and excessive commitment to the architecture and landscape demanded by the urban-industrial complex. A cybernated society will require blueprints which show how modern science, technology, cybernetics, and automation can be adapted to small-scale communal existence without sacrificing the more important social, educational, cultural, and scientific advantages which have been the concomitants of the

17 Percival and Paul Goodman. *Communitas. Means of Livelihood and Ways of Life.* New York: Vintage Books, 1960. 248 pp.
18 E. A. Gutkind. *The Twilight of Cities.* New York: Free Press (Macmillan), 1962. 201 pp.

large-scale, urban-industrial complex. I have expanded on this point elsewhere.[19] Some advantageous technologies in this connection are miniaturization and microminiaturization, polymorphic computer setups, small-size units for the exploitation of solar and wind energy, thermal energy of the seas and geo-thermal sources of energy, to name but a few examples. The literature on small industry construction for underdeveloped economies is now substantial [20] and a cybernating society, wishing to adapt some of the ideas employed for the development of small industry in economically backward countries, to small-scale community development in the West, will have few difficulties in this connection.

Blueprints may have to be developed which can provide small-scale communities which are able to cultivate cultural cross-fertilization and ecological interdependency without tying themselves to any type of political subordination to a central source of political power. In a world of this sort ecological interdependency will be achievable only through *intermittent federation* based on a modernized version of the principle of voluntary association. A world of such quasi-independent communities which are, in effect, scientific, intentional micro-communities, can be serviced by stations and power units not within the communities themselves to provide utilities, communication, and transportation. Research and development, freed from considerations of monetary gain, and reinforced strictly by such intellectual motives as curiosity, creativity, social altruism, a passion for managed social change, a love of system and theory, and a commitment to the methods and thoughtways of science, can be set up regionally. The manning of research and development institutions can be a collective function, each community providing talent for limited periods and taking as its payoff priorities in claims to new products and new forms of leisure, travel, and recreation. I strongly suspect that in a cybernated society, morally sensitive to human rights and responsibilities, *many new kinds* of motives will have been developed to encourage participation in the creation of new ideas, new knowledge, new things, new services, and new forms of cultural and

[19] Henry Winthrop. "Bureaucratization and the Rebirth of Community." *American Journal of Economics and Sociology.* Vol. 23, No. 2, April, 1964. 113–30. Henry Winthrop. "Some Proposals Toward Experiments in Peaceful and Non-Competitive Living." *Darshana International.* Vol. 4, No. 2, April, 1964. 74–97.

[20] S. Nanjundan, H. E. Robinson, and Eugene Staley. *Economic Research for Small Industry Development. Illustrated by India's Experience.* Menlo Park, California: Stanford Research Institute, International Industrial Development Center, 1962. 316 pp. This research was done under the auspices of the Stanford Research Institute. The volume was published by the Asia Publishing House, Bombay, India. The reader who is interested in this subject should familiarize himself with the many items in the program which bears the following series title: *Publications of the International Industrial Development Center, Stanford Research Institute, On Small Industry.*

creative activity. The profit motive will, of course, be a museum piece in such a world.

This is clearly not the place to enumerate the many kinds of blueprints which will have to follow the public education programs which will have been developed for the initial stages of the coming cybercultural age. It is the proper place, however, to emphasize for the experts and for all those committed to the vision of a cybernated world that such blueprints must be forthcoming if cybernation is to gain the attention and the respect of the *Realpolitikers* of our time.

This chapter has been on the whole cautiously optimistic about the possibilities of achieving a cybernated society once we get beyond programs and think in terms of economic and sociological needs. However, even if all our economic and social expectations were fulfilled, there would still be five needs which, if not met, might help to prevent the successful creation of a cybernated society: (1) a viable relation for the transition period between present corporate power which controls cybernation and the institutional framework of a cybernated society; (2) the need to develop a type of social and economic planning which is appropriate for a cybernated society; (3) a national understanding with respect to our resource problems which will not disappear in a cybernated society but may, in fact, be aggravated; (4) a workable solution concerning the uses to which the enormous gains in leisure in a cybernated society are to be put; and (5) an understanding and agreement on how to preserve the legacy of our humanistic ideals in a cybernated society, so that the state of technology releases man for activities which are not dictated by the need to keep the society going economically.

It will not be easy to meet these needs because there are certain roadblocks to their achievement. Chapter 4 will therefore be devoted to a discussion of the nature of these roadblocks. Thus the discussions of Chapters 3 and 4, together, will provide us with an assessment of those of our current assets and liabilities which may be relevant to the achievement of a cybernated society.

# 4

# Some Roadblocks on the Way to a Cybernated World*

## I. THE VISION OF A CYBERNATED SOCIETY

With the publication of the *Manifesto* of the Ad Hoc Committee on the Triple Revolution,[1] both popular and professional interest in cybernation has risen markedly and an expanding literature has been appearing. This indicates an increasingly favorable reception to those ideas which are intrinsic to what has come to be referred to as the coming *Age of Cyberculture*. The leading ideas of cybernation have been discussed in Chapter 3.[2] It will be sufficient to stress here only that cybernation, defined as the combination of the computer and the automated self-regulating machine, has broken the link between work and income. According to cyberculturists, if the West is therefore willing to take advantage of the technical and social possibilities inherent in cybernation, certain dramatic consequences must inevitably follow—consequences which will require drastic social and institutional innovation in the future. Let me mention briefly some of these major consequences.

Production in the future will require a new type of social and technical organization, and technically advanced countries, particularly the United States, will have to recognize that only a small percentage of its citizens would have to work at all. Under the new social dispensation promised by cybernation a high standard of living is guaranteed, without any need for the type of backbreaking toil which has historically been recognized as the prerequisite for economic survival. A Great Society is emerging whose dominant characteristic will be leisure for all, and if we have the foresight to use that leisure intelligently, along intellectual, cultural, educational, spiritual, and aesthetic lines, there is literally no limit to what men can accomplish socially. Partisans of the

* Chapter 4, with adaptations and modifications, has been taken from the following source: Henry Winthrop. "Roadblocks on the Way to a Cybernated World." *American Journal of Economics and Sociology*. Vol. 25, No. 4, October, 1966, 405–414.

1 See footnote 2 of Chapter 3.

2 See Chapter 3, pages 60–66.

social and technical possibilities inherent in an *Age of Cyberculture* describe a vision of the human community which surpasses in desirability and novelty anything dreamed of in most of the utopias which have thus far been advanced by thinkers in the West. Such Utopias have always constituted a cultural legacy which has moved most educated people to express their discontent with the imperfect present and have always tended to prompt them politically to try to usher in an improved future, socially speaking.

In July 1964 an *Institute for Cybercultural Research* was proposed by Alice Mary Hilton and described in a document [3] which may subsequently prove of some historical importance. The essential purpose of this new institute was described as twofold:

1. To foster interdisciplinary and multidisciplinary study of: the immediate and future problems and conflicts arising from the acceleration of technology coupled with the continued and increasing lag in adapting social, cultural, economic, political, and other institutions and ethical concepts to new conditions; of the potential created by modern science and technology to create a great civilization and a humane society provided the lag is closed; and of the most practical means to close the lag.
2. To serve as a reliable and independent source of information to government, industry, labor organizations, and other groups and individuals in need of accurate and reliable information, whether they realize their need and consult the Institute or require the institute to make them aware of existing problems as well as possible solutions.[4] (p. 1)

From this statement it should be clear that an important set of new ideas has arisen concerning the future roles of science and technology. Readers of imagination, vision, and knowledgeability cannot fail to be sympathetic to these new ideas. However, there are certain roadblocks to the consummation of the vision of our social cyberneticians—roadblocks which, if not dealt with seriously, could abort the great potentialities of that vision. The need to examine these roadblocks honestly and to face up to their implications is then the purpose of the present chapter. We shall examine and evaluate five of these major roadblocks in the section which follows, in the hope that such an examination and evaluation of the prospects for a cybernated society will prompt an Institute for Cybercultural Research to give these roadblocks more serious consideration

[3] Alice M. Hilton, "Preliminary Proposal to Establish the Institute for Cybercultural Research." Mimeographed separately, 6 pp.

[4] *Op. cit.*, p. 1. The statement continued: "The Institute for Cybercultural Research is named to designate its purpose, *i.e.*, the concern of the founders with the beginning Age of Cyberculture. Cyberculture is the era in human history when the way of life of the society (culture) will be predicated upon the discovery of the science of cybernetics, *i.e.*, the study and knowledge of communications and of the complex relationships within a system of increasing complexity."

and ensure that its proposed research and planning objectives will subsequently take cognizance of them.

## II. SOME ROADBLOCKS IN THE WAY OF CYBERNATION

1. *Cybernation—Master or Slave?* Two immediate practical tasks face cyberculturists, for which they seem to have no plans whatsoever. One is the framing of legislation and proposals for the development of new institutions which will keep the industrial corporation from controlling the uses to which cybernation is to be put. The other is the promulgation of social theories which describe how cybercultural leadership may wrest such control institutionally from the corporate centers of power in a free enterprise system, without falling into a totalitarianism of either the Left or Right. It seems both foolish and naïve to overlook the great historical truth that no group has ever given up its power voluntarily. To expect those in corporate control in our society to do so is absurd. The cybercultural dream will never become a reality without political action, lobbies, pressures, propaganda, and organization. To date experts in cybernation are yoked to the goals of decision-makers who compose what C. Wright Mills [5] has called the power elite. To make matters worse, our institutions—particularly the courts and the antiscientific bias of the legal mentality—will support the continuation of a yoke of this type. The stronger a cybercultural movement should become, the greater will be the legal and corporate resistance it can expect to meet. For this reason continued, large-scale public education, over radio and television and in newspapers and periodicals, will be necessary. To effect these, "cybernation angels" will have to be found who will furnish the needed finances. Even strong support by a small government contingent will still be only moral support, for the social outlook of the corporate empire is, by and large, reflected in the thinking of Congress and in our administrative agencies.

If we assume that entry into the field of the mass communications media has succeeded, then the fight will only have just begun. It is at this point that social cyberneticians can expect to face the struggle to determine whether cybernation is to be the master of, or slave to, our present industrial complex. At that point if the type of legislation and planning whose necessity I have emphasized above is not forthcoming, along with a popular program of education to make them comprehensible to the public, the age of cyberculture will be sufficiently aborted to remain a program only. All organizations which are directly or indi-

5 C. Wright Mills. *The Power Elite.* New York: Oxford University Press, 1956. 423 pp.

rectly devoted to the cybercultural dream will have to create committees to work on such detailed legislation and planning schemes, with or without the help of farsighted, socially conscious members of the legal profession.

2. *Cybercultural Planning.* Many enthusiasts at the conference spoke glibly about planning. What was generally overlooked is the fact that most planning today is either planning for economies of scarcity or planning for better distribution of goods and services within economies exhibiting sectors of wealth and poverty, as in some of the Scandinavian countries. A reading of some of the major works devoted to planning, such as those of, say, Tinbergen [6] or Chenery and Clark,[7] and the reading of articles describing the techniques of planning, such as we find in some of the United Nations publications,[8] will quickly convince the reader of this fact. But cybercultural planning will have to be something entirely different, intended as it must be for economies of abundance and superabundance. Planning will have to have almost an entirely different meaning in a cybernated society which has eliminated poverty and which confers status, influence, and prestige on what a man is and does rather than on what he acquires in the way of wealth and power. If devotees of cybernation intend to plan for a rational and humane society—as indeed they must—they will have to devote themselves *right now* to the development of econometric models and planning techniques based upon acceptable sets of assumptions concerning the cybernated, continuous-flow production of a cybercultural age and the patterns of distribution appropriate to such an age.

Instead of talking about the futility of economics, cyberculturists will have to recognize that many of the processes and phenomena studied by the economist will be basic to all societies from the pre-scientific to the cybercultural. The nature and meaning of such economic phenomena as investment, changeovers in the composite of production, preference schedules, rational distribution and expectation will have to be drastically revised for a cybernated economy, but revised or not, these phenomena will still exist. The cyberculturists will have to recognize that new meanings will have to be given to such concepts as gross national product and production costs if a cybernated society is to dispense with the traditional credit system, a conviction which is now a

[6] Jan Tinbergen. *Economic Policy: Principles and Design.* Amsterdam: North Holland Publishing Company, 1956. 276 pp.

[7] Hollis B. Chenery and Paul G. Clark. *Interindustry Economics.* New York: Wiley, 1959. 345 pp.

[8] See, for instance, in this connection, the following publication: *Industrialization and Productivity*, published by the United Nations, Department of Economic and Social Affairs. Of particular interest will be Bulletins 1, 4, and 5, especially Bulletin 5.

central feature in the thought of the economist, Robert Theobald.[9] In a sense cyberculturists have been hoist by their own petard. Instead of dispensing with economic theory and economic analysis, they will have to recognize that they cannot do without it. They can win only a moral victory—one that derives from switching from conventional modes of economic analysis to new modes of economic analysis. Instead of burying economics, they will have to realize that the corpse must be given a new lease on life. They will be plunged more profoundly into economic analysis than economists are at present, but the economic analysis will be appropriate for cybernated economies rather than economies of scarcity.

Cyberculturists will have to develop, as it were, a new science of "cybermetrics," the econometrics of the age of cyberculture. At the present time those alert to the social potentialities of cybernation are not doing this at all. If, as they insist must be the case, orthodox economic analysis will be irrelevant to the characteristics of a cybernated society, then it is incumbent upon them to lay the groundwork at present for the type of economic analysis and social and economic planning which the cybernated society of the future will surely need. If the knowledgeable and competent academic, business, or government economist is to be convinced of the deficiencies of conventional postures in economics, if he is expected to change the framework of his thinking, he *may do* so when crushed by the weight of a relevant and perceptive technical economic analysis. I say "may do so" because outmoded professional ideologies sometimes continue to function merely as cultural residues. Some economists will, no doubt, be humble before the weight of a cogent and practical cybermetric analysis and reverse their position. Many will probably remain unconvinced and recalcitrant to the end. None, however, can be expected to enter the cybercultural camp unless the new type of economic analysis appropriate to the assumptions of cybernation and to the anticipated characteristics of cybernated economies is made both explicit and substantial. Such analysis at present is not the unfinished business of cyberculture. It has not even been placed on its agenda.

3. *The Problem of Resources.* Participants at the conference, in their enthusiasm for the productive potentialities of an age of cybernation,

9 Robert Theobold. *Free Men and Free Markets.* New York: Crown Publishers, 1963. 203 pp. In order to take care of distribution and purchasing power, Theobold proposes to distribute credit claims on GNP as free goods in a cybernated society. His credit claims would consist basically of two devices: Basic Economic Security Payments for all and, in addition (perhaps in recognition of the fact that Americans can be persuaded to adopt a drastic social innovation only if it preserves the social stratification to which they have grown accustomed), what he calls Committed Spending. This latter, in a sense, provides for the continuation of discretionary income in a cybernated society. The former type of payment will average $3,200 per family, the latter, $10,000, approximately.

allowed themselves to be blinded to fresh aspects of the problem of irreplaceable resources which cyberculture implies. The potentiality for superabundance commanded by a cybernated world would eat up irreplaceable natural resources at a faster rate than they would be consumed if the entire world were to demand certain critical materials at the present U.S. rate of consumption. In order to see what this would mean, I attach a brief table adapted from a fuller table which appears in the *Proceedings* of a United Nations Conference.

*Table 4-1.*     World Reserves of Selected Metals and Minerals, Based on the Assumption
That World Consumption is Equal to the Current
United States Per Capita Rate [a]

| Metal or Mineral | Years of Supply Remaining |
|---|---|
| Iron ore: | |
| Actual | 25 |
| Potential | 74 |
| Manganese ore | 50 |
| Chromite | 8 |
| Tungsten | 34 |
| Copper | 5 |
| Lead | 4 |
| Zinc | 6 |
| Tin | 6 |
| Bauxite | 31 |
| Petroleum: | |
| Proved and indicated | 2.5 |
| Ultimate | 18 |
| Coal | 340 |

*Adapted* from the following *SOURCE: Proceedings* of the United Nations Scientific Conference on the Conservation and Utilization of Resources (UNSCCUR), II, *Mineral Resources,* 4. The full table was presented by Robert A. Brady in *Organization, Automation, and Society,* Berkeley And Los Angeles: University of California Press, 1961, pp. 481. The full table in question is given on p. 47 of Brady's volume.

[a] Unadjusted for population trends.

The data in Table 4-1 refer to years of remaining supply. They were presented at a Conference held at Lake Success in 1949 and published by the United Nations Department of Economics Affairs over the period, 1950–3. Because of their age they are not up to date and should be used with caution. More accurate, current estimates would have to take stock of the amounts of these resources used up since 1949 and new sources of supply discovered since then.

In order to appreciate the significance of Table 4-1 the reader should note that the data shown were gathered at different times and in earlier periods than the present. Consequently the projections shown are not as serious as they would be if the same type of data were gathered today. Brady, himself, notes that they are admittedly incomplete and subject to many corrections. The limitations upon consumption which they suggest can be reversed if *new sources* of exploitable raw materials should be discovered. This, of course, is precisely what happens from time to time. One instance of this is the fact that the sources from which the data in the table were garnered, allowed only 15 billion tons of "potential" iron ore for the USSR at the time, whereas official Russian reports, we are told, were claiming 250 billion tons sometime later. These data uncertainties *change the time* at which the reserve picture will begin to fail the world. They will not change the fact, however, that a reserve picture may emerge *for some materials,* sooner or later, which is as unsanguine as the table suggests.

Clearly the figures in column 2 of this table would be far smaller than those presently shown if the ratio of consumption which would be characteristic of a cybernated world came into play. In fact, some of these figures would definitely dwindle to zero. If this were to occur, then, to the extent that the age of cyberculture would not be universally achievable unless these and other critical materials were in good supply, the enthusiasm of the devotees of cyberculture would be seriously misplaced. The resource problem will be with us even in a cybernated world and even if we begin to tap the resources of the seas. Vogt's [10] formula for the carrying capacity of the environment will still remain an applicable constraint upon human production and ecological expectations. Clearly a successful cyberculture will demand limitations upon population, limitations upon the standard of living, and therefore limitations upon productive capacity as a long-term growth phenomenon. Any detailed realistic planning for the world, executed by the devotees of cybernation, will clearly be valueless unless such planning is sobered by the realities of resource limitations and unless the plans evolved are meshed with projections concerning world supplies of those materials which will be critical even for a cybernated society in the very near future.

4. *Political and Economic Difficulties.* Partisans of the cybernated society do not face up sufficiently to the political and economic problems which cybernation would thrust upon us, with perhaps no more than a few decades notice to adjust to coming events. The information-revolution bids fair to create a very complex society and, perhaps, a world which has thrown up rather hurriedly a variety of new and bewildering institutions. In this complex society that cybernation may generate, how can the issues facing the body politic have much meaning for the average man? If the understanding of the issues facing the national community depends upon the citizen's ability to keep dozens of functionally related variables in mind, in order to achieve a genuine

[10] William Vogt. *The Road to Survival.* New York: William Sloane, 1948. 335 pp.

understanding of a pressing national problem, how will the average man rise to the occasion? The average man usually shows great difficulty in riveting his attention on more than two or three variables *simultaneously* rather than *sequentially*. If the interdependence of the factors which create real community problems are to be understood only in terms of complex modes of analysis—the province of the econometrician—what chance will the ordinary citizen have to understand the complex cybernated society of the future? These modes of analysis are alien to him now. How much more alien will be the more intellectually demanding approaches to his socioeconomic milieu in a society that has traveled far along the road to cybernation!

Even his betters will rely on the computer to come up with decisions and with solutions to problems of national importance. Lacking the training in the analytic skills associated with mathematics, symbolic logic, programming languages like Fortran or its descendants of the future, how will the average man even begin to understand the *methods* by which his community's problems are tackled? How much emotional faith will he have in the computerized results which are meaningless for him unless translated into measures whose direct impact on his life is immediately discernible? And where, in all of this, do we find the political expression of the popular will—the pivot-ideal of democracy? If the grass-roots society forever disappears, if folk wisdom becomes irrelevant to the comprehension of a world he never made and if the "conventional wisdom" is a sociopolitical fossil in the metademocracy of the future, then the average man cannot avoid becoming a political fifth wheel.

He will be a fifth wheel in relation to the political activities and decisions of the social cyberneticians of tomorrow. The political decisions that will be required in a cybernated society which has to live with an accelerating knowledge explosion, cannot depend upon folk knowledge or folk wisdom. In such a complex society, as Boulding [11] emphasizes, what will be needed is a social science which is as taxing intellectually as astronautics. Only in terms of such a social science and its associated types of expertise, can men adapt to the cybernated society to which, it appears, the information-revolution is now acting as midwife. But in such a society the average citizen will be completely left out in the cold and the notion that government belongs to the people will achieve the status of a quaint myth. One has to remember that there is an enormous amount of information now needed to understand one's world. In an indirect sense one can obtain a crude notion of this maelstrom of information which modern man must draw upon by noting the percent of GNP which is due to what has been called the "knowledge industry." This figure runs anywhere from 30 to 43 percent.

[11] Kenneth E. Boulding. "The Knowledge Boom." *Challenge. The Magazine of Economic Affairs.* Vol. 14, No. 6, July/August 1966. 5–7.

*Political disfranchisement and political alienation* from a society he has never made, is then clearly an eventuality which may be an everyday occurrence for the average man in the cybernated society of the future. As Wilkinson [12] puts it

The contention that persons ignorant of technology can function in a democracy to any effect when the society is a technological one is dubious. Understanding is not only a prerequisite of control, it *is* control. We are not living in classical Athens, a society in which informational couplings were, for the most part, weak . . . (p. 23)

But economic disfranchisement will surely come before political disfranchisement. Wilkinson, in talking about Noodles—the middle-class individuals with no special skills—points out that they cannot all sell real estate or insurance, once they are dispossessed from more pertinent skills and occupations, by advancing cybernation. When our middle-class Noodles begin to show up on the relief rolls, the political repercussions will be far more serious, says Wilkinson, than they were when we tossed middle-aged coal miners, packinghouse workers, teenagers, Negroes, and Puerto Ricans on the junk heap. What plans will a cybernated society make for absorbing the gradual, occupational obsolescence of our Noodles during a period of economic transition?

Sylvia Porter [13] quotes Buckminster Fuller in this same connection. Fuller thinks the rate of obsolescence of all workers—production and service workers alike—is so great that 50 years from now the word "worker" will have disappeared from the American language. But, at least, Fuller has a plan, even if it is only a far-out one, for dealing with this rapid labor obsolescence. He would have industry grant fellowships to individuals to go to school, to learn, to explore, to invent, and, perhaps, thereafter to contribute to society in some way. If a youngster had no academic aptitude, Fuller would advocate that he be given a fellowship to "study" fishing. He might teach us something in this area that we never knew before. Fuller has not, of course, worked out the details of such an Elysian economy. Perhaps no basis can be found for such an economy. And then again, maybe it is something that can be done in the future when affluence is overwhelming. In learning and exploring, says Fuller, lies the real wealth of the future. Those who learn are those who will contribute to the world's wealth.

Cyberculturists must come up with plans for political and economic adaptation to the economic heaven and affluent cybernated society which they envisage. They may be "wild" plans or "temperate" ones, economically informed plans or economically half-baked ones, and technologically

[12] John Wilkinson. *The Quantitative Society or, What Are You to Do with Noodle.* Santa Barbara, California: Center for the Study of Democratic Institutions, 1964. 32 pp.
[13] Sylvia Porter. "Future 'Workless' World Can Concentrate on Increasing Wealth." *The Tampa Tribune,* September 16, 1964.

feasible plans or technologically absurd ones. But they must come up with *some* plans for effecting a politically democratic transition and an economically humane changeover, if their visions and their claims are to be taken seriously.

5. *Cyberculture and Existentialism.* Existentialists may differ in many respects, but most of them share a few postures in common. These are a concern for the individually unique and a fierce love of freedom for the individual qua individual rather than as a component of a social aggregate abiding by certain rules. In addition they recognize the major importance of feeling in the human condition and exhibit an ever-present awareness of the role which the subjective and the inner dialogue play in experience. Existentialists are naturally suspicious of those who think in terms of abstractions, even when these are the paraphernalia of various forms of technocratic ideology. The cybercultural framework for social change and the prevailing modes of thought which characterize devotees of cybernation are very much anti-existentialist in this sense. Cyberneticians, interested in social transformation, thus far are tending to think in terms of aggregates rather than in terms of individual differences. Their technological passions in this sense seem to flare up more fiercely than they do for other types of technicians who are enthusiastic over the social possibilities for creative altruism in science and technology. They see men in terms of social aggregates and social processes, thereby tending to lose sight of the fact that the individual human beings involved do not enjoy being manipulated as inanimate entities.

Above all, they have neglected the role which feeling will play in human affairs. The neat social designs which human reason and applied science create and the neat technocratic categories into which individuals are allocated in the model building for a cybernated society both overlook the tragic sense of life. Social cyberneticians also seem to be overlooking the need for individuals to find personal meaning as well as social meaning in life, the need to relate to others more deeply than perhaps the themes of a cybernated society may encourage in the initial throes of its technocratic successes, and the need to relate to others in ways which may seem alien to the good citizen of the cybercultural age. It may prove to be the case that a cybernetic society will be flexible enough to make a place for the fast-disappearing individuality which many no longer mourn. The tendency, however, for cyberculturists to think in terms of grand theory, aggregate modes of analysis, and sets of individuals who are both depersonalized and cyberculturally bureaucratized does not augur well for the future relationship of men and women of feeling and sensitivity to the world of computerized decisions. I strongly suspect that heartbreaks await cybercultural planners who may be flabbergasted to find that human beings will reject certain forms of salvation when it is handed to them on a silver platter. This heartbreak can be avoided if cybercultural planning makes more provision for the expression of the life of feeling—even irrational feeling—than it appears likely to do. Man does not live by bread alone. He may also, of course, never learn to live by reason alone, whether in the form of regulatory computers or strategic, technological intelligence. This is as it should be.

Not all the vast amount of social change which we can expect as a result of the impact of science and technology, will derive from cybernation. Space technology which now plays so important a role in scientific research is likely to bring about social changes which will be quite different from those deeply involved with the progress of computer technology. Types of social change which may derive from advances in space technology, are also of great interest to us. A perfect example of the types of new technology, resulting from research devoted to the conquest of space, was furnished by a recent conference held under the auspices of the National Aeronautics and Space Administration.[14] In this one conference alone, developments which might be germane in the future to American industry and our civilian economy, were discussed. All of these developments had emerged from research which had been preoccupied with the problems surrounding the exploration of space. They included such research areas as fabrication, materials, electric power generation, lubrication in difficult environments, liquid-metal technology, cryogenic and superconducting devices, ion and plasma technology and instrumentation for measurement and control. These new developments do not by any means exhaust all the frontier areas of research in space technology, which are likely to have a decisive impact on society in the future, when they receive industrial and economic expression. They are sufficiently representative, however, to illustrate the claim that we can expect much forthcoming social change to have its roots in the discoveries flowing from efforts to develop space technology, both currently and in the recent past.[15]

[14] *Conference on New Technology.* Cleveland, Ohio: Lewis Research Center: Scientific and Technical Information Division, *National Aeronautics and Space Administration,* June 4–5, 1964. 156 pp.

[15] In this same connection—space technology—and with reference to still other important types of technologies which will have a substantial bearing on the creation of social change in the decades ahead, the reader should consult the following: 1. John McHale (editor). *2000+. Architectural Design* (London). February 1967. 101 pp.; and 2. John McHale. *World Design Science Decade 1965–1975. Document 6. The Ecological Context: Energy and Materials.* Published by *World Resources Inventory.* Carbondale, Illinois: Southern Illinois University, 1967. 136 pp.

# 5

# The Space Sciences
# and Social Change*

I have chosen to deal with the effects that I believe space science and space exploration will have on three matters that I regard as of unusual importance. The first has to do with the effect that certain aspects of space science will have on one of America's current and important industrial practices, planned product obsolescence. The second is concerned with an important possible use to which communications satellites may be put in dissipating international misunderstanding and increasing the fund of good will among nations and cultures over the globe. The third and most important of the three is the increased possibilities for social change, social experimentation, and the improvement in human relations in the not-too-distant future that are inherent in space exploration and human settlement elsewhere in space. The particular aspects of them that I have chosen to emphasize are aspects and emphases that, to the best of my knowledge, have either received no treatment elsewhere or have received treatment by others in a fashion that is quite different from that which I have given them.

## I. SPACE TECHNOLOGY AND PLANNED
## PRODUCT OBSOLESCENCE

In recent years we have heard a great deal about an economic phenomenon that has been christened *Planned Product Obsolescence*—the industrial habit of ensuring that buyers will accept consumer durables with a useful life far less than that which current science and industrial technology can provide. One of the contradictions that inheres in a free-enterprise economy is the conflict between the ideals of providing service

* Chapter 5, with adaptations and modifications, is taken from the following sources: Henry Winthrop. "The Space Sciences and Social Change." *Journal of Human Relations*. Vol. 12, No. 1, First Quarter, 1964, 127–141, and Henry Winthrop. "Space Colonization and the Quest for Community." *Dalhousie Review*. Vol. 46, No. 2, Summer 1966, 233–248.

to the consumer and of seeing to it that our productivity, measured in terms of Gross National Product, shall be forever on the increase. This latter ideal entails either expanded markets for whatever comes out of the industrial hopper or expanded consumption within those markets that have already been established. When foreign markets do not expand fast enough and the extra volume of goods and services that we have produced are not taken up by domestic demand, unemployment increases, prices fall, and capital investment declines. This threatens stagnation and, when severe enough, even collapse of the economy.

One means of getting the consumer to absorb unexportable increases in the volume of GNP is to increase the speed of dysfunctioning of consumer durables—a fancy way of saying that if we define operationally a *unit of service* obtainable from a consumer durable item, then more units of that item will have to be purchased and consumed per unit service as time goes on. If prices remain stable or if they decline at a rate such that the total cost to the consumer per unit service rises with the passage of time, this will enable the manufacturer to dispose of a large portion of the increase in domestic goods that cannot be absorbed by foreign markets alone. This industrial makeshift represents one form of what has come to be called planned product obsolescence, a practice widely bemoaned by manufacturers themselves.

Typical results of this unhappy industrial habit are razor blades that can serve perhaps for only two good shaves, automobiles whose parts wear out much sooner than is necessary in terms of modern automotive engineering techniques, and radio and television sets that require both repairs and replacements earlier than is warranted in terms of the length of life and efficiency we could bestow on their components. Similar examples could be supplied for other durable items of many major American industries.

There are other forms of planned product obsolescence not considered here. One is to get the consumer to part with an item that still has a large part of its useful life before it in order to purchase another that will confer upon him an increased measure of social status. Another is a result of competition and is highly desirable. This occurs when industry tries to make a model of an item that will do what the existing market model does more efficiently or more cheaply, or both. It is the first unhappy and undesirable industrial habit, that puts a premium upon shoddy work and is under indictment almost everywhere, that is our concern here. What then does space technology have to do with this matter of planned product obsolescence? More than is apparent at first glance. Let us see why.

It is now recognized that the space technology of communications satellites holds the promise of revolutionizing our currently existing communications industries. If we are to believe such men as L. V. Berkner, the impact of space technology will be felt on such processes as radio, telephone and television transmission of messages sent by the teleprinter, wirephoto and radiophoto, and on still other but lesser-known means of communication.[1] The impact that space technology, in the form of both passive and active relay systems, is likely to have on all of these may result in the creation of one or more new industries. The number of radio channels suitable for long-distance communication by presently existing technologies is severely limited. Transmission by cable is likewise limited and quite costly. All this can be changed by facilitating communication through the use of properly oriented, suitably designed, and efficiently equipped communication satellites. Telstar was merely the first of these that was put on a commercial basis. The efficiently equipped communications satellite of the future will probably condemn Telstar to that graveyard of those technologies that reflect crude beginnings, namely, The Smithsonian Institution, provided our crude beginnings in communications satellites can ever be recovered and prevented from cluttering up the skies.

Space technology is affecting planned product obsolescence, thus, by demanding component parts of electronic circuits that must achieve a high reliability in performance and, even more importantly, a very long life. Communications satellites may have to last for decades. If anything goes wrong in a communication satellite, no repair work or replacement can be done, or the cost of such repair work and replacement would be prohibitive, and the operation would be both risky and impractical. Barring unforeseen technologies of self-repair and replacement for communications satellites of the future, we shall have to pin our faith on components of lasting durability. In this connection let us note that the Soviets have now developed a technology which minimizes the need for maintenance of parts in space. The Russians have developed a nuclear reactor, capable of being used as a power station in space, which requires a minimum of maintenance in space as a source for long-term power supply. This nuclear reactor, called the "Romashka" or "Daisy" reactor, achieves its advantage because it has no rotating parts.

This requirement of high reliability will mean that the users of capital goods—in which category I think we can legitimately classify all types of space hardware, but particularly communications satellites—will demand production specifications that contravene an industrial philosophy of planned product obsolescence. The demand that component parts of delicate equipment be highly reliable and long-lasting will also have to be made for artifical satellites intended as space probes for nearby bodies and that carry equipment for continuously recording a variety of

---

1 L. V. Berkner. "Are Space Probes Worth It?" 33–9. In *Issues of the Sixties* (Leonard Freedman and Cornelius P. Cotter, editors). San Francisco: Wadsworth Publishing Company, 1961. 412 pp. A reprint from *The New York Times Magazine*, August 28, 1960.

data to be relayed back to earth. The same demand must be anticipated for unmanned space ships that will be expected to land on the moon and on other bodies in the solar system, only to see if successful landings can, in fact, be achieved. Demanding standards of reliability for the coming age of robot technology can also be foreseen. We have to look forward to robots that can collect samples of various kinds of substances and gather various kinds of data, after they have emerged from a space ship that has landed at its celestial destination. Such robots will then have to televise back to earth pictures of objects or substances, if this has been made technically feasible by some sort of an orbiting relay system. They will also have to transmit data readings by some sort of a long-distance communications system. High component reliability and durability will also become pressing necessities when we want *unmanned* space ships to land, pick up samples of various substances, accumulate data for a given period, and then be capable of relaunching themselves to earth, perhaps through a present timed signal, while carrying their prizes with them.

Finally, and of current practical urgency, the *manned* space ships that will presumably follow the unmanned will have to be blessed with highly reliable circuitry, subassemblies and components that are long-lasting in nature. This demand will, of course, be inevitable where human lives are at stake. The occupants of manned space ships, because of their unusual abilities and the expensive training that has been necessary to equip them for their tasks, represent almost irreplaceable resources. We cannot afford to lose the enormous investment that such persons and their space ships represent through the failure of one or more components of their space vehicle. Component reliability and durability must then become one of the most essential requirements for space technology and space research.

One consequence of all this emphasis on excellence in craftsmanship and design is that thousands of workers will become directly familiar with good, industrial workmanship and that millions of citizens not directly connected with space activities will be educated in a philosophy of *planned product durability*. It will further mean that engineers' ideals and engineers' dreams of high performance standards, admiration of good workmanship for component parts, and knowledge of extended life for complex assemblies will all come to the forefront. It will also mean that the type of industrial production associated with space technology will never give rise to the shoddy and the quickly dysfunctional with the loss of professional self-respect that usually accompanies the aiding and abetting of jerry-built goods. It will finally mean that all those associated with the production and design of space equipment will not have to wrestle continually with the moral problems that accompany productive activity in which the profit motive supersedes the fulfillment of contractual obligations to the buyer and also supersedes the highest scientific and professional ideals. In short, at least in those industries associated with space technology, it means the eclipse of planned product obsolescence forever.

Can we then expect that industrial countries, operating under free-enterprise ideals, will allow a double standard of industrial morality to exist in their economies? Do we really believe that when the capital goods needed for space technologies, instrumentation and activities of every sort, have entered the era of mass production—perhaps under some type of United Nations planetary coordination—that this will have no effect on the consumer durables industries? The question is, of course, a rhetorical one. I believe that the intelligent citizen of the not-too-distant future will stage a buying revolt, with respect to consumer durables, until the standards of planned product durability, which will then be so characteristic of the space goods industries, will be applied to the consumer durables industries themselves. When this socioeconomic phenomenon takes place on a large scale, planned product obsolescence will go. When it does, all our Western economies that now function in terms of what the economist W. W. Rostow calls high mass-consumption will have to be revamped on an entirely new institutional basis.

The problem that will have to be met is that of planning for and coordinating a series of objectives that at present do not cohere too well. These objectives include the maintenance of high industrial productivity, the achievement of a longer life for consumer durables, population control, the satisfaction of the profit motive, and the ability to maximize human energies and human ingenuity within the framework of our industrial system. This will have to be done without producing waste, without slowing up the rapid pace of industrial change, and without altering our designs for living. Admittedly this is a tall order, and I do not envy the social experts whose responsibility it will be to deal with social problems of this complex nature. But one consequence does seem to be in the offing. Space technology and space activity should result in some drastic institutional and economic changes, some pervasive changes in our notions of a functional standard of living, and in the eclipse forever, let us hope, of planned product obsolescence. Thus do great economic trees from spatial acorns grow.

## II. COMMUNICATIONS SATELLITES, SEMANTOGRAPHY AND INTERNATIONAL UNDERSTANDING

My second topic of concern has to do with *one way* in which communications satellites in space may be so exploited as to increase universally the fund of international good will in our time. The effort to achieve international understanding *is in part a function of a common language.*

Needless to say, we have none such today. Any modern language can serve as propaganda for a given way of life, whether that of the West or that of the Communist East. As a result, for a long time to come, we can expect that no *existing* language will be allowed to take "squatter sovereignty" and become the first international language deliberately adopted in the hope of achieving a common global understanding.

The international artificial languages, like Esperanto, Ido, and Volapük, have required intense effort and some linguistic background for adoption only by an educated elite. Even Interglossa and Interlingua, much of which can be read at sight by most educated people, still assume a familiarity with the linguistic roots of various languages, particularly Latin and its derivatives. What would be most useful is a language of symbols, a great part of which could immediately be understandable by all peoples, that required hardly any instruction and that was capable of extension to some of the abstract ideas and concerns of modern man. If such a language could be found, it could be used for international communication and, hopefully, understanding through the instantaneous, *visual* transmission of messages in its terms, using telecommunications systems like Telstar and its coming progeny. Such a language being visual, and therefore relayable, would also have the advantage of being immediately receivable on the screen of a receiving set anywhere. It would be easier to transmit information via the communications satellite in such a language, and far less costly than to try to transmit the same information via the printed word. The presence of such a language, together with the prospects of communication by space satellites, would force the competition for reception to go from the objective of blocking information and propaganda to trading information and propaganda. Ideas would have to slug it out, as it were, trading the punches contained in their information content on the principle, "Let the best relayer win."

Is there a universal language of symbols now available for such use? There is. C. K. Bliss,[2, 3] an Australian, had set out to realize the dream of the philosopher, Gottfried Wilhelm Von Leibniz, namely, to produce a symbolism that would provide a system of universal communication. Leibniz, himself, christened such an international language a *characteristica universalis.* Bliss was convinced that he had achieved this in the form of a symbolism that is called *Semantography.* It is an auxiliary, simple Picto-Ideography for interlinguistic communication. It is intended not only for people who do not understand each other's language but

[2] An example of a few symbols which Charles K. Bliss feels can be used as part of a universal language, is given on p. 78 of Oliver L. Reiser's book, *The Integration of Human Knowledge* (see footnote 4 of this chapter). The material on semantography, dealt with in this chapter, is based *in part* upon the discussions of this language, scattered throughout Oliver L. Reiser's, *The Integration of Human Knowledge.*

[3] Charles K. Bliss. *Semantography, a non-alphabetical symbol writing, readable in all languages.* Sydney, Australia: Institute For Semantography, 1948. 3 Vols. 700 pp.

(and this is perhaps equally important) also for scientists, technicians, and businessmen who cannot communicate with one another. Lord Bertrand Russell, a logician and mathematician as well as the twentieth-century's best example of a universal mind, praised highly the possibilities that seem to be inherent in Semantography. He is one man whose opinion should carry some weight in this matter.

Bliss and his supporters believe that Semantography is the answer to an international-minded idealist's prayer. The inventor of Semantography had for a long time been fascinated by cuneiform and picture writing. He made a study of the ideographs of the Chinese, Babylonians, and Egyptians. In these studies he even included the cave paintings of Aurignacian man. Bliss's objective was to separate out, if possible, from all picture writings any unitary elements of symbolism that they might contain. By analyzing the ideographic elements of symbolism with which he became familiar, Bliss succeeded in limiting the number to 100 symbol elements that could be used by hand or with a special typewriter and could be understood by everyone who was, in any sense, familiar with them. This offers a kind of literacy to millions of persons throughout the globe who have not had a formal education of even the most elementary sort. It is the considered judgment of some thinkers that peasants everywhere could master Bliss's *Primer for Children*.[4] Semantography, therefore, could become not only an invaluable aid to the technical assistance programs of specific countries or of the United Nations but, what is even more important, it could be used for purposes of disseminating important news and information all over the globe, thereby hopefully increasing the fund of international understanding and good will. It is felt by many who have become familiar with Semantography that its units of symbolism can prove of real worth in the realm of generally accepted human relations and can be used as a basis for communication in relation to the common needs of peoples of diverse cultures. By extending its development over the course of time, it might even prove useful in communication that is concerned with matters involving high-level abstractions.

In the present context, however, I am suggesting that televised visual communications, using communications satellites, could take full advantage of so important an invention as Semantography. The period of learning would be short for all. The effort required to learn Semantography, either within the schools of each country or via spatial communications using a United Nations channel, would not be very taxing. At the same time no current language is a casualty if space technology suc-

4 This judgment is made by Oliver L. Reiser in his book, *The Integration of Human Knowledge,* Boston: Porter Sargent, 1958, 478 pp. Dr. Reiser also refers to the primer mentioned in this chapter. However, the author has been unable to locate the standard publication data with respect to the volume by Bliss, namely, *Primer for Children.*

ceeds in making an international language of Semantography. The jamming of messages becomes a highly impractical affair because of the lead time that will probably occur between presentation of a program and the time required to succeed in jamming a visual message telecast from great distances in space. Most important of all, the peoples of the earth can begin to communicate with one another in earnest—politics or no politics—and with or without the accompaniment of the physical presence of the communicants. In the long run, this may reduce the amount of international misunderstanding and ill will. Should this possibility become a reality, we shall owe an immeasurable debt of gratitude to the space technology which made it possible. It would then become a dramatic triumph of good will in which the technological product of man's newest ideas will have combined with a technique of communication which is among the oldest of man's artifacts, to reduce social and cultural parochialism. In so doing it may provide that millennial type of understanding which, until now, has seemed to be only an idle dream.

If we are thinking of a common language *for developed countries only*, then a drastically different picture emerges. It would then become possible to develop a universal computer language which could be relayed by communications satellites to any country on earth and translated into the natural language of the receiving area. That this possibility for widespread international understanding through an international computer language, is not a pipe-dream, was indicated, to some extent, by the fact that very similar ideas were advanced by David Sarnoff, Chairman of the Board of the Radio Corporation of America, in a talk he gave before the 1964 American Joint Fall Computer Conference (October, 1964). In that talk Sarnoff—speaking about the computer of the future—had this to say:

> Its vocabulary will extend to thousands of basic words in the language of its country of residence, and machines will automatically translate the speech of one country into the spoken words of another. . . .

## III. THE INTERSPATIAL TRANSPORTATION OF HUMAN ECOLOGIES

We turn now to an additional possibility for increasing international understanding and good will. This is the possibility for utopian social experimentation in space on sites settled by human beings. I propose to examine the feasibility of such a dream.

Historians and sociologists are accustomed to interpreting conflict among terrestrial cultures in one of two ways. One of these may be called The Top-Dog View. The other should be called The No-Hope View. Let us briefly examine each of these in turn.

According to the first mode of interpretation—The Top-Dog View—some one terrestrial culture sooner or later may become globally dominant. This may occur either through military penetration short of nuclear war or through peaceful, cultural conquest. In either case the top cultural bidders at the moment appear to be either a *pax Americana,* a *pax Anglo-Saxonica* or a *pax Sovietica.* For the time being a *pax Sinica* does not appear to be in the offing because China is not yet an immediate threat. Each of the three real possibilities which we have mentioned, bothers certain prominent national groups no end. The French, of course, fear a pax Americana. Knowing the American's fondness for Coca-Cola, they see this beverage as the symbol of all that is coarse, unimaginative and materialistic in our culture and they are determined to resist our urge to spread *The American Idea* which they refer to as "la coca-colaization du monde," that is, the *coca-colaization of the world.* While they are not looking, however, let us hope that they do not succumb to the *vodkaization* of France.

The Latins, both in Europe and south of the border, dread a pax Anglo-Saxonica more than they dread a pax Americana. This is because of the widespread stereotype they hold that Anglo-Saxons are bent upon a paranoid mission to remold the world a little closer to their hearts' desires. Many intelligent Latins have taken Henry L. Mencken's lampoons of the American scene to heart and have also taken very seriously our own criticism of our national foibles. They do not realize that the gripe —particularly of the intellectual variety—is a national pastime. As a result Latins are deeply convinced that the Anglo-Saxon is an incorrigible Puritan in many ways. As for themselves, they prefer the fleshpots of the bacchanalian revel and the sidewalk cafe. Since they hold Puritanism to be beneath contempt, they will tolerate a pax Anglo-Saxonica only over their own dead bodies.

In the West the most general fear is that of a pax Sovietica. The Communist way of life is judged to be completely inimical to our ideals and to our democratic designs for living. We may be willing to consume *shashlik* and *caviar* but we intend to avoid the consumption of any Marxist ideas and of Soviet habits of living, until the last breath, if need be, has expired from the body politic. We may not be as enthusiastic as the Russians are over the prospect of class-bred societies withering away, but we utter twenty-six *paternosters* every night, metaphorically speaking, in public prayer and hope that dialectical materialism, proletarian literature, and party lines in genetics will wither away—and fast!

The No-Hope View which some historians and sociologists cultivate, assumes that no single terrestrial culture will ever succeed in becoming dominant. The No-Hope View assumes that all contemporary cultures will continue to exhibit a venomous antipathy towards one another rather than move towards a planetary, cultural melting pot. In this view international understanding and good-will will be achieved only by a minority educated elite, the great majority of us on this planet being doomed to be forever embedded in the unimaginative parochialisms and provincialisms of our own cultures. This is seen as inevitable as a result of the xenophobic propaganda furnished by our political masters. Advocates of the No-Hope View are strongly convinced of the longevities which lie ahead for our current provincialisms which, if anything, have been aided and abetted by the emergence of the new nations and which will be furthered by those cultural groups still seeking a place in the firmament of national sovereignties. Global travel has failed to make much of a dent upon the virus of cultural egocentricity because of the fact that such travel is limited. The number of people who will have had the broadening advantage of travel, will be awfully small, relatively speaking, in relation to those billions doomed to a narrow cultural perspective as a result of the population explosion which now perturbs the intellectually sophisticated West. In addition many who go abroad seek only confirmation of their national pride. If, of course, the No-Hope View should be confirmed by the passing of the years, then certainly our "time of troubles" which has been a lifelong concern of the historian, Toynbee, bids fair to be prolonged.

An increasing use of social imagination may prove that the above dichotomy is a false one. The difficulties of cultural conflict are in part associated with mass societies and the high degree of political centralization and administrative bureaucratization that they thrust into our daily lives and activities. Centralization and bureaucratization thrive on certain laws of large numbers that were never even dreamed of by either Tshebysheff or Markoff. The effects of these laws of large numbers can be wiped out or, at least, diminished by certain types of social experimentation. I am referring here to what certain writers call "the intentional community." Precisely what is meant by this phrase?

An intentional community is deliberately formed by a group of relatively few individuals with the express purpose of achieving a pre-planned way of life. Such groups hope to realize in action some design for social living that has been well thought out and that, hopefully, will reduce the extent of alienation in human relationships. The psychologist, Burrhus F. Skinner, for example, has furnished us with a description of one such mythical but possible community in his well-known novel, *Walden Two*. In this mythical intentional community, understanding and good will are achieved by the prevalence of what I am tempted to call the rat's-eye point of view. Skinner has faith that the laws of operant behavior will do for man what religion, time, and history have thus far failed to do for him. I do not wish to enter into the merits and weaknesses of his position. But there are also many actual intentional communities throughout the world today, some of which are successful and going concerns. Any community design for living subscribed to and practiced by numbers of people that embodies ideas for living together in greater happiness and mutual trust and understanding is an intentional community.

In passing it is interesting to note that Robert Theobald anticipates that a cybernated society may give rise to a special type of intentional community which he calls a "consentive." Consentives will consist of productive groups formed by individuals who will come together on a voluntary basis simply because they wish to do so. Members of these consentives will produce goods which will not compete with those produced by cybernated firms. Instead, they will produce custom-designed goods which are fast disappearing from an economy based upon the principle of mass production.

Members of intentional communities tend to be decentralist in their political and social outlooks, although cosmopolitan in their ideals. They invariably reject the consequences that would follow if the Top-Dog View proved to be correct, precisely because they believe that a world culture, regardless of its vintage, must intensify the evils of centralization and bureaucratization. They clearly reject the No-Hope View—a rejection that is self-evident in any experiment with intentional community. In the past, intentional communities tended to withdraw from the social and institutional complexities of their host milieus—complexities that they felt were unamenable to group control and were inescapably bound up with the increasing complexities of science and technology, themselves. This was equivalent to throwing out the baby of scientific and technological advantage and progress with the bathwater of such evils as social conflict, excessive centralization and standardization, demands for unreasonable amounts of social conformity, and ubiquitous and unenlightened administrative bureaucracy. This was, of course, a mistake, since there is no necessary conflict between social idealism and social altruism, on the one hand, and scientific and technological progress, on the other. Space sciences make it possible to look forward to the "scientific intentional microcommunity"—an intentional community engaging in daring experimentation in community living and human relationships, precisely by exploiting all the available scientific and technological means for ensuring the success of such experimental ventures. Since the members of such a community would tend to be both cosmopolitan and scientifically educated, altruistic as well as practical, they would have a much greater chance of succeeding in achieving social and cultural pluralism than almost any other group that one can imagine. Such social and cultural pluralism is almost a guarantee of the kind of understanding and good will that we now seek on an international scale and that is so conspicuously absent terrestrially. *Internationally-minded* intentional communities, however, whether scientific in outlook or not, would have a difficult time of it if they sought to set up house-keeping in the middle of the fratricidal atmosphere that now rules the terrestrial roost.

But suppose in the decades that lie ahead or in a century or two it became feasible technically and socially for hardy bands of altruistic and scientifically trained individuals to establish scientific intentional micro-communities on the moon or elsewhere. This would appear as an ideal only if the advanced social thinkers of the age were convinced that the fratricidal social and political atmospheres on terra firma did not provide much chance for terrestrial success in such experimentation because the greater the success achieved by such experiments, the greater the likelihood of social and political interference. Many scientists are looking forward to lunar cities as a feasible future possibility. Should such lunar settlements ever become a joint venture of existing nations, each of which is given the right to furnish a quota of its own scientists in order to help forward their realization, we would have all the ripeness for social experimentation except the intentional dream, itself. This last has a good chance of emerging also from the hearts and minds of any group of lunar pioneers, once they are freed from home directives and are on their own. In fact, home directives will not be very meaningful on the moon or on a far-away planet where intelligent, kindly and civilized souls face the task of constant adaptation to new physical and social circumstances. Planetary social pioneers are hardly likely to signal terra firma for advice.

Even without the prefabricated, intentional dream, it seems highly likely that the first settlements on the moon or other heavenly bodies will result in the unintended appearance of scientific intentional micro-communities. Their formation may prove to be an intrinsic social necessity. It may even prove to be the case that the world organization assigned the task of planetary exploration and colonization in the future may officially decide to subsidize settlements in space for purposes of social experimentation just as much as for purposes of scientific advance. That these latter two objectives are likely to go well together in the future seems almost assured. It seems equally likely that such extraterrestrial settlements, considering the enormous financing they will require, will have to be underwritten by national or international support. The only possible exception to this that can occur is if several multimillionaires or billionaires in the near future should share a common, intentional dream —a not very likely prospect—and jointly finance such ventures themselves. In general the terrestrial costs of such ventures could not possibly pay off in commercial terms, as we use this phrase today. The payoff would have to be chiefly in terms of the increase in man's knowledge and, hopefully, the improvement of society.

I have said nothing about time expectations in relation to the probable realization of extraterrestrial settlements. Excessively enthusiastic scientists on both sides of the Iron Curtain envisage the lunar colony as a possibility towards the closing years of this century. More conservative and cautious scientists, both in the U.S.A. and the U.S.S.R., play it safe and assert that the lunar colony may be a practical possibility perhaps sometime in the twenty-first century. In these matters realities generally make the science-fiction writers appear to have been unimaginative and overcautious, and soothsaying is a risky business because technological progress accelerates very rapidly and the stock of scientific knowledge appears to double every ten years. We should therefore not be surprised if the timetable of expectations in these matters shrinks in the decades that lie ahead. Should the possibility of lunar colonization become a reality, let us say no earlier than in the first years of the twenty-first century, this perhaps will be just in time. Roughly 40–50 years is the estimated time period which some specialists in the social sciences think is required for China to become an economic, industrial, and military threat. If they should be right—and considering that Mao Tse-Tung and Chou En-Lai are not showing any signs that they are prepared to let a hundred cultures bloom—then the technical feasibility of lunar settlement will perhaps have come none too soon.

Let us suppose, however, that as a result of several early and successful efforts to land isolated astronauts on the moon, a group of technically trained, socially idealistic, and inspired men and women have gotten together in order to try to establish a quasi-social utopia on that satellite. We shall make no assumptions as to how they are financed. We shall assume also that such a body of men and women have expressed an intense wish to establish a scientific intentional microcommunity on the moon in the hope that it will serve as a pilot experiment and guide for the dissolving of political and social follies on terra firma. We shall further assume that such a group of pioneers are moved somewhat by the Wellsian dream of someday creating men like gods, through social training and personal aspiration. What are the technical possibilities for success in such a venture? What does space technology, space research, space exploration, and scientific imagination have to say with respect to the feasibility of such a venture?

When the quest for community is translated into terms of colonization on other celestial bodies, certain fundamental considerations have to be emphasized above others. The first of these is that man, in the not-too-distant future, may be able to transport an entire human ecology to other heavenly bodies. Technologically a human ecology on the moon becomes possible because we can transport packed earth, fertilizer, a simulated terrestrial atmosphere, and the necessary flora and fauna to maintain an edaphological balance, while yields per unit of a given depth would probably be greater than on earth because of the absence of insect pests and plant blights of every sort. Lunar agriculture can simulate the terrestrial variety of such technologies as hydroponics and chlorella culture or might develop new technologies locally which in a lunar situation could render materials found on the moon's surface fertile. In fact, man can transport equipment for utilizing subsurface material on the moon so as to render it productive, perhaps by the addition of chemicals and chemical fertilizers that may be processable from materials to be found upon the moon itself. Man now possesses the possibility of seeding the moon or any other habitable planet, for that matter, with plants of terrestrial origin, since he can create or transport terrestrial atmospheres isolated from local atmospheres or from the local absence of any atmospheres at all. The solution of the problem of nutrition other than by import from earth can surely be licked eventually, provided only that we are willing to disregard prime costs.

The atmospheres to which we have referred in the previous paragraph—and which would be necessary for growing plants—will be atmospheres which, we are assuming, will be confined within a lunar city that has been enclosed beneath a man-made dome. We shall shortly describe this type of city. There is reason to believe, however, that someday the moon *as a whole* may be given an atmosphere such as that of the earth's, and this, in spite of its low gravity. That this is a future possibility may be seen from the following words of Theodore Gordon.[5]

. . . even on the moon, where gravity is too small to hold the atmosphere indefinitely, it may someday be possible to build an atmosphere which will never escape, by covering its furthest extremity with a retaining gaseous membrane. What a resort it could become, with every motion almost effortless, weather tailormade, with month-long days and deep peaceful month-long nights. As suggested before, the moon could become the busiest port the world has ever known, with freighters heading out to the planets, quarantine stations set up for returning cargo and passengers; the commerce of the solar system flowing by our satellite. What a lot of work man—earth's man—has left to do. (p. 175)

We are, of course, assuming that scientific, intentional microcommunities will have been established successfully and will have demonstrated the feasibility of various experimental notions of community, long before the kind of take-over envisaged by Gordon.

A second necessary consideration for lunar settlement is that man

5 Theodore J. Gordon. *The Future.* New York: St. Martin's Press, 1965. 184 pp. Gordon is now director of advanced large launch systems at Douglas Aircraft Co. and was formerly chief engineer for the upper stage of the government's Saturn rocket. In 1962 he was selected by *Life Magazine* as among the one hundred "red hot" young Americans—leaders in all fields of endeavor. He served at Cape Kennedy (then Cape Canaveral) as a test conductor for early Thor rocket launches and was test conductor of the world's first lunar probe in 1958, described in his earlier book, *First into Outer Space,* written in collaboration with Julian Scheer.

will likewise possess the means for transporting any existing social structure elsewhere or for initiating on another celestial body the social expression of any new ideas concerning the nature of community. If, in the minds of any group of intrepid, socially minded cosmonauts, the ideals to be given social expression far outweigh the biological and technical difficulties that will be initially encountered, then the sacrifice of terrestrial standards of mass culture and gracious living are not likely to daunt them at all. It will be possible for small groups of men to establish entire facsimiles of existing terrestrial culture which are composites of existing terrestrial cultures, and where these parts will cohere and maintain a given value-system. Best of all, of course, will be the possibility, to which we have already alluded, of establishing new designs for living via intentional communities adapted to the small-scale use of science and technology.

The notion of a lunar base or a lunar city is familiar to scientists and scholars on both sides of the Iron Curtain. We have already stressed the fact that within a matter of less than a hundred years, and perhaps only several decades, the technical possibility of establishing a lunar city may become a full-fledged reality. Donald Michael, a social psychologist with a background in the physical sciences and author of the Brookings Institution report to the National Aeronautics and Space Administration entitled "Proposed Studies on the Implications of Peaceful Space Activities for Human Affairs," has commented on the possibilities of lunar colonization.[6] He feels that the most important technological essential for this venture is the space ship run by nuclear power that is obtainable from fusion processes. The second most important essential, as Michael sees it, is the rapid development of robot technology on an unprecedented scale—a technology that can supply robots for exploration and specialized work functions both before and after men land on the moon. The third most important essential is the development of psychological tests that will identify those individuals who are capable of living together, both in the forbidding psychological milieu of the space ship and the even more forbidding, shut-in environment of the lunar colony. These elite souls, besides medical screening, would be subject to this psychological screening-out. But in addition, there could be the self-screening that resulted from their commitment to some form of intentional ideal. We shall suppose that at some not-too-distant date all these requirements will have been met. Let us then picture a lunar colonial establishment as imaginatively previsioned by the Russian scientist,

---

[6] Donald N. Michael. "Prospects for Human Welfare. Peaceful Uses." 31–63. In *Outer Space. Prospects For Man and Society* (Lincoln P. Bloomfield, editor). Englewood Cliffs, New Jersey: Prentice-Hall, 1962. 202 pp.

Nicolas Alexandrovich Varvarov. President of the Astronautical Institute of the U.S.S.R. and consultant to the armed forces of that country.[7]

A good many of the moon's craters are natural sites, as our real estate developers might put it, for land development. One of these, for example, would be the famous lunar crater of Eratosthenes. A specially built and hermetically sealed car would take the freshly landed space traveller to the lunar city, presumably located in Eratosthenes or in another of the moon's many craters. This car is hermetically sealed and air conditioned in order to avoid having its passengers roasted by direct solar radiation while they are covered by the metal envelope that constitutes its shell. The city to which they will be travelling is a city of glass and plastic domes, possessing an artificial atmosphere, gigantic greenhouses, helioelectric stations and, for that matter, everything else that will have been found necessary to accommodate living terrestrial organisms to the basic changes required for adaptation to lunar conditions.

I shall not enter here into an extended description of the technical details of construction of a lunar city, as these are generally given by knowledgeable writers. Such prospective details are to be found in tentative technical plans incorporated in professional books and periodicals, although the technologies that are actually likely to be employed in the near future are probably regarded as classified information at present. Here let us simply state the functions of the multi-layered transparent domes, some consisting of glass and others of plastics, that are expected to house the lunar city. The elastic glass roof of such a city must allow the same proportion of solar rays to come through as that which reaches terra firma from the sun itself. This glass roof, together with its auxiliary operating devices, must also capture and transform solar radiation into electrical energy, and the proportion of solar radiation that must thus be transformed is almost exactly equal to the proportion of the sun's rays that is caught by the earth's atmosphere. Finally these same glass roofs will have to serve as protection against falling meteorites, since these do not burn up in the nonexistent atmosphere of the moon. Some meteorites will succeed in crashing through these glass and plastic coverings. For this reason some devices will have to be employed that will restrict damage to certain zones.

The shrubs and vegetables of a lunar city will come as somewhat of a surprise to the space traveller. Although these will be familiar, they will not be easy to recognize. Because of the lesser force of gravity on the

---

[7] Chapter 28. "In the Lunar City." 213–6. Based upon an interview with Nicolas Alexandrovich Varvarov. In *Russian Science in the 21st Century* (Sergei Gouschev & Mikhail Vassiliev, editors). New York: McGraw-Hill, 1960. 222 pp. The material of this chapter, describing the nature of a lunar city, has been adapted from the ideas of Varvarov.

moon, we are told that a normal radish will achieve the height of a date palm and that an onion will have a stalk thirty feet long. Whether onions of this expected lunar size will keep the inhabitants of these cities in a permanent state of tears, we are not told. Within the lunar city the space traveller will find aluminum, glass, plastic materials, water, and soil. All these materials will be capable of being either mined or processed on the moon itself. In the long run, aluminum can be mined economically on the moon. Glass and plastic materials can be made in lunar factories. Water can be extracted, we are told, from the depths of our satellite, thus taking care not only of human needs but also of the humidity needed for cultivation of the soil or for use in hydroponic cultivation. Oxygen and nitrogen are equally obtainable from lunar materials so that we can create an atmosphere that simulates our terrestrial one and that is equally healthy. The lamps that will burn during the long lunar nights will be fed from batteries that, at the same time, will supply heat for residential living and power for industrial production. It is also expected that local atomic power stations will be available to supply energy in addition to that captured from the sun.

Such a lunar city will not only be economically self-supporting but will be able to manufacture synthetic fuel for rockets departing from earth as well as rockets themselves. Assuming that rocket-propulsion by nuclear power has already been achieved, raw materials for nuclear power may eventually be found in lunar deposits. The needed equipment for exploiting these may likewise eventually be producible by a lunar colony itself. Wharfs for cosmic ships can be attached to lunar cities. Lunar cosmodromes will themselves become the starting point of long-distance space journeys. Such then are some of the technological possibilities for lunar colonization envisaged by scientists. In short, lunar colonies will eventually be able to become what the economist calls a "closed economy" and what the sociologist and philosopher call an "open society." [8]

Of such stuff can be our dreams of space and society. We can only hope that the discoveries of space technology and the results of space exploration may be translated into social forms constituted of nobility and grandeur—forms that are completely undreamed of at present. Such are the possibilities of the activities of space research and exploration.

These three themes constitute, in my opinion, possible and important effects that space technology and space exploration may have upon human society. Social prediction in such matters always seems far-fetched at the time of its inception, but scientific realities and social change may make our most daring dreams prove to have been too conservative. The

[8] Some of the technologies alluded to are also described in Gordon's volume, pp. 158–61. *Op. cit.*

reader's judgment is as good as my own, perhaps better. I shall not retreat from my predictions, since I sincerely believe in their practical possibility. Proof or disproof of their correctness lies in the limbo of time. One thing is certain. The relation of space science and space exploration to human society augurs changes so drastic that the type of social and economic relations we take for granted today will seem almost infantile to the men of tomorrow and will, no doubt, raise a smile on the lips of future historians. This is to the good. Our fondest hope should be that the directions of social change that will be imposed by the space sciences will carry the promise of human relations more in line with eternal peace and the brotherhood of man.

# SUMMARY OF PART I

The purpose of the five chapters of Part I has been to show the variety of ways in which science and technology make their impacts on our lives. We have singled out for attention automation, cybernation, and space technology. We do not wish to convey to the reader the impression that there are no other major changes in science and technology which will affect our social future. The three we have selected, however, are both dramatic and representative and, perhaps, closest to our lives.

A seminal use of automation and cybernation will probably call for *indicative planning*[1] in the near future. Indicative planning begins when government economists select a rate of growth that is reasonable for the nation's economy. This growth rate is related to forecasts of the growth of the labor force and the rate at which labor productivity can be expected to increase at full employment. Data of this sort are combined with past experience and future policies and from this combination technicians project broad outlines of the economy for several years. This projection is examined, criticized, and reshaped by key representatives of industry, labor, agriculture, consumers, government officials whose decisions affect the economy and academic experts. Representatives of the public, together with unions, speak for the *unrepresented, the unemployed, the unemployable, and the nonaffluent.* When a general consensus has been achieved the projection is translated into action programs for industries and government departments.

A thoughtful consideration of the facts and arguments presented in Part I should explain and dramatize the overwhelming role which science and technology will play in our lives for the indefinite future, but,

[1] For a discussion of *indicative planning,* see the following: Bernard Nossiter. *The Mythmakers*. Boston: Houghton-Mifflin, 1964. 244 pp.

at the same time, should also serve to suggest some of the ways in which this is likely to happen. The material presented should be taken less as prophecy and more as a venture in social interpretation, that is, an appraisal of possibilities whose beginnings are sprouting in our very midst.

# II

# Culture, Leisure, and Education

## ORIENTATION TO PART II

If we move towards a cybernated society this will automatically guarantee an Age of Leisure. Leisure may be used fruitfully or pathologically. If used pathologically men may find themselves more unhappy in a world in which toil has been considerably reduced than in the world of The Protestant Ethic, of whose inhabitants Thoreau could say "the mass of men lead lives of quiet desperation." If such a world is to be supplanted by one in which the majority of men will lead lives only of noisy rather than quiet desperation because they have not learned to use leisure fruitfully and maturely, then nothing will have been gained and much will have been lost. Thus we can see that the problem of leisure, that is, the problem of how to use it maturely and fruitfully for most people, can be one of the major social problems in the decades which lie ahead. This problem of leisure arises, of course, only in technologically advanced societies.

Part II has, therefore, for its purpose the examination of certain major aspects of this problem of leisure. There are numerous aspects of this problem. We have chosen to deal only with the following considerations: the problems of leisure and mass culture in a cybernating society; the pitfalls and deficiencies of middlebrow culture; the examination of the meaning of culture and the formulation of a philosophy of culture for an age of science and technology; and the functions of the teacher and the intellectual in the transmission of culture and in making culture relevant to the good life, particularly in technological societies.

The over-all purpose, then, of Part II will be to tie together the existing relationships of those aspects of civilized life, which we refer to as culture, leisure and education. These relationships in their own right are of central importance in the lives of most intelligent and sensitive men and women. They are also of importance in setting the stage for Part III which is devoted to an examination of the effects upon our lives of having to adapt to a world whose social complexity increases day by day.

# 6

# Leisure and Mass Culture in the Cybernating Society*

## I. FORMS OF LEISURE

The problem of leisure is receiving increasing attention. How will Americans use their free time as the amount of such time increases with the reduction of the work week? The four major forms in which leisure time is used today are *rest* or *recuperation, relaxation, recreation,* and *renewal*. By *rest* we refer to time used for recovery from physical or mental fatigue caused by, e.g., work, ill health, sorrow, or extended worry. By *relaxation* we refer essentially to the use of free time to escape boredom either by a change in the pace or type of one's activity. The individual who, perhaps, has been working hard for hours, goes to the movies, tunes in on radio or television, joins a bowling team, takes an adult education course or joins a choral group. The new activity is *mentally* relaxing even though it may be more strenuous physically. By *recreation* we refer to a use of free time in which an activity is enjoyed for its own sake rather than to reduce or eliminate the ennui produced by one's daily routine. The usual methods of obtaining recreation are sports, games, hobbies, play, and sociability. By *renewal* we refer to time used for the expansion of intellectual, spiritual, and cultural horizons, which the individual may find taxing but which in a sense serve to unfold his potentialities and enlarge his appreciation of life. The enlargement of horizons is most likely to come via study, scientific research, creative activity in the arts, religious meditation, "participant" travel versus "observer" travel, and so on.

Two of the preceding four forms of leisure, namely, *recreation* and *renewal*, require special comment. Let me first take up recreation. *Games* and *play* are not to be identified solely with such activities as playing cards or playing scrabble. People play games even more frequently in the

* Chapter 6, with adaptations and modifications, has been taken from the following source: Henry Winthrop. "Leisure and Mass Culture in the Cybernating Society." *Journal of Human Relations*. Vol. 13, No. 1, First Quarter 1965, 93–109.

sphere of human relationships and these games take up a fairly large fraction of adult, free time. They emerge as a result of role-playing, role-expectancy, and role-strain in the lives of most adults, particularly in middle-class life.

Berne [1, 2] has developed a thesaurus of 36 such games broken down into seven major categories: Life Games, Marital Games, Party Games, Sexual Games, Underworld Games, Consulting Room Games, and Good Games. In order to get the full flavor of games as a recreational device let me illustrate three of them here. A *marital game* may be one which two people may utilize to sustain a frustrating or unrewarding life. One favorite form of marital game is "Frigid Woman," in which one of the two parties provokes an argument, leading to anger and alienation of feelings, in order to avoid sex. A *sexual game* occurs when A provokes sexual reactions in B and then, as in the particular sexual game called "Rapo," acts as though he (or she) is the innocent victim. A *consulting room game,* played by a patient with a doctor, has for its objective the task of avoiding a cure. This form of a consulting room game is called "Psychiatry." Another form of a consulting room game is called "Wooden Leg" and enables a patient to avoid responsibility by claiming illness, or insanity, for example. All of the preceding games must, *unfortunately,* be classified as recreational forms of leisure.

Caillois [3] uses a classification which is wholly different from that of Berne's but which is equally applicable to modern adult games which are employed for a recreational use of leisure. Caillois classifies games four ways: games of competition, chance, mimicry or simulation and vertigo. These are further classified by the amount of tumult they arouse and the amount of rulemaking they require, but the important point is that it can easily be shown that much adult recreational game-playing can, in the last analysis, also be allocated to an appropriate category within Caillois' classification, as well as Berne's.

In a way *renewal* is the equivalent of striving to fulfill the Greek ideals of *paideia*. Let us make clear what the proper content of the Greek ideal of "paideia" is. The term, *paideia,* possesses a meaning which sums up chiefly the content of the English words "civilization" and "education." The Greeks, in contrast to many other peoples and nations, past and present, believed that men advanced in civilization, not through the acquisition of power or wealth, but by educating themselves. Their great masterpieces—tragedies, epics, histories, speeches, philosophical works—are distinguished by the fact that they aim to bring to fruition our most

[1] Eric Berne. *The Structure and Dynamics of Organizations and Groups.* Philadelphia: J. B. Lippincott, 1963. 260 pp.

[2] Eric Berne. *Games People Play. The Psychology of Human Relationships.* New York: Grove Press, 1964. 192 pp.

[3] Roger Caillois. *Man, Play and Games.* Glencoe, Illinois: The Free Press of Glencoe, 1961. 208 pp.

distinctive human potentialities. They are preoccupied with encouraging what Maslow [4] would call "self-actualization." In addition, the term, paideia, also meant for the Greeks the desire to cultivate the ideals of "sophrosyne" or sweet reasonableness and "spondaitos" or appropriate seriousness.

More important, however, was the fact that in addition to insisting that culture and education enabled men to enlarge their horizons intellectually, spiritually (in the sense of value-seeking) and aesthetically, the Greeks also felt that culture and education possessed a second purpose which was just as important as the first one, if not more so. This second purpose was one which emphasized that culture and education were also social, both in their nature and in their consequences. The Greeks expected the cultured and educated man to do everything he could, according to his lights, to improve his community and to contribute his talents and services to the solution of its problems, to the fulfillment of its needs and to the formulation of such ideals as would contribute to a richer culture and to a social order which would be more just and more humane. In short, a truly cultured and educated man made every effort to see to it that—before he passed away—his community would be a better one than he had found it. The improvement he left behind would, hopefully, have been brought about *in part* by the contribution of his own efforts and the generosity with which he applied whatever talents he possessed to that improvement.

The ideal of *paideia* could be cultivated in depth because the civilized and educated Greek had some pretty sharp notions of what constituted the good life; therefore both ideas and politics could be viewed critically from that standpoint. This critical posture is unavailable to the members of such an institution as The League of Women Voters because, in spite of the social worth of this group, political issues and proposals are discussed within a limited framework. By this we mean that a notion of the good life allows us to think of different rosters of social value each of which is presumably achievable within different types of social structure and different types of social philosophy. Obviously, it would be some kind of questionable sociocentrism to assume that the good life is attainable only within a democratic, political, institutional and economic framework. The questionability of this assumption can be raised when we take note of the existence of clear-cut public philosophies of the good life in such countries as Sweden and New Zealand which pursue a *socialistic* outlook and India which pursues a political outlook which has properly been described as *democratic socialism*. In an organization such as that of The League of Women Voters, political issues and proposals are most likely to be discussed within the

[4] Abraham H. Maslow. *Motivation and Personality.* New York: Harper, 1954. 411 pp.

framework of a conventional, democratic philosophy. If portions of such a philosophy should be outmoded for any reason, there would be little tendency for the members of this organization to question our allegiance to such outmoded ideals. A challenge, however, to their most deeply cherished values would have been accepted by the civilized and educated Greek, influenced by the ideals of *paideia*, without batting an eyelash. In making this assertion we must, of course, recognize that the democratic credo in the Greek city–state did not have the same meaning and objectives in all senses, which that same credo has for us.

The ancients were deeply persuaded that the content of such modern expressions like *civilization, culture, tradition, literature,* and *education* are *not* distinct from the objective historical structure of a nation's spiritual life. In the United States politics and social values are largely separated from considerations such as these, and our national activities in all of these five areas are likewise compartmentalized. By contrast, the opposite of such separation and compartmentalization occurs in the USSR in the name of "socialist realism" and the still omnipresent Stalinist philistinism which regards the writer as an "engineer of souls." Work intending to influence a reader's thinking and feelings in each of the five categories I have mentioned, is expected to assume the correct ideological-political positions. But this sense of involvement in the Communist world likewise fails to reflect either the Greek ideal of *paideia* or any bastardized version of it.

The expectation that ideas and ideals should have a bearing on a nation's spiritual life is a most creditable one. But when that nation's way of life is not, itself, subject to reexamination, modification, renewal or overturn, then one's involvement with that way of life is pathological and occurs in a spirit which is quite opposite to the ideals of *paideia*. The truth of this will be conveyed fairly quickly to any reader of a work concerned with contemporary communism, such as the fine book of readings edited by Swearer and Longaker.[5]

## II. THE LEISURE-TIME DILEMMA OF AMERICANS

Americans are familiar with the leisure-time use of rest (recuperation), relaxation, and recreation. Renewal or *developmental leisure,* however, is a relatively alien concept to many Americans. We are expected to see the value of an activity before we can give it our blessing. Anyone can see the value of recuperation, relaxation, and recreation. The first is medically recognized, the second is seen as a psychological necessity in order to make sure that work and responsibilities do not "get us down"

[5] Howard R. Swearer and Richard P. Longaker (editors). *Contemporary Communism. Theory and Practice.* Belmont, California: Wadsworth Publishing Company, 1963. 405 pp.

and the third satisfies our sense of gregariousness, sharpens our skills at social adjustment, and keeps alive the spirit of play in a world in which work and responsibility are the dominant leitmotifs. Renewal, concerned basically with ideas, with enriched aesthetic perception and social feeling, with personal growth and the sharpening of a sense of social justice and community responsibility, is another matter entirely. The results of self-development in these senses of the term "renewal" are difficult to notice and are even more difficult to understand, unless one is, himself, fairly well-cultivated in these respects. As a result developmental leisure to the unimaginative, the unfeeling, the thoughtless, does not seem to have a visible payoff function. Also aiding and abetting American indifference to developmental leisure is our historically deep-rooted anti-intellectualism.[6]

One very important reason for our national, relative indifference to developmental leisure is the fact that *mass culture* provides substitutes which demand less effort for the hard work which would be involved if we seriously pursued the ideals of *paideia*. We cannot be devoting all of our leisure time to rest, relaxation, and recreation. We regard it as imperative, however, that we provide ourselves with pursuits which furnish the form but not the substance of developmental activity. This aim is guaranteed by the entire gamut of activities which are subsumable under the rubric, "mass culture." This is not the place, of course, to discuss the findings with respect to mass culture and the analyses which have been undertaken of this phenomenon (see references 7 through 11 below). Two aspects of mass culture, however, must be emphasized here—aspects which seem to diminish the prospect that Americans will use their free time for the purposes of developmental leisure—*homogenization* and *kitsch*.

When these two aspects of mass culture are predominant in the forms of leisure pursued by the individual, they lessen considerably his ability to discriminate between uses of leisure which will promote renewal and uses which will not. When such capacity for discrimination is reduced, a real loss has been incurred. Because homogenization and kitsch are so germane to certain major technological developments which will be discussed in the next section and which presage a new world-a-

---

6 Richard Hofstadter. *Anti-Intellectualism in American Life*. New York: Alfred Knopf, 1963. 434 pp.

7 Bernard Rosenberg and David Manning White (editors). *Mass Culture*. Glencoe, Illinois: The Free Press & The Falcon's Wing Press, 1957. 561 pp.

8 Eric Larrabee and Rolf Myersohn (editors). *Mass Leisure*. Glencoe, Illinois: The Free Press, 1958. 429 pp.

9 Richard Hoggart. *The Uses of Literacy*. Boston: Beacon Press, 1961. 319 pp.

10 Norman Jacobs (editor). *Culture for the Millions?* Princeton, New Jersey: Van Nostrand, 1961. 200 pp.

11 Russell Lynes. *The Tastemakers*. New York: Harper, 1949. 362 pp. See particularly Chapter XVII, "Highbrow, Lowbrow, Middlebrow."

coming, so far as leisure is concerned, they must be separately treated.

Homogenization refers to the failure to discriminate among the values of the different materials brought to the reader's or listener's attention. Thus an issue of a popular magazine will devote an equal number of pages to the following features: famous stars of the stage and screen who have made a comeback from alcoholism, courtship customs in the islands of the Pacific, recent discoveries in nuclear physics which promise to revolutionize our understanding of matter, the political views of retirees who live in Bellyache, North Dakota, and the latest hobbies of teenagers in Harlem. The significant is lumped with the sensational, the lasting is coupled with the transient, the noble is married to the debased. The presentation and style tend to imply that everything is just about as important as anything else and that the educational and cultural value of one feature is just about the same as any other.

A similar phenomenon occurs during news broadcasts. With no change of tone the announcer will slip from comments on an earthquake and tidal wave which destroyed 20,000 lives in northern Japan to the observation that Stan Musial sprained his leg in the ball park in today's game and may be unable to play for several days. In the same flat and deadpan voice he will remark that during the first six months of this year one million children died of starvation in underdeveloped nations and that a waitress in Hollywood accuses Rock Hudson of being the father of her child. About the same amount of time will be given to all news items. It matters not that one news item seems to carry the threat of an uprising and civil war in Bolivia while another suggests only that women's skirts will be an inch shorter this year. Everything has the same momentous significance or the same boring unimportance.

MacDonald [12] has furnished us with an excellent illustration from *Life* magazine of what homogenized reading fare looks like. He says

> *Life* is a typical homogenized magazine, appearing on the mahogany library tables of the rich, the glass cocktail tables of the middle class, and the oilcloth kitchen tables of the poor. Its contents are as thoroughly homogenized as its circulation. The same issue will present a serious exposition of atomic energy followed by a disquisition on Rita Hayworth's love life; photos of starving children picking garbage in Calcutta and of sleek models wearing adhesive brassieres; an editorial hailing Bertrand Russell's eightieth birthday (A GREAT MIND IS STILL ANNOYING AND ADORNING OUR AGE) across from a full-page photo of a matron arguing with a baseball umpire (MOM GETS THUMB); nine color pages of Renoir paintings followed by a picture of a roller-skating horse; a cover announcing in the same size type two features: A

---

12 Dwight Macdonald. *Masscult & Midcult*. New York: *Partisan Review*, 1961. 78 pp. The British use the term, "trivialization," where we use the term, "homogenization." For a very valuable discussion of trivialization, see the following: Philip Abrams. "Radio and Television." In *Discrimination and Popular Culture* (Denys Thompson, editor), Harmondsworth, Middlesex: Penguin Books, 1964, 199 pp.

NEW FOREIGN POLICY, BY JOHN FOSTER DULLES and KERIMA: HER MARATHON KISS IS A MOVIE SENSATION. Somehow these scramblings together seem to work all one way, degrading the serious rather than elevating the frivolous. Defenders of our Masscult society like Professor Edward Shils of the University of Chicago—he is, of course, a sociologist—see phenomena like *Life* as inspiriting attempts at popular education—just think, nine pages of Renoirs! But that roller-skating horse comes along, and the final impression is that both Renoir and the horse were talented. (pp. 12–3)

*Kitsch* is the term we apply to those products of mass culture in which all the aesthetic and intellectual work is done for the recipient. The message is built into, rather than drawn out of, the product. Let us illustrate what this means by reference to a novel or play. The author or playwright has thought and felt deeply about some problem or condition. He has so organized his experience and his material, so chosen his words and phrases, and so distinguished between what he takes to be relevant and irrelevant, that usually the distinct message and mood which he wishes to convey has been well achieved. The reader or spectator, however, will not experience the message and the mood, as intended, unless in some substantial measure he works through the material being presented, as the author or playwright has done, and unless he keenly senses the dilemmas as these have been felt by author or playwright. When, however, one views a movie, let us say, which is a canned version of a novel, the spectator is, in effect, told what to feel or think, by the wooden cliches put into the mouths of the actors, by the tricks and montage of the camera work, by the splicing and reorganization of the cutting room. Often the effects upon a main character of some of the ongoing action and circumstances, are produced for the moviegoer by telling him what he ought to be thinking and feeling and this is done through the remarks of the actors themselves.

Likewise, a radio or television drama may take a sensitively done play and denature it to suit the tastes of an uncultivated audience— usually by eliminating words and action involving complexities of message and feeling. To make up for the significant, excised material, a commentator will tell the audience between the acts and scenes not only what the characters are supposed to think and feel but also what the audience is supposed to think and feel. Thus, in the case of the cinema, the sweep of symbol and allegory of the original novel is replaced by the visually concrete image of the screen. Intellectual depth in the radio or television drama is eliminated for an artificial simplicity of treatment and falsification of plot, locale, and character, which bear little resemblance to the events which they are supposed to mirror. The consumer of mass culture must never be emotionally taxed or swept up in nuances of mood and conflicts of personality which are not a familiar part of his own daily life. The objectives and techniques of mass culture must flatten intellectual and moral complexity, so that dilemmas are seen in terms of moral blacks and whites. If a classic is brought to the attention of a mass audience, its meaning must be either explained in a corrupted and distorted fashion or it must be explained away entirely. This, then, is *kitsch*.[13]

Just as there is a *"kitsch"* of high culture and high art, so there is a *"kitsch"* in the life of the mind and the spirit. Any efforts of education which hope to create understanding without intellectual strain in the student, without developing habits of intellectual organization and analysis, are *"kitsch"* in this sense. Likewise all the efforts to play at culture by providing students with rapid surveys of literature and the arts are equally doomed. This is *"kitsch"* of the spirit which hopes to convey the existentialist content of frustration, suffering, disappointment, human struggle, and shattered and renovated ideals, through abstractions rather than through personal experience. None of the passion and power of great art, none of its capacity to probe into the motivational grounds of personal striving and to convey the gap between our real and our alleged motives, can become part of the spiritual warp and woof of any individual who has not experienced significant tensions which have been worked through. Such growth tensions cannot be provided by what we now call "gracious living." Nor can gracious living establish a vital center nor promote the full expression of a personal idiom.

It is such lack of experience that makes it utter folly to expect a boy who has thus far been interested only in baseball batting averages to analyze *avant-garde* literature or be sensitive to its intentions, content, or purpose. It is absurdity to the *n*th degree to try to teach economics, science, mathematics, or philosophy to youngsters who have no comprehension of the four fundamental operations of arithmetic. The analysis of *avant-garde* literature, which will then be only a meaningless chore and the bored submission to literary content which is not even minimally grasped, are both guaranteed to make the development of seriousness impossible. Yet without such seriousness the use of free time for developmental leisure, that is, for renewal, is completely out of the question. Cultivation of the Greek ideals of *paideia* must depend on *"spondaitos"* or appropriate seriousness.

The one time in the average American's life when he *may escape* *"kitsch"* of the spirit and move towards the content of the Greek ideals of *paideia,* is when he is an undergraduate. I am referring particularly to undergraduate ideals of radicalism, evangelism, and Bohemianism,[14]

13 In this connection the reader will find the following reading matter worth consulting. Clement Greenberg, "Avant-Garde and Kitsch," 98–110. In *Mass Culture.* *Op. cit.*

14 David Matza. "Subterranean Traditions of Youth." 102–18. *The Annals of the American Academy of Political and Social Science. Teen-Age Culture.* (Jesse Bernard, Special editor). Vol. 338, November 1961.

although these ideals rub off soon enough when undergraduates who hold them "go secular." However, *"kitsch"* of the spirit is built into the *intellectual goulash* which we now call the liberal arts tradition, and it is quite fair to say that the liberal arts atmosphere of the modern college or university is not, in most cases, conducive to the later appearance of a concern for developmental leisure.

Other American institutions contribute to the intellectual and spiritual superficiality of the times. Book-of-The-Month Clubs and amateur theatricals in which the playwright is never understood and the emotions with which he is so deeply concerned are run through by stage-struck lasses with neuro-muscular gifts but little empathy, will also provide the possibility for playing at culture without being serious. The playing at culture by "listening to good music" and "looking at great paintings" while never becoming involved with the materials, theme, mood and message, as did the composer or the artist, are further cases in point. Popular books on science which humanely pretend to help the reader to understand very difficult matters without any effort greater than that required to discriminate between two diagrams or pictures, also help to provide the shadow as a substitute for the substance and leave the reader unable to see the intellectual forest of science for the factual trees so gratuitously provided by the author. At the same time the spirit of the intellectually disciplinary methods of science is never caught at all.

I am aware that we have exceptional educational institutions which have not betrayed the pursuit of excellence and which inculcate the necessary respect for intellectual and spiritual discipline without which our culture cannot be inherited. One result of institutions not like these, however, is that our population is becoming bimodal with respect both to seriousness and cultural depth. Those who receive such exceptional training or manage to provide it for themselves, form one mode or group, and a very small one at that. Most of the remainder who pride themselves on "having been educated" and who are the great consumers of non-serious, middlebrow culture, continue to deceive themselves with a variety of cultural and intellectual shadows and continue to wade into a host of literary and artistic shallows. We do not have to worry about the minority but the intellectual and cultural inertia of this middlebrow majority augurs ill for the democratic future of the west. If the blight of middlebrowism can be halted or reversed, both in and out of academic life, perhaps the pessimism expressed here will become only a matter of historical amusement, which I shall be glad to see it become if I am wrong.

I firmly believe that techniques can be developed both to halt and to reverse the inroads which middlebrow culture has made on our capacity to be serious in contexts where seriousness is called for. I firmly believe such techniques, applicable to the average student and adult, can be developed. If I am right, however, that nothing will be done to halt the march of middlebrowism—in fact that much will be done to increase its tempo—then I think its consequences will have to be taken seriously and assessed. If we wish to stop this march of middlebrowism, education must revamp both its philosophy and its objectives. I mean by education all forms of it, though chiefly, of course, the institutional forms. Such a revamping will not only have to include the pursuit of excellence in ways which require effort but also the inculcation of seriousness which both the themes of our culture and modern social, economic, and political problems, demand and deserve. Without that seriousness we can only look forward to the triumph of the shadow and the shallow and with their triumphs there is not much democracy we can look forward to at all.

I have taken pains to emphasize the outstanding roles played by homogenization and kitsch in mass culture because, as I have already remarked, they are both phenomena which reduce the possibility of using leisure time for renewal. They reflect the kind of stimulation which mass man has come to expect from mass culture and they determine the nature of the activities which he is likely to pursue in his free time. They are thus diametrically opposed to the Greek ideals of *paideia*. The leisure-time dilemma of American culture and civilization lies in the fact that, under the impact of science and technology, we are rapidly moving towards a civilization in which leisure may increase rather rapidly and substantially. The question which would then naturally arise is whether this substantial increment of time was to be devoted to more mass culture which promotes homogenization and kitsch or more free time for developmental leisure in the sense of renewal. The former would give us a civilization which would be an air-conditioned nightmare. The latter would give us a civilization which moved rapidly towards the fulfillment of the Greek ideals of *paideia* with the promise of fulfillment of all the millennial dreams which have moved men in their quest for the good life.

The promise of greatly increased leisure is now upon us with the dawn of the Age of Cyberculture and the fruits of cybernation upon which it rests. A cybercultural society will aggravate the dilemma which leisure-time creates for Americans. The nature of that dawning society and the problems which it poses with respect to the use of leisure must be understood. It is to this matter then that we shall now turn.

## III. THE PROBLEM OF LEISURE FOR A CYBERCULTURAL SOCIETY

The problem of the appropriate use of leisure in a cybernated society has hardly been touched upon by enthusiasts of cybernation. The notion of leisure, that operates within our existing philosophy of "having fun," is clearly not one which puts the emphasis on what we have called *developmental leisure*. A recommendation that he make a close study of Plato or Aristotle, to see if any of their ideas may have relevance to the modern world, would cause the average man to yawn. A course on the work of Cyril Connally or Dylan Thomas, would soon make him run to the nearest tavern for relief. The typical, American "joiner" is hardly likely to welcome a production by his organization of a play by Sartre, Genet or Anouilh, that is, a play in the tradition of the theatre of the absurd.[15] Mass-man is not likely to run panting to France in a frenzy of aesthetic excitement over the opportunity to see the famous Bayeux Tapestry. He is not likely to give a plugged nickel to hear the musical compositions of Gustav Mahler or Bela Bartok. Nor would he be caught dead in the Louvre or the Uffizi Galleries, except as part of a guided tour and only after having made certain that none of the "boys from back home" were in his party.

Not for him, these high-flying cultural pursuits. He will protest that he is no "long-hair." As a down to earth, red-blooded, American citizen, this *is not* the way to "have fun." If he has any spare time and he seeks enjoyment, give him one of the following: Mardi Gras; the drive-in movie which can serve as a "passion pit" for him and his girl friend; civic parades devoted to nothing in particular but which provide color and martial music; football and baseball games; penny arcades; the Coney Island "chamber of horrors"; the musical charisma of the Beatles; the beer guzzling, shouting and singing at an urban Rathskeller; a good burlesque show if he can keep this enthusiasm from his wife; a motor-cycle club if he is young and single; stock-car racing; hunting and fishing on weekends; and the comics when he wants to relax. Nor should it be thought that this sample of "having fun" activities, exhausts the spectrum of possibilities for the average man.

Cyberculturists, that is, partisans of a Great Society which shall depend upon cybernation as a main technological means for releasing the human spirit, recognize the tremendous amount of leisure which a cybercultural society promises to those who will be lucky enough to be part of it. They have, however, insufficiently emphasized the Pandora's Box of troubles which tremendous increases of leisure in a mass society are likely to generate. They assume that the transition to a cybernated society would present no insuperable difficulties but that the real problems men would face, would be the question of what to do with "vacant time." This, of course, refers to "neutral time," that is to say, to "time that has to be killed" or to "leisure time" as that phrase is misused in the United States today. Time that has to be killed is *endured time*

---

[15] In this connection the reader might wish to consult the following. Martin Esslin, *The Theatre of the Absurd*, New York: Doubleday, 1961, 364 pp.

whose inevitable accompaniment is boredom. Leisure time is properly understood only in two senses,[16] namely, the negative sense of freedom from the necessity of labor and, even more importantly, the positive sense which refers to the fact that a man of leisure gives the best of himself to his community and spares no pains in the cultivation of the mind, which includes the expression of the religious impulse. For a discussion of these two senses, see Sebastian de Grazia. Enthusiasts for cybernation rightly recognize that leisure in this latter, dual sense will be available to all in a cybernated society where work is no longer necessary and the link between work and consumption has been broken.

But—and this is the tragic note—they fail to recognize that there are two major factors which will limit most men's participation in the benefits of leisure. The first of these is the distribution of human intelligence, itself. For people of less than average intellectual capacity (25 percent of humanity, to be exact) spiritual goods rightly understood and intellectual goods rightly employed, are out of bounds, generally speaking. Even, however, for those of average intelligence (IQ: 90-110), potential participation in leisure is defunct. This is the range of intelligence characteristic of those individuals in mass society who tend to become cheerful robots,[17] that is, the mass-men of the European critics of an older generation or the Babbitts and conformists of disgruntled American intellectuals. Unfortunately in the average range of human intelligence, we also find large numbers of people with a total incapacity for the cultivation of the mind and who lack a sense of responsibility for the fate of their communities.

Of what avail will it then be if a cybernated society produces vacant time for all and then, perhaps, it finds that more than 50 percent of its beneficiaries have only learned to kill time through passive submission to mass media of communication. If a mass culture is cybernated out of existence, will the mid-range of human intelligence, aptitude, and sensitivity rise to the occasion and enjoy the activities which will come so much more easily to their intellectual betters? The fear that this will not take place has been expressed through the scholarly labors of a large number of critics. Let us even suppose that the answer is in the affirmative. There will remain the problem of participation in the fruits of cybernated leisure on the part of the intellectually disfranchised, that is, IQ's below 90. Unless some of the portentous biological techniques described for improving human characteristics,[18] particularly intelligence,

16 Sebastian de Grazia. *Of Time, Work, and Leisure.* New York: The Twentieth Century Fund, 1962. 559 pp.

17 C. Wright Mills. *The Sociological Imagination.* New York: Oxford University Press, 1959. 234 pp. See, in particular, Chapter 9, "On Reason and Freedom," and Mills' discussion of "The Cheerful Robot" in Section 3.

18 Jean Rostand. *Can Man Be Modified?* New York: Basic Books, 1959. 105 pp.

are adopted by a cybernated society or other means have been found for improving the genetic quality of the race, a cybernated society will face a most unusual problem. This will be the problem of finding a place in the scheme of things for a large sector of the population which cannot achieve the high-flying cultural pursuits of the rest of the society. This sector is, in effect, permanently exiled from the culture—a substratum which is in, but not of, the cybernated society. This, in a sense, is a graver demographic problem than some of those which presently worry our population experts.

Partisans of cybernation do not seem to realize that for those culturally disfranchised from a world they never made, a restlessness would arise and a resentment ever be present, which would be troublesome, indeed. This disfranchised sector would, in a cybernated society, have nothing to kill time with and, even if they did, most of their neighbors would disapprove of it. These helots to boredom could, indeed, become an atavistic minority. Their representatives at the present time can at least find a way to kill time, through alcohol, radio, television, the comics, spectator sports, gambling, variety in fornication, and a whole host of what are primarily indoor sports. All such outlets would be denied them in the cybernated future.

Cyberculturists then may live to see the day when they have kicked material poverty out of the front door only to find cultural poverty climbing over the backyard fence. Unless a blueprint for a cybernated world contains proposals for dealing with those who cannot make a fruitful use of inescapable leisure, the cyberculturists are headed for trouble. There does not at present seem to be any plan for the intellectually underprivileged in a cybernated world. Staring at us bleakly is a future cybernated world we never made, containing a new proletariat—a psychological proletariat rather than an economic one. The grim future which leisure in a cybernated society seems to threaten may be a time for weeping and a gnashing of teeth. Will we be able to prevent this bleak eventuality?

That the preceding pessimistic picture is not unreasonably drawn is somewhat corroborated by Michael.[19] The forcefulness of his analysis of the effects of abundant leisure on the masses in a cybernated society and the cogency of his conviction that the values we live by will have to be drastically changed, is best conveyed in his own words.

In twenty years, other things being equal, most of the routine blue-collar and white-collar tasks that can be done by cybernation will be. Our schools will probably be turning out a larger proportion of the population better educated than they are today, but most of our citizens will be unable to understand the cybernated world in which they live. Perhaps they will understand the rudiments

---

[19] Donald N. Michael. *Cybernation: The Silent Conquest*. Santa Barbara, California: Center for the Study of Democratic Institutions, 1962. 48 pp.

of calculus, biology, nuclear physics, and the humanities. But the research realm of scientists, the problems of government, and the interplay between them will be beyond the ken even of our college graduates. Besides, most people will have had to recognize that, when it comes to logic, the machines by and large can think better than they, for in that time reasonably good thinking computers should be operating on a large scale.

There will be a small, almost separate, society of people in rapport with the advanced computers. These cyberneticians will have established a relationship with their machines that cannot be shared with the average man any more than the average man today can understand the problems of molecular biology, nuclear physics, or neuropsychiatry. Indeed, many scholars will not have the capacity to share their knowledge or feeling about this new man-machine relationship. Those with the talent for the work probably will have to develop it from childhood and will be trained as intensively as the classical ballerina.

Some of the remaining population will be productively engaged in human-to-human or human-to-machine activities requiring judgment and a high level of intelligence and training. But the rest, whose innate intelligence or training is not of the highest, what will they do? We can foresee a nation with a large portion of its people doing, directly or indirectly, the endless public tasks that the welfare state needs and that the government will not allow to be cybernated because of the serious unemployment that would result. These people will work short hours, with much time for the pursuit of leisure activities.

Even with a college education, what will they do all their long lives, day after day, four-day week-end after week-end, vacation after vacation, in a more and more crowded world? (There is a population explosion to face in another ten to thirty years.) What will they believe in and aspire to as they work their shorter hours and, on the outside, pursue their "self-fulfilling" activities, whatever they may be? No one has ever seriously envisioned what characteristics these activities might have in order to be able to engross most men and women most of their adult lives. What will be the relationship of these people to government, to the "upper intellectuals," to the rest of the world, to themselves?

Obviously, attitudes toward work, play, and social responsibility will have changed greatly. Somehow we shall have had to cope emotionally with the vast gap in living standards that will then typify the difference between us and the have-not nations. We shall presumably have found some way to give meaning to the consumption of mass leisure. It would seem that a life oriented to private reaction might carry with it an attitude of relative indifference to public responsibility. This indifference, plus the centralization of authority, would seem to imply a governing elite and a popular acceptance of such an elite.

If this world is to exist as a coherent society, it will have to have its own "logic," so that it will make sense to its inhabitants. Today, for most of our population, our society makes sense, even though some other eyes hardly see us as logical in the formal sense of the word and the eyes of some of our own people look on us as a more or less pointless society. We make and solve our problems chiefly by other than mathematical-logical standards, and so must the cybernated generations. What these standards might be, we do not know. But if they are inadequate, the frustration and pointlessness that they produce may well evoke, in turn, a war of desperation—ostensibly against some external enemy but, in fact, a war to make the world safe for human beings by destroying most of society's sophisticated technological base. One thing is clear: if the new "logic" is to resolve the problems raised here, it will have to generate beliefs, behavior, and goals far different from those which we have held until now and which are driving us more and more inexorably into a contradictory world run by (and for?) ever more intelligent, ever more versatile slaves. (pp. 44–6)

All the preceding then represents the leisure-time dilemma of American society, both as it exists now and in the immediate future. The values of leisure as renewal and the emphasis on developmental leisure are alien to mass culture in America. The effort to spread developmental values presents great difficulties when most men and women are habituated to a culture of homogenization and kitsch. The difficulties are aggravated by the fact that the lower quarter of the distribution of human intelligence is probably separated from the values of developmental leisure because these demand aptitudes which are not part of the natural gifts of the poorly endowed. Will a cybernated society then be facing a civilization of two cultures—the culture of the alpha-moron, on the one hand, and the epsilon-normal and beta-bright, on the other? Will a cyber-cultural society controlled, as it inevitably must be, by the beta-bright, even permit the continuation of a mass culture for the alpha-moron? How will the epsilon-normals and the beta-bright of a cybernated society protect themselves against the smoldering and destructive resentment of a psychological proletariat disfranchised from participation in a world they never made? Must the historian of the future be prepared to describe a new age of revolution known as *The Revolt of the Low-IQ's?*

Nor are dangers absent for those of us in the middle range of intelligence, the epsilon-normals. Here too homogenization and kitsch hold their sway via "gracious living" and middlebrow culture. Among the several antidotes to such tendencies must be one which recognizes that we shall have to revamp modern education in the direction of some of the cultural and community ideals made famous by William Morris and other Utopian thinkers. In addition, we shall probably have to learn how to inculcate a taste in the average man for ideas and theories of the type characteristically provided by science, mathematics, philosophy, etc. Does the possibility of the existence of the twin dangers I have mentioned, mean that the beta-bright will be left alone to pursue their cybernated outlooks, come hell and high water? I think not. The outlook of the technician in an Age of Cyberculture will have to be tempered by an education which promotes the fusion of facts and values.[20] Instead of insisting that, *in order to be truly scientific,* facts and values should be separated, particularly in matters concerning the behavior of man, we

[20] Abraham H. Maslow. *Religions, Values, and Peak-Experiences.* Columbus, Ohio: Ohio State University Press, 1964. 123 pp.

shall have to recognize that such a separation is, in fact, both impossible and undesirable. When the proper relationship between facts and values have been worked out for an education for an age of cyberculture, the cybernetician and technician of the future will then have to be immersed in it. He will have to make humane values part of the warp and woof of his own inner being rather than dealing with them as mere abstractions. The needed revamping of modern education is long overdue in this respect. When it comes it will have to be concerned with those matters best expressed in the following words of Maslow.

The final and unavoidable conclusion is that education—like all our social institutions—must be concerned with its final values, and this in turn is just about the same as speaking of what have been called "spiritual values" or "higher values." These are the principles of choice which help us to answer the age-old "spiritual" (philosophical? religious? humanistic? ethical?) questions: What is the good life? What is the good man? The good woman? What is the good society and what is my relation to it? What are my obligations to society? What is best for my children? What is justice? Truth? Virtue? What is my relation to nature, to death, to aging, to pain, to illness? How can I live a zestful, enjoyable, meaningful life? What is my responsibility to my brothers? Who *are* my brothers? What shall I be loyal to? What must I be ready to die for? (p. 52)

When, and only when, the educational matters referred to above have been properly dealt with, will leisure come into its own. Until then, the use of leisure-time will continue to be a fundamental problem for Americans—spiritually, intellectually and culturally.

In this chapter we have stressed the problem of leisure as it appears to be emerging for a society which is rapidly moving towards an era of cybernation. The problem of leisure, of course, reflects a situation which will be more aggravated for the *alpha-morons* than for the *epsilon-normals* and the *beta-brights*. This is because these latter two groups in society are substantially more self-conscious about culture than are the alpha-morons. To be self-conscious about culture, however, provides no guarantee that one will pursue the life of culture in the sense of *paideia*. The notion of what it means to be cultured has, in fact, undergone a transformation in the hands of many epsilon-normals and beta-brights—a transformation which, many thinkers feel, represents a deterioration. The general name for this deterioration is "middlebrowism." Middlebrow culture, as practised by most members of the epsilon-normal and beta-bright groups, is regarded by a number of writers and thinkers as shallow and unprofitable, precisely because middlebrows have either never possessed the cultural vision which is reflected in the ideals of *paideia* or—if this vision has ever been truly understood—because it clearly has been abandoned.

This abandonment and betrayal of the ideals of genuine culture (paideia) can be said to be most clearly indicated in the lack of seriousness with which cultural concerns are presumably pursued by middlebrows. This lack of seriousness has produced many undesirable intellectual and social consequences. These consequences, therefore, also create a problem of leisure for middlebrows, that is, for most of those who can be classified as epsilon-normals or beta-brights. The problem of leisure for these two groups, however, takes on a different form from that which holds for alpha-morons—insofar as we are concerned with the use of leisure for mature and culturally fruitful ends. It behooves us, therefore, to examine the nature of the leisure-time situation and its cultural accompaniments, which is created by the increasing lack of seriousness exhibited by middlebrows and by the deflection from the ideals of paideia which such lack of seriousness has produced. We shall therefore return to an examination of the alleged cultural deterioration created by the decline of seriousness among those whom we have called middlebrows.

# The Disappearing Art
## of Being Serious*

A mature participation in those aspects of the democratic *ethos* which depend upon a willingness to understand the nature of the complex social processes and problems with which we have to deal, demands a seriousness and a concern which is proportional to the gravity of these problems. In a wider context, a genuine democracy demands a general intellectual seriousness whose transfer to the concrete issues of our time will be assured. In our own time such seriousness is to be expected more from members of the educated classes than from any other group, and this means the great American middle class and the intellectual elite of the upper class—but chiefly among the former. It is the members of these classes who should be expected to create the intellectual tone and climate of our age and encourage communication, both emotional as well as intellectual, in depth and breadth. Somewhere Bertrand Russell has said that the proper aim of education is to develop minds sensitive enough to perceive, to feel the shock of tragedies taking place thousands of miles away and somehow communicate a feeling to the heart. An event, however, of importance in this connection, is the appearance of a social psychology with roots in these classes, which appears to wish to abdicate the responsibilities of intellectual leadership and moral feeling and action. Among many of our educated an issue is essentially a conversation piece. This growing psychology avoids the exploration of issues in depth and seems to be moving towards the adoption of an attitude which regards communication in depth as a species of Original Sin. In view of this increasing phenomenon, the time is right for a description and partial analysis of it.

A description is quite separate, of course, from a cultural analysis of the roots of this phenomenon and even more importantly is quite separate from a discussion of methods for dissipating it. Inasmuch as this

* Chapter 7, with adaptations and modifications, has been taken from the following sources: Henry Winthrop. "The Disappearing Art of Being Serious." *Journal of Human Relations*. Vol. 10, No. 1, Autumn 1961, 84–95, and Henry Winthrop. "Social Zombieism—The Anti-Existential in Modern Life." *Journal of Existential Psychiatry*. Vol. III, No. 12, Spring 1963, 343–60.

nascent psychology is to be found among pretenders to intellectuality and cultural sensitivity, both in and out of academic life, we have a threat here to the best features of the humanistic and scientific traditions—features which are absolutely essential to the life of both the intellect and the spirit. This creeping paralysis of the mind and heart affects the middle class educator even more than it does the middle-class culture-hound. It is therefore a major tragedy that the educational adventure (perhaps, we should say misadventure), is to be placed increasingly in the hands of many who are almost completely untouched by learning, love, or logic. The first is noticeable by the degree to which it is shunned currently by many who have taken to the academic hills—more for the soft berth this promised them than because of any passion for or dedication to teaching. The second is merely a word to those who have never *felt* the *emotional meanings* attached to the concept of "agape" and a word whose compass is best described by the Fitzgerald heroine who said, "I'm hipped on Freud and all that; but its rotten that every bit of *real* love in the world is ninety-nine per-cent passion and one little soupçon of jealousy." As for the third, it is conspicuous by its absence from the cocktail party circuit and the small-talk conversational gambits of those who prefer the light fantastic intellectually. These attributes of middlebrow culture in the United States are in marked contrast to the atmosphere which prevailed for the Renaissance or Enlightenment scholar. Even the patron of the arts and culture of those two periods and the culture-oriented members of his or her entourage, pursued these interests with a seriousness which is beyond question.

There are few aspects of social change in basic current attitudes which will have as much impact on the quality of our human relations in these United States as this growing lack of seriousness. It will profoundly affect our outlook and for the worse. The understanding of the human condition, the need to explore that condition thoroughly, objectively and honestly—these can be expected to go by the board. The need to feel how the world affects others, particularly when its effects contain the possibilities of high tragedy, can be expected to dwindle. Finally, *without seriousness,* the current shibboleth which issues from so many lips, "I couldn't care less," can result in a diminishing number of individuals who will really feel moved to change things.

If seriousness should disappear from the life of culture, the need for communication would itself become an archaic cultural expectation. Without communication the best in our heritage would perish. Lack of communication in all senses of the word, goes to the roots of most human misunderstanding, creates the tragic elements of life, and serves as poisonous soil for the growth of attitudes, values, and aspirations which, given concrete expression, become so many variants of our current social pathology. In a very valid sense it can be argued that many of the complex social, economic, political, cultural, and religious issues of our time are simply the offshoots in given contexts of our general failure to cultivate communication—in the humanist's, philosopher's, and scientist's senses of this term, rather than in the advertising man's craven sense or the stultifying sense which the journalist imparts to it. This changing social psychology towards the original meaning of communication, a meaning which had been demonstrated in action by Socrates surrounded by the youth of Athens and by the dialectic of exploration cultivated by Adler [1] and Hutchins,[2] is then our current concern. This oldest meaning of communication involves continued, taxing, and probing analysis in the realm of ideas. It also involves the presence of imaginative sympathy, the quest for empathy, and the capacity to translate ideas into action through an understanding of their emotional meaning, their implications for the ongoing values of individuals, and the cultivation of a sensitivity for recognizing the personal and social contexts which call for their application. Today our middlebrow culture flees from these themes, and a good many educators make a social vice out of the play of ideas in depth or the profound expression of social reality and personal commitment via the arts. Moments of truth are abhorred like the plague. Intellectual sloppiness and intellectual disorganization become social virtues; superficiality and ignorance masquerade as the widest extension of shared communion; shallowness of feeling and woodenness of purpose parade as social and administrative tact, and routine without imagination, as efficiency. These are all forms of a breakdown in communication which, themselves, stem from a lack of seriousness. What are some of the factors which have generated this undesirable situation—and why?

In discussing the answer to this question I should like to paraphrase the late Franklin Delano Roosevelt by saying that in discussing seriousness our attitude should not be that we must be serious about everything except seriousness, itself. It would require a volume to do justice to the many factors which contribute to a changing social psychology which repudiates seriousness. Perhaps the most cogent factor is the *fear of seriousness, itself.* This is expressed in various, current anti-intellectual forms. Culture—in or out of the classroom—is not expected to be taxing.

1 The meaning of dialectic as, perhaps, the basic skill in communication, has been extensively examined in the following volume: Mortimer Adler, *Dialectic,* New York: Harcourt, Brace, 1927, 265 pp.

2 Hutchins has emphasized the importance of dialectic to serious discussion, through his emphasis on metaphysics and, in general, the disciplines associated with the highly refined, consciously directed skills of reason. See, for instance, Chapter 4 "The Higher Learning," 89–119, in the following volume: Robert Maynard Hutchins, *The Higher Learning in America,* New Haven: Yale University Press, 1962, 119 pp. He has also emphasized the importance of serious discussion and communication in the following volume: Robert M. Hutchins, *The University of Utopia,* Chicago: The University of Chicago Press, 1953, 103 pp. See particularly chapter 3 "Philosophical Diversity," 49–74.

Conversation must be light and flutter from one topic to another and deal only with the surface of ideas. The analysis of ideas is simply not regarded as cricket. It makes the hearer uncomfortable. Any use of information relevant to the issue being discussed is regarded as offensive, egocentric, and a display of intellectual one-upmanship. To follow whither the argument leadeth, as Socrates suggested, is felt to be a strain on sociability, and both heavy and boring. A conversation is defined as *stimulating* when it consists of an exchange of countless platitudes, when it succeeds in massaging the listener's ego, and when it has no bearing on anything. The middle and upper classes in each generation have, perhaps, their own changing notions of good conversation. In the Victorian period the polite raconteur was held in high esteem. In the Depression Thirties, at least in the East, serious evaluations of current situations and what meaning they might hold for the listener and the groups to which he belonged, were well received. Today in an atmosphere consisting overwhelmingly of sleek and fat cultural cats, the purpose of conversation is meant only to be fraternal.

No one can criticize this objective if this is really the purpose for which individuals engage in a verbal exchange. The tragedy occurs only when a confusion of purpose arises; that is, when it is assumed by some that everyone wants to *learn from others and to share his own ideas with them.* The results are, of course, bleak when this assumption is unsound because some of those who are gathered together have done so strictly and only for reasons of sociability. If no one present is serious, then all are self-deceived—which serves them right. If some are and some are not serious, then the pretense of an interest in communication by those who are not serious results in wasting the time and effort of those who are. What the serious have to say will fall on deaf ears. What the nonserious have to say will generally constitute twaddle which purports to be serious, and no one profits thereby. When conversation has a social rather than an intellectual purpose—no one can take offense. But the moment the emphasis turns to *serious* exchange and the moment anyone can safely assume others wish also to be *serious*—then at that moment communication must abide by the dictates of logic and the constraints of fact rather than by the conceits of fancy. This means signing the oath of loyalty, metaphorically speaking, to Aristotle and applying the constraints of modern, scientific method to the exchange of ideas. Few are willing to abide by these classic restraints.

The ennui, the waste of time, the educational follies which result from attacking a serious topic with the techniques of the drawing room, parlor car, and the whiskey and soda overtures of the gentlemen's club, are farcical to the intellectually sensitive. If one intends to be serious, one should be. If not, there should be enough maturity not to try to discuss complex and weighty issues with the fol-de-rol of literary conceits, epigrams, and the well-turned phrase. This is the bastard version of the humanist in action. The obtuseness which this represents has been only too well catalogued by others. Lundberg[3] has dealt at great length with the barriers to communication which arise from the prescientific thought-ways of most humanists—particularly the literary variety—barriers which stem largely, though not wholly, from the *expressive language* of the humanities. A dozen years later C. P. Snow,[4] extending the same theme concerning the lack of seriousness of the literati, has stressed their indifference to the methods, principles, and findings of science. Those of us who, through intellectual indiscretion, have made the mistake of attending cocktail parties and literary teas, can remember with amusement how hastily a retreat will be made by the middle-class culture hound, the upper-class dilettante and the academic pretender to the intellectual life, when the going really gets serious rather than scintillating. Yet, *if we really wish to be serious,* certainly the methods of being so should be no different outside the classroom than those used in it. When I speak of the classroom in this context, I envision a forum presided over by a distinguished philosopher, a distinguished scientist, or an astute social critic, any one of which has dedicated himself to disciplined thought and humility in the face of facts. The irony of modern mass education is that the intellectual atmosphere of the fraternal order is invading the classroom on serious issues, when instead, the atmosphere of genuine learning should be temporarily adopted extramurally by those who pretend to a live interest in the complex issues of our time. It is hard to exceed an educational obtuseness which naively presumes to deal with intellectually difficult matters via the sloppiness of thought and superficiality of information characteristic of the middlebrow garden party or the ladies' auxiliary.

A lack of intellectual seriousness tends to produce a condition which —for want of a better phrase—we may call "social zombieism." The dictionary defines "zombie" as a supernatural power by which a corpse may be reanimated. Derivatively a "zombie" *is* such a corpse. I wish to maintain in this chapter that our *current middlebrow culture* has all the trappings of a supernatural power in that it takes "cultural corpses," metaphorically speaking, namely, our fellow-citizens, and re-animates them through prevailing patterns of motivation. What are some of these prevailing patterns of motivation which constitute zombie behavior and which reflect that lack of seriousness without which a genuine concern for culture must necessarily be severely aborted?

3 George A. Lundberg. *Can Science Save Us?* New York: Longmans, Green, 1947. 122 pp.
4 Charles P. Snow. *The Two Cultures and the Scientific Revolution.* New York: Cambridge University Press, 1959. 58 pp.

The first form of *zombieism* in social life which is of major significance is "rubricization." This is the term employed by Maslow [5] to refer to the habit of looking at one another and assessing one another in terms of labels or stereotypes. As Maslow puts it, stereotyping is a process which not only serves social bias and prejudice but is also a process that is applicable to the way in which we perceive people and events. Social perception is not simply a matter of a camera recording of what is passing before our eyes. The recording is filtered through our own consciousness, that is, it is subject to interpretation by our *cognitive maps,* to use an expression from psychology. This filtering results in an *evaluation* and *classification* of the persons and events before us. The classification is likely to be glib and hasty, indicating our own feelings, judgments and values. For just this reason our classification is likely to be both incomplete and, to some extent, in error. Yet stereotyping is escapable. It is not a psychological constraint upon the human organism. One can look at another human being and react to him as he is, noting his authentic qualities rather than reading into him qualities, usually negative, which reflect our own indifference, insecurity and hastiness. Intellectual laziness and moral irresponsibility, however, frequently prompt us to ticket or "rubricize" him. We then see a Chinaman, instead of Lum Wang, an individual unlike any other, possessing his own dreams, ambitions, fears, aspirations, and interests. We escape the need to press for an authentic encounter by the use of such labels as millionaire, Marxist, dame, Babbitt, confused adolescent, Jew, and many other labels too numerous to mention here. People prone to stereotype in this fashion are best described in Shakespeare's words: They have eyes and see not, ears and hear not.

Maslow lists some of the qualities which occur in rubricized perception. In rubricized perception we perceive the following: (1) the familiar and hackneyed rather than the unfamiliar and fresh; (2) the schematized and abstract rather than the actual; (3) the organized, structured, the univalent rather than the chaotic, unorganized, and ambiguous; (4) the named or namable rather than the unnamable; (5) the meaningful rather than the meaningless; (6) the conventional rather than the unconventional and (7) the expected rather than the unexpected. Furthermore, says Maslow, if an event is unfamiliar to us, if it is concrete, ambiguous, unnamed, meaningless, unconventional, or unexpected, we make use of what the psychologist calls perceptual distortion and perceptual selectivity. This means that we twist, classify, or interpret what we see until it can fit into some neat category with which we are familiar. And always, unfortunately, this blinds us to that which is idiosyncratic, unique, authentic and different in the person or event before us.

[5] Abraham H. Maslow. *Motivation and Personality.* New York: Harper, 1954. 411 pp.

Common examples in social life of rubricization occur when the reformer is called a "communist" or when the citizen whose outraged sense of social justice prompts him to action, thereby earns for himself the label of "troublemaker" or "non-cooperative." A still more obvious example is the individual who shuns certain personalities because of their pettiness or habits of intrigue, thereby earning the monicker of "skizzy," "paranoid," "psychopath," etc. A literary familiarity with psychoanalysis often prompts the unserious middlebrow to employ such glib labels. The middlebrow addiction to labels, however, is not confined to their clinical misemployment. The habit of slapping down the intellectually gifted and the creative, who tend to remind us of our own mediocrity, by dismissing them with such labels as "aggressive," "too ambitious" and "professional climber" are still further examples but in the opposite direction. By this I mean that the preceding traits which are being devalued because the labels in question are meant to cast aspersions on their victims, are traits which, in reality, are socially approved. By contrast, the clinical conditions previously referred to through the use of ill-understood, clinical labels, are not socially approved and they are all too frequently applied to social critics whose ideas seem to rock the boat of tranquillity of middle-class existence, thus tending to make many middlebrows uncomfortable, both socially and intellectually.

The important consideration in all these cases, however, is to examine the existential meaning of such rubricization. Essentially it is the intellectually lazy man's device for avoiding thought. Avoiding thought seems to be a national pastime to which such an institution as the cocktail party seems to be perfectly geared. A predilection for rubricization, however, is more than just intellectual laziness. It represents even more significantly an unwillingness to seek to know others in their full, idiosyncratic concreteness. A willingness to do so would be a form of "involvement." Unfortunately socially approved forms of alienation discourage this willingness which, if properly manifested, would help us to go places. These socially approved forms of alienation encourage us to see others as "on hand" when our paths cross theirs, as "useful and friendly" when they can serve our purposes but, on the other hand, describable by any number of pejorative terms when they appear as a threat or block to our secular ambitions. This *must be* the behavioral repertoire when one's motives are basically egoistic rather than altruistic. Thus if people are seen as means they vary in merit in relation to their potential exploitability and demerit in relation to their frustration potential. A ready-made vocabulary, both honorific and pejorative, is at hand to earmark these differentials in merit and demerit. As a result rubricization has a field day. This tendency is the form which Buber's [6] I-and-It relationship

6 Martin Buber. *I and Thou.* New York: Charles Scribner's Sons, 1957. 137 pp.

takes when an I–and–Thou relationship has never been developed. A rubric is the perfect device for the "Itness" of the "Other."

Studies on *visual* perception have revealed the degree to which we fail to notice background elements in the visual field because only the foreground elements are of interest to us. The ease with which background elements of importance can be overlooked in the visual field, is aided by the use of broad labels which help to dismiss that amorphous background from our attention. Analogously, this also happens in *social* perception. We overlook important elements in the make-up of the human personality by viewing him or her through a rubric of some sort. This rubric then brings to the fore an interest in only limited aspects of the person. More important aspects will then be lost sight of, because these are not crucially related to the verbal or psychological meaning associated with the rubric.

In social life perhaps the one type of activity which most succinctly betrays social zombieism is our middlebrow effort to play at culture. Whether it is the Civic Cultural Committee, the local PTA lecture circuit, the intellectual light-fantastic of the cocktail party, the cultural katzenjammers of faculty wives or the cultural bosom-heaving of the Ladies' Club, the zombies are animated by a thousand and one substitutes for the genuine life of culture. What the genuine life of culture means has been the subject of a vast literature among which some representative writers are Arnold,[7] Powys,[8] Eliot [9] and Cowell.[10] The familiarity with this literature and even more, its spirit, is conspicuous by its absence among the devotees of such groups as I have mentioned above. The United States, under the new, middlebrow dispensation, is full of cultural pretensions of a thousand varieties, mostly existential failures. This is so because the characteristic profile of the middlebrow is one in which one never learns to live one's values or even to feel them as something more than cognitive abstractions. The middlebrow's code, a sort of *bushido of retreat,* results in a variety of escape devices most of which require the synthetic forms of animation which convert the cultural corpse into the social zombie of the present. I should like to provide a bill of particulars by merely mentioning these escape devices here without expanding on any of them. They include the sanctification of pretense, role-playing, running along with the herd, life adjustment, cooperation, the attitude of "I don't want to get involved," self-preoccupa-

[7] Matthew Arnold. *Culture and Anarchy. An Essay in Political & Social Criticism.* Cambridge: Cambridge University Press, 1957. 241 pp.

[8] John Cowper Powys. *The Meaning of Culture.* New York: W. W. Norton, 1929. 275 pp.

[9] Thomas Stearns Eliot. *Notes towards the Definition of Culture.* New York: Harcourt, Brace, 1949. 128 pp.

[10] Frank Richard Cowell. *Culture in Private and Public Life.* New York: Frederick A. Praeger, 1959. 357 pp.

tion, a preference for an irrelevant and bloodless gentility, a malaise in the face of tendenciousness which is regarded as a species of Original Sin and the namby-pambyism to which we have already alluded. On the cultural side the dead hand of zombieism is reflected in a whole pattern of life-denying characteristics which are mistaken for the earmarks of being civilized, in lack of spontaneity in intellectual and aesthetic matters (enthusiasm is suspect and is characteristic only of naive and low-class Latins), a consciousness of class shored up by a pronounced xenophobia and a preference for the passive and the spectator role in all forms of entertainment.

What then are the psychological perturbations of those who plead for this sort of thing? The individual who is made uncomfortable by genuine thought may have any or all of the following characteristics: (1) A lack of sincerity which is an inevitable derivative of chronic role-playing. This results in fear of forthrightness which forever presents a threat to a Babbittry and conformity which must be disguised and/or protected. Issues must be hidden and, if thrust upon him, the middlebrow must evade them by *intellectual deviousness*. Chronic cultivation of the latter makes seriousness impossible. (2) The middlebrow may be intellectually lazy, given to what we have already mentioned, namely, "rubricizing," that is, the tendency to label situations, people, and ideas, and then obviate the need for dealing with them fairly and honestly by virtue of having classified them. (3) The middlebrow may actually be *incapable of genuine thought,* having become habituated to what Ogden and Richards [11] have called *expressive language,* the language of literature, poetry, religion, and the arts, rather than *ratiocinative* or *representative* language, which is the handmaiden of rigorous, conceptual thinking. (4) The individual who is not serious intellectually is also likely to prove to be a poorly informed individual. If he is an academic pretender he will thrive on borrowed capital; that is to say, given a reputation for being learned, he will prefer the manners to the matter of the sage, the role to the product, the reputation to the reality, and the status to the capacity. (5) The nonserious middlebrow is often an individual who is shallow intellectually and emotionally, accustomed to stereotyped and cliché thinking, almost completely alienated from a sensitivity to the exquisitely rational, and therefore unable to discriminate between genuine thought and its disjointed shadows. This middlebrow type is often the tweedy, pipe-smoking character who conceals his shallowness behind an advertising man's stereotype of wisdom and urbanity, who can impress the misguided, naive and uninformed—as well as his fellow middlebrows—but rarely the thoughtful and knowledgeable individual.

[11] Charles K. Ogden and Ivor A. Richards. *The Meaning of Meaning.* New York: Harcourt, Brace, 1959. 363 pp.

We cannot, of course, assert that these are the only factors which create an abhorrence for genuine thought and feeling. The common thread running through these and other factors we could mention, is the threat to one's shaky self-image which *seriousness of thought and feeling would produce.* It is difficult to discover instances of genuine thought and feeling which can be expressed via a role or some form of intellectual self-deception. Satire is always effective in puncturing pretension, deflating pomposity, and making role-playing impossible, because a false self-image easily yields blood to the shafts of wit. This is inevitable because the moment of truth created by satire fits the observer's or reader's sense of social reality in a way which no amount of reinforcement of a phony self-image could ever do. One barb tinged with acid and truth does more effective work than role and status, and renders the sheltering warmth of one's clique and the fine art of the "evasive," powerless to protect one. When this happens self-reconstruction is intellectually and spiritually in order for the victim. Failing this, the pretender indulges in one of three traditional reactions to the shafts of irony. The pretender will show fright, fight, or flight. In a middlebrow culture like our own which emphasizes "gracious living," fright must be concealed by the irrelevantly urbane, and fight is simply unthinkable. The typical middlebrow reaction—an extension of the mood of nonseriousness—is to make one's excuses and leave the table, the room, or the party.

Lack of seriousness shows up also in the educational pabulum of the modern curriculum. The very course titles betray the emptiness, discontinuity, and lack of organic cohesion in the offerings: *The Meaning of Culture, Main Threads of Western Civilization, Living Ideas of Our Time, The Greek Way of Life, etc.* Here superficiality and the tendency to play at culture, together with a determined effort to avoid seriousness, are served up through a variety of intellectual smorgasbord. By tasting everything on the menu in small quantities, one presumably becomes an intellectual gourmet. This is the type of curriculum which, marching under the banner of a liberal education, adds the confusion of four years of college to the bewilderment and naiveté of high-school graduation. Any insistence that one pursue some of the topics of such an intellectual hasty pudding more deeply is usually frowned upon by the nonserious. The usual excuse is that of insufficient time. Courses such as these cultivate every intellectual vice in the books. When they are accompanied by an educational philosophy which insists that the students "participate" or even run the show via "bull-session panels," with neither teacher nor student equipped to be serious about the complex matters under discussion, the vices are compounded. Any resemblance between the prevailing atmosphere and an educational process is purely coincidental and, I might add, purely inconsequential.

Under the social dispensation which discourages seriousness, it becomes clear that no two individuals can ever have an "encounter" in the existentialist sense of this term. By this we mean that no two individuals will ever get to explore one another's *ideas* and *feelings* deeply and meaningfully. No two individuals will ever develop the capacity to touch one another at their respective centers. The reasons are obvious enough. A full probing of the presuppositions of the other party is regarded as offensive, discomforting, and boorish. Intellectual shallowness is difficult to conceal and role-playing is difficult to continue when there is an insistence on intellectual honesty and disinterestedness. The pleasant but unwarranted intellectual self-image is maintained only through psychological defenses of one sort or another. The middlebrow will don impenetrable, Reichian armor-plating of character and insist upon an intellectual form of Bushido in which being a gentleman is the important thing rather than being a thinker. The probing personality who does not cease and desist arouses outraged feelings of dignity, and soon learns that the maintenance of the unjustified self-image is more important than truth and accuracy. Furthermore, this reaction will occur even when the prober is well intentioned and friendly in his approach. The difficulty arises from a situation in which the assertions which are being probed are so bound up with the questionee's weak self-image that even the deftest and most benevolent of approaches are seen as threatening.

There is something worse, however, than the inability to achieve an encounter because of lack of intellectual seriousness. This is the permanent wall between two souls which a mutual or one-sided unwillingness to reveal one's deepest feelings, guiding values, and cherished emotions, produces. There are many reasons why two nonserious individuals hesitate to share the worlds of feeling. Let us note a few of these. (1) All of us feel it necessary to keep back a core of our deepest selves from public view. Each of us finds it difficult to bare his or her innermost self without, at the same time, risking the submergence of his ego so deeply in that of another that the danger may arise of becoming completely dependent emotionally upon one who has called every turn in the books on us. Self-revelation is a difficulty even for the open characters of a Russian novel. In a culture like our own which stresses the importance of role and adjustment, the sharing of any but the shallowest of emotions becomes almost an impossibility. (2) The very stress on role-playing which is encouraged by middle-class gracious living makes the stripping of habitual pretense and affectation difficult. Such unmasking is not part of the *ethos* of a deeply ingrained middle-class outlook and is certainly not approved of at all in the middle and upper classes. Its suppression thus results in a modern version of a species of psychological Victorianism in which the revelation of nakedness of soul rather than nakedness of body is abhorrent and improper. (3) The modern middlebrow has learned that success is obtained by projecting an acceptable public image of himself. This public image is invariably false or distorted but, for social purposes, it gains entree into social contexts for which the nonserious middlebrow is ill equipped. In these contexts he protects himself from discovery by various approved *social skills*—the new humor of togetherness, stressed by Henry Steele Commager,[12] the glib phrase, the evasive reply, and the effort to be all things to all men. Thus the modern middlebrow winds up as one of the lonelier souls in the lonely crowd, with no habits, abilities, or inclinations that would create a capacity for touching others at their vital centers. This dries up the capacity for deep feeling and comprehending emotional projection so that personal encounters become completely foreign to the middlebrow's experience. (4) Social displays of genuine emotion leave the modern middlebrow visibly embarrassed. He has rarely met with this kind of thing outside of the play, the novel, or the cinema. He does not have a repertoire of socially-learned responses and skills for meeting it. His first and last impulse, as a relief from embarrassment, is to escape from any form of breast-beating and personal emotion exposure. All the preceding considerations, and others besides, preserve the individual who is fearful of seriousness from having to make any personal encounters. In this way the middlebrow locks himself forever in a web of alienation.

[12] Henry Steele Commager. *The American Mind*. New Haven: Yale University Press, 1950. 476 pp.

# 8

# Towards a Philosophy of Culture[*]

## I. PROLEGOMENON

It is beyond the power of any man, no matter how erudite and perceptive, to begin to give a complete picture of the factors which are basically responsible for the increasing social complexity of our age. I do believe, however, that scientific, technological, and economic factors are certainly among those most central to the production of that social complexity of which we are today distinctly aware.

Now it is well enough, of course, to recognize this increasing social complexity of our age but it is even more important to consider the education, both formal and informal, which is needed for grappling with that complexity properly. I am referring to the education which is needed by the average citizen if he is to participate meaningfully not only in the life of his local community but, even more importantly and less provincially, in the life of the world community. It is this latter community which faces most of the large-scale social, economic and political issues of our time. If the reader feels that it is overly sanguine to speak of the education needed by the average citizen then let him think of the education needed by the above average citizen who is defined psychometrically as any citizen whose IQ is above 110. I do not want it thought that I believe intellectual capacity alone should define the type of responsible citizen we seek to produce. A concern with ideas and ideals, the capacity to be intellectually, culturally or socially productive, the possession of attitudes, values, interests and levels of aspiration germane to a dispassionate but humane concern with the problems of world community, are even more important defining criteria of responsible citizenship. Furthermore and frankly I believe that most average citizens, again speaking psychometrically, can profit from the proper education needed to grasp the social complexities of our age, provided the nonintellectual consid-

[*] Chapter 8, with adaptations and modifications, has been taken from the following source: Henry Winthrop. "Towards a Philosophy of Culture." *Darshana*. Vol. 2, No. 4, 1962, 24–40.

erations we have mentioned, are fully present and operative. But to avoid digressing let us note that the important question is that of determining the nature of the college curriculum to which our prospective good citizen should be exposed. I say college curriculum because I believe that in the immediate future here in the U.S., almost everyone of average capacity will both seek that education and hopefully be influenced by it to some degree.

Curricular development in education, as we all know, is a hotbed of controversy. Some educators wish to plan the curriculum in relation to the abilities of the clientele and others to its probable vocational needs. Some wish to offer a curriculum adapted to the needs of a world which is not the presently complex one, the world, perhaps, of 1910 or 1920, to which their curricular offerings would have been highly relevant, but not the world of the Sixties. Some scholarly educators, egocentric in their points of view, ask for a curriculum which would be germane only if all our students were prospective scholars. In the present context I think the proper question is simply to ask what studies are germane to a proper understanding of the social complexity of our time, to an understanding of what is happening in the world today, and to the acquisition of those skills and that information without which it is pointless to expect the average citizen to participate intelligently and meaningfully in the democratic process.

Here, I believe, the more dispassionate, better-informed and more thoughtful answers are coming from scholarly individuals who are not in educational administration and curriculum planning. I am thinking particularly of C. P. Snow and George Lundberg. Snow has emphasized the impact that education has on the human condition, which receives far less treatment than it deserves. The world labors on under the notion that a proper education for its prospective leadership is a humanistic and belletristic one, aided and abetted preferably by legal training whenever the individual seriously intends a career in politics or statesmanship. The fact is missed that scientific thoughtways and some knowledge of natural and social science are imperative if one is to achieve a better and more relevant understanding of social change, modern history, the economics of rising expectations, and the aspirations of subject peoples everywhere. The prejudices of the literary mind have been fought in the past in such excellent volumes as George Lundberg's [1] *Can Science Save Us?* Lundberg is a distinguished social scientist, and perhaps his criticisms were less telling than they should have been, because of the ambiguous scientific status with which the layman tends to view the social sciences. These are everybody's pastures in lay eyes. A second attempt was made by Snow to overcome the scientific ignorance of decision-makers with a

[1] George A. Lundberg. *Can Science Save Us?* New York: Longmans, Green, 1961. 150 pp.

monolithic, humanistic bias. C. P. Snow [2] addressed himself to the same task that Lundberg set for himself some years ago. Snow is peculiarly fitted for this task. He is both one of Britain's outstanding novelists and outstanding scientists; he can, therefore, not be accused of ideological, educational bias towards either group. Snow feels that world political and moral leadership and the administrative effort to tackle the large issues of our time should be infused not only by the imagination, sympathy, breadth, perspective, feeling, and the wide-ranging cultural identifications of the humanists, but also by a knowledge of some of the basic fundamental principles of modern science, which find universal application in technology, invention, and planning, and whose social and economic impacts on the lives of all of us have to be clearly grasped if we are to guide properly our own destinies. Snow can best be understood in his own words:

". . . I believe the intellectual life of the whole of western society is increasingly being split into two polar groups . . .

Literary intellectuals at one pole—at the other scientists, and as the most representative, the physical scientists. Between the two a gulf of mutual incomprehension—sometimes (particularly among the young) hostility and dislike, but most of all lack of understanding. They have a curious distorted image of each other. Their attitudes are so different that, even on the level of emotion, they can't find much common ground. Non-scientists tend to think of scientists as brash and boastful. . . . Then they hear a much louder voice, that of another archetypal figure, Rutherford, trumpeting: 'This is the heroic age of science! This is the Elizabethan age!' Many of us heard that, and a good many other statements beside which that was mild; and we weren't left in any doubt whom Rutherford was casting for the role of Shakespeare. What is hard for the literary intellectuals to understand, imaginatively or intellectually, is that he was absolutely right. . . .

The non-scientists have a rooted impression that the scientists are shallowly optimistic, unaware of man's condition. On the other hand, the scientists believe that the literary intellectuals are totally lacking in foresight, peculiarly unconcerned with their brother men, in a deep sense anti-intellectual, anxious to restrict both art and thought to the existential moment. And so on. Anyone with a mild talent for invective could produce plenty of this kind of subterranean back-chat. On each side there is some of it which is not entirely baseless. It is all destructive. Much of it rests on misinterpretations which are dangerous. (pp. 4–6).

Snow points out that most scientists are ignorant of literature and the arts, of books with sweep, power and ideas which have the strength to move men and make history. On the other hand, the literary intellectuals are tone deaf to the significance of science, deliberately so and

2 Charles P. Snow. *The Two Cultures and the Scientific Revolution.* New York: Cambridge University Press, 1959. 58 pp.

rather cocky about it, completely unwilling to face up to its meaning for the human condition. Says Snow:

> As with the tone-deaf, they don't know what they miss. They give a pitying chuckle at the news of scientists who have never read a major work of English literature. They dismiss them as ignorant specialists. Yet their own ignorance and their own specialisation is just as startling. A good many times I have been present at gatherings of people who, by the standards of the traditional culture, are thought highly educated and who have with considerable gusto been expressing their incredulity at the illiteracy of scientists. Once or twice I have been provoked and have asked the company how many of them could describe the Second Law of Thermodynamics. The response was cold: it was also negative. Yet I was asking something which was the scientific equivalent of: Have you read a work of Shakespeare's?
>
> I now believe that if I had asked an even simpler question such as, What do you mean by mass, or acceleration, which is the scientific equivalent of saying, Can you read?—not more than one in ten of the highly educated would have felt that I was speaking the language. So the great edifice of modern physics goes up, and the majority of the cleverest people in the western world have about as much insight into it as their neolithic ancestors would have had. (pp. 15–16).

Snow is, of course, interested in closing the gap between the two cultures. If this is not done, he feels, man will learn to control his own ecology without even knowing what purposes and values he is trying to achieve. Inasmuch as the humanist tradition has had a long headstart, the process of closing the gap will consist of a heavy injection of modern science, mathematics, and the scientific thoughtways into *general education*. The educational ship will have to lighten its ballast in the literary direction and take on board another load of ballast in the scientific direction but—and this is most important—both kinds of ballast will have to be on board.

## II. THE INFORMATIONAL IMPERATIVES OF MODERN CITIZENSHIP

Modern man fails in responsible citizenship for a variety of reasons. A brief mention of these will be to the point here although the order in which we shall comment on them is not necessarily the order of their importance. First is the fact that the variety of activities and pursuits opened up by the industrial and urban community is tremendous and that a sensible choice from among these to which to dedicate oneself is well-nigh impossible to the self-alienated individual who has never possessed a vital center. When man was close to the soil and in organic relationship with his community, the problem of separating the essential from the trivial in achieving the more abundant life, rarely arose, particularly where he owned the land beneath his feet and where wrestling a living from it was not too hard. The sense of community and the way of life which was traditional in that context gave rise to patterns of behavior which gave him roots and meaning. Unfortunately the similarity between the patterns of life of the simple, agricultural community and those of the modern, industrial-urban center, is purely coincidental. Without question many of the activities and pursuits of modern life are spiritually and intellectually pathological. Many, of course, are not. But the problem of separating the healthy from the pathological is difficult for the individual who has no set of relevant criteria for separating the wheat from the chaff. Since such a separation is essential if one wishes to talk sense about the good life, the bewildering variety of urban distractions makes the task well-nigh insuperable for modern man, especially where roots to the past have been lost and these have not been replaced by the development of a vital center which can guarantee a modicum of wisdom. Here then is one obstacle to the task of formulating the good life.

A second consideration which makes for difficulty in the development of responsible leadership is that the average man has a very poverty-stricken picture of the activities and characteristic purposes of the groups and institutions by which he is surrounded. To make matters worse, he is so alienated from himself and a sense of community that he does not feel any need to acquire this type of information. In a sociological sense he finds himself in utter confusion, embedded in a milieu whose workings, history, purposes and changes, are foreign to him. Whether he likes it or not he is forced to be a member of a lonely crowd. The conflicts for power and the competition of purpose he reads about can therefore take on so little meaning for him that there is no reason for him to make his voice heard. In desperation he insulates himself against the attendant confusion through "having fun," the modern version of wine, women, and song. If his purse is limited he takes the vicarious equivalent of these from the sensational stories of the modern tabloid. Our modern passion for the sensational is certainly in part the result of our withdrawal from participation in the flow of social forces which are so little understood. There is an increasing tendency for the socially bewildered and alienated citizen to pursue some of our safer equivalents of modern forms of escapism. Among these are a number which receive a good deal of social approval: (1) the business conference which accomplishes nothing but contributes an ersatz sense of relatedness to its participants; (2) the humbug fellowship and communion of the country club; (3) the do-it-yourself activities which confer a false sense of power and personal meaningfulness upon their devotees; and (4) the pretended satisfactions of suburban living which provide a shallow sense of family life in which one is a hero to one's uncritical offspring and from which one derives a sense of accomplishment which in reality was lost a long time ago with the disappearance of the American frontier.

Consider a third phenomenon which makes for rootless citizenship. Modern life in the West is very complex. The consequences of group action, institutional behavior and legal, administrative policy, often cannot be understood without the closest type of analysis, currently relegated to experts. To determine the future impacts of the social artifacts and policy decisions for which we, ourselves, are responsible, requires exhaustive thought and much specialized knowledge, and even these often fail in predictive value. The mathematical and analytical training needed in order to try to determine the consequences of human action, requires years of preparation. The fund of knowledge to employ these skills demands additional years. The average man has neither the training nor the inclination to submit to intellectual regimens of this sort. Yet it will become a mockery to talk of the good life, of responsible citizenship and participation in the democratic process, if these skills and this information do not eventually become the property of the average citizen. We cannot reconstruct society nearer to our heart's desire on the shifting sands of a population divided into intellectual "haves" and "have nots." In spite of the average citizen's willingness to "let George do it," direct participation in the matters spoken of here will, in the generations to come, have to become a must for us all. If this participation fails to occur, the fragmentation of modern man will go on its merry way to a chaos which will bury us all.

A fourth consideration which merits our concern and is somewhat corollary to the preceding one, is very basic. This is the fact that when problems hit a modern community the democratic process is frequently vitiated by the fact that both leaders and followers have frequently never acquired the type of information which is germane to decision-making and which would be suitable for proposing one or another type of social change that might be in order. Nor can we always expect the public-spirited statesman or citizen to acquire this information under an accelerated program, no matter how feverish his efforts. An excellent example of the type of adjustment and single-mindedness needed can be seen in the efforts of some of our more forward-looking senators and congressmen, to acquire sufficient information concerning the nature of atomic and nuclear physics to deal adequately with pending legislation surrounding both military technology and proposals for the peacetime uses of atomic energy. In general, then, our ignorance of necessary types of information on all sorts of matters can make a shambles of all our talk of the good life. The great open spaces of ignorance in our lives will have to be irrigated by study and reading and the burning of much midnight oil, if the achievement of educational wholeness is truly our objective.

There are many other important factors and phenomena a lack of knowledge of which makes modern citizenship febrile. Unfortunately we have neither the time nor the space to discuss these. However, the fourth factor mentioned above is of major importance. It leads naturally and easily to a recognition that there are types of information and types of skill which the intelligent and responsible citizen must acquire to some degree in order to understand his milieu and to manipulate it effectively in order to realize his values. This will be true regardless of what his conception of the good life may be. But in America our intelligent and responsible citizen is being shunted away from these tasks by what has come to be called "middlebrow culture." Middlebrow culture gives the impression that one is fulfilling one's social and cultural responsibilities when, in fact, one is distinctly avoiding them. What then is middlebrow culture?

## III. THE CULTURAL BLIGHT OF MIDDLEBROWISM

As our culture grows more complex and the social determinants of human nature become more varied, the pursuit of the good life requires not only greater mental health than ever before but also greater knowledge and greater wisdom. This means that more than ever the mature, responsible citizen must acquire a vast fund of information and think harder, longer, and more wisely than ever about the problems he faces and the manner in which the good life is to be achieved. Assuming that our understanding of what we mean by the good life has been sharpened, we find that our fellow middlebrow Americans have taken a direction which prevents us from sharing any sharpened convictions and objectives with them. Americans are fast becoming a nation of middlebrows and middlebrowism is characterized by the following sins: a dislike of difficult and sustained thought; resentment of high seriousness and purpose; annoyance with, and flight from, high moral indignation; and a refusal to acquire the extensive information and the sharp analytical skills required for enlightened and mature, responsible citizenship. Instead the middlebrow becomes a cultural dilettante. He or she prefers the conversational bilgewater of the cocktail party or the standard, social visit. To furnish a jest and to obtain a laugh are infinitely more important than to try to raise one's spiritual or intellectual stature in any degree.

For the middlebrow the sharpening of intelligence as a worthwhile activity is unwanted and depreciated. It is regarded as proper for the classroom but most inappropriate for the drawing-room. The close examination of the values we live by in order to establish bonds of agreement and possibilities for reformation, where reformation is needed, is regarded as offensive. Such efforts are simply not cricket and both social visitors and party-goers will close ranks to prevent you from engaging in such unsociable action. No effort must be made to introduce people to their own subconscious. The middlebrow insists on being left fragmented and if his fragmentation eventually leads to conflict, why everyone knows what to do. Just visit the nearest psychiatrist at fifty bucks a throw, provided his couch has clean slip-covers and the spiritual baptism he gives us never gets beyond verbal total immersion. Serious thinkers who have found this deculturation repugnant, have explained it to themselves by asserting that the art of good conversation has been lost. This is a mistake. It has died. Lost articles may be recovered but dead entities leave only memories. Clearly the logical and dialectical efforts which mature people must make to spell out the nature of the good life for changing needs and circumstances, will never be made by those hapless middlebrows afflicted with the coctkail-party conversation virus. Clearly the translation of a way of life into action which may succeed in eliminating the pathological from our individual lives and from the social fabric in which we are immersed, is impossible for those who have no sense of felt values and whose most ennobling and renovating experience consists of a new way to mix highballs. The middlebrow loves to remain a heathen intellectually because he is so used to being one. He can, indeed, persuade himself that he is above the common herd by playing parlor games which tax four of his cortical cells, or less. It is common even in university circles to see middlebrows passionately concerned over "ghost" or "scrabble" or bridge, while the world goes to pot. Today the middlebrow may identify with the contestants in a huge give-away program but he will rarely identify with a reading list aimed at improving his intellectual and psychological stature. I have said that these experiences are common. They are also depressing and doubly so because most Americans today seem more anxious to achieve and retain middlebrow status than to achieve and retain anything else.

Middlebrows are expected to relate to each other in terms of what Riesman [3] calls other-directedness, which demands that we massage one another's egos, avoid treading spiritually or intellectually on each other's toes, and do and say only those things which will create an atmosphere of the familiar. Conversation is reduced to what the general semanticists call phratric communion, the exchange of trite phrases and stereotypes of thought, in order to achieve warmth, security, and friendship only, while carefully avoiding conversational gambits which would tax the other fellow intellectually and thereby render him uncomfortable. At the same time role-playing must be present to a maximum. At the cock-

[3] The nature of other-directedness as a cultural character-type is discussed in the following volume: David Riesman et al, *The Lonely Crowd*, New York: Doubleday, 1953, 359 pp. See, particularly, Chapter 1, "Some Types of Character and Society," pp. 17–53.

tail party or the social visit we are all expected to behave as though we have the manners of a philosopher and thinker—but not the matter. To be poised, to possess charm (if a male) or sex appeal (if a female), to smile and grin perpetually and meaninglessly, to drip verbal idiocies in syrupy accents and inflections which suggest nonexistent sensibilities and resources—in short to cultivate Heinz's 57 varieties of animal magnetism —this seems to be the order of the day. The earmark of culture and intelligence is to drop a generality, a name or a bloodless banality, and preferably all three. An idea must be discussed at the level of the high-school book review and the most complicated problems are to be solved by mentioning without understanding and without relevant information some doctrinaire credo or by discussing these problems in emotionally charged language rather than through extended and exhaustive analysis. Conversation is not only confused and ambiguous but to be acceptable it must zigzag from point to point.

I can best illustrate the middlebrow addiction to conversational zig-zag by quoting a passage from *The Autobiography of Lincoln Steffens*, even though the middlebrows of whom he speaks were in their prime several decades ago. This passage serves at least to show that the middle-brow art of zigzagging intellectually has not been completely lost al-though it must be confessed that many middlebrows of my acquaintance have lost even this ability, preferring to discuss any topic with a series of grunts interspersed by an occasional exclamation which sounds like middle C. Steffens [4] is describing the conversation at Holly House, an art colony in Cos Cob, Connecticut, frequented by writers and artists whose intellectual level is characteristically middlebrow, although to give them their due they are certainly more serious than contemporary middle-brows. He says

. . . We dined all together at one long table in a fine, dark beflowered dining-room. The game was always the same. Twachtman would whisper to me as he passed on to his place, "I'll say there can be no art except under a monarchy." Waiting for a lull in the conversation, he would declare aloud his assertion, which was my cue to declare the opposite. "You are wrong, Twachtman. Art is a flower of liberty and blossoms only in republics." Others would break in on his side or mine, and marking our followers, he and I led the debate, heating it up, arousing anger—any passion, till, having everybody pledged and bitter on a side, we would gradually change around till he was arguing for the republic, I for the monarchy. Our goal was to carry, each of us, all our party around the circle without losing a partisan. The next night Twachtman would whisper and later declare that "foreign women are not beautiful; only American women have real beauty," and again we would try to lead our heelers around to the opposite view. It was amazing how often we could do it. We had difficulty with

4 Lincoln Steffens. *The Autobiography of Lincoln Steffens*. New York: Harcourt, Brace, 1931. 884 pp.

only one man, Mr. Frederic Dow, a lawyer, not merely an attorney, but a trained mind. He did not take part in the argument; he only listened and suffered. "How illogical!" he would exclaim. "You are arguing yourselves around! You are changing sides. Can't you see it? Don't you know it?" Even his exposure did not halt many of our followers; they were more loyal or more combative than they were reasonable. But the game hurt Dow so much that he got up from the table once to run away, with his hands holding his head. "I can't stand it," he cried. Twachtman took mercy on him and told me to tell him what we were up to. After that the only logical mind there used to sit at the table and join us afterward on the veranda, where, abandoned and betrayed by their leaders, the artists, writers, and their wives fought it out alone till the night air calmed them or somebody saw or said something else . . . (pp. 437–8)

American middlebrowism then, in contrast to, let us say, Russian cultural and educational seriousness, clearly stands in the way of a mature and responsible examination of the good life. American middlebrowism is characterized by cultural dilettantism and educational poverty, by intellectual laziness and social herd-mindedness, by other-oriented conformity and conversational claptrap. It is also characterized by the pursuit of comfort, the cultivation of all forms of alienation and role-playing and a rise in the number of our personal conflicts. We are a nation of headless horsemen and if we look carefully even the horses are only rockinghorses. The social bunting in which we love to wrap ourselves is proving to be a shroud.

These unhappy characteristics which we have so sketchily touched upon constitute a very tiny fragment of our middlebrow culture. The middlebrow characteristics we have mentioned here, as well as others we have not even touched upon, stand in the way of any serious examination of what we mean by the good life, and even more, stand in the way of any possibility of leading it.

## IV. THE SUBSTANCE OF CULTURAL MATURITY

What can the middlebrow do to change his direction, assuming he wishes to change it? What can the salvageable minority which deplores middlebrowism do to increase Isaiah's remnant? We must reeducate ourselves along avenues which will build up states of consciousness without which there can be no meaningful concern with the good life—either philosophically or in action. There are five such states of consciousness which, I believe, are the *sine qua nons* of maturity and which I wish to mention most briefly here. These are dialectical consciousness, empathic consciousness, value consciousness, methodological consciousness, and integrative consciousness.

Dialectic consciousness makes us fit for articulate and profound communication. It is characterized by being a balanced blend of logic, semantics, and a sense of the value system and metaphysics which underly the manner in which we actually propose to pursue the good life, to contemplate it or to criticise it. It enables us to examine all aspects of an issue or problem and yet never lose sight of the core meaning predicated by that problem and which nevertheless influences its peripheral aspects.

Empathic consciousness is concerned with developing techniques for the thorough intellectual understanding of the other person's predicament, with developing in ourselves the feelings with which that predicament becomes charged and with a show of compassion for the individual in that predicament, which the occasion requires. Add to this the recognition that the sufferer is ourself in another corporeal frame and add the earnest wish to eliminate that suffering by one means or another, and we come closer to what is involved in empathy. Add further that in a psychological sense we feel we are our brother's keeper and that a workable morality of sentiment and feeling demands that we help the other fellow to grow and realize himself, both when he is aware of his conflicts and frustrations and when he is not, and the cup of empathy is nearly full. Ideally there should be no limit to the mutual aid which empathic consciousness involves. We may fall short of how much empathy we can give but we must do no bookkeeping in advance as to the amount of empathic credit we are prepared to extend. We give what our limitations, circumstances, and insight allow us to give—no less and no more.

Value consciousness arises when we make a conscious effort, both intellectually and emotionally, to translate the pattern of values to which we subscribe, into action, either in relation to our own personal growth, in relation to the growth and needs of our fellow-men, in relation to our human ecology, that is, Nature, or in relation to the unresolved mysteries of life and matter which is sometimes called the sense of the mystery of Being. We must commit ourselves to actions which fulfill or implement the values we profess, and if we clearly understand the implication of our values we may understand what these implications demand in action for a variety of contexts. It is this type of commitment which philosophical existentialists stress and which they describe as a resolve to "engage ourselves." We must seriously avoid a gap between the values we hold and the behavior which so often works against them. It is this difference between conceived and operative values which marks the greater insanity of our time, in contrast with human behavior in the past. This gap is widening rather than narrowing with middlebrow culture whose most characteristic feature is to cultivate as a virtue the socially approved schizophrenia of our time. This it succeeds in doing very largely through the widespread, smug appreciation of role-playing. The psychologist, Festinger, calls the awareness of the fitness of our actions and our values— cognitive assonance. When we develop cognitive assonance we are developing one sense of value consciousness. When we are almost completely unaware what we mean by our values, even verbally, and when we are almost completely unaware that our actions are out of joint with our expressed values, even where we are clear as to what these mean, then we suffer from cognitive dissonance which is the absence of value consciousness entirely.

One of the essentials for escaping the claptrap of middlebrow culture is to cultivate a capacity to think clearly and to think scientifically. The first is generally a product of the development of logical and semantic penetration into the issues which move us. The second is an awareness of the manner in which research must be undertaken or designed in order to arrive at natural or social truth. If we add to these an awareness of the metaphysical and value presuppositions which underly even our scientific ventures and an awareness of the relationships between our theoretical constructions and the world as given, we have what I am calling *methodological* consciousness. Taking all these matters in the aggregate, we can speak of them as the "philosophy of science." A good familiarity with the philosophy of science and a readiness to approach problems of human communication in its terms, together with the realization that systematic inquiry into anything demands a deep and firm understanding of scientific method, will save us from much error and frustration and certainly from middlebrow confusion. Deliberate efforts to function in these terms represents what is meant by methodological consciousness.

Finally no real cultivation of intellect and spirit and no intelligent employment of action is possible without integrative or holistic consciousness. This refers to the studied effort on our part to avoid compartmentalization of different theories concerning the same phenomenon or the fragmentation of knowledge into disparate data whose relationships do not arouse our interest. When we make an effort to coordinate different theories dealing with the same or different aspects of a common problem or phenomenon, this is one type of integrative consciousness, particularly when the coordination achieves a new theoretical unity. When we coordinate different data which are related to each other, so as to see the relevance of these data to a common phenomenon or problem, we have a second type of integrative consciousness. The first we call coordinative integration and the second existential integration. The two types together make up integrative consciousness. When integrative consciousness is deliberately cultivated in our contacts both with human knowledge and theory and in our experience with different aspects of nature and self, we have laid another brick in the temple of human development and we have added another weapon to the armory with which we can avoid middlebrow obtuseness.

If each of us takes seriously an education devoted to the development of these five types of consciousness, we can make sense of our common concern with the good life. If not, we shall continue to develop intellectually in an aborted fashion—our confusion and middlebrow fragmentation increasing all the time—with no prospects, whatsoever, of succeeding in reformulating the great ideals of *paideia* for an age increasingly dominated by science and technology.

Until now we have stressed chiefly the negative aspects of the pursuit of culture, that is to say, we have been preoccupied with those departures from the ideals of *paideia*, which can be found in the pursuit of culture as practised by middlebrows. We have not as yet attempted to define explicitly the meaning of culture in a positive sense. We are now fully aware of some of the leading but mistaken ideas concerning the content of culture. What, however, may be said to constitute the positive content of culture? What can we say is the *true meaning* of culture for an age whose quality and pace of change are chiefly determined by the advances and discoveries of science and technology? Of equal importance is another sort of question which we have not as yet faced. What difference does a genuine sense of culture make for the relationships which govern men? The intent of such a question is to explore in a general way those improvements which presumably may be made possible in the sphere of human relationships when a culture seeks to express the ideals of paideia in a modern context.

In Chapter 9 we answer some of these questions in a general fashion. In this way we can somewhat justify the position that it is worthwhile for the average person to be concerned with the problems of leisure and of culture and that such concerns are, in fact, meaningful in his own life. With Chapter 9 we close our discussion of the nature of the problems which leisure and culture constitute for modern man. The remainder of Part II concerns the bearing which a genuine sense of culture has for the reconstruction of modern education—a reconstruction which must unswervingly serve the ideals of paideia but do so, however, in a society which is being increasingly shaped by the social and economic changes produced by new technology and, above all, cybernation.

# 9

# The Meaning of Culture:
# Culture as Human Relations*

## I. WHAT CULTURE IS NOT

Perhaps the most appropriate way to begin a treatment of my theme would be to try to be clear about what culture is not. There are many things, of course, which might mistakenly be called culture, but the most ridiculous error to be avoided in this connection is what, for want of a better term, I shall call the *aesthetic pretense*. By this I am referring to the most dishonest of all meanings of the term "culture." This is the meaning which includes *talking* about books, plays, and films of a high artistic level, without ever having genuinely worked through the aesthetic, moral, or socially critical intent of their creators. The aesthetic pretense includes the postures of the culture-hound, such as the ersatz swooning over classical music at a concert in order to demonstrate to the onlooker one's superior but phony sensitivity. It includes attendance at such affairs as art exhibits, film and dance festivals, and poetry readings, followed by a gathering of people into little knots to discuss the experience with a meaningless and pretentious vocabulary as fuzzy as the program notes at a concert. It brings within its compass name-dropping in literature and quotations from poems and novels which are intended to prop up the quoter's ego rather than to amplify the context of the discussion. Perhaps the most bastardized aspect of the aesthetic pretense is the notion that to be cultured, one must be "refined." The examples of refinement made popular by Metro-Goldwyn-Mayer, using the Hollywood version of the *snobismus* of the international set as a prop, come in two models. In one of these the "refined" lady or gentleman must employ cultivated speech, mellifluous accents, an icy stare when ruffled, and a patter which suggests nothing so much as a mouth full of mush. The other model of refinement requires a proper lady or gentleman to respond to the rude stupidities of one's inferiors by learning to titter at them

---

* Chapter 9, with adaptations and modifications, has been taken from the following source: Henry Winthrop. "The Meaning of Culture: Culture as Human Relations." *Journal of Human Relations.* Vol. 11, No. 1, 1962, 105–122.

through one nostril. All these immaturities, and many others besides, are examples of the follies underlying the great American middlebrow notion of culture with its worship of the attenuated posture in manner and speech. The aesthetic pretense is fundamentally the Reichian armor of the male middlebrow namby-pamby and his pretentious and fatuous wife who has very little between the eyes and even less beneath the sternum.

Almost as great a disaffection as the aesthetic pretension is the "precious" literary-humanistic approach which prefers to treat culture as a hothouse product. This is a stance of the highbrow snob as well as that of some other types of snob so cleverly caught in the thumbnail sketches of Lynes.[1] It is also the posture of the educated anglophile who mistakes a "veddy, veddy" British accent for the earmarks of a "CULT-yored" soul, "don't you know!" We also find this posture in the sheltered, ivory-tower version of culture *disembodied* from the mortal battles and the pursuits of men. We are given versions of this above-the-battle humanism in such standby pre-Georgian and Georgian interpreters of culture as Matthew Arnold,[2] T. S. Eliot [3] and John Cowper Powys.[4] The deficiencies of the "literary-humanistic" approach to culture are first, that it is irrelevant to the great issues of our time where it is strictly literary; second, that it is psychologically separatist when it is class-conscious or snobbish; and third, that it is myopic about those aspects of the human condition which can be understood only by appreciating the impact of science and technology on our lives and the greater relevancy of scientific thoughtways over our literary heritage for the problems of the age.

The reader should not assume that there is some contradiction between the remarks made in the text above, in connection with the authors mentioned, and our reference to these authors in Chapter 7. In Chapter 7 we indicated that these writers understood the meaning of a genuine sense of culture. The most conspicuous *deficiency* of their viewpoint is that it plays down social and political involvement. This deficiency is seized upon by middlebrows and erected into a virtue. Culture, when thus transmogrified, is not regarded as something relevant to the great social and moral issues of our time. This is what we mean by the phrase, "above-the-battle humanism." The attribute which receives poverty-stricken treatment in the writers mentioned then becomes the *sine qua non* in the cultural posture of the middlebrow.

[1] Russell Lynes. *Snobs. A Guidebook to your Friends, Your Colleagues and Yourself.* New York: Harper, 1950. 54 pp.
[2] Matthew Arnold. *Culture and Anarchy.* Cambridge: Cambridge University Press, 1957. 241 pp.
[3] Thomas Stearns Eliot. *Notes towards the Definition of Culture.* New York: Harcourt, Brace, 1949. 128 pp.
[4] John Cowper Powys. *The Meaning of Culture.* New York: W. W. Norton, 1929. 275 pp.

The last counterfeit posture which I should like to mention here is that of the *liberal rhetoric* and the *liberal ritual*. This is also the most dangerous posture because it is usually disguised, sometimes well and sometimes poorly. This is the stance which equates being socially conscious with being cultured. Properly speaking, I should have said *"talking about social consciousness"* rather than *being* socially conscious. I make this discrimination because in this extravagance of attitude one is expected to be "in the know" about social corruption and social injustice of every sort and to be prepared, *verbally only,* to take a stand which may variously be called "liberal," "progressive," or "independent." In actuality those who pursue the liberal rhetoric and the liberal ritual most of the time, display the following characteristics: (1) They are poorly informed about the nature of the problems on which they declare themselves. (2) They do not plunge into any genuine involvements and tend to be merely ideologically oriented to issues, although the ideology is, in almost all cases, a denatured and spotty version of what they imagine constitutes the democratic philosophy. By this I mean that they have some vague notions and some equally vague sentiments concerning what it means to be on the side of the humanistic angels when it comes to social and political issues, but they lack almost completely any of the technical and analytical skills required for dealing properly with the complexities which these issues pose. (3) They make certain to keep at a safe distance from the consequences *in action* which are entailed by their liberal rhetoric and liberal rituals. (4) They can be counted upon to violate the vaguely held notions and sentiments of their "liberal" credo in their daily face-to-face relationships at work, in political crises, and in their constant efforts to curry favor with "squares" who are in a position to help them advance themselves. (5) They are the spiritual Quislings of our time, for in order to go places, they will perpetrate any sell-out and develop the lamest of rationalizations for doing so, as befits the intellectually and spiritually crippled who suffer from character disorders which are, as yet, uncatalogued in any psychiatric nomenclature.

These epigonoi of liberalism are more dangerous in the long run than our ambitious authoritarian personalities because their anti-Christ potentialities are concealed by the masks of a humanitarian credo. A good many of them flourish remarkably well among the "professoriat" of American institutions of higher learning. But in or out of the university, they are found *chiefly* (not solely) among the members of that generation which was *roughly* 10 years of age or less in 1939, provided this pinpointing of age is not taken too literally. Many of their members have never been subject to economic and social stress and strain in a period of adulthood, such as was characteristic of the depression generation. A good many members of the loose group to which I refer are social nincompoops in that halfway house of the spirit which fell between World

War II and the thermonuclear Doomsday which presently faces the world. Many of them, if they had their way, would begin to write books on the care of parents, a possibility which Michael Young's [5] glimpse of the immediate future, suggests could be a reality a few decades hence, to judge from his mock-serious sociological report of a future nightmare world in which presumably these liberal jelly-rolls could practice their one-upmanship.

The preceding remarks should not be misconstrued. Many members of this generation are among today's genuine and altruistic leaders. I simply wish to emphasize that there are more members of this generation alienated from a genuine liberalism than the members of any other American generation. This is true for at least two reasons. (1) They became adult in an Age of Opportunity and rarely directly experienced any major social pathologies or economic and educational difficulties in reaching adulthood. (2) They escaped the major disasters of our time—unemployment in the Depression, service in World War II, the job anxieties of the McCarthy Era and freedom from being drafted for service in Vietnam. For reasons such as these, the liberalism of many members of this generation tends to be a verbal posture rather than a way of life.

The liberal rhetoric and the liberal ritual are not confined to this age group. That type of rhetoric and ritual is often more rigidly exemplified in members of a much older group. It is a depressant to the human spirit to hear many of these "liberals" remark in the face of an injustice which they judge to be minor, whether or not the victim so regards it, that justice is only an ideal and not to be regarded as something attainable in this world. Here we hear the apologetic voices of those who live on the surface of things. One's optimism concerning the dynamism of the liberal rhetoric and ritual is considerably reduced at receiving the sage advice not to fight too hard to rectify injustices tolerated by large numbers, where these are created by false gossip and slander, downright prevarication, social misinterpretation and misjudgment, inaccuracy, personal prejudice, or character assassination—even where these exact a toll from their victims, a toll which these same victims would like to avoid. What shallowness of understanding is revealed by an attitude of this sort! Where is this "liberal's" sense of history, that he forgets how much the human condition has been improved because there were people at all times who possessed a sufficient fund of social altruism to be concerned over wrongs done to others as well as to themselves.

---

[5] Michael Young. *The Rise of the Meritocracy. 1870–2033. An Essay on Education and Equality.* London: Thames and Hudson, 1958. 160 pp. The general protest of the young towards the way of life of their elders, is described by Young in Chapter Four, Section 3, entitled *Challenge to Age.* The revolt against their elders by the young, described in this section, constitutes, by inference, a critique also of their parents—a critique which could conceivably be incorporated in manuals for the proper redirection of parents in general.

Many liberals of this stamp have developed a standardized cant to justify their stasis of soul. They insist that the wrongdoing and mistakes perpetrated upon individuals, must be rectified by better behavior on the part of their victims and by insisting that these victims improve their sense of good human relations. One does not know whether to laugh or to cry at this effort to twist the meaning of the phrase, "good human relations," into a credo for the justification of servility, obsequiousness, and resignation—a credo which asks those who are wronged to provide an unnecessary and despicable apology for being wronged, by cultivating any form of social hypocrisy which will convince the wrongdoer that the victim realizes the wrongs were deserved, by turning over a new leaf. This "new leaf" is to be called "improved human relations." The liberal who practices this cant is the same type that refuses to accept the need for communication to straighten out a misunderstanding between two individuals on the ground that this only exacerbates the already existing misunderstanding. He prefers to use the chain of administrative and executive authority. The truth of the matter is, of course, that he is running from an honest solution of the perennial problem of "authority versus responsibility." He prefers authority and loyalty because social and ethical responsibility might force him to disagree with or reprimand an ally or acknowledge that his judgment of men is poor. Under these circumstances the best motto, of course, is "Don't rock the boat!" and the best "philosophy" is that "justice is only an ideal." This is the Platonism of the moral apologist who wishes to forget that it is men and men only who usher into being justice or its opposite. The whole outlook described here is a part of that type of behavior which supports any tissue of social lies, so long as it makes one's own situation a comfortable one and leaves one's false and inflated self-image unshaken. This is, however, the self-image of the "square" who looks into the mirror and sees a fighting champion for justice and humanity, albeit a wiser one than most, because this type of liberal fancies himself politic, temperate, and free of self-defeating passion.

It is the existence of a bourgeois mentality of this sort which gave rise to the Western type of radicalism of the 19th and 20th centuries. This was a radicalism which rejected the "organized system" of social injustice, repudiated the leadership which had no genuine feeling of outrage over the existence of such injustice, and repudiated those intellectual pretenders who developed a variety of apologetics for it. The essence of these apologia was that a little injustice, like a little inflation, might be a good thing. It is this Panglossian mentality which fundamentally makes its peace with the social imperfections of this world and which it holds are tolerable, that has given rise to an existentialist sense of outrage from Kierkegaard to the existentialists of our own time, whether in literature, social philosophy, or psychiatry. These "liberals" are the good boys who allow themselves to be manipulated by those who hold power—but for a price, usually the advancement of one's career. It is precisely this type of false liberalism, precisely this type of "bleeding heart" without blood vessels, which makes it so necessary for anyone sincerely concerned with human relations, to wish to have no truck with the liberal rhetoric and the liberal ritual.

The American professoriat is shot through with these milksop attitudes. Under no circumstances then can one rationally and humanely hold a posture of this sort to be one of the genuine and basic meanings of the term, "culture." This is the type of liberalism which, whether it recognizes the fact or not, is destined to be the midwife at the birth of a Western type of authoritarianism. The most charitable remark that one can make about it in this connection, comes from Lerner.[6]

. . . But I agree with Ortega y Gasset that the modern liberal mentality suffers from the disease of tendermindedness in its fear of facing the reality of power. This has paralyzed much of our educational thinking, and has recently led by recoil to a brand of educational policy proposals which would make the schools and universities merely the instrument of the state, and would make the test of truth not whether it is valid and verifiable but whether it makes the existing power-structure viable—a position not substantially different from the Party-line truth of the Communists. (p. 15)

These then are three of the postures which are currently regarded as synonymous with the meaning of culture and which are, in one way or another, natural antitheses to the true meaning of that much abused term. There are other shoddy meanings of this term, held by substantial numbers of people in each case, and which emasculate its true content almost completely, but this is not the place to deal with them. I have emphasized the three mentioned here simply because I feel they represent the most frequent and mistaken abuse of the meaning of culture.

## II. HOW SHOULD WE DEFINE CULTURE?

Having cleared the atmosphere of some of the false and noxious notions surrounding the meaning of culture, it is now time to turn to those meanings which I regard as distinctly creditable. There are, of course, many ways of defining culture, each of which would find some acceptability on the part of an educated and sensitive public. Many of them will be found to share *some* common ground. This will likewise be true of the definitions which I wish to bring to the fore here.

Our first definition of culture defines the term by a flank attack rather than a frontal assault. It recognizes that there are three kinds of people in the world—those who do not know what is happening around

[6] Max Lerner. *Education and a Radical Humanism. Notes toward a Theory of the Educational Crisis.* Columbus: Ohio State University Press. 1962. 63 pp.

them, those who do and let it happen, and those who—having a Christian and a democratic vision of the good life—see to it that they make things happen. A justifiable catch-all definition of culture, then, might be one which characterized culture as all those activities which can prompt people to move from the first two categories into the third. This will be serviceable provided we understand that this occurs when the spirit hath been moved and the shift is entirely voluntary. A person who made the shift under coercion would really be a member of our second category.

This first definition has chiefly its pithiness to recommend it. If, however, we mull over those aspects of human experience which have moved us profoundly, in either an intellectual or an emotional sense, our definition will be considerably different. If we consult our inner selves with utmost honesty I think most of us will agree that a genuine sense of culture refers to the following matters:

1. It refers to every type of experience which expands the horizons of consciousness of people, enlarging their understanding of the world, of others, and of themselves.

2. A genuine cultivation of the intellect and of human sensibilities should implant *a feeling for the implications* ideas and sentiments have for social action as well as for humanity's collective movement towards various forms of the good life.

3. Only that culture is genuine *which we intend to live and express in action,* and genuine culture must arouse a willingness to remake ourselves in the light of the implications to which I have just referred, as well as *a desire to try to remold the world a little closer to these same implications.* These implications are our guidelines for voluntarily produced social change.

It is this third aspect of our second definition of culture which is most important for the *area of human relations.* What are the ways in which we succeed in remolding others? First, we may enlarge their horizons via *personal contact* socially, via educational contact in or out of the classroom, via contacts in civic and cultural groups and via groups of one sort or another with a mission which has some significance for the human condition. Second, we can fan the flame of the human spirit by actively translating our enlarged horizons into support for the battles waged for official but worthy causes, but particularly for those on behalf of social justice and personal freedom of all kinds. Those who joined the Freedom Riders in the Sixties were striking out for one form of social justice. Those who fought in the Sixties to find a place somewhere in the world for the refugees from Red China who steamed into Hongkong, were striking out for one form of personal freedom. Third and last, we must keep alive through all the personal influence which we can muster, all important biases *on behalf of* Man. Some of these biases may change over the course of the decades, due to altered social circumstances and unforeseen contingencies of a dramatic nature. There are certain social and political biases, the products of either our recent history or the American ideological past, which bid fair to be relevant to the social issues and struggles of the next few decades. These should be reinforced in a culture which is to be meaningful. I should like to discuss some of these at this point.

The New Deal spirit of effective liberalism is one of the major biases which men and women, wishing to express a genuine and lived culture, can try to preserve. The New Deal tradition in the United States was essentially a task-oriented tradition which insisted upon taking stock of pressing and unsolved problems rather than pretending they did not exist. The New Deal insisted upon a genuine fulfillment of the traditional ideal of opportunity for all instead of merely giving lip service to it. It tried honestly to remember the import of Lincoln's words "New times demand new measures and new men." Having captured the essence of this apothegm, it tried to create a congeries of new opportunities throughout the land to the extent that existing skills, the current state of technology, the popular state of psychological readiness, and the political circumstances of the time, would allow. It earned unpopularity, hostility, and misunderstanding as a result, particularly from vested interests which had some selfish privileges to protect and some inertia to justify. Such reactions never deterred those New Dealers who had thoroughly understood what Aristotle meant when he defined politics as the art of the possible. The New Deal likewise remembered some of our traditional egalitarian ideals, in the only sense in which such ideals could have meaning—equality before the law and in the face of public opinion. Through some of the early New Deal administrative agencies, it tried to translate these egalitarian ideals into a form workable in the face of the economic, industrial, and social complexities of the 20th century. But it was most lavish in its efforts to provide the equality of opportunity already mentioned and right within the government's own preserves. In this form the New Deal took stock of Napoleon's principle—*"une carrière ouverte aux talents"*—and Civil Service doors were opened to the best brains of the country. Talent was enlisted to deal with the pressing problems of the day.

The effort at selection and screening did not succeed completely. How could it be expected to in a less than perfect world? Politics still played a major role in the choice of decision-makers—some were called because of the old school tie, some were called because they had been faithful party hacks. But more talent and ability than was ever before summoned on behalf of our national democratic destiny, fell between these two stools. The New Deal's efforts also fell short in that there was less than perfect relationship between the intelligence and educational achievement of those who were called and the decision-making power which was actually put into their hands—power to make decisions of a political, social and community nature. Essentially, those who were called received the power to implement policy and inaugurate a small measure of it. Major policy changes were still, of course, in political hands. Nevertheless a less than perfect relationship between talent and decision-making power may have had certain advantages. Hindsight suggests that a perfect relationship between these two factors might have contained the threat of the worst aspects of a rigid "meritocracy," as described by Michael Young.[7] So, perhaps, a little imperfection in this respect was a blessing in disguise. We would not have been ready for such perfection at the time.

The New Deal also conserved the traditional, liberal ideals concerned with the struggle for increasing the amount of justice in this vale of tears. This it brought about by social action rather than by the lip-service of exemplars of the liberal rhetoric and the liberal ritual and by an enlargement in the scope of the nation's democratic practices. It is all these biases on behalf of Man, on behalf of the effort to remold the thinking and the actions of others a little nearer to the implementation of the good life, which a genuine culture must try to preserve. It is an expression of historical, cultural ideals *which are to be lived,* that commends the New Deal bias as one of the ways of reinforcing the third aspect we have set forth in our second definition of culture.

There is still another important bias on behalf of common humanity which a culture that is to be meaningful on a day-to-day basis cannot afford to lose sight of. Lerner [8] has remarked that Americans, who were once a revolutionary people, have in recent years begun to deny vehemently this aspect of their cultural heritage. I am referring, of course, to our traditional support of popular revolutions which arise on behalf of an effort to ensure an extension of social justice and democracy. Lerner makes the following remarks:

It is a curious fact that Americans, whose nationhood came out of revolution and whose whole history distills the authentic revolution of modern times, should today be so fearful of the word and idea of revolution, which has dominated world history ever since the American and French revolutions and which forms today the essential world climate. The image we present to a large part of the world is that of an acquisitive and tenacious people, sitting on top of a pyramid of wealth and power, fearful of having it taken away from us, but also doomed by the laws of history to give it up, the only question being whether we give it up with good or bad grace, and after or without a world nuclear war.

I have had occasion, in the past fifteen years to concentrate much of my energy on a study of the American civilization pattern, and more recently of the challenges offered to that civilization by the nature of contemporary world politics. What has emerged clearly from my studies is that American civilization

---

7 Michael Young. *Op. cit.*
8 Max Lerner. *Op. cit.*

has been in continuous revolutionary change, especially in the two generations since the start of Roosevelt's New Deal—which makes it even more ironic that Americans, in their conscious attitudes, at some point lost sight of the gleaming image of a people continually transcending and transforming the conditions of their lives, the values they believe in, the means and instruments for achieving their goals. If I say that America embodies the authentic revolution of our time, I do not say it rhetorically, as a Department of State official or an ambassador to India or to Guinea might say it, but out of the American tradition and the recent changes in American life and a sense of the American cultural potential. (pp. 25–6)

In gradually giving up a social psychology which regarded democratic revolutions as worthy of support, we are losing the capacity to translate our cultural heritage into social action. We are most reluctant to support revolutions in despotic countries in Asia and Latin America— countries which are just now struggling towards a first taste of democracy and social justice. It upsets our comfortable preoccupation with gracious living and our unharrowed concerns with the three false notions of culture of which we spoke in the first section of this chapter, to face up to the fact that there are areas in the world which require violence before some justice can be achieved. We demand without reason that dissidents and protestants in such areas show respect for *democratic gradualistic procedures,* as we understand them, when in fact they lack entirely any traditions or way of life which would encourage such genteel perspectives. We will support revolutions, of course, when they are "nice" revolutions—far away geographically and possessing no tangency to American interests, like that which took place in Hungary. Such "nice" revolutions are anti-Communistic or pro-Western, or both, and are therefore virtuous. Other kinds of revolutions are, of course, "bad" revolutions. These are defined as anti-Western in nature where often they are non-Communistic but not oriented towards Western *forms* of democracy. Towards these we often take a "wait and see" attitude, which was our posture towards the *early phase* of the Cuban revolution, or we try to contain them and reverse them in countries where, we feel, they may swing too far to the left. This bifurcation of revolutions into "nice" and "bad," depending upon whether they appear to be pro or anti-Western, is one of the great middlebrow vices of our age. Obviously the mere fact that a revolution is politically pro-Western is no guarantee that its aftermath will foster ideals of social justice and democracy. By the same token the mere fact that it is anti-Western is no guarantee that democratic ideals, as we understand them, will not be given expression. One of the biases then on behalf of Man, which a lived culture can support, is to rekindle moral support for revolutions on behalf of democracy and social justice, even if such support unsettles the even tenor of American life.

A corollary to this support, of course, which the genuine expression of a meaningful cultural attitude demands, is that we help underdeveloped countries to better themselves even if they are moving only towards *humanistic, democratic socialism.* This point has been well justified by Fromm [9] and I will not labor it again here. A cultured attitude, however, which exhibits understanding, demands that we take stock in other countries of their histories, circumstances, and ways of life, where these are vastly different from our own. If *our* political forms and procedures would be a poor fit to these histories, circumstances, and ways of life, let us not demand that they be adopted. This would be as silly as trying to wear another man's oversized overcoat. A true cultured understanding would demand only that change elsewhere move clearly in the direction of more democracy and more social justice. These, as Fromm puts it, have three major characteristics which should satisfy us. These are (1) an atmosphere of personal freedom; (2) an economic system which works for the vast majority of the population; and (3) a social system which furthers rather than hinders individual development, responsibility, and decentralization; a social system which discourages conformity and discourages the formations of bureaucratic atmospheres which are without heart, intelligence, skill, altruism and imagination. Here again is a bias on behalf of a greater fund of social decency, which, if reinforced, would be expressing part of the terminal meaning of our second definition of culture.

## III. THE CONTENT OF CULTURE

In the last analysis no definition of culture, no matter how well it may be expanded, is sufficient to come to grips with the meaning of the term. No definition of culture, no matter how broad-gauge it may be, and no description of what we might reasonably call "anticulture," by which we refer, of course, to a description of those attitudes and those kinds of behavior which are "off limits," so to speak, will be sufficient to deal with the meaning of culture. The meaning of culture is most truly reflected when we can refer to some degree to its categorical content. It would, of course, be both impractical as well as superfluous to try to enumerate either all of the categories subsumable under this badly treated term or all of the content actually includable within its domain. We can abbreviate our task, however, if we recognize that all culture can be divided up basically into "soft culture" versus "hard culture." Let us discuss the nature of soft culture first.

9 Erich Fromm. *May Man Prevail? An Inquiry Into the Facts and Fiction of Foreign Policy.* New York: Doubleday, Anchor Books, 1961. 252 pp.

Soft culture is concerned with the way in which man pours meaning into life. It is concerned with the human and personal aims of individuals and with ushering into being those social aims and those social values which most of us hope will eventually inhere in the human condition. Soft culture is concerned with exploring the many alternative ways available for achieving personal growth and spiritual salvation in the face of human error and fallibility of judgment. It is concerned with the cultivation of the arts and sciences to the extent that they open up new horizons of consciousness, new dimensions of feeling, and new perspectives on a developing future. This aspect of culture is concerned more and more with the establishment of a perfect sense of community, with the provision of a greater fund of social justice in historical time and with the continual reconstruction of society in an eschatological sense. Furthermore soft culture works unceasingly for the diminution of unnecessary social pathology in any given period and place while at the same time trying to expand the horizons of freedom, both for individuals and groups. It encourages the continual experimentation with changing value patterns aimed not merely at improving the human condition but also at bringing mortals a little nearer to the earlier Wellsian dream of men like gods.

Here, in the good old U.S.A., men and women of culture and intellect, are presently concerned with trying to get their fellow citizens to switch from a pattern of values concerned chiefly with externals to a pattern of values concerned chiefly with internal matters of the spirit. The task of soft culture in the United States at the present time can best be stated in Lerner's [10] words:

In describing the life goals of Americans in the course of my *America as a Civilization,* I adopted the going sociological classification of the five-goal system: success, money, power, prestige, and security. I added to them the 'fun imperative' and the over-all permeating commitment to happiness. Together these form what can only be called sawdust goals, and the values associated with them leave the taste of sawdust in our mouths. It has become a shopworn commentary to note that as a consequence of these goals and values, the dominant drives in the American character are toward conformity, playing-it-safe, and status-seeking; the personality has become vendable; we make a cult out of bigness and numbers and do not value authenticity; we avoid conflict and fear the controversial; and we are beset not only by the man with the gray flannel suit but even more by the man with the gray flannel mind. (pp. 58–9)

Instead of these sawdust goals, says Lerner, certain substitutions are absolutely necessary. Instead of success, we must put the emphasis on facing whatever life presents, good breaks or adversities. Instead of seeking power over others we would do better to seek power over ourselves. In an existentialist sense power over ourselves refers to the development

[10] Max Lerner. *Op. cit.*

of our various potentialities, our skills and our sensitivities—and to an effort to make concrete our noblest dreams. Instead of what Lipton [11] calls our "moneytheism," our preoccupation with pecuniary canons of choice and action, we need to shift to values which enrich our inner selves. Our preoccupation with prestige based upon our phony public images should give way to efforts to make these false self-images *real,* or better still, should be superseded by our efforts to achieve ideal self-images *not* based upon the sawdust goals of *homo boobiens,* if I may be allowed to reincarnate a phrase made famous by Henry L. Mencken. Our overconcern for security should be replaced by the acceptance of some dimension of risk somewhere in our lives. There is nothing, of course, holy about risk. Its value in the mainstream of existence comes from human struggle to reduce that risk and to overcome the challenges associated with it. Victories over these are the tempering forces of character and personal resourcefulness. Instead of "having fun," let us adventure among ideas, explore the realm of taste, and cultivate what Edmund Burke has called "the unbought grace of life." Though soft culture is an affirmation of life, it makes this affirmation in a very special way. It suggests that, rather than go whoring after happiness all the time, that men face up also to the tragic sense of life; that is, to those inescapable bereavements, frustrations, deprivations, and disappointments of the human condition, which are the lot of all. It asks men to steel themselves against the whole range of unimaginative stupidities which take a toll of human happiness and which existentialists often ticket off under the category of the "absurd." Though Thoreau had probably never heard of this abstraction, nevertheless he was aware of its significance—a significance which prompted him to emphasize that the majority of men lead lives of quiet desperation. Finally, says Lerner, we ought to try to liquidate the current pathological forms of the cult of individuality and cultivate their proper replacements. Among such replacements would be a more genuine sense of fellow feeling, more sincere forms of the religious impulse, more concern with a healthy and altruistic sense of community, and more capacity to appreciate the ways of life of other cultures—what Allport [12] calls ego-extension. It is not by means of social xenophobia and cainotophobia that we will succeed in junking our sawdust goals, but only by a sincere and passionate openness to new experience. It is with needed transformations such as these that soft culture must be concerned.

Hard culture has quite a different set of meanings. It refers in general to all those matters which are of significance for the human condition, which largely help to create it and which are of such a nature that knowledge of them is difficult to come by. The difficulty is not due to the

---

11 Lawrence Lipton. *The Holy Barbarians.* New York: Grove Press, 1959. 318 pp.
12 Gordon Allport. *Becoming. Basic Considerations for a Psychology of Personality.* New Haven: Yale University Press, 1955. 106 pp.

fact that in any sense these matters are hidden but rather because they are intellectually taxing and demand a high level of intellectual self-discipline for mastery. For these reasons the content of hard culture includes such matters as the following:

1. It involves *some* technical understanding of the manner in which science and technology make their impact on human life and help to generate some of our current forms of the human condition.

2. It demands some familiarity with the presuppositions, the methods, and the findings of modern science, in the areas of both the natural and the social sciences.

3. In our search for truth it entails a somewhat more than nodding acquaintance with such disciplines as the philosophy of science, symbolic logic, the role of scientific methodology, statistics, and experimental design. These are particularly needed for those truths which we hope will usher in a better understanding of the nature of man and to frame more humane, workable, and manageable communities of mature dimensions.

4. Hard culture makes it absolutely necessary that the cultured individual have some familiarity with the grammar of mathematics. In this way the man or woman of culture can be expected to think both functionally and causally about the problems of modern life and bring the requirements of the logico-empirical tradition to bear upon the community's collective problems as well as those of humanity, itself.

There have been some intellectual revolutions in our time which have dealt with man's enlarged self-consciousness over the way he uses language. This therefore brings us to the next concern of hard culture.

5. The man or woman of culture has to become familiar with some of these different revolutions in the *rational* or *representative* uses of language. Each of these has focused on different problems and different content in exploring the proper functions of language and therefore the different names for these different revolutions reflect these differences in emphasis. Among these revolutions in the use of language with which a proper meaning of culture demands some familiarity are the following: logical positivism, philosophical analysis, general semantics, modern quantitative studies in linguistics, modern technical studies of the communication process, the analysis of the functions of language into their semantic, syntactical, and pragmatic forms and the rival theories concerning the functions of signs and symbols. There are, of course, many other breakthroughs of importance besides those mentioned here, for anyone wishing to obtain some fundamental knowledge of the functions of representative language. These would be too numerous to deal with in this discussion. We must, however, also add to all the above some of our modern anthropological studies of the manner in which language reflects the individual's phenomenal and cultural fields, using the word

"culture" here in the anthropologist's sense of that term. One of several good references along this last line, particularly in relation to what anthropologists call the Sapir-Whorf hypothesis, is a collection of papers edited by Hoijer [13] and the reader should find these of real interest.

There is also some very important social content to hard culture, a content which brings us to our sixth and seventh categories of it.

6. One of the fundamental necessities of hard culture is its emphasis on "modern perspective," sometimes called "the cult of contemporaneity" by ignoramuses with strictly humanistic leanings. I am referring to an understanding of those social revolutions which are taking place now all around us: the revolutions in industrial and social organization; the second industrial revolution of cybernetics with all the new technologies which this revolution is giving birth to—general systems theory, new approaches to systems analysis, bionics, etc.; the vast changes in the nature of work and leisure which have been generated by the revolutions in automation and data processing; the revolutions in management and administrative science which can help to usher in either a secular paradise, or if uncontrolled by soft culture, a world so inhumane as to make *1984* look like a Sunday school picnic.

7. Hard culture also demands some knowledge of the unfinished social revolutions of our time and Goodman [14] has given an excellent summary of these. The reader, I believe, will be interested in deepening his own knowledge along these lines.

In this section I have tried to characterize the *content of culture* in as broad a fashion as possible. We have avoided enumeration and description of that content in detail as both impractical and unnecessary. Instead we have tried to characterize that content in terms of a basic dichotomy of hard and soft culture. The one fact that we must never lose sight of is the relationship between these two. Hard culture must implement soft culture—not the other way around. This implementation takes the form of helping soft culture to receive expression via the social circumstances of the time and the potential relations of production and distribution which the then current state of technology make possible. It must be soft culture, however, which should give direction and purpose to the pursuit of hard culture. The great tragedy to be avoided in the relationship between these two great aspects of modern civilization is one which unfortunately modern man is allowing to shape up under his very eyes, without offering much conscious resistance to it at all. This is the mistake of accepting the current social trends and direction of

---

13 Harry Hoijer (editor). *Language in Culture.* Conference on Inter-relations of Language and other Aspects of Culture. Chicago: Chicago University Press, 1954. 286 pp.
14 Paul Goodman. *Growing Up Absurd. Problems of Youth in the Organized System.* New York: Random House, 1960. 296 pp.

technology, applied science, and industrial research, allowing these to congeal into set social and institutional patterns, and then becoming indifferent to the fact that his acceptance forces soft culture to make its peace with these institutional trends and frozen patterns. This is the equivalent of asserting implicity that soft culture must serve hard culture, the reversal of a great social truth. The great danger in this is that certain characteristics inhere in hard culture which, if allowed to sprawl unchecked over the human scene, and if undirected by the great aims of soft culture, will generate values and objectives which are antithetical to the traditional humane biases of soft culture—biases which must be preserved at any cost. Such trends must be reversed and such patterns broken up. This is one of the central meanings of culture. It is soft culture which is the breath of life and only soft culture which can pour meaning into it. This is the great lesson to be learned.

Until now our concern has been strictly with the twin problems of leisure and culture. But education which is, perhaps, the major contributor to the spiritual enrichment of our lives, will also be affected by computer technology. In particular one wonders whether the new technology of the teaching machine or, more accurately, that of programmed instruction, is likely to become the major basis of formal education. We must therefore consider carefully in what ways the distinguished flesh-and-blood teacher is indispensable for the promotion of a genuine culture. This is the focus of attention in Chapter 10.

# 10

# What Can We Expect from
# the Unprogramed Teacher?*

The literature these days on computers in general and programed learning in particular conveys an undisguised enthusiasm over the possibility that the machine will make man obsolete. The zest is sometimes hard to understand. Devotees of cybernetics and automated teaching occasionally create the impression that they see no limitations in the scientific revolution opened up by the Age of Computers. They seem to consider that there is no skill, no aptitude, no trait, no quality, and no function of man which cannot be taken over by the machine and which, in some instances, can be exercised better than by man himself.

A paper by Vandenberg,[1] for example, suggests that computer enthusiasts not only look forward to psychiatric diagnosis by machine, but that some of them may even feel that a machine can be programed to furnish the empathy which a good clinical counselor can provide. Some of them seem to hope for a machine which will provide a reasonable facsimile of the emotionally supportive functions of the psychologist or psychiatrist. Presumably, we may even be able to program a machine which will cluck sympathetically, wipe away the patient's tears, and give her a comforting pat on the shoulder. The literature on computers is full of such conceits and conceptual extravaganzas.

To be fair to the partisans of the computer revolution, it must be admitted that the original claims for the possibilities of simulating human behavior were, indeed, modest. Berkeley,[2] who was one of the pioneers of the simulation of human behavior, envisaged address books, libraries, translators, typists, stenographers, and various forms of recognizers and controllers, all of which were to be automated. He looked

* Chapter 10, with modifications and deletions, has been taken from the following source: Henry Winthrop. "What Can We Expect from the Unprogramed Teacher?" *Teachers College Record.* Vol. 67, No. 5, February 1966, 315–329.

1 S. G. Vandenberg. "Medical Diagnosis by Computer: Recent Attempts and Outlook for the Future." *Behavioral Science,* Vol. 5, 1960. 170–174.

2 Edmund C. Berkeley. *Giant Brains or Machines that Think.* New York: Wiley, 1949. 270 pp.

forward to mechanical prognosticators of the weather, psychometric machines capable of psychological and educational diagnosis, devices capable of providing training, including our modern teaching machines, and data-processing equipment for business and management decisions. Finally, he anticipated portable, auxiliary brain-machines—essentially huge mechanical memoranda devices—for enabling men to store information and to retrieve it easily, thus avoiding the cluttering of human brains which, presumably, could serve nobler purposes and more significant functions.

## I. THE PARTISANS SPEAK

With the advances in cybernetics, the possibilities of simulating human behavior, chiefly of the motor-adaptive and sensory-discriminative types, are considered enormous. These possibilities have been described in a flood of semi-popular works (see references 3–6, inclusive, below). Several learned compendia dealing with the range of accomplishments of computer applications in the behavioral sciences, like that of Borko,[7] have also appeared. Enthusiasm for cybernetics and the simulation of human behavior has carried over into the concerns of psychologists and educators, Smith and Moore,[8] for instance, and Galanter.[9] Finally, advances into the territory of strictly psychological functions, wholly subjective and central in nature, have been assembled in the journal, *Behavioral Science.* Other advances along these lines have given rise to the new science of bionics, and the Bionics Symposium [10] bids fair to become an annual affair at which cyberneticians, general systems theorists, and other interdisciplinary workers convene to advance the state of the art.

The literature critical of the excesses and extravagant claims of the more enthusiastic partisans of these developments is oddly scanty. In his last book, the distinguished thinker, von Neumann,[11] warned that the

[3] David A. Bell. *Intelligent Machines. An Introduction to Cybernetics.* New York: Blaisdell, 1962. 98 pp.

[4] Pierre de Latil. *Thinking by Machine. A Study of Cybernetics.* Boston: Houghton Mifflin, 1957. 353 pp.

[5] Georges T. Guilbaud. *What is Cybernetics?* New York: Grove Press, 1960. 126 pp.

[6] Gordon Pask. *An Approach to Cybernetics.* New York: Harper, 1961. 128 pp.

[7] Harold Borko (editor). *Computer Application in the Behavioral Sciences.* Englewood Cliffs, New Jersey: Prentice-Hall, 1962. 633 pp.

[8] Wendell I. Smith and William J. Moore. *Programmed Learning.* New York: Van Nostrand, 1962. 240 pp.

[9] Eugene Galanter (editor). *Automatic Teaching. The State of the Art.* New York: Wiley, 1959. 198 pp.

[10] Wright Air Development Division. *Bionics Symposium. Living Prototypes—The Key to New Technology.* (Technical Report 60–600). Wright-Patterson AFB, Ohio: Air Research and Development Command, USAF, 1960. 499 pp.

[11] John von Neumann. *The Computer and the Brain.* New Haven: Yale University Press, 1958. 82 pp.

brain uses a statistical language unlike that employed in the operation of man-made computers, but the warning was unheeded. Other severe critics of exaggerated expectations concerning computers in general and thinking and teaching machines in particular, like Taube,[12] have generally received critical and unsympathetic reviews, many of them executed by obvious enthusiasts and supporters of cybernetics. Wiener,[13] himself, who may be called the father of cybernetics, has warned against the possible abuse of both the philosophy and accomplishments of the computer revolution.

The important point here is not that the enthusiasts are in error, philosophically speaking. The liabilities lie entirely in another direction, the tendency to overlook what men can do which the machine cannot. Educationally, the sins of omission consist of not taking stock of the values inherent in a good teacher who is also a man, in not taking stock of what a great teacher can accomplish which a machine cannot, and in overlooking the indispensable contributions to the total context of learning, education and culture which only the human spirit can provide. It is of these distinctively *human* potentialities that we need to be reminded.

## II. THE TEACHER AS MENTOR

All education which has left an impact upon those exposed to it bears witness to the fact that an inspiring teacher who can convey his enthusiasm for his subject leaves an indelible impression upon the memories of a large number of his students. The history of Western culture confirms this, from the personal magnetism of Socrates to the platform charm exercised by William James. Though we pay tribute to the stimulus value of a programed question, how does it compare with the stimulus value of the unprogramed teacher? I am willing to concede to the supporters of automated instruction that perhaps a good teacher should be defined as a well programed human being. But he also has the additional virtue of being multiply branched: that is, he can go off in any direction which he can demonstrate is related to the main topic in hand and can create a recrudescence of attention and interest which no machine and no programed text can supply. Furthermore, the stimulus value of an inspiring teacher has the following to commend it. If we look at several good programs of automated instruction, defined as those which possess built-in safeguards against muddy, incomplete, illogical teaching, we will notice that they possess one of two intellectual virtues. Some

12 Mortimer Taube. *Computers and Common Sense. The Myth of Thinking Machines*. New York: Columbia University Press, 1961. 136 pp.
13 Norbert Wiener. *The Human Use of Human Beings* (second edition). New York: Doubleday, 1954. 199 pp.

programs are built like a funnel standing on its spout; others like a funnel standing on its mouth. If the former is the case, the program proceeds from factual minutiae to generalizations. If the latter is the case, the program begins with some well established and well understood generalization and then proceeds to *interpret* that generalization by applying it to a variety of relevant contexts. In either case the logical rectilinearity of the program prevents its branching out into domains of meaning *apparently* remote from the main area of concern.

If a good teacher is merely a good program which happens to be animated and talkative—a point of view which sometimes appears to inspire the worshippers of the mechanical calf—he at least can branch off into matters quite remote from the groove in which programed questions or frames constrain the student. Such branching off has perhaps been necessitated by a student's question, by his bewilderment, or by the challenge he throws down concerning the *value* of the topic being discussed. Sometimes this branching off is the product of a lively imagination in either the student or the teacher. Sometimes it results from an inspiring and irresistible teacher who meets a perceptive but immovable student. Regardless of the genesis of the tangent, however, if it creates relevancy in a Gestalt sense for the main line of inquiry, that is to say, if it makes the latter seem to matter in a larger context of intellectual interest which exists for both student and teacher, then it is doing something which no straitjacketed, teaching-machine sequence can accomplish.

We have not as yet built this quality of imagination into our automated programs, but its usefulness in the instructional process is hardly to be questioned. Imagination may be an attribute which an unimaginative programer would define in terms of electronics as analogous to a mixed-up circuit, a blown fuse or a non-conforming relay. The analogy may be just but I do not think this or any similar analogy would warrant *devaluing* the attribute itself. In any case the *branching* provided by a stimulating teacher can unquestionably pour emotional, social and aesthetic meaning into our lives—in addition, of course, to the cognitive experience he can and does provide—and this is something which I believe no amount of self-instruction by machine can furnish. To use the jargon of programing itself, every good teacher creates his own *multiple tracks* and these need not always be *subdivisions* of the sequence with which he began.

### III. MEDIATING TRANSFER

A top-notch teacher's capacity to shift attention to the relation of the topic at hand to a quite different one is clearly relevant to the problem of how one concept influences the learning of another or, to put the matter in more familiar terms, to the *problem of transfer of training*.

Kendler [14] has shown that transfer of training seems to be more a matter of individual differences rather than of programed instruction. He believes such transfer to be a matter of centrally mediating factors in behavior. He reports the following:

> Experimental results seem to indicate that problem solving is intimately related to the ability of organisms to generate appropriate response produced cues. These cues mediate the transfer from one situation to another with the *amount* and *kind* of transfer, depending on the implicit responses of the subject. (p. 181)

The gifted teacher, I submit, possesses the ability to generate such appropriate response produced cues. If to this ability we add a rich mine of information whose content has been well monitored and knit together (the implicit responses to which Kendler refers), we get a teacher who can set the mind to racing by the prodigal way in which he can establish contexts of relevancy and relatedness for a plethora of concepts. In this respect he cannot be simulated by a teaching machine at all.

Kendler also points out an aspect of a mass, standardized, educational program, to which, it is reasonable to assume, teaching machines may someday lead. This is the threatened decline of the gift of imagination, a quality which I hold to be an extremely important ingredient in inspired teaching. One piece of evidence as to how imagination has been flattened by human exposure to *another* type of mass education, is revealed by Kendler. He notes that, as a result of the probable influence of our mass media programs, the American college student's capacity to employ free association, using the Kent-Rosanoff Free Association Test, has declined considerably from 1929 to 1952. A result of this sort is, perhaps, an *indirect measure* of declining imagination in our national loadings in Thurstone's V (verbal) and W (word-fluency) factors. By contrast, the response variability of French and German subjects in word association is much greater than ours and perhaps it may be reasonably argued that this is because the *content* of education in these countries is less regimented than in our own.

One additional cause for educational lament in the present instance, indicating the enfeeblement of imagination as well as the effects produced by the limitations inherent in mass media vocabularies, is Kendler's report that our national language habits are becoming less abstract and more concrete. The probability is slight that this will occur in the classroom when instruction is received from a group of good teachers all of whom are very different from one another. By contrast this is likely to be one of the unwanted and unanticipated effects of automated instruction. Kendler's remarks appear to emphasize one basic danger, namely, that the selection of a particular teaching machine or a pro-

14 Howard J. Kendler. "Teaching Machines and Psychological Theory." 177–85. In Eugene Galanter (editor). *Automatic Teaching. The State of the Art. Op. cit.*

gramed textbook may place severe limitations on the type of variables and aptitude development which the student can make the focus of his attention. By contrast, the wraps are off in the form of a competent and inspiring flesh-and-blood teacher.

## IV. THE TEACHER AS MAN

We must also not overlook, I think, the value which the living teacher possesses by virtue of the fact that he can point out the relevancy of his subject to the *personal* and *social concerns* of the student. Again in the spirit of *noblesse oblige* and also, I might add, *sang-froid,* I will concede the opposition that, if the living teacher can be said to have this advantage, it is only because he has a *larger storage capacity* and a better *monitoring system.* But the live teacher has one other virtue which even a super-duper teaching machine will probably never possess.

Since an *ideal,* automated teaching device (admittedly not yet produced) would have to be asked a clear question or, at least, be given a clear answer before it could proceed, a confused question or an unclear response would most likely gum up its works. This is precisely where the programing of the biped is of a superior type. He is programed to furnish answers to unclear questions and vague or muddled answers by *knowing how to recast these.* These he can recast precisely because he is *sensitive to the intent* of the speaker or the questioner and precisely because he can be sympathetic to the concerns, anxieties, groping and *Weltschmerz* of the student whose reach unfortunately exceeds his grasp. Perhaps the first-rate teacher creates an existential sense of understanding for the student listener by the tone of his voice, by the expression on his face or by the touch of his hand upon the student's shoulder. It matters not. But create it he does. No teaching machine to date has been endowed with the tragic sense of life, and yet without this sense much of human learning must be as ashes in the mouth. As for the future, I am definitely *not* expecting to see the day when a rubber pad at the end of a steel arm, comes down upon the shoulder of a student and a taped voice, speaking in sepulchral tones from the remote electronic interior of some marvelously advanced teaching machine, says "Yes. I know *just* how you feel!"

## V. THE GREATNESS OF BOOKS

Even at second remove, in the form of the printed book, the humane teacher can create an atmosphere of understanding of the student's personal and social concerns, which is highly inspiring and conducive to the learning process. All our contact with great books furnishes living testimony to the fact that motivation can be kindled and human energies galvanized by a greatness of mind and soul which speak to us across the centuries. The writer who can pour meaning into our personal lives, either through his capacity to use expressive language, his demonstration of beauty and precision in intellectual organization, or a style which creates an air of intimacy and rapport, is also doing something which lies outside the range of effects producible by a teaching device.

Where a book deals directly with the *importance* and the *nature* of true education and true culture, the use of expressive language may be of even greater value to the student who is struggling to find himself intellectually than the unadorned prose of straightforward exposition. Such prose, stripped bare of emotional content and the stimulation provided by a preoccupation with values, often furnishes only a shell without the husk. No teaching machine can do for a student, for instance, what the little known classic of Hamerton [15] did in the past for those of us who were struggling to enlarge our horizons, both intellectually, aesthetically and socially. In the same way one gets a feeling of what a superb teacher can be like and what life's intellectual adventure can provide, through two highly interesting books by Barzun [16, 17] or through a recent volume by Hadas.[18] Finally, a sense of the atmosphere which might be created for a student by a genuine community of scholars, and which no series of teaching machines providing a variety of programs could possibly confer, can be dimly glimpsed, I believe, from the picture of an ideal university as described by Hutchins.[19]

There is a major disadvantage of the teaching machine, in contrast to the good teacher, which is hardly ever mentioned in the literature. This is the fact that programed material which is as extensive as that of Holland and Skinner [20] whose program deals with human behavior, will rarely be devoted to pulling together all that has been learned. Such a pulling together provides an organic unity and perspective for the student, in which everything tends to fall into its proper place. This is something which the student usually has to provide for himself by mulling over what he has learned. Occasionally the needed recapitulation is provided by a good teacher. Once again we may concede the devotees of automated instruction, using their own terminology, that such recapitulation and such unifying activity as we refer to here, is merely *selective playback*. So be it. I have not, however, read of any program which has

15 Philip G. Hamerton. *Intellectual Life*. Boston: Little, Brown, 1902. 573 pp.
16 Jacques Barzun. *Teacher in America*. New York: Doubleday, 1955. 280 pp.
17 Jacques Barzun. *The House of Intellect*. New York: Harper, 1959. 276 pp.
18 Moses Hadas. *Old Wine, New Bottles*. New York: Simon & Schuster, 1962. 137 pp.
19 Robert M. Hutchins. *The University of Utopia*. Chicago: University of Chicago Press, 1953. 103 pp.
20 James G. Holland & Burrhus F. Skinner. *The Analysis Of Behavior*. New York: McGraw-Hill, 1961. 337 pp.

so highly sophisticated a *scanning operation* of its *storage content* as to be able at the end of an extensive learning sequence, to provide the same type of playback. Let us therefore not devaluate this important function which as yet only the live teacher can perform. Within the framework of our Western, cultural legacy there are certain pithy sayings which indicate a general recognition of the importance of a unified perspective upon life and learning. One of these apothegms is "Let us not lose sight of the forest for the trees." Another is "Let us view life steadily and view it whole." There are few aspects of great teaching that are more important than this unifying function which is completely outside the performance of any type of programed instruction.

## VI. THE FULL MAN AS TEACHER

Finally let us consider the teacher as a person. What does it mean to be a *full man* as well as a teacher in the classroom? Such a question is a roundabout way of emphasizing certain highly valued instructional gifts which belong to the unprogramed biped. These are gifts which by no stretch of the imagination will ever be exercised through the invasion of the precincts of learning by technological barbarism.

As a full man, the really outstanding teacher sees to it that, wherever possible, learning is related to life. Much and perhaps most of man's learning has sprung from problems with which he has been preoccupied. These sometimes have a *contingent* character, as when he is concerned with wresting maximum productivity from the soil. Other problems, however, with which he wrestles are perennial, such as his concern with the answers to such questions as "What is the good life?" or "What is the ideal society?" The first seeks to define a personal ideal. The second is always raised in connection with the quest for community and Utopia. The instructor as *compleat teacher* eschews concern with the accumulated learning and skills of the race, when these are presented only as a set of abstractions to be found between the covers of a textbook and memorized. He has no patience with the worship of information for its own sake, divorced from the everyday concerns of men. No matter how beautiful the foliage may be overhead and no matter how interesting some of the individual leaves may appear to be, all of it leads back to the roots at the base. These roots are almost invariably concerned with finding the means for the solutions of both man's contingent and man's perennial problems. They are basic to man's daily struggle to create meaning, value and purpose in his life, particularly in the presence of a universe which, as Russell has phrased it, is completely neutral to man's efforts, a universe which, left to work out its own grand and accidental designs, might even succeed in making a mockery of those efforts.

These functions of creating meaning, purpose and value by building ladders between abstractions and their earthbound bases, the dedicated and charismatic teacher never loses sight of. The teaching device obviously will never be able to assume these roles. We too easily forget this fact. What is worse, we too easily devaluate it. Without someone with intellectual presence, such as the *compleat teacher,* to help us move familiarly and with sure foot up and down the ladder of scholarly abstractions, the process of learning would rapidly degenerate into a series of tortured and meaningless drills. Too great a dependence upon the automated program carries a similar educational threat which we would do well not to overlook.

## VII. SHAPING *PAIDEIA*

Consider the original function of education or *paideia* as conceived by the Greeks. The ancients were convinced that education and culture cannot be separated from the historical and social structures which underly a nation's spiritual life. *Paideia* involves a conscious ideal of education and culture, which combines a concern for self-development and the enrichment of all our human potentialities with the inculcation of the obligation to serve one's own community and to bring it somewhat closer to whatever notions of the good life move the mass of its citizens. For a long time this ideal was incorporated into the humanistic heritage of the West. It is only now growing slowly moribund, as de Grazia [21] has amply demonstrated in a recent volume, being displaced by shoddy and superficial ideals of gracious living and high mass consumption.

A true education and culture must provide for the unfolding of the moral grain in every man. Few question the great importance of this task. All of us, at some time or other, have been deeply impressed by the examples of greatness of soul, deriving from a conspicuous concern with the education of character, as held up to us, for instance, by Plutarch. In the past the young in the West have frequently been urged to emulate the Plutarchian virtues. For those of us who have not lost sight of the ancient, cultural ideal of *paideia,* the molding of character is still one of the major goals of education. In what respect, may I ask, can automated instruction, providing chiefly facts clothed in representative language rather than ideals of character described in expressive language, help to achieve the great educational goal of *paideia?* In what respect can automated instruction provide the emotional tone and admiration which Plutarch's word pictures can convey? These questions may be rhetorical but their intent, I believe, requires an educational instauration.

21 Sebastion de Grazia. *Of Time, Work, and Leisure.* New York: Twentieth Century Fund, 1962. 559 pp.

In what sense then can the moving description of a great human soul be simulated by automated instruction? Better still, in what sense can the impact of nobility of life and purpose, given by a great man we have been privileged to know or a great teacher at whose feet we have been privileged to sit, ever be furnished by a teaching machine? Only written descriptions of such great souls, delineated in expressive language, have the power to move us and to serve as models for our moral development. The very techniques of programing destroy the inspirational function and the moving drama which are frequently the virtues of great prose. This function is forever lost in the fractionation of information which a proper program requires and in the matter-of-fact, unadorned style which the items of automated instruction require. The moving power of great novels, distinguished plays, poetry which touches us in depth, and even the nonfictional classics are clearly alien to the objectives of automated instruction. Every form of aesthetic catharsis, producible in the theatre or by great forms of art, is eternally foreign to the mission of a teaching machine. What then can replace the great teacher who can give life to all those elements of education and culture which depend for their powers on the expressive rather than the representative functions of language? These depend more on the student's sensitivity to the power of words to bring out the best in each of us than upon their information content. What can a teaching machine do here?

Morris [22] has made a case for the existence of 16 different types of discourse with which men relate to themselves, to each other, to society, to work, to nature and to God. Leaving the language of technology aside, only two of these are employable in programed instruction, namely, the designative-informative discourse which belongs to science and to descriptive prose and formative-informative discourse which belongs to the analytic disciplines, such as logic and mathematics. If Morris is correct, then surely we have to cast about for ways of preserving the other functions of language and human relationship. But the solution, of course, is at hand and was obvious all the time. It is the competent, dedicated and inspired teacher, in love with learning, who is seeking to pour meaning into life and who wishes to share that meaning with his students, who will have to be our chief source of reliance in these matters.

## VIII. CREATING AND COMBINING

A teacher is essentially a means for fulfilling what the great Italian sociologist, Pareto, called the *instinct for combinations*. He can combine ideas in a highly novel fashion, bringing together notions, processes and attributes into relationships hitherto unnoticed. The inspiring teacher

[22] Charles Morris. *Signs Language and Behavior.* New York: George Braziller, 1955. 365 pp.

can do this by creative processes which have been richly described in recent years by such writers as Bruner,[23] Crutchfield,[24] Gordon [25] and others. These creative processes are, in many respects, unlike anything within the armamentarium of programing techniques. Creative teachers, possessing this instinct for combination, like creative writers, artists, scientists, philosophers and thinkers in general, have qualities of mind and heart—amply described in the research literature on creative personalities —which, *in the main,* cannot yet be programed. On the other side, let it be said that Simon [26] *et al.* is one researcher who is convinced that within ten years we shall have computers which will discover and prove an important mathematical theorem and compose music which will be regarded as aesthetically significant. Few are as optimistic as he. Even were he to prove to be correct, however, this would only be a modest triumph, for the qualities of mind and heart which are reported to be attributes of the creative personality exist along several dimensions and not merely the *cognitive* one.

It is these very qualities, used to highlight the relations of learning to life, which are indispensable for good teaching and which cannot be built into even the most advanced type of computer. By these creative functions a good teacher can undo or, at least, loosen the twisted character structure of a student whose *social programing* leaves much to be desired. He can do this effectively by showing the relationship of different aspects of his subject matter to the pathological and the undesirable values, attitudes, ideas and ideals of the deviant student whose community orientation has been badly short-circuited. To show the bearing of one's subject matter on some individual's social philosophy or upon those current problems and issues which press heavily and personally upon each of us—this is certainly one major function of an outstanding teacher. What teaching machine, may I ask, will branch off to provide such connections? What teaching machine will accompany the ability to branch off, with the sense of outrage and human concern, which the flesh-and-blood teacher can provide? What operant *Deus ex machina* will turn existentialist and provide the student with a sense of the emotional and social significance of what would otherwise prove to be a congeries of bloodless facts and alienated abstractions? In contrast with

23 Jerome S. Bruner. *On Knowing. Essays For the Left Hand.* Cambridge: Harvard University Press (Belknap), 1962. 165 pp.

24 Richard Crutchfield. "Conformity and Creative Thinking." 120–140. In Howard E. Gruber, Glenn Terrell, and Michael Wertheimer (editors). *Contemporary Approaches to Creative Thinking.* New York: Atherton, 1962. 223 pp.

25 William J. J. Gordon. *Synectics. The Development of Creative Capacity.* New York: Harper, 1961. 180 pp.

26 Herbert A. Simon, Allen Newell and J. C. Shaw. "The Processes of Creative Thinking." 63–119. In *Contemporary Approaches to Creative Thinking.* Howard E. Gruber, Glenn Terrell, and Michael Wertheimer (editors). *Op. cit.*

the warmth and concern of the great teacher the computer can only provide *rigor mortis* of the spirit.

## IX. THE LIFE OF FEELING

Only the human being can provide a sense of what a lived culture can be. This, he does, not only by example but also by bringing to the fore the importance of the dimensions of feeling and sensitivity for the human condition. Knowledge is not enough. One must distinguish, as Archibald MacLeish once put it, between a fact and the feel of a fact.

Knowledge divorced from its significance for the life of feeling, knowledge disentangled from the social matrix to which it must have relevance, knowledge which does not determine the postures we take towards ourselves and each other can provide only an alienated type of education. This is precisely one of the greatest dangers in teaching by machine, for the automated program will frequently deal with abstractions completely alienated from the human context which gives them relevance. Alienated learning is a modern Frankenstein and it is tragically on the increase. Learning which cannot become part of the warp and woof of one's own inner being, is learning which, from the viewpoint of a philosophy of existentialism, is without commitment. Programed instruction *cannot* escape increasing the fund of alienated learning and education in our time. It could be argued, I believe, that the central function of a great teacher is precisely that of preventing the process of alienation in education. In this sense he has no substitute and remains an eternal bulwark against the twin dangers of the Scylla of over-intellectualization and the Charybdis of emotional and sentimental surcharge.

## X. THE TEACHER AND ALIENATION

Today the perceptive social philosopher, the insightful literary critic and the acutely sensitive teacher observe the human condition and note the amazing amount of suffering which is reflected in myriad forms of alienation all around us. The ideals of Western learning demand that if one is to regard oneself as truly cultured then one must devote oneself to fighting all forms of alienation, both in oneself and in others. To accept the inevitability of alienation as a result of our modern, complex, bureaucratic society and, at the same time, to talk about the need to develop an individual psychology, is a contradiction in terms. The latter development must in large measure feed on a social psychology which has been effective in liquidating or diminishing forms of alienation which inhere inevitably in the depersonalizing, dehumanizing and deindividuating features of a technique-worshipping civilization. This is the spirit which permeates the recent work of such truly cultured individuals like Fromm,[27] Ortega y Gasset [28] and Marcel.[29] Each of these in his own way is trying to fight the standard forms of alienation in our time: alienation from self, from the opposite sex, from one's fellow man, from work, society, Nature and God. In this context I am invoking the notion of Godhead, not in some secular, anthropomorphic and institutional sense, but rather as a well established sensitivity to the need for self-transcendence in this vale of tears and a capacity to preserve a sense of wonder and awe concerning the mystery of Being, Time, Matter and History.

Poets, novelists, playwrights, social critics, social philosophers and charismatic teachers alive to the social currents and pathology of our age, who genuinely feel the unrelieved anguish of those of their fellow men who are victims of modern alienation, have a very special task to perform. They have to cut through to the root sources and institutional follies which produce the excesses and absurdities of the human condition. They have, as their first duty, the task of exercising their talents in an effort to dissipate the traditional forms of alienation which have resulted from these same excesses and absurdities. These are all figures who by destiny are men with a mission, a mission which, in part, is concerned with helping each of us in his quest for personal identity. These frontiersmen of Western culture must, in a sense, be among those who make a flank attack rather than a frontal assault on alienation. The frontal assault is the duty of the psychiatrist and psychologist. In serving in this undeclared war such frontiersmen are, in their own way, furthering the development of an individual psychology.

## XI. THE CENTRALITY OF HUMOR

I turn finally to that quality so characteristic of man, which, in a sense, clearly distinguishes him from the brutes. I refer to his sense of humor. The capacity to laugh at human foibles, to see the incongruity between human behavior and human ideals, to see the unexpected and surprising relationships of similarity between what at first glance seem to be disparate elements of human experience—all these are of inestimable value in moving ever closer to our definitions of the good life. I do not, of course, wish to pretend that every form of wit and humor known to us, is capable of being ticketed under one of the descriptive phrases I have just employed. But, of course, that is not the point. What is to the point is the remarkable fact that good teachers usually also possess a good sense of humor. This is a major asset in literature, the humanities, the behavioral, social and management sciences and, in fact, in all the dis-

27 Erich Fromm. *The Sane Society.* New York: Rinehart, 1955. 370 pp.
28 Jose Ortega y Gasset. *Man and People.* New York: W. W. Norton, 1957. 172 pp.
29 Gabriel Marcel. *Men Against Humanity.* London: Harvill Press, 1952. 205 pp.

ciplines which have to do with man. It is also, of course, very welcome when it is used as cement for training the young in the natural sciences, but it can most effectively be brought into play in those disciplines concerned with the affairs of men.

There is no limit to what a fine teacher can do with a good sense of humor. One barb which punctures a pattern of intellectual or social affectation, is worth a mint of dull chapters in a textbook. A single satire may do more to change the course of history than a mountain of learned monographs. An epigram or a humorous anecdote may sometimes undo more academic gibberish in a flash than all the ponderous proofs of pedants and a shaft of wit often quickly dispels the most effectively disguised forms of the learned ignorance. The teacher, with a touch of an Erasmus or a Nicolas de Cusa, is armored against folly. The devices of wit and humor are as much tools in the hands of a great teacher as his knowledge or his skill at some of the functions which I have already described. When I look back in memory and try to recall the most impressive wisdom of those teachers who meant the most to me, I find that I can remember more material which was accompanied by the use of wit than material which was delivered with an air of sobriety unrelieved by humor of any sort. This, of course, may be a personal idiosyncrasy rather than a representative result of instruction. I am not sure. But to the extent that humor can provide the common touch and sweep up both instructor and student in a bond of mutual appreciation, there are few substitutes for it.

Automated instruction, I am strongly convinced, will never provide a commodity which is competitive with an outstanding teacher's sense of humor. I will apologize for the strength of this conviction on the day when I hear the first side-splitting, belly laugh emerge from the interior of a teaching machine. All my doubts will be completely resolved on that day when, in response to a student's pressing a button or turning a crank, a teaching machine will stop running true to programed form and insert a risqué story in the stimulus frame it calls home. Until that great day I shall continue to place my bets on that poor but neglected biped known as a good teacher. Until then let us never allow ourselves to forget, in the excesses of our educational follies, an ancient adage. If I remember correctly that adage reads "Whom the gods would destroy, they first make mad."

The teacher is primarily a transmitter of culture. The intellectual, by contrast, is the social conscience of humanity. His traditional functions have been to reveal and to try to dissipate injustice, inhumanity, obtuseness, waste and folly in the affairs of men. This he does through his writings. On the positive side he formulates visions of a more perfect, social order which, he hopes, will capture the enthusiasm and support of his fellow men. If a cybernating society is not to become a caricature of the dreams of human reason and a source for the drying up of human hope, it is the intellectual who can be counted upon to exercise the vigilance which the maintenance of a genuine culture requires. Chapter 11 takes stock of the intellectual's functions in the life of culture, since these are more needed than ever in an age of science and technology.

# 11

# Practitioners of Culture:
# The Vanguard of the Procession *

## INTRODUCTION

The role of the intellectual in public life in the United States is on the increase. The participation by intellectuals in public life in this country was a relatively rare matter prior to the advent of the early New Deal years. Active immersion in politics on the part of European intellectuals is somewhat less novel than it has been here. Examples of European intellectuals who played a significant part in politics and social change and whose names were once household references, are Eamon de Valera in Ireland and Trotzky in Russia. There are, of course, many other European intellectuals who have cut a figure in politics but with less dramatic consequences. Joll,[1] who is a contemporary historian, has given us some pen-portraits of three distinguished European intellectuals—Leon Blum, Walter Rathenau and F. T. Marinetti—who, as decision-makers, reflected rather well some of the traits historically associated with intellectuals. The traits associated traditionally with intellectuals have been classically drawn by Julien Benda [2] in his *The Betrayal of the Intellectuals*. The intellectuals are, for Benda, men who devoted their lives to unworldly causes—to the cultivation of the mind and the spirit. They were disinterested thinkers, men who pursued knowledge oblivious of the social and economic tendencies of their age. What Benda meant by "disinterested" was not a penchant for withdrawing from the secular issues of the times. The intellectual definitely was expected to strike a political posture as a critic of his society. But the form in which that posture was to be expressed was in moral terms. Benda abjured political partisanship and political hatred. If the intellectual entered politics

* Chapter 11, with adaptations and modifications, has been taken from the following source. "The Intellectuals, the Educated, and the Trained." *Darshana International.* Vol. 5, No. 3, July 1965, 32–42.

[1] James Joll. *Three Intellectuals in Politics.* New York: Harper & Row, 1960, 203 pp.

[2] Julien Benda. *The Betrayal of the Intellectuals.* Boston: The Beacon Press, 1955. 188 pp.

Benda demanded that he be free of party ties, that he function in terms of what would now be called an "independent voter and thinker," in the American context.

But while intellectuals are being increasingly accepted today by the body politic, the historical characteristics of intellectuals, particularly as critics of their society—and whether or not they are in power—is a matter that is still not widely understood. This misunderstanding has been very succinctly brought out by Richard Hofstadter [3] in his book, *Anti-Intellectualism in American Life*. The ignorance and misunderstanding of the traditional functions of the intellectual are brought into focus by this author in his last chapter "The Intellectual: Alienation and Conformity." But the anti-intellectualism that Hofstadter mourns is increasing even among brain-workers who *are not* intellectuals but who have either entered politics or serve the American community within some of the governmental, bureaucratic structures now found everywhere on the American scene. Donald C. Hodges [4] goes into quite some detail in order to show this in a critical article which attempts to present a bird's-eye-view of the changes in the status of brain-workers in American life and the relationship of the traditional intellectual to these changes. He has written an article that makes it clearer than ever that the authentic intellectual has a harder row than ever before to hoe.

There is, of course, a wider range of functions which the true intellectual performs than only that of calling the follies and injustices of his society into account. We have to be reminded of what these are, particularly when the forces arrayed against intellectuality today, in and out of academic life, threaten to obliterate from public consciousness the difference between the analytic, critical, and social functions of the intellectual and the socially useful, intellectual functions performed by other types of brain-worker. The intellectual functions of other types of brain-worker are significantly different from those of the intellectual *qua intellectual*. If these distinctions are not brought home to roost we may, in fact, lose the historical functions of the socially critical intellectual entirely. This risk is likely to increase as our society becomes more and more complex and increasingly oriented to technological ideals, while continuing to move away from the humanistic legacy of the West. It is therefore important to restate the functions of the intellectual, particularly in a technologically dominated society that is likely to forget them completely and certainly when these functions are needed more than ever before.

[3] Richard Hofstadter. *Anti-Intellectualism in American Life*. New York: Knopf, 1963. 434 pp.

[4] Donald C. Hodges. "Anti-Intellectualism in a Society of Eggheads." *The American Journal of Economics and Sociology*. Vol. 25, No. 4, October, 1966. 427–37.

Part of the confusion with respect to the authentic functions of the intellectual is traceable to the fact that the generations which have been educated in the affluent society, consist of many who, even though quite sophisticated, have come to apply the rubric "intellectual" to a variety of brain-workers. Distinctions, however, must be made between intellectuals and other types of brain-worker. Such distinctions will be attempted in this chapter. Some important discussions of the range of the intellectual's functions will be found in the work of de Huszar [5] and Molnar.[6] Considering the role which the contemporary intellectual plays in political and social life and the increasing effort he makes to understand and grapple with current issues and problems, it is essential, I believe, to obtain a clear understanding of some of those functions which discriminate the different categories to which I have already referred. I therefore wish to turn to a brief discussion at this point which may provide an opening wedge in making the necessary discriminations.

## I. THE FUNCTIONS OF THE CONTEMPORARY INTELLECTUAL

There are certain characteristics which most intellectuals share in common and this will be true in spite of the fact that a taxonomy can be provided for making discriminations within the very group which we tend to subsume under the rubric "intellectual," itself. Among those characteristics, then, which can be ascribed to the modern intellectual, I would include the following as fairly central.

The intellectual exhibits a tremendous personal interest in and enthusiasm for ideas and for the clash between and counterpoint among ideas. He enjoys examining ideas critically, not only from a logical standpoint but even more from the standpoint of how well or how poorly they will stand up when subjected to the touchstone of collective, social experience. This critical posture will be exhibited whether or not the intellectual is also a direct actionist concerned with translating novel ideas into hoped-for, beneficial social change. The genuine intellectual is not made uncomfortable by logical or "interpretive" analysis, no matter how extensively an idea is probed. He will stick doggedly to such probing, will refrain from premature intellectual foreclosure with respect to the truth or value of ideas, and he will enjoy and encourage a pluralism with respect to them.

Many intellectuals have a deep conviction, in Max Lerner's [7] phrase,

[5] George B. de Huszar (editor). *The Intellectuals. A Controversial Portrait.* Glencoe, Illinois: The Free Press, 1960. 543 pp.

[6] Thomas Molnar. *The Decline of the Intellectual.* Cleveland and New York: The World Publishing Company, 1961. *Meridian Books.* 369 pp.

[7] Max Lerner. *Ideas are Weapons.* New York: Viking Press, 1939. 553 pp.

that *ideas are weapons* for the organization of social life and for the determination of the needed changes which such reorganization may require. As a result they are insistent that when social consensus has been reached intellectually with respect to the merits of an idea, that we express and fulfill that idea through social action. Intellectuals abhor the emasculation of ideas, that is to say, they have no patience with middle-brows whose allegiance to an idea extends no further than a conversation piece for cocktail-party palaver, and who will rarely do anything financially, educationally, morally, or politically to act as midwives to the social and institutional expression of an idea. This gap between *asserted conviction* and *expressed indifference* is, of course, part of the socially approved schizophrenia of our time. Intellectuals dominated by social concern insist that we must *live our values* and give concrete expression to our ideas.

Intellectuals by and large are probably characterized by a conviction that life is not worth living without those artifacts of the human spirit which we speak of as culture. For the ordinary man the ability to obtain love, sex, friendship, social esteem and health, will suffice for this vale of tears, although not necessarily in the order just given. These same considerations also move the intellectual but often he is even more driven by the daemon of creative activity. Such is his nature that he must add his contribution to the cumulative fulfillment in historical time of what Teilhard de Chardin [8] calls "hominisation," that is, the fulfillment of those potentialities of man's being which are distinctively human and which separate him from all other living, terrestrial forms. The creative activities in which the true intellectual engages are highly varied. They range from activity in literature, the humanities and the arts, through novel social inventions, to research and discovery in the natural and social sciences. The intellectual recognizes that leisure should be used for self-fulfillment and for the expression of the Greek ideal of *paideia*. This is the ideal which encourages the enlargement of our intellectual, spiritual, emotional, aesthetic, social and educational horizons of understanding while, at the same time, demanding that we accept increasing social responsibility in our quest for community. Central to the leisure-time activities of most intellectuals is the need to expand and deepen awareness and this expansion and deepening is promoted by the life of culture. The importance of such a life of culture has been attested to in various ways by T. S. Eliot, Cowell, Arnold, and Powys, whose work we have referred to in Chapter 7.

For over two thousand years the Western intellectual has exhibited a deep concern for the elimination of human suffering and the establishment of social justice for all. He has been among the first to attack social

[8] Pierre Teilhard de Chardin. *The Phenomenon of Man.* New York: Harper, 1961. *Harper Torchbooks.* 318 pp.

pathology in all its forms, by harangue, by pleading with the powerful on behalf of the oppressed, by tracts and through political pamphleteering. He has fought oppression and injustice through the novel and through the arts, through Utopian forms of social philosophy and through social criticism of the oppressive and unintelligent customs, manners, attitudes, values and erroneous ideas prevailing in his own time. With the coming of the Industrial Revolution in the West, the intellectual has made it his concern to note the new forms of social pathology and injustice which have been produced by the morally unregulated impact of science and technology on our lives. Recent examples of the expression of this function are evident in the work of such figures as Juenger,[9] Arendt,[10] and Ellul,[11] to select a trio of protestants from literally hundreds of social critics preoccupied with the effects of science and technology on human life.

Intellectuals tend to exhibit a lifelong preoccupation with questions of appropriate action and choice in given contexts and with questions concerning the relevancy of traditional, social objectives to the ongoing human condition. They show a deep concern for the proper hierarchical ordering of social values. They devote much of their thought, time and energies to a passionate effort to eliminate ongoing values which they regard as anachronistic and which, they feel, create unnecessary human suffering. Driven by concerns such as these, the modern intellectual tends to be cosmopolitan and therefore impatient with the obstructive (not the *constructive*) values of traditional society. As a result of such cosmopolitanism the intellectual is rarely ethnocentric, provincial or limited in outlook. Freed from the fetters of every variety of parochialism, he is able to survey his own culture and to note its faults just as readily as he can call the shots on the immaturities of other cultures. A marked freedom from ethnocentrism tends to produce certain historically interesting phenomena. Among Western intellectuals and largely as a result of historical accident, the Jew as an intellectual is, perhaps, more singularly free from ethnocentrism than most intellectuals who are non-Jews. A highly plausible explanation of this phenomenon has been furnished by Veblen [12] and, to some extent, by Samuel.[13, 14] This freedom from ethnocentrism, so marked among intellectual Jews, is what is, perhaps, tacitly recognized by the cultural authoritarians who are now so

9 Friedrich Georg Juenger. *The Failure of Technology*. Chicago: Henry Regnery, 1956. *Gateway Editions*. 189 pp.

10 Hannah Arendt. *The Human Condition. A Study of the Central Dilemmas Facing Modern Man*. New York: Doubleday, 1959. *Anchor Books*. 385 pp.

11 Jacques Ellul. *The Technological Society*. New York: Knopf, 1964. 449 pp.

12 Thorstein Veblen. "The Intellectual Pre-Eminence of Jews in Modern Europe." *Political Science Quarterly*. Vol. 34, March, 1919. 33–42.

13 Maurice Samuel. *You Gentiles*. New York: Harcourt, Brace, 1924. 221 pp.

14 Maurice Samuel. *I, The Jew*. New York: Harcourt, Brace, 1927. 275 pp.

rampant in the USSR. It is this liberation of the spirit which, I suspect, leads in some measure to an increasingly virulent form of anti-Semitism in that country.

But whether as Jew or non-Jew, the Western intellectual recognizes that contemporary man is guaranteed a limited span of time in this flicker between eternities which man calls "his life." In this limited period, he feels, we should make the most out of life by developing a deep sensitivity to questions of value and to problems of choice. When men fail themselves in this sense, the intellectual engages in social jeremiads, trying to remind his fellow men of the ways in which they are wasting their lives and of the worthier ends to which they can put their time. In taking the long view with respect to a concern for human values, the intellectual is a man with a mission. In fulfilling this mission he does not count the costs. His sense of relatedness to his fellows drives him on. He demands that all human activity minister to both human and humane ends.

Many intellectuals are not "social." Such intellectuals seem to have a congenital incapacity for teamwork, *not because they* are *anti-social* but rather because they do their best work alone. By and large creative activity is an *individual matter,* although when it comes to creative activity in *science and technology,* we now have abundant evidence that group processes can lead to highly desirable forms of inventiveness and creativeness. This, for instance, has been well attested to by Gordon and by Gruber, Terrell, and Wertheimer, whose work has been mentioned in Chapter 10. Inasmuch as so many intellectuals, however, tend to be preoccupied with the improvement of the human condition, either in terms of the formulation of explicit social philosophies and highly systematic, social criticism or in terms of the *cathartic function* of art and literature, they tend to be critical "loners." Intellectuals of this calibre are what Schultz [15] calls *counter-personal types.*

Such intellectuals travel alone not because of unfriendliness towards their fellow men but rather because they feel their critical effectiveness is optimum when they are detached from (not unsympathetic to) conflicting loyalties. This detachment leaves them free to criticize and to snipe at (if that is the appropriate phrase) what they take to be error, folly, rationalization and selfishness. It also exempts them from the restrictions upon their work which would inevitably follow if they made the mistake of pursuing credos for conquest, power and prestige. Sooner or later such pursuit would force them into conventional policies of hypocrisy, self-deception and a thousand and one other forms of conventional folly. Such policies would also soon put an end to the maintenance of intellectual integrity. For all these reasons it is natural for many intellectuals to work alone and to pay the price for this non-intimate mode of related-

[15] William C. Schultz. *Firo. A Three-Dimensional Theory of Interpersonal Behavior.* New York: Rinehart, 1958. 267 pp.

ness to others, through the misunderstanding with which their work is often received and the spiritual loneliness which so often accompanies that misunderstanding.

Finally, let us note that the functioning intellectual—like Sartre, for instance—tends to exhibit *a lifelong dedication to his dreams.* This will be true whether his dreams are concerned with the establishment of social justice, the achievement of personal nobility or the arousal of the religious impulse in man. It will equally be true when his dreams are the dreams of reason and contain the hope of what reason may accomplish towards the perfection of man or when those same dreams express a yearning only for enlarged, individual experience or enhanced, personal consciousness. With ordinary mortals these dreams vanish with the passing of the years and the ordinary pressures of life. The conventional citizen forgives these dreams in the young on the grounds of both their youth and inexperience. He is enraged, however, when he encounters an adult in his middle or late years, who has retained these dreams. He tends to assume that such an adult must be either emotionally ill-balanced, impractical or immature, in spite of age.

The adult intellectual who steadfastly holds on to these dreams and who can defend and justify them from a wealth of experience and a store of learning, perhaps enrages the conventional citizen most of all. To the philistines of the world such intellectuals are an enigma as well as a thorn in their sides because of the fact that such intellectuals remind them of how profoundly they have betrayed the dreams and promises of their own youth. In the philistine the dreams of youth give way to the accumulation of personal frustration over the years and the social disillusionment and accommodation which comes with the increase of worldly experience. For the intellectual, on the other hand, the dreams of youth are polished, enriched and intensified as a result of frustration and worldly sophistication and they come more and more to serve as permanent guidelines for him at any stage of his life.

The preceding characteristics, then, are only a few of the dominant motifs of the Western intellectual. Many more characteristics would be needed to round out a description of the intellectual, if space permitted. However, since my original intention was to distinguish the intellectual from the professor and educator, the technician and the professional man, I shall now return to that task.

## II. SOME CONTRASTS BETWEEN INTELLECTUALS AND ACADEMICS

The *typical* professor or educator is a purveyor of information or of skills, in a given area. There is no dearth of literature which deals with the characteristic picture of the educator—literature which extends from the acid attack of Upton Sinclair,[16] through the many satirical novels on academic life of the last five decades, to some of the recent critiques formulated by Paul Goodman.[17, 18] The academic is typically without vision and without dedication. He has little interest in seeing life steadily and seeing it whole. He is generally of a timid and cowardly disposition. He rarely exhibits the intestinal fortitude and the moral courage of the intellectual. The latter often sacrifices a variety of worldly gains for principles and ideals, which *are not only to be understood but which must also be lived from day to day.* Where the intellectual *is not* egocentric—and unfortunately some of them are—he is moved by the plight of his fellow man. He will be outspoken over wrongs done to others. The typical academic, in contrast, will mark time and retreat into the ivory tower of specialization, far from the madding crowd's ignoble strife. This accusation, by the way, is the same charge that was leveled by MacLeish [19] against intellectuals when, in fact, MacLeish was largely referring to academics.

Many of the world's intellectuals—not all to be sure, by any means—are men of courage, who will not compromise with principle and decency where such compromise would be self-defeating and a betrayal of social interest. Intellectuals are therefore likely to sacrifice their careers and lay down their lives in periods and situations of crisis. This is in marked contrast to the professor and educator whose dominant concern is his or her career and whose yearning for social acceptability by the powerful, the wealthy and the "practical," is the keystone of his social attitudes. As a result of this contrast, the genuine intellectual may succeed in playing an effective role in social change, either in the drastic form of revolution and social upheaval, or through social reform and the taking up of particular causes and movements. Frequently the intellectual, feeling the pulse of popular concern and frustration, is able to command men and to exhibit true leadership in periods of social crisis. Such attitudes and actions, however, are conspicuous by their absence in the lives of most academics who prefer to observe and describe social change rather than to help create it. Many academic types rarely have the necessary common touch, vision, concern, honesty, courage, wisdom, or sense of political and social realities, to be cast in an activist mold or to develop any perspi-

---

[16] Upton Sinclair, *The Goose-Step. A Study of American Miseducation.* Pasadena, California: Published by Upton Sinclair, 1923. 448 pp.

[17] Paul Goodman. *The Community of Scholars.* New York: Random House, 1962. 175 pp.

[18] Paul Goodman. *Compulsory Miseducation.* New York: Horizon Press, 1964. 189 pp.

[19] Archibald MacLeish. "The Irresponsibles." 239–46. In *The Intellectuals. A Controversial Portrait.* George B. de Huszar (editor). *Op. cit.*

cacity regarding actual relationships and processes either in the political arena or in the marketplace.

Professors and other educators frequently share the value patterns of the middle classes and, not rarely, of the social elites of their own society. The forms of protest which they are willing to make against unjust and oppressive conditions, are limited. These protests will take such forms as speaking abstractly in the classroom against doctrinal bigotry and superstition. The academic can acquire a cheap sense of moral courage in trying to dispel the ignorance of his students. He may criticize the worst forms of mass culture from the lofty and established vantage point of that which is recognizably best in the Western cultural legacy. He can be aroused over what he takes to be an infringement upon "academic freedom." When the problem arises of getting the community to extend to him more prestige, more concern and more salary for his role and for the importance of education in general, he will register his opinion. But when fists are flying and bullets are whizzing by, metaphorically speaking, the typical academic runs for cover and his voice is stilled. This will be particularly true where large-scale social issues are concerned and which may involve a large sector of the general population. Up to the time of this writing, there were no conspicuously large contingents of professors among the Civil Rights marchers concerned with the plight of the American Negro and the deep injustice he is forced to suffer.

I am not, of course, asserting that there are no professors or educators who are intellectuals. This would be absurd. What I am asserting is that the *typical* academic *is not* an intellectual and rarely exhibits those characteristics of the intellectual which have been described in the preceding section. The public may be unaware of the distinction which I am making here, but it is a distinction, nevertheless, which ought not to be lost sight of by the intelligent reader. In short, the academic is, himself, rarely an agent of social change or a bitter protestant against existing evils and social injustices of which he is usually fully aware. His *knowledge and skills* are, of course, of primary importance in the *creation of social change,* as we can see in the case of the many economists and technicians who are helping underdeveloped countries to come abreast of the twentieth century. Many of these academics, possessing a broad and creative vision and a wide spectrum of interests, are also intellectuals. Gunnar Myrdal [20, 21, 22] and Walt W. Rostow,[23] the economists, are cases in

20 Gunnar Myrdal. *Value in Social Theory. A Selection of Essays on Methodology.* New York: Harper, 1958. 269 pp.

21 Gunnar Myrdal. *An International Economy. Problems and Prospects.* New York: Harper, 1956. 381 pp.

22 Gunnar Myrdal. *Beyond the Welfare State. Economic Planning and Its International Implications.* New Haven: Yale University Press, 1960. 287 pp.

23 Walt W. Rostow. *The Process of Economic Growth.* London: Oxford University Press, 1960. Second edition. 372 pp.

point. There is likewise a small group of academics, like Linus Pauling and Bertrand Russell, who are also intellectuals but who differ from the kind just mentioned in that *they have not been formally trained in the social sciences.* By and large, however, figures such as those we have just mentioned, are not the rule in academic life.

The manner in which the unrepresentative academics to whom we are referring, depart from the academic esprit, lies in their accentuated willingness to adopt a moral posture, to refuse to alienate themselves from contemporary and significant, extramural issues and, on occasion, to participate in wordly struggles for a more just social order. By contrast the typical academic will not be *actively* preoccupied with the plight and the needs of his fellow man, except in the abstract and safe sense of the classroom, the professional meeting, the conference, the lecture forum, the panel, and the debate. The emphasis lies then in the continued display of an active moral posture, whether or not great learning has been acquired in the social and behavioral sciences. More important, perhaps, than extended learning is genuine and *intimate* knowledge of the issues about which one is concerned, particularly where that knowledge is to be made relevant to the world outside of academe. When this occurs the learning may be said to be free from alienation. It is these latter attributes which the authentic intellectual displays. These same attributes are too often conspicuous in the run-of-the-mill academic by their absence.

### III. THE INTELLECTUAL AS A TRAITOR

The distinctions we have made thus far are reasonably workable. That is to say, by and large and in a gross, descriptive sense, we can distinguish between the functions of the intellectual, the typical academician, the technician and the professional man. In short, we can describe with a fair degree of accuracy what we have called "class structure in the world of ideas." But intellectuals may betray their functions. They may forget them, muffle them or compromise them. This is more likely to be true now than ever before, because of the fact that intellectuals are now entering politics in increasing numbers—as "brain-trusters," as consultants to government agencies and congressional bodies, as fact-finding critics who formulate proposals for social reform and as liaison agents between politicians and statesmen, on the one hand, and the intellectual community on the other. Our technological civilization which generates increasing social complexity and thereby is becoming more difficult to understand than ever before, has belatedly begun to make use of its intellectuals, although grudgingly to be sure. Their talents and their capacity for disinterestedness, that is, for freedom from partisanship, when trying to improve the society they so frequently criticise, are increasingly recognized. The extent to which this is so has been dramatically described by one

American intellectual, namely, Daniel P. Moynihan,[24] formerly our Assistant Secretary of Labor, in a distinguished article entitled "The Professionalization of Reform" (*The Public Interest,* Fall 1965).

If in their efforts to get along with men of power, whether that power be political or industrial, if in the flush of newly won social esteem and recognition of their talents, usefulness and ideas, the intellectuals who are serving their community should cease to become its critics and, instead, become its advance, partisan agents and advocates, then, indeed, they will have failed both society and themselves. Loren Baritz,[25] a social scientist by early training and now a professional historian, asserts that intellectuals who serve society do, in fact, abandon their traditional function of being its critics. He has posed the dilemma facing the intellectual who enters the market place, in the following way.

Frequently an intellectual has been described as one whose most essential job depends on resistance to his society. Thus, the argument goes, any intellectual who accepts and approves of his society prostitutes his skills and is a traitor to his heritage. One question this work attempts to answer is whether or not such a conception is right: whether, by definition, a man of ideas must maintain the posture of the critic, and whether that intellectual who sincerely believes in and approves of the larger movements of his society can reconcile the demands of his mind and those of his society. Is even the suggestion of a potential antagonism between mind and society justifiable? (pp. ix–x)

Using as a sample of intellectuals, social scientists who have served industry (a group which, in terms of the distinctions made in this paper, would largely consist of "academics" and "technicians") but who, prior to doing so, were critical of American society, Baritz makes the following observation. He concludes that the intellectual who plunges himself into the problems of any important sector of the American community—in the present example the American business and industrial community— absorbs the values of that community and does, in fact, prostitute not only his talents but also his basic posture. That posture, for Baritz, is the quality of mind of the intellectual, that quality which, when he is free to exercise it dispassionately and honestly, enables him not only to call into account the questionable values of his society and to emphasize its persistent errors but also to try to dissipate some of the terrible and escapable alienation that his society is *unnecessarily* producing.

Because the intellectual who absorbs the secular concerns of the American community is first trapped into being an apologist for its values and finally brainwashed into serving them uncritically and with

24 Daniel P. Moynihan. "The Professionalization of Reform." *The Public Interest.* Vol. 1, No. 1, Fall 1965. 6–16.

25 Loren Baritz. *The Servants of Power. A History of the Use of Social Science in American Industry.* Middletown, Connecticut: Wesleyan University Press, 1960. 273 pp.

enthusiasm, Baritz has, himself, answered the question raised in the passage quoted above. He calls for a conscious and principled withdrawal of intellectuals from social institutions, from relevance, responsibility and power. It is this author's sober conviction that if the intellectual is absorbed in promoting and supporting the secular values of his community, he will finally end up by being digested by that community. If he permits himself to touch power, it will, in turn, touch him and blight his traditional and authentic function of engaging in social criticism. Baritz declares that when the intellectual becomes an agent responsible to his society's institutions and its ways of life, rather than intellectually responsible for maintaining his critical postures towards his society, his mind will lose part of that freedom and resiliency which is his most useful and necessary gift.

The proper posture for intellectuals, seeking to be both morally committed and activist without being politically partisan, has been best expressed, I believe, by Raymond Aron [26] in his book, *The Opium of the Intellectuals*. He puts it this way.

. . . The intellectual who sets some store by the just and reasonable organisation of society will not be content to stand on the side-lines, to put his signature at the bottom of every manifesto against every injustice. Although he will endeavour to appeal to the consciences of all parties, he will take his stand in favour of the one which appears to offer humanity the best chance—a historical choice which involves the risk of error which is inseparable from the historical condition. He will not refuse to become involved, and when he participates in action he will accept its consequences, however harsh. But he must try never to forget the arguments of the adversary, or the uncertainty of the future, or the faults of his own side, or the underlying fraternity of ordinary men everywhere. (p. 303)

Criticism of one's society need not, of course, always be executed in a serious vein. There are intellectuals who do this best in terms of satire. One example of this type of intellectual was Franz Schoenberner [27] whose autobiography, *Confessions of a European Intellectual*, illustrates vividly the value of a satirical, critical posture. Schoenberner was the editor of the internationally distinguished, German periodical, *Simplicissimus*, devoted to political satire. The chief characteristic of *Simplicissimus*, as Schoenberner, himself, describes it, was its absolute independence. It was at liberty to comment on all political and cultural events, without being tied to any political party or to any commercial interest. It can clearly be seen that this is precisely the advantage that we are stressing as the life-blood of the detached but socially critical intellectual.

[26] Raymond Aron. *The Opium of the Intellectuals*. New York: W. W. Norton, 1962. 324 pp.

[27] Franz Schoenberner. *Confessions of a European Intellectual*. New York: Collier Books, 1965. 338 pp.

One of the best indictments against the intellectual who betrays his true function, has been formulated by Hans J. Morgenthau [28] in an article entitled "Truth and Power" (*The New Republic,* November 26, 1966). Not only has Morgenthau systematically restated the valid functions of the intellectual in the sense emphasized by Baritz and Benda but he has also presented the case against American intellectuals, both of the academic and nonacademic variety, who have entered politics and betrayed their trust. Morgenthau's indictment against American intellectuals is intended not only for those who actively participate in politics but also for those who seek to influence political decision-making, either from the university or the marketplace. It is clear by his reference to Benda that Morgenthau takes his stand alongside that of this distinguished, French intellectual and that he feels American intellectuals in recent years have betrayed both their functions and the needs of the American community, itself.

Morgenthau's theses with respect to intellectuals as traitors are not difficult to understand. He asserts that *historically* there has been and still is a fundamental incompatibility between truth and power. Morgenthau, himself, puts it this way.

. . . In his search for the truth, the ideal type of intellectual is oblivious to power; in his pursuit of power, the politician at best will use truth as a means to his ends. Yet the two worlds are also potentially intertwined; for truth has a message that is relevant to power, and the very existence of power has a bearing both upon the expression and recognition of truth. (pp. 8–9)

In the face of both the *historical* incompatibility of truth and power as well as their *potential* interconnectedness, the intellectual, says Morgenthau, can respond in any one of four different ways: by retreat into the ivory tower, by prophetic confrontation, by expert advice or by surrender. The first of these is, of course, The Way as seen by Baritz. The second reflects the viewpoint of Benda, Aron and Schoenberner. The third reflects precisely the situation for the American intellectual and academic who have entered the political arena, either by actively serving in a government post or as academic consultants to governmental agencies. These are the intellectuals who have advanced what Moynihan would call the professionalization of reform. The fourth mode of response to the relationships between truth and power is to serve supinely and uncritically the interests of business, labor, the government or the military. This, of course, is the indictment levelled by Baritz against those social scientists who have abandoned their critical functions and allowed themselves to become the servants of power.

[28] Hans J. Morgenthau. "Truth and Power." *The New Republic.* Vol. 155, No. 22. November 26, 1966. 8–14.

Morgenthau indicts American intellectuals in relation to the moral considerations which should underly the political sphere, by stating that those intellectuals who are now concerned with political matters, have become the advocates of an unsystematized, American ideology. They have transformed themselves into agents of political partisanship, thereby subjecting themselves to the dictates of power. They have allowed themselves to become, in effect, the public relations men of official policy. In this latter role they may sometimes have to make the worst appear the better reason. This means that they may have to rationalize popular passions so that they appear to be intellectually sound and socially just and, at the same time, they may on occasion have to invest the exercise of power with the appearance of truth. This latter will occur in two ways: first by apologies which work both sides of the political street, and later by arguments which leave no room for doubt that official actions are without moral blemish. When intellectuals do this, this is their betrayal.

Men of power, says Morgenthau, can react to unpleasant truth which reveals questionable motives underlying their official actions, in four different ways. They can heed, silence, discredit, or corrupt it. What usually happens is that those in power first try to corrupt truth. If this fails they try to discredit it and if efforts to discredit it are not, themselves, successful, they will be followed by attempts to silence it. With respect to a great deal of official action on various issues, those holding political power have done just this in recent years and have done so, argues Morgenthau, *with the connivance of American intellectuals, themselves.* In the process the American intellectuals, by and large, have become silent and corrupt. Their willingness to be silenced and morally corrupted can be explained, according to Morgenthau, by three factors. These are the moral and social conformity which now dominate American society, the personal ambitions and career considerations of American intellectuals, particularly those of an academic stamp, and a variety of inducements and temptations held out to the academic intellectuals. These inducements are in the form of consultantships, research contracts and grants, the subsidizing of foreign travel for American intellectuals who have adopted the official viewpoint on pressing issues, and through a variety of honors and rewards which The American Establishment has at its command. As a result, says Morgenthau, academic intellectuals are weaned away from the authentic functions of the true intellectual. To bridge the conflict between truth and power and in order to pursue truth without sacrificing personal ambition, the academic intellectual must play it safe. He must, says Morgenthau,

. . . concern himself with issues, and deal with them in ways, which are non-controversial because they neither deviate from the standards of society nor invite dissent from the policies of the government. Thus the intellectual deals with "safe" subjects in a "safe" manner. Yet on the great issues of political life, which are controversial by definition, he must remain silent. He does not need to be silenced; he silences himself. Silence with regard to these issues is the passive manifestation of conformity. (p. 13)

Morgenthau spares no pains in making pungent his indictment of most academic intellectuals. With Baritz, Benda, and Aron, he pleads for a return to those practises which have always been the valid functions of intellectuals, namely, the pursuit of truth and social justice and the ever-watchful maintenance of a moral posture. If the price of liberty is eternal vigilance, then it is the intellectual who must stand watch longer and more faithfully than any other type of citizen. Until men become angels, that vigil is an absolutely indispensable function of the intellectual. It has to be exercised most intensively in relation to the official acts of men of power, no matter how well-intentioned such men are or seem to be. It is only in this way that the intellectual can remain faithful to his calling and to his public trust. Anything short of this is treason.

These, then, are distinctions which I hold to be fairly important. Let me emphasize that the desire to deal with the social complexity of the modern world, to alleviate the unnecessary evils and suffering of the human condition and the desire to see ideas and knowledge transformed into the direct action required for needed social change, are likely to be most characteristic of the intellectual. An intermittent concern with some of these matters is occasionally found among professors and educators but they are rarely the constant themes of concern for academics which they are, in fact, for intellectuals. The same passions, of course, may occasionally move some technicians and professional men but, in a statistical sense, these social passions are even less likely to appear in these groups than among academics. On the whole, as Lerner [29] indicates, technicians and professional men are apolitical and proud of it. When the concerns which are the life-blood of the intellectual do appear among the educated and the trained, they are usually not integrated into the individual's picture of the *total life* by which he is surrounded.

In contrast, the desires which we have already mentioned, constitute the intellectual's way of life, his "character" as Mounier [30] would put it. It may be true that these concerns and this way of life, result in a *variety* of proposals from intellectuals for improving the human condition. Such pluralism is all to the good. But the important thing is that it is the intellectual who is concerned with the good life, not the academic, the tech-

---

[29] Max Lerner. *America as a Civilization. Life and Thought in the United States Today.* New York: Simon and Schuster, 1957. 1036 pp. See Chapter IV "The Culture of Science and the Machine," particularly Section 3, *Big Technology and Neutral Technicians,* 227–238.

[30] Emmanuel Mounier. *The Character of Man.* New York: Harper, 1956. 341 pp.

nician, or the professional man. It is the intellectual's vision and his passion which, in the long view, enable man's reach to exceed his grasp. It is his projections of perfection which gradually mold this world a little nearer to the heart's desire. The academic, the technician, and the professional man will, by and large, take things as they find them. It is chiefly the intellectual, however, upon whom we must depend for that larger vision without which stagnation of every sort would be the inevitable lot of man.

# SUMMARY OF PART II

In Part II we have explored the manner in which culture, leisure, and education are interwoven into a pattern of a sort. We have also discussed in a general way the bearing which the impact of science and technology in the modern age can be expected to have upon the strands of this pattern. Let us highlight our main points here. The most significant aspect of *paideia* is *leisure as renewal*. Mass and middlebrow culture work against a fruitful expression of this theme. Certain separations in culture are dangerous in a cybernating society. One of these is the separation of the humanities from science or—to put the contrast somewhat differently —"soft culture" from "hard culture." Another is the relegation of culture to a genteel, hothouse pursuit divorced from life in the raw. A third undesirable separation is that which occurs when academic learning is separated from the problems of community.

The legacy of liberal education must be preserved in spirit but given new forms for a cybernating society. In particular, we have to be clear about what we can and ought to expect from good teachers of large vision and what we can and ought to expect from the information-processing revolution in the classroom, made feasible by computer technology. In addition, we should be alerted to the fact that learning is due for some interdisciplinary syntheses—inescapable in an age of growing social complexity produced by science and technology—but that these syntheses will complement specialization rather than eliminate it. Finally, many of the advancements of society towards greater social justice and a more perfect social order have come from "intellectuals." We have to be clear about the meanings which can be attached to this term. We have to be aware of the long-run, social functions performed by intellectuals. Above all we must not lose sight of two major and contemporary functions of intellectuals. One of these is to act as watchdogs for the moral and social functions of the human community, a task which now demands greater knowledge and sensitivity than ever before. The other is to work at the task of restating those functions in terms which will be appropriate for an age of science and technology.

# III

# The Burden of Social Complexity

## ORIENTATION TO PART III

Social complexity is a difficult burden for people of average and superior intellectual endowments. It is probably a veritable cross of Calvary for the intellectually underprivileged. It is, of course, the intellectually average and superior citizens who constitute the life-blood of democracy. Consequently, if modern man is to exhibit a well-developed sense of social responsibility, both average and superior citizens have to be helped to understand the burden of social complexity and be shown ways in which to deal with it. The perennial quest for community can be made almost impossible if social complexity is excessive. Since men *do* seek community they must be prepared to minimize and deal with the social complexity created by science and technology. The purpose of Part III is to examine the burden of social complexity facing modern man—a burden which will clearly be aggravated as we move toward an era of cybernation.

# 12

# The Complexity of
# Our Social Environment[*]

### INTRODUCTION

The problems of community are relatively simple ones when men live in communities which are based essentially upon agriculture. Almost any citizen of an agrarian community can participate to some extent in running it. Even when a community is partly industrial and partly agricultural, it is not difficult to manage so long as it is *small in population and size*. When, however, as in the recent history of technologically advanced Western countries, the community has become overwhelmingly industrial, swollen in population and very large in area, a new kind of problem arises for its residents. This is the problem of dealing with the burden of the increasing social complexity generated by a number of important factors.

In the first place our lives are being complicated socially by applied science in the form of modern industrial technologies. A great deal of social complexity is the result of the impact of such factors as the following: new patterns of consumption, new modes of residential living, new methods of transportation, changed forms of leisure and recreation, new ways of engaging in trade and commerce, new types of education for an increasing variety of new professions and occupations, and so on. The difficulty of understanding the "social-go" of things—if we may be permitted to coin a neologism—has also been increased because of the bewildering variety of new social, economic, and political institutions which have been invented to cushion and regulate the impacts of all this novelty.

Aiding and abetting the difficulty of comprehension are the many new laws, legal theories and legal philosophies which seek to manage social and technological change. Due to the fact that the roots of the

---

[*] Chapter 12, with adaptations and modifications, has been taken from the following source: Henry Winthrop. "The Dilemma of Modern Man." *Journal of Human Relations.* Vol. 11, No. 2, Winter 1963, 276–288.

legal mentality and the legal outlook lie in a pre-scientific, pre-technologi-
cal past, it is highly doubtful that they are the most appropriate postures
for grasping and dealing with the burdens of current and expected social
complexity. It must be remembered that those who control our destinies,
the politicians, are chiefly ex-lawyers, and says Goodall,[1] politics suffers
from the fact that there are "so many stuffed shirts in positions where a
vivid sense of reality is the major requirement."

All of the preceding factors we have mentioned—and a good many
we have not—have introduced enormous social complexity into the life
of the modern community at all levels. In effect, they have generated
several "complex systems" in the design-engineer's sense of this phrase.
Each of these systems possesses component parts which affect one another
in ways too little understood, even by the expert. In such a system what
we would ordinarily call a "social problem" is essentially a malfunctioning of the entire system and this malfunctioning is likely to be the result
of parts whose functions work in opposing ways and often in opposite
directions, socially speaking. This is largely because these component
parts were introduced at different times independently of each other.
Unfortunately, when these systems break down they do so within the
framework of our modern democracies. Within our democratic traditions,
the average citizen is expected to make his voice heard and his influence
felt in trying to solve our social problems—our system breakdowns, as it
were. He is expected to do this by means of the vote, by lobbies and civic
groups, by commission studies, by the use of the initiative, referendum
and recall, by "passing a law," and in many other ways. The most powerful of all these response mechanisms is, of course, the popular vote.

In order, however, to exercise the vote intelligently and to participate meaningfully in the democratic process, the voter needs to become
aware of the *social complexity* of the system in which he has his being
and on behalf of which he casts his decision-making votes. He needs a
fuller understanding of what we have called the "social-go" of things.
Such an improved understanding of the complexity of the issues faced
in modern society would be helpful on several counts. First, it would
give the serious and mature citizen some idea of the homework he had
to do before he could participate intelligently in the democratic process.
Second, there is surely a relationship between intellectual capacity and
the community's interrelated issues and problems. This relationship provides a rough indication of how many votes could *potentially* be "thoughtful votes." Third, there is a similar relationship between the fund of

[1] Marcus C. Goodall. *Science and the Politician.* Cambridge, Massachusetts: Schenk-
man Publishing Company, 1965. 83 pp. Goodall, whose publishers are proud to emphasize that he is not confined to narrow specialization, has worked at different times on
radar research, on the foundations of relativistic quantum mechanics, muscle biophysics,
and the theory of cognitive systems. This author tries to relate science to modern politics
because of his strong interest in the human condition.

information at the voter's disposal and his capacity to understand the community's difficulties. This relationship provides a rough indication of the amount of *potential* homework that would be required in order that a vote be truly an "informed vote."

In a sense some foreknowledge of the homework the voter would have to do in order to participate intelligently in the social responsibility of voting, would be fairly obvious if only we had some sort of a *measuring device* which could indicate the social complexity of the system in which the responsible voter has to function. This would be realizable if we had one or more *indices of social complexity*. Such an index of social complexity would have the further advantage of allowing us to know in advance what percentage of the citizenry can meaningfully participate in the democratic process because they are in fact able to grasp the bio-ecological and institutional realities of their daily existence. Where social welfare is both measurable and capable of being either maximized or optimized, as has been ably demonstrated by Rothenberg,[2] *an index of social complexity*, as it were, would be of maximum help in trying to achieve such maximum or optimum welfare. It would furnish us with some notion of the number of citizens who could responsibly and mutually be expected to be able to put their heads together not only to deal intelligently with the issues faced by the body politic but also to understand the factors which generate the grave problems before us today.

All systems are of differing complexity and there are clearly several values—particularly educational ones—which would inhere in our being able to recognize, measure and describe the relative differences in complexity of different systems. There is one difference, however, between the complexity of natural systems and those of a technological sort, on the one hand, and man's social systems, on the other. Most systems in nature possess fixed properties and are unchanging. It can be argued that the properties of man-made systems, like an airplane motor or a telephone communications system, are, for all practical purposes, fixed once and for all. But when it comes to man's social systems their properties are changing all the time. This is because in effect the system, itself, is being constantly changed by the introduction of new components (institutions), new legislation, new motivations and newly created human wants. As a result of these constant changes our social system (or systems, if you prefer) grows more complex all the time. Precisely because it grows more complex all the time it becomes more and more difficult to understand.

If we could measure in some sense the growing complexity of that system, by means of one or more indices of social complexity, we would obtain a lot of socially useful information. In particular, knowing the

---

2 Jerome Rothenberg. *The Measurement of Social Welfare.* Englewood Cliffs, New Jersey: Prentice-Hall, 1961. 357 pp.

distribution of human intelligence, the distribution of years of education in the population and even the variation to some extent in the quality of the education of different groups in the population, we could obtain some idea of the prospective efficiency with which different groups of our population could understand and adapt to the workings of our social system. This, of course, is another way of saying that we could obtain some idea of how well different groups would be able to understand the problems of the American community and deal with them via the vote and other democratic processes. This would be prized information for those who sincerely wish to see the democratic process function both intelligently, humanely and knowledgeably.

Unfortunately, no sociologist has as yet dedicated himself, so far as I know, to the construction of such an *index of social complexity*. It is to be understood, of course, that such an index would have to be some sort of *composite measure*. Operational definitions of complexity would have to be furnished for each separate *type* of social phenomenon, social process, or social difficulty which it was felt *consensually* would have to be included in the composite. These definitions would vary with the context involved, the techniques for measuring the different types of complexity involved would likewise vary, and the *weights* attached to the separate component measures of complexity entering into the composite index would also vary. Methods for determining these weights and for properly aggregating the component measures most judiciously and usefully would present a separate set of problems. But considerations such as these are methodological difficulties *in principle* only, far from insuperable, and do not differ in any way from similar considerations which have entered into other types of social measurement. Nor is it to be denied that more than one type of index of this nature could, in principle, be constructed. Once constructed, the fruitfulness of such an index in connection with the possible uses we have emphasized above, can be exploited so as to determine the extent to which the citizen *can truly participate meaningfully in the democratic process*.

Let the reader imagine that such a reliable index has already been developed. Then for *one* proper and significant use of this index we need to make only one assumption, namely, that for some time to come the distribution of human intelligence is likely to remain what it is today. This assumes a frequency distribution of intelligence quotients which run roughly from zero to some figure in the neighborhood of 200. If there is a relationship between intelligence and the degree of social complexity which may be grasped, that is to say, if the degree of social complexity which is to be understood depends upon a minimum, critical IQ level, then it becomes possible *at any time* to determine the absolute numbers and percentage of the total, eligible, voting population that are *theoretically* disfranchised from the possibility of intelligent participation in the democratic process or, at least, from intelligent participation in the solution of a given issue. This theoretical disfranchisement in terms of intellectual qualifications says nothing, of course, either about the willingness of the citizen to participate or his good intentions and altruistic stance towards his fellow citizens and their problems. This predicted percentage disfranchisement rests on the fact that there would be little difficulty in establishing empirically a positive correlation between a critically needed minimum IQ and measures of social complexity for any given issue or problem. Such a correlation would clearly justify the assertion that any community that arrives at the consensus conviction that its problems can properly be grasped and dealt with only by those endowed with a given, minimum critical IQ or better, is equally in a position to assert that those who fall below this minimum cannot *adequately* participate meaningfully in democratic processes and problems. The presence of a critical minimum implies that the further below this critical minimum an individual's intellectual capacity falls, the less adequate he or she is to deal with the social complexity of modern life.

Inasmuch as in the preceding paragraphs we have talked about meaningful participation in the democratic process, we should end this section by stating what we mean by "democracy." Our intended meaning is a refinement of the commonly understood content of this term. We refer to all those processes and functions by which men living together in community propose to govern themselves. Some of these processes and functions men delegate to others, particularly in a large and complex community. Still other processes and functions are undertaken directly by the citizens, themselves. These include such matters as voting, the use of the initiative, the referendum and the recall, the use of write-ins on ballots, the use of citizens' petitions in order to accomplish certain objectives, the use of citizens' lobbies, citizens' councils and citizens' study groups, the formation of civic organizations to achieve given ends and make certain that as-yet, unfulfilled needs of the community are met, and a host of similar considerations in which the ordinary citizen may make his thinking felt and his voice heard.

In all of these processes and functions, the activities involved are purposeless if those who engage in them do not really understand the issues and problems they are dealing with. When the citizen genuinely understands the political and civic concerns which he pursues, then we can speak of this as meaningful participation in the democratic process. When the citizen does not understand the nature of the problems on which he wishes to be heard, then he is only going through the "forms and trappings" of the democratic process. In that case his participation is not meaningful. As our social milieu becomes increasingly complex, meaningful participation becomes *increasingly difficult*. This difficulty can be met only when the citizen makes himself knowledgeable and is willing—and hopefully, able—to do the hard thinking required in order to understand the problems of his community and comprehend the nature of various solutions which are being proposed for dealing with them.

## I. THE CONSEQUENCES OF SOCIAL COMPLEXITY

Let us now suppose that *one or more* indices of social complexity have been constructed and made available to any community, democratic or otherwise. In the light of the institutional and technological realities of modern society and extrapolating recent trends into the future—a not unreasonable procedure in this context—what is likely to be the nature of the mathematical curve describing the change of such an index with time? I venture to suggest that the expected growth curve will not be linear but exponential in nature. This is obviously equivalent to asserting that, for any arbitrary time interval of measurement, the increases in social complexity will, themselves, be getting larger and larger in successive units of the time interval chosen for measurement. This is a reasonable expectation since it is recognized that knowledge in general is now doubling every ten years and that equal, if not greater, rates of acceleration are occurring just for science and technology alone. If we assume that the complexity of our social issues and problems will be proportional to these growth rates—since the periods between the discovery and application of new knowledge are now growing smaller with the passage of time—we can expect the difficulties which attend the average man's efforts to wrestle with the concerns of his time to be aggravated. Inasmuch as the effects of the applications of new science and technology tend to destabilize already achieved social equilibria, and inasmuch as political, social, and legal institutional changes are instituted to recapture such lost equilibria—albeit on a different basis—we would expect an understanding of proposed new measures for restoring equilibrium to be more difficult to attain. This, of course, is only another way of saying that the issues and problems with which we shall have to deal will grow more complex with the passing of time.

However, it is not to be expected that the change in an index of social complexity will be *directly proportional* to the changes in the rates of acceleration of new knowledge. Human effort to restore lost equilibria will tend to simplify the effects of the impact of new knowledge but the simplification achieved will rarely leave the complexity of any problem exactly the same as it was before. To some degree it will have grown more complex. All of these considerations can then be summed up by saying that in any society which permits an element of decision and choice for the average citizen—and clearly enough this is the major, pristine ideal of democracy—we can expect that it will become more and more difficult for the citizen to understand the problems and issues on which he is expected to exercise that choice. This will have to be true if our assumption is sound that the social complexity of our lives will increase with the passage of time, regardless of whether a trend line for an index of social complexity is exponential or not. *A fortiori,* this is a reasonable assumption if the present do-nothing attitude continues, concerning the growing difficulty of comprehending social change.

We must then relate human intellectual capacity to the growing social complexity of this not-so-distant human ecology. The phrase "intellectual capacity" can mean different things to different people but I am using it here to refer to the well-known *intelligence quotient.* This is not because I believe that no other operational definition of this concept can be given that is superior to the concept of the IQ. Rather it is because no other *has been given,* so that the IQ is simply the best, even if quite crude, measure to date of intellectual capacity. For the psychologically sophisticated reader who is aware that the use of the IQ as a crude measure of intelligence has received much professional criticism in recent years, and who, therefore, feels somewhat uneasy over using it, let me suggest an alternative. Let us imagine that some *superior* measure of intelligence or intellectual force will be developed in the future and let us christen this measure *in advance* as the IC or "intellectual capacity." [3]

[3] The concept of "intellectual capacity" or IC will, of course, prove to be a *composite one.* This is brought out very succinctly in the following paper. John L. Horn. "Intelligence—Why It Grows, Why It Declines." *Trans-action.* Vol. 5, No. 1, November 1967. 23–31. This author shows that there are two broad types of intelligence: *fluid intelligence* (FI) and *crystallized intelligence* (CI). The former is relatively independent of education and experience. The latter is directly derived from experience. Both kinds of intelligence are formed by about *30 more elementary abilities.* These 30 abilities, which are highly variable from one person to another, constitute the *composite* of our mythical, aggregate *measure of intellectual capacity, IC.* Horn further points out that there are three processes essential to the development of both kinds of intelligence: *anlage function,* the *acquisition of aids,* and *concept formation.* The first refers to the *physiological base* of intelligence and includes heredity but is, of course, wider than heredity in its meaning. The second refers to techniques which are aids and short-cuts to learning, such as mnemonic devices or the rules of algebra. The third refers to the categories by which man grasps and generalizes experience and through which he discovers or invents relationships. Language is the major handmaiden to concept formation, particularly its *structural* or *ratiocinative* aspects. *Maturation, acculturation,* and the *physiological status* of the individual, affect the *development* or *status* of both (FI) and (CI), so that either or both of these may decline with age. If it were not for neural damage with age and some of the deleterious effects of our environments, *acculturation,* alone, might make it possible for intelligence to increase, not decline, in adulthood.

Horn's summary of the nature and development of intelligence is relevant to the concerns of the present chapter, chiefly in relation to our fictitious concept of "intellectual capacity" or IC. Social complexity (SC) increases with time. (CI) can grasp increasing SC through acculturation, where there is little or no neural or other physiological damage and a favorable (FI) and *anlage* to start with. (CI) can do this with aids and concept formation. But—and this is the point—the combinations of (FI) and (CI) to be found in the present distribution of human intelligence, appear to be increasingly insufficient to grasp the present levels of SC and these levels will apparently become even more dysfunctional as SC increases, as revealed by any ISC. This dysfunctionality can be offset by a biological raising of the level of human intelligence and this will be the concern of the last part of the present chapter. It can also be offset by improvements in the acquisition of aids and concept formation (acculturation) and the possibilities for improvements of this sort will be the concern of Chapter 13.

Then if the reader will substitute IC for IQ every time he meets the latter concept, no harm will be done, and the nature, structure, and cogency of the exposition will remain unaltered. For the more hard-bitten type of reader who might feel that adaptation to social complexity is even more likely to be a function of *educational achievement or performance,* such as that measured by the National Merit Scholarship Test, then I suggest that in his mind's eye he substitute the score on such a test for the concept of IQ whenever the latter is mentioned in the course of this chapter.

It is also recognized that the efficiency with which one uses one's native intelligence depends on the quality of one's education. Discussion of the relation between intelligence and educational method, particularly where the quality of response is important in relation to human adaptation to social complexity, has been reserved, however, for chapter 13.

Using the IQ, then, as a rough measure of intellectual capacity we require *only one assumption* in order to relate measures of IQ to an *Index of Social Complexity* which we shall hereinafter refer to as the ISC. That assumption is this: *any problem or issue of a given degree of social complexity requires in principle a critical, minimum IQ for its complete comprehension.* This is certainly the case for some traditional subject matter in modern education, e.g., plane geometry, Latin, or chemistry, and the evidence is substantial in this connection. The difficulties which students at or below a given IQ level have in these subjects, are due essentially to the difficulty inherent in the subject matter itself, and this will be true even when such material is presented by excellent teachers using *optimum* pedagogical methods. In practice, a critical minimum required for given difficult subject matter, will be found to vary slightly, but this variation really reflects a deficiency of the test yardstick rather than an invalidity of our underlying assumption. That assumption really asserts that there is a one-to-one correspondence between a given level of complexity of subject matter, where that complexity is accurately measurable, and a minimum IQ needed to deal with that level of complexity, where the IQ is accurately measurable. Those familiar with the nature of intelligence testing theory and construction know that the practical difficulty of assigning a fixed IQ to any single individual is due to variation in results. This variation arises both from the fact that different tests measure somewhat different things and the same test given many times has inescapable error variance. For reasons such as these, we have to think of a minimum, critical IQ as an average of several values over a small range. In spite of such variation, our assumption is sufficiently heuristic for both practical as well as theoretical purposes.

Suppose the complexity of the social environment of a small community has been measured in some way for the first time in, say, 1960. Let us arbitrarily set the *value* obtained for the measure in question equal to 100, since we are going to use the year of first measurement as our base year for an ISC. Then the *value* obtained for the social complexity of the environment of that same community in a *subsequent* year—using the same method of measurement—divided by the value that was obtained in the base year, will give us the value of the ISC in that subsequent year.

Now consider the relationship between a social environment which is growing more complex all the time—as measured, of course, by an ISC—and a fixed level of human intelligence which, we will assume, is used at top efficiency. Let us assume that we are dealing with a group of citizens of *average intelligence* and let us further assume that it has been shown that when the ISC = 100, the understanding of the socioeconomic environment of the small community in question is perfectly within the grasp of citizens of average intelligence. Suppose, however, in the subsequent year, the ISC = 115 and it has been shown in one way or another that an overwhelming percentage of our citizens of average intelligence now have great difficulty understanding the socioeconomic environment to which they must adapt through political decision-making and the issues generated by that environment. Then clearly it is beyond their intellectual capacity to deal with their, then current, social environment. As time passes this will become truer since the ISC will rise above 115. In short, if the level of intelligence of the members of a given group is fixed but the complexity of their environment increases all the time, there is less and less likelihood of their being able to use the democratic process most fruitfully. Matters, of course, will be even worse if they do not use their general intellectual capacity at top efficiency.

Relationships such as these, and similar considerations, can be presented quantitatively and more precisely for the mathematically minded reader. When presented quantitatively they provide a better insight into the burden of social complexity which is the concern of Part III. In the light, then, of these considerations the relation between the IQ and the ISC can be brought out via Figures 12-1 through 12-5. Although these figures oversimplify the relationship between IQ and the ISC—a relationship which must be emphasized for a participant democracy—they do bring out the essential considerations involved.

Figure 12-1 emphasizes, of course, the fact that the values of the ISC can be expected to increase with time.

Let $IQ_{min.}$ designate the *critical, minimum IQ* required to comprehend one or more issues or problems of a specified degree of social complexity. Then Figure 12-2 emphasizes that the *critical floor* of intellectual

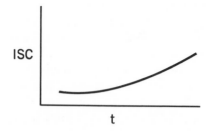

*Figure 12-1.*     The change in ISC with the passage of time

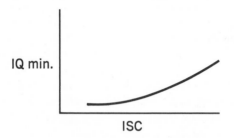

*Figure 12-2.*     The change in *minimum IQ* ($IQ_{min.}$) required to deal with a social
environment whose complexity is increasing,
as indicated by a rising ISC.

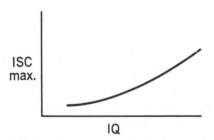

*Figure 12-3.*     The variation in the *maximum value* of the ISC ($ISC_{max.}$) which can
be dealt with by IQ's of increasing magnitude.

capacity required to deal with a *composite* ISC that measures the overall
difficulty of dealing with some set of major issues and problems which
press upon the democratic community at any given time, will, itself, have
to be larger and larger as the ISC increases over time.

   Let $ISC_{max.}$ represent the *maximum degree of social complexity* which
can be dealt with by an individual of specified IQ level. Then Figure
12-3 reflects the fact that the maximum value of the ISC with which the
citizen can hope to deal will increase as the IQ, itself, rises. It should also
be clear that the entire range of values of the ordinate, that lies above

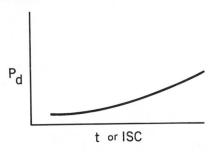

$P_d$

t or ISC

*Figure 12-4.* The increasing percentages of voters who would be intellectually disfranchised ($P_d$) from meaningful participation in democratic processes, as time passed or as the ISC increased.

that point of the $ISC_{max.}$ which corresponds to a *given* IQ level, represents degrees of social complexity which an individual of the given IQ level in question, will not be able to handle.

As the critical floor of IQ needed for grasping the essential nature of our social issues and problems rises, more and more citizens are automatically disfranchised from effective, that is, meaningful participation in the democratic process. The votes of these disfranchised citizens on various issues are *miscast* because all voters possessing an intellectual capacity (measured in IQ or otherwise) below the critical minimum needed for grasping the issues in question, cannot be said to understand properly the issues involved. If, for a long time to come, the distribution of human intelligence remains what it is today, roughly a theoretical range from 0-200, then the percentage of the total population disfranchised from meaningful participation in the democratic process, $P_d$, increases with time or—what amounts to the same thing—increases with a rise in the ISC. This is shown simply in Figure 12-4.

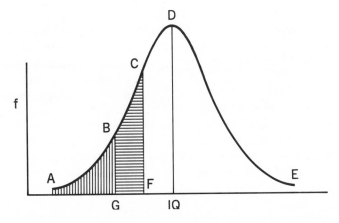

*Figure 12-5.* The change in the number of disfranchised voters as an increasing percentage of the distribution of human intelligence (IQ).

In Figure 12-5 we are shown the well-known normal or bell curve, which describes the distribution of human intelligence. The *frequencies* or *numbers,* f, of individuals of a given IQ, are shown. At time, $t_o$, when an ISC is first constructed, the level of complexity of social issues and problems is such that a certain number of the voters are disfranchised from meaningful participation in their solution. This number would be all those voters whose IQ's were below the needed $IQ_{min}$. These voters will be included in the area, ABG. At a later time, when the ISC has risen, an additional number of voters will now be disfranchised in the sense we have been describing, and this additional number falls within the area, GBCF. The total number who will have been disfranchised by this time will fall, of course, under the area, ACF.

Clearly enough if the ISC were to increase with time, theoretically a larger and larger percentage of our population would fail to participate intelligently in the democratic process. Long before this could happen there would be enough popular revulsion over the political and civic bewilderment that followed increasing complexity, to create a demand that something be done about it. Quite obviously it would be absurd to allow the process of disfranchisement to go to completion. The point at which this revulsion would set in is, of course, unpredictable. One can venture the guess, however, that it is likely to occur when the decisions of controllers in a highly centralized body politic, cannot be made clear to an electorate that put them into office in the first place. This, itself, is likely to happen when there are too few intermediary human channels to provide the effective volume of communication which would be required to convey, if only in oversimplified, dramatic and popular form, the complex nature of the problems faced by the citizen. Social and political instability, I think, is bound to result when the ratio of competent decision-makers to controllees in the community-at-large is too small to provide effective translation of the decision-making process. There is no current sociological theory that will provide us with any ideas as to what the magnitude of such critical ratios would have to be before destabilization occurred. There is likewise no type of research along these lines in either sociology or political science, that is to say, no effort to arrive at such ratios in community studies. This may be because community breakdown in the sense of intellectual disfranchisement has never as yet been of concern. It may likewise be due to the possibility that community breakdowns of this political type have not as yet occurred. Such breakdowns apparently lie in the future. But even though such breakdowns may only be a threat in the near future, the importance of trying to prevent them before they occur is, I think, beyond question.

## II. THE LONG-TERM SOLUTIONS

In order to avoid the impasse to the functioning of democracy that increasing social complexity threatens, we have to consider possible alternatives that will head off political meaninglessness. There are probably many avenues that democracy will be able to take to avoid the dilemma of well-nigh universal disfranchisement that would result if man were to allow his own social ecology to become increasingly more complex. I should like to discuss only a few of these alternatives here. All solutions of the dilemma will be either of a long-term nature or short-term nature. Inasmuch as the long-term type of solution will always appear "impractical" to men who have no sense of the urgency of the problem we are trying to describe, let us deal with that type first. The long-term solution is one which assumes that the degree of political simplification open to a civilized, democratic community is limited in the short run and that, for this reason, whatever measures are taken will have to be novel and nongradualistic in nature.

If we assume that the critical ratio at which social instability will set in will not occur for one to two centuries, if we further assume that the proposal I am about to discuss can be consummated before that time, and if we also assume that no degree of social complexity is too much to wrestle with for those who are at the upper reaches of intellectual capacity (say an IQ of 170 and up), then a long-term solution *may be* possible. The long-term solution which I wish to mention is not, of course, a grassroots solution. Furthermore, since it is long-haired in nature it would be regarded by "practical" men who wish to concern themselves only with familiar possibilities as out of the question. Men who would balk at opposing popular notions of what constitutes proper democratic methods of social change will draw back from the solution in question. Nevertheless it is a technical possibility. I am referring to techniques for raising the mean IQ of a population through genetic controls. It is conceivable that such techniques may become established over the next 200 years, provided required changes in current moral outlook occur that will permit the exploitation of these technical possibilities among human beings. Clearly a population possessing a considerable number of individuals with an IQ of 170 or higher may be able to deal with the increasing social complexity which future human communities face.

Rostand [4] has described several of these techniques. One that has been made popular through Aldous Huxley's *Brave New World,* involves the use of *ectogenesis* (the ability to keep an embryo alive outside the womb) followed by the use of certain procedures on the motherless embryos to control the heredity character and quality of the adult orga-

4 Jean Rostand. *Can Man be Modified?* New York: Basic Books, 1959. 105 pp.

nism. Among these procedures could be special microsurgeries, the use of chemical agents for bringing about a tailor-made, predetermined onto-genesis, or the use of *selective feeding* similar to the process by which bees transform a larva into a queen bee. Assuming moral and social repugnance to such procedures have been overcome, Rostand then assumes they could be used to control human heredity and produce intellectually superior men and women. *For the present* ectogenesis is not a technical possibility on human embryos, but has been successful for short periods on the embryos of rats, mice, rabbits, and guinea pigs. Rostand also conceives of techniques which might produce fatherless births by parthenogenesis in human beings as a possibility in the future, presumably with the consent of a human mother of outstanding genetic composition. It has also been found that there are techniques for fertilizing the eggs of salamanders, frogs and other animals, so that the nucleus of the zygote contains two sets of maternal chromosomes and one set of paternal chromosomes. If such techniques are ever developed for human conception and the resulting adult organisms prove to be viable, then perhaps the present intellectual limitations of the human population will be surmountable. This would be doubly so if females of outstanding genetic composition were impregnated, using artificial insemination, by male spermatozoa of equally outstanding genetic composition. Artificial insemination, itself, becomes an independent technique in its own right since, treating the semen of cocks and bulls with glycerine, their spermatozoa can be preserved at low temperatures without losing the power to fertilize. In fact vitrified human semen has already been used to produce human births. Here again the value of the technique is assured if semen banks contain only spermatozoa of outstanding hereditary pedigree and human female receivers are themselves of superior vintage genetically. It should be carefully noted that artificial insemination as a technique lends itself to *telegenesis* and *palaeogenesis,* that is, to conception across space, (the donor in the United States, the receiver in Europe) and to conception across time, (the donor being a male who lived and died generations before the receiver).

There may also be available *in principle* a technique of *human propagation by cuttings,* which would extend Hullin's Law.[5] This technique, when applied to frogs, consists of removing the nucleus of an egg and putting in its place the nucleus of a cell from the embryo of another frog. The receiving egg then starts developing and the frog which develops possesses the chromosome make-up of the donor embryo. Rostand believes that someday this same type of result may be obtained from a cell

---

[5] Hullin's law describes the frequency of multiple-birth in human beings, that is, the frequency of occurrence of twins, triplets, quadruplets, and quintuplets. This frequency is given by the ratio $(1/85)^{n-1}$, where $n$ stands for the total number of children born to a human mother at any one time.

of any of the tissues of a donor. In that case if we took the nuclei of cells of outstanding men, exchanged them for the nuclei in the eggs of female receivers and found some way to ensure the development of these eggs into full human beings, we would in effect be able to reproduce the genetic makeup of great geniuses indefinitely. All such human beings would, of course, be twins or, more correctly, *n*-tuplets. If we can ever couple this technique of nuclear transplantation with ectogenesis, the possibilities are staggering, assuming always, of course, that social and moral attitudes have been modified sufficiently to permit the use of such procedures. All the procedures we have just described are strictly genetic techniques. We are omitting entirely such techniques for controlling the quality of an organism, as hormone treatments, psychogenic drugs or chemicals, such as orthedrin, maxiton, and glutamic acid, special types of nutrition, or psychosurgery.

The optimistic possibilities for novel biological change as envisaged by Rostand, can best be delineated in his own words.

For the moment, biology is incapable of satisfying the principal requests addressed to it by the man in the street. It does not prolong life, it does not determine sex, it does not control heredity, it does not procure intelligence for fools. . . . But it is possible that all these powers may belong to it tomorrow, and many others as well, which people do not dream of expecting from it: the procreation of twins at will, test tube pregnancy, the modification of the embryo, controlled mutation, the production of a superhuman being. . . .

Under the magic wand of biology, man is now gradually becoming quite different from what he was. Here and now he is changing into a new and paradoxical animal, unknown to those who assign names to things, an animal with a special, pied physiology, borrowing features from the most diverse families of the animal kingdom. Here and now *Homo sapiens* is in process of becoming *Homo biologicus*—a strange biped that will combine the properties of self-reproduction without males, like the greenfly, of fertilising his female at long distance like the nautiloid molluscs, of changing sex like the xiphophores, of growing from cuttings like the earth-worm, of replacing its missing parts like the newt, of developing outside the mother's body like the kangaroo, and of hibernating like the hedgehog. (pp. 33–4)

It may, of course, be the case that Rostand is overly optimistic concerning technologies available for human modification. He does not make the explicit judgment that these will be within our grasp within a few centuries. Such an anticipation is only a hope—a hope that may be relevant to the problem of how a democratic ethos may learn to deal with the increasing social complexity of the immediate future. Even if the democratic community were to sanction the use of some of these techniques, so that we might find some of them in use in 200 years, this gives us at most eight voting generations in which to adapt to the social complexity with which we are concerned. Still this is a period which was regarded as long enough to produce intellectual genius by *artificial selection* alone, according to the anthropologist, Lapouge. The feeling that *something can be done,* without specifying precisely the period of time which must transpire before a payoff function occurs, is shared by the palaeontologist, Simpson.[6] This author feels that a rational, humane, and unsnobbish eugenics plus an enlightened use of artificial selection (and of mutation followed by selection) will help to improve the intellectual level of the human population. The following quotation from Simpson makes clear not only his conviction that human IQ must be raised but also that present levels of IQ are insufficient in relation to the existing degree of social complexity.

Some differences in degree of intelligence may be desirable, but the point is debatable and in any case the raising of the average nearer to the present maximum is evidently desirable. Such changes as these would require provision of optimum environmental conditions, but could not be achieved by this means alone; genetic selection in the existing variability of the species would also be required. There is ample evidence that intelligence is if not strictly determined at least strictly limited as to potentialities by inheritance. Even temperament is apparently to some degree hereditary and correlated with physical structure, better knowledge of which would facilitate selection.

Such changes, involving differences in distribution of existing characters within the human population, are evolutionary but they are of limited scope. Ultimate progress beyond these limits would necessarily involve the development of new characters in the human organism. Probably the new character most surely necessary for evolution beyond the present limits is an increase in intelligence above the existing maximum. Human progress depends on knowledge and learning, and the capacity for these is conditioned by intelligence. Most scientists are already aware that the progress of science is being impeded by the fact that the most brilliant men simply do not have enough learning capacity to acquire all the details of more than increasingly narrow segments of the field of knowledge. Only a very stupid person can believe that mankind is already intelligent enough for its own good. (pp. 170–1)

I find it interesting that Simpson in effect believes that an IQ of 200 (the theoretical maximum) is closer to what society needs. His conviction that the learning capacity of even our highest IQ's is still insufficient to acquire the knowledge that presumably they must have in their own fields, supports indirectly my own opinion that, *a fortiori,* the understanding of complex social issues and the wide range of information needed to deal with them meaningfully, is also becoming increasingly difficult. Such a difficulty, of course, holds even more for the average man than it does for the gifted one. It is obvious that Simpson seems even more pessimistic than I am in his guess as to how numerous the politically elect may be, even at the present time.

[6] George Gaylord Simpson. *The Meaning of Evolution.* New York: Mentor Books, 1951. 192 pp.

The next chapter considers the question of short-term proposals for improving man's capacity to deal with our growing social complexity. Some of these proposals will be found acceptable by people who think of themselves as practical; others will undoubtedly be rejected out of hand as "Utopian." Regardless of how these proposals may be catagorized, it is important to get some idea of what is meant by a short-term solution, that is, one which does not and cannot wait for men to become like gods in foresight and wisdom.[7]

[7] Additional papers describing short-term proposals for dealing with our growing social complexity—proposals which are not taken up in Chapter 13—will be found in: "Bibliography of Publications By Henry Winthrop, 1932–1966." 181–203. In *Sociologia Religiosa. Rivista Di Storia E Sociologia Delle Religioni* (Padova, Italy), Anno X,º 15–16, 1967, Edizioni C.S.S.R., 208 pp.

# 13

# Education, Science, and
# Social Complexity*

## I. THE SHORT-TERM SOLUTIONS

The variety of short-term solutions which are available are less dramatic but some of these too would be likely to meet with resistance and misunderstanding. The first of these of interest would be the formation of an *IQ oligocracy* which, of course, is not to be confused with an oligocracy of intellectuals. This would be equivalent to allowing only high IQ's, properly trained and educated for their tasks, to get into positions of policy-making, governmental power and administrative execution of such policies. What we envisage is a screening procedure by which large numbers of individuals of high IQ, broad and deep range of information and special aptitudes, would be selected for these positions after years of appropriate training. The screening devices would be, of course, in addition to years of training, a psychological battery of relevant tests. In effect this would be equivalent to *euthenic selection* of individuals fitted by ability and training to deal with the increasing social complexities of our time. The empty forms of democracy would be adhered to only in the sense that the citizen casts his vote for competitors who seek political responsibility and power, all of whom have been selected by the screening process just described. If we assume character, disinterestedness and social benevolence in such candidates, we have a pool of talent which would probably be equipped to deal with community affairs, regardless of the magnitude of the ISC. This solution simply ignores the unprepared voter and holds him unfit to participate meaningfully in the democratic process. In effect, the results of such a novel solution have been lampooned by Michael Young [1] in a mock-sociological description of a future Britain operating under just such a policy. Young, however, does not assume a fund of social altru-

---

* Chapter 13, with adaptations and modifications, has been taken from the following source: Henry Winthrop. "Education, Science and Social Complexity." *Darshana International.* Vol. III, No. 4, October 1963, 53–75.
1 Michael Young. *The Rise of the Meritocracy 1870–2033. An Essay on Education and Equality.* London: Thames and Hudson, 1958. 190 pp.

ism among the elect but instead sets the expression of superior intellectual ability in the same "dog eat dog" atmosphere of status-seeking, prestige and power, which are *leitmotifs* in the world of today. Members of his "meritocracy" which, in Young's parlance refers to the high IQ's selected for administration and policy-making, are primed by the same motivations that exist throughout most of the world today, particularly in the West. They are interested in status-seeking, job prestige and influence and they hope to take care of number one via the existing rat-race by the same methods of jockeying for power with which we are chiefly familiar. As a result Young, looking back on British history over the period 1870–2033, describes in a mock serious vein, a United Kingdom that got rid of class differences based on hereditary nobility, mercantile influence or sheer political advantage, only to wind up with a society in crisis—a society deeply conscious of *caste,* albeit caste based upon IQ.

Clearly enough, unless a selection and screening procedure put equal weight upon character, disinterestedness and social benevolence, a mere high IQ would be a necessary but certainly an insufficient condition for effective participation in the democratic process. As someone has put it in another context "Any dope can have a high IQ." An appropriate selection procedure would also have to make use of devices, based upon a combination of tests, interviews, case histories of candidates and situational probing of their dispositions, resourcefulness, fellow-feeling and other important characteristics, which would ensure a different type of motivational pattern. The meritocratic pattern described by Young leads to a psychological separatism which, as a cure for democratic mobocracy, is worse than the disease. A motivational pattern which aimed to help the individual achieve what Maslow [2] calls "self-actualization," which sought to find new forms of a sense of community and which brought most human beings closer to the pursuit of nonmaterial and cultural goals rather than bogging them down chiefly with economic and prestige-seeking concerns, would be more to the point. If individuals who were brought to the top in such a society not only possessed very high intellectual capacity but also the motivational pattern we have just described, this joint play of factors would come much closer to giving us a ruling elite who would be well-adapted, from every point of view, to dealing with the increasing social complexity of our time.

A second short-term solution would be one which took advantage of modern computer technology and our contemporary revolution in information-processing. It would be a solution which rested on the recognition that social complexity is going to increase to such a point that the bleak picture, described by Donald Michael in Chapter 6, will come true. In that picture the average man and even the citizen of above average ability, will simply not be in a position to deal directly with our

[2] Abraham H. Maslow. *Motivation and Personality.* New York: Harper, 1954. 411 pp.

growing social complexity at all. Michael has emphasized that in a world growing increasingly complex, the discoveries and methods of science, the problems of government, and the degree to which the former generate the latter, will surpass the understanding of college graduates. As a result, thinks Michael, most people will have come to recognize that, to the use of methods of analysis applicable to complex issues, and to keeping the dozens, sometimes hundreds, of variables in mind when a difficult but socially important problem is to be solved, the modern computer has no peer and can exercise these skills faster and more efficiently than any human being.

But, as Michael sees it, the programing of such computers and the interpretation of the results of their data processing, will depend upon a small band of extremely intelligent individuals with a thorough knowledge of computer technology and programing expertise. The work that they will do, the methods of analysis which they will have to employ, the range of information that they will have to possess, and the technical innovations in computer technology which they will be introducing from time to time, will all be matters which cannot be shared with the average man. These are matters and activities, says Michael, which are as much beyond the average man's grasp as are problems of molecular biology, nuclear physics or neuropsychiatry. The competent grasp of such matters and the successful termination of such activities are achievable only by those fortunate enough to be at the upper reaches of human intelligence and who have been trained intensively for a long time in the exercise of the highly esoteric know-how which we now call computer technology, data-processing and programing.

The existence of this kind of situation, however, would, in effect, disfranchise most of the population from *participating intellectually* in the democratic process. Yet it need not disfranchise them from *participating politically* in that process. Although the average citizen would be unable to translate the important social problems of a cybernating society into the language of the computer and into its underlying mathematical or logical structure, he is still in a position to make his aggregate desires and concerns known and to demand that they be met. Furthermore, he is in a position to understand the nature of the alternative solutions to the community's problems, which the computers and their masters can supply, once these alternative solutions have been translated for him into the everyday language of common experience. Finally, he is in a position to express his preferences when he is called upon to choose from among such translated alternatives, by having their respective social costs explained to him.

In a sense this kind of participation in the democratic process accomplishes three things. First, it converts the science of information-processing and social problem-solving into a form of *indicative planning* in which the public is the most important sector. Second, it enables the average man to deal *indirectly* with the social complexity by which he is surrounded, by demanding that his aggregate desires and concerns receive expression and fulfillment. In this way his inability to understand the social complexity of his environment would be irrelevant. His concerns could still be satisfied. Social conditions could still be improved. Popular choices and preferences could still be made known. Third, this kind of participation would make science and technology the servant rather than the master of the average man—a condition which is absolutely essential if democracy is to be made viable.

## II. ADAPTING TO SOCIAL COMPLEXITY THROUGH EDUCATIONAL REFORMS

A third approach concerns itself with the citizen before he becomes a voter. It looks forward to more intelligent voting by looking forward to a revamping of the process of education, itself. It assumes that perhaps average as well as superior citizens can learn to deal with the social complexities of our age, if they have been exposed to a type of education which prepares the individual to feel at home in the presence of complexity. Among educational theories and practices there are, of course, many candidates which claim fitness for such a task. Let us briefly examine some of these.

The standard, educational vice of our time is one which emphasizes routine drill, memorization and the fragmentation of the content of learning. An approach which is most polar to this would be a Gestalt emphasis on learning. A Gestalt approach to productive and creative thinking would be most in order. We shall have to insist that methods which encourage the learner to see the *total structure* of a situation or problem, will probably give the greatest return on time invested. This has recently been given renewed emphasis by Bruner.[3] We shall have to devise methods which encourage functional thinking in the young, encourage them to see relationships among elements of their experience instead of keeping these compartmented, and prompt the learner to develop the habit of relating anything new which he is learning to items and areas which are already matters of interest to him. In a sense we already see the fruits of this last mentioned stance in the field of operations research where the novel and original idea is frequently interdisciplinary in nature and often reflects the adequacy of a conceptual scheme, originally strictly developed for a traditional discipline, for problems in another discipline. This often happens when a deliberate effort is made

---

[3] Jerome Bruner. *The Process of Education.* Cambridge: Harvard University Press, 1961. 97 pp.

to try out the intellectual fit, so to speak, an effort which has often been preceded for a long time by no suspicion that such connections could be established at all.

There are even techniques which can develop the habit of looking for relationships between items which ordinarily are not conceived of as related. These tend to help in the discovery of the structure of events in precisely the fashion which is needed to grasp and deal with complex social variables which are connected by mathematical functions as yet unknown. They are worthwhile techniques not only for the heuristic value of the cognitive structures which we impose on the complex social realities which we are trying to grasp, but also for the attitude which they instill of being willing to face up to complexity and the perfecting of intellectual skills for dealing with these. I remember one of these well which was used by the most brilliant and versatile man I ever knew. His technique was to open up Roget's Thesaurus, close his eyes, and make a random stab with a pencil at any word on the printed page. He would then repeat this operation for another page chosen by a random flicking of the leaves. Since it is axiomatic that some relationship can be found between *almost any pair of words* chosen at random and very often between their referents, where these are nouns, the party of whom I speak would then force himself to find *at least one such relationship,* either between the two randomly chosen words or their respective, empirical referents. The point, however, is not to arouse the reader's wonder or skepticism but to reemphasize that an intellectual habit or game of this sort, established early, is one of several devices which may accustom even the average child to face up to complexity and get a "kick" as well as a sense of mastery in dealing with it. This habit of looking for relationships can aid considerably the type of creativity in children, studied by Torrance.[4]

That the effort to relate things helps at least the memory, if not the act of learning, has been attested to in another context. A highly effective memory is a very necessary adjunct to quicker learning of the range of information required to understand the functional nature of social complexity, where we hope this latter will be made easily available to the active intellect. Bruner [5] has done a series of experiments which indicate quite clearly that when new material which has to be remembered is deliberately learned by trying to relate component portions of what has to be learned, the act of memorizing is much superior than when a subject tries to learn the components separately without any effort to create some relation between them. In particular, *pairs of words* were presented to

4 Paul E. Torrance. *Guiding Creative Talent.* Englewood Cliffs, New Jersey: Prentice-Hall, 1962. 278 pp.

5 Jerome Bruner. *On Knowing. Essays For the Left Hand.* Cambridge: Harvard University Press, 1962. 165 pp.

twelve-year olds. One group was merely told to remember the pairs which they would be asked to repeat later. Others were told to remember the pairs by producing a word or idea that would tie them together in a way that would make sense. The results are best made clear in Bruner's own words.

. . . The word pairs include such juxtapositions as 'chair-forest,' 'sidewalk-square,' and the like. One can distinguish three styles of mediators, and children can be scaled in terms of their relative preference for each: generic mediation, in which a pair is tied together by a superordinate idea: 'chair and forest are both made of wood;' thematic mediation, in which the two terms are imbedded in a theme or a little story: 'the lost child sat on a chair in the middle of the forest;' and part-whole mediation, in which 'chairs are made from trees in the forest' is typical. Now the chief result, as you would predict, is that children who provide their own mediators do best—indeed, one time through a set of thirty pairs, they recover up to 95 percent of the second words when presented with the first ones of the pairs, whereas the uninstructed children reach a maximum of less than 50 percent recovered. Also, children do best in recovering materials tied together by the form of mediator they most often use.

One can cite a myriad of findings to indicate that any organization of information that reduces the aggregate complexity of material by imbedding it into a cognitive process a person has constructed for himself will make that material more accessible for retrieval. We may say that the process of memory, looked at from the retrieval side, is also a process of problem solving: how can material be 'placed' in memory so that it can be obtained on demand? (pp. 95–6)

For Bruner and others the basic problem of human memory is not the task of increasing the storage of information. Rather it is that of finding a variety of techniques for encoding it so that informational retrieval is improved. When our educational methods from kindergarten to graduate school are drastically revamped so that memorizing and learning are achieved by deliberately looking for relations among factors which are the focus of attention, then several things are likely to be achieved. The range of information immediately available to the cerebrating subject is increased, the cognitive structure of complex situations is more readily perceived and functional relationships between variables are more likely to be understood. When improvements of this type occur as a result of educational innovation extended over the entire length of the educational process, then we are likely to have adult citizens who are prepared to deal with the increasing social complexity of the modern world. Such expectations may even be reasonable for what we now call the normal range of intelligence. It is not that such methods of learning and memorizing raise the individual's intellectual stature. It is more reasonable to suppose that they merely allow all levels to operate more efficiently. It is therefore no idle dream to assume that a rise in intellectual efficiency for the average man will considerably increase his "civic fitness" for dealing with social complexity.

Critics of modern mass education have tended to make four major criticisms of it. It is first of all to some degree joyless and overdisciplined by adults, particularly in the lower elementary school where the teacher's chief role seems to be that of *Magistra Ludens*. Second, it fails to inculcate a habit of persisting at trying to master instructional materials, so that youngsters become bored with intellectual tasks rather quickly, even when these tasks, from an adult viewpoint, are rather fascinating. Furthermore, the more complex the task the earlier will the boredom set in and the more readily will the learner discontinue with them. Third, teachers tend to neglect what Mayer [6] has called the *persistence of error* in the teaching process as conducted in U.S. schools. The student moves from one class to the next, retaining incorrect concepts of basic and significant ideas and skills, and becoming more and more confused and falling more and more behind as he moves from one class to the next. No doubt, the popular demand for social promotion makes its contribution to this unhappy situation. Finally, curricula and procedures often tend to be planned unrealistically, with little relation to what can be expected from the growing youngster at his particular stage of intellectual development, conditioned as it is by maturational considerations. These four types of appraisal represent some of the more widespread criticisms which the intelligent layman reads about. There are, of course, many others. There is no doubt that an individual subjected to an educational regime of this sort cannot be expected, as an adult citizen, either to be continuously interested in the issues which face the community perennially or to exhibit that intellectual persistence and effort which the complexity of these issues demand, if one is ever to understand them properly and participate in their solution responsibly. The average adult has had the necessary habits, interest and concern thoroughly weeded out of him by a dysgenic education with faults such as those we have just mentioned.

This need not, however, continue to be the case. Interest, perseverance and independence of mind have been shown to be well encouraged by certain types of educational techniques, some new, some old. Among these are the Montessori Methods and a renascence of these has been interestingly described by Rambusch.[7] Indirect support for some of the Montessori claims, at least with respect to preschool learning, has come

6 Martin Mayer. *The Schools.* New York: Harper, 1961. 446 pp.
7 Nancy McCormick Rambusch. *Learning How to Learn. An American Approach to Montessori.* Baltimore: Helicon Press, 1962. 180 pp.

in recent years from the experimental researches [8] of Moore [9] who is in no sense a devotee of Madame Montessori. Recognition of the differences in learning which go with the different, maturational stages of intellectual development, has been thoroughly confirmed by the research of Piaget,[10] an extremely brief summary of which has been available for some time. All these types of research, I believe, suggest methods for learning and intellectual development, which will increase conceptual rigor, interest and perseverance and which hopefully will promote a life-long habit of facing up to complex problems, wrestling with them, remaining with them and enjoying the sense of mastery and accomplishment which result from a break-through. Since these advantages hold for the average as well as the gifted learner, we can expect that much of the complexity of the issues which must be faced by adult citizens will be more amenable to treatment and more likely to win their concern, if they have had the advantages of an early education which is greatly different from the present one. The education of the future, if we are determined to have it, will show many differences from the present one—differences which reflect some of the attributes we have just mentioned.

These differences will be differences both in content and in method. Content must address itself to the requirements for understanding work, place and people in an age of science and technology, for understanding such matters as industrial organization, new types of community planning, quantitative advances in the social studies as well as a wholly new set of phenomena with which the social sciences have to deal. In addition, content must address itself to the impact of science and technology on human relations and a set of social problems and social issues which represent themes that are wholly new under the sun. Differences in method, however, will be almost wholly related to the learning process. The newer methods of learning and teaching aim not only to shorten the periods needed for learning given amounts of material but, even more importantly, they aim to increase conceptual understanding and rigor, interest and mastery, perseverance and independence in the learning process. Perhaps the most revolutionary development in the newer methods of learning is the teaching machine, a device which, according to most of the available reports concerning the results of its use, really promises

---

[8] Unpublished separates on his research were made available by Dr. Moore to the present writer and these warrant a substantial optimism concerning what some of the newer educational techniques may accomplish in the way of developing a high order of learning capacity in the average child. If the reader is interested in an up-to-date, simplified, journalistic account of one of Dr. Moore's accomplishments, let him turn to the following reference. C. P. Gilmore. "Omar Khayyam and His Talking Typewriter." *The Saturday Evening Post,* November 20, 1965, Issue No. 23, pp. 40–1.

[9] Omar Khayyam Moore. "OK's Children." *Time.* Vol. LXXVI, November, 1960, 103.

[10] Jean Piaget. *Logic and Psychology.* Manchester: Manchester University Press, 1953. 48 pp.

to make the average subject use his abilities to the full, with the unexpected result of a fringe benefit years later.[11] This fringe benefit may be an increased capacity for, and willingness to deal with, social complexity, a capacity which will be needed more and more as time goes by, if we are serious about demanding a mature, meaningful and intelligent participation in the democratic process on the part of the average citizen. Let us therefore take a look at some of the accomplishments which have been claimed for the teaching machine by most of the authorities who have attempted to evaluate its potentialities objectively. I mention these only because of their relevance for democracy's expectation that the average citizen will make the effort to understand the issues of his time and the further effort to cope with them intelligently, so that his participation in community life will not be merely "the still small voice" which it is today.

Research results tend to show that the average human being is using only a tiny portion of his abilities. Many so-called "slow learners" are found to be only the victims of poor teaching. The art of programing has reached the point at which almost all students can get 95 percent of the answers right. This provides the interest and pleasure which are alleged to be missing from the modern classroom for many of the young. Programs are so constructed as to prevent muddled, half-baked and illogical cerebration. Thus the preparation for the conceptual rigor needed for the handling of complex matters, is assured. The great social and democratic hope which resides in instruction given via this new device, is emphasized for us in the surprising finding that children with low IQ's get just about as many correct answers as do the gifted children. It is only their rate of learning which is slower. The degree to which learning time is reduced is perhaps best exemplified by reports of students doing a year's work or more in half the regular time. More able students in high school mathematics, for instance, have covered in one year a program involving axiomatic algebra, solid geometry and calculus. One anecdote reports the case of a boy who completed a semester's work in solid geometry in four days and who received a score of 100 on the final examination which covered the whole course. Shortening of the time for instruction has also been achieved in other programs, such as one covering English in a school in Manhasset, Long Island, and one covering high school algebra in Nutley, New Jersey. Time-savings have been reported

---

11 The reader should not assume that the emphasis on the value of the teaching machine, which we are making in the present chapter, is inconsistent with the stand we have taken in Chapter 10. In that chapter we acknowledged the educational value of programmed instruction but sought to emphasize, instead, those values of the live teacher which no teaching device could supplant. When it comes, however, to creating speed and efficiency in learning the logical structure and development of various types of subject matter, the teaching machine has definitely proven its great worth. It is these achievements of programmed instruction which are being emphasized in the text at this point and such an emphasis in no way detracts from the stand taken in Chapter 10.

over a whole spectrum of material, from spelling in the lower grades and arithmetic for retarded youngsters to elementary psychology at Harvard. Results of this sort seem to indicate that we can abolish what has been called *the persistence of error* in our educational system—a gain which augurs well for the expectation that we can have adult citizens who are sufficiently well informed to face the issues of their time. The hope that we can employ such revolutionary inventions like the teaching machine, to bring out fully human, intellectual potentialities, so that the complex problems of democracy may be met by the citizen of the future, has perhaps been well expressed in the following quotation from *Look*.[12]

Beyond its utilitarian applications, the new movement holds out a rare new faith in the untapped abilities in every human being. For several decades, the world's leading philosophers and poets have preached of man's weakness, helplessness and despair. It has been a long time since there has been any serious talk of the perfectability—or even the improvability—of man. Now, a buoyant, busy group of psychologists and educators are refusing to set any limit on what the average human being can accomplish. If they are right, they will give this nation a big boost in what H. G. Wells called 'the race between education and catastrophe.' And they will prove to the whole world that the human race has been selling itself short. (p. 70)

In recent years pedagogical techniques have been developed which not only arouse intellectual curiosity but make it possible for the young to perform intellectual tasks which once were felt to be within the capacity of only gifted adults. The more distinguished of these pedagogical innovations have been worked out with respect to mathematics, the field most obviously presenting maximum intellectual difficulties from a traditional point of view. Ingenious methods, for instance, of teaching high school mathematics and occasionally of teaching arithmetic in such a way as to prompt young children to discover new ways of seeing arithmetical relationships and occasionally discovering new mathematical theorems, have been developed by a series of experimental projects at various universities.[13] A revolutionary new method of teaching mathematics, known as the Cuisenaire technique, making use of colored rods of unequal length and a device called a Geo-Board for creating quick changes in geometric figures, whose mathematical consequences can be immediately detected visually, have respectively resulted in the discovery that complex portions of algebra and geometry can be learned by the

[12] George B. Leonard. "Revolution in Education." *Look*. Vol. 26, No. 12, June 5, 1962. 58–70.

[13] Projects for the reform of mathematics teaching are widespread. The most active experimental groups have been the University of Illinois Committee on School Mathematics and the Arithmetic Project at the same institution, the University of Maryland Mathematics Project, the Ball State, Indiana State Teachers College Experimental Mathematics Program, The Boston College Mathematics Institute, and the Minnesota Laboratory for the Improvement of Secondary School Mathematics.

very young, and that algebra can be taught before arithmetic. This technique has been described in many articles, but one highly representative one is a paper published by Gattegno.[14] A device known as The Psi Apparatus, developed by John and Miller,[15] will yield a picture of an individual's method of working intellectually, of his efficiency in the acquisition and handling of information in solving a problem, as well as his consistency and appropriateness of approach. It thus not only offers an early opportunity to diagnose undesirable intellectual working habits but also provides the teacher with enough information to correct them. The Psi Apparatus has been found promising with grade school children from six to ten, and may therefore encourage those intellectual stances needed to deal with complex problems, social or otherwise.

Other techniques which would probably encourage a full use of the individual's intellectual potentialities, would be the introduction of general semantics into the elementary and high school curricula. This, we believe, would tend to sharpen the analytic propensities of the average youngster fairly early. The use of visual models of social processes and social equilibria could be expected to make a significant contribution to the development of sustained thinking on complex social matters. Pictographs, pie-charts and other visual materials can often be the first steps in the presentation of complex, social structure. A host of pedagogical devices too numerous to mention here, all work in the same direction. They serve to make subjects more efficient at grasping intellectual complexity, convert the solution of a complex problem into a fascinating game, and finally eventuate in habits of thought which improve the intellectual efficiency considerably of the adult who has been exposed to all such educational innovations. The net result is that various IQ levels operate more intensively, that is to say, generate more power for the cerebral plant than might otherwise be expected.

The items mentioned in the preceding two paragraphs represent only a few approaches, but these are a small sample of many techniques which are currently being developed as the result of a creative ferment in education—a ferment aimed at showing how much the intellectual potentialities of the average person have been neglected. From our point of view, once we start developing these intellectual potentialities as early as possible, we increase the possibility that the average citizen, years later, will be able to rise to the political demands of an increasingly complex social milieu. In terms of our social and political concerns, this is a promise which can

14 Caleb Gattegno. "The Cuisenaire Discovery: Notes on a Radical Transformation in the Teaching of Mathematics." *Main Currents in Modern Thought.* Vol. 14, January, 1958. 51–54.

15 Erwin R. John and James G. Miller. "The Acquisition and Applications of Information in the Problem-Solving Process." *Behavioral Science.* Vol. 2, October, 1957. 291–300.

only increase democratic morale. Such educational efforts obviously should be encouraged, for they are among those techniques which can counter the possibility of intellectual disfranchisement which an increasingly complex social environment, threatens.

In Chapters 12 and 13 we examined the strain which the growing social complexities of our time are bound to have on our intellectual effort to understand the social difficulties in which we find ourselves. In particular, we focused attention on either the level or the efficiency of human intelligence. Both will apparently have to be raised in order to master the social complexities of our age. We further pointed out that there are essentially only two ways of doing this: either by improving human intellectual capacity in a biological sense, or improving it through novel techniques of an educational and psychological nature. The purpose of Chapters 12 and 13 was to provide some of the possibilities for human intellectual improvement which exist within these two frameworks.

We have said little, if anything, however, concerning some of the ways by which social complexity, itself, might be measured. This is the subject of Chapter 14. We are also interested in the relationship between political innovations which may be needed for future forms of a democracy and the social complexity which will be found in a society which is increasingly moving in the direction of cybernation. A thoughtful citizen cannot help wondering how much political innovation will be allowed by a society which makes the level of understanding and the outlook of the average citizen the chief determinant of whether suggested changes in political procedures and institutions, are or are not truly democratic. These are matters to which we must now devote some attention if we are to achieve a fuller understanding of the burden of social complexity.

# 14

# Political Innovation and
## Social Complexity*

## I. CONSIDERATIONS CENTERING ABOUT
## AN INDEX OF SOCIAL COMPLEXITY

It is now pertinent to ask what broad operational definitions might conceivably be supplied for obtaining measures of social complexity—and preferably indices of this attribute. In Chapter 12 *we assumed that we had such a measure at hand* and then tried to relate the increase in the value of such an index over time, to intellectual capacity and intellectual disfranchisement from *meaningful, political participation in the democratic process.* Now we turn to some suggestions for developing *measures and indices of social complexity,* if only because such measures and indices suggest the difficulties we are likely to have in reducing the average man's areas of social ignorance and social misunderstanding.

There are limits, of course, on the potential amount of such reduction—even if we introduce the most superior educational methods imaginable—and these limits are set for the average man, by the existing degree of complexity found in his society. It therefore behooves us to discuss how we might talk about operationally defining an index of social complexity (ISC).

I do not wish to enter into the technical details concerning the probable nature of indices of social complexity or the statistical and mathematical requirements which would enter into their construction. The problems of measurement and weighting which would be thrust upon the sociologist who undertakes the task of constructing such an index, will be analogous, I feel sure, in many respects to standard problems of current index number theory. In other respects, such as the dimensionalities of certain indices or the choice of a common unit for several such different indices, new problems may arise. I do think, however, that it

* Chapter 14, with adaptations and modifications, has been taken from the following sources: Henry Winthrop. "Political Innovation and Social Complexity." *Sociological Inquiry.* Vol. XXXIII, No. 1, Winter 1963, 78–96, and Henry Winthrop. "Education and the Problems of Community." *The Educational Forum.* Vol. XXIX, No. 2, January 1965, 171–177.

would be of value to spend some time discussing some of the possible meanings which could be attached to the concept of "social complexity." Inasmuch as complexity is an attribute which describes our difficulty in comprehending the given and therefore expresses a relation between the structure [1] of events and processes, on the one hand, and the ease or difficulty with which we can grasp that structure, on the other, we should mention the type of content which, precisely because it reflects in some sense what is meant by structure, would be reflected in some way in an index of social complexity. We are, of course, using the term "structure" here as the Gestalt psychologists use it, to refer to the invariant pattern of relationships which, once understood, enables us to pose properly a problem in any context which displays the same pattern. An extensive treatment of this concept can be found in Wertheimer.[2] The relationships are generally of a logical or mathematical nature although the structure of a pattern or Gestalt may involve other cognitive characteristics, such as a grasp of cause and effect relationships, and frequently enough may reflect some important non-cognitive characteristics centering about psychological and social attributes of persons. Since an index of social complexity then should refer to the difficulties we are likely to meet with in trying to understand properly a significant social issue or problem, the requirements involved in trying to grasp the nature of the problem are precisely what we mean by its complexity or difficulty. Let us discuss briefly some of the considerations which are sure to be among these requirements.

One of the first considerations on which the struggle to understand properly the nature of a problem, would turn, would clearly be the minimum amount of information one needs to comprehend the bare essentials of its structure. In order to understand, for instance, a major number of the economic and social conflicts of our time and the problems to which they have given rise, a citizen does well to understand both the moral as well as the economic issues involved in trying to determine the proper distribution of wealth in a democratic economy. All efforts to think about this matter are referred to generically as the *problem of distributive justice*. This problem not only has a given structure in a mathematical sense but there are also many possible alternative answers. No matter what may be our choice a tremendous amount of information of all sorts is needed to make that choice. This information will include economic, technical, sociological, psychological and philosophical considerations, to name only some of the relevant categories involved. The enlightened and thoughtful citizen should have some understanding of the problem of distributive justice, both analytically and informationally,

---

[1] For the meaning of the concept of "structure" as used here, see Jerome S. Bruner, *The Process of Education*, Cambridge, Mass., Harvard University Press, 1960, 97 pp.

[2] Max Wertheimer. *Productive Thinking* (Michael Wertheimer, editor). New York: Harper, 1959. 302 pp.

if his participation in the democratic process is to be meaningful. Let me then try to describe *one form* of this problem as briefly as I can, before returning to its relationship to an index of social complexity.

An *increase* in this year's total national output of all goods and services, over that produced last year, is, by definition, *an increase in Gross National Product (GNP)*. For all practical purposes most of such an increase can be regarded as flowing directly from improved science and technology. For the sake of vivid imagery let us liken this year's increase in GNP to the baking of an *extra national pie* which is to be added to another baked pie which is equal in size to that which was baked last year. Basically we can regard this extra national pie as having been produced by six cooks. These cooks are—in economic terms—the six sectors of our economy which have, in one way or another, contributed to the baking of the extra national pie: *management, labor,* the *technicians* responsible for improved science and technology, the *investors,* the *consumers* and the *government,* of course, not necessarily in that order. Each of these sectors or cooks might try to make out a case for claiming the whole pie on the grounds that it is his services which, in reality, produced the extra national pie. In actuality the claims will be more modest than this. Each may claim only that he is entitled to the largest share of that pie, on the grounds that his services were *more indispensable* than the services of the other cooks, in producing the extra pie.

The first three of our cooks could state that this largest slice could be handed to them in a form which is really a larger share of profits after taxes. Management could ask for this larger slice in the form of either increases in salary or through an extra end-of-the-year bonus. Labor could ask for it in the form of increased wages or profit-sharing. The technicians could make the same claims as management. Investors could demand the lion's share of the extra national pie in terms of increased dividends from profits. The consumers would make their claims in terms of a demand for lowered prices of available goods and services. This would be equivalent, of course, to asking corporations to accept smaller net profits. Finally, the government could claim the lion's share of the extra pie through a larger tax slice of gross profits. It is important to remember that rather strong arguments could be marshalled by each cook to justify his claim.[3]

3 The reader should realize, of course, that the argument presented above on behalf of the *increment* to total national output, applies with equal force to the total volume of national output. Conflict occurs more readily over the manner in which an increase in national output is to be divided. We tend to become resigned to what we regard as the inequities of previously existing divisions of the social product. One can, of course, divide up the claimant sectors of the economy in other ways, so that there may be more or fewer than six cooks. For a nontechnical discussion of this problem the reader should consult the following: Kenneth E. Boulding. *Economic Analysis.* New York and London: Harper & Brothers, 1941, 809 pp. See particularly, pp. 784–7. For a more technical discussion of matters related to this problem, see Jerome Rothenberg, *The Measurement of Social Welfare,* Englewood Cliffs, New Jersey: Prentice-Hall, 1961, 357 pp.

These claims tend to be incompatible. One can distribute the extra national pie equally among all the claimants—or unequally. All claimants reject the first alternative. In order to satisfy the second alternative one must find a mode of distribution which does not ask that the satisfaction resulting from it be *maximized* but rather that the dissatisfaction resulting from it be *minimized*. We seek a mode of distribution which will rank the six claimants in an *order* which reflects the decreasing portions of the extra national pie which is to be served. The quest for this rank-order of distribution *is one form of the problem of distributive justice.* In passing it might be mentioned that the number of possible *rank-order distributions* involving six claimant sectors of the economy, amounts to 720, which is the number of possible permutations based upon rank order. The distribution finally selected must be justified in terms of its present and foreseeable future consequences for all six sectors, as well as the criterion of minimizing dissatisfaction.

Many of our current controversies surrounding proposed new tax measures, particularly in relation to the allocation of the tax burden among all six claimant sectors mentioned, are bound up with the manner in which the competent citizen answers the problem of distributive justice. Any answer regarded as the *optimum* alternative which should be chosen to deal with this problem can be shown, without too much difficulty, to be highly relevant to a whole series of problems. Among these would be: the public role of corporate management, the proper regulation of investment, the proper returns to labor and management, the question of how much inflation should be controlled through price regulations, various issues surrounding consumer economics and what would be a reasonable expectation as to how fast the standard of living should rise, the role and domain of government services and powers, the place and responsibility of research and development in an expanding economy and the proper length of the work day in relation to a specified standard of living and the existing state of technology. These, and many similar problems, can be shown to be bound up with a *consensus* agreement concerning an adequate solution of the *problem of distributive justice.* Unfortunately, however, from the standpoint of lending one's voice to the making of decisions within the democratic framework and in order to arrive at the *consensus* I have mentioned, a vast range of information, particularly economic, historical, legal and technological, is needed. This range often includes areas of exploration frequently unknown to the citizen voter and, where known of, all too often arouses more inertia than we know how to deal with.

One of the constituent features then of an index of social complexity will involve some *measure* of the *changing* amount of information, such as is needed for the understanding of the problem of distributive justice or, for that matter, any other problem. The amount of information needed for the understanding of any given social problem will, in general, increase with time. In principle this measurement will not be difficult to make for the construction of a standard achievement test is all that it calls for. In general such an achievement test would become longer and longer but any score, related to some base year score, would provide the needed index.

## II. SOME CENTRAL FACTORS IN THE MEASUREMENT OF COMPLEXITY

In addition to the needed range of information which creates much of the social complexity of a given problem, there is a sheer intellectual factor which is rarely mentioned. This has to do with the *number of variables* one has to deal with in order to comprehend the structure of a complex problem properly. Although I know of no research specifically addressed to the problem of defining a *standard situation* which can be modified so as to have it change only in terms of the number of variables which would be required to understand it as it went from one modification to another, such a research technique would be useful in developing norms for the conceptual attention of human subjects. It would be a step in the direction of determining the relationship between the *number of variables* an individual could keep in mind in trying to solve a problem and a given IQ level. Bruner [4] tells us that adults can handle about seven independent items of information at a time, although he fails to specify the IQ level of the adults involved. These results are probably derived from the types of experiment which Bruner [5] and his associates performed on thinking and other cognitive processes. If this is correct then the adults involved would be chiefly Harvard students all of whom are selected by the Dean of Admissions precisely because of an unusually high intellectual capacity. Our ordinary experience, however, suggests that the *average man* rarely seems to keep more than two or three variables in mind at a time when tackling a problem. This is certainly less promising than Bruner's observations. However, the difference may be due to a semantic difficulty. Ordinary experience may reflect what the average man does by habit and inertia—grapple with two or three variables and then let his approach to a problem jell into a rigid mental set involving possible relations among the few variables initially selected for attention. This tells us, of course, nothing about what he could do, that is, nothing about the *potential* capacity of an average adult to handle many more than three variables. In the case of the average citizen we may be dealing with what he *does do* rather than what he *could do*, if the proper training

4 Jerome S. Bruner. *Op. cit.*

5 Jerome S. Bruner, Jacqueline J. Goodnow, and George A. Austin. *A Study of Thinking*. New York: Wiley, 1956. 330 pp.

and education were provided early enough. As Bruner would put it, we are dealing with the way in which the average citizen handles a *learning episode,* rather than how he might be taught to do so.

Now the complexity of a problem can also be said to be related to the *number of variables* which must be dealt with in trying to grasp its structure. Many of the highly significant issues of our time involve such complex structures, when properly formulated, that dozens of variables may be involved in being able to grasp merely the bare essentials of such problems.[6] Unless the mathematical relations between these are grasped, it is not very likely that the problem will really be understood. The scholar and technician refer to a complex system of such mathematical relationships as one which involves *multivariate analysis.* This refers to those *theoretical* or *practical* aspects of a problem which involve the need to keep in mind a large number of factors. Complex economic phenomena are of this nature and the average man, thinking about economic issues, tends in fact to pull two or three factors out of a congeries of relevant variables and will try to limit his analysis to the relationship between these. So ingrained is this habit of oversimplification that many a Ph.D. in the social and behavioral sciences will also exhibit this tendency, in spite of all his training in behavioral science methodology, mathematics, statistics and experimental design. Artificially isolated and fragmented phenomena may be treated as real and significant if we pretend that they can be properly understood only by assuming that the quantitative and process relationships inherent in them involve just a few variables. What is a comfortable assumption for many a research man in the behavioral and social science areas is clearly an intrinsic necessity for the average citizen. If this charge is true and if it is equally true that most of the significant issues of our complex society involve large numbers of variables for proper analysis, then certainly one of the components which measure social complexity must be a figure expressing the complete number of variables involved. Here again, since our ability to grasp any given social problem will change with time because the number of variables involved also changes with time, a component index can always be formed by relating this number to the number which was involved for some given base year and for that same problem.

Most genuine problems of a social nature possess cognitive structure. It may be true that often considerations of value and humanity are relevant to a problem—considerations which far outweigh its cognitive and abstract features. These are, of course, the considerations which would

---

[6] Warren Weaver has discussed problems of "organized complexity," that is, those problems involving large numbers of variables which call for unusual methods of approach. His discussion is apposite to our context and appears in a paper entitled "Science and Complexity," *The Scientists Speak* (Warren Weaver, editor), New York: Boni and Gaer, 1947, 369 pp.

be stressed by the philosophical, psychological and literary existentialists. Even where these existentialist features of a large-scale social problem are given their due weight, nevertheless from the standpoint of national planning, institutional analysis or remedial legislation, the *structural* features of this same problem must be understood before they can be dealt with intelligently in a democracy. These features are akin to mathematical expressions of true relationships among the variables which contribute to its structure. These relationships, of course, *may,* but need not, always be couched in mathematical terms. Although ideally expressible in these terms they can fortunately also be expressed in terms of words, pictures, diagrams, pictographs, animated film techniques and other devices. Such structural descriptions are also able to exhibit the genuine nature of the relationships involved, whether causal or merely associated in the statistical sense. These structural descriptions vary in difficulty. They can often be represented in terms of *system analysis,* a major tool of analysis not only in the physical sciences but also in the biological sciences, and the behavioral, social and management sciences as well. It would be possible *in principle* to develop a *scale of difficulty* for different types of systems which can be represented, as they usually are, by flow diagrams. If such a scale were applied to the structure of any given problem, as represented by a system employing flow diagrams, and bearing in mind that the difficulty of dealing with this same problem over time would be reflected by a system whose difficulty would also be changing *numerically* as reflected by an *applicable scale of difficulty,* this would yield us another component index of complexity. The index of difficulty would be given by dividing the current scale value of difficulty by the scale value obtained for some base year. Not only would such a component index reflect changes in the difficulty of understanding a complex problem or issue as time passed but it would also enable us to see the relative difficulties at any given time in any batch of social problems with which the responsible citizen would have to wrestle in any effort to deal with contemporary issues. The construction of such a scale assumes, of course, that the structure of each social problem can be represented by some type of system which skeletalizes it.[7]

Another rough measure of the complexity of a social problem is, of course, the *time required to master its essentials.* It would clearly not be difficult to devise a standard achievement test which centered about a given social problem. It would also not be difficult to arrive at *consensus agreement* among specialists as to what *minimum score,* that is, what critical score could be regarded as providing evidence that the problem was understood, at least with respect to its basic structure and the mini-

---

[7] The index described would be valid only for a *ratio scale.* For other type scales the index would have to be derived differently.

mum amount of information essential to its comprehension. Next it would only be a routine professional matter to take a large sample of the voting population and, using the intelligence quotient as a measure of intellectual capacity, determine the mean scores on the achievement test which correspond to all the IQ levels from say 90 IQ and up. From this array of mean scores we could determine the IQ level corresponding to the preset, *consensus, critical minimum.* Finally we should want to ascertain the *mean length of time* required by a pilot population with a mean IQ which just achieved this critical minimum, to complete the achievement test in question. In this way clearly enough we are using the achievement test as a *power test* in the psychometric sense of this term. As the social problem with which we were dealing became more complex, the achievement test based upon it would not only become longer but the items would become more difficult to comprehend and master. An index could then be established by dividing the mean length of time obtained in any given period by the mean length of time of some chosen base period. If we were interested in obtaining a composite index for a melange of social problems for each of which we had the index number, we would have to apply an appropriate statistical technique and achieve some consensus agreement concerning the proper weight for each index.

It would be possible to expand at length on the nature of the factors which, in some way, could be expected to be reflected in some composite index of social complexity. I do not wish to enter into a lengthy or technical discussion of the nature of that composite. Instead I think the purpose of the theme which I am considering will best be served, I believe, by mentioning some of the remaining elements which might enter into the definition of an index of social complexity. A characterization of some of these, without elaborating upon how each of these would be expressible quantitatively for index number purposes, would aid in the further clarification of the nature of such an index. Among these remaining factors would be included, I feel certain, the *difficulty* of the mathematical *concepts* which are inherent in the structure of a particular problem or inherent, at least, in its cognitive aspects. As we have already emphasized, most of the significant social issues of our time possess such cognitive aspects which can be described mathematically. In principle it would be possible to formulate a *hierarchy* of the relevant mathematical concepts required to deal with the cognitive aspects of any given problem. The hierarchy to which I refer is a *hierarchy of difficulty* in relation to the task of intellectually mastering the concepts in question.[8] The diffi-

[8] A method for dealing with *different levels of conceptual complexity,* which *might* be adaptable to the present context, is given by Myron Woolman, Richard Bloomer and Lawrence Schlesinger in a paper entitled "The Conceptual Graph: A Method for Coding Complex Domains," read at the Tenth Anniversary Meeting of the Operations Research Society of America, Washington, D.C., May 9–11, 1962.

culty of any concept in the hierarchy would be determined by the fact that it could be understood only if a subject had intellectually mastered all the concepts of lower rank in this same hierarchy. We are thus defining the attribute of difficulty of a mathematical concept, needed in order to understand the structure of a given social problem, in terms somewhat similar to those employed for a *unidimensional or cumulative scale* as developed by Guttman.[9] The Guttman-type scale, of course, is used for *attitude research* purposes and would have to be adapted in some fashion to the purpose with which we are here concerned, namely, the problem of measuring conceptual difficulty in relation to the larger problem of measuring social complexity. No matter by what method an appropriate scale was finally developed, it could clearly be converted to a *power test* if the concepts of the hierarchy were transferred to a series of problems of graded difficulty, although, of course, such a transfer would clearly change the nature of the context to which the attribute of difficulty is applicable.

The concept scale thus derived would provide, for any given problem and the hierarchy of concepts relevant to its structure, a picture of the median scale value of difficulty of the concepts involved. In later periods the same problem would become increasingly complex and the mathematical concepts needed to grasp its structure would increase. The concepts needed for this later period would in part include some of the concepts which were needed in the base period and some which were not. It would therefore be necessary to reestablish a scale of difficulty which made use of *all of the concepts of the base period* as well as all those which cropped up *for the first time* in the later period. The division of the new median scale value of difficulty thus found, by the base period median scale value, would provide one method for determining an index number of difficulty.[10] This index number, of course, refers only to the difficulty of grasping those mathematical concepts which are needed for understanding the *structure* of the particular social problem with which we are concerned. If, at the same time, we were interested in a composite index of the difficulty of any *sample* of problems with which we were concerned at any given time, we could represent this by the median of all the respective, median scale values.[11] These medians of medians over time can also be used to furnish a composite index number. This composite

9 Louis A. Guttman, "Questions and Answers About Scale Analysis," Research Branch, Information and Education Division, Army Service Forces, *Report D-2,* 1945; Louis A. Guttman, "A Basis for Scaling Qualitative Data," *American Sociological Review,* 9 (April, 1944), pp. 139–150; Louis A. Guttman, "The Basis for Scalogram Analysis," in S. A. Stouffer, *et al., Measurement and Prediction,* Princeton University Press, 1950, pp. 60–90.

10 The same considerations apply here as in footnote 7.

11 This would be true only if some way could be found for referring all such scales to a *common zero point of difficulty* or, at least, to *equivalent zero points of difficulty.*

index now, however, refers to a sample of social issues and problems, rather than any single problem of this sample.

Still other factors which would create complexity for the understanding of the major issues and problems of our time—and these can only be mentioned in passing—are: (1) the *unfamiliarity* of the mental set required to deal with an issue, an attribute which could, of course, increase with time; (2) the *nature* and *variety* of the intellectual skills needed for the comprehension of a given problem—a matter to which the growing use of the theory of games in the study of our defense postures or in international politics, as undertaken by Kaplan,[12] and a variety of other methodological approaches, bear witness; (3) the *multiordinality* of the analysis required for the successful comprehension of a problem, a term first employed in general semantics by Korzybski [13] to refer to the level of abstraction on which an analysis is being conducted; (4) the personal energy which individuals have to expend in order to overcome the inertia which stands in the way of a direct frontal and continued attack upon a problem, a concern which has been basic in the work of Zipf; [14] (5) the *interdisciplinary* background fundamentals needed as the intellectual base of operations for approaching a given problem, a situation which has been well recognized in the work of Reiser; [15] (6) the subtlety of an analysis which is required for the successful comprehension of a problem's structure (not to be confused with what is meant by multiordinality) and which must be confronted when analyzing economic problems in depth, as in the work of Arrow,[16] Koopmans,[17] Leontief [18] and in econometric problems in general; (7) the difficulty of spotting or *intuiting* the relevant causes of a given problem, particularly when it can be *overdetermined* by a large variety of factors in a large number of possible combinations, a difficulty to which Simon [19] has addressed his classic papers on causality; and (8) the difficulties which are resident in trying to understand the nature of various types of statistical and experimental design which social scientists have employed in trying to isolate causal relations or associated

---

[12] Morton A. Kaplan. *System and Process in International Politics.* New York: Wiley, 1957. 283 pp.

[13] Alfred Korzybski. *Science and Sanity: An Introduction to Non-Aristotelian Systems and General Semantics.* Lakeville, Conn.: International Non-Aristotelian Library Publishing Company, 1948. 3rd edition. 806 pp.

[14] George K. Zipf. *Human Behavior and the Principle of Least Effort: An Introduction to Human Ecology.* Reading, Mass.: Addison-Wesley, 1949. 573 pp.

[15] Oliver L. Reiser. *The Integration of Human Knowledge.* Boston: Porter Sargent, 1958. 478 pp.

[16] Kenneth J. Arrow. *Social Choice and Individual Values.* New York: Wiley, 1951. 99 pp.

[17] Tjalling C. Koopmans. *Three Essays on the State of Economic Science.* New York: McGraw-Hill, 1957. 231 pp.

[18] Wassily W. Leontief. *The Structure of American Economy, 1919–1939.* New York: Oxford University Press, 1960. 2nd edition. 264 pp.

[19] Herbert A. Simon. *Models of Man.* New York: Wiley, 1957. 287 pp.

changes, or both. Where this last type of sophistication is highly relevant to the satisfactory analysis of a major social problem of wide, popular concern, the perplexity of the average citizen can be well imagined. In principle each of these eight factors and others which have not even been mentioned, could be quantified by one or another type of procedure, in order to establish some useful index of their changing complexity with time. A measure of such changing complexity is relevant to the issues which men must face as a result of the haphazard ecology which they, themselves, have produced.

### III. POLITICAL DISFRANCHISEMENT

Let us consider one proper and significant use to which an index of social complexity may be put. First, it can be used by test experts to determine the number of citizens who are *intellectually disfranchised* from *meaningful participation* in the democratic process. This type of disfranchisement was discussed in Chapter 12. Second, it could be used to create *political disfranchisement,* that is, it could be used improperly and unethically by *political* leadership imbued with *totalitarian propensities.* This could occur if it was used to withdraw the voting privilege entirely from those citizens who were found to be intellectually disqualified from being able to comprehend the complexity of the sociopolitical milieu in which they found themselves. Apart from the fact that the effort to foist such permanent political disfranchisement upon the electorate is almost certain to fail in a democracy, I would personally abhor such a totalitarian move and would be among the first to oppose it. A third use, however, of the ISC lies in the fact that it can be used to create what may be called *intermittent, political disfranchisement,* that is *temporary* withdrawals of the voting privilege from those who cannot use it meaningfully. At the present time intermittent, political disfranchisement does not have the ghost of a chance. But what about the future?

In the distant future, however, such political disfranchisement may come about by means of a third alternative which would probably not be entirely alien to some of the more progressive forms of democracy. This would involve the ability to devise achievement tests with social, economic and political content, which are known to reflect the same degree of complexity which the experts have found exists for the issues and problems that face members of the body politic. A long process of education might bring the electorate around to accepting as a criterion for the voting privilege, the need for a voter to achieve a minimum critical score on such a test. In effect, these tests would be *issues tests* rather than *literacy tests,* these latter, of course, being our current, limited device for deciding whether some citizens should be extended the privilege of voting. The literacy test indicates that we are really concerned with "civic fitness." The irony of our current situation, however, lies in the folly of believing that such civic fitness is established merely by a test of literacy. What I am asserting here is that such fitness depends more realistically upon the citizen's level of intelligence and in particular his capacity to deal analytically with complex issues and problems demanding hard and prolonged thought. In addition, in order to cope adequately with these problems, the average citizen must possess *a vast range of sound and accurate information pertinent to them.* Literacy alone confers neither of these benefits.

One aspect of the original intent of democracy, namely, the principle of "one head—one vote," is still with us. The original supposition of this principle was that each voter would be familiar with the issues involved in voting and would acquaint himself with the information needed to exercise his vote intelligently. The ability to do this, however, becomes more and more difficult because of increasing complexity brought about indirectly by the impacts of science and technology and directly by the institutions men create to deal with these impacts. This complexity is in part a function of the lack of that intellectual integration concerning social issues and problems which future interdisciplinary research institutes will, hopefully, supply.

The exercise of the vote where one does not understand the issues involved, as with a referendum, or where one does not possess the requisite information to make an intelligent choice, is wasted. In fact it is worse than wasted. A miscast vote may have consequences which will so plague the voter as to make him regret deeply having made a particular choice. Under our increasing social complexity, therefore, it would seem to make good sense to demand that the would-be voter pass some sort of Issues Test instead of just a Literacy Test. We have already spoken in a general way of the possible use of an Issues Test as a kind of political innovation. At this point I should like to speak about an Issues Test in somewhat greater detail and indicate some of the ways in which a test of this sort might be used politically so as to enable a renovated democracy to deal with the increasing social complexity of our age.

An Issues Test can be an objective instrument which varies with different elections. Its construction could be the joint effort of several social scientists. Its administration would be costly but probably no more costly than a great deal of contemporary, administrative boondoggling—in fact, probably less so. Research teams of psychologists and other social scientists could construct such Issues Tests prior to elections on the principle of sampling the minimum range of information and the minimum amount of analytic ability which appear to be demanded by voting on issues, alternative solutions to which have been proposed by different candidates running for office.

From a psychological standpoint an Issues Test would have the effect of guaranteeing that the fate of the country, insofar as it is decided by the voter, would be in the hands of only voters conscientious enough, informed enough, and thoughtful enough to exercise intelligent citizenship by finding out in advance what the voting was all about. We would still be employing the principle of "one head—one vote," but in a modified sort of way with the corollary, so to speak, of "no head—no vote." There is nothing totalitarian about this. It is the exercise of a good management principle applied to government—let him who can, do.

The use of an Issues Test as part of the redesigning of democracy entails certain other considerations. The fate of a democratic community should never be settled by a fraction of the potential voters which is smaller than a critically-settled-upon ratio, that is, proportion. If, however, we are to institute an Issues Test, how can we tell in advance of an election that the number of competent voters (assuming that the number of them who stay away from the polls is negligible) will be equal to or greater than this critical ratio? The answer to this involves a type of research, hardly as yet begun in social science, which is also part of the unfinished business of democracy. We know that the social complexity of our culture increases as time passes. An Issues Test will directly reflect this increasing social complexity. Because we also know that the distribution of human intelligence is fairly constant, this fact can be combined with the results available from administering Issues Tests to the citizen, so as to determine two important matters: (1) the decision as to who should be allowed to vote *in any given election* and (2) an estimate of the number of competent voters who will be going to the polls. This latter estimate would then make it possible to determine whether the eligible bloc of voters is large enough to equal or exceed the *critical election ratio* of which I have already spoken.

The *difficulty* of any Issues Test can be measured by either one of the methods discussed in the preceding section or by some other, appropriate method. The first time we do this we can set the measured difficulty equal to 100. This is equivalent to establishing a base year for the difficulty in the comprehension of the issues faced by the community. For any year thereafter for which an Issues Test has been constructed, we can do the same thing, that is to say, we can obtain a measure of the difficulty in comprehension posed by the issues in question. If we divide this *later* measured difficulty of an Issues Test by the measured difficulty of the Issues Test in the base year, we have an *Index of Social Complexity* (ISC). The measured difficulty directly reflects the difficulties of the sociopolitical environment faced by members of the community. This ISC can be useful in a way which we are about to describe. Here, however, let us note that this ISC would be no different in use than an economic index, although the manner in which it would be contructed would be considerably different. It should be clear that the principles on which an Index of Social Complexity would be constructed—such as the one to which we are now referring—would be a principle which was either identical with one of those discussed in the previous section of this chapter or one which was similar in nature to approaches such as those so briefly discussed in that section. In addition, of course, such an Index of Social Complexity would probably have to be a composite one so as to reflect more than one criterion of intellectual difficulty.

A group of social scientists who are expert at the task of dealing with the issues sampled by an Issues Test, would next have to agree upon a minimum critical score which must be obtained or exceeded by a would-be voter on an Issues Test in order to earn the privilege of voting. Next we would have to establish by a separate type of research program, a mathematical or statistical relationship between this particular Index of Social Complexity and the Intelligence Quotient (or some other measure of "intellectual capacity"). This established relationship would have to be based upon a good sample of the adult citizenry. We would then be able to show that, on the average, a given level of intelligence or better could be expected to achieve the consensually desired, minimum critical score, where we know the given degree of social complexity reflected by a particular Issues Test.

Knowing the value of our Index of Social Complexity for a currently administered Issues Test and knowing the distribution of human intelligence, we should be able to predict the percentage of the would-be voting population which can be expected to achieve the minimum critical score or better. In this way we would know in advance of an election whether the voting bloc would be *sizeable enough for democratic purposes.* As the social complexity of our culture increases, this bloc may decrease in percentage if the community decides not to compromise on the level of the expected minimum critical score, but numerically it may grow larger as our population increases.

What we have in mind when we speak of a voting bloc sizeable enough for democratic purposes, is, of course, the kind of information supplied by Figure 12-5. From Figure 12-5 we can always state the percentage of the human population which would be *intellectually* unable to understand a social environment of a given ISC. From Figure 12-5 one can always say that, *on the average,* if the complexity of our social environment (ISC) is X, then all people with an IQ less than the $IQ_{min.}$ —that is, the minimum critical IQ needed to comprehend that environment—will be unable to understand it. Since the IQ distribution of our prospective voters would be the same as that for the general population, then it is equally true that if the ISC = X, all voters with an $IQ < IQ_{min.}$ would be unable to understand the nature of their social environment. They would, therefore, be likely to be the voters who would be *tempo-*

*rarily* disfranchised from voting in the then, current elections. This would be the case because they would be the voters most likely to obtain scores on an Issues Test, which fell below the acceptable minimum critical score achieved by consensus agreement among the experts constructing the test.

But from Figure 12-5 we also know the percentage of the population which possesses an $IQ > IQ_{min}$. Therefore it is this percentage of our prospective or would-be voters that would constitute the bloc of citizens who could meaningfully participate by vote in a democratic settlement of issues. This percentage is either less than, equal to, or greater than *the desired percentage* of the voters whom, it is felt, should be making democratic decisions for the community as a whole. The *desired percentage* is, of course, what we mean by the *critical, election ratio*.

Two matters must be emphasized here. No voter would be disqualified because of his or her IQ. Only the failure to obtain a score equal to or greater than the minimum critical score on an Issues Test, would disfranchise a prospective voter. As a result many prospective voters with an IQ less than the $IQ_{min}$ would still be able to achieve an acceptable score on the Issues Test by hard study, that is, by doing their political homework. The prediction of the percentage of voters who could be expected to understand the issues of the coming election—using the relationship between IQ and ISC—would only be used for determining whether or not the *critical, election ratio* could be met. There would always, then, be voters of more limited intellectual endowments who would make the grade. Likewise, there would always be voters with endowments above the critical minimum IQ, who *would not pass* the Issues Test. This would happen when such voters refused to learn what they should have learned in order to understand their social environment and the problems facing their community.

The second matter which should be emphasized here is that one can substitute for the IQ a measure of *general achievement or performance*, a point which was made in Chapter 12. If we did so, we would then be interested in the relationship between such a performance score and the ISC rather than between IQ and the ISC. The former relationship would probably be an equally valuable relationship, since many performance scores are normally distributed like the IQ, itself. However, we would have had to have done some previous, independent research on the relationship between such performance scores and the ISC, for the population as a whole.

# 15

# The Inconsistencies of
# Community Expectations*

## INTRODUCTION

In Chapter 14 we were concerned with some broad suggestions as to how social complexity might be measured and with the complications which our increasing social complexity may have upon some of the political practises of a modern democracy. We stressed the fact that, because our modern democracies would become increasingly complex as they became cybernated societies, men would experience increased difficulty in making them viable. In particular, we ventured to predict that voting might become a privilege rather than a right in the future and that this could come about if a technologically complex community tried to make certain that the voting which was intended to deal with its difficulties and problems, represented enlightened political activity. The spirit which underlies voting in a contemporary, complex democracy reflects chiefly an effort to allow each voter to have an influence on community change, regardless of whether or not he understands the technological bases or the needs of his community.[1]

* Chapter 15, with adaptations and modifications, has been taken from the following source: Henry Winthrop. "The Inconsistencies of Community Expectations." *Darshana International*. Vol. 6, No. 4, October 1966, 32–41.

[1] A major inroad into national consciousness concerning the technological basis of a modern, socially complex democracy, took place not so long ago as the result of an accident which occurred on Tuesday, November 11, 1965. This occurred in the form of a dramatic power failure which affected the Northeastern section of the United States. In the days that followed, a rash of articles by journalists and by prominent figures in all walks of life, appeared throughout the country in the nation's newspapers. The burden of these articles and comments was to stress the utter dependence of the advanced, democratic community of the West, on modern technology. The radio and television likewise developed this theme. If one had to choose a single date as a dividing line between a period of national unawareness, relatively speaking, concerning the technological base of modern, democratic life, and a period just beginning in which it appears that a new awareness will begin to occupy the center of national consciousness, the date of November 11, 1965, would be an excellent choice for that dividing line. It took a technological drama, however, affecting 30 million people in seven highly developed American states, to produce this new awareness.

In Chapter 14 we went out on a limb, as it were, and predicted that sometime in the future, if a democracy which faced bewildering social complexity as a result of overpowering technological complexity, expected to remain viable, it would have to convert voting into a privilege rather than a right, by means of an Issues Test. We stated that, if that should happen, the primary gain would be that the fate of the community —to the extent that an Issues Test really dealt well with the issues and problems the community had to face—would be in the hands of enlightened voters. Such voters, hopefully, would, at the same time, be chiefly citizens of goodwill, imbued with civic and social concern. This, of course, would be all to the good. A secondary gain—if this is, indeed, the proper phrase to use in the present context—would be the reduction in political influence of both those who are intellectually marginal and those who, though able, are not willing to do their political homework and thereby improve the functioning of the human community. The latter group consists largely of those who have not been touched by the ideals of *paideia* at all.

The burden of social complexity would not, of course, cease even if all our intellectually competent citizens did their political homework. This is because an enlightened vote accomplishes only two basic aims, namely, to put into office enlightened candidates of goodwill and to record the voter's wishes with respect to proposed legislation. The voter has always had the opportunity in our own type of democracy to make his wishes directly known through the initiative, the referendum, and the recall. Essentially, however, these are not devices which will guarantee that either the voter or the candidates in office are really enlightened with respect to the community's problems. But the ability to cast an enlightened vote in the two senses just mentioned, is only the first act of the political drama. The rest is much more significant than the opening, first act. In the next two chapters we wish to take up two themes in connection with the burden of social complexity: practical difficulties and theoretical difficulties. The first theme—the present chapter—will be a concrete discussion of the manner in which the American citizen asks for community objectives which are either utterly incompatible under any circumstances or—and this is more frequently the case—incompatible in the light of the present operating characteristics of the American economy or of some of its existing community institutions. The second theme— and the *raison d'être* of Chapter 16—will be a discussion of the problems which planners must face when the solutions to a community's problems have to be complementary, in short to spell out the meaning of the concept of coordination in social planning.

## I. ASKING FOR THE ECOLOGICALLY IMPOSSIBLE

The American citizen tends to ask for the moon as he approaches his community's difficulties. This arises sometimes as a result of ignorance, sometimes as a result of short-sighted selfishness, and sometimes merely thoughtlessness concerning his socially complex environment; usually as a result of all three combined. The burden of social complexity receives, perhaps, its major manifestation in our frantic effort to deal *piecemeal* with major problems. The typical American, moreover, does not plan to *prevent* a condition which is foreseeable and which will almost surely come about if he fails to act. Rather he prefers to attack it after it has become a reality. Thus, for example,[2] to ask that "something be done" about air pollution over some of our major cities and at the same time to ask that traffic congestion in these same cities be "relieved" by constructing highways which run through them or even around their outskirts, is to ask for the impossible. This is because the air pollution is, itself, the product, to a great extent, of the innocent-looking tailpipe (idling motors also contribute to air pollution) which spews forth numerous air pollutants. In the course of using up a thousand gallons of gasoline, motor vehicles typically discharge 17 pounds of sulfur dioxide, 18 pounds of aldehydes, 25 to 75 pounds of oxides of nitrogen, and more than 3,000 pounds of carbon monoxide. In Los Angeles, in the recent past, it was learned that 80 percent of the pollutants in Los Angeles smog was produced by the city's three million privately owned motor vehicles. Thus, we can see that if we build more highways to service the transportation needs of our existing cities, these will increase the density per unit time of motor vehicles traveling through these same cities. Such an increase of motor vehicle density per unit time will, in turn, increase the intensity of the air pollution over these same cities.

Another example of impossible community expectations is the urban demand that the amount of pollution of its water sources be reduced by conventional water-treatment methods while, at the same time, welcoming the increasing conurbations with their resulting overpopulation densities. The latter phenomenon, moreover, results in an expansion of industrial activity and in new industries which produce an unprecedented variety of new water-pollutants as industrial waste, in the form of such chemicals as detergents, insecticides, herbicides, plastics, abrasives, food and food

---

2 If, of course, current motor vehicle design is changed by introducing the direct-flame afterburner into motor vehicles, as well as blowby devices which, incidentally, reduce the hydrocarbon emissions of *new* automobiles by only 25 to 35 percent, the problem of air pollution from motor vehicles as a source will be somewhat reduced. In general, if a concerted effort is made to introduce devices of any nature which will cut down pollutants from motor vehicles, the problem of air pollution may yet prove manageable.

additives, pharmaceuticals, petroleum derivatives and radioactive materials. These eventually find their way into the water supply and many have proved to be physiologically harmful. Serious effects of others are almost certain to be "discovered" later. It is impossible to break down many of them by existing and conventional methods of water-treatment, in order to prevent possible damage to humans and marine life. As a result the fact that most citizens accept community development through ribbon urbanism but, at the same time, demand more fresh water and, most important of all, more fresh water uncontaminated by industrial wastes, reflects simply inconsistent demands.

The crisis in our cities is largely the result of incompatible demands such as the two already mentioned. Even worse is the fact that the crises in our cities are also the result of *incompatible solutions* to different problems. Thus Von Eckardt,[3] commenting on the incompatible proposals which the new Department of Housing and Urban Development will be saddled with, as a result of having had placed under its official jurisdiction various existing agencies which have, in some respects, been working at cross-purposes, has pointed out the existence of the following headaches.[4] At the time of this writing the federal highway program has so far *alloted* $20 billion for cities while the federal mass transportation program has *authorized* $375 million—a sum which cannot even meet the transportation needs of Chicago alone. Urban renewal is supposed to keep taxpayers and jobs downtown but the freeways and suburban mortgages lure them out. Freeways take taxable land and displace people and thereby result in aggravating the municipal problem of finding ever-more parking space for cars for people who moved "out" and still work "in." Slum clearance and building code enforcement programs actually help spread the slums because those who are emptied out of the slums by government action are forced into other existing poor neighborhoods which then tend to deteriorate even more rapidly as a result of increasing congestion. In the name of conservation the American will support demands for the preservation of the country's greenbelt areas but, at the same time, supported by a local booster psychology, he will demand more housing developments to accommodate population influxes, more suburban developments which will enable him and his family to escape urban sprawl and more land for new industry so that his community may wax more prosperous. The inconsistencies of these expectations do not register deeply on our national consciousness.

3 Wolf Von Eckardt. "The Department of Headaches." *The New Republic*. Vol. 153, No. 19, Issue 2659, November 6, 1965. 19–22.
    4 Incompatibility in objectives may also crop up between the new Department of Housing and Urban Development and many federal agencies which will be independent of the new department—agencies whose activities, to quote one small example, are devoted to education, public welfare, water supply, power needs, or the elimination of pockets of poverty.

Incompatibility in public choices and in the elements of our disjointed public philosophy as well as incompatibility among the proposed solutions to different urban problems, show up in many other concrete ways. Housing legislation seems somehow to equate the welfare of the building industry with the "public" welfare. Urban renewal programs tend to favor downtown business so that the housing needed for the poor is supplanted by the building of corporation palaces and high-rise luxury apartments. Agencies at different levels of government often work at cross-purposes. In Baltimore the highway department tried to run an expressway through an area which had been set aside by the housing and urban renewal agency for public housing. The highway department had sought to run the expressway smack through one newly completed and one nearly completed public housing project. It would seem that public agencies would make every effort to see to it that their official objectives meshed, yet impasses such as the above have become normal in almost every community.

Perhaps one of the most tragic inconsistencies in American attitudes towards our native ecology is the conflict between private greed in the pursuit of agriculture for profit and our desire to preserve natural areas of great beauty, abundant wildlife and tourist appeal. A recent and tragic example of this is the selfishness of growers in South Florida who demand water from already limited sources of that natural commodity. They demand this water for new tomato patches which they wish to cultivate—tomato patches which would probably, in no sense, constitute a local, regional, or national necessity. If their demands continue to be met this may destroy more of an already economically ravaged Everglades National Park. Much of the Everglades has already been wiped out by pressures on and from the U.S. Army Corps of Engineers, to provide water chiefly for various growers or because the Corps has dumped water in the past into areas where nothing profited from it. Out of ignorance and apathy the public will support both the growers (are they not giving expression to free-enterprise initiative?) and the public-spirited citizens who wish to preserve the Everglades—citizens consisting in part of members of the National Park Service, biologists, conservation-minded individuals, and responsible Washington officials. For a succinct account of this ecological inconsistency the reader should consult "Last Chance for the Everglades" by Wallace Stegner (*Saturday Review,* May 6, 1967).

We also exhibit inconsistency in public choice, public philosophy and proposed solutions to our community problems by the eagerness with which we turn *short-range solutions* into *long-range problems*. Where we have to deal with chronic traffic jams we plunge into the construction of highways which, themselves, will later produce effects which will create new problems or aggravate existing difficulties. If suburban commuting becomes difficult, we establish heliports on the rooftops of our downtown buildings. Should such a practise ever become widespread—not a likely eventuality considering its current costs to individual beneficiaries—there would be fresh problems to deal with. To increase the flow of traffic per unit time into our crowded cities, we build underground or multi-storied garages. These will later pose fresh problems as the community expands physically and its activities and services multiply. We hope to maintain small greenbelt areas, like parks, in our cities but make this impossible by increasing the number of throughways and urban, four-lane highways associated with them. We plead for the aesthetic preservation of the landscape and then deface it by sweeping, steel-girdered "parkways" and by separating pedestrians from our river banks by a maze of twisting highways. Finally, let us note that most of the *solutions* to our problems tend to conflict with one problem which is frequently regarded as central to them all: the problem of reducing municipal costs of government per capita or per taxpayer. As a result of unchecked urbanism and expanding industrialism these costs must inevitably rise in spite of the outraged protests of many citizens who sincerely believe they can be reduced.

The incompatibilities among our community expectations and among the solutions we propose for dealing with our community problems, are not confined merely to economic matters, to community modes of living or to health problems of a physical nature. They also arise in connection with problems of mental health. One major incompatibility in this category is our willingness to increase population densities in our large urban centers, in order to meet problems of urban renewal and public housing, while demanding a reduction in the amount of mental illness in our midst. The extent to which this last pair of demands is equivalent to asking for the ecologically impossible, has been revealed by the Midtown Manhattan Study undertaken by Dr. Thomas A. C. Rennie and his associates in the early 1950's, an account of which has been furnished by Leo Srole [5] *et al.* In this study it was found that in a highly congested urban area, such as mid-Manhattan, *4 out of every 5* people have symptoms of psychiatric disorder and *1 out of 4* have neuroses severe enough to disrupt their daily lives. In contrast, a low-density, stable, agrarian community, such as that of the Hutterites,[6] showed that 97 out of every 100 Hutterites have never experienced a major, mental disorder. Urban stress, it seems, is largely responsible for the high incidence of metropolitan ill health. The detailed results of each of these studies have come under some professional criticism but there is no denying that, even if the quantitative biases with respect to the incidence of mental ill health are corrected, there is no gainsaying the fact that *distinct and*

[5] Leo Srole *et al. Mental Health in the Metropolis. The Midtown Manhattan Study.* New York: McGraw-Hill, 1962. 428 pp.

[6] Joseph W. Eaton and Robert J. Weil. *Culture and Mental Disorders.* Glencoe, Illinois: The Free Press, 1955. 254 pp.

*contrasting trends* are shown by the two studies. One of these trends indicates that increased mental ill health and mental disorder are associated with the congested urban center. The other indicates that increased mental health is associated with a low, community population density.[7] The apathetic acceptance of the continued rise of urbanism, and popular demand that something be done to lower the amount of urban mental ill health and disorder, reflect simple incompatible expectations.

Medical and public health problems in general provide a fertile matrix for the types of incompatibilities which we have been stressing. Specific examples have been provided by Dubos [8] who has attempted to show that technological advances approved by the citizenry, create public health problems which are difficult to eradicate. Although not mentioned by Dubos, the ever-growing acceptance of the use of chemicals in agriculture and in the processing of food—in order, in the former case, to meet the food requirements of a growing population and, in the latter case, to avoid waste in the food supply by methods of food preservation— has led to the appearance of hypovitaminoses as a common form of nutritional disease. In addition, hypovitaminoses have led to other types of nutritional disorders, disturbed metabolism in various forms of physiological malfunctioning and ill health. Dubos, himself, mentions the extent to which hypervitaminoses, too, are a common form of nutritional disease in the Western world. The use of detergents and various synthetics has increased the incidence of allergies in modern man. Advances in chemotherapy and other therapeutic procedures have created a new staphylococcus pathology and given rise to mutant microbial forms resistant to chemotherapeutic agents. The effort to escape or forget the modern rat race for success and security and the effort to reduce the tensions of modern living, have increased alcoholism and addiction to various tension-reducing drugs the effects of which are not really known, in the twentieth century. The conditions which produce air pollution have also produced an increase of chronic bronchitis. In England chronic bronchitis claimed 37,000 lives in 1951 and accounted for the certified loss of 26.6 million working days among the insured population. In general air pollution gives rise to trivial infections of the respiratory tract which are impervious to drug treatment and other methods of therapy.

Other unexpected and undesirable consequences of advances in medical and other fields are reported by Dubos. Mutant forms of bacteria are now becoming resistant to penicillin and other chemotherapeutic agents and new nutritional diseases, associated with agricultural and

[7] In addition to low population density the Hutterites possess a distinct way of life. This latter is undoubtedly also playing a significant and major role. However, it should also be pointed out that the expression of a satisfying way of life for an entire community, is not likely to be easily attained in a highly congested one.

[8] Rene J. Dubos. "Medical Utopias." *Daedalus.* Vol. 88, No. 3, Summer 1959. 410–24. Issue entitled *Current Work and Controversies.*

industrial technology, are appearing, such as hepatic toxicity of unknown mechanism and various types of cancer from alleged carcinogenic agents in food, water and air. There is some evidence that the boredom created by automation, is creating new forms of psychosis. As medical science becomes increasingly effective in preserving the lives of biologically defective individuals, there will be an increase in the frequency of detrimental genes which are allowed to accumulate in our population. The modern community seems to provide a protective ecology for the biologically defective individual, particularly the poorly endowed intellectually.

Research has also indicated that the domesticated rat of the laboratory has lost the ability—ever present in its wild ancestor—to provide for itself, to fight, and to resist fatigue as well as toxic substances and microbial diseases. It is possible, Dubos points out, that human communities, made up of well-domesticated citizens, comfort-loving and submissive, may not prove to be the ones which will be most able to survive. Research has also indicated that animals born and raised in a germ-free environment, exhibit extraordinary susceptibility to infection. By implications the "gracious living" so ardently sought by the American middle class, may likewise tend to unfit its members for biological stress and, perhaps, also psychological stress.

All of the preceding, then, indicate that as our citizens demand that the quality of life be improved in the short-run by advances in science and technology, they should not, at the same time, expect improved health *in the long run*. How such inconsistent expectations are to be ironed out in the future will call for considerable, human ingenuity. There may be several feasible alternatives. One is increased decentralization of modern life, the virtues of which will be examined in Part V of this volume. Decentralization works in the direction of reducing the number of incompatible demands which a community is likely to make. Another could be an extended and refined use of social planning in order to avoid the types of inconsistency in community expectations, which we have been describing.

In Chapter 16 we shall be discussing a type of social planning whose chief virtue is that it takes cognizance of the inconsistencies in community demand and which employs techniques for reducing or eliminating such inconsistencies. Before we do so, however, it is important to recognize that America is in the midst of a vast, social revolution— invisible to the average man—but one which will be making it increasingly necessary *in the future* to be aware of the manner in which our problems tend to be related. This revolution will also demand a greatly more realistic, public consciousness concerning what is ecologically possible in the huge metropolitan areas in which so many choose to live. This revolution is producing more social change in a year than men formerly could create for themselves in a lifetime: it is occurring in such a way that the average citizen is playing a very small role in its creation, although he is its chief beneficiary. This revolution is taking place in three steps.

In Step 1 each of the community's problems is being studied by groups of experts who are highly knowledgeable with respect *to the one problem in question*. These studies may be undertaken for congressional committees, for a government official, for a national organization like the AFL–CIO, for a nonpartisan body which is civically dedicated to improving community life, or for some other enlightened agency or public body. When these studies are finished they are usually accompanied by one or more expert proposals for dealing with the problem. This phenomenon in which social change is being introduced into American life by professional social scientists, welfare workers and knowledgeable, legal experts, has been called by Moynihan,[9] "the professionalization of reform," since all the techniques of social problem-solving are in the hands of professionals.

In Step 2, after these studies have been placed in the hands of congressmen or of other public officials who are interested in doing something to solve the problem in question, *a solution which seems to have a chance of being accepted politically is chosen*. This solution is incorporated in the form of proposed legislation for dealing with the problem. In Step 2 the chief activities are the political and legal maneuverings which accompany the composition of the proposed legislation by a congressional or other legislative committee which has the task of dealing with the problem, followed by the activities involved in ensuring its introduction to the legislature. This, in turn, is followed by long debates which precede its adoption or rejection. This description is, of course, highly over-simplified but essentially correct. Step 2 is the only part of the process of producing social change which is visible to the average citizen and much of even that process is not, in fact, visible.

These first two steps reduce considerably the influence of the voter, as voter, but not necessarily as a citizen. He can make his voice heard and his influence felt in the organizations of which he is a member. These are the organizations with whom the professionals make their contacts. The professionalization of reform—really, of social change—if continued, would mean that if an Issues Test were ever adopted as a political innovation in American life, the voter's influence would be confined to choosing those candidates whom he felt to be most knowledgeable and legally competent, with respect to the task of successfully dealing with the community's major and significant social problems. It is quite obvious that under a novel, political innovation such as an Issues Test, a candidate for political office would really have to be sound in his social thinking and

9 Daniel P. Moynihan. "The Professionalization of Reform." *The Public Interest.* Vol. 1, No. 1, Fall 1965. 6–16. In the recent past Moynihan functioned as Assistant Secretary of Labor.

his social judgment, and well prepared informationally to use power wisely, if he hoped to be elected. Under an Issues Test the effective voters would, in a sense, almost be the equals of the running candidates. From the political wisdom contained in the expression "you can fool all of the people some of the time and some of the people all of the time but you cannot fool all of the people all of the time," we would move to a position in which we could with justice say "you can fool none of the people (effective voters) none of the time." This certainly would be a real gain in the existing expression of democracy.

The third step by which revolutionary social change can be produced is a step still to be taken on a widespread scale and still to become part of the focus of national consciousness. That step will call for *effective national planning.* "Planning" is still a dirty word to many Americans and, although some planning does take place nationally *on a limited scale,* it is not played up as planning but rather as good, practical, government administration. Effective national planning, however, has certain specific meanings. Just what are some of these meanings? In the chapter which follows we turn our attention to a description and discussion of those meanings which are specific to the concept of effective national planning.

# 16

# The Meaning of
# Structure and Coordination
# in Social Planning*

## I. PREVIEW [1]

The ideal approach to planning involves the recognition that usually we are dealing with a context in which several problems have to be solved. The solutions of these problems are invariably related in two senses. First, the measures which solve one problem may help in the solution of another, may have no effect upon the solution of any other problem, may worsen another problem or may work against measures taken to solve a different problem. Second, the consequences which are the aftermath of the solution to one problem, whether foreseen or not, and whether desirable or not, may prevent or speed up the realization of those consequences which are the aftermath of the solution to a different problem, whether or not these latter are desirable or were foreseen. The *ideal set of solutions* to any set of problems would have the following characteristics. First, each solution to each problem would be, *in some sense which was variable from problem to problem,* that solution which was *the optimum solution* from among all the alternatives which can be shown to be a *feasible set* of solutions to that problem. Second, any such set of *optimal solutions* should be such that *the consequences which can be foreseen* for each solution are *reciprocating.* By this term is meant the following. Since, in general, every optimal solution will produce both *desirable* and *undesirable anticipated* consequences, the best we can hope for is a situation in which both types of consequence from the solution of any problem *reinforce* the *foreseen desirable* consequences of the solutions to the remaining $n$-1 problems and work against (that is, dampen the magnitude

* Chapter 16, with adaptations and modifications, has been taken from the following source: Henry Winthrop. "The Meaning of Structure and Coordination in Social Planning." *Sociological Inquiry.* Vol. XXXIII, No. 2, Spring 1963, 144–156.

1 The planning discussed in this chapter includes both social planning as well as economic planning.

of or slow up the appearance of) the *foreseen undesirable* consequences which flow from the solutions to the remaining $n$-1 problems.

In any type of planning, whether industrial, economic or social in nature, an optimum solution to a problem is generally chosen without reference to the optimum solution of other problems and without any expectation of meeting the ideal conditions mentioned above. This is particularly true if the body of individuals responsible for meeting different problems, varies from one problem to another, and if these bodies confer haphazardly or fail to confer at all. The meaning of the concept of *coordination in planning* refers to any *conscious attempt* to approximate an ideal set of solutions—where the sense of the word "ideal" is that briefly mentioned in the preceding paragraph—whether or not the ideal outcome was actually obtained. In terms of the definition of an ideal set of solutions it would, no doubt, also be possible to devise an operational measure of the *degree of coordination* achieved by a set of solutions which was less than ideal. In addition to the unilateral approach to problems which occurs in planning operations, any body of planners which was given the responsibility for achieving coordination in the sense just defined, would be up against the fact that the *highly varied contexts* in which the different problems occurred, made an understanding of the functional relationships of the variables peculiar to these contexts, very difficult to achieve. The *degree of complexity* of a system of interrelated contexts which are difficult enough to understand separately as subsystems and which involve phenomena and variables from universes of discourse which we are accustomed to think of as independent of one another, would prompt any group of practical planners to eschew the global or coordinative approach and seek, instead, to achieve efficiency on a piecemeal basis.

In seeking to achieve such piecemeal solutions the temptation is to assess the quality of the solution to a given problem and its probable aftermath and to do so by invoking the *ceteribus paribus* shibboleth. Unfortunately the complexity of interrelated but qualitatively different contexts makes the assumption of "other things being equal" a highly erroneous one. The illegitimacy of such an assumption for complex milieus is well brought out by Ashby in his discussion of the importance of cybernetics. He says:

> Science stands today on something of a divide. For two centuries it has been exploring systems that are either intrinsically simple or that are capable of being analysed into simple components. The fact that such a dogma as "vary the factors one at a time" could be accepted for a century, shows that scientists were largely concerned in investigating such systems as *allowed* this method; for this method is often fundamentally impossible in the complex systems. Not until Sir Ronald Fisher's work in the '20s, with experiments conducted on agricultural soils, did it become clearly recognized that there are complex systems that just

do not allow the varying of only one factor at a time—they are so dynamic and interconnected that the alteration of one factor immediately acts as cause to evoke alterations in others, perhaps in a great many others. Until recently, science tended to evade the study of such systems, focusing its attention on those that were simple and, especially, reducible.

In the study of some systems, however, the complexity could not be wholly evaded. The cerebral cortex of the free-living organism, the ant-hill as a functioning society, and the human economic system were outstanding both in their practical importance and in their intractability by the older methods. So today we see psychoses untreated, societies declining, and economic systems faltering, the scientist being able to do little more than to appreciate the full complexity of the subject he is studying. But science today is also taking the first steps toward studying "complexity" as a subject in its own right.[2] (p. 5)

The present chapter is an attempt to recognize that planning generally proceeds in the face of such complexity and to *analyze the structure* of planning in relation to the desirability of *coordination in planning methodology*. Inasmuch as we are interested in the structure of the complex milieu for which planning is intended and the structure of the methodology which is appropriate for complex milieus, we shall restrict ourselves to *schematizations* only. That is to say, our analysis will try to present only the *framework* of the considerations that planning technology must recognize in relation to the problem of coordination. No detailed mathematical analysis of any of the considerations spotlighted, will be attempted in this chapter.

Finally it should be noted that when we speak of the context of planning as involving a system of *n interrelated problems,* we assume that the planning treats these n problems as endogenous to the system. Any disturbance to the planned-for-system from effects or factors outside of the states of affairs which constitute the context of planning, are exogenous in nature and will clearly affect the quality and results of the planning involved. If such effects have not been foreseen the planning is poor in the sense that the planners involved have misjudged the context of planning. This misjudgment is reflected in taking the context of planning or the system of interrelated problems too narrowly, so that its boundaries have been ill defined. In good planning the judgment as to the proper context is either perfectly accurate in connection with the specification of boundaries, or, *more practically,* the boundaries are never perfectly specifiable and the context of planning is never perfectly isolated. The most that good planning technology can hope to achieve is that the context of planning and the sense of boundaries, in terms of the interrelationships of the different problems planned for, is so well chosen that exogenous disturbances to the results of the planned-for solutions are both minimal and negligible.

[2] W. Ross Ashby. *An Introduction to Cybernetics.* New York: Wiley, 1956. 295 pp.

## II. THE RELATIONSHIPS AND ATTRIBUTES
## AMONG THE EFFECTS OF PLANNING

In this section we propose to try to make clear the nature of the relationships and attributes which hold *between pairs of effects or consequences* which must occur as a result of planning operations. We can do this in part by constructing a useful classification in this connection, one which will serve the purposes of explanation. Let us assume that a body of planners is given a set of interrelated problems, $A_1$, $A_2$, . . . $A_n$, in some planning context of a social, economic, industrial nature, etc. In less abstract terms this is equivalent to asserting that we have $n$ separate *states of affairs* which we wish to manipulate so as to transform these into n states of affairs whose characteristics will be quite different. In the context of planning this is precisely what we mean when we speak of the needed solutions to n different problems. This way of speaking should be taken to mean in general that the transformation of any given state of affairs will involve either the addition of one or more new attributes to the given state of affairs, the elimination of one or more existing attributes, or both these contingencies. In any such planning operation it will be recognized that either all the separate states of affairs are interrelated, some are interrelated or all are completely independent. In a complex context the first of these considerations will most probably obtain and in what follows we will assume this is the case. In such a context to assert that two states of affairs are interrelated will mean that the attributes of one of these affects the attributes of the other and that this interrelationship may be either *unilateral* or *reciprocal*. In the considerations which follow we shall assume both these types of interrelationship. *The attributes planned for* by any group of planners and which are clearly the major goals of all planning operations will be spoken of hereafter as *primary consequences*. It is the unambiguous achievement of such *primary consequences* (states of affairs) which is central in all planning. This must be emphasized.

In planning for problems in a complex context, it will also be recognized that following any transformation of a given state of affairs, due to the solution imposed upon the problem (state of affairs) at hand, *secondary consequences* or *side-effects* will flow from the transformation. These will be over and above the attributes sought for in the transformation and/or the attributes which the planners seek to remove from the existing state of affairs. These *secondary consequences* which may appear shortly after institution of the solution or which may unfold gradually over time, will, in planning worthy of the name, be foreseen and, where they are not of the all-or-none variety, their magnitude will have to be *estimated* by any one of several planning techniques or *metrics* which have become available. To the extent that such secondary consequences *are not* foreseen, planning will be *less than perfect* and the more complex the context of planning, the more likely is this to be the case. In the matters discussed below, however, we shall assume that the planning involved is of such high reliability that no *unforeseen* secondary consequences occur or that those which do, have a negligible effect on the achievement of the overall objectives of the planning operations. Finally it is to be noted that even the best solution to a given problem may entail, in the total context of all problems, the realization that secondary consequences will inevitably involve both desirable and undesirable results. In well thought out planning, the optimal solution finally chosen for any given problem, will be ideally one which is foreseen to have facilitation effects upon the desirable primary and secondary consequences of all the problems involved, as well as inhibition effects upon the undesirable primary and secondary consequences of these other problems.

Whether consequences are primary or secondary, it is assumed that their effects can be determined, that is, estimated or predicted. This is the fundamental task of planning technology. The effects to be predicted will be of several kinds. Ordinarily the primary consequences planned for in a problem which is the focus of attention, can affect the primary consequences planned for a different problem, can clearly affect some of its own *later* secondary consequences or the later secondary consequences derived from another problem. In addition the foreseen secondary consequences of the solution to a focal problem may *later* have a disturbing effect upon its own primary consequences, the primary consequences sought for in a second problem, or the secondary consequences of a different problem. Finally some of the primary consequences of the solution to a problem affect some of the remaining primary consequences of that solution and likewise some of the secondary consequences of a solution to a problem may affect other foreseen secondary consequences of that same solution. The first group of effects may be called *extrinsic*, the second, *intrinsic*.

If the effect of any consequence, whether primary or secondary, is to increase the magnitude of a primary or secondary consequence or merely helps to sustain it, this will be spoken of as a *facilitation effect*. If the effect of any consequence, whether primary or secondary, is to decrease the magnitude of a primary or secondary consequence or serves to eliminate it, this will be spoken of as an *inhibition effect*. Planning of any merit which aims to *coordinate* the solutions to two or more interrelated problems will aim at optimal solutions which either facilitate desired primary consequences of other problems or desirable secondary effects, or which diminish or eliminate entirely undesired secondary affects. Obviously, planning is never aimed at achieving undesirable primary consequences. If these considerations cannot be ensured, the planning will, *at least,* aim at establishing balances in which the price to be paid for the advantage of living with minimal inhibition effects on some desirable consequences is offset by the disadvantage of obtaining limited facilitation effects on some other desirable consequences. Likewise the disadvantage of living with only limited inhibition effects on some undesirable consequences is offset by the advantage of knowing that the facilitation effects upon other undesirable consequences are limited.

The considerations stressed in the preceding paragraphs can be rendered somewhat clearer synoptically by a glance at Table 16-1.

In columns (2) and (3) of the table we distinguish between the consequences of the solution to the same or different problems. The upper-case letters, "P" and "S," will refer to a primary and a secondary consequence, respectively. The primary and secondary consequences in question and which are referred to under columns (2) and (3) of Table 16-1, may both have emerged from dealing with a single, given problem or one of these two types of consequence may have emerged from dealing with one stated problem, $A_1$, while the other may have emerged from dealing with a second, stated problem, $A_2$. From any row of Table 16-1 these two letters will always be read in pairs, the pair in question always occurring under columns (2) and (3) of the table. In any given row of Table 16-1, columns (2) and (3), one may find either both letters, each occurring but once, or one may find one of these two letters occurring twice.

The lower-case subscript letters, s and s', always refer to *two different solutions* to either *two different problems* or to *two different plans* for achieving *two different objectives.* If the letters, s and s', modify the letter, P, twice, as in rows 5 through 8 of Table 16-1, they refer to the *primary consequences* of *two different solutions* to *two different problems.* If they modify the letter, S, twice as in rows 21 through 24 of the table, they refer to the *secondary consequences* of *two different solutions* to *two different problems.* If they modify the upper-case letters, P and S, respectively, as in rows 13 through 16 of the table, this indicates that s is to be taken as referring to the primary consequence of a *solution* to one problem, while s' is to be taken as referring to a secondary consequence of a *solution* to another problem. When the *superscripts* (1) and (2) appear above the letter, P, which occurs twice, as in rows (1) through (4) of the table, this indicates that we are referring to *two different primary consequences* flowing from *one given solution* to a certain problem. When the same superscripts appear above the letter S, which occurs twice, as in rows (17) through (20) of the table, this indicates that we are referring to *two different secondary consequences* flowing from *one given solution* to a certain problem.

*Table 16-1.*    Relationships and Attributes of Primary and Secondary Consequences

| Num- ber | Type of Conse- quence Pro- ducing Effect | Conse- quence Pro- duced or Affected | Type | Quality of Effect | Nature | Nature of Relation- ship | Cate- gory into which Conse- quence Falls |
|---|---|---|---|---|---|---|---|
| 1 | $P_s^{(1)}$ | $P_s^{(2)}$ | F and PF | D or D' | I | R or U | V or A |
| 2 | $P_s^{(1)}$ | $P_s^{(2)}$ | I and PF | D or D' | I | R or U | V or A |
| 3 | $P_s^{(1)}$ | $P_s^{(2)}$ | F and NF | D or D' | I | R or U | V or A |
| 4 | $P_s^{(1)}$ | $P_s^{(2)}$ | I and NF | D or D' | I | R or U | V or A |
| 5 | $P_s$ | $P_{s'}$ | F and PF | D or D' | E | R or U | V or A |
| 6 | $P_s$ | $P_{s'}$ | I and PF | D or D' | E | R or U | V or A |
| 7 | $P_s$ | $P_{s'}$ | F and NF | D or D' | E | R or U | V or A |
| 8 | $P_s$ | $P_{s'}$ | I and NF | D or D' | E | R or U | V or A |
| 9 | $P_s$ | $S_s$ | F and PF | D or D' | I | R or U | V or A |
| 10 | $P_s$ | $S_s$ | I and PF | D or D' | I | R or U | V or A |
| 11 | $P_s$ | $S_s$ | F and NF | D or D' | I | R or U | V or A |
| 12 | $P_s$ | $S_s$ | I and NF | D or D' | I | R or U | V or A |
| 13 | $P_s$ | $S_{s'}$ | F and PF | D or D' | E | R or U | V or A |
| 14 | $P_s$ | $S_{s'}$ | I and PF | D or D' | E | R or U | V or A |
| 15 | $P_s$ | $S_{s'}$ | F and NF | D or D' | E | R or U | V or A |
| 16 | $P_s$ | $S_{s'}$ | I and NF | D or D' | E | R or U | V or A |
| 17 | $S_s^{(1)}$ | $S_s^{(2)}$ | F and PF | D or D' | I | R or U | V or A |
| 18 | $S_s^{(1)}$ | $S_s^{(2)}$ | I and PF | D or D' | I | R or U | V or A |
| 19 | $S_s^{(1)}$ | $S_s^{(2)}$ | F and NF | D or D' | I | R or U | V or A |
| 20 | $S_s^{(1)}$ | $S_s^{(2)}$ | I and NF | D or D' | I | R or U | V or A |
| 21 | $S_s$ | $S_{s'}$ | F and PF | D or D' | E | R or U | V or A |
| 22 | $S_s$ | $S_{s'}$ | I and PF | D or D' | E | R or U | V or A |
| 23 | $S_s$ | $S_{s'}$ | F and NF | D or D' | E | R or U | V or A |
| 24 | $S_s$ | $S_{s'}$ | I and NF | D or D' | E | R or U | V or A |

All the preceding should become somewhat clearer by summarizing our notation as follows. Two different primary consequences of a solution to the same problem, are referred to as $P_s^{(1)}$ and $P_s^{(2)}$. Two different primary consequences, each of which was an objective of respective solutions to two different problems, are referred to as $P_s$ and $P_{s'}$. A primary and secondary consequence both of which were the result of applying a given solution to a given problem, are referred to as $P_s$ and $S_s$. A primary consequence flowing from a solution to one problem, coupled with a secondary consequence flowing from a solution to a different problem, are referred to as $P_s$ and $S_{s'}$. Two secondary consequences which have resulted from a solution of the same given problem, are referred to as $S_s^{(1)}$ and $S_s^{(2)}$. Finally, two secondary consequences one of which resulted from a solution of a given problem and the second of which resulted from a solution to a second problem, are referred to as $S_s$ and $S_{s'}$. Certain cases which would seem to fall under columns (2) and (3) of Table 16-1 are really *structurally equivalent*. Thus the following cases are structurally equivalent. $P_{s'}$ and $S_s$ is structurally equivalent to $P_s$ and $S_{s'}$; $P_{s'}$ and $S_{s'}$ is structurally equivalent to $P_s$ and $S_s$; $P_{s'}^{(1)}$ and $P_{s'}^{(2)}$ is structurally equivalent to $P_s^{(1)}$ and $P_s^{(2)}$; and $S_{s'}^{(1)}$ and $S_{s'}^{(2)}$ is structurally equivalent to $S_s^{(1)}$ and $S_s^{(2)}$.

Entries under columns (2) and (3) are to be read as follows. Consider row 4. It refers to a primary consequence of a solution to a given problem which *affected* another primary consequence of the solution to that same problem. When we speak of one consequence affecting another we mean that either the first altered the second in some qualitative fashion, changed the magnitude of the second, completely obstructed the work which ordinarily might have been done by the second, or had some impact upon the second so that the effects it would otherwise have had, have been altered in some fashion. Consider row 8. It refers to a primary consequence which was achieved as a result of the solution to a given problem and which either *produced* a side-effect which was, itself, the primary consequence originally planned for in a solution to a different problem, or it refers to a primary consequence of a solution to one problem which *affected* a primary consequence which was a result of a solution to a second problem. Consider row 12. It refers to a primary consequence which was planned for in the solution of a given problem, which has, itself, *produced* a secondary consequence, or it refers to a primary consequence which has affected a secondary consequence that resulted from another primary consequence which flowed from the solution to that same problem. Consider row 16. It refers to a primary consequence of a solution to a given problem which has had an effect upon a secondary consequence which, itself, resulted from a solution to another problem. Consider row 20. It refers to two secondary consequences which resulted from a solution to a given problem. These secondary consequences are related in the following way. Either the first of these *produced* the second at a later date or *affected* the second in some way at that later date. Finally consider row 24. Each of these two secondary consequences has appeared as the later result of two different solutions to two different problems but they are related in precisely the same way as the two consequences in row 20.

The manner in which an entire row of Table 16-1 is to be read will be taken up at the conclusion of this chapter, after the various other types of entry in the table have been separately explained.

The remaining symbols of Table 16-1 are more easily explained. The letters F and I designate respectively a facilitation and inhibition effect. The symbols, D and D', refer to desirable and undesirable consequences, respectively, as this attribute is judged consensually by the community as client of the planning body. The meaning of "desirable" and "undesirable" are self-explanatory. However, the meaning of the phrase, "a facilitation effect," refers to the fact that a given consequence serves to increase, reinforce or sustain another, while the meaning of the phrase, "an inhibition effect," refers to a situation in which one consequence or factor serves to diminish another, eliminate it or impair its work drastically. The letter, R, refers to a relationship between consequences which is *reciprocal,* while the letter, U, describes a *unilateral* relationship between consequences. Most forms of positive and negative feedback between pairs of consequences, will involve reciprocal relationships. However, some forms of relationship are *unilateral* in that a change in one factor may produce a change in another, but not vice versa. Thus an increase in the population in a given area *must* result in a decrease in the *average dietary per capita,* if food resources are fixed or increasing more slowly than population. However, a decrease in the average dietary per capita in a given area may not be associated with an increase in its population. A decrease in the average dietary clearly can be associated with education surrounding diet and nutrition. Such unilateral associations will, of course, occur in general when changes in the first of two factors must be due to changes in many others, including the second, while increases or decreases in the first need not *necessarily* affect the second. When a consequence has actually been planned for or has been recognized as an inescapable side-effect, we shall speak of it as *intrinsic* to the solution of the problem. When a consequence, whether desirable or not, has not been planned for but is inescapable as the result of the solution to some problem other than the one which is the focus of attention, we shall speak of it as *extrinsic.* Finally we must note that some consequences of planning are in the nature of attributes which are *variable,* while others are of an *all-or-none variety.* A population's purchasing power would clearly be variable but the location of a firm's only industrial plant at point A rather than at point B is in the one-shot class. In Table 16-1 if a consequence is a variable, this is indicated in column (8) by the letter, V, and if it is of the all-or-none variety, this is symbolized in the same column by the letter, A.

Let us illustrate the kind of concrete situation to which the preceding, necessarily abstract, discussion is relevant. The example furnished will illustrate only *part* of the taxonomy employed in Table 16-1 for discussing the results of planning. That partial discussion, however, should serve to make clear the taxonomy we have presented.

Imagine a community faced with only three problems, $A_1$, $A_2$, and $A_3$. Problem $A_1$ is how to reduce overcrowding in schools. Problem $A_2$ is the question of how to lessen unemployment by reducing the number of cases on the community's welfare rolls. The concern of Problem $A_3$ is with the question of how to raise money to meet certain community needs. The solution, s, decided upon for $A_1$, is to lower the age for leaving school, say from 16 to 15. The solution, s', decided upon for $A_2$, is to try to create jobs in the community for eligibles on the relief rolls. The solution, s'', proposed for $A_3$, is to inaugurate certain new taxes which will be more burdensome on groups with modest incomes than on groups with good incomes.

The application of s is easy. A student merely has to prove that he is 15 years of age or older and he can leave school if he wants to. The application of s' is achieved by means of a survey of cases on the relief rolls and the business community decides it can create $x$ new jobs, after that survey has been completed.

It is then found over the course of the next two or three years that $2x$ students, aged 15, are leaving school annually who would have had to stay on if the age for leaving school had not been lowered. Quite unforeseen, these students compete for the $x$ new jobs and—since, in most cases, it is their first full-time job—they are quite happy to accept a low wage level. It has also been ascertained that the clients on the relief rolls have refused to accept the low wage level offered, because it was not much more than they could get from their relief checks, after allowing for the losses occasioned by the imposition of new taxes.

The community has also found to its sorrow that the $x$ students who left school but did not get jobs are now turning increasingly to juvenile delinquency. In addition the new taxes have begun to come in for sharp criticism because a substantial fraction of them have had to be earmarked for *additions* to the relief rolls and for additions to the police force in order to deal with the increased juvenile delinquency. Finally, it is widely reported that many of the $x$ unemployed dropouts who are also now delinquents, are from families on the relief rolls and that they are embittered over what they take to be a "raw deal" given their fathers or mothers or older siblings, with respect to the promise of a "good job."

We shall now relate this situation to *some* of the symbolism we have employed for the *structure of planning*. The following were the primary consequences planned for: $P_1$, *reduction* of the overcrowding in schools—problem, $A_1$; $P_2$, *creation of new jobs* by the business community in order to reduce the relief rolls—problem, $A_2$; and the imposition of new taxes *to meet community needs*—problem, $A_3$—a fiscal imposition which proved to be more burdensome on low income groups than on high income groups. The solution, s, for $A_1$ produced the *undesirable* (D') secondary consequence, $S_s$, namely, that *some* of the $x$ students who were unable to find jobs turned to juvenile delinquency. The solution, $s'$, for $A_2$, produced the undesirable (D'), secondary consequence, $S_{s'}^{(1)}$, that the low wages offered for the $x$ new jobs that had been created quickly returned nearly all relief clients interested in working, to the relief rolls. Then, too, $s'$, produced the undesirable (D') secondary consequence, $S_{s'}^{(2)}$, of embittering the $x$ unemployed school dropouts from relief families whose would-be breadwinners felt that they were not receiving a living wage. In addition, $S_{s'}^{(3)}$, the inadvertent creation of $x$ jobs for school dropouts, proved to be a desirable (D) secondary consequence. The solution, $s''$, for $A_3$, produced $S_{s''}^{(1)}$, one undesirable (D'), secondary consequence, namely, complaints from the taxpayers concerning the way new tax funds were being used. In addition, $s''$ produced $S_{s''}^{(2)}$, the additional taxpayer criticism that the relief rolls were being *increased* rather than *diminished*.

We must also note that s worked against $s'$, to the extent that it created more unemployment, so that s can be said to have *inhibited* $s'$. Ironically $s''$ also *inhibited* $s'$ by providing some new tax funds that were subsequently used *in part* for additional welfare relief. Note, too, that s also *facilitated some* reduction of relief rolls (intended by $s'$, the creation of new jobs) to the degree that *some* of the $x$ dropouts who obtained jobs were from families on relief. Most of the secondary consequences we have mentioned are *intrinsic*. $S_s$, however, is an *extrinsic consequence,* since it was not the intention to increase community unemployment or juvenile delinquency by lowering the school-leaving age. There are also certain feedback situations to be noticed. Increased unemployment will mean increased juvenile delinquency which, in turn, will mean more taxes for increased police surveillance. More taxes will mean greater encouragement of unemployed or marginal workers to apply for relief and this increased volume of relief will require more taxes. Both of these situations are examples of positive feedback. The second of these two examples also illustrates a reciprocal (R) relationship. All the consequences mentioned above are of the variable (V) type. No all-or-none (A) consequences have been described. The reader can, by now, create some fresh examples for himself of the applicability of the *structural classification* set forth in Table 16-1.

### III. THE RELATION OF THE NOTION OF FEEDBACK TO COORDINATED SOCIAL PLANNING

Because feedback in general is of central importance in social planning due both to the *facilitation* and *inhibition* effects which the consequences of social planning will usually have upon one another, as well as the frequent relation of such effects to feedback action, itself, some comments are in order.[3] The reader can best appreciate the difficulties created by the facilitation and inhibition effects of anticipated and unanticipated consequences of planning, if he obtains a bowing acquaintance with the nature of feedback. These facilitation and inhibition effects take place within systems which have either already achieved equilibria at several points or are exhibiting progressive disequilibria at many points.

It is, therefore, important to remember that, in general, *negative feedback* is associated with the *stability* of a complex system, social or otherwise, while *positive feedback* may be associated with *increasing instability* in a system. Ashby[4] has shown that the stability or the instability of a system may be quite independent of what we are calling the facilitation or inhibition effects between a pair of factors or consequences. What social planning must aim for is the stability of the community system which is to be subjected to a multiplicity of planned for effects over time. For this reason column (4) of Table 16-1 must not be misinterpreted. Thus rows, 1 and 2 of column (4) refer, respectively, to facilitation and inhibition effects between variables, where both these types of effect are occurring within a social system undergoing positive feedback, that is, tending to move away from a position of equilibrium, if nothing is done to restore the original equilibrium. On the other hand, rows 3 and 4 of column (4) refer to the same two types of effect within a social system characterized by negative feedback, that is, by one which oscillates minimally about various and presumably desirable equilibria.

Both primary and secondary consequences in planning *usually* appear in the form of states, conditions, or attributes which are variable, therefore measureable, and, above all, therefore able to affect one another. Let us designate a set of such variable primary consequences as $P_1, P_2, \ldots P_n$ and a set of such variable secondary consequences as $S_1, S_2, \ldots S_m$, without specifying the problems, $A_1, A_2, \ldots A_r$, from whose treatments (that is, from the solutions to which) these consequences emerged. It is quite true that some consequences which social planners would take as their objectives are of the all-or-none variety, that is to say, they would be consequences which are *not variable* in any sense. This is, of course, recognized in column 8 of Table 16-1 by means of the letter, A, and when a consequence is of the all-or-none variety it may produce effects elsewhere but frequently other types of consequences cannot produce effects upon *it*.

The example already given of the location of a plant would be one such non-variable effect for, no matter what effects other consequences may have on the newly located, industrial plant, *the location, itself,* of that plant *cannot be changed by these consequences*—not, at least, as a

---

[3] For a detailed and technical exposition of feedback in economic systems, see Arnold Tustin, *The Mechanism of Economic Systems*, Cambridge, Massachusetts: Harvard University Press, 1953. 161 pp.

[4] Ross Ashby. *Op. cit.* See especially pp. 53–61.

direct result of their free play. The minds of the firm's managers may be changed after awhile as a result of these effects and they may decide to relocate once again. But this is not what we have in mind when we think of variables or factors which immediately affect one another. As a result of what we have just said, it is to be recognized that in the discussion which follows, the reader must bear in mind that we are talking about only such consequences—whether primary or secondary—which are variable and which can therefore affect one another immediately or, at least, after a modest time lag.

Variable pairs of consequences such as, for example, $P_1$ and $P_2$, which are so related that $P_1$ affects $P_2$ but $P_2$ has no effect upon $P_1$, have been given a special name by Ashby.[5] In the example given, $P_1$ is said to *dominate* $P_2$. A pair of variables which shows the relationship that Ashby speaks of as *dominance* is identical with the relationship which, in column 7 of Table 16-1, is spoken of as *unilateral* (U). A pair of variables, $P_3$ and $P_4$, such that changes in the measureable value of one of them affects the magnitude of the other, and vice versa, may be said to exist in a *feedback* relationship. This type of relationship is spoken of as *reciprocal,* in column 7 of the table. Variables in a feedback relationship may be said to show circularity of action between themselves.

Relationships of dominance or unilaterality are, of course, commonplace and the stuff of conventional mathematical analysis, particularly when our equations are meant to be applicable to events in the physical or the social world. When the physicist says that

$$s = \tfrac{1}{2}\, gt^2 \tag{1}$$

where $s$ is the distance which a body falls from rest and the constant, $g$, is the gravitational acceleration with which an unresisted body falls, he calls $t$, the independent variable, that is, the dominant variable, and $s$, the dependent variable. By this he means that the value of $s$ is dependent upon $t$ and that it would make no sense to speak of the value of $t$ as dependent upon $s$. Although $s$ is *dependent* upon $t$, $t$ is not the *cause* of $s$. In the present context such a statement would make no sense. All we mean is that as $t$ increases, $s$ increases.

Similarly, a social scientist may be interested in the number of people, $n$, who have heard a given rumor after the lapse of a certain amount of time. If he assumes that the rumor was started by one person and that each person in a population, who hears the rumor, passes it on *immediately* to $m$ other persons per unit time who have not as yet heard the rumor, he will express the growth or propagation of that rumor by means of the following equation.

$$n = (m + 1)^t \tag{2}$$

---

[5] Ross Ashby. *Op. cit.* Chapter 5.

Here again we find an expression of the relationship of dominance or unilaterality. The independent variable is again $t$, the dependent variable is $n$ and $m$ is a constant. The social scientist would now mean that the magnitude of $n$ would be dependent upon the value of $t$ and, once more, it would make no sense to speak of the value of $t$ as dependent upon $n$. Furthermore, $t$ is not the cause of $n$. All the social scientist means is that as $t$ increases, $n$ increases.

Relationships of circularity or feedback between variables are also commonplace both in nature and society but are usually the relationships which hold between variables which exist in large and complex systems.

The preceding discussion should provide the reader with a rough idea of the nature of feedback relationships. The relevance of such relationships to the task of achieving a coordinated type of planning in dealing with the burden of social complexity, should now be clear. The network of consequences which planners must face—both the primary consequences for which they plan and the secondary consequences which they foresee as inevitable accompaniments to the achievement of their objectives—constitute a tissue of factors which can facilitate or inhibit one another in unforeseen ways. These facilitation and inhibition effects may be such as to aggravate existing problems while simultaneously reducing or eliminating a number of conditions which the community finds both desirable and necessary for its healthy functioning. But even more important than these facilitation and inhibition effects, however, is the fact that many of the primary and secondary consequences of planning may mesh in the form of complex interdependencies which produce positive feedback. Such feedback may create nodes of disturbance in a complex social system. These nodes of disturbance become points of growing disequilibria in that system. In turn such disequilibria threaten the stability of the system and make its management exceedingly difficult.

In order to avoid the threat of such disequilibria it should be obvious that planners face a very special and difficult task. That task can be defined as the problem of finding a set of $r$ solutions to the $r$ problems of the community (all of which, hopefully, can be put into operation within a relatively short span of time), such that the $n$ primary consequences planned for and the $m$ secondary consequences which are the anticipated accompaniments of these $r$ solutions, yield the fewest possible points of subsequent disequilibria in the community regarded as a complex system. This is clearly not an easy matter. Because there is no unique set of $r$ solutions to the $r$ problems of a community, the formidability of the task of achieving coordinated social planning lies precisely here. The planners are, in effect, forced to find that set of $r$ solutions to the problems of the community which will (1) create a minimum amount of disequilibria due to positive feedback and (2) create a maximum amount of stability at important points in the functioning of a socially complex milieu, through the achievement of negative feedback [6] mechanisms of a socioeconomic nature. Most important of all, the finally chosen, *optimum* set of *r* solutions should (3) not only *solve* the *r* problems of the community—at least, for a reasonable stretch of time—but should also, at the same time, give rise to useful secondary consequences. These should be secondary consequences which not only support the primary consequences planned for but are also maximally facilitative with respect to other desirable and anticipated secondary effects and maximally inhibitory for undesirable but unavoidable secondary effects expected throughout the socioeconomic system.

Clearly, then, coordinated social planning is no easy matter and the burden of social complexity tends to become a staggering one to deal with, for planning which is meant to be taken seriously. Coordinated planning cannot escape these difficulties, largely because the interactions of many primary and secondary consequences in a complex social system, increases the likelihood that we will obtain many closed loops or sequences which will interact. The analysis and *management* of systems made up of many closed loops which interact then becomes considerably more complicated than the analysis and management of a socioeconomic system containing many closed loops most of which are independent and *do not* interact with one another.

The last emphasis which must be made is to remind the reader that coordinated social planning takes a variety of social goals for its objectives as well as economic goals. The network of consequences sought are both economic and *noneconomic* in nature. As a result the complexity of the task of providing solutions to the community's problems through coordinated, social planning is increased many times over. When all variables are economic, we are familiar with the types of units or dimensions by which they can be measured. But when the system contains variables of a social nature they are often of a kind for which units of measurement have not as yet been provided. To make matters more difficult we are often unfamiliar with the functional relationships, in a mathematical sense, which exist (1) among some of our social variables and (2) between some of our social variables and some of our economic variables. All of the preceding, then, indicate rather clearly the gravity of the task involved in coordinated, *social* planning.

---

[6] When we say that a system exhibits *negative feedback,* we mean that as the feedback effect travels round the system as an output, it operates later on at some point in the system and in such a way, as to diminish any displacements or changes which have occurred in the system. In short, it acts so as to bring about a condition in which certain variable attributes of the system operate within fixed limits. In this sense *negative feedback* is a prime characteristic of a self-regulating system. When we say that a system exhibits *positive feedback,* we refer to one in which an output or the change in, deviation of or displacement of some variable factor, is *amplified* or *increased* over time.

In view of all that has been said in this chapter, it is now appropriate to wind up our discussion of Table 16-1 by indicating how that table is to be properly read. Before leaving this section we shall therefore *briefly* illustrate in general the manner in which Table 16-1 is to be read by interpreting row 8. This row states that a primary consequence of a solution to a given problem may either *later produce* one of the primary consequences planned for in a solution to a second problem, but not sought for in the first, or the primary consequence sought for in the solution to the first problem, may have an effect upon a primary consequence which actually resulted from a solution to a different problem. This latter alternative is, of course, realistically, the more likely eventuality. Column (4) states that, regardless of which of these two eventualities occurred, the subsequent relationship between these two consequences is that one inhibits the other within a going system which is characterized by negative feedback, that is, by stabilities at many points within the system. Column (5) states that the inhibition effect may, from the standpoint of either the community or the planning body, be found desirable or undesirable. Column (6) notes that the effect(s) is *extrinsic* by definition, where two consequences resulted from solutions to different problems. This, of course, would be the *more likely eventuality*. Where they resulted from a solution to the same problem, they would, of course, be *intrinsic* by definition. Column (7) asserts the inhibition effect mentioned in column (4) may be either *unilateral,* in that one consequence impedes the play of the other but not vice versa, or the inhibition effect may be reciprocal, in that the play of each consequence tends to dampen the play of the other.[7] Column (8) indicates that the *effect produced* may be variable in nature or be of the all-or-none variety. In the same way the reader should be able to interpret for himself any other row of the table, with little difficulty.

What are some of the changes ahead in science and technology which promise to generate additional social complexity for modern man? Chapter 17 answers this question. It therefore makes use of a number of distinguished projections of future science and technology—science and technology which is bound to increase further the social complexity of the human environment. In order, however, to handle the increasing social complexity of our human environment, experts and planners have developed many techniques in recent years for managing that complexity in planning operations. A sample of these techniques is, therefore, briefly discussed in the following chapter.

[7] Perfect examples of such reciprocity occur when two opposing armies face each other and reduce one another's strength over time or when two political factions vie for the same limited amount of political power and tend to weaken each other as time passes.

# 17

# New World-A-Coming: The Promise of Science and Technology*

## I. INTRODUCTION

Basically social complexity is a function of two broad sets of causes: (1) the manner in which human ingenuity in the form of science, technology and invention change man's ecology, his resource future, his modes of production and his wants and (2) the ingenuity he expends in devising institutions to deal with the impacts of science and technology, the complexity of the procedures, activities and symbolic manipulations which are the going concerns of these same institutions, and both the foreseen and unforeseen relationships which these institutions exercise upon one another. The social complexity which has been the concern of Part III is being created to a large extent in our time by the types of technology which were stressed in Part I—automation, cybernation, the revolution in information and data-processing technology and the coming social and industrial applications of space technology.[1] Though this group of scientific and technical developments occupies the center of the stage at the present time and is, indeed, making life for modern man unbearably

---

* Chapter 17, with adaptations and modifications, has been taken from the following source: Henry Winthrop. "The Significance of Scientific Specialization and Interdisciplinary Developments for Higher Education." *Journal of Human Relations*. Vol. II, No. 5, Autumn 1963, 575–598.

[1] For some excellent examples of technological developments which have emerged from space technology and research but which are bound to have industrial, economic and social impacts, see the following volume. National Aeronautics and Space Administration. Scientific and Technical Information Division. *Conference on New Technology.* Held at the Lewis Research Center, Cleveland, Ohio, June 4–5, 1964. Published in Washington, D.C., 1964. 156 pp. This volume covers such matters as newer methods of fabrication, new materials, electric power generation (it contains a special section on magnetohydrodynamic converters which are mentioned later on in this summary), lubrication in difficult environments, liquid-metal technology, cryogenic and superconducting devices, ion and plasma technology and instrumentation for measurement and control.

complicated—and will surely continue to do so—the technologies in this group are certainly not the only sources of contemporary and coming social change.

It is equally true that the current picture of the social complexities facing modern, Western democratic man—of which only a few limited aspects have been discussed in Part III—does not even begin to indicate the complications in store for us. These current and coming social complexities are being dealt with by information-processing techniques using computers of ever increasing ingenuity and by certain developments in mathematics, logic and scientific method—developments which will be briefly discussed later on in this chapter.

## II. EMERGING SCIENTIFIC DEVELOPMENTS AND TECHNOLOGIES OF THE FUTURE

Analyses of the probable states of advanced societies are increasingly being made by both natural and social scientists and by technicians. These forecasts are based on voluminous data and on the sober and cautious analyses of thinkers who are painstakingly conservative in their projections. Conservative though they may be, the glimpses into the future which such thinkers provide is almost invariably more fascinating than many of the extravaganzas of either science-fiction Utopias or space-operas. As stimulating as writing in these genres may be, the prosaic descriptions of scientific and technical developments to come, together with their anticipated social consequences, prove to be even more fascinating.

In the meantime it should be mentioned that there exists a vast literature of systematic projections of this sort. It would be pointless to try to mention some of the leading contributions to this area. Apart from the fact that this would only constitute a form of scholarly name-dropping which serves no useful purpose, there would not be enough space to begin to do justice to developments which bid fair to change the course of human history. More will be gained, we believe, if we provide in connection with future scientific and technological developments, a few tables which sum up much of the exposition which would otherwise consume space. We shall *present one* of these tables and *refer* to several others and we shall say something about the information contained in all of them. Data in the form of tables, charts and graphs which present projected scientific and technological developments are not at all rare. The value of such systematic projections is that they frequently furnish synopses which will give the general reader a well organized and easily remembered picture of emerging developments. They will thus serve to increase his grasp of the subject and particularly of the relation of science and technology and their consequences to the complex future into which man is inescapably moving.

Let us, then, mention some of these well organized projections. Calder,[2] editor of the British journal, *New Scientist,* had furnished a series of tables outlining scientific and technical trends from 1964 to 1984. In one table he has provided a list of the major technical revolutions to be expected over this period, in terms of the character of the technical change, its technical aspects, the industrial, economic and service possibilities which may arise from it, its expected effects on individuals, some of its social consequences and the global changes it can be expected to produce. The same author has also provided a table of evolutionary changes over this same period, showing the expected patterns of change, some of the factors which will be deeply associated with these patterns and some of the consequences—social and otherwise—that these patterns are sure to produce. Finally, Calder has also provided a table showing at a glance the coming conflicts and choices which will be faced by modern man, in terms of the points at issue, the scientific and technical developments relevant to the settlement of these conflicting situations and some of the social and political issues and consequences which will be associated with human choice in these matters. Calder's projections are among the richest the author has seen to date.

Calder provides a table of *Major Technical Revolutions* which illustrates rather well the nature of some of our emerging technologies—other than those mentioned in Part I—and some of the social consequences to which they are more than likely to give rise. Thus Calder imaginatively but realistically notes that the revolution in information technology will, in the long run, probably produce the following social consequences: (1) the 'abolition' of libraries, paperwork and typists and (2) the end of newspapers as we know them. He notes that the rise of marine technologies to exploit the resources of the oceans must eventually result in ownership of the ocean floor by the UN or some other world organization which might conceivably supplant it in the future. In addition he points out that, because of the importance of the world's oceans (which occupy five-sixths of the earth's surface) in the production of weather, there will probably also be UN surveillance of climate-control experiments which are bound to be made in the future. He further points out that new forms of energy, including magneto-hydrodynamic generation (MHD),[3]

[2] Nigel Calder (editor). *The World in 1984.* Baltimore, Maryland: Penguin Books, 1965. 2 vols. V. 1, 215 pp.; V. 2, 190 pp. See Tables A, B, and C in the section entitled *Summing Up,* at the close of volume 2.

[3] A device which generates electricity from a moving, electrically conducting working fluid is called a magneto-hydrodynamic (MHD) converter and is used in place of the turbogenerator in a conventional cycle. In a MHD converter a moving fluid that is an electrical conductor moves at right angles to a magnetic field and serves to generate power.

the wide use of fuel cells as small power units and for energy storage, and the use of nuclear fission and fusion power, seem likely to lead to shifts of populations to regions where water and conventional energy sources are scarce. The opening up of such presently uninhabitable regions would, in a sense, be as historically significant as the discovery of the new world by Columbus.

*Evolutionary Changes,* another table supplied by Calder, presents some interesting projections concerning some of the social consequences of *patterns of science and technology.* Thus Calder sees the pattern of general industrial progress, including automation, as providing opportunities for decentralization with small-scale automated plants. Because industrial decentralization increases the possibility of community decentralization and because community decentralization is one of the major themes taken up in Part V, we feel that a projection of this sort may be an important augury of coming social change.

Projections of emerging scientific and technological developments and some of their possible social consequences, have also been made by what has come to be dubbed the Delphi Technique, first used at the Rand Corporation by Theodore J. Gordon [4] and Olaf Helmer. Bell [5] has given us a brief description of this technique and of some of the projections derived from its use. The intention of the Delphi Technique is to *systematize* the intuitive judgments of experts in science and technology with respect to projections of scientific and technological developments in the future and some of their social consequences. Gordon and Helmer used 82 experts: 20 engineers, 17 physical scientists, 14 logicians and mathematicians, 12 economists, nine social scientists, five writers, four operations analysts and one military officer. The members of this group were asked to make their predictions in the following six areas: (1) scientific breakthroughs, (2) population control, (3) automation, (4) space progress, (5) war prevention and (6) weapon systems. They were also

[4] Theodore Gordon is also the author of the following volume which is apposite in this connection. *The Future.* New York: St. Martin's Press, 1965. 184 pp.

[5] Daniel Bell. *"The Study of the Future." The Public Interest.* Vol. 1, No. 1, Fall 1965, 119–30. Professor Bell is also chairman of the American Academy of Arts and Sciences' Commission on the Year 2000. This Commission consists of a group of scholars and thinkers who are trying to anticipate what life will be like by the year, 2000. At the time of this writing this Commission had prepared for private circulation, four of five planned volumes, bearing the general title, *Working Papers of the Commission on the Year 2000.* The five volumes carry the following individual titles: I. *Preliminary Statement. Transcripts of Commission Meetings;* II. *The Next Thirty-Four Years, a Context for Speculation;* III. *Questions and Caveats about Forecasting the Political Structure;* IV. *Values and Rights;* and V. *Intellectual Institutions. The Life-Cycle. The International System.* A condensed version of these working papers appeared in the following source: *Daedalus. Journal of the American Academy of Arts and Sciences.* Summer 1967. Issue title: *Toward the Year 2000: work in progress.* 639–994. This is to be followed by an issue entitled *America's Changing Environment,* which will be the first volume to emerge from the Academy's Project 1976. Actually the Commission prepared six volumes, designated as I, II, II-A, III, IV, and V.

asked to predict the probable time of breakthrough. The possibilities they listed were resubmitted independently to each member of the group twice, that is, three submissions in all. The resubmissions were made for methodological refinements. This laborious panel technique was employed in order to achieve independence of judgment by having each expert participate independently of the others. The resubmissions were employed in order to achieve a feedback effect which enabled a respondent to reconsider his choices, reassert abandoned choices or predict new probabilities for his already declared choices. Predictions were made for three different periods: up to 1984, 1984 to A.D. 2000 and A.D. 2000 to A.D. 2100.

A substantial but brief picture of developments to come, made by the 82 experts, and which will increase enormously the social complexity of man's future, is suggested by the following brief enumeration of *some* of the predictions made. They are listed without comment. The reader should note, however, that some of these eventualities have been among the themes of Part I. Others will be taken up *in extenso* in Part V.

*The World of 1984.* Automation in agriculture, desalinated sea water, population fertility control, medical transplantation of natural organs and implantation of artificial plastic and electronic organs, widespread use of personality-control drugs, sophisticated teaching machines, automated libraries, worldwide communication by satellite relay systems and automatic translating machines, the establishment of a permanent lunar base, deep-space laboratories, and a considerable number of highly novel weapons of warfare.

*The World of 2000.* Large-scale ocean farming and the manufacture of synthetic protein, *controlled* thermonuclear power, raw materials from the ocean, the beginnings of regional weather control, general immunization against bacterial and viral diseases, the correction of faulty heredity through molecular engineering, advances in automation from robot-machines performing menial services to sophisticated, high-IQ machines, a universal language derived from computer technology, the mining and manufacturing of propellent materials on the moon, terrestrial ballistic transport and continued advances in military technology.

*The World in the Year 2100.* Chemical control of the aging process, the growth of new limbs and organs through biochemical stimulation, man-machine symbiosis enabling a person to raise his intelligence through direct electromechanical tie-in of the brain to a computer,[6] household robots, remote facsimile reproduction of newspapers and magazines in the home, completely automated highway transportation,

---

[6] The reader should note that this method of improving human intelligence to deal with increasing social complexity, was not discussed in Chapter 13. Also not discussed in that chapter was the possibility for improving intellectual capacity through recent advances in brain chemistry.

international agreements with respect to the distribution of the earth's resources and establishment of a permanent lunar colony with regularly scheduled traffic between the earth and its satellite.

Limitations of space prevent a detailed discussion of the projections that were achieved by the Delphi Technique. There are, however, according to Gordon and Helmer, four areas in which—if we are to take the predictions seriously—a major effort will have to be concentrated in order to avoid disaster. Bell [7] describes these four areas as follows:

*War prevention.* While the odds against another war within the next generation are considered to be 80 percent (within 25 years), a 20 percent chance is intolerable. The main danger appears to be in mutually undesired escalation and downright inadvertence; hence a major effort to seek improved ways of forestalling such disaster becomes necessary.

*Equitable distribution of resources.* While there is a consensus that eventually there will be an abundance of resources in energy, food, and raw materials, there is no foregone conclusion that such resources will be available in time for the increasing world population, or that effective means of an equitable world distribution will have been found and agreed upon. To solve such problems would clearly be a great contribution toward the prevention of big or small wars.

*Social reorganization.* The anticipated growth in the amount of automation is likely to reshape the industrialized nations. While improved and highly automated methods of education will make the acquisition of technical skills available to a larger fraction of the population, only the very ablest people are likely to be needed to manage the new, automated economy. Since robots are apt to take over many of the services, especially the more menial ones, large segments of the population may find themselves without suitable employment within an economy of potential abundance. Farsighted and profoundly revolutionary measures may have to be taken to cope with this situation.

*Eugenics.* Finally, a problem, though not yet upon us, which will require much forethought and wisdom. There is the possibility—within a generation or two—of selectively extending an individual's life span through biochemical methods and of selective eugenic control through molecular genetic engineering. (p. 130)

Arthur C. Clarke, fellow of the Royal Astronomical Society and former chairman of the British Interplanetary Society, has constructed a *Chart of the Future*,[8] which attempts to look ahead scientifically and technologically, stopping at the year 2100. For the period between 1970 and 2100, Clarke lists a series of developments in transportation, communication and information, materials manufacturing, biology and chemistry, and physics. Because Clarke's projections are among the most interesting,

[7] Daniel Bell. *Op. cit.*

[8] Chart "The Future" (Page 233) PROFILES OF THE FUTURE by Arthur C. Clarke. Copyright © 1962 by Arthur C. Clarke. Reprinted by permission of Harper & Row, Publishers.

while being at the same time among the most controversial, I have chosen to reproduce it in this chapter. A caution is expressed by Clarke, himself.

The chart given is not, of course, to be taken too seriously, but it is both amusing and instructive to extrapolate the time scale of past scientific achievement into the future. . . . (p. 234)

The following items in Clarke's table are important, regardless of whether or not one feels he has to strain at them.

1. The achievement sometime between A.D. 2070 and A.D. 2080 of speed near that of the speed of light.

2. The achievement of robots sometime between A.D. 2020 and 2030 —robots which will presumably be even more intelligent than the creations of science fiction.

3. The creation between A.D. 2080 and A.D. 2090 of machines whose intelligence will exceed that of man's. A development of this sort would give rise to dilemmas never before faced by man. Could man control machines or simulacra which would be more intelligent than he was? Would not such machines attempt to refashion terrestrial society in a manner which they felt to be an improvement over human arrangements—a refashioning which might not at all please their creator, man? Finally, would the kind of a world which could be brought into doing by creatures more intelligent than man but which might not possess feelings, emotions and compassion, be one in which men could feel secure, comfortable and happy?

4. The creation of "Cyborgs" by A.D. 1990. These are cybernetic organisms, that is, human bodies which have machines hitched to them or built into them, to take over or modify some of their functions.

5. A package deal which includes the control of heredity sometime between A.D. 2020 and A.D. 2030, the development of bioengineering [9] between A.D. 2030 and A.D. 2040 and the production of intelligent animals sometime between A.D. 2040 and A.D. 2050. The latter will, of course, make a reality out of the fantasy-theme which H. G. Wells [10] incorporated into *The Island of Dr. Moreau*.

6. The creation of artificial life around A.D. 2070. This would mean that for the first time in human history man will play at being God.

[9] Bioengineering refers to the science and art of redesigning the human body so as to improve its present functions and eliminate its present shortcomings and defects—sensory, motor, perceptual, neurological, etc. The scientific and technological possibilities in this direction are now enormous. See in this connection the following volumes. 1. D. S. Halacy, Jr. *Cyborg: Evolution of the Superman*. New York: Harper & Row, 1965. 207 pp. 2. Richard R. Landers. *Man's Place in the Dybosphere*. Englewood Cliffs, New Jersey: Prentice-Hall, 1966. 266 pp.

[10] H. G. Wells. *The Island of Dr. Moreau*. pp. 79–182. In *Seven Science Fiction Novels*. New York: Dover Publications, 1934. 1015 pp.

*Table 17-1.*   The Scientific and Technological Future as Envisaged
by Arthur C. Clarke *

### NOW

| Date | Trans-portation | Communication Information | Materials Manu-facturing | Biology Chemistry | Physics |
|---|---|---|---|---|---|
| 1960 | Spaceship | Communication satellite | | Protein structure | Nucleon structure |

### THE FUTURE

| Date | Trans-portation | Communication Information | Materials Manu-facturing | Biology Chemistry | Physics |
|---|---|---|---|---|---|
| 1970 | Space lab Lunar landing Nuclear rocket | Translating machines | Efficient electric storage | Cetacean languages | |
| 1980 | Planetary landings | Personal radio | | Exobiology | Gravity waves |
| 1990 | | Artificial intelligence | Fusion power | Cyborgs | |
| 2000 | Colonizing planets | Global library | "Wireless" energy Sea mining | Time, perception enhancement | Sub-nuclear structure |
| 2010 | Earth probes | Telesensory devices | Weather control | | |
| 2020 | Interstellar probes | Logical languages Robots | | Control of heredity | Nuclear catalysts |
| 2030 | | Contact with extra-terrestrials | Space mining | Bioengineering | |
| 2040 | | | Transmu-tation | Intelligent animals | |
| 2050 | Gravity control "Space drive" | Memory playback | | Suspended animation | |
| 2060 | | Mechanical educator | Planetary engineering | | Space, time distor-tion |

| Date | Trans- portation | Communication Information | Manu- facturing Materials | Biology Chemistry | Physics |
|------|------------------|--------------------------|---------------------------|-------------------|---------|
|      |                  | Coding of artifacts      |                           | Artificial life   |         |
| 2070 |                  |                          |                           |                   |         |
|      | Near-light speeds |                         | Climate control           |                   |         |
| 2080 |                  | Machine intelli- gence exceeds man's |               |                   |         |
|      | Interstellar flight |                       |                           |                   |         |
| 2090 | Matter transmitter |                        | Replicator                |                   |         |
|      | Meeting with     | World brain              |                           | Immortality       |         |
| 2100 | extra- terrestrials |                       | Astronomical engineering  |                   |         |

* See footnote 8, this chapter.

7. The biggest bombshell in Clarke's table is his guess that man will be able to achieve immortality sometime between A.D. 2090 and A.D. 2100. The human mind, *as we know it at the present time,* is simply unable to grasp the social problems which such a situation could produce.

For those who are more interested in projections of the immediate future which are less overwhelming to the imagination, Diebold [11] has produced an interesting timetable of expected changes in information technology from 1965 to 1975. These are changes of interest solely to modern industrial man. The effects of these technological changes have been classified into the following six categories: changes in business structure, specialized applications, emergence of new information-oriented businesses, information system developments, communicating with the computer and impact on everyday life. The constellation of consequences which are of prime interest to Diebold, is, of course, the effects of the "second industrial revolution" on management policies and practices.

Some of the forecasts made by Diebold in the six categories mentioned, and in the form of what he calls an *Information Technology Timetable, are the following.* (1) *Changes in Business Structure:* widespread use in entrepreneurial decision-making and strategy development; important changes in organizational structure; (2) *Specialized Applications:* machine intelligence applied to system design (optimization) prob-

11 John Diebold. *Beyond Automation. Managerial Problems of an Exploding Technology.* New York: McGraw-Hill, 1964. 220 pp.

lems; legal research; automated newspaper publishing; (3) *Emergence of New Information-Oriented Businesses:* data processing as a public utility service; automated information services—a new form of publishing; (4) *Information System Developments:* integrated communications switching under computer control; huge low-cost file memories; integrated circuitry; information storage and retrieval-powerful indexing approaches; (5) *Communicating With the Computer:* visual presentation with optional hardcopy output; spoken commands to computer; (6) *Impact on Everyday Life:* weather prediction; medical diagnosis; patient monitoring in hospital beds; centralized medical records (large cities only); automatic language translation; visual communication (picture phone); enhanced productivity—more leisure time.

It would be well nigh impossible to enumerate all those emerging technologies which are bound to create drastic social change in the decades ahead and, even more importantly, increasing social complexity. *The gap is increasing between this growing social complexity which, as we tried to point out in Chapter 14, is in principle measureable, and our willingness to recognize its significance and do something about it.* Clearly the most important thing that we must do is to so control that growing social complexity as to make it serve the democratic tradition rather than to allow it to interfere with the benefits which democracy can offer. The control of the social and economic complexity which is being generated by modern science and technology is meanwhile being attempted by new methods of analysis which are increasingly becoming part of the stock in trade of the planning expert, social scientist and social engineer but which, unfortunately, are matters which are completely unfamiliar to the average citizen of a modern democracy. It is important to be made acquainted in a very general sense with *some* of the newer methods which are being employed to deal with this growing social complexity. We shall therefore now turn to a brief description of some of these newer methods.

### III. METHODS CURRENTLY BEING EMPLOYED FOR DEALING WITH OUR INCREASING SOCIAL COMPLEXITY

It would, of course, be impossible literally to list all methods of dealing with social complexity, but some can be given through the representative items listed in Table 17-2.

We shall discuss only the first four items in the Table. These will be sufficiently representative to give the reader a rough idea of the ways in which the modern social technician and planner are able to deal with the social and economic complexities of human ecology.

The term *cybernetics,* as originally introduced by the mathematician,

*Table 17-2.*     A Sample List of Some of the Newer Methods of Analysis for Dealing
with Social and Economic Complexity

---

1. Cybernetics
2. Operations Research
3. General Systems Theory
4. New developments in economic theory and their applications, e.g., input–output analysis, linear programming, activity analysis, etc.
5. New mathematical developments and their applications in the social sciences, e.g., game theory, theory of convex sets, polygons and polyhedral cones, as used in activity analysis, graph theory, Monte Carlo theory, etc.
6. Administration and Organization Theory
7. Mathematical models in the social sciences
8. Science and Information Theory
9. Decision-Theory
10. Operant learning and conditioning and their educational and social implications
11. The use of symbolic logic in scientific research in the natural and social sciences
12. Data-Processing and Computer Theory and Its Applications
13. Human Engineering and Human Factors Analysis
14. Systems Analysis in the Natural and Social Sciences
15. Simulation technique in the behavioral and social sciences
16. Recent developments in the Philosophy of Science
17. New interdisciplinary fields in the natural and social sciences, e.g., zetetics, the unity of science movement, etc.

---

Norbert Wiener,[12] was defined as control and communication in the animal and the machine. Its subject matter ranges from such control mechanisms as servomechanisms, mathematical calculators, automatic pilots, and homeostatic physiological mechanisms to the nerves and brain of the human body and to societies that regulate themselves by highly rationalized, smooth-working institutional arrangements. All of these are feedback mechanisms in some sense. Ross Ashby describes cybernetics as a change of attitude towards a machine, in which one asks not "What individual act will it produce here and now?" but "What are *all* the possible behaviors that it can produce?" As a discipline, cybernetics possesses two great advantages: it offers a single vocabulary and a single set of concepts suitable for representing the most diverse types of systems, and it offers a method for the scientific treatment of that type of system in which complexity is outstanding and too important to be ignored. Cybernetics has been interdisciplinary in nature since its inception.

Because of its applicability over a wide area, it has captured the interests of physiologists, psychologists, biologists, medical researchers, mathematicians, linguists, electrical engineers, radio engineers, sociologists, philosophers, anthropologists, psychiatrists, physicists, and many other types of specialists. It has also found wide application in these areas and even more in problems that often cut across the range of informa-

---

[12] Norbert Wiener. *Cybernetics or Control and Communication in the Animal and the Machine.* New York: Wiley, 1948. 194 pp.

tion and concerns of several traditional disciplines. As one of the most exciting developments of subject matter and method that aims to provide intellectual integration, cybernetics has revolutionary implications for modern education. Inasmuch as it represents an intellectual approach that stands at the crossroads of the sciences, providing great opportunities in cross-fertilization, it is able to deal with a variety of what appears at first glance to be highly disparate questions. Among these are such questions as: How does a machine "think"? How does an unmanned missile find its predetermined target? By what means does a modern electronic computer monitor its own errors? By what means can we predict the different courses of alternative behavior available to human subjects or to whole societies? What common set of rules are equally applicable to the decisions of gamblers, chess players, or businessmen operating in a specified context? Cybernetics is in a position to give some sort of an answer to these and many other questions of even greater importance. For these reasons it will have to be reflected very substantially in the curriculum of the future.

*Operations research* may be defined in several ways. One definition would define it as the scientific study of complex organizations aimed at identifying problems and giving decision-makers a quantitative basis for decisions that will increase effectiveness in achieving objectives. Another definition would lay a somewhat larger stress on method and define operations research as the application of scientific methods, techniques, and tools to problems involving the operations of a system, so as to provide those in control of the system with optimum solutions to their problems. Operations research is interdisciplinary both in *method* and *content.* Among its *methods* are such classical procedures as algebra, calculus, differential equations, geometry, mathematical statistics, probability theory, symbolic logic, and so on. More important, however, are recently developed mathematical tools that it uses extensively. These include model-making, game theory, Monte Carlo procedures, linear programming, servo theory, waiting-line or queueing theory, information theory, and many other new types of methodology too numerous to mention here. With respect to *content* it draws upon information in all the natural, social, management, and administrative sciences. With respect to the types of study it undertakes, one of the better classifications of operations research objectives, chiefly of interest to industrial organizations, has been given by Goodeve. This author classifies operational research studies as follows: [13]

I. *To do with people alone*
   (a) Organization and management
   (b) Absenteeism and labor relations

[13] Charles Goodeve, "Operational Research as a Science," *Operations Research for Management.* Baltimore: The Johns Hopkins Press, 1954. Pp. 50–51.

      (c) Economics
      (d) Market research
  II. *To do with people and machines*
      (a) Efficiency and productivity
      (b) Organization of flow in factories
      (c) Methods of quality control, inspection, and sampling
      (d) Organization of technological change
  III. *To do with movement*
      (a) Transport
      (b) Stocking, distribution, and handling
      (c) Communications

However, operations research has been just as extensively used in the provision of health services, in administration, in military logistics and tactics, the improvement of agricultural practices, systems analysis, design requirements and arrangements of machines, signals, controls, and so on, and economic and social planning. Furthermore, it shows great promise of extension to many other fields. The variety of these fields can be gleaned from a rapid survey of the contents of its leading American journal, *Operations Research,* which is the journal of the Operations Research Society of America. It is hard to see how the complex problems generated for the human condition by a society based on science, technology, and its industrial applications can be solved in the immediate future without the widespread application of operations research methods. It is also difficult to envisage the possibility of higher education claiming to be able to fulfill its function of turning out individuals who have some comprehension of the problems and issues of their time and of the means for dealing with these unless they have been introduced to some extent to the nature and methods of operations research. For these reasons it seems fairly certain that curricular revisions of the future will probably have to make an ample effort to recognize the far-reaching importance of this newer, interdisciplinary field.

*General Systems Theory,* highly interdisciplinary in nature, was developed by the distinguished biologist, Ludwig von Bertalanffy. Its subject matter is the formulation and derivation of those principles, theories, and relations that are valid for systems in general. It seeks to develop a consistent body of theory that will account for the appearance of structural similarities or *isomorphies* in different fields that are now the standard and traditional areas of study in higher education. Bertalanffy has, himself, given a succinct account of its objectives, which recognizes its importance for integration in scientific education. He has put it this way:

Summarizing, the aims of General Systems Theory can be indicated as follows:

(a) There is a general tendency towards integration in the various sciences, natural and social.

(b) Such integration seems to be centered in a general theory of systems.

(c) Such theory may be an important means for aiming at exact theory in the nonphysical fields of science.

(d) Developing unifying principles running "vertically" through the universes of the individual sciences, this theory brings us nearer to the goal of the unity of science.

(e) This can lead to a much-needed integration in scientific education.[14] (p. 2)

One of the finest accounts of the nature and purposes of General Systems Theory was furnished by Kenneth Boulding in a paper that appeared in the first yearbook of the Society. It should be a must for every reader who wishes to understand the objectives of this multidisciplinary endeavor, its social significance, and its relevance to problems of curricular revision in higher education. I cannot refrain from drawing a few excerpts from this paper because of the succinct way in which it brings out the purposes of General Systems Theory.

. . . The crisis of science today arises because of the increasing difficulty of . . . talk among scientists as a whole. Specialization has outrun Trade, communication between the disciplines becomes increasingly difficult, and the Republic of Learning is breaking up into isolated subcultures with only tenuous lines of communication between them—a situation which threatens intellectual civil war. The reason for this breakup in the body of knowledge is that in the course of specialization the receptors of information themselves become specialized. Hence physicists only talk to physicists, economists to economists—worse still, nuclear physicists only talk to nuclear physicists and econometricians to econometricians. One wonders sometimes if science will not grind to a stop in an assemblage of walled-in hermits, each mumbling to himself words in a private language that only he can understand. In these days the arts may have beaten the sciences to this desert of mutual unintelligibility, but that may be merely because the swift intuitions of art reach the future faster than the plodding leg work of the scientist. The more science breaks into subgroups, and the less communication is possible among the disciplines, however, the greater chance there is that the total growth of knowledge is being slowed down by the loss of relevant communications. The spread of specialized deafness means that someone who ought to know something that someone else knows isn't able to find it out for lack of generalized ears.

It is one of the main objectives of General Systems Theory to develop these generalized ears and, by developing a framework of general theory, to enable one specialist to catch relevant communications from others. Thus the econo-

14 "General Systems Theory." *The yearbook of the Society for General Systems Research.* Vol. 1, 1956. 1–10, by Ludwig von Bertalanffy, Department of Zoology and Center for Advanced Study in Theoretical Psychology, University of Alberta, Edmonton, Canada. This publication is issued under the auspices of The Society for General Systems Research, Ann Arbor, Michigan and is edited by Ludwig von Bertalanffy and Anatol Rapoport.

mist who realizes the strong formal similarity between utility theory in economics and field theory in physics is probably in a better position to learn from the physicists than one who does not. Similarly a specialist who works with the growth concept—whether the crystallographer, the virologist, the cytologist, the physiologist, the psychologist, the sociologist or the economist—will be more sensitive to the contributions of other fields if he is aware of the many similarities of the growth process in widely different empirical fields.[15] (pp. 11–12)

*Linear programming* may properly be defined as the techniques used to find the optimum relationship between a number of interdependent variables—or the means of obtaining the very best course of action where many courses of action exist. Put in more prosaic fashion, linear programming is concerned with the selection of rational means of an optimum course of action from among a set of such courses of action. It is highly mathematical in nature and has been successfully applied to problems in the following industrial areas: product allocation, distribution and shipping, market research, job and salary evaluation, the manufacture of blended products in industry, materials handling, and production planning. Its applications, however, are not restricted to modern industry. It has also been applied to national social and economic planning, particularly in underdeveloped countries, to the construction of optimum diets in the field of nutrition, to problems in the optimum allocation of limited resources, and to scheduling problems of every sort. The Berlin Airlift, for instance, as a scheduling problem, was successfully dealt with in part by linear programming. Linear programming has also been applied to many other types of problems too numerous to list here. It is highly interdisciplinary in method and content, an attribute that the literature on the subject quickly reveals.

The term *activity analysis,* or *linear activity analysis,* should be mentioned in this connection. It refers to the application of linear programming techniques to such problems as the allocation of scarce resources to a finite set of objectives, the allocation of scarce resources over time (in connection with welfare economics), newer methods of establishing models for the analysis of international trade, and the application of linear programming methods of analysis to what economists refer to as general equilibrium theory and to models of expanding economies. One of the contributors to this field who may legitimately be regarded as having pioneered in it is Tjalling C. Koopmans.[16, 17] Also in connection with linear programming one should mention *input–output analysis,* pio-

---

[15] Kenneth Boulding. "General Systems Theory—The Skeleton of Science." *The yearbook of the Society for General Systems Research.* Vol. 1, 1956. 11–17. This article was originally published in *Management Science,* Vol. 2, No. 2, 1956, 197–208.

[16] Tjalling C. Koopmans (editor). *Activity Analysis of Production and Allocation.* Cowles Commission Monograph 13. New York: Wiley, 1951. 404 pp.

[17] Tjalling C. Koopmans. *Three Essays on the State of Economic Science.* New York: McGraw-Hill, 1957. 231 pp.

neered by Wassily F. Leontief.[18] Input–output analysis is concerned with the analysis and control of an entire economy through the use of mathematical methods as applied to the basic empirical features of a going economy. These features are essentially the supply and purchase relationships of industries to each other, the relation of levels of production to consumer demand, and the ratio of the cost of raw materials purchased by one industry from another industry to the dollar value of the total output of the former.

To the extent that modern economic and social planning probably cannot be successfully carried on without the application of linear programming methods, higher education should be prepared to provide the young with some intellectual contact with this field—a contact that emphasizes its importance for a philosophy of liberal education. To the extent that liberal education in a democracy insists that the average citizen have some understanding of the nature of our current issues and problems and of the intellectual means for their solution, it would be the height of educational neglect not to give some emphasis to this new field. Both these objectives can reasonably be met by curricular revision that makes an explicit attempt to furnish some knowledge of the intellectual synthesis provided by linear programming.

The preceding material, then, on new scientific developments and technologies which are emerging [19] and on some of the newer methods

18 Wassily F. Leontief. *The Structure of American Economy, 1919–1939. An Empirical Application of Equilibrium Analysis* (second edition). New York: Oxford University Press, 1951. 264 pp.

19 The reader should not fail to consult one of the most distinguished publications in this connection, which has come to the author's knowledge. I am referring to the Ciba Foundation volume entitled *Man and His Future,* edited by Gordon Wolstenholme, Boston: Little Brown And Company, 1963. 410 pp. The galaxy of distinguished scientists and Nobel Prize winners contributing to this volume, includes the following well known names: Julian Huxley, Colin Clark, Gregory Pincus, Albert Szent-Györgyi, Hermann J. Muller, Joshua Lederberg, Hudson Hoagland, Brock Chisholm and J. S. Haldane. Also of value in this connection will be the following: Dennis Gabor. *Inventing The Future.* London: Secker & Warburg, 1963. 231 pp.

For more technical source materials along this line, see the following items. Robert O. MacBride. *The Automated State. Computer Systems as a New Force in Society.* Philadelphia: Chilton Book Company, 1967. 407 pp. William H. Davenport and Daniel Rosenthal (editors). *Engineering: Its Role and Function in Human Society.* New York: Pergamon Press, 1967. 284 pp. Edgar L. Morphet and Charles O. Ryan (editors). *Prospective Changes in Society by 1980. Including Some Implications for Education.* Denver: Project: Designing Education For The Future, 1966. 268 pp. See also the volumes published by NASA based on the various conferences devoted to recent science and technology and to their possible effects. In particular see the *Conference on Space, Science, and Urban Life* (NASA SP-37), 1963, *Peaceful Uses of Space* (NASA SP-51), 1964, *Space-Age Planning* (NASA SP-40), 1963 and *Conference on New Technology* (NASA SP-5015), 1964. For an untechnical approach to this whole area, the following material is to be highly recommended: *Kaiser Aluminum News,* 1966. Six special issues devoted to the future social impacts of science and technology. 1. *The Dynamics of Change.* 2. *The Promised Land.* 3. *Telemobility—When Far is Near.* 4. *Life with a Little Black Box.* 5. *The Theory of the Leisure Masses.* 6. *Foreseeing the Unforeseeable.*

being employed for the analysis of social and economic complexity, should provide some food for thought on the *relationships* between the social complexities created by science and technology and the methods democracies must employ for dealing with such complexity. Any effort to understand social change in a technologically based democracy must clearly take stock of the relationships just mentioned.

# SUMMARY OF PART III

The reader by now will realize only too well the burden which social complexity creates for modern man. That burden is clearly relevant to the distribution of human intelligence and to man's efforts to guide the human community, through purposeful planning. We have shown what can be done to improve human intelligence and what kind of thinking will be required for coordinated social planning that is intended to make community life workable and humane. Finally, we have indicated those changes in science and technology [20] which can be expected to increase social complexity in the near future and some of the modes of analysis men now use to deal with social complexity.

[20] The reader who is *deeply* interested in some of the more recent scholarly work along these lines should consult the following materials. Erich Jantsch. *Technological Forecasting in Perspective.* Paris: Organization for Economic Co-Operation and Development, 1967. 401 pp. John McHale and Buckminster Fuller (editors). *World Design Science Decade 1965–1975.* Carbondale, Illinois: World Resources Inventory, Southern Illinois University, 6 vols. Published over the period, 1963–7. John McHale (editor). *2000+.* London: February 1967. 101 pp. This is a reprint of the British journal, *Architectural Design,* which appeared in February 1967. Robert W. Prehoda. *Designing The Future. The Role of Technological Forecasting.* Philadelphia: Chilton Book Company, 1967. 310 pp. Olaf Helmer. *Social Technology.* New York: Basic Books, 1966. 108 pp. Bertrand de Jouvenel. *The Art of Conjecture.* New York: Basic Books, 1967. 307 pp. Henry Winthrop. "The Sociologist and the Study of the Future." *The American Sociologist,* Vol. 3, No. 2, May, 1968. 136–45.

# IV

# The Pathologies of
## Overurbanization

## ORIENTATION TO PART IV

Part IV opens with a discussion of what constitutes an *authentic* community. It is important to have a clear picture of the attributes of a genuine community in order to be able to *contrast* community authenticity with some of the leading characteristics of the modern, large-scale, urban center. In this way we can get a glimpse of what we have lost. We shall therefore select for attention urban pathologies of a social, psychological, cultural, and political nature. This will be followed by an extensive discussion of the *physical* pathologies which are deeply associated with *overurbanization*. When one's milieu is chronically pathological, there is a danger that the pathological will be taken as normal. Part IV is intended to provide a bill of particulars against urban life as we know it now. If man, in the near future, should seek to *restore* a genuine sense of community to social life, the pathologies discussed in Part IV are among the many urban pathologies he must remove permanently from the community. Most current trends are towards increased urbanization. However, authentic communities on a small scale are now possible which will have to depend on modern developments in science and technology and on the physical design of new types of community. A discussion of what can be done in this latter direction is the theme of Part V.

# 18

# In Quest of Community*

A sense of community is essentially a psychological matter. We may think of it as an extension of the I–Thou relationship—which is essentially dyadic—to a larger group of persons. We cannot enumerate *all* the attributes and processes which collectively would testify to the fact that a genuine sense of community is being shared by a given population. We can, however, mention here some of the focal considerations which indicate the presence of an authentic sense of community.

Among the characteristics of a true community, then, we may list the following. (1) The people in it share similar activities, and the development of similar values, attitudes and beliefs. (2) They share common problems and act jointly and amicably to solve them. (3) They may individually engage in dissimilar activities but many of these prove to be interdependent. (4) There is a strong identification among members of the community with one another or, at least, intellectually and in principle this identification can be aroused on behalf of people whom one has never met face-to-face. This identification is a major ingredient in what the German sociologist, Tönnies, called *gemeinschaft*. Self-interest may be achieved through *gemeinschaft* but, nevertheless, the individual tends to locate the sphere of self-interest within the framework of community needs, practices and expectations. This does not mean that his *weltanschaaung* is some variant of that of the community. What it does mean is that no matter how original and radical a departure his phi=losophy of life may be—as contrasted with that of the community—nevertheless he finds some way of giving expression to it within the operating community to which he already finds himself attached psychologically. In short, a true communal spirit which is, at the same time, an enlightened and knowledgeable one, does not demand too much conformity in anything except mutual affection, mutual aid, social altruism and fellow-feeling. (5) Shared experience is sought and found to be very satisfying. (6) A pattern of adaptation to both familiar and unfamiliar events is common and if the sense of community which exists, is a mature

* Chapter 18, with adaptations and modifications, has been taken from the following source: Henry Winthrop. "In Quest Of Community." *Journal of Human Relations.* Vol. 14, No. 3, Third Quarter 1966, 457–472.

one, that pattern of adaptation will be intelligently modified as the occasion requires.

There is another way of thinking of the psychological sense of community. That is the recognition that in a genuine community fellowship exists in depth—not the superficial, polite, back-slapping and role-playing camaraderie which is so often mistakenly called fellowship, but rather those human relationships in which people understand and appreciate one another's life styles. Likewise in a true community, mutual aid is conspicuous, that is to say, people help one another, trust one another, and underwrite one another, so that if misfortune falls upon one individual, others will do what they can to relieve his plight, liquidate his adversities and enable him to make a fresh start. In a true community certain traits are conspicuous, even if they are not found everywhere in the community—such traits as goodwill, neighborliness, fair play, courage, tolerance, open-minded inquiry, and patience. Where a valid community exists we also tend to find a common background of experience and a shared history as well as the habit of cooperation.

The life-style of a true community is often the result of generations of shared experience and a behavioral repertoire which is the by-product of a fairly stable environment. A community life-style, however, may also be the joint creation of a number of like-minded people who have voluntarily associated together to give concrete expression to what they hold to be the elements of a good life. In this case there will also be a common behavioral repertoire and a spectrum of shared satisfactions, but these are more likely to be the product of conscious planning aided and abetted by intelligence, education, social maturity and social altruism.

One of the remarkable things about the collective behavior of the persons in a genuine community is the amount of democracy that is generated in dealing with their common problems. This democracy, whether conducted by a village council guided by the village elders or by the tried and tested, wise and fair-minded judgment of members of the little hamlet involved, often reflects the fact that nearly everyone has a pronounced sense of fellow-feeling for most of the other members of the community. A "we-mindedness" is often present, which bespeaks a genuine sense of empathy, social altruism and social concern. It is a by-product of a common understanding that all will be heard, that all opinions will be respected, even if all are not given equal weight. There is a common understanding that any community decision finally arrived at will reflect a genuine consensus rather than the "phony" type of consensus reached at a committee meeting in which one gauges what one says by the possible consequences—favorable or unfavorable—one's words may have upon one's standing and one's future.

In fact committee consensus in our time often seeks to give the appearance of an organizational, institutional or neighborhood cooperation. It tries to do this when—in fact—each person present seeks his own personal, departmental or group advantage. In seeking such advantage the effort is made to try to give the impression, through established roles, modulation of voice, stereotypy of phrase and close adherence to the rules of parliamentary procedure, that he is a "member of the team" and thinking of the good of the whole.

Some readers may have a feeling for this brief résumé of the psychological attributes of a genuine sense of community, if they have been fortunate enough to have known a close family life. There are few things which can convey the quality of genuine community more than the warmth of a healthy, nuclear family—provided that such a family has conducted its group activities and decisions with intelligence, understanding, imagination, respect for the rights of other family units, and the communion of a felt democracy. Unfortunately these are qualities fast being lost to the nuclear family in mass society. The reader may be luckier still if he has had the experience of being a member of an *extended family*—such as we find among Greeks, Italians and, frequently, pre-World War II Jews—for here the psychological atmosphere of the genuine community is nearly always omnipresent. If the atmosphere of the extended family is preserved with intelligence, imagination and humane feeling, wisdom and patience, goodwill and concern for others, rather than with rigidity of outlook and restraint in community expectations and demands, then there are few things which can match it for its humanizing qualities. The extended family can then provide the security and the capacity to define oneself and to conduct one's affairs with a sense that one will be backed up, while encouraging the individual to pursue his personal talents and dreams. A genuine community—if not too large in numbers—can be regarded as an amplification of the intelligent and sympathetic atmosphere of the extended family or it can be regarded as a larger unit which seeks psychologically to approximate the virtues and warmth of the extended family.

Extended families—uncles, aunts, cousins, parents, grandparents and grandchildren—have been described by anthropologists. Some extended family systems are admirable and some are only pocket-editions of unthinking tribal and group restraints. Occasionally the spirit of the warm and wise, extended family may be enlarged so as to embrace an entire community. When this occurs the psychological attributes of community now describe a larger cluster of persons. One such augmentation of the extended family existed among the Jews of Eastern Europe, prior to World War II, in the form of the *shtetl*. The shtetl was the small-town, Jewish community of Eastern Europe. Zborowski and Herzog [1] have given us a magnificent description of the culture of the shtetl, and it is easy to see that here we have an authentic, communal expression of

---

[1] Mark Zborowski and Elizabeth Herzog. *Life is with People. The Culture of the Shtetl.* New York: Schocken Books, 1964. 452 pp. See especially, Part III, Chapter 2, "Life is with People," 214–38.

many of the psychological attitudes associated with the genuine community. The functions of the shtetl were confined to religious, educational and welfare activities. Any event that required group action or consensus was dealt with by debate, dispute, disagreement and exhaustive exploration of all aspects of the matter at hand. Majority decisions were executed with the reservation that the minority was always free to reopen the matter under contention at any time. Taking stock was a constant process. Disagreements were over ideas rather than with individuals. This was the Jewish equivalent of "hating the sin but not the sinner." It is to be contrasted with our middle-class, Western habit of regarding a criticism of one's ideas as an impugning of one's personal worth and abilities. Orders were willingly executed in the shtetl, but not blindly. They had to be shown to be reasonable and just, where any individual had any doubts on this score. This again must be contrasted with our Western habit of demanding unquestionable compliance with an official order.

The judgments of such a community leader as the Rabbi were never backed up by physical force. Those judgments had to be shown to be reasonable in order to command respect. The shtetl was run by the men of heart and mind, that is, those who know—the learned—and those who gave of themselves. Sometimes a leader fitted into both of these categories. Leaders were expected to lead open lives, so that people could assure themselves of the honesty, integrity and good judgment of their leaders. Public opinion was extremely compelling. A leader had to validate his Jewishness, his honor, integrity, religious piety, sound judgment, and common sense, before inquisitive, civic-minded and, hopefully, responsible and intelligent laymen. Everybody in the shtetl was ready to demand an accounting of a leader's behavior or to express an opinion concerning it. There was little alienation of the type found in the overurbanized and bureaucratized, Western community, so aptly expressed in the saying "Let George do it!" The great urge among all members of the shtetl was to share and communicate. It was normal and natural to mind everyone's business—not in the sense of morbid curiosity but in the sense of responsible, civic-minded commitment. The freedom to observe and to pass judgment on one's fellows, the need to communicate both emotionally and rationally and to share events and emotions, were ubiquitous. *All of this proceeds from a strong feeling that individuals are responsible to and for each other.*

Under the Covenant people are interdependent because the acts of one may affect the fate of all. The Jew in the shtetl was, therefore, forever trying to avoid the necessity for being forgiven because he did not know what he had done. He developed the habit of looking ahead as a moral and social duty. He *intended* to be his brother's keeper. The underprivileged in the shtetl depended on the privileged for all sorts of help—instructions, advice, services, and material assistance. The privileged depended on the underprivileged in order to validate themselves as "real Jews," that is, in order to share this world's material bounty as well as its spiritual values and to exhibit the fellow-feeling which was so basic to the religious impulse. This interdependency is remotely analogous to the virtuous woman's need to have prostitutes in this world, in order to validate her virtue—a fact which Oscar Wilde had emphasized. Wilde's example, however, differs in spirit from the interdependency of the shtetl, in that the underprivileged—unlike the harlot—were not social outcasts.

In spite of the close, spiritual and communal linkages of people in the shtetl, nevertheless they remained individuals. It is a remarkable fact that a ubiquitous sense of community never became a constraint upon personal freedom, thus providing that balance between freedom and authority which is still a Western ideal. The citizen of the shtetl was merged *with* the community but never *submerged* in it. Nearly everyone in the shtetl had his or her own distinct and separate character and was recognized for any talent, learning or knowledge which distinguished him from others. One's abilities and ideas were determined by demonstrated behavior and the quality of one's decisions. They were never determined *artificially* and once and for all, by one's professional status, degrees, popularity or false image, so characteristic of middle-class life in the West. Anyone was free to challenge a specialist's claims, an authority's rulings or the claims of a pretender to learning and ideas. The challenger did this by *showing* that he was, indeed, more gifted, more knowledgeable and more thoughtful in the area of the other's "intellectual squatter sovereignty." Strangely enough, this did not promote the tiresomeness of cranks. The *nyudnik* (a combination of a pest, bore and fool) and the *kibbitzer* or mere talker were properly squelched and put in their place. Everyone had to validate his status and claims, if challenged, by delivering the goods rather than pulling social or educational rank.

The Jews of the shtetl took care of one another. They donated money, food and clothing to widows, orphans and the poor. They were concerned with the problems and troubles of their fellows and did what they could to dissipate them. They shared good fortune. They participated in and enjoyed the high moments in the lives of their fellow Jews. They were ever conscious of the need to dispense justice and mercy towards one another, to be fair and reasonable, to place the individual above all legal and bureaucratic abstractions, to make learning serve life, community values and an omnipresent but enlightened morality. All of this was summed up in the ever-present dictum "Müss sein ein mensch," that is, "you have to be a human being." This was the *first rule* of communal life.

There was, to be sure, a debit side to the shtetl's ledger. No community is perfect and the glowing account we have furnished here of the assets of one type of authentic community is not intended to overlook deliberately the liabilities of social life in the shtetl. The one-sided emphasis we have given here is purposeful. It is done solely to illustrate one form of the expression of a genuine, communal life. It is, after all, only the assets of the communal psyche which will make our point clear.

The Eskimos are another people who have managed to achieve an authentic expression of community, although this achievement has been breaking down under the impact of Christianity and the fur trade with the white man. In the Eskimo community of northern Canada, natural resources and raw materials were held in common. Fabricated articles, however, were privately owned. The only law was public opinion. There were no formal authorities but the influence any person had upon the community was determined by the respect its members had for him. The degree of such respect depended, of course, upon being known to as many members of the community as possible, but widespread familiarity was easily achieved because of the limited size of these Eskimo communities.

It appears that the small community is particularly well adapted to *gemeinschaft*. The Morgans [2] have shown the extent to which this is so by an account of some genuine expressions of community which were or are characteristic of other cultures and which appear to have been aided and abetted by the small size of the communities in question. Among the genuine but small communities included for brief discussion by these authors are the following: the Hutterite communities of the American West; the Buddhist communities of Burma; the communities of the American Indian; and the little forest communities of Germany, similar to those described by Tacitus in his History of the Germans, written about A.D. 100. As the Morgans put it—after selecting a number of small communities which demonstrate the psychological attributes of an authentic community—the problem of community is to preserve the organic unity, the soul of the community, while also making it possible to develop the capacity for independent thought and self-actualization in the individual. One has to strike a balance between a fulfilling sense of relatedness and the ability to withstand the unthinking onslaughts of mass opinion, as these are created by centers of power. What the shtetl was able to do, a modernized but genuine, small community should be able to do—namely, preserve the *communal virtues* of the traditional society, while giving them the backing of the advantages offered by mod-

[2] Arthur E. Morgan and Griscom Morgan (editors). *The Heritage of Community. A critique of community living based on great ways of life practised by small communities over the world.* Yellow Springs, Ohio: Community Service, Inc., March, 1956. 64 pp.

ern science and technology, education, social responsibility and civic enlightenment.

By virtue of its limited size, the small community may also be best able to preserve the pristine ideals and spirit of democracy. First of all the small community approximates face-to-face relationships better than does metropolis. Second, its problems are more manageable than those of metropolis. Third, it can exercise the principle of voluntary association more frequently than is possible in the highly centralized structures of our big cities. Fourth, it can plan for *stability* or *flexibility* rationally, rather than being rendered impotent by political and technological changes beyond the control of its civic-minded members—a major defect of the conurbations of our time. Fifth, its problems are fewer, by virtue of its size, and the information that has to be disseminated to its citizens is not overwhelming, so that most of the small community's inhabitants can receive access to the kind of information which would make their participation in the democratic process, both feasible and meaningful. Sixth, it can exercise so much local autonomy in dealing with its problems, that there is little excuse for encroachment on its way of life by central authorities. There are many other features of the small community, ready to take advantage of modern science and technology, which can aid the democratic process, but space forbids an extended discussion of them here. The Morgans [3] have also provided us with some readings to illustrate the manner in which the small community can generate genuine types of democracy. These involve processes and institutions which eliminate the need for the chronic promotion of unnecessary amounts of centralization and bureaucratization in our lives.

Arthur Morgan [4, 5, 6] has, in fact, taken the position that the small, primary community is the model for democratic life and the expression of *gemeinschaft*. He feels that in a community of this kind rather than in any other type of community, the good life can be defined and pursued. It is his conviction that conurbations prevent our living on the human scale. We are losing the sense of authentic community because modern man is bluffed by the prestige of bigness, by the alleged efficiencies of both centralized controls and excessive industrialization. Morgan believes that the present day, small community—where it still survives—is being

[3] Arthur E. Morgan and Griscom Morgan (editors). *Bottom-Up Democracy. The Affiliation of Small Democratic Units For Common Service.* Yellow Springs, Ohio: Community Service, Inc., December, 1954. 64 pp.

[4] Arthur E. Morgan. *The Small Community. Foundation of Democratic Life. What It is and How to Achieve It.* New York: Harper & Brothers, 1942. 312 pp.

[5] Arthur E. Morgan. *The Community of the Future and the Future of Community.* Yellow Springs, Ohio: Community Service Incorporated, 1957. 166 pp.

[6] Arthur E. Morgan. *It Can be Done.* Yellow Springs, Ohio: Community Service Incorporated, 1959. 63 pp. This publication constitutes Nos. 1–6 of Vol. XVI, March, 1959 of the publication, *Community Comments.*

dissolved, diluted, and submerged by modern technology, commercialism, mass production, propaganda and centralized government.

For Morgan it is the small community, the intimate group or, at least, the group whose members are somewhat familiar with one another, even if socially out of contact, which must remain the primary pattern within which the effort to achieve the good life must be made. The moral sensibilities of men, their integrity, their capacity for devotion and fellow-feeling, flourish only in the roots of neighborliness and shared experience. Morgan does not, of course, want to turn the clock back or declare a moratorium on large-scale, industrial organization and centralized controls. He does, however, insist that we have to rethink through the place of these highly organized activities in our lives, so that instead of inhibiting the formation of authentic communities, the latter, instead, can find a way of bending advanced science, technology and industrial organization to a democratic expression of the good life. In the three volumes mentioned in the footnotes given he has tried to think through the methods of dealing with this problem and to show how a modern, streamlined, small community can be designed so as to achieve both democracy and a communal expression of the good life.

Morgan's point about propaganda is important and should not be overlooked. The extent to which mass propaganda is creating world attitudes has been described in a recent volume by Ellul,[7] which is practically the definitive work on the subject of the evil effects of mass propaganda. For those interested in the small community one can draw an important conclusion from Ellul's work. Mass propaganda in favor of urbanization, industrialization, centralization and bureaucratization, is bound to create discontent and doubts about the benefits of their way of life, in the minds and hearts of citizens of genuine but small communities. Ellul's volume explores in detail the many ways in which mass propaganda is destructive of both individuality and authentic expressions of community life. He regards propaganda as the Siamese twin of misused technology in our society and to the extent that, thus far, technology and industrialization have been used to destroy true community, to that extent propaganda tends to destroy the I–Thou relationship among human beings. The sense of the word propaganda in Ellul's work is not limited just to lies. Half truths, truths of limited application, truths that hold conditionally only for certain contexts—all these are part of the contagion of psychic destruction by mass propaganda, associated with the uncritical extensions of urbanization, industrialization, centralization, and bureaucracy.

---

[7] Jacques Ellul. *Propaganda. The Formation of Men's Attitudes.* New York: Alfred A. Knopf, 1965. 320 pp.

Unfortunately, the psychological sense of true community is disappearing from the modern world. Technology has accidentally ushered in industrialization. Industrialization in turn has helped heavily to produce urbanization. Urbanization has tended not only to destroy the small community—particularly, the genuine, small community—but what is even worse it has produced the mass society and culture of the metropolis. Mass society is the negative side of the ledger dealing with the steady erosion of community in the modern world. Mass society is accompanied not only by a variety of social pathologies but also by a variety of psychological illnesses. These illnesses have been named and these names have given rise to what Nisbet [8] calls the vocabulary of alienation. This vocabulary includes such terms as *disorganization, decline, insecurity, breakdown, frustration, anxiety, dehumanization, depersonalization, bureaucratization, anomie, acedia, homogenization, kitsch* and other types of social psychopathology, which are among the leading concerns of both sociologists and psychologists. These are the psychological diseases of the urban-industrial complex.

A stream of criticism of mass society has been produced in recent years, by virtue of the intensification of these social psychopathologies, and there is much pessimism concerning the mental and social health of mass society if present trends continue. Some critics urge some form of urban decentralization to stave off the day of reckoning. Some critics think that the conditions of mass society can be ameliorated—if there is a public will to do so—and people encourage various institutional inventions for unscrambling the damage that has already occurred. But in either case, the pessimism concerning the *contemporary* trends of mass society and its anti-communal expressions, is increasing all the time. We find such pessimism either *reported* or *expressed*—to give but one small sample of the critics involved—in the work of writers like Fromm,[9, 10] Larrabee and Meyersohn,[11] Rosenberg and White,[12] Stein,[13] Olson,[14] and the Josephsons.[15]

[8] Robert Nisbet. *The Quest For Community. A Study in the Ethics of Order and Freedom.* New York: Oxford University Press, 1953. 303 pp.

[9] Erich Fromm. *Escape From Freedom.* New York: Avon Books, 1965. 333 pp.

[10] Erich Fromm. *The Sane Society.* New York: Holt, Rinehart and Winston, 1955. 370 pp.

[11] Eric Larrabee and Rolf Meyersohn (editors). *Mass Leisure.* Glencoe, Illinois: The Free Press, 1958. 429 pp.

[12] Bernard Rosenberg and David Manning White (editors). *Mass Culture. The Popular Arts in America.* Glencoe, Illinois: The Free Press & The Falcon's Wing Press, 1957. 561 pp.

[13] Maurice Stein. *The Eclipse of Community. An Interpretation of American Studies.* Princeton, New Jersey: Princeton University Press, 1960. 354 pp.

[14] Philip Olson (editor). *America as a Mass Society. Changing Community and Identity.* New York: The Free Press of Glencoe, 1963. 576 pp.

[15] Eric and Mary Josephson (editors). *Man Alone. Alienation in Modern Society.* New York: Dell Publishing Company, 1962. 592 pp.

Some writers on the subject of mass society see it as an agent of freedom—one which more than ever allows the expression of both communal and individual themes. These writers argue that because the communal spirit now receives expression in new types of social settings, that spirit is hidden from us. It is hidden from us, they assert, because of our traditional mental sets which prompt us to look for old and established evidences of genuine community. When we fail to find these familiar indicators of community we declare the communal spirit to be nonexistent. A second group of writers sees mass society as restrictive on personal freedom, destructive of personal identity, productive of the spiritual malaise of mass culture and mass taste, a sponsor of regimentation, irrationality and ignorance in social and economic life, and the generator of impersonal, large-scale organization and meaningless and sometimes dangerous, social conformity. As Olson stresses, however, the weight of the evidence appears to favor the pessimists.

A few of the theses of the pessimists may be mentioned at this point. (1) It does appear that community is being dissolved. (2) Personal survival appears threatened and since identity is now being defined in terms of the themes encouraged by mass culture, it is more and more probable that a "mass man" will emerge. (3) Alienation of every sort is on the increase. (4) The imperatives of technology are determining group adaptations to changing circumstances. (5) Political democracy is becoming less and less meaningful in the mass society. Mills [16] is particularly preoccupied with this last thesis. The pessimists feel that if present trends continue, Western civilization as we have known it, will be a thing of the past—a fossil of freedom.

In addition to the psychological disturbances created by overurbanization, a number of writers, like Kapp,[17] Herber [18] and Harrison [19] have stressed the serious, *social costs* of unplanned and unregulated industrialization and urbanization. Among these social costs they have included the following items:

1. Impairment of the human factor of production
2. The social costs of air pollution
3. Depletion and destruction of animal resources
4. The premature depletion of energy resources
5. Soil erosion, soil depletion and deforestation
6. The social costs of technological change

[16] C. Wright Mills. *The Power Elite.* New York: Oxford University Press, 1956. 423 pp. See particularly chapter 13 "The Mass Society," 298–324.

[17] K. William Kapp. *The Social Costs of Private Enterprise.* Cambridge: Harvard University Press, 1950. 287 pp.

[18] Lewis Herber. *Our Synthetic Environment.* New York: Alfred A. Knopf, 1962. 285 pp.

[19] Ruth Harrison. *Animal Machines. The New Factory Farming Industry.* London: Vincent Stuart, Ltd., 1964. 186 pp.

7. The social costs of unemployment and idle resources
8. Monopoly and social losses
9. Social costs of distribution
10. Social costs of transportation
11. Urban life and health
12. The problem of chemicals in food
13. Environment and cancer
14. Radiation and human health
15. Industrial farming

Certain writers like Gutkind [20] have stressed the relation of the *physical pathologies* of mass society to the improper environmental relationships which characterize it and to the excessive and irrational urbanization and industrialization of our time. Gutkind has stressed the need for urban and regional decentralization. If decentralization is ever to be feasible, that is, if we are ever to obtain the authentic, communal spirit by a return to the small-scale community, without sacrificing the cultural and social advantages of metropolis, then, clearly, community redesign will have to lean heavily upon new, ingenious and untried adaptations of science and technology. These will have to be adaptations which move away from the urban-industrial complex in the direction of the small community.

To the extent that science and technology have been heavily associated with overurbanization, it is important that we take a look at that same science and technology in relation to its potentialities, in the future, for ensuring the possibility of physical decentralization, should large blocs of humanity ever wish to try decentralization on a substantial scale. No doubt physical decentralization will be tried to some extent, once modern man realizes that excessive urbanization as a handmaiden to mass society tends to destroy genuine community. There are many ways to achieve physical decentralization and many different types of technology which may be exploited to this end. A rough understanding of such possibilities must be part of the equipment of the civic-minded citizen of our time.

In the chapters which follow we shall first of all describe some of the *sociopsychological* and *physical* pathologies of urbanism, both contemporary and projected. We shall then deal with some of the proposals for the physical decentralization of mass society. We shall close our volume by trying to state a social philosophy for an age of technology. The reasons we shall stress decentralization and innovation in community formation are many. It is widely felt that the sociopsychopathologies of mass society are in large measure a product of its overcentralization and

20 E. A. Gutkind. *Community and Environment. A Discourse on Social Ecology.* New York: Philosophical Library, 1954. 81 pp.

excessive urbanization. Reduce the intensity of both of these, it is argued, and this will help considerably to restore a condition of genuine community. Schemes of decentralization are, of course, aimed at achieving this reduction. We shall therefore discuss some of those schemes and the technology which may help to usher them into being.

# 19

# The Psychological Costs
of Overcentralization in
Urban Life*

## I. THE PSYCHOPATHOLOGY OF URBANIZATION

There are many thinkers and writers [1] who have pointed out the psychological disadvantages of highly centralized and congested urban living. Anyone wishing to see the case for decentralization made against the urban center because of what it does to the human being, will have no difficulties, whatsoever, in finding numerous, fair-minded and effective statements of the case. Space forbids our going afield and collecting a large number of these. We therefore turn chiefly to a single statement of the case which, in our eyes, does it justice. George Simmel,[2] the sociologist, has done a classic criticism of the psychological disadvantages of living in a large, urban center. It is his indictment which we use in presenting the psychological disadvantages of the great urban center. Let us, therefore, turn to the bill of particulars which he has furnished in this connection.

* Chapter 19, with adaptations and modifications, has been taken from the following source: Henry Winthrop. "The Psychological Costs of Urban Life." *The Western Humanities Review.* Vol. XXI, No. 2, Spring 1967, 155–162.

1 The following names and categories represent a few of the outstanding figures of protest against modern urbanism: architects: Frank Lloyd Wright and E. A. Gutkind; engineers: Arthur E. Morgan; intellectuals: Paul Goodman, Roderick Seidenberg, Friedrich Georg Juenger, Hannah Arendt, and a group of distinguished American thinkers whose criticisms are examined in the volume entitled *The Intellectual Versus the City* by Morton and Lucia White, New York: Mentor Books, 1962, 271 pp.; social critics and social reformers: Lewis Mumford, Aldous Huxley and Ralph Borsodi; philosophers: Martin Buber and Gabriel Marcel; biologists: Patrick Geddes; psychiatrists and psychologists: Erich Fromm; and sociologists: George Simmel and Pitirim A. Sorokin.

2 *The Sociology of George Simmel.* Translated, edited and with an introduction by Kurt H. Wolff. New York: The Free Press, 1964. 445 pp. See, particularly, *The Metropolis and Mental Life*, pp. 409–24.

Simmel first emphasizes the tendency of the metropolis to *intensify nervous stimulation* which results from the rapid and uninterrupted change of stimuli occurring both around us and within us when we live in metropolis. This makes for heightened consciousness and awareness and an intellectualization of responsiveness—which are, of course, assets—but, at the same time, this alienates metropolitan man to some extent from the deeply felt, emotional relationships with other people, which rural life or life in a small community can generally provide. The distinction Martin Buber [3] has made, between human relationships of the "I–It" and the "I–Thou" variety, is relevant here. When A and B relate to each other in terms of the manner and degree to which each can serve the purposes of the other, that is to say, only in terms of the personal or social utility they potentially bear for each other, this is what we mean by the I–It relationship. The common expression "What can I do you for?" is a cynical reflection of the motivation underlying the I–It relationship. It is an expression which will be heard more often in the big city than in a rural area or small community. The I–It attitude is the civilized and masked form of the ancient observation "Homo homini lupus."

When, however, A and B relate to each other both in terms of the affection and respect each feels for the qualities of the other and in such a way that each voluntarily behaves so as to promote the expression of these qualities in the other, we have the I–Thou relationship. When the I–Thou relationship holds between A and B, each contributes to the other's development, without expecting anything in return—that is to say, each provides affection and does what he can to promote the needs and aid the self-selected activities of the other. When this is done on a non-bookkeeping basis—that is, when it is done freely and without expecting any return—this is what we call the I–Thou relationship.

The metropolis, of course, overwhelmingly promotes the I–It relationship and, in so doing, fosters the heightened awareness and sophistication which Simmel has emphasized. It does this, however, at the tragic cost of intensifying the alienation between man and man. The small community and the rural milieu, at their best, promote by contrast the I–Thou relationship. In emphasizing this contrast we are not unaware that there is a liability side to the ledger of small-town life. Given the advantages of goodwill, enlightenment, modern education and emerging developments in science and technology, it would not be difficult to either eliminate these liabilities or to reduce them considerably in the small community. From the decentralist's standpoint, however, even if all these same advantages were introduced into metropolis, they would be of little avail in increasing the number and quality of I–Thou relationships prevailing in the highly centralized, urban center. There is a reason for this. The very bigness of megalopolis, the excessive centraliza-

[3] Martin Buber. *I and Thou.* New York: Charles Scribner's Sons, 1958. 137 pp.

tion which is the inevitable price it must pay for functioning smoothly and the inescapable bureaucratization of the civic functions it must dispense—all these make the intensification of the I–It relationship the constant price that must be paid if big city life is to avoid a breakdown. The price would have to be paid even if the advantages we have mentioned were injected into urban life. To be blunt about the matter, they *have* been injected into urban life by civic groups in our time. The pay-offs, however, have been disappointingly slim.

In this sense the decentralist questions the value of the heightened intelligence and awareness created by metropolis, when such intellectuality only upsets the balance between man's rational functions and his emotional and compassionate qualities. The self-centered sophistication which the metropolis provides, does so only at the cost of blunting our capacity for social altruism. It also blunts our concern for a type of practical self-transcendence—the ability to think of the needs of others as well as of our own—without which the achievement of a genuine sense of community is impossible.

Let us now elaborate to some extent upon the charge Simmel has made, namely, that the urban center intensifies "nervous stimulation." The more modern and scientific term for this is "stress." [4] The distinguished scientist, Hans Selye,[5] has done the world's leading research on stress and for an account of the vast range of psychological and biological meanings and manifestations of this phenomenon, the reader should acquaint himself with the fascinating volume mentioned in the footnote below. In the present context, however, we are interested in some of the manifestations ("bodily changes" in Selye's terminology) of stress created by urban living—or, at least, those manifestations whose incidence is distinctly greater for urban life than in the small community or rural milieu. A number of these have been brought together and discussed by Herber.[6] It is to be understood that the stress of urban life *contributes heavily* to these manifestations rather than being the *cause* of them. Here we shall simply enumerate them. These manifestations, then, include the following: allergies, asthma, arteriosclerosis (especially in the form known as atherosclerosis in which the large arteries are thick-

[4] "Stress" is defined by Selye as the manifestation of the "stress syndrome." Selye defines the latter, in terms of *bodily changes,* as follows. *"The stress syndrome consists* of ALL the nonspecifically induced CHANGES. Why do we have to specify *all* changes? By this we mean that whenever an agent acts upon the body and produces several nonspecifically induced effects, no one of them in itself—but the totality of the changes—is the stress syndrome." For a full account of what is meant by stress the reader is urged to read chapters 6 and 7 of the volume mentioned below. Chapter 6 is entitled "Inventory of Assets: (A) The facts." Chapter 7 is entitled "Inventory of Assets: (B) The abstractions." The fullest understanding of this concept can, of course, be obtained by a full reading of the volume in question.

[5] Hans Selye. *The Stress of Life.* New York: McGraw-Hill, 1956. 324 pp.

[6] Lewis Herber. *Our Synthetic Environment.* New York: Alfred A. Knopf, 1962. 285 pp.

ened by deposits of cholesterol and other fatty-like substances), cancer, coronary heart disease, hay fever, mental illness, muscular tension, peptic ulcers and rheumatoid arthritis. These manifestations, however, do not exhaust the undesirable medical conditions which prolonged psychological stress helps powerfully to reinforce. For a fuller discussion of the many pathologies to which the stress of highly centralized, urban living may reasonably be said to contribute, the reader is urged to read Selye's work, already mentioned. So much for the nature and the consequences of the nervous stimulation produced by overcentralized, urban living.

Let us now return to some of the other elements in the bill of particulars furnished by Simmel. Before we do so, however, let us bear in mind that Simmel has tried to pull together the major mental and psychological changes which appear to be produced by the excessive centralization of large-scale, urban life. The phrase "mental and psychological changes" will, therefore, include such intangible elements as values, attitudes, interests, ideas, ideals, biases, levels of aspiration, intellectual habits and many other similar examples of the psychological content of the human mind. Having thus cautioned the reader, let us then note a second charge made by Simmel, namely, that the metropolis has always tended to measure all human values in terms of money. This unidimensional habit is closely related to what Veblen [7] has called pecuniary emulation, the pecuniary standard of living, pecuniary canons of taste, dress as an expression of the pecuniary outlook and the higher learning as an expression of the pecuniary culture. According to Simmel, the pecuniary canon of judgment which the big city pushes to the center of human consideration, translates all human individuality and all intimate emotional relationships into such questions as "How much?" "Does it pay?" "What is there in it for me?" One must notice that this monetary standard of judgment crops up much less frequently in the small, intimate circle of social intercourse where warmth, the acceptance of the individuality of others and the I–Thou relationship is predominant. If one reduces persons, places, things, events, situations, relationships, ideas and so forth, to monetary terms, the inevitable consequence is an alienation in which these same persons, places, things, etc. are seen and felt as abstractions. Once this occurs the possibility of maintaining or creating I–Thou relationships is considerably reduced, if not eliminated. In this sense again human relations tend to become similar to those of the beehive rather than a network of relationships dominated by fellow feeling.

In order to sense the truth of Simmel's charge that the prevailing themes people live by in the metropolis, sponsor the translation of most values into monetary terms, consider the following. (1) If a workman

[7] See Chapters 2, 5, 6, 7, and 14 of the following volume: Thorstein Veblen, *The Theory of the Leisure Class. An Economic Study of Institutions.* New York: Mentor Books, 1953, 261 pp.

suffers accident or injury, his first thought—if the accident is not too serious—will be how best to obtain workman's compensation. (2) If an individual suffers an accident at home or on street or highway, one of the early and major concerns he will experience will be that of instituting a legal suit so as to translate the consequences of his accident or injury into dollar values. The dockets of American courts are notoriously overburdened with pending cases and many of these, perhaps most, are due to suits instituted by litigious citizens seeking to translate some type of situation—sometimes serious, sometimes not—into dollars for themselves. (3) If educators, statisticians and journalists wish to impress the public with the value of a college education, they do so by translating education into dollar terms. This will frequently be done by showing what the average, high school graduate can earn in a lifetime, what the holder of a BA, MA or Ph.D. degree can expect to earn in a lifetime, and contrasting the rise in lifetime income which occurs as one goes up the educational ladder. But the emphasis on the great, Greek, educational ideal of *paideia*—education for self-development and civic responsibility— is nowhere visible.

(4) If a husband seeks a divorce our courts reason that the "discarded" wife must be compensated by money for the affection which has been lost. This is given in terms of "alimony" and it will be given even where the wife asks for the divorce (being tired of the husband) and even where the husband is the injured party. This last occurs because an "injured" husband often cannot legally bare his injury, since an archaic, social code of gallantry and chivalry demands that he pretend to be the "sinner"—at least, in the courts. (5) If a man dies his wife is said to be entitled to a given fraction of his estate, even if she has been a "hellion" for years, refusing to give him a deserved divorce and making his life miserable. Legally and socially, it is argued, she is entitled to compensation for the "services" and "companionship" she rendered him while he was alive and for any "suffering" this may have entailed for her.

(6) Many physicians and surgeons require that prospective patients fill out certain forms which directly or indirectly reveal their annual incomes and then they graduate the fees for their services accordingly. They thus relate their professional services less to patients' medical needs and more to the variations of their patients' incomes. (7) Funds for the conduct of political campaigns generally come from financially comfortable individuals or wealthy, business enterprises. The purpose of such funds is to translate some prospective legislation desired by donors into dollar values expressed in campaign contributions. Later, successful candidates will equate the dollar value of campaign contributions into dollar values of certain legislation which is desired by previous donors and these legislators will then push this desired legislation through the governing body involved.

Thousands of additional examples could easily be furnished of how life in our overcentralized cities is conducive to the translation of many of our values and activities into pecuniary terms. Space forbids the dreary enumeration of these examples. What the examples mentioned above, and the dozens of examples *which could be furnished,* illustrate, is that Simmel is, in no sense, exaggerating when he emphasizes the degree to which mental life in the metropolis is dominated by pecuniary standards of behavior.

The metropolis also *standardizes* habits and values, thus offering its greatest rewards to the inflexible type of personality. The device which has lent itself most to the standardization of habits and values is, says Simmel, the clock. What began as a device to give order to devotional activities in monasteries, as Mumford [8] indicates, has turned into a tyrant which smoothes the way in metropolis for depersonalization, deindividuation and dehumanization. The clock forces on urban man an overvaluation of punctuality, calculability and exactness, in order to enable him to adapt to the social complexity and close demands of urban life. These traits are needed, of course, in order to adjust to a money economy. However, they also tend to destroy human spontaneity and the human ability and need to examine inwardly many of the most basic aspects of the human condition, such as birth, love, death, sex, friendship, loneliness, unreasoning ambition, the obsession with power rather than creativity and the intellectual passions,[9] etc. Since such matters as social routine, the rationalization of work habits, and the standardization of personal habits and personal values do not provide every one with the same satisfactions and cannot be equally appropriate for all, urbanization is not an unmixed blessing. Many thinkers, such as Ruskin and Nietzsche, have felt that the deepest values of life lie in its unschematized aspects. It is for this reason that such thinkers abhor those attributes of megalopolis which promote the standardization of habits, values and ideas.

Simmel has also charged that metropolitan life may encourage a greater intellectuality than that of the small community or the rural milieu. Unfortunately, however, the type of intellectuality which the metropolis fosters is highly impersonal and therefore highly undesirable for genuine human relations of the I–Thou variety. The best example of

---

[8] Lewis Mumford. *The Human Prospect.* (Harry T. Moore and Karl W. Deutsch, editors). Boston: The Beacon Press, 1955. 319 pp. See the selection entitled "The Monastery and the Clock," 3–9. This selection is Section 2 of Chapter 1 "Cultural Preparation" in Mumford's *Technics and Civilization,* New York: Harcourt, Brace & World, 1963, 495 pp.

[9] For a discussion of what is meant substantively by the phrase, "intellectual passions," see the following volume: Michael Polanyi. *Personal Knowledge. Towards a Post-Critical Philosophy.* Chicago: The University of Chicago Press, 1958. 428 pp. See, particularly, Part Two, Chapter 6 "Intellectual Passions," 132–202.

this type of impersonal intellectuality is what we call "the blasé attitude." It is expressed in such statements as "I couldn't care less." "Go fight city hall!" "I don't want to get involved." "So what's the difference—half a dozen of one, six of the other." "So what!" No doubt the reader can think of many other expressions which betray the blasé attitude. The blasé attitude, resulting from the numerous, fleeting and often contradictory stimulation of urban life, blunts discrimination. It also liquidates what existentialists refer to as *concern, genuine encounter, commitment* and *engagement*. This is equivalent, in ordinary garden variety of language, to improper and unfeeling reactions to novel situations in which human needs must be met.

The blasé person experiences everything as of equal importance or unimportance. Thus we can see that what we have earlier called *homogenization* is the direct consequence of the blasé attitude which, in turn, is part of the pathology of metropolitan life. The blasé attitude is, of course, a protection against the deleterious effects of the overintensified, nervous stimulation provided by megalopolis. This self-preservation, says Simmel, "is bought at the price of devaluating the whole objective world, a devaluation which in the end unavoidably drags one's own personality down into a feeling of the same worthlessness." If, of course, the association between urban congestion and the blasé attitude, is inescapable, then, argues the decentralist, the solution to its elimination lies in the decentralization of our cities to human scale—a scale in which the overintense stimulation which is excessive for our humane thresholds of response, is simply either liquidated entirely or reduced to manageable proportions.

Simmel has recognized that the anonymity of the individual in the large urban center enables him to cultivate a protective reserve which would be impossible in the neighborly small town and would only lead to a type of social ostracism if practised in the small community. He also recognizes that this anonymity frees the individual from the restraints and expectations of small groups such as we find in the traditional small town or uncongested rural milieu. Given this freedom in the large city *some* men are able to develop their individual potentialities and to specialize in function—all of which give scope to the expression of talent if, indeed, such be present. The same freedom is far less likely to be conferred in the traditional, small community. In the big city such freedom is of real and maximum value *chiefly to men of talent and genius.*

But many men lack talent and special gifts. Nevertheless they seek to individuate themselves in some fashion. It is the anonymity of the metropolis which furnishes conditions which enable such "hollow men" to "stand out," as it were, and to make themselves conspicuous by extravagances in mannerisms and through caprice and preciousness. Where this kind of individuation leads to a violation of the social mores and leads to deviancy, it is seen as *degeneration* and—seen this way—was the focus of attention for a famous study by Max Nordau.[10] If this same kind of individuation is accompanied by some *modest* talent coupled with literary dissatisfaction with prevailing ways of life or is accompanied by a Bohemian hostility to the bourgeoisification of society, it then emerges in the form of an unconstructive protest against the social order. It is then that literature is seen as decadent, as growing moribund and as characterized by what Joad [11] has called "the dropping of the object." By this phrase we refer to the growing tendency (1) for men to play God, that is, to feel that they can do all things if they only will to do so, (2) to conceive of progress as the increase of power over man's physical environment, (3) to seek to expand experience and sensation without limit as though this constituted the enlargement of the self, (4) to become convinced that only science and rationality are the keys to the understanding of man and nature and (5) to conceive of the religious and moral impulses of man as merely ballast from his socially infantile past, which must be thrown overboard.

In general, when the freedom provided by the large, urban center is seized upon by the slightly above average man, standards are thrown overboard and the conviction arises that one man's opinion is as good as another's and that all values are relative and of equal, logical status and objective relevance. This roughly describes what is meant by "the dropping of the object" and leads to works of art and extravagant philosophical positions which—in spite of their superficiality—appeal to large numbers of people precisely because they reflect commonly understandable views or postures. The metropolis enables men of little profundity but with enough aggressiveness, to strike flamboyant literary, philosophical or political postures and thus to be seen as "individuals." Again these are forms of the extravagances, mannerisms, caprice and preciousness which Simmel has emphasized.

It was at just about the turn of the century that Simmel was developing his ideas about the metropolis and mental life. Almost seven decades of the twentieth century have elapsed since he made his observations. Since then a new note has been sounded with respect to techniques by which "hollow men"—taking advantage of the anonymity offered by the metropolis—may appear to be individuals and personalities when, in fact, they are not. The new technique, which has been highly developed in our day, is the technique of creating a public, "ersatz" image for oneself. More accurately our image-merchants and public relations men

---

10 Max Nordau. *Degeneration*. London: William Heinemann, 1913. 560 pp. This volume is a classic study of personal and social decadence and degeneration and the forms in which these states manifest themselves in Western society.

11 C. E. M. Joad. *Decadence. A Philosophical Inquiry*. London: Faber and Faber Limited, 1948. 430 pp.

create it for various types of urban nonentities. Those who seek to pre-serve an acceptable and respected public image of themselves—as con-trasted with what they often truly are—prove to be, all too often, the kind of men who would prefer to have the *manners* of a philosopher rather than the matter. The twentieth century term for these cultivators of the image is, of course, "phonies." The creation of the public image is frequently our *up-to-date form* of that type of infantile individuation which Simmel has referred to as the "specifically metropolitan extrava-gances of mannerism, caprice and preciousness." It is obvious that the "phony image" would not be very viable in a small community, since it thrives on social distance and lack of contact. These latter two condi-tions are exactly what the metropolis provides. It is equally obvious that the "phony image" would make little headway in the minds and hearts of men and women of intelligence, discrimination, and spirit.

It is for this reason that many decentralists are convinced that only a new type of small community—making use of many of the advances of modern science and technology and many of our advances in culture, education and knowledge in general—can prevent the type of phony lead-ership which so often appeals to mass-man. The image-merchant is a psychological plague, devoted often to the task of creating and sustaining improper leadership—a luxury which we can ill afford in so complex a world as the one which is now emerging. It is this type of leadership which has prompted Bertrand Russell more than once to remark on the ignorance and irrationality of the figures to whom most men entrust their fates. The metropolis then creates the mass-men who are taken in by the extravagances and poses of the false leader. The metropolis also produces the demogogue who claims to provide authentic leadership. The anonym-ity of large-scale urban living thus proves to be a blessing in disguise for "hollow men." Their emptiness is rarely realized. It is only their tinsel images which sustain them and capture public support.

# Culture and the
# American Metropolis*

## I. MASS CULTURE AND THE METROPOLIS

The metropolis—as one of the leading expressions of overcentralization in the twentieth century—is also the chief, if not the sole, source of what has come to be called "mass culture." In the most general sense mass culture consists of all those activities, interests and concerns, which occupy the overwhelmingly major portion of the leisure-time of the average man, as well as of many men and women who may be characterized as less than average. Because this is so, the phrase, "the average man," in the present context, should be made clear. It may have any one, or all, of several distinguishable meanings. Most commonly it refers to men and women who are average *intellectually*. Quite frequently it may refer to men and women who are simply commonplace with respect to their aesthetic and social sensitivity or—what is more to the point—the lack of such sensitivity. Perhaps the phrase "mass culture" is most apposite when it has reference to the activities of men and women who *placidly* and *uncritically* welcome and enjoy the values, interests, attitudes, biases, ideas, ideals and levels of aspiration which are offered to them by their cultural milieus and where what is welcomed and enjoyed is, by and large, cut off from tradition and the humanistic heritage of the West. The uncritical acceptance to which we have just referred is invariably accompanied by both an unwillingness and often an inability to take stock of the intellectual, psychological, educational, social, aesthetic and moral consequences of indulging an appetite for the foci of interests which are regularly supplied and emphasized by these same, cultural milieus.

* Chapter 20, with adaptations and modifications, has been taken from the following source: Henry Winthrop. "Culture, Mass Society, and The American Metropolis. High Culture and Middlebrow Culture: An Existentialist View." *Journal of Existentialism*, Vol. 7, No. 27, Spring, 1967, 359–380.

In this all-too-brief clarification the emphasis should, perhaps be placed upon the factor of intellectual status in talking of the average man or average woman but, in doing so, it should be remembered that *any one* of the other considerations we have mentioned may define *mass-man* and, usually, some combination of these considerations describes him. Quite often, of course, intellectual mediocrity will pave the way for being average in one of the other senses we have employed, although occasionally we find men and women of average intellectual attainments who are unusually gifted and discriminating along some of the other dimensions we have emphasized. Most often, however, the mass man is one who appears to be limited along *all* of the dimensions and considerations which we have just stressed.

Overcentralization can be indicted *indirectly* but *strongly* as a condition which promotes mass culture. This is because overcentralization achieves one of its paramount expressions in modern urbanization and mass culture is the expression, *par excellence,* of cultural life in the metropolis. Mass culture—in a society boasting a mass communications technology—may be said to be the *"cultural law* of large and congested numbers," if we may paraphrase an expression from statistical theory. In expressing the concerns and the interests of a large and congested population, mass culture expresses largely the concerns and the interests of the *least common denominator* of such a population—both intellectually and spiritually. If we therefore propose to state the case against centralization through its ubiquitous *urban expressions*—particularly in terms of the psychological, the intellectual and the cultural shortcomings of the metropolis—we must be prepared to examine the pathology of mass culture. Mass culture will be an additional indictment on the bill of particulars which must be levied against overcentralization. In examining the pathology of mass culture we must be prepared not only to examine the forms in which it appears and the consequences which it produces but also the educational, spiritual and cultural aims which it fails to fulfill, which it departs from or which it ignores. We must also remember that modern communication technology, that is, mass communications, is the chief handmaiden to mass culture and that mass communications can only be viable within the framework of the overcentralized, overcongested, modern, urban community.

In order to talk sensibly about mass culture it behooves us to distinguish a variety of different cultures which are shared by different publics in technologically advanced, Western countries. Many classifications of such distinguishable cultures could be advanced in order to display the tendency for different levels of human interest, spiritual sensitivity and intellectual awareness to fly apart and receive separate expression through the activities of different blocs in the community. For purposes of the present chapter, however, we shall choose a taxonomy for culture which distinguishes *five,* qualitatively different types of culture to be found in the United States, only three of which are *heavily* promoted *at present* by the overcentralized conurbations of our time. These five *levels* or *types* of culture may be designated as follows: (1) *High Culture;* (2) *Middlebrow Culture;* (3) *Mass Culture;* (4) *Lowbrow Culture;* (5) *Folk Culture.* Admittedly this is only one possible taxonomy and, perhaps, not even the most illuminating one in the last analysis. We propose to use it here, however, because we think it will be quite useful in making some of the discriminations which we deem to be essential in dealing with group expressions of cultural concern in the overcentralized, modern, large-scale community.

## II. HIGH CULTURE

We have spoken above of the necessity to examine the educational, spiritual and cultural aims which mass culture either fails to fulfill or from which it departs or which it ignores. We are then implicitly referring to cultural norms from which mass culture has become uprooted. These norms are those of "high culture," itself. These norms must be made explicit. If we therefore begin with an examination of the nature of high culture we will not only be initiating the discussion of the taxonomy of culture to which we have already referred but we shall be devoting ourselves, at the same time, to a description of those traditional spiritual and cultural aims from which mass culture has become alienated.

The reader should not assume that those who express a concern for high culture are necessarily snobs. Some, indeed, undoubtedly are. High culture, however, can be pursued with sincerity and passion while retaining the most respectful, amiable and concerned attitudes towards one's fellow men. High culture is quite consistent with the democratic spirit but not with a bastardized, bowdlerized, or denatured version of that spirit. It demands, however, a seriousness which is rarely present in the average man and which is *insufficiently* reflected in the cultural life of most people who can be said to be blessed with more than average intellectual capacity, talent, or sensitivity.

### High Culture as *Paideia* and *Catharsis*

High culture can be expressed in many ways. One of these is, of course, the Greek ideal of *paideia.* Since we have discussed the meaning of this ideal in the earlier portions of this volume, we shall say no more on that score here. A more traditional meaning of high culture has been associated with Aristotle's aesthetic doctrine of *catharsis.* For Aristotle art possesses a socially valuable function. When catharsis is successful at its best, as in drama, it relieves the members of the audience of the oppressive emotions of pity and fear. These emotions may be *initially* aroused as we watch the unfolding of the action of a drama but a play is great to the extent that these emotions—which cloud judgment and understanding—are purged away or liquidated by the play. In their place, according to Aristotle, a great drama provides us with the understanding of how misfortune is the result of frailties and defects of character, thus providing the auditor and viewer with a better balance of judgment with respect to the human condition. The production of catharsis, then, may be regarded as one of the functions of a genuine, high culture.

Later writers have extended the meaning of catharsis, defining it so as to include the functions of both irony and pity or compassion, and applying Aristotle's concept generally to all forms of art but particularly to the novel, the short story, the narrative or epic poem and biographies. In an extended meaning of catharsis irony is used to deflate the onlooker's poses, affectations and self-deceptions. It may be used to dissipate irrelevant, maladaptive and deleterious emotions, moods, sentiments, attitudes, ideas, ideals, biases, and exaggerated and false beliefs, as well as any unrealistic aspirations which may be associated with any of these states. Such deflation and dissipation occur first, by intensifying the onlooker's awareness that these are states which he shares with the characters in a play or novel, and finally purging him of them because of the sense of shame and the ridiculous which they generate. In this way, it is felt, the onlooker or reader is left with balanced judgment and a better understanding both of himself and of others.

The mechanism by which irony functions in this extended meaning of catharsis is to enable the onlooker or reader to *identify* himself with the frailties of the characters presented. This same psychological mechanism, of course, will operate when purgation is achieved through pity. It is more difficult, however, to achieve catharsis through irony because of the tendency of spectators at a play or movie or readers of a book, to continue to try to deceive themselves by identifying only with heroes and heroines rather than with villains and witches.[1] In either case, however, the Socratic dictum that the unexamined life is not worth living, is the dominant motive behind the artist's work and one of the central purposes of the artist's communication. Another central purpose of catharsis in its extended meaning, is frequently to raise questions by indirection,

---

[1] This difficulty is recognized by a number of avant-garde playwrights who write in the traditions of *The Theatre of the Absurd*. A few such playwrights deliberately construct characters, plots and situations which will make audience identification difficult, precisely because there are no traditionally recognizable heroes or heroines on stage. Presumably this would intensify emotional objectivity and balance in judgment. In this connection see the following volume. Martin Esslin. *The Theatre of the Absurd*. New York: Doubleday, 1961. 364 pp.

concerning the nature and the acceptability of the values and the themes men live by. This can be done in the context of the drama, novel, film, poem, biography, etc. High culture is held, then, to be concerned with these matters and irony and pity are held to be capable of dealing with them effectively in work of great merit.

## High Culture as the Pursuit of the Good Life

High culture has also been held to be committed to the objective of try-ing to answer the question "What is the good life?" This, of course, can be attempted more forcefully by philosophical analysis and, to some ex-tent, by scientific inquiry. When, however, high culture refers strictly to belles-lettres and the arts, the effort to answer the question "What is the good life?" is done suggestively, through the delineation of character, through the manner in which the characters choose the values they in-tend to live by and through the artistic exploration of the consequences of their choice. In addition, the writer may be trying to indirectly answer the question "What is the good life?" through the manner in which the characters relate to each other, by the way in which they deal with frus-tration and tragedy and learn from their experience, in the manner in which they mull over their own deeds and those of others, by the hon-esty, integrity and clarity with which they seek self-expression and try to enter into I–Thou relationships with one another if, indeed, they try to do so at all, and so on.

For the novel, play, film, biography, poem, etc. to be able to do this most successfully, both the writer, on the one hand, and the reader or onlooker, on the other, have to be serious and mature. If only the writer is mature, much will be lost to the reader or onlooker, but great art should, hopefully, add an increment to the maturity even of the ill-prepared reader or spectator. When the mission of high culture is to raise questions concerning the good life, the writer's purpose is to try to pour as much meaning as possible into that flicker between eternities, which we call "our lives." In this sense of high culture we are concerned with *injecting* value into human experience. Nature, herself, gives us no clues as to the proper conduct of life and is perfectly neutral with re-spect to what men call good and evil. When we, therefore, speak of a play or a novel as "powerful" we generally mean that it is in this sense of high culture that the play or novel has been executed.

## High Culture from the Existentialist Point of View

Perhaps one of the better senses of the meaning of high culture is con-veyed in terms of the *existentialist outlook* in literature and philosophy.

There are five separate considerations which may be singled out as indicating the mission of high culture from an existentialist point of view. All of these five emphases are aimed at promoting conditions which will improve human relations, that is, bring us nearer to an I–Thou attitude in the relationship of man-to-man.

The first of these considerations encourages an art and literature which delineate and plead for *authenticity* in human relations rather than for the *cultivation of roles*. This emphasis encourages honesty and candor in human relations, depth in self-analysis and in the exploration and understanding of the motives of others, integrity in the quest for self-identity and openness in communication with those who become a significant part of the network of our lives.

The second emphasis in high culture, which is encouraged by the existentialist posture, is the portrayal of relationships between human beings which illustrate a *genuine encounter*. A genuine encounter serves to maximize spiritual understanding between the characters of a play or novel, between the writer and the reader and ultimately between one person and another, following the impact of a significant, aesthetic experience. Such a genuine encounter, however, calls for honesty and trust between individuals when a relationship is begun. The purpose of an atmosphere of honesty and trust is that candor facilitates a straightforward, reciprocal disclosure of one's true being and renders unnecessary any tendency to engage in psychological fencing. This latter is promoted by an atmosphere of fear or distrust and tends to maximize interpersonal misunderstanding. Both the social and the physical conditions by which men have been surrounded historically make the *genuine encounter* difficult in human relations, but not impossible. High culture tries to encourage men to approximate in their relations an atmosphere which will be as close as possible to that of the genuine encounter. Greatness in belles-lettres is said to flow in part from a treatment of the human condition in which the warmth and affection of the *genuine encounter* becomes apparent through the lessening of conflict and misunderstanding. Any treatment of human relations in literature which makes the *genuine encounter* appealing—bringing out the best in men and women—is regarded as fulfilling one of the missions of high culture.

There are two other emphases in the existentialist outlook which promote high culture. This is the artistic task of delineating the nobility, utility and power which flow from adherence to humane ideals of justice, compassion and intellectual honesty. Such adherence is called *commitment* and lesser ideals than those just mentioned may also move individual men and women. These ideals are self-selected rather than thrust upon one. They guarantee the emotional meaningfulness and humanity of the themes men choose to live by. However, men stand in danger of losing both themselves and one another, by too great a reliance upon abstract ideals, words and phrases. We therefore expect them to give flesh-and-blood concreteness to these ideals by behaving in conformity with their expressed *commitments*. We hold that anything less than this is absurd and emotionally meaningless. In this sense we look forward to a follow-through in human behavior, which expresses a man's commitments. This we call *involvement*. Part of the existentialist outlook is the conviction that high culture will both advocate and portray men and women who, in their relations with one another, are committed and involved. Behavior and human relations which lack commitment and involvement are absurd, uninteresting and a constriction, rather than an expansion, of the human spirit.

The fifth and last existentialist consideration which we choose to emphasize here—in connection with the characteristics of high culture—is that a mark of greatness in literature is that it seeks to dissipate all forms of alienation in human affairs. High culture shuns all those habits and relationships which separate men from the emotional understanding of other men, of the opposite sex, of places, situations, ideas and things. A sense of organic relatedness to all of these tends to enlarge the horizons of human consciousness and understanding. High culture emphasizes the universality of our human relatedness rather than those deficiencies in human nature which make for separatism. There are, of course, many ways in which alienation can exist for modern man. Seven of these ways should be emphasized here, namely, alienation from oneself, one's fellow man, the opposite sex, from work, society, nature or God. Each of these has been described extensively in the existing literature, but space forbids such a detailed description here. High culture, then, tries to break down the alienation which exists in the human condition and it is a mark of cultural and artistic greatness when this is done well, leaving an emotional impact upon the reader or spectator, and increasing his sense of kinship with others after he has read a great novel, attended a great play or seen a distinguished film.

All of the preceding then provides the reader with some notion of what is generally meant by high culture. It should help to some degree to reduce the ambiguity which generally surrounds the use of this phrase.

### III. MIDDLEBROW CULTURE

The essential features of middlebrow culture were discussed in Part II, Chapter 8 of the present volume. The reader is urged to reread that discussion at this point. In the present context, however, the point to be emphasized is that the *shallowness* of middlebrow culture is a peculiarly urban product. Urban man tends to be organically related to very little with respect to persons, places, ideas and things. The megalopolis promotes alienation, with respect to the substance of both ideas and ideals. In the small community any tendency to separate learning from life would be both seen and felt as absurd. So too would the tendency to skate *on the surface* of all those manifestations of the human spirit which give life its value, savor, and adventure, as well as its mystery, uncertainty and the surprises which always seem to open up fresh horizons of consciousness.

An urban, middlebrow culture soon loses sight of the forest for the trees. It begins to prefer the shadow to the substance. It is pleased with words and slogans, with the well-turned literary phrase and the pungent epigram, with the vague cliché rather than the genuinely understood idea and with superficiality of treatment rather than depth and completeness in approach. The inevitable result of this rootlessness in the approach to the genuine life of culture is a loss of spiritual depth and the failure to achieve a meaningful expression of a culture that counts. Any person of average intelligence can learn the art of participating in a conversation piece, of learning to talk for the sake of effect, and of nauseatingly parroting statements without genuine conviction. Communication of this sort is conspicuously lacking in the emotional tone that would make it meaningful and therefore encourage its translation into personal and social action.

It is precisely the deficiencies which we have just described that are the glaring sins of the middlebrow cultural posture. The excessive social and intellectual stimulation of the metropolis, singularly rewards middlebrow alienation and intellectual shallowness. The middlebrow man in megalopolis has no time for a genuine, spiritual and cultural pilgrimage. There is too much to taste and sample, too many distractions and too little perspective and contemplation projected upon the things to which he devotes his time. The last thing that the varied stimulation of urban life—crowding in upon the urban middlebrow—is likely to stimulate, is a clear-cut sense of value, spiritual direction, intellectual purpose, and emotionally fruitful relationships with others. For most men living in metropolis, urbanization promotes the I–It attitude rather than the I–Thou attitude. The former develops cunning and career shrewdness, the latter understanding. All in all, then, the sins of middlebrow culture can with justice be declared to be deeply related to the rat-race of metropolitan living.

Having made the preceding observations concerning middlebrow culture—observations which must be added to those already made in Chapter 8—we can further extend the reader's understanding of the nature of middlebrow culture, by briefly discussing a fresh type of middlebrow posture which is peculiarly urban in origin. It is a species of middlebrow outlook that receives its fullest expression among the decadent artificialities of an urban civilization which has lost contact with the sincere and emotionally significant expressions of the human spirit. It illustrates only too well the tendency of the middlebrow outlook to move towards a type of "cultural gamesmanship." The middlebrow stance to which we are referring will be discussed in the section which follows.

## IV. MIDDLEBROW CULTURE AND "CAMP"

There is a somewhat pretentious variant of middlebrow culture, called "Camp," which deserves separate discussion. The importance of Camp in the present context is that it is peculiarly and unmistakably the product of degenerate trends in urban civilization—trends which are found among certain middlebrow cultural pretenders, particularly artists of various kinds, some film directors with "advanced" ideas of technique and some "avant-garde" writers. Camp has been discussed by Susan Sontag [2] but its importance in the present context is the degree to which it illustrates the enervating characteristics and effete effects of the metropolis upon mental and cultural life. It shows these effects both in the blasé attitude, emphasized by Simmel,[3] and in the decadent dropping of the object, emphasized by Joad.[4] Camp is essentially a degradation of the moral sensibilities and the need for communal concern with social values, so characteristic of high culture. It is likewise an abandonment of the quest for social justice and the loss of the awareness of a tragic sense of life. The tragic sense of life creates an interest in the plight and remediable suffering of concrete individuals and such concern is likewise part of the *raison d'être* of high culture. Middlebrows who have either given up the struggle for honest self-identification or who have never taken up that struggle at all, and the intellectually lazy and socially indifferent who are looking for a justification of a cultivated alienation, find in Camp a ready-made ideology for their irresponsibilities.

Sontag defines Camp in general as a love of the unnatural: a preference for the artificial, the aesthetic pose, the social role, the exaggeration, the extravagance, and the monolithic style. It is a pose, expressed in every artistic medium, in which form and style are emphasized as the important attributes and content is devalued. It is a pose which turns its back

2 Susan Sontag. *Against Interpretation and Other Essays.* New York: Farrar, Strauss & Giroux, 1966. Second printing, 304 pp. See particularly the chapter "Notes on 'Camp,' " pp. 275–92. See also "The Sensational Susan Sontag." *The Atlantic Monthly.* Vol. 218, No. 3, September, 1966, 59–63.

3 *The Sociology of George Simmel.* Translated, edited, and with an introduction by Kurt H. Wolff. New York: The Free Press, 1964. 445 pp. See Part V, Chapter 4 "The Metropolis and Mental Life," 409–24.

4 C. E. M. Joad. *Decadence. A Philosophical Inquiry.* London: Faber and Faber Limited, 1948. 430 pp. The reader is urged to read Part II "Applications. Decadence in Our Time," 251 *et seq.*

on the problem of good and evil and on the artistic task of wrestling with that problem. Camp makes a virtue out of detachment and non-involvement, both of which are so central to the existentialist outlook. To be a Camp buff—if such a harsh-sounding phrase is permissible—a middlebrow must be disengaged and be apolitical. To possess the sensibility which goes by the name of Camp is to convert the serious into the frivolous, to deal in such a way with serious matters that they don't quite come off or to deal with serious matters in such a way as to ridicule them deliberately. The former stance is likely to be inadvertent, the latter, deliberate Camp.

To illustrate the wide variety of matters which reflect the cold enthusiasm of Camp, Sontag lists the following: Zuleika Dobson, Tiffany lamps, Scopitone films, The Brown Derby restaurant on Sunset Boulevard in Los Angeles, *The Enquirer,* headlines and stories, Aubrey Beardsley drawings, *Swan Lake,* Bellini's operas, Visconti's direction of *Salome* and *'Tis Pity She's a Whore,* certain turn-of-the-century picture postcards, Schoedsack's *King Kong,* the Cuban pop singer, La Lupe, Lynn Ward's novel in woodcuts, *God's Man,* the old Flash Gordon comics, women's clothing of the twenties (feather boas, fringed and beaded dresses), the novels of Ronald Firbank and Ivy Compton-Burnett, and stag movies seen without lust. What is to be noticed as characteristic of all these motley items is that they have "style," although this need not necessarily be a virtue. Hitler had style but this did not commend him to civilized people. In general, middlebrow enthusiasts of Camp are interested in "Campy" movies, clothes, furniture, popular songs, novels, people, buildings, ideas of some lunatic fringe, professional showmanship instead of solidity, the mouth-filling phrase instead of the transforming idea, and so on.

Simmel spoke of the metropolis as creating men and women who loved the pose, the role, the extravagance of mannerism, caprice and preciousness, in order to "stand out." To such metropolitan types, substance or content in one's life does not mean a thing. To catch the attention of others is what is important. The "phony" image and the histrionic hamming of those in the public eye—these are the inverted moments of truth. Such attitudes are pure Camp and many middlebrows love it. As a result, if it is the role that we seek, we can get it in the corny, female flamboyance of movie sexpots or the frozen character-structure of George Arliss or George Sanders. If it is extravagance that we seek, we can get it in a movie portraying a woman walking around in a dress made of three million feathers, in a movie dealing with a good guy who discovers a money-tree growing in his garden, in a movie theme concerned with a London draper's assistant (courtesy of H. G. Wells) who has the power to remake the world by his every wish or in a film showing the last man on earth surrounded by millions of idolizing women—a natural monopoly which has been created by the fact that all other men have become the victims of a strange disease which thus far has been sexually selective.

Many middlebrows imagine themselves to be highly cultured and inside-dopesters of the arts, by cultivating a "pure" aestheticism. Not for them the moralistic concerns of high culture or the tension between a moral predicament and an aesthetic passion—a tension so frequently found in avant-garde literature. Camp is wholly aesthetic. The earmarks of high culture are its concern with truth, beauty, goodness and seriousness. The earmarks of Camp, by contrast, are aesthetic preciousness, style and, if possible, a comic vision of the world. The middlebrow with a taste for Camp wishes only to enjoy and appreciate or—as Joad would have put it—he values experience for its own sake and "to hell with where it leads." The dropping of the object, aesthetically speaking, has now become a virtue.

Camp illustrates the superficiality with which middlebrows with cultural pretensions will attack the question of the purpose of aesthetic experience and the general problem of the quest for meaning. Insofar as Camp is concerned with aesthetic and cultural experience, it is not indifferent to the dictum "Man does not live by bread alone." Insofar as Camp fails to exercise discrimination and seriousness, prefers the pose to the reality, the extravagance and conceit to any real effort at understanding, and prefers immediate enjoyment rather than a sense of direction, it is mindless. Camp is merely an up-to-date version of the degradation of cultural life which the modern metropolis makes possible. It provides a comfortable operating position for the rootless intellectual and for those who have either lost sight of or never understood the mission of a genuine culture.

## V. MASS CULTURE

Mass culture has to be distinguished, on the one hand, from middlebrow and, on the other hand, from lowbrow culture. A little later we shall spell out the difference between mass culture and lowbrow culture. Here let us discriminate between middlebrow and mass culture, remembering that the lines we are trying to draw between them are not always hard and fast. At certain points these two types of culture tend to merge into one another. In general, however, middlebrow culture exhibits a definite interest in ideas and the arts. This interest is a self-conscious one but it is also a superficial one. Neither rigor of thought, sustained attention, intellectual perseverance nor deep seriousness characterize the middlebrow posture in cultural matters. Fantasy, the inability to make fine but necessary distinctions, and an often chronic failure to distinguish between the genuine and the phony in many intellectual and artistic contexts, are all noticeable in the middlebrow treatment of themes. Intellectual and artistic pretensions abound in the middlebrow approach to most matters. A topic is less a driving and sustained challenge to increase one's power of understanding than it is a conversation piece for the tedious good humor of a dinner or a cocktail party.

Mass culture, by contrast, has a much thinner interest in ideas and these must almost invariably be oversimplified to an absurdly concrete level. This may be done by means of pictures, slogans or analogies all of which usually have only the remotest of relationships to the original ideas they were intended to convey. In mass culture there is no pose at all that ideas really matter and no preoccupation with them at all. In literature, the arts, the cinema and mass entertainment via radio, television or the theatre, there is no pretense at being genuinely interested in cultural experiences of quality. The end sought by those who enjoy mass culture is entertainment, distraction and escape from the seriousness of life. Subtlety is to be avoided at all costs, in human concern as well as in serious ideas. The object of mass culture is to fill up time, that is, to while away free time as pleasantly as possible and without taxing one's mind or having one's convictions and values challenged. In mass culture the more the stimulation is varied, the more it is appreciated. One cannot say that mass culture is mindless and entirely lacking in aesthetic sensibility. The attributes of thought and feeling are present but at so low a level that they can rarely be said to enlarge the understanding, promote emotional balance or improve the individual's judgment.

With the preceding brief distinction, then, in mind, let us note that in mass culture we come to the nub of those leisure-time concerns which the communications technology of the overcentralized metropolis has, in part, reinforced. Before going on to provide a taxonomy for mass culture, let us first *enumerate* some of the cultural manifestations which are subsumable under this rubric. Mass culture will include, but without limitation, the major programs on radio and television, particularly soap operas, horse operas, Western operas and space operas. The themes of mass culture are also reflected by the sensationalism of the tabloid newspaper and low-tone, brassy periodicals such as *True Confessions*. Also part of mass culture are spectator sports, vaudeville, Broadway musicales, barber shop quintets, potato races at club picnics, the gambling of card-playing buffs in such areas as Miami and in some communities in Los Angeles county, the social activities and parades of Rotarians, Kiwanis, Elks and dozens of other social organizations, and the activities of retirees who are chronic fishermen and shuffleboard enthusiasts.

If we are looking for the element of humor in mass culture, we shall find it quite varied but lacking always, as we have already said, any element of subtlety. That humor will vary over a whole spectrum of possibilities, from the situational humor of Donald Duck and Jerry the Mouse, through the antics of Red Skelton and the cinematic horseplay of the Marx Brothers, thence to the newspaper caricature carrying a politically obvious meaning and finally to the sometimes harsh, sometimes grisly and sometimes Rabelaisian touches of the *Mad* pocketbooks. Above all, mass culture includes the productions of the movie industry or what Hortense Powdermaker [5] has called "The Dream Factory." The influence of the movies in creating distractions which turn people away from the serious business of life—distractions which produce a tinsel happiness and cover a gnawing despair in the life of the average man and woman—cannot be underestimated. There is still some question as to whether television will succeed in replacing the cinema in the production of satisfying distraction, since the unlimited context of action offered by the film, makes for a much wider scope in the possibility for distractions. The fundamental role which such distractions play in meeting the moods of the average man and woman has been explored in a classic paper by van den Haag.[6]

## VI. LOWBROW CULTURE

Mass culture—we have already noted—is not to be confused with the culture of lowbrows. It is therefore necessary to digress for a moment in order to make the distinction between mass culture and lowbrow culture, which we promised earlier. It is necessary that we make this distinction, because it is *chiefly* mass culture and middlebrow culture which are widely disseminated by our highly centralized, large-scale communities. Lowbrow culture, by contrast, is less frequently offered on radio and television programs of our mass media. When lowbrow fare is offered there, it is usually material which is inoffensive, that is, not regarded as in bad taste for *family viewing,* and therefore not likely to offend a middle-class audience or a working-class audience with a middle-class psychology. Thus the presentation of a beauty contest, a bicycle race or an amateur, golden gloves boxing match all represent cases in point. The reason that we find lowbrow fare ill represented on radio or television—except for such material as noisy jazz songs executed by shouting Negro singers or intended for adolescents whose hormones are popping violently—is related to our national social psychology.

5 Hortense Powdermaker. *Hollywood the Dream Factory.* Grossets Universal Library. Boston: Little Brown & Company Edition, 1950. 342 pp.
6 Ernest van den Haag. "Popular Culture." 167–91. In *The Fabric of Society. An Introduction to the Social Sciences,* by Ralph Ross and Ernest van den Haag. New York: Harcourt, Brace, 1957. 777 pp.

American society is increasingly a middle-class society and the leisure-time activities of middle-class society find their chief expression through middlebrow and mass culture. The former is chiefly an outlet for the more educated, upper income, middle-class groups. The latter is chiefly confined to the less educated groups with more modest incomes. These two cultures merge at the fringes with the less educated and economically less privileged groups aspiring to the cultural interests and pretensions of American middlebrows. The aesthetic biases, the values, attitudes, interests, ideas, and levels of aspiration which characterize America, stem largely from the themes of either middlebrow or mass culture and *not at all from lowbrow culture.* Because this is so, it is important to take time out to distinguish mass culture from lowbrow culture. After the brief discussion of lowbrow culture which we shall take up in a moment, the distinction between middlebrow and lowbrow culture will hardly be missed by any reader, particularly in the light of the examination of middlebrow culture, which we entered upon in Part II of this volume. The distinction, however, between mass culture and middlebrow culture is less likely to be obvious and therefore has been made.

Lowbrow culture is characterized by greater vulgarity and crassness than mass culture. Its contents include such items as the following: low-grade comic books which appeal almost wholly to quasi-illiterates; mud-slinging, pie-throwing comedies; zany movie antics such as those provided by the Keystone Cops in the comedy films of the Twenties; penny arcades; boardwalk shows, boardwalk entertainment and boardwalk "chamber of horrors" exhibits; sensational stunts such as those provided by marathon dancers, flagpole sitters, pie-eating contests, or cigar-smoking contests in which the object is to retain without its crumbling, the longest possible ash at the end of a cigar; burlesque and girlie-shows; the improvised fun at working-class picnics; beer-hall and basement-tavern entertainment and the activities of juke joints and taxi dance halls.

The main reason, however, that prompts us to state that lowbrow culture is not synonymous with mass culture, is its *complete mindlessness.* This can be seen from some of the more recent innovations in lowbrow culture, such as motorcycle clubs for adolescents, the "chicken" games of immature, teen-age hot-rodders, the hoop-craze of the late 50's and, perhaps, the go-go craze of the mid-60's. Furthermore, in the quest for aesthetic satisfaction, lowbrow culture exhibits such extreme limitations of taste as to be as close to zero in this respect as one could possibly get. The flat and repetitive, musical range of hill-billy music and the neuromuscular excitement of hootenanny melodies, are cases in point. There is no lowbrow literature unless it be that of the pulps with their action stories. The Baby Jane Holzer craze, rock 'n' roll, stock-car racing, television teenage dances and the craps-table culture of Las Vagas are all additional examples of what might properly be included under the rubric of lowbrow culture. For a description of some of these culturally marginal aspects of the American scene, the reader will find the work of Tom Wolfe [7] most illuminating.

There is a basic need which lowbrow culture fulfills for its devotees. All men require some sort of excitement and interest in their lives in order to give them zest. But the low intellectual level of most lowbrows frequently excludes them from sharing the satisfactions of *any* type of culture—even those of mass culture. Lowbrow culture exhibits extreme limitations in taste and makes no pretense at being concerned with ideas at all—a pretense which is found to some extent even in mass culture. The actionist tendencies of lowbrows and the remarkable fact that they are often individuals with little emotional balance and even less aesthetic sensitivity, closes the door to the appreciation of even the relatively untaxing, unsophisticated music, plays and literature for which mass culture has succeeded in creating an audience. The lowbrow is so often the creature who has the eyes that see not and the ears that hear not, that he automatically becomes marginal even to mass culture. Like the rest of us, however, he too requires zest and savor in his life and he finds it in the varied, action fare of the lowbrow culture of our time.

[7] Tom Wolfe. *The Kandy-Kolored Tangerine Flake Steamline Baby*. New York: Farrar, Straus and Giroux, 1965. Third Printing. 339 pp.

# 21

# Pathologies of Culture
## in Urban Life*

### I. KITSCH IN MASS CULTURE

Having tried to distinguish, then, between mass and lowbrow culture, let us now return to the task of describing more extensively than before, one of the most conspicuous features of mass culture—*kitsch*. In Chapter 6 we defined kitsch in a general way and then dealt with a few brief examples of it in operation. Again we suggest that the reader take a fresh glance at the material already presented in that chapter. We did not, however, stress in that chapter the more depressing consideration that kitsch is one of the leading cultural products of an urban civilization. This is what we must do now, that is to say, in this chapter we return to kitsch as an expression of the artificial, shallow and denaturing processes which the mass society of the metropolitan milieu accepts as part of its explicit definition of culture. Almost everything which is deeply associated with the excitements of our pathological forms of urban living tends also to be something which is transient rather than something which is supposed to take sustained root in the heart and mind of mass man.

Cultural interests which are transient are also very likely to be cultural interests which are second-hand. The denatured products of high culture, which we have called kitsch, and the childish fantasies concerning life and its many complexities and inescapable tragedies—which are also part of what is meant by kitsch—easily receive pathological expression in the leisure-time activities provided by a culturally rootless, urban civilization. The relation of the kitsch of mass culture to the themes of high culture is about the same as a sign in a man's home, reading "God Bless Our Home," to the spiritual regimes a monastic order lays down in order that a deeply religious subject be able to purify his soul and become a model of the genuine expression of the religious impulse. Or, to

* Chapter 21, with adaptations and modifications, has been taken from the following source: Henry Winthrop, "Culture, Mass Society, and The American Metropolis. Mass Culture, Lowbrow Culture, and Folk Culture: An Existentialist View." *Journal of Existentialism*. Vol. 7, No. 28, Summer, 1967, 505–528.

put the matter another way, kitsch in mass culture resembles the themes and motivations of high culture in about the same way that the prescription given in the old saw, "If at first you don't succeed, try, try again," resembles a management counselor's analysis of why a firm's decisions and activities resulted in a net loss for the firm. Kitsch deceives its enthusiasts by leading them to believe that a cultural gimmick of some sort is providing the profound insight into human struggle, frustration and striving, that can be provided by an earnest effort to lend oneself to the stream of consciousness of a great writer or the tight and involved exposition of a great thinker who is trying to get us to see a certain situation in a fresh light.

The material that follows is an extended discussion of the forms of kitsch in mass culture which are provided by the pathological, leisure-time activities of an urban civilization. Before we begin, however, let us briefly recapitulate the nature of kitsch. Kitsch refers to those products of mass culture which make it possible for the reader or the onlooker to avoid the task of giving a cultural product the true intelligent and critical handling of the emotional themes presented to the reader or spectator. What must be emphasized is the fact that kitsch denatures the individuality of a work of art, that it treats character and plot rather woodenly and that it presents human conflict and struggle in flat, moral blacks and whites. The great aim of kitsch is to avoid taxing the reader or onlooker either intellectually or emotionally, to help him avoid the seriousness which is the *sine qua non* of high culture, to make a virtue out of superficiality and to place a premium upon simplicity and artificiality of treatment. We now wish to explore the attributes of kitsch in mass culture a little more closely by looking at a number of instances of kitsch in full flower. It is important that we do this since kitsch is one of the most conspicuous attributes of mass culture.

First consider an example from the drama. Whenever the producer or director of a play whose setting and characters are from an earlier, historical period, recasts it in modern dress by having the action take place in a modern context and by allowing the characters to speak with current locutions rather than the original dialogue and speech forms used by the playwright, kitsch is likely to be the result. The world of learning, perhaps, provides the most frequent examples of the denaturing characteristic of kitsch and the large, urban center the widest market for that denaturing. Consider the following examples of kitsch from the world of learning—examples which depend upon *popularization*. In the 20's the American public was furnished with a popularization of philosophy, which took the country by storm. This was Will Durant's [1] *The Story of Philosophy*. This book was written both interestingly and entertainingly. It was, however, more the *story of philosophers* than of philosophy.

[1] Will Durant. *The Story of Philosophy*. New York: Simon & Schuster, 1926. 577 pp.

The complex and profound themes of philosophy were oversimplified and denatured considerably, so that although the average reader could understand what Durant was saying, the material presented left the philosophical matters being considered at so superficial a level that one could not say that they were really grasped by the reader.

Furthermore, to maintain interest, Durant made use of a good deal of anecdotal material and of material which gave glimpses into the personalities of the great philosophers. The object, of course, was to make them seem human. This is an important aim to realize since, for the average man or woman, philosophers are stereotyped as creatures who "are out of this world." Such material is, of course, intrinsically interesting in its own right and, perhaps, effectively brings philosophy within the framework of interest of the average man. What it decidedly does not do, however, is impart a real understanding of philosophical issues and problems or inspire the reader to plunge more deeply into philosophy by continued reading. Popularization of this type clearly runs the danger of convincing the reader that he has understood some very difficult matters bristling with both perplexities and complexities. He is thus satisfied with himself intellectually when, in fact, he has only touched the surface. This encouragement of superficiality is the risk which is run by all well-intentioned kitsch in the sphere of learning. The rash of books we have had since Durant's *The Story of Philosophy,* such as the many simplified accounts of this or that subject matter, all attempting to introduce the reader painlessly to various fields of learning, or the many books bearing titles such as *Chemistry For the Millions* or *Economics For the Millions,* and so on, are further examples of the deplorable effects of kitsch.

Other examples of kitsch from the world of learning are equally numerous and likewise stem from the effort at popularization. One of these is the effort to rewrite the Bible in modern prose. An early attempt in this direction was made by Hendrik Willem Van Loon.[2] This may unquestionably make the Bible more understandable and may even make the television or movie presentation of a Biblical theme more interesting. At the same time, however, the *poetical quality* of the original King James version is wholly lost—a quality which has, perhaps, more than anything else made the Bible a moving vehicle for the best impulses in the spirit of man.

Examples of kitsch are, of course, very common in the arts. We meet kitsch in the romantic love story of the typical, Hollywood film, in which the action is governed by the well-known, scenario formula of Sam and

---

2 Hendrik Willem Van Loon. *The Story of the Bible.* New York: Permabooks, 1953. 448 pp. This work was originally published in 1923. Its value in bringing home to the reader, the historical events which surround monotheism and Christianity cannot be denied. The price, however, is the loss of the moving quality of the English prose into which the Bible was originally translated.

Bella Spewack, namely, "Boy meets girl—boy loses girl—boy gets girl." By this we refer to the cinematic story which usually unfolds in three stages. In the first stage the hero and the heroine meet and fall in love. In the second stage through some misunderstanding or some unforeseen circumstance, they are forced to part in anger or in disappointment. In the third stage something happens to resolve the misunderstanding or eliminate the circumstances which separated them, and they find each other once more. In an earlier day Hollywood also supplied a customary kitsch ending to every love story—an ending in which the lovers kissed and lived happily ever after.

In popular music, such as jazz, we likewise have kitsch both in words and music. We have it both in the hackneyed rhymes of the lyrics and in the hackneyed content of the love themes, in which love is almost invariably equated with sex appeal. We also meet kitsch in the honky-tonk music of such performers as Andy "Plymouth" Rocke, in which classic pieces are denatured in order to produce melodic and rhythmic effects only, omitting the development, counterpoint, thematic variations and innovations in musical structure of the original classic compositions.[3] Kitsch also occurs in the effort to teach beginners to play a simple instrument by following numbers on an instruction sheet. We often find it in the "schmaltzy" or sweet, mood music of the dance floor. Many other examples could be furnished of kitsch in music. All of them, however, would have one element in common, and that would be an avoidance of the intellectual and aesthetic elements of composition in depth.

Numerous examples of kitsch abound in the other arts. We find it in popular newspaper poetry which equates rhymed material and doggerel with poetry and the poetical image. Kitsch is the basis of the do-it-yourself art kit which attempts to teach the beginner the art of painting by filling in numbered parts of a presketched composition, with colors indicated by the instructions given. We meet kitsch in the phony Greek columns of public buildings whose original designs were approved by accountants and politicians. These will be columns which either carry no weight or carry very little weight. They are meant to be decorative in some public edifice for which the Greek column was never intended in the first place. Kitsch abounds in collages and montages exhibits which are without meaning but use the potpourri technique of the collage and the montage—easily acquired by the artistic pretender—to suggest some profound, artistic merit which is not really present.

3 In this connection it is suggested that the reader listen to the following record. *Honky Tonk Classics* by Andy "Plymouth" Rocke. *Curio Records* (Curio C-3). The classic pieces which are denatured into kitsch on this record are the following: Rachmaninoff's Second Piano Concerto, Danube Waves, Liebestraum, Barcarolle, La Cinquantine, Minuete in G, Melody in F, Tchaikovsky's Pianto Concerto Anitra's, Dance, Tchaikovsky's Pathétique Symphonie, Chopin's Polonaise in A Flat, Brahms's Hungarian Dance #2. All these are the titles *as printed* on the album cover.

Kitsch assails us every day in popular efforts to achieve painless learning. The "digests" of articles and books in popular periodicals constitute abundant examples of kitsch. Advertisements for records which will enable one to learn a foreign language while sleeping, is sheer educational kitsch. We meet with kitsch in advertising which claims to increase one's reading speed and comprehension by certain novel methods of instruction. These are methods, however, which really provide only reading schemes that increase superficiality, particularly for material which deals with ideas. They reflect a monstrous form of kitsch to which the intellectually uncritical are easily susceptible. The most glaring evidence of the worthlessness of these speed-reading methods is the fact that those who swear by them give no evidence, whatsoever, of improvement either in the ability to think rigorously, to be creative or to develop any originality in ideas. Finally, we are presented with kitsch in the popular newspaper attempts at psychological counseling, whether we are dealing only with advice to the lovelorn or with other types of individual problems. The complexities of emotional difficulties and the nuances of an individual's motivational vicissitudes are completely denatured out of each correspondent's problems in counseling, which is usually given by some woman newspaper columnist. For this reason such advice is generally worthless. Kitsch in counseling may even be personally destructive.

All the preceding then reflect examples of kitsch in mass and—to some extent—also middlebrow culture. Let us now turn to a classification of the major attributes of mass culture, since it is mass culture which is made omnipresent in our time by the development of an urban, mass communications technology.

## II. A TAXONOMY FOR MASS CULTURE

The attributes of mass culture which provide a workable classification of its functions have been suggested by Leo Lowenthal.[4] These attributes may be characterized as follows: (1) standardization, (2) stereotypy, (3) conservatism, (4) mendacity and (5) manipulated consumer desires. We shall here try to demonstrate these attributes by example rather than enter upon an extended discussion or analysis of them.

[4] The taxonomy we are employing here has been suggested by some observations of Leo Lowenthal. These observations have been slightly revised and extended here. This revision and extension is the basis of the classification we are employing for mass culture. See Lowenthal's *Literature, Popular Culture and Society.* Englewood Cliffs, New Jersey: Prentice-Hall, 1961. 169 pp. Lowenthal's observations occur on p. 11 of this volume. It should be made clear here that I have used the categories of Lowenthal's five-point classification *in my own way.* There is no certainty that the meanings Lowenthal would have attached to these categories would jibe with the meanings I have attached to them. It is likewise more than probable that Lowenthal might not give them the identical content I have given them here.

Examples of *standardization* in mass culture occur in many forms. Let us enumerate some of those forms here. (1) The movie "happy ending" which is often so false to the tragic sense of life. (2) A movie shot is frequently standardized to last not more than 45 seconds. (3) The choruses of most popular songs usually possess the same number of bars. (4) A movie scenario, as we have already noted, is almost invariably built on the Sam and Bella Spewack formula "Boy meets girl—boy loses girl—boy gets girl." (5) The canned greetings—birthday or otherwise—which Western Union will deliver in song for a price, are the same for all.

The use of the *stereotype* in mass culture is very common, although it is not always easy to distinguish the *standardized* theme from the *stereotyped* theme. The former depends for its effect on a *formula,* the latter on thoughtless suggestibility and ignorance. The following represent a cluster of examples of stereotypy. (1) Many cartoons and caricatures seek to convey a false image of an *idea* or a movement, as in current caricatures of *Reds* or *Communists* and in the caricatures of *Drys* or *Prohibitionists,* which were so characteristic of the *Prohibition Period* in American life. (2) In the movies men and women are almost always handsome and glamorous, a device which is absurd, as reality, but perhaps pleasant as an ideal. (3) In poetry the message must be canned and clear, as in popular doggerel, barrack room ballads or the poems of Edgar Guest or it must be "cute" as in the messages on greeting cards. (4) Art reproductions are almost invariably sold in drug stores for color and decorative purposes and rarely for the artistic education of the purchaser. The message, social background and artistic problems which existed for the artist are never made clear to the buyer—but only the price. (5) Jazz music of the canned variety (not the improvisations of jazz which we hear at the Newport Jazz Festivals) depends only on rhythm, melody and harmony. Counterpoint is banished forever because this would constitute an intellectual strain.

*Conservatism* is a trait which is fairly easy to detect in mass culture. It is revealed when certain beliefs are held both uncritically and tenaciously. Examples of such beliefs are the following. (1) If you work hard, success is sure to attend your efforts. (2) If your grandfather voted Republican this is reason enough for you to vote likewise. (3) What's good enough for General Motors is good enough for the USA—an outlook made famous by Charlie Wilson of General Motors.

*Mendacity* is an outstanding characteristic of mass culture. It reveals itself in chronic lying, exaggeration and absurd claims—particularly in advertising. Three well-known examples of mendacity in mass culture in the United States are the following. (1) The tendency to lie about human nature and social reality in radio and television soap operas and various other fantasies of the radio and television script writer's art. (2) The false claims in advertising and the cynicism with which it is asserted that such claims are supported by scientific research. (3) The lying in cinema advertising and the chronic use of such superlatives as "colossal, stupendous and magnificent" in recommending and praising a film.

We come now to a category of mass culture which has to do with our American standard of consumption, that is, our love for increasing amounts of goods and services without which most Americans would feel life is not worth living. We are referring to the great American dream which Fromm [5] has described as follows.

Man today is fascinated by the possibility of buying more, better, and especially, new things. He is consumption-hungry. The act of buying and consuming has become a compulsive, irrational aim, because it is an end in itself, with little relation to the use of, or pleasure in the things bought and consumed. To buy the latest gadget, the latest model of anything that is on the market, is the dream of everybody, in comparison to which the real pleasure in use is quite secondary. Modern man, if he dared to be articulate about his concept of heaven, would describe a vision which would look like the biggest department store in the world, showing new things and gadgets, and himself having plenty of money with which to buy them. He would wander around open-mouthed in this heaven of gadgets and commodities, provided only that there were ever more and newer things to buy, and perhaps that his neighbors were just a little less privileged than he. (p. 135)

This love of gadgetry leads to a set of activities characteristic of mass culture which might be designated as the *manipulation of consumer desires*. Such manipulation takes place in four ways: (1) through the promotion of false wares; (2) through the creation of false needs; (3) through the creation of milady's fantasies; and (4) through the creation of public fantasy. Let us try to give examples of each of these four modes in turn.

*The promotion of false wares* refers to the tendency of the consumer to satisfy his needs for goods and services so uncritically and thoughtlessly that he actually encourages manufacturers to create a market for items which really betray these needs. The following constitute examples of situations of this sort. (1) The sale of drinking glasses with false bottoms in establishments which dispense refreshments. (2) The purchase of false, antique furniture by collectors. This may be, for instance, furniture which is made to look wormy and by inference, aged, by a special process in which wormholes are produced by bullets shot into arms and legs. (3) The sale of poisonous, processed foods made to look fresh chemically. (4) The willingness to purchase jerry-built houses, just as long as they appeal to the eye.[6] (5) A fondness for ready-made men's ties in which the fabric frays after two wearings. (6) The universalization of Coca-Cola which is so powerful chemically that it will dissolve nails after awhile. One can

---

[5] Erich Fromm. *The Sane Society*. New York: Holt, Rinehart and Winston, 1955. 370 pp.

[6] In this connection see John Keats. *The Crack in the Picture Window*. New York: Ballantine Books, 1956. 158 pp.

readily imagine what it must do to the human stomach, given enough time.

Coca-Cola is now sold nearly everywhere on earth where one can find Americans or their representatives. It is done largely through ads picturing pretty girls. To many foreigners Coca-Cola has become a *symbol* of American standardization. The French who fear American standardization refer to it as "la coca-colaization du monde."

Advertisers and commercial sponsors who are responsible for the dissemination of mass culture, have been accused of creating false needs for mass-man. These are desires for goods and services which are successfully implanted because of the fears, vanities, and status-seeking of the prospective consumer. They are usually for goods and services which are either nonessential or—if there is a genuine need which has given rise to them—are more properly met by other means. The following list constitutes a small sample of what is meant by *the creation of false needs*. (1) *Arid* for milady's sweating armpits. (2) *Sen-Sen* for a lover's fetid breath. (3) Annual fashions in women's wear in which change for the sake of change has become a habit and in which feminine bodily narcissism is almost invariably strengthened at the expense of almost all other attributes —intellectual, spiritual and even physical, such as carriage and exercise. Walter Pitkin calls woman "that economic imbecile" because of the strong tendency of the American woman to engage in the aimless purchasing of unnecessary goods and services. The woman buyer is usually responsible for about 85 percent of national retail sales. (4) Feminine susceptibility to the use of chemicals to remove the body odor which the lady doesn't have in the first place, so that she may become kissable, squeezable and hugable. (5) The presence of Planned Product Obsolescence in everything, that is to say, the tendency to throw away or discontinue the use of many consumer items which are still in good condition—like cars, refrigerators and washing machines—in order to own the latest models of these same items.

The type of advertising by which these false needs are created is a fascinating cultural phenomenon in itself. Jules Henry [7] has furnished us with excerpts from a series of advertisements which promote false needs and this series is reproduced at this point. Henry asks whether it is literally true that

. . . everybody's talking about the new *Starfire* (automobile)?
. . . Alpine cigarettes "put the men in menthol smoking"?
. . . a woman in *Distinction* foundations is so beautiful that all other women want to kill her?
. . . *Hudson's Bay Scotch* "is scotch for men among men"?
. . . if one buys clothes at Whitehouse and Hardy his wardrobe will have "the confident look of a totally well-dressed man"?

[7] Jules Henry. *Culture Against Man.* New York: Vintage Books, 1965. 495 pp.

. . . *Old Spice* accessories are "the finest grooming aides a man can use"?

. . . 7 *Crown* whiskey "holds within its icy depths a world of summertime"?

. . . "A man needs *Jockey* support" because Jockey briefs "give a man the feeling of security and protection he needs"?

. . . one will "get the smoothest, safest ride of your life on tires of *Butyl*"?

. . . the new *Pal Premium Injector* blade "takes the friction out of shaving" because it "rides on liquid ball bearings"?

. . . *Pango Peach* color by Revlon comes "from east of the sun . . . west of the moon where each tomorrow dawns" . . . is "succulent on your lips" and "sizzling on your finger tips (And on your toes, goodness knows)" and so will be one's "adventure in paradise"?

. . . if a woman gives in to her "divine restlessness" and paints up her eyelids with *The Look* her eyes will become "jungle green . . . glittery gold . . . flirty eyes, tiger eyes"?

. . . a "new ingredient" in *Max Factor Toiletries* "separates the men from the boys"?

. . . when the Confederate General Basil Duke arrived in New York at the end of the Civil War "Old Crow (whiskey) quite naturally would be served"?

. . . *Bayer* aspirin provides "the fastest, most gentle to the stomach relief you can get from pain"? (p. 46)

Henry has analyzed the characteristics of this advertising language of mass culture. He finds it possesses three characteristics: (1) *pecuniary pseudotruth,* (2) *para-poetic hyperbole* and (3) *pecuniary logic.* Any advertisement may possess one or more of these three attributes. Henry defines the first as a false statement which is offered as though it were the truth but which no one is really expected to believe. The second characteristic is defined as language or phraseology which is something like poetry—containing high-flown figures of speech—but which, likewise, no one is expected to believe literally. By *pecuniary logic* Henry refers to phraseology which, it appears, wishes to convey conviction for commercial purposes, but fails to do so to the mind of the critical reader.[8]

We come now to the third category in the manipulation of consumer desires. This is the category which involves *the creation of milady's fantasies.* The phrase, "milady's fantasies," refers to devices, appliances, gadgets and inventions which will make Mrs. Middle Majority happy. Mrs. Middle Majority, a term employed by merchandisers, designates the typical American female consumer whose buying habits are discussed by Vance Packard.[9] Mrs. Middle Majority is the woman who feels that it is

---

[8] *Op. cit.* Pp. 47–8.

[9] Vance Packard. *The Hidden Persuaders.* New York: David McKay, 1957. 275 pp. See particularly Chapter 11, "Class and Caste in the Salesroom," 114–35. According to one writer, Mrs. Middle Majority is the "typical American housewife" who "has a fine moral sense of responsibility and builds her whole life around her home. On the other hand she lives in a narrow, limited world and is quite timid about the outside world. She has little interest in civic work or the arts, she tends to fall into accepted patterns of conformity readily and feels no need for originality." (p. 116)

possible to take household work and drudgery totally out of the kitchen. A convenient way to illustrate the nature of milady's fantasies is to suggest a paradigm of one of her fantasies. The following paradigm—having to do with her work in the kitchen—would, in our opinion, be representative of the type of dream which ever lurks on the surface of Mrs. Middle Majority's consciousness.

The *creation of milady's fantasies* in our paradigm, is a series of dreams. They consist of the following:

1. The dream of a cake mix so universal in its scope that one does not have to mix, knead, stir or batter.

2. The dream of a micro-wave oven which times baking, roasting and cooking and which speeds up these processes.

3. The dream of attachments to these ovens which will slide out the finished product, roll it on to a serving table, set the china and silverware on that same table, slice the food if such slicing should be necessary, salt and pepper it automatically, and so forth.

4. The dream of a push-button device on the serving table just mentioned, which moves it to the dining room area, extends an artificial lever-arm which places the china and silverware in position in front of each diner and finally dishes out the food, without any mess, whatsoever.

5. The dream of an electrical dishwasher which cleans up the dirty dishes and silverware and transports them to a mechanical incinerator which crushes and packages the garbage and then transports it in turn to an appropriate refuse receptacle.

In all of the preceding, of course, the main drawback is that one has to do one's own eating, belching and excreting. Presumably even this limitation will eventually be overcome by advancing technology.

The last category in the manipulation of consumer desires has to do with the provision of services to mass-man and mass-woman. We refer to what we have called *the creation of public fantasy*. This involves such educational functions as the presentation of news of the world in news-reels shown in theatres, in which for a few fleeting seconds a scene or a personality associated with a critical event, is shown, but no effort is ever made to analyze the event for its social or historical significance. Everything shown the onlooker is left unanalyzed and unexplained. Then the rest of the "newsreel" is devoted to sports, fashions, and human interest material like the birth of quintuplets. To the mind of the mesmerized onlooker, this is taken to be the news of the world.

A similar type of fantasy is created by the movie travelogue in which the breathtaking features in the scenery or architecture of a foreign country or of one of its cities, will be shown, leaving the onlooker with the impression that this is a fairyland he would like to visit some day. Never shown at all are the slums, ghettos, favelas and other ghastly areas of the same country or city—areas which are often the price which has been paid for the preservation of the beauty spots shown. The indifference to areas of squalor on the part of those who dwell in the beautiful sections of the cities shown or in the scenic country areas over which the camera lingers, helps considerably to sustain the human misery never shown by the travelogue. Public fantasies make the more sordid, unreal and absurd features of mass culture and urban ugliness, somewhat more bearable.

### III. MASS CULTURE AS "HAVING FUN"

There is an important area of mass culture which lies wholly outside of the classification we have employed. It is properly subsumable under a category which might be called "having fun." Traditional examples of cultural activities within this category would be the following: Mardi Gras; block parties; the masque ball; the Greenwich Village nightclub catering to the out-of-town curious, the uptown-slummer and the restless young suburbanite on Saturday night; the drive-in movie which serves as a "passion pit" for youngsters whose hormones are uncontrollable; the smoke-filled Harlem basement nightclub for white and colored jazz buffs; the Thanksgiving and Christmas parades put on by big city department stores; the planned and the "unplanned" entertainment activities of the "borsht circuit" in the Catskills; the sexually far-out big city club used as a hangout for homosexuals and lesbians and featuring a stage-show or floor-show which is nothing but sugar-coated obscenity; the wife-swapping parties of young, suburban couples, which—although hardly to be condoned—are regarded as livening the tedium of suburbia; the Broadway, sidewalk canteen; the beer guzzling, shouting and singing patrons of an urban Rathskeller, etc. Inasmuch as these are not activities which are popularized *by our mass media,* they deserve separate mention. They are concerned with release from the restraints of everyday life and, I suppose, can be regarded as forms of recreation.

The latest wrinkle in the mass culture of "having fun" is "discothèque" which has been called "total recreation." Discothèque has been honored by a description in *Life* [10] magazine and it is clearly a style of release (or insanity, depending upon your point of view) which only our large urban centers, can offer. *Life* describes it as follows.

To enjoy the latest thing in discothèques, you had better wear ear plugs, dark glasses and shin guards. Otherwise, you may be deafened, blinded and bruised in an electronic earthquake that engulfs you completely in an experience called

[10] "Wild New Flashy Bedlam of the Discothèque." *Life,* Vol. 60, No. 21, May 27, 1966. 72–6.

"total recreation." It has developed out of the tamer discothèque clubs, and its common ingredients are blinking lights that look like Broadway signs gone berserk, canned or live music, dancing and far-out movies flashed on small screens. One place has a boutique, where you can buy nutty clothes to wear so you really fit into the picture. In these new clubs everybody looks like a kook in a Kubla-Khanteen. (p. 72)

The discothèque is a species of "having fun" which has been infiltrated by certain middlebrow, cultural pretensions. For this reason it bids fair to become a sterile, cultural hybrid. Among these cultural pretensions we find such stimuli as those furnished at a private club in Chicago. This Chicago discothèque offers an automated, abstract light-painting called *The Translator*. This device offers a change of colors and patterns produced by the pitch of musical notes. Presumably this device caters to the aesthetic pretensions of its patrons. The Translator apparently marries the virtues of the telharmonium with an animated type of Neoplasticism in which nonrepresentational colored forms and patterns are given constant motion. Some discothèque clubs make extensive use of "pop art" in far-out costumes for both guests and entertainers. In one New York discothèque club the dancers gyrate to mood created by "pop music" and "light paintings" on background screens. Another New York discothèque provides a library, movie room and color TV for "discopooped" guests. In all these small ways the cult of total recreation offers its patrons a marginal contact with culture. One result of such cultural pretension is that neuromuscular ecstasies, generated by sensory stimulation, don a mask of mild, cultural respectability.

In the widening and deepening of that aspect of mass culture which we have categorized as "having fun," we may be witnessing a form of decadence which is dependent upon the hectic life of the metropolis. The spread of such decadence will undoubtedly be facilitated as urbanism, itself, continues to flourish on an ever-increasing scale.

## IV. "TEEN-AGE" CULTURE AS MASS CULTURE

The description of mass culture furnished here would not be complete without mentioning the growth in our time of one of its varieties, namely, "teen-age culture," sometimes called "youth culture" and sometimes called "adolescent culture." This teen-age culture (which we describe briefly below) is that type of culture which is coterminous with the mass culture of the older generation, the culture of the parents of these teen-agers, and all those who follow, by and large, with enthusiasm, the fare offered by our mass media. Teen-age culture is not to be confused either with the culture of social protest of the "upbeat" generation [11] or with the lowbrow culture which we have already described. It is a variant of the "having fun" philosophy of the older generation and, therefore, similarly lacks seriousness, is apolitical and is minimally preoccupied with ideas, the expression of social discontent and programs for social reform.

The expression of these characteristic lacks varies somewhat with the class backgrounds of the cliques of youngsters who enjoy or give active expression to teen-age culture. Nevertheless, teen-age culture must be classified as a variant of mass culture—regardless of the varying class backgrounds of its enthusiasts and practitioners—because of (1) its uniform and relatively nonintellectual *esprit* which cuts across all classes, (2) its lack of seriousness and unconcern over the grave, civic and social problems of the contemporary American community and (3) its central *leitmotif* which everywhere can be summed up as "having fun." It is a culture that can be regarded without question as the junior version of "having fun," the immature facsimile and edition of that type of activity and entertainment fare which the older citizen enjoys in radio, television, movies, the "funnies" and other media of mass communication.

A brief description of the content of teen-age culture has been provided by the sociologist, Jessie Bernard.[12] She has given us the following abstract of the features of teen-age culture.

Teen-age culture is a product of affluence: we can afford to keep a large population in school through high school. The teen-age culture of younger adolescents is characteristically lower class, that of older teen-agers, upper middle class. The material traits of teen-age culture include certain kinds of clothes, automobiles, and the paraphernalia of sports and recreation. Teen-agers constitute an important market; advertisers are in a coalition with them if parents protest. The nonmaterial culture traits include a special language. There is also great ememphasis on fun and popularity. Popular songs reflect the preoccupation of teen-agers with love in its various stages. Political concern is not characteristic of teen-age culture, but, when they are asked for opinions, teen-agers reflect those of their class backgrounds. Class pervades all aspects of teen-age culture from clothes to taste in moving pictures to hangouts to activities. In teen-age society, as in the larger world, a substantial proportion are alienated—outsiders, rejected. At the college level, the old "rah-rah" culture is giving way to more serious vocational and academic cultures. If this trend continues, teen-age culture

11 For a description of the more serious, more socially conscious philosophy and culture of the "upbeat" generation—largely young college and university students—see the following report: *The Young Americans. Understanding the 'Upbeat' Generation.* A *Time-Life* Special Report. The Editors of *Time* and *Life* and nonstaff consultants. New York: Time Incorporated, 1966. 112 pp. This Report discusses both the representatives of teen-age culture as well as the members of the 'upbeat' generation on the American campus—those concerned with transforming and improving the world.

12 Jessie Bernard. "Teen-Age Culture: An Overview," 1–12. In *Teen-Age Culture. The Annals of the American Academy of Political and Social Science.* (Jessie Bernard, special editor). Volume 338, November 1961. 210 pp.

may end with high school graduation; at the college level, young people will be more adult. At the same time, however, it appears that children enter teen-age culture at an earlier age. So long as we can afford to support a large leisure class of youngsters, teen-age culture in some form or other will continue. (p. 1)

Space forbids an extended discussion of the various manifestations of teen-age culture. Among these manifestations, however, let us mention the following: the teen-age magazine, the teen-age musical records and addiction to the high-fidelity phonograph and bongo drums, the rock 'n' roll mania, the teen-age preoccupation with clothes, style and personal glamor (extroversion is "in" and introversion is "out"), automobiles, cosmetics, travel, camping, photography, sports, athletics, the swinging dance, occasional marijuana jags and the use of other materials for kicks, the community "hangout," the early dating and, sometimes, the "steady" date, the high school cheerleader and majorette, the passion for "action" and "ain't love gLand" movies of the drive-in lot, the "petting parties" in parked cars on lonely roads and the associated "bushwacking" or "hunting" in which the peers of teen-agers find the parked cars and flash their headlights on the petting couples, and many other teen-age cultural activities too numerous to mention here.

The middle-class affluence of contemporary America—which Bernard has stressed—has given rise to a host of spoiled youngsters and a round of hedonistic, egocentric activities which are a large part of the content of teen-age culture. This round of activities has been described by Wyden.[13] The clientele may be a *product* of suburbia but the *activities* and *fare* offered this clientele can be provided only by the highly commercialized, overurbanized metropolis and the regimented and canned distractions and entertainment the metropolis can organize. The teen-agers of this public are familiar chiefly with their neatly manicured, fumeless, and comfortably monotonous bedroom communities. They know nothing of the hustle-and-bustle world which creates and caters to their "cultural" demands. They know nothing of life as it is—of a world in which people are unemployed, frustrated and wasted. They know nothing of the live social issues and pressing problems of our time. They know nothing of social tensions, management-labor conflict, international ideological struggle, tax headaches and the worry which attends a bread-and-butter position threatened by the possibility that technology may displace one's economic skills.

These teen-agers know nothing of a world their elders made and left behind. They have been deprived of social perception through extensive living in a suburban community of young families—a community in which there are almost no old people, no poor, no Negroes, no Jews, no places to explore except those chaperoned by mother acting as chauffeur,

13 Peter Wyden. *Suburbia's Coddled Kids*. New York: Avon Books, 1962. 142 pp.

while using the family car. In their communities almost all families have similar incomes, similar homes, similar gadgets and similar interests and before long the suburban teen-agers follow suit with similar attitudes, similar interests, similar social values and similar cultural tastes. Suburbia, indeed, has become the breeding ground of cultural uniformity and behavioral conformity.

The atmosphere or *zeitgeist* of teen-age culture can, perhaps, be well illustrated by its taste for music and the manner in which it expresses itself in this medium. Let us here refer only to *one of the most recent innovations* along this line, since the reader is already familiar with the teen-age song and dance programs transmitted both by television and radio. *Life* [14] not so long ago discussed the rise of the teen-age combo. These are groups of teen-agers who form combos—featured by electric guitars—and these combos enjoy servicing their own peer groups for pay. Occasionally they will play "for fun" with groups with which they may identify closely. *Rock 'n' roll* is, of course, the dominant fare, with a liberal sprinkling of other musical styles. These combo groups range from elementary school youngsters to college groups. The latter tend, however, to cater to the tastes of high school teen-agers, whether these are actually in high school or have started going to college but have not, as yet, cut the cultural umbilicus chord leading back to the musical tastes they acquired in high school. The popularity of these teen-age combos is so great that one of them—called Dino, Desi, and Billy—made up in part of a son of Desi Arnez and a son of Dean Martin, will refuse to go to any city which will not provide police protection from their hysterical and effervescent fans. This particular combo makes $5,000 per performance.

The names assumed by some of these combos reveal real imagination and occasionally that slight pretension towards culture, which middlebrows show more persistently and more avidly. One such combo group of four girls calls itself, *The Freudian Slips,* an excellent example of imagination on the margin of middlebrow culture. Other titles are equally imaginative but make no pretense, whatsoever, at entering the middlebrow cultural park. *Life* has furnished some of the "coolest" combo titles it could find. These read as follows: The Bird and the Worms, Joe Banana and his Bunch, Little Caesar and the Romans, Judas and the Traitors, Dow Jones and the Industrialists, Mogen David and the Grapes of Wrath, The Four Gone Conclusions, What Four?, The Hairy Things, Big Brother and the Holding Company, Studs and the Bearcats, Deluxe and De Bagels, The Baskerville Hounds, The Mixed Emotions, Six and the Single Girl, Jay Walker and the Pedestrians. As the reader can note, there is not a middlebrow cultural pretension in a carload of these titles.

14 "Teen-Age Money Music." *Life.* Vol. 60, No. 22, June 3, 1966. 102–10.

We must again emphasize the fact that teen-age culture, as a junior edition of mass culture, could not have arisen except as an offshoot of the fare and entertainment sponsored by the mass media of an urban civilization. The small community with an independent cultural life of its own—mature and serious—would not be likely to give rise to teen-age culture. The latter demands the mass audience of the communications media of the metropolis and its highly bureaucratized procedures for putting teen-age, cultural entertainment on a paying basis. To be commercially profitable huge advertising and production costs must be incurred. These can only be offset by the mass audience which can be created through the large-scale, communication facilities and centralized commercialization of the big city; whether in the form of paying guests in a theatre or nightclub or in the form of the hopeful payoff in retail sales of his product, which moves the commercial sponsor. The relationships between teen-age culture and the centralizing processes of large-scale urbanization are, therefore, immediately apparent.

## V. FOLK CULTURE

We come finally to our fifth type of culture—*folk culture*. It is easy to distinguish folk culture, on the one hand, from mass culture and middlebrow culture, on the other. Folk culture, which consists of such items as ballads or folklore and legend concerning such heroic figures as Paul Bunyan, Johnny Appleseed, Jesse James, Davey Crockett, springs from the collective consciousness of the people, themselves. It reflects an authentic picture of their yearnings, their values and their everyday way of life. By contrast mass and middlebrow culture consists almost wholly of material created commercially by others—producers, directors, writers, artists and composers—and material which may be fairly alien to the everyday struggles and problems of the average man or woman. Other parts of folk culture prove occasionally to be the creation of particular individuals—comic strip characters, the hero of a play or the image of a movie star—but here again the personality which is admired has been taken to heart by people because that personality has been cast in their own image. It will be a personality or character which reflects the strivings, ambitions, attitudes, interests, biases, ideas, ideals and levels of aspiration of the common man and not those of the more educated, middle class producers of most of the products of mass or middlebrow culture.

The themes of folk culture are neither sophisticated nor high in the level of their spiritual aspirations. They dwell on the satisfactions of only limited portions of the human psyche. They admire only a limited range of heroism. But they are authentic in that they portray the yearnings of the average man or woman. They are understandable in reflecting the trials and tribulations, the fears and struggles, the frustrations and perplexities of men and women who live *in this world* rather than in the dream factories of our mass media. By contrast the themes of mass and middlebrow culture are more ambitious, more extensive and more aspiring, but they function more as ideal and unreal grafts upon the consciousness of the average man and woman rather than as genuine projections of his or her yearnings.

Once more we must remind the reader of the emphasis which has underlain the execution of the present chapter. We have argued that some of the advances of science and technology lead to an intensive development of mass communications and communications technology. We have then gone on to assert that when these are exploited by the mass communications industry which, itself, tends to become highly centralized and bureaucratized,[15] they interlock with the excessive centralization of our large, urban centers. In so doing they act all too often to produce uniformities in the life of culture. These uniformities we have called mass culture and middlebrow culture. The meshing of these two highly centralized situations—the provision of culture and entertainment and the regulation and conduct of life in the metropolis—results in a degradation and denaturing of genuine culture and the abandonment of the Greek ideal of *paideia*. This degradation and degeneration are measured against the ideals of genuine culture, that is, high culture, itself.

It is in these senses that the existence of mass culture constitutes an additional item in the bill of particulars against the excessive centralization of life in the twentieth-century metropolis. The metropolis cannot pace a changing environment which is growing increasingly complex socially, due largely though not solely, of course, to a rapidly changing technology. One of the ways in which the metropolis seeks to distract twentieth-century man from the realities and pathologies of his milieu is through mass culture. It is in this sense that mass culture can be traced in large measure—though not completely—to excessive centralization. It is a major grievance which must be brought to attention in the case against centralization.

15 The type of personality and situations to which excessive centralization can lead in a mass communications industry, is well illustrated in novels dealing with such a milieu. One such representative novel is the following: Donald Stacy. *The God of Channel 1*. New York: Ballantine Books, 1956. 184 pp.

# 22

# Political Overcentralization in a Complex Society: Three Types of Resulting Pathology*

The increasing exploitation of modern science and technology to enrich our modern standard of living and the unplanned extension of urban industrialization as the habitual form in which to meet the growing composite of human wants, has greatly contributed to the formation of the large-scale, human community. The latter in turn has determined the intrinsic nature of the governing political structures and the types of control required by the community. Whether political machines, law-making bodies or law-administering agencies, these structures tend to be bureaucratic. They tend all too often to be complex, top-heavy, unimaginative and unfeeling and easily subject to internal breakdowns in communication. The modern, large-scale community which tends to be host to political centralization and which encourages the bureaucratic conduct of public business, has inevitably become "dystopian" rather than utopian, that is to say, it is a poor place to live in, if one seeks to preserve concerned and humane relationships among men.

Perhaps the gravest charges against large-scale centralization is that the preservation and augmentation of democratic values become more and more difficult as political centralization increases. This will be just as true for capitalistic democracies as it is for political totalitarianisms of the *Left* or *Right*. In order to see why so many thinkers and intellectuals [1] are in despair over "creeping centralization"—a greater menace than "creeping socialism" which, therefore, has been only a special variant and subspecies of the former—let us discuss some of the social pathology which

* Chapter 22, with adaptations and modifications has been taken from the following source: Henry Winthrop. "Political Overcentralization in a Complex Society: Three Types of Resulting Pathology." *Il Politico* (Italy). Vol. XXXI, No. 2, 1966. 239–261.
    [1] In this connection the reader should acquaint himself with the following volume: Morton and Lucia White, *The Intellectual Versus the City*, New York: Mentor Books, 1964, 271 pp.

is almost invariably associated with excessive centralization. The pathologies to be taken up below are, of course, not due solely to centralization but centralization is either *sometimes* their major cause or a factor which distinctly intensifies the pathology in question.

## I. LACK OF DEMOCRACY

Fundamentally a democratic relationship is one in which what Buber [2] calls an I–Thou attitude exists either between two individuals, between two small groups or between an individual and a small group. In the I–Thou relationship A and B each seek to promote the Being and the needs of the other—not, of course, by ignoring their own needs in a saintly fashion—but only in the reasonable sense of mutual aid. In this relationship both A and B will make a genuine effort to achieve mutual understanding. The I–Thou relationship is contrasted by Buber with the I–It relationship. In the latter A and B relate to each other in terms of the use each can make of the other and the degree to which they can effectively manipulate one another. The I–Thou relationship can only thrive in some form of intimacy or face-to-face relationship. A centralized bureaucracy—for the sake of achieving alleged efficiency in its functions—must automatically demand a relationship between one of its employees, A, and a recipient, B, of some of its agency services, in which automatically the I–Thou relationship has to be liquidated if institutional and procedural bedlam are to be avoided. Thus human relationships, at least with respect to community services, cannot be democratic in the I–Thou sense. They can only be instrumental in the sense that people serve to provide each other with needed inputs and outputs.

If overcentralization and bureaucratization are to be regarded as the potential enemies of democracy in spirit, it behooves us to define our terms. If *unimpeachable rigor* of definition is sought for the vocabulary of politics—particularly for such words and phrases in the democratic vocabulary as "democracy," itself, and, in addition, "authority," "rights," "law" and "the rule of law," "freedom," "justice," "social morality"—then, we had better give up before we start. The difficulties inherent in trying to impose logical and scientific rigor on the language of politics, has been amply demonstrated by Weldon.[3] If, however, we allow ourselves the luxury of talking about "democracy" in prescriptive-valuative language whose functions have been succinctly described by Morris,[4] then, at least, we can achieve a first approximation to agreement, or, perhaps,

[2] Martin Buber. *I and Thou.* New York: Charles Scribner's Sons, 1958. 137 pp.

[3] T. D. Weldon. *The Vocabulary of Politics.* Baltimore: Penguin Books, 1953. 199 pp.

[4] Charles Morris. *Signs, Language and Behavior.* New York: George Braziller, 1955. 365 pp. See especially Section 11, *Political Discourse,* 145–6 in Chapter 5, "Types Of Discourse."

we should say, a feeling about a common intention. By prescriptive-valuative language Morris means language which neither makes pretense at logical rigor nor pretends to be describing a state of affairs. Instead, such language frankly possesses the aim of prescribing a given organization of society on the grounds that the proposed organization will best minister to a stated budget of individual and social needs. The purpose of those who use such language is to win social approval for the proposed social organization or reorganization. Wherever possible, those who employ such language will use facts and logic to support their valuative-prescriptive missions. The facts employed may—to cite but one example—be research data about human nature. The logic employed may take as a context some economic laws which have been well tested by short-range, historical experience. The over-all purpose, however, of those who employ language of the prescriptive-valuative type, is persuasion. They seek to get others to share a set of political values and to move them to implement these values by programs and methods which are made explicit.

It is in this way that one should discuss the meaning of democracy. Here, however, I must allow myself to make only brief, characterizing statements which could, *in principle,* be recast into prescriptive-valuative language, if they were carefully elaborated upon. At the same time it must be pointed out that, of necessity, if such brief, characterizing statements were cast into extended discussion in prescriptive-valuative terms, they would inescapably need a plurality of meanings. There is not one meaning to democracy which characterizes it but several, each possibly legitimate for a given context which may or may not be made explicit and some which are legitimate for more than one context.

In the Periclean Age the Greek notion of democracy received, perhaps, its major emphasis in the mechanism for registering political opinion and conviction. The ideal was that kind of society and political structure in which all free men participated in the social and political decision-making processes of the community. In our own time we realize that this is a necessary condition for social welfare but not a sufficient one, since we recognize prior to the registration of political opinion the desirability that it be informed. This demand is obviously inescapable in a complex society whose social processes are not easy to understand. Where voting is not informed we have a mockery of political and social effectiveness and of the task of organizing social welfare. Freedom of political expression which is uninformed leads to demagogy, corruption, tyranny and social breakdown. That is why intellectuals and social critics have always despaired of immature political conceptions of democracy and have originated a flood of political and social protests against the inequities, injustices, travesties and tragedies which a politically immature conception of democracy creates. A politically immature conception of democracy is one which stresses everyone's participation in the political process, regardless of the quality of understanding each citizen shows and regardless of the presence or absence of social altruism and goodwill which should be manifested on behalf of the community. Many social philosophers, social critics, intellectuals and, in general intelligent and civic-minded men of goodwill, feel that the *"numerical"* conception of political democracy can degenerate into rule by cliques, gangs, mobs or—in terms of social structure—by in-group, power elites.

John Locke identified democracy with rule by the majority but the same criticisms which can be made against the Greek conception can be made here, since the size of a voting bloc is no guarantee that its politically registered opinion is informed with respect to the issues involved. Furthermore, the motives behind votes—even where the motives are accompanied by an understanding of public issues—can reflect selfishness, fear and other immature impulses. In fact the eventuality could arise in which a minority of 49 percent could be an enlightened minority and yet by Locke's rule an unenlightened or less enlightened majority would have to be allowed to prevail politically. A common and popular conception of democracy thinks of it as present when citizens govern themselves through elected and appointed representatives. Again the critique of the Greek conception will also apply here.

The philosopher, John Dewey, saw democracy not as merely a political process but as a way of life. Democracy, for Dewey, referred to a socially altrustic outlook as well as an I–Thou posture, one or both of which receive expression *in all human associations*—the family, the school, industry, government or religion. Again, one can go along with Dewey in sponsoring and supporting the ideal which he has mentioned and yet recognize the *alienation* produced by the large-scale, political structures which are the normal vehicles through which the associations just mentioned, get their work done. The basic objective of such associations (with the exception of the family) is to achieve their stated ends as economically as possible and in a spirit which thinks of people as objects to be manipulated on behalf of these ends (the I–It relationship of Buber). Such large-scale relationships, by virtue of their pronounced tendency to treat human relationships in an abstract manner, must not only often play down social altruism but cannot, by their very structure, sponsor the I–Thou posture at all. Many other notions of democracy could be characterized here if space allowed, but the accumulation of such characterizing statements would not really serve our purposes.

The important point in the present connection is that the overcentralized community makes *almost any notion of political democracy* impossible. By political democracy we are referring to some substantial degree of the I–Thou attitude between individuals, between small groups, and between an individual and a small group. Even more importantly, we are referring to the demand that our institutions meet the needs and services of most—and sometimes all—members of the community. That political and community overcentralization and institutional bureaucratization do prevent various forms of political democracy from meeting human needs and services, can be attested to, I believe, in the following ways.

Political bureaucracy concentrates power. Decision-making falls into fewer and fewer hands. Thus Michels [5] iron law of oligarchy is unquestionably facilitated by large-scale, political structures. Decision-makers begin to represent special power groups and often only a power-privileged clique of their own. The pretense that the wishes and needs of the community at large are being serviced is often abandoned. Altruistic and fair-minded individuals and minorities can be suppressed on the grounds that they weaken the proper functioning of the bureaucratic agency or organization involved. A demand for a uniform Group-Think replaces the ideals of democracy and this demand is made in the name of loyalty. Dissent is perceived as a threat to efficiency. The demand for institutional stability is used to stifle initiative. A demand arises for narrow forms of administrative planning—administrative planning which worships fidelity to established procedures and loses sight of the human ends to be served. A not unexpected by-product of this worship of red tape is regimentation. The *principle of voluntary association*—which Mills has recognized as the *sine qua non* of any democratic enterprise—is disregarded.

In our society people are buttonholed to join organizations, persuaded to believe in them through propaganda and myth-making and expected to support them with dues. Sometimes through political apathy [6] and moral irresponsibility and sometimes through ignorance, members default on the task of running their own organizations. A bureaucratic clique runs the organization, makes all decisions for its members and definitely dictates policy. Communication and decision-making tend to be from the top down in bureaucracies. Political parties and political machines tend to belong to political managers rather than to the people. Voters may think they are members of the team and that it operates on their behalf. In reality, however, they usually vote yea or nay to the decisions and alternatives presented by a bureaucratic power clique or a political power elite.

All the preceding and many similar phenomena are largely aided and abetted by large-scale centralization. Many apologists for bureaucratic and political centralization emphasize its virtues, such as economic

[5] Robert Michels. *Political Parties. A Sociological Study of the Oligarchical Tendencies of Modern Democracy.* New York: Collier Books, 1962. 379 pp.

[6] An excellent study of political apathy, with which the reader should become familiar, is the following: David Riesman and Nathan Glazer. "Political Apathy: Its Social Sources and Subjective Meaning." 535–58. In *Mass Society in Crisis. Social Problems and Social Pathology* (Bernard Rosenberg, Israel Gerver, and F. William Howton, editors). New York: Macmillan, 1964. 663 pp.

progress. Often, however, the factors which they are pointing to as examples of the efficiencies introduced by bureaucratic organization are basically only the advantages created by science and technology. We must never forget that—using this same science and technology—a totalitarian Germany under Hitler exhibited an efficiency equal to, if not surpassing, our own.

The reader will have misinterpreted the purpose of this section if he sees it as a criticism of democracy. This it decidedly is not. The author sincerely believes that democracy is the best possible atmosphere for achieving the I–Thou attitude in personal relations and for achieving a genuine sense of community. What we have been trying to say is that the fulfillment of various types of democratic ideals becomes impossible under the aegis of large-scale political and administrative organization. Some social processes, such as democratic ones, cease to be viable when they embrace too many persons in too complicated or too deficient a communication network.[7] The culprit is overcentralization and not democracy.

Although the democratic atmosphere is more likely to be realized when practiced on a small scale, we still have to recognize, unfortunately, that world trends will, for some time, be in the direction of ever more centralized political units and institutions. This trend aborts some of the best features of small-scale, community life.[8] Small-scale community life which is not too strongly affected by the centralizing processes of mass society is far less subject to the type of criticisms which have already been made in this section.

When the love of bigness in politics, institutions and community formation has run its course, then, perhaps, we shall see some real thinking done on the possibility of feasible decentralization. By the phrase, "feasible decentralization," we mean small-scale community and institutional life, relatively autonomous, which preserves all the advantages of large-scale living, provided by modern science and technology, but which manages to liquidate (or manages never to give rise to) the various forms of social pathology now produced by overcentralization. The ideal, decentralized community would then have the best of both worlds—up-to-date exploitation of advances in science, technology, education and culture— and wholesale elimination of those social relations, social processes and social effects, which now embitter human life, and which are deeply

---

[7] For an analysis of some of the communication difficulties involved when dealing with large-scale communication networks, see the following volume: Josephine Klein, *The Study of Groups*. London: Routledge and Kegan Paul, 1956, 200 pp. See specifically Chapter 12 "The Larger Society and Social Change," 153–62.

[8] For a discussion of the problems which arise when small-scale community life has to struggle with some of the phenomena produced by overcentralization, see the following volume: Arthur J. Vidich and Joseph Bensman, *Small Town in Mass Society. Class, Power and Religion in a Rural Community*, New York: Doubleday, 1960, 337 pp.

bound up with the overcentralization and bureaucratization of modern large-scale community life.

## II. INJUSTICE AND CORRUPTION

The development of large-scale, administrative organization—whether in the form of national or urban governments, corporate, judicial or academic institutions, professional or communication monopolies or any other type of bureaucratic entity—must inevitably make for injustice. The injustice which is perpetrated as a result of the growth of bureaucratic Molochs takes many forms. Let us briefly remind ourselves of some of these.

There is first of all the long record of political corruption found wherever centralization of government goes on unchecked. Such corruption can be found in England, France, Germany, Italy, China, Russia, Latin America or the United States. We are, of course, interested here only in our domestic forms of it. If we take the case of urban government we have seen historically that the injustices of overcentralization show up in the form of political bosses, machine politicians and party hack workers whose job is to get out the votes for the machine's candidates. In return for "persuading" voters to vote the straight machine ticket, stuffing the ballot box with returns from fictitious voters, offering drinks to stumble-bums from skid row if they would vote and food to the politically ignorant poor for voting right, the political hack received his rewards either in the form of money, a job on the city payroll, an opportunity to collect minor forms of graft or the advantage of being able to get matters "fixed" when necessary. Graft in connection with the administration of justice, the disbursement of contracts or the granting of franchises has a long history. The tremendous tie-up between urban government and crime is also notorious.

The elementary facts about politics, politicians, and political machines were long ago presented by Frank Kent.[9] Although times have changed, we have Senator Javit's word for it that the message of Kent's book "is as pertinent today as the day it was written." The corruption in urban politics has been beautifully illustrated historically from the exposés of Lincoln Steffens [10, 11] to those of Reid and Demaris [12] or even the depressing fictional account of big city politics furnished by Edwin O'Connor.[13] Even the reading of *recent* "clean" accounts of politics—

[9] Frank R. Kent. *The Great Game of Politics*. Buffalo: Smith, Keynes & Marshall, 1959. 322 pp.

[10] Lincoln Steffens. *Shame of the Cities*. New York: Hill and Wang, 1963. 214 pp.

[11] Lincoln Steffens. *Autobiography*. New York: Harcourt, Brace, 1931. 884 pp.

[12] Ed Reid and Ovid Demaris. *The Green Felt Jungle*. New York: Pocket Books, 1964. 244 pp.

[13] Edwin O'Connor. *The Last Hurrah*. New York: Bantam Books, 1957. 376 pp.

municipal or otherwise—on the analogy with a "clean" bomb, still leaves us in an unexhilarated mood. Two examples of such "clean" accounts are the political autobiography of Bullitt,[14] a figure with some political experience, and a discussion of urban problems by the dean of American public administration, Luther Gulick.[15] If the reader wishes to convince himself that corruption in the overcentralized society is as commonplace as ever—exhibiting itself in new forms but generated by the same old motives—he has only to read Cook [16] in order to have his convictions settled on this score. Corruption at the state level, in particular, has changed in form and appearance over the last few decades, but not in spirit. The style in which corruption among the states now exhibits itself in the political arena is put most succinctly as follows by Wilson,[17] in referring to some of the industrial states of the Northeast as a revealing sample.

". . . about all that seems to have happened in the last fifty years is that, on the whole, their governors have become more respectable and their political parties more disorganized, thereby transforming what once was well-organized, machine-like corruption into disorganized, free-lance corruption." (p. 30)

It is interesting to note in passing that Wilson discusses briefly three major theories of government corruption. These are the following. (1) There is a particular political ethos or style which attaches a relatively low value to probity and impersonal efficiency. The counterpart of this style is to stress personal forms, loyalty and private gain. (2) The second theory holds that corruption occurs when ordinary men face extraordinary temptations. Corruption is then seen as a consequence of a social system which offers power, wealth and status for the taking and where the means of seizure are often morally questionable and almost always kept from the public gaze. (3) The third approach to a theory of governmental corruption is that when the doctrine of governmental separation of powers into legislative, executive and judicial, was sponsored as a form of checks and balances, its sponsors never foresaw the jealousy over prerogatives which could prompt the three different branches to obstruct one another's activities. To get all three governmental horses to pull together —according to this third theory—the professional politicians *must use corrupt practises.* Wilson fails, however, to emphasize the obvious fact that the bureaucratization of large-scale political entities and agencies, exercising their functions, duties and prerogatives through numerous,

---

14 Stimson Bullitt. *To Be a Politician.* New York: Doubleday, 1961. 215 pp.

15 Luther Halsey Gulick. *The Metropolitan Problem and American Ideas.* New York: Knopf, 1962. 167 pp.

16 Fred Cook. *The Corrupted Land.* New York: Macmillan, 1966. 352 pp.

17 James Q. Wilson. "Corruption: The Shame of the States." *The Public Interest,* Vol. 1, No. 2, Winter 1966, 28–38. Wilson is Professor of Government at Harvard University and Director of the M.I.T.–Harvard Joint Center for Urban Studies.

detailed, complex and often uncoordinated procedures, makes the expression of each of the conditions emphasized in the three major theories, an easy matter.

There has been a long tradition of muckraking and exposé literature on the forms of injustice, graft and corruption which occur on the national level and which are greatly fostered by overcentralization. These run from the exposes of the muckraking period, whose heyday ran from 1902–1910, to the unearthing of the injustices, corruption, graft and malfeasance in office which have been made public by the latest Congressional hearing. Examples of modern muckraking, exposing the many forms of injustice which political overcentralization creates, are exemplified, for instance, in Blair Bolles's [18] description of how the rich exploit the welfare state for themselves, in Eugene Castle's [19] account of how Uncle Sam wastes billions of dollars of the taxpayer's money in trying to save other countries, while trying at the same time to create favorable grounds for the reception of a flattering American image, or in Bruce Catton's [20] description of national mismanagement and cynicism among members of the early, military-industrial complex of this country. These, of course, are neither the most significant, outstanding nor interesting examples of modern muckraking, but they *are* representative.

Overcentralization also lends itself to the expression of many institutional forms of injustice which need not be "political" in the narrow sense of that word but rather in the worst senses attached to the term "bureaucracy." A random selection of examples of institutional injustice and corruption—as such injustice and corruption is initiated and sponsored by administrative structures which serve cliques rather than the public—would be quite varied. Such a random selection might, for instance, include the spectacular forms of corruption associated with big business—a type of corruption which draws into its net politicians, account executives, big corporation heads, salesmen, labor bosses, ordinary small-fry, business men, market speculators and influence peddlers. One author who looked into this type of corruption is Frank Gibney.[21] A picture of injustice and corruption in the labor-management field was furnished by no less a distinguished figure than Senator Robert F. Kennedy.[22] The injustices, immoralities, lies and tragedies perpetrated by the American press should receive an honored place in any sample of

[18] Blair Bolles. *How to Get Rich in Washington. Rich Man's Division of the Welfare State.* New York: Norton, 1952. 309 pp.

[19] Eugene W. Castle. *Billions Blunders and Baloney.* New York: The Devin-Adair Company, 1955. 278 pp.

[20] Bruce Catton. *The War Lords of Washington.* New York: Harcourt, Brace, 1948. 313 pp.

[21] Frank Gibney. *The Operators.* New York: Bantam Books, 1961. 229 pp.

[22] Robert F. Kennedy. *The Enemy Within.* New York: Popular Library, 1960. 320 pp.

how administrative centralization can work against social decency and democracy. An excellent treatment of the role of the press in this connection has been furnished by that prominent critic of American journalism, A. J. Liebling.[23] The extent to which the alienation of organizational life and the struggle for success within the impersonal framework of an industrial, overcentralized society, bring about the destruction of personal character, has been frankly described by Mark Caine [24] and somewhat philosophically surveyed by Alan Harrington.[25] Finally the institution of the confidence man, the aristocrat of the underworld, is important here. Those who operate in the shadowy realm of the confidence man, find that their nefarious activities are considerably facilitated by the social distance created by bureaucratic agencies and institutions which they often make use of to accomplish their ends. It has taken a professor of linguistics, David W. Maurer,[26] to give us one of the better accounts of this shady institution.

This citation of institutional corruption which derives in large measure from the basic features of overcentralization in our lives, would not be complete without an accounting of the sordid injustices which arise in relation to marriage and divorce. Here unfeeling, uninformed, unimaginative and frequently stupid bureaucracy operates at the lowest depths of psychological hell. The manner in which lawyers batten on the life-situations of men who are in the process of obtaining a divorce and the manner in which the "great American bitch" is allowed to destroy a man's future—even in those cases where he is an exemplary citizen and an individual of integrity—only because he is a man, still require telling. The lies, hypocrisies, deception, cynicism and immorality involved in seeking legal fees for clients who have been tied legally hand and foot—even before legal proceedings have begun and who know nothing of these matters—has to be experienced to be believed. The manner in which many (though not all, of course) stupid, vicious or ignorant judges make a routine mockery out of the psychological traumas which marital failures produce and make a divorced man the slave of both a woman and the

---

23 A. J. Liebling. *The Press.* New York: Ballantine Books, 1961. 284 pp.

24 Mark Caine. *The S-Man.* New York: Pocket Books, 1962. 179 pp.

25 Alan Harrington. *Life in the Crystal Palace.* New York: Knopf, 1959. 263 pp. Harrington's book provides an excellent insight into the kind of mentality and American middle-class pattern of values which, in the present writer's estimation, may lead to an American form of authoritarianism. That form will perpetrate its injustices by less visible and stringent methods than those of totalitarian governments but the blighting effects on human life and character may prove to be just as great. Americans worry about the effects on their lives of the welfare state. They seem far less worried about the social psychology which can be created by the welfare corporation. The changes in American life may yet take off in the direction of a welfare corporatism—a corporatism which may eventuate into a kind of highly decentralized type of authoritarianism.

26 David W. Maurer. *The Big Con. The Story of the Confidence Man and the Confidence Game.* New York: Pocket Books, 1949. 316 pp.

court, in the name of the hypocritical slogan that the court's "natural sympathies are with the woman," has not yet been studied with proper objectivity.

The degree to which legalized slavery in terms of alimony [27] can be a worse condition than the whipped and chained captive of the Roman galley or trireme, is something of which the average citizen is, as yet, unaware. Something of this picture has been provided by Charles Wilner [28] in a book which has failed to make headway precisely because it exposed the operations of the worst legal "shysters" and female "gold-diggers" in American life. We can be grateful for the fact that many American women are too decent, honorable and self-respecting to go along with the legal tide. Enough of them, however, so lack these qualities as to make a nightmare out of divorce, particularly when they are encouraged to do so by Frankenstein attorneys and judges. When this story has been properly told, some of the injustices and horrors of divorce will surely have to be chalked up to the evils of an impersonal and overly bureaucratized, judicial process which makes a virtue out of alienation and a vice out of understanding and compassion.

What is it that allows us to say that the bureaucratization of modern life creates injustice and corruption? Essentially it is the fact that the over-organization of our procedures for supplying services to mass society makes such injustice and corruption inevitable. Let us consider the case of corruption first.

Our procedures for providing institutional services are complex, detailed and frequently irrelevant to the case at hand. The fragmentation of what is called the "processing of an action" involves so many hands, so many decisions and such a division of responsibility, that it is fairly easy to bend existing regulations to selfish purposes. Since the legal language of administrative regulations is semantically open and ambiguous as compared with the more rigorous and highly structured language of science, it can be so stretched as to make it serve personal gain rather than public welfare. Because of reasons such as these—and many others too numerous to mention here—corrupt practises are often easy to pull off. They are easily hidden and are often not discovered except through congressional

27 This same criticism may occasionally apply to legal situations of child support. Although this writer strongly believes that there are practically few circumstances in which an able-bodied, employed but divorced father should be relieved of child support, nevertheless even here unreasonable, legal tyranny may creep in. The phrase, "child support," can be stretched to the breaking-point not only legally but also socially and psychologically, metaphorically speaking, until a perfectly responsible, ex-husband is ruined economically. In order to acquaint himself with the hundreds of ways in which this can be, and has been done legally, the reader has to develop a special interest in the sociology of divorce and become acquainted with the actual behavior of the courts in this connection.

28 Charles Wilner. *Alimony. The Tragedy of Marriage.* New York: Vantage Press, 1952. 329 pp.

or public hearings, journalistic sleuthing, exposure by reformers or research by scholars who make their findings public.

When the public furor is over, when the particular corruption which
was under fire, has ended, and when the bureaucratic captains and the
kings who were involved, have departed, the same situation continues but
in new forms of corruption. No matter how well the relevant legislation
may be modified, the weaknesses mentioned—the inescapable accompaniment of bureaucracy—remain. *"Plus ca change, plus c'est la même chose,"*
continues to apply. A new set of rapscallions will eventually emerge to
take advantage in new ways of the total administrative situation, including
the new legislation as well as the revision of the faulty administrative
regulations which facilitated the exposure of the previous, public scandal.

If we turn to the question of how bureaucratization facilitates injustice, we find ourselves on both old and new grounds. The old grounds
are those we mentioned in the preceding paragraphs, that is to say, the
complexities and ambiguities of our procedures create unhappy situations
for individuals—unhappy situations which could not have been foreseen
by those well-intentioned lawmakers who originally framed the legislation. Inasmuch as there is no place for the individual exception when
"actions have to be processed" routinely, much bitterness may flow from
this fact. The exceptionality of the individual's circumstances are "details" which the majesty of the regulations cannot be concerned with.
This attitude is starkly revealed in the legal, Latin adage *"Lex de minimis
non fit"*—which can be freely translated as "The law is not concerned with
trifles." If we add to all of these difficulties the difficulties which arise for
an individual in trying to redress a personal wrong, matters become even
more depressing.

This can best be seen in the bureaucratization of the legal process.
First, the would-be plaintiff will discover that in order to recover or protect $1000, he may have to spend many times that amount. Second, if this
does not deter him—since, perhaps, he may feel he has to fight for a principle—then he may find that the dockets are in so crowded a state that he
must suffer additional injustice until his case can be reached. If this does
not deter him he may then discover that his case is held up because a
judge has ruled that his attorney did not operate in a correct fashion
*procedurally* or with respect to the required forms to be filed. If even this
does not discourage the plaintiff from seeking justice, he may find that the
trial or hearing will do so. His case may involve a time-consuming trial,
entailing previously unforeseen expenses. If his case requires only a
hearing before a judge he may find—as in a divorce suit—that the complex
circumstances of his life, relevant to his case, will be ignored and that the
judge will evince no real interest in getting at the facts in relation to the
claims of the adversaries involved. He may be staggered to discover that

in 15 or 30 minutes a bored judge, playing God, will hand down a decision —based frequently on nothing solid—which is not only inhumane and unfair but which will affect the plaintiff's life and that of others who depend upon him, for the rest of his days. If justice is not obtained after a trial or a hearing and the injured litigant seeking relief makes use of the appeals system, a whole new chain of bureaucratically farcical activities will be initiated, perhaps costlier than before.

Finally, while we are on the subject of the effects of bureaucracy and overcentralization on the judicial process, let us not overlook the extent to which the law can be abused by scoundrels—whether litigants or their lawyers—so as to stretch the meaning and intent of legislation and thereby harass or impoverish both individuals and corporations. The latter are usually rich enough to defend themselves. The former often are not. Then, too, legal procedures and legal forms can be misused so as to tie up innocent and defenseless people in legal knots, push them around or incarcerate them occasionally without a trial. Legal folderol has been and can be used to prevent subjects from being given an opportunity to defend themselves properly, by denying them the time needed to gather important facts and witnesses.

It is now no longer rare to read of individuals who have been pushed around and railroaded through the *esprit de corps* with which corrupt politicians help one another and often the essential problem of the ill-intentioned lawyer and/or politician is to find a good statutory and legal excuse for making the victim miserable and crushing him. The wheels of the law not only grind slowly but even more often they grind so obtusely and in such an involved procedural manner—with no one, except the victim, apparently interested in either the facts involved or in the expectation of justice—that it is difficult to know whom to fight, how to fight, the nature of the accusation or how to begin one's defense. The long arm of the law often proves to be a pitchfork for injustice rather than an avenging angel. Frequently an abused party is stopped dead in his tracks when the appalling magnitude of the costs required to defend himself, are made known to him.

And now that police officers, private eyes, government sleuths and various other forms of snooper and Peeping-Tom have been permitted to bug the average citizen and snatch up features of his private life to be used against him, the possibilities for legal tyranny have been considerably enhanced. I am here, of course, referring to the rapidly disappearing right of individual privacy under the onslaught of modern investigative techniques and listening devices, described so fully and so depressingly by Packard [29] and Brenton.[30] To the extent that material gathered in this

[29] Vance Packard. *The Naked Society*. New York: David McKay, 1964. 369 pp.

[30] Myron Brenton. *The Privacy Invaders*. New York: Fawcett Publications, 1964. 176 pp.

way may be allowed in the courtroom, governmental hearing, or personnel inquiry or can be used behind the scenes to guide an effort to harass the individual citizen, judicial and quasi-judical processes can be corrupted beyond measure. All of these hounds of Satan may increase immeasurably the untold possibilities for enhancing legal tyranny and mistreatment by those in a position to "dispense" justice in one form or another.

Abuses of all these kinds increase to the extent that legal and judicial organization grows unwieldy and overcentralized. The more complex such organization becomes and the more alienated and abstract becomes the body of the law which is drawn upon, the richer become the hypocritical legal excuses for violating individual and democratic rights and the more numerous are the scoundrels who can hide under the umbrella created by the nooks and crannies of judicial overcentralization.

## III. INCOMPETENCE AND THE CULTIVATION OF MEDIOCRITY

As the technological society becomes more complex and more centralized, the difficulty of administering it—not to speak of understanding it—becomes greater than ever. Efficient administration and planning—whether humane or otherwise—requires intelligence, information, special aptitudes and a capacity for what educators call functional thinking. Efficient administration requires, in addition, imagination, the ability to foresee the consequences of decision-making, an interest in the impact which new developments in science and technology can have upon the market, an awareness of the impact which economic invention and managerial practises [31] can have upon one's administrative functions, and many similar considerations. Many are needed to carry and direct the burden of corporate or social management but few have the cluster of abilities which it takes to assume these necessary burdens.

However, the bureaucracies which have the responsibility thrust upon them of dealing with some of the processes which are part of our growing social complexity, fill up all too often with time-servers who have

---

[31] The new managerial skills which are becoming increasingly vital both for the total management of the economy, for regional management, for industrial or military planning and for corporate control, are now part of what is called *operations research*. For a *technical* introduction to this subject the reader should consult the following: C. West Churchman, Russell L. Ackoff and E. Leonard Arnoff, *Introduction to Operations Research*, New York: Wiley, 1957, 645 pp. For a *non-mathematical* introduction to linear programming which is a central development in operations research, see *New Decision-Making Tools for Managers. Mathematical Programming as an Aid in the Solving of Business Problems* (Edward C. Bursk and John F. Chapman, editors), New York: Mentor Executive Library Books, 1965, 413 pp. For a very simple, *mathematical* introduction to linear programming, see Kurt Meisels, *A Primer of Linear Programming*, New York: New York University Press, 1962, 103 pp.

only the manners and the studied air of competent administrators. In point of fact many of them are "hollow men" or, in harsher language, "phonies." Thus bureaucracy, as one form of pathological centralization, not only lowers the aggregate level of competence in contexts which are, at the same time, becoming increasingly complex and more difficult to understand, but the maladministered bureaucracy becomes an excellent refuge for mediocrities of every sort—for windbags, pretenders, *poseurs*, rubber stamps, and those who enjoy having authority without the corresponding and necessary competence and sense of responsibility. Administrative "goof-offs" are swept under the rug, regarded as "inevitable in a big operation of this sort," seen as due to "failures down the line" or to "growing pains."

The administratively incompetent are fertile in excuses and rationalizations which preserve their unrealistic self-images but are fallow in the ability to foresee and prevent further "goof-offs." The bureaucratic *luftmensch* has to have an almost infinite capacity for both repression and regression in order to sleep peacefully and to forget his costly and accumulated mistakes. He has to have a limitless ego, free of self-doubts, at least on the surface, in order to have the effrontery to continue to make decisions in a complex milieu which he is unable to see steadily and unable to see whole. He has to have colossal cheek to pick the brains of competent subordinates and technicians and then take credit for the outcomes of their decisions, where these prove to be sound, or to blame subordinates and technicians for the harmful and wasteful outcomes of his own uninformed and ill-advised decisions. Above all, the mindless functionary has to capitalize upon a socially approved form of schizophrenia in order to play God all the time, smug and certain that he knows he can pick good men for assistants from all those who wish to operate at the right-hand side of God.

Nevertheless the overcentralized bureaucracies and administrations of the modern world do cultivate mediocrity and reward it frequently, regardless of the quality of its performance. In fact, the men at the top, separated from the administratively *gauche* underlings and middle echelon incompetents, soon come to defend a "good" performance in terms of the wasteful and inefficient performance of these underlings. They would, indeed, be surprised at the degree of waste and incompetence which would be revealed after the typical organization or institution was raked over by management specialists and consultants. It is quite true that the charges being made here apply *minimally* to scientists and technicians who not only have to deliver but whose mistakes can be laid at their feet by reports and inspection techniques. But for the great mass of mediocrities who shield their poor performance by defining administration as an art, responsibility can be evaded. This tendency of bureaucracy and centralization to cultivate and shield mediocrity has, of course, been amusingly described in terms of *Parkinson's Law, Injelititis* and other pathologies of administration by C. Northcote Parkinson.[32]

What are some of the ways in which bureaucratic incompetence manifests itself? Whole libraries of books have been written on this subject and the reading public, interested in governmental incompetence, has been familiarized with literally thousands of examples of this phenomenon, not only from books but also from reports of governmental incompetence appearing in congressional hearings and in the well-documented stories which are furnished both in the press and in popular magazines over the years. For these reasons there is no point in indulging the reader in a long catalogue of bureaucratic follies generated in the day-to-day work of government functionaries, and which can be gathered from various documented sources. In order, however, to convey—if ever so briefly—the flavor of such incompetence, let me cite some examples here.

Brady[33] reports the following fact which was unearthed by the Hoover Commission's Task Force. This Commission noted the failure of the Armed Services to coordinate food purchases by citing the fact that the Army shipped 807,000 pounds of canned tomatoes from California to New York while the Navy shipped 775,000 pounds from the East Coast to California. It also pointed to an instance in which the Army shipped 1,120,000 pounds of canned tomatoes into Texas from five Midwestern states at the same time that the Navy was shipping 933,000 pounds out of Texas to destinations at which its East Coast activities were being carried out. Brady is inclined to see a situation of this sort as evidence of mismanagement rather than to attribute it—as did the Commission—solely to the independent but uncoordinated records on inventory kept by the two branches of the Armed Services in question. He notes with justice that these situations clearly reflect poor warehouse location as well as poor shipping arrangements but that a knowledge of the new managerial skill of linear programming might have prevented their occurrence.

Brady also reports the following bureaucratic types of dysfunctioning which would be comical if it did not reflect the huge waste of time and money involved, when we remember that it is multiplied a thousandfold in government. (1) A West Coast shipyard during World War II required more than 16 copies of documents whenever materials had to be requisitioned. It was found that these documents were going nowhere at all. A popular wisecrack was making the rounds to the effect that if all the paperwork required to build a 20,000-ton troopship were loaded on it

[32] C. Northcote Parkinson. *Parkinson's Law and Other Studies in Administration.* Boston: Houghton Mifflin, 1957. 113 pp.

[33] Robert A. Brady. *Organization, Automation and Society. The Scientific Revolution in Industry.* Berkeley and Los Angeles: University of California Press, 1961. 481 pp. See particularly Chapter 13 "Recapitulation and the First Sum of Consequences," 387–424.

when it was launched, it would sink. (2) During the Korean War a bored civilian officer noticed flypaper in a barroom. In order to amuse himself he turned in a report on flypaper inefficiency. Receiving no comments on his reports he sent on additional ones regularly. On the first occasion when he failed to route one on to Washington he received an official reproof reminding him that his report was in arrears. Shortly thereafter, to his surprise, inquiries came from other military headquarters, asking how to make such reports and in almost no time at all such reports had become part of standard operating procedure.

In this second instance, one sees the hand at work of that type of incompetent at headquarters, who is trying to learn the ropes and make his own job, that is, to fill up time according to Parkinson's Law. The fact that no questions are asked as to the purpose of the item or process being incorporated into standard operating procedure and the humorlessness and wooden conformity shown, are both par for the course.

An excellent measure of bureaucratic waste lies, I believe, in the opinion of one management expert referred to by Brady. This expert believes that in the United States as a whole, one file-case drawer is filled each year for every man, woman, and child in the country and that more than half of this total is unnecessary. It is argued that the wasted manpower employed in producing the paper and typewriters used is very great but that the labor going into filling out the forms, typing, filing and maintaining records, is greater still. Brady recognizes rightly, that as free market phenomena tend to be taken over by bureaucratic agencies, they tend also to produce bureaucratic problems and inefficiencies of the type we have mentioned.

It would be a mistake, I think, to imagine that the ineptitude of government bureaucrats is not matched by that of executives in private industry. If it were important to do so, case histories of incompetent decision-making in the modern corporation, could be liberally supplied here. In a sense one measure of such inept decision-making would be the savings in costs, time and energy which typically follow the application of the new skilled managerial techniques to modern industry—techniques such as those of operations research and particularly linear programming. A description of the traits of the incompetent, corporate functionary whose prolonged malpractises are well protected by the compassionate, corporate practise of spreading the responsibility created by ineptness through having it shared by committees, is furnished by Harrington.[34] A discussion of some of the actual advantages which are derived from being bureaucratically inept are humorously described by Samstag,[35] but unfortunately the

---

[34] Alan Harrington. *Life In The Crystal Palace.* New York: Alfred A. Knopf, 1959. 263 pp. See Chapter X, "Social Justice *v.* Efficiency," pp. 160–171.

[35] Nicholas Samstag. *The Uses of Ineptitude or How Not to Want to do Better.* New York: Ivan Obolensky, 1962. 147 pp.

administratively incompetent are already familiar with the art of defining professional vices and failings as personal and administrative virtues. The corporate and public cost of tolerating ineptness is far too great—especially the public cost—and the consequences are far too risky for a world growing increasingly complex, to be tolerated.

If the author's government experience is any index of the traits of the bureaucrat, then all one can say is that there are far too many people of the wrong kind into whose hands large-scale centralization puts effective power, the opportunity to affect the lives and destinies of millions [36] and to create unnecessary havoc. In a government agency we stumble upon men whose task it is to apply the content of administrative law, expressed in the form of publicly available regulations, to the solution of a major national problem or to the handling of a major, national emergency and the control of economic processes associated with that problem or emergency. What do we find? All too often the men given major power to interpret the regulations in order to deal with national difficulties cannot understand the very regulations about which they are supposed to be more knowledgeable than the average taxpayer or than most people in the industries to which the regulations apply.

We should not assume that bureaucratic mediocrities in government express themselves only in the bungling, ill-informed and publicly costly, day-to-day decisions associated with the exercise of their basic functions. Bureaucratic ineptness is, to be sure, *chiefly* expressed in the routine services which are the staple features of the functionary's job. Incompetence, however, occurs in other directions. It occurs in hiring new personnel who are sized up by colleagues-to-be in the shallowest of interviews. It occurs in the treatment of employees who are in some way or other different from the motley crew of organization men by whom they are surrounded. One way in which bureaucratic folly expresses itself in this direction is in the absurd overconfidence in the efficacy of psychological tests to detect intellectually and psychologically wayward employees who may have "dangerous thoughts" and "un-American" ideas.[37] The

[36] As part of his government experience, the author has served as an industrial and labor economist with the Department of Labor, as an administrative price economist both with the Office of Price Administration during World War II and the Office of Price Stabilization during the Korean War, as an economic, research and financial consultant to the Housing Commissioner of the State of New York, and as an Analyst for the War Assets Administration.

[37] The absurd bureaucratic faith in psychological tests has, of course, been catalogued by William H. Whyte, Jr. See his *The Organization Man*. New York: Simon and Schuster, 1956. 429 pp. In this connection the reader will also find the following two volumes of some value. 1. Martin L. Gross. *The Brain Watchers*. New York: Signet Books, 1963. 256 pp. 2. Banesh Hoffman. *The Tyranny of Testing*. New York: Collier Books, 1962. 223 pp. *The New Republic* ran a series of articles in 1965 by James Ridgeway on the Federal misuse of psychological testing, which the reader will find invaluable. See also this author's book review entitled "How to Take a Test" in *The New Republic*, Vol. 154, No. 9, Issue 2635, February 26, 1966, 31–2.

bureaucratic incompetent often tends to be a poor judge of men, investing the role-playing poseur—with whom, no doubt, he identifies more easily—with virtues and abilities which he, himself, lacks, while failing to credit a man of substance with possessing these same qualities, if the life-style of the latter is conspicuously different from that of his colleagues.

All of the preceding then explains in part the constant criticism of American bureaucracy. Referring to the traditional nature of this type of criticism, Lerner [38] has commented on it in the following way.

. . . the withering barrage of criticism directed against the tax-fed bureaucrats stressed only the obvious negative aspects—the red tape, the routineering, the stuffiness and self-importance of men with power attaching to their office, the frequent cases of sheer incapacity for the job. (p. 410)

What must not be overlooked, however, in such criticism is the fact that complex technology has created a complex economy and a complex social life and that these, in turn, have reinforced the tendency to create a complex, overcentralized, governmental process organized to deal with the problems generated within a complex and technologically based society. Again, as Lerner puts it.

. . . What first made a government bureaucracy necessary was the spate of scientific inventions which in turn created a vast industrial organization that needed regulation from without as well as order from within. (p. 408)

Lerner notes that there is always a danger that the relationship of technology to bureaucracy may be misunderstood, which prompts him to stress the following considerations.

. . . What is missed is the fact that the welfare state, with its bureaucratic base, came in America as a response to the felt urgencies of modern industrial society. There was the need of setting a floor under economic insecurity; there were clashes of interest groups, which required the intervention of the government as umpire and as equalizer of unequal bargaining conditions. There were new industrial practices which had to be regulated if chaos was to be prevented; there were concentrations of economic power which had to be kept in check, lest they lead to the growth of a state within a state; and there were actual failures of functioning in various segments of the economy which brought the government in as entrepreneur and investor. Added to all these were the war economy and war services which could be run only through the state. (p. 410)

[38] Max Lerner. *America as a Civilization. Life and Thought in the United States Today.* New York: Simon and Schuster, 1957. 1036 pp. See Chapter VI, "The Political System," 355–464 and particularly Section 6 of this chapter, entitled "The Government Managers," 407–15.

# 23

# Political Overcentralization in a Complex Society: Additional Types of Pathology*

## I. THE FLIGHT FROM INDIVIDUALITY OF CIRCUMSTANCE

The desire for order and the cultivation in mass society of what Ellul [1] calls technique, dampens the recognition of the great variety of circumstances which surround the lives of individuals and tends to oppose the differentiated treatment of such individual circumstances. In a small community there is no great strain involved in approaching a man's problems on an I-Thou basis. It is practically possible and often psychologically appropriate. In mass society a basic purpose of centralization, bureaucratization, and the institutional manual of procedure, is to avoid the necessity for dealing with that which is unique to the individual's circumstances. It would be absurd even to try to do so. One has to deal with the problems of individuals in terms only of the characteristics common to their problems, not the characteristics *unique* to these same problems. Furthermore, since these problems have to be met by uniform procedures, any attempt to deal with individuality of circumstances would not only be a luxury but almost an impossibility. In bureaucratic, mass society and in the relation of the governmental agency to the individual citizen, the individual is *just another case*.

As a result the Internal Revenue agent cannot consider those circumstances in the citizen's life which may make certain aspects of existing tax law irrelevant or unfair, when applied to the citizen's situation. The

* Chapter 23, with adaptations and modifications, has been taken from the following source: Henry Winthrop. "Some Social Pathologies of Political Overcentralization." *Journal of Human Relations.* Vol. 14, No. 4, Fourth Quarter, 1966, 605–619.
[1] Jacques Ellul. *The Technological Society.* New York: Knopf, 1964. 449 pp. By "technique" Ellul refers to every objective procedure and process of rationalization applied to human relations, human productivity, the dispensation of justice, the process of education, selection for employment, execution of bureaucratic objectives, etc.

admissions officer in a graduate school cannot listen to the reasons why a student's grade-point average is mediocre, even though such reasons may amply and truly indicate that the student's grade-point average is unrepresentative of his abilities. Even if the student should have a high IQ and even if he may have already published *as an undergraduate* some respectable papers in his chosen field of interest, these facts may not offset a low grade-point average in the eyes of the admissions officer or committee. If the admissions cut-off point is 3.0 and if the student is below that cut-off point, then the bureaucratic admissions requirements are rigidly applied and the student is denied admission.[2]

The judge who asks the citizen why he does not pay his wife the alimony due her and hears the citizen reply that he is unemployed, will shrug his shoulders. A court decision is a court decision. The paramount concern is respect for, and obedience to, the law. He will therefore—and usually in the privacy of his chambers—tell the citizen to go out and beg, borrow or steal the amount by which he is in arrears. If he refuses, or if he cannot do so, he will be thrown into alimony jail. Often it is the ex-wife's attorney who will behave this way, rather than the judge, but the judicial behavior of the judge involved, will support in every way the attorney's actions.

But whether such actions proceed from the judge or the attorney is not the point. What is to the point is their absurdity. This absurdity is driven home when one realizes that if, under the same circumstances (unemployment) a citizen was still domiciled with his ex-wife, he would be the object of compassion and social welfare. To be unemployed while married—say, during the great depression when events such as we are describing actually occurred—is to be a victim of circumstances and the community argues that it is responsible for feeding and sheltering the family through some type of welfare provision. To be unemployed after being divorced—and in identical circumstances—is to threaten to be a burden upon the taxpayer and therefore, by implication, a wrongdoer, in which case incarceration in an alimony jail is the answer.[3] The spirit of the legal maxim, *Lex de minimis non fit,* translated as "The law is

---

[2] In fairness to admissions officers and committees it should be stated here that a good many of them *are* flexible and *would* make an exception to the rule, if individual circumstances appeared to warrant it. What we are trying to stress here is that *rigidity* in the application of bureaucratic rules is probably *most often* the characteristic form of institutional behavior in the graduate school.

[3] The absurdity of this procedure can be further seen from the fact that in a large city like New York, if the *unemployed* citizen who owes alimony is childless, but has fallen into arrears, he is often put in jail. If, however, he has children, he often is left alone—with a judicial reprimand at most—since to throw him into alimony jail would be to cut off his ex-family's source of prospective, economic support. This would automatically throw his family on the relief rolls, thus adding to the taxpayer's burden. The definition of sin and legal misbehavior in these cases is clearly a matter of public expediency.

not concerned with trifles," is here seen in all its naked, bureaucratic inhumanity. It becomes an appropriate legal phraseology for bureaucratic indifference towards individual circumstances which are not covered by the wooden use of legal statutes and ordinances.

To the extent that the democratic ethos is dependent upon a proper expression of the I-Thou relationship which in turn accommodates to individual differences, and to the extent that routine, centralized procedures cannot take care of individual differences in circumstances, the bureaucratic spirit is a natural enemy of that which is unique to the individual conditions of men. It is a traditional dream of the democratic philosophy that, as we move towards a more perfect society and a more just social order, everything will be done to contribute to self-fulfillment and to individuality of expression. But to the extent that the centralizing and bureaucratic trends of our time demand uniformity in the procedures by which we deal with individuals and conformity in the outlook and values of men and women in the community, then those same centralizing tendencies are in conflict with the democratic ideal of, and emphasis upon, the recognition of that which is individual and unique. Such centralizing tendencies are also in conflict with the ideal which has traditionally aimed at giving free play to the expression of individuality when such expression in no way harms the community. Since all trends point to an increasing centralization throughout the world, before mankind turns to experiments in decentralization, things will get worse before they get better. We must expect more conformity in behavior to occur and more standardization in the expression of human relations.

## II. THE PROMOTION OF BLUNDERS

In a small community of *intelligent citizens* the individual who is "phony," incompetent, a time-server or simply the man on the citizen's back, is not likely to be trusted with community responsibilities for very long. Nearly all citizens soon come to know him and they are not likely to exercise bad judgment and ask a "bad apple" to assume a commanding position. Even if they did make such a blunder, however, they would soon remove such a person from a position of influence, as a result of his many "goof-offs" and misdemeanors which would soon come to light. People of this calibre, however, have a field day in the political atmosphere generated by the *large-scale community* and the unwieldy administrative organization which the latter generates. Their incompetence, mistakes and dishonesty are well hidden under the anonymity and procedures of large-scale organization and the diffusion of responsibility which a pork-barrel, top-heavy, administrative organization promotes. It is difficult to pinpoint responsibility in a bureaucratic, administrative apparatus and sometimes it is even difficult to know what is going on when decision-making tends to be polycentered. Thus the incompetent is often protected from the watchful gaze of the responsible citizen and the critical bystander and outsider. Those who are exploited by the politically overcentralized "apparatus" often can neither prevent the abuses which are foisted upon them nor ascertain who the culprits are. More often than not they find it difficult to determine who is running interference for these same culprits. This is the type of situation which is the exact analogue of that in which Kafka's main character found himself in *The Trial,* only in this case the individual is exploited rather than accused of some crime.

The Danes have an institution called the "ombudsman." This is a publicly accepted individual whose job it is to investigate all citizens' complaints about bureaucratic mistreatment or bureaucratic mishandling of their problems. The ombudsman is an administrative watchdog whose job is to help prevent abuses or to assist in their elimination, once they are brought to his attention. The use of an ombudsman will obviously work rather well in a relatively small community of honest citizens. In communities, however, which are excessively large or which, if modest in scale, are more than overburdened with dishonest citizens, the presence of an ombudsman will probably not help too much to stave off incompetence and corruption.[4] If both these evils should be present—that is, excessive size, on the one hand, and indifference, apathy or lack of integrity in a large body of the citizens, on the other—the situation will be even worse. Both these evils, unfortunately, are present politically in many of our large urban communities.

The equivalent of the ombudsman in the large-scale democracies, is the congressional committee which conducts public hearings or the committee of review. The most the congressional hearing committee can do

---

[4] It would probably be worth some research effort to ascertain the relative efficiency and achievements of the ombudsman by comparing the consequences of his work in such a large city as Copenhagen with the outcome of the ombudsman's efforts in some of the smaller cities of Denmark. In the meantime, however, so distinguished a labor leader as Walter Reuther has decided—based on his observations during a trip to Sweden—that what large American communities need is an *ombudsman.* Reuther wishes to see this institution become a permanent part of our national life. The Auto Workers Union recently passed a resolution in this direction. That resolution calls for the following: "Establishment of an Office of Complaints administered by a Commissioner whose responsibility would be to protect the ordinary citizen against governmental neglect or abuse of power, and whose office, operating nationally and regionally to serve purposes similar to those for which the UAW Public Review Board was created, would investigate citizen complaints against the civil service, administrative tribunals, regulatory commissions, and possibly, as in the case of the Swedish Ombudsman, against the courts, prisons and police as well."

That the figure of the *ombudsman* could become a part of the institutional characteristics of English-speaking democracies, is credible when one realizes that Great Britain has recently conferred the ombudsman's functions on Sir Edmund Compton, the former Auditor General. The British have seen to it that only Parliament can fire the individual assigned this role.

is to unearth corruption, expose it to public view and frame legislation to prevent the revealed abuses from continuing. But in large-scale democracies which continue to shelter many individuals who either lack integrity, are apathetic or are, in no sense, public-spirited, new ways will be found to achieve the same old violations of both human rights and property rights. The function of public investigation and public review within the framework of politically oversized units, inevitably amounts to locking the stable door after the horse has been stolen.

Similar abuses in the *small* but *bureaucratically run* enterprise— whether it be a corporation, a government agency, a church, a foundation, a school, or university—also occur and there should be no illusions on this score. It is the *bureaucratic ethos* which is the cancer rather than the absolute size of the organization, although the larger the absolute size of the organization, the more easily does the cancer spread. A large political or administrative unit, however, does tend to make the bureaucratic ethos well-nigh *invincible*. Top-down direction of the type which Goodman [5] writes of and complains about so extensively, is the culprit here. This top-down direction often refuses to function in some sort of a partnership with the lower administrative echelons. It often refuses to function in some sort of a partnership with that part of the public which consists of the "beneficiaries" of its services and which the bureaucratic entity is supposed to take care of efficiently and honestly. As a result top-down direction in the smaller, bureaucratic, enterprise can lead to the same evils we have been describing in the large-scale organization, namely, "goof-offs," the encouragement of "phonies," incompetence, malfeasance on the job, and so forth. These evils can be expressed in many ways in the small bureaucratic unit. Let us mention two of these ways here.

One way to ensure blundering in the small but bureaucratically run enterprise, is to make it easy for an incompetent to climb to the top by processes such as those described so amusingly by Parkinson.[6] By these processes the blunderer at the top can ensure his security by often surrounding himself with faceless incompetents and rubber-stamps who can always be counted upon to go along with the top man's mistakes. Such "hollow men" can be counted upon to share the top man's fear and dislike of genuinely competent underlings. Such underlings might be open in their criticism of organizational mistakes. Incompetent administrative associates can always be counted upon to say nothing if the top man uses their ideas—if they have any—without giving due credit for them. Such resigned silence is all too often called "loyalty" and the administrative puppet who is willing to be a good "organization man" is described as be-

---

[5] Paul Goodman. *People or Personnel. Decentralizing and the Mixed System.* New York: Random House, 1965. 247 pp.

[6] C. Northcote Parkinson. *Parkinson's Law and Other Studies in Administration.* Boston: Houghton-Mifflin, 1957. 113 pp.

ing a *member of the team*. Such organization men need have no fear of being called to task for their mistakes. Such mistakes will usually be swept under the rug.

The other technique for hiding the evils of the bureaucratic ethos when they crop up in the small political unit or administrative enterprise, is the use of *"esprit de corps."* An "in-group" or oligarchy invariably arises which runs the establishment. Since members of this oligarchy tend to be like-minded, if the topman is a mediocrity then members of the in-group also tend to be mediocrities. Members of the oligarchy develop a mutually reinforcing, self-protective *esprit de corps* and a bond of secrecy concerning their true values, administrative objectives, plans and procedures. If, then, a mistake is made by one of them it will be quickly covered up by the others before it comes to public attention. If, however, it should come to public attention in spite of the efforts to conceal it, it will be quickly whitewashed or rationalized so as to make light of it. A dozen rationalizations will be found for explaining it away or making it seem unimportant. The most damaging aspect of administrative *esprit de corps* is what Joad [7] calls "the dropping of the object," that is, the tendency, in the present context, to lose sight of the public to be served and to act as though self-commendation of the behavior and careers of public servants is the central reason for the existence of the bureaucratic unit. This behavior and these careers therefore continue and as a result the *esprit de corps* of small men and small minds promotes the indefinite extension of incompetence or malfeasance in office. Thus is political blundering served.

## III. CENTROPHILIA

The most frequent and inveterate habit of the dyed-in-the-wool bureaucrat is his love of bigness and the fact that, when the evils of bureaucracy are brought to his attention, his idea of curing those evils is to demand more administrative centralization than ever before. The confirmed bureaucrat's idea of political therapy is essentially homeopathic. His idea of the universal cure for sociopolitical difficulties is "centrophilia." If things are going wrong municipally he calls for tighter state controls. If bureaucratic corruption in several states has become outrageous and led to a public hue and cry, he demands Federal intervention and regulation of the behavior which is leading to abuse of the public welfare. If difficult problems, the waste of public resources, or unnecessary conflict are occurring among members of a group of contiguous nations, he calls for a regional council or for some other type of institution which is to have

---

7 C. E. M. Joad. *Decadence. A Philosophical Inquiry.* London: Faber and Faber Limited, 1948. 430 pp.

absolute power to regulate these problems which he sees as strictly regional difficulties. Finally, if the social and economic difficulties which are brought to his attention are universal, he finds the panacea in some form of world government.

There is no question that centralization tends to eliminate many abuses and to reduce waste. That is not the point, however. What is to the point here are really two other questions. The first of these is the question of whether the social and economic gains achieved by greater centralization are worth the price that has to be paid for them. Increasing centralization magnifies the bureaucratic, political evils which are the source of chronic public complaint and which provide the sophisticated criticism which comes in a steady stream from social critics, social philosophers, social reformers and alienated intellectuals. Many writers who seek to be fair and stress the social and economic advantages brought about by bureaucracy, often take absurd positions. Thus Bonner, Hill and Wilber [8] after admitting that bureaucracy endangers the democratic process—point out that it was precisely the bureaucratic organization of the automotive industry that made it possible for every American to own an automobile. As a consequence, these authors argue, Americans "are far more mobile, which means that our freedom of movement is vastly increased."

The irrelevance of this consideration to the dangers which threaten democracy through modern bureaucratization, should be patent to all. Sheer physical mobility is no virtue and can aid or destroy the institutional expressions of democracy. Some of the undesirable consequences of such mobility have been ironically described by Keats.[9] The catalogue of social furies unleashed by the automobile, which Keats has furnished, causes the intended defense of bureaucracy, in the terms suggested by Bonner, Hill and Wilber, to boomerang somewhat. Even more important, however, than the question of physical mobility, is the fact that in a democracy it is not *freedom of physical movement* which is important but rather freedom of intellectual movement, freedom to cultivate self-actualization, freedom in the quest for variety in human values and freedom to achieve social pluralism in the quest for community. It can easily be shown that the automobile tends to lessen these freedoms considerably.

The second question which is to the point is whether we should not be looking into the possibility of establishing new social institutions which can achieve the same efficiencies of public administration which have been achieved in large-scale societies, while dissipating the abuses

8 Thomas N. Bonner, Duane W. Hill, and George L. Wilber. *The Contemporary World. The Social Sciences in Historical Perspective.* Englewood Cliffs, New Jersey: Prentice-Hall, 1960. 594 pp. See particularly pp. 418–19 of this volume.

9 John Keats. *The Insolent Chariots.* New York: Fawcett World Library, 1959. 176 pp.

which bureaucratic institutions in such societies seem to promote. After all, to respond blindly to difficulties, in the form of new legislation and new institutions which have to increase the amount of centralized control in our lives, in order to do away with abuses of the democratic spirit and the inefficiencies of existing operations, is only to fall back upon fixed and uncritical habits of thought and action. It is neither a law of nature nor of society that social organization must eternally run to ever larger scale and that complex and unwieldy bureaucratic procedures are *the only answer* to human self-government and the quest for community in technologically advanced societies.

A consequence to which a cybernated or managed economy may lead, would be one which exploited the advances in computer technology and in data-processing, in order to reduce bureaucratization and increase the possibility for democratic decentralization in our lives. This can be done by arranging for decision-making and problem-solving on a local or more limited scale but permitting a central computer to check in advance on the smooth coordination and interlocking of the multiple decision-making plans and processes which are being prospectively suggested at local levels. Under such an arrangement inconsistencies among locally made decisions concerning *proposed* social and economic action, could be ironed out in advance by a central computer and a *set* of reasonable modifications for various types of local planning could also be suggested by a central computer. Under this second eventuality people would be free to achieve democratic consensus concerning both local ends to be achieved and local ends to be coordinated into some larger, perhaps regional, plan. The computer would then be the *servant* of the democratic process rather than its master and regulator.

In a certain sense what we are suggesting here is a modification, by means of the techniques available to the computer, of what has been called *indicative planning*. This is a democratic type of planning, described by Nossiter,[10] in which representatives of different sectors of the economy—labor, management, government, agriculture, the unemployed, etc.—have the right to modify a central plan so that, after all the suggested modifications are in, the original plan can be modified to meet the needs of all those who are properly classified as belonging solely to the separate sectors in question. Using the proposed sectoral modifications the central planning body then adjusts the original, over-all plan so as to embody the sectoral modifications and *coordinate* them. In this way everybody is happy and the planners are the servants of the several publics represented in the economy. Indicative planning has been successfully used in a number of countries today, of which France and Japan are representative.

[10] Bernard Nossiter. *The Mythmakers.* Boston: Houghton-Mifflin, 1964. 244 pp.

What we are saying here is that a type of democratic decentralization by computer is available which will be *analogous* to the procedures used in *indicative planning*. In this analogy the local computer takes the place of a public sector, the local program reflects the needs, decisions and preferred procedures of the small-scale community, and the central computer acts as an overseer *to coordinate* local plans. Furthermore, the central computer functions so as to suggest *without any partisanship, whatsoever,* needed modifications of local plans—modifications in the form of several alternatives, so as to provide a choice for each local community involved. In this way, again, everybody is happy, no single bloc's decisions are forced on any community, democracy is served, the computer becomes the servant of man, and the oppressive atmosphere of a human bureaucracy is gradually eliminated. In addition, freedom of personal expression and the establishment of a community idiom is greatly facilitated and we wind up with technology serving human aspirations, leisure and political ideals, rather than dominating these with imperatives of its own. At the same time this enrolls technology in the service of a workable decentralization and enables us to meet head-on the growing social complexity of our modern communities and the inescapable complexities which must be faced politically in managing such complex organisms.

The trends described above and which are visible to all may prove to be one of the major factors in the future which will reduce considerably the viability of "centrophilia." In the meantime, however, the type of unimaginative bureaucrat in Western society, who has overlearned the repertoire of bureaucratic impulses which promote increasing political centralization, will continue to try to deal with the complex political problems of a technological civilization in the fashion to which he has grown accustomed. He will continue to recommend increasing the amount of bureaucratic control which is to be placed in his hands and those of his associates. As a result the amount of social pathology and dislocation which will be produced in the immediate future will grow by leaps and bounds. This very increase, however, may hasten both the day when computer control of government business will be inaugurated as well as the *extent* of the government's services which will be subject to handling by computer technology.

## IV. THE DROPPING OF THE OBJECT

The English philosopher, Joad,[11] has proposed that decadence exists when the view is widespread among thoughtful persons, that experience is to be valued for its own sake, regardless of its quality or content. Derivatively, according to this philosopher, decadence may be said to exist

11 *Op. cit.*

*in a society,* when its convictions about the good life, about morals, politics, art and society, are simply expressions of this same point of view about experience, but modified for special contexts. Finally, for Joad, decadence will include those scales of values and those modes of taste which are associated with the expression of the view already stated about experience. Joad has criticized the modern posture which approves of decadence and which expresses it by what he calls the "dropping of the object." By this phrase Joad refers to the refusal to ask oneself to what ends the experiences one seeks are to be put and the even more important refusal to recognize that some ends are appropriate to the quest for experience, while others are not. In this way one avoids the moral problem of a choice between good and evil or even the problem of having to ask the question "What values are most worthwhile?" There are three consequences of such a posture, as Joad has noted. These are (1) experience will be valued for its own sake, since it cannot be for the sake of anything else; (2) experience will be judged only by the standard of how much pleasure it provides; while (3) we shall tend to hold that the more intense and varied our experience, the better it is.

Joad then goes on to show that the dropping of the object is expressed in a variety of contexts. It occurs in *politics* where the pleasurable experience sought is the increase of power and where only rarely does the power-seeker ask himself to what ends he proposes to put all the increases in power which he hopes to achieve. Even more rarely does the power-seeker—alienated from moral ends—count the consequences which his exercise of power produces upon thousands of individuals who are remote from him in space, social conditions and ways of life. As Joad sees it, if the use of political power is to be socially beneficial it must be *impersonal* and, in order for the exercise of power to be impersonal, it must satisfy three conditions. These are (1) power should not be used for its own sake, (2) the purposes to which it is put should be capable of being fulfilled without depriving or harming others and (3) the means adopted to fulfill one's ends should not bring more evil, suffering and frustration, than the happiness or helpfulness or humanity ushered into being by the fulfillment of those ends.

Modern bureaucracy and specialization, says Joad, lead to increasing centralization and the dropping of the object wherever political power has been placed in bureaucratic hands. In addition, the dropping of the object through the blind use of political power has tended increasingly to deprive modern man of a sense of personal and social responsibility. Joad puts it this way.

. . . The more functions the State takes over from the individual, the fewer the individual becomes capable of exercising for himself. Thus, modern man who does not bring up his own children and only partially feeds them, who does not choose his own doctor, who has no voice in the spending of half his income, and whose mind is made up for him in regard to the disposal of most of the other half by advertisements, who is liable at any moment to be bidden to surrender both body and mind to the control and service of the State, who is dependent upon the community for support when he is old and for partial support for his wife at some and children at all times, for insurance against injury and sickness and for all the varied benefits of an advanced social legislation, modern man, I say, diminishingly acts as a responsible individual, freely exercising his judgment and following his inclinations in the planning and living of his own life as seems good to him. (p. 404)

The dropping of the object is everywhere observable in the bureaucratic unit dominated, as it usually is, by politics and the struggle for power. The official who is constantly manipulating underlings for the purpose of serving his own career instead of cooperating with them in providing a common service to the community, provides one illustration of this phenomenon. The frequent overemphasis on "going by the book," that is to say, the demand that bureaucratic rules and regulations be observed in some way, even if the plight of the citizen fails to reflect particular circumstances which are subsumable under the prevailing administrative procedures, is another. Still a third example of what Joad calls the dropping of the object in a political context, occurs when the bureaucrat insists on applying existing regulations to the situation of a given individual even though the original legislation which set up his agency in the first place, was never intended to cover that situation. A context of this sort clearly reflects a compulsive-obsessive passion for order in the means even at the price of disorder over the ends to be served.

A state university administration which takes as its central responsibility the task of catering to the educational and political prejudices of state politicians, rather than concentrating on the task of improving both the quality of the education and the quality of the teachers it provides for its students, furnishes a prime example of the dropping of the object. The political machine which makes appointments and throws elections only to those who will safeguard the selfish concerns of those vested interests which support it—forgetting that the purpose of government and political organization is to safeguard the general welfare—provides another illustration. The executive or administrator—in government, industry, the university and the church—who insists on the right to make decisions beyond his competence and play god with the lives of men, is likewise a sinner in this connection. The administrator who arrogates to himself the right to carry out public services, governed by regulation, but which are beyond his competence to understand, has clearly placed his ego-satisfactions and status-striving above the public purposes of his functions. The bureaucrat who rationalizes a selfish abuse of his powers, who rewards loyal mediocrity and keeps down the critically competent, has placed his self-esteem above the quality of public servant to which the community is entitled.

The politician and administrator who blithely squander public funds because there is no check on the good sense with which they are disbursed, illustrate a common example of the dropping of the object. Each has forgotten that the citizen expects the best quality service for the least expenditure of public monies and that "free spending" by bureaucrats is a waste of other peoples money. The waste cost-wise of taxpayers' money, the diversion of it to publicly questionable purposes—all this is equivalent to the waste of other people's time—the time that was required to earn the tax payment which is wastefully spent by a large-scale, political bureaucracy. Such wasted time is, therefore, quite clearly a waste of part of the all-too-finite lives of the taxpayers. Mismanagement of public funds, whether through corruption in urban government or Federal pork-barrel projects, are the commonest examples in public life of the dropping of the object when political centralization becomes excessive.

The dropping of the object, then, clearly occurs in political life as well as in other spheres. The point to be emphasized here, however, is that the tendency to drop the object is considerably reinforced in the overly centralized, large-scale, human community. The fragmentation of service functions in the typical bureaucracy promotes a tendency among employees *to lose sight of the welfare functions* which the agency is supposed to provide and which is the reason the agency was set up in the first place. This myopia arises out of a rigid desire to observe faithfully the procedural rules of operation. In this way error is avoided and thereby punishment. The situation frequently degenerates rapidly into a case of being unable to see the forest for the trees but one in which this inability occurs in a political context.

Changing technology will, in the foreseeable future, be producing even more unmanageable social complexity than is the case now. As social complexity becomes less manageable, efforts will be made to stem the tide of resulting disasters by the traditional response of trying to increase the amount of bureaucratic control which government is permitted to exercise over social, economic, and political processes. This extended, bureaucratic control will, itself, have to become increasingly fragmented and so long as this fragmentation provides an operating atmosphere for *human, decision-making functionaries,* the tendency to drop the objects of human concern will, itself, be widened and deepened.

Some writers thoughtlessly imagine that the displacement of unimaginative bureaucrats by the even more unimaginative computer, will reduce considerably those faults of bureaucracy about which all of us constantly complain. The use of the computer, however, will not help matters here. The computer may, of course, be superior in dealing with the complex planning and problem-solving of the large-scale, political and governmental community. But this is not the point. The nub of the matter in trying to avoid an abstract treatment of the problems of individuals, is the inability of bureaucratic procedures to take cognizance of the uniqueness of the individual's circumstances. This is often a uniqueness to which bureaucratic regulations may be quite irrelevant. In this respect the rigid computer program is hardly the answer, since such a program will be even less likely to take stock of individual circumstances than the unimaginative, government bureaucrat. If any improvement is to arise in an administrative, operating atmosphere, it can only do so when the operating atmosphere allows more free play of judgment to the content and style of the decision-maker's actions. What is it about the bureaucratic atmosphere which inhibits such free play of judgment? This is a question worth exploring. Let us try to answer it in the section which follows.

## V. THE IMPERATIVES OF BUREAUCRACY

Is bureaucratic behavior *chiefly* an artifact of large-scale, social organization, is it more an attribute of human nature *when organized collectively* or is it more than anything else a situational matter which depends upon the operating characteristics of a certain type of human context? Clearly bureaucratic behavior is a function of all three of the considerations mentioned and many others besides. Furthermore, we have been emphasizing all along the observation that large-scale, social and political organization must give rise to bureaucratic structures. This observation has been a matter of central concern to us. The question which we wish to raise now is precisely what is it about large-scale organization which gives rise to both the bureaucratic atmosphere and bureaucratic behavior? In other words what are the *motivational dynamics* which are uniquely created by large-scale organization.

The anonymity of the bureaucratic milieu is achieved by providing a service for the citizen which is completely accomplished by legislation, rules and regulations, and standard operating procedures. These rules and regulations are meant to cover circumstances which are thought to be uniform, and expected to continue to be uniform, for all individuals. At the least, bureaucratic procedures must rest on the *"fiction"* that the circumstances of all individuals to which they are relevant, are identical. This assumption satisfies the perfectly well-intentioned desire of the bureaucrat to achieve the feeling of certainty that his judgment will be free of error if he adheres faithfully to the letter of the regulations. In this way, from his own standpoint, he acts with an abstract impartiality towards all. From the standpoint of his superiors, he will not have to exercise thought and judgment on each new situation which may arise for an individual who has a slightly different problem from the fictitious, typical one which underlay the framing of standard operating procedures in the first place.

From the administrative standpoint this latter contingency would open up the flood-gates of chaos, allowing the bureaucratic functionary to exercise judgment in each service-situation, creating a thousand different and incompatible criteria for the exercise of that judgment and leading to public bitterness over the inequities created by "capricious," institutional decision-making. Clearly, no one—neither the public nor the public servant—would be happy with a situation in which the ground rules changed all the time.

The concern of the bureaucratic overseer with the behavior of his bureaucratic underling is matched by the habits of the underling, himself. The average human being is neither inclined to extensive thought nor capable of it. This ideophobia is reinforced in a bureaucratic setting. The more complex the problems with which administrators have to deal, the truer is our statement about ideophobia likely to be for officials down the line. Since the trend of the times is towards increasing social complexity which, itself, is being met by increasingly, large-scale political and administrative organization, the penchant for avoiding thought through bureaucratic, standard operating procedures is, itself, on the increase. A second consideration which clearly aids and abets the avoidance of individual judgment on the part of a bureaucratic underling, is, of course, the fear of the punishment which will attend mistakes in judgment. The employee's job tenure, itself, may be threatened as a result of any temerity he dares to exercise in departing from the operating rules which have been laid down for all.

What would happen if—in spite of the considerations already mentioned—top administrators in a bureaucracy were willing to take the risk involved, reverse themselves and encourage the employee to trim his judgment to the circumstances of individuals rather than to classify their situations in order to apply existing regulations to them in the usual, wooden, bureaucratic fashion? Let us suppose that a bureaucratic agency did, in fact, wish to humanize its procedures by allowing the underling to use the regulations *only as guide-lines* or *norms* for the solution of its clients' problems. Let us suppose further that it did this by encouraging the minor official to be *flexible* in the exercise of his judgment. This flexibility would then be achieved by trying to see in what ways the client's circumstances departed from the statistically typical situations on which the governing law and the detailed agency regulations were based. The minor bureaucrat would then be encouraged to steer somewhere between the feeling of certainty and confidence which the rigid application of the agency regulations could provide and the desire to be flexible, humane, imaginative and involved. This he would endeavor to do by recognizing the unique aspects of the client's circumstances and tailoring the agency's decision to the unrepresentativeness of these circumstances.

The effort to strike such a balance, even if it were followed by no punishment, whatsoever, would call for a great deal of knowledge, refinement in judgment and a willingness to devote time to the individual case. If either of these three virtues were lacking, the granted flexibility would serve no purpose. The recognition that the road to hell is paved with good intentions, would certainly apply in this instance. All the goodwill in the world would then not prevent mistakes, unconscious favoritism and unforeseen consequences in which the cure in many cases would be worse than the disease. On the other hand, suppose the bureaucrat were, in fact, some sort of an administrative demigod, with perfect knowledge, judgment and patience. Nevertheless it would still be true that the willingness to devote the amount of time required for dealing properly with each individual case, *would make it impossible to service all the clients who came with their pressing, individual problems.* If one increased the number of employee demigods needed for the proper treatment of all, the costs would surely become prohibitive.

This last contingency emphasizes another aspect of the problem of trying to be humane, moral and involved in an increasingly complex world in which bureaucratic administration is the chief handmaiden to the task of meeting the needs of large-scale, social organization. If the decision-making official wishes to be humane he must weigh the cost to the community of providing welfare to the client *against* the value of the increased welfare which he hopes to create for that same client. What is a proper balance between these two? When should the individual's welfare be sacrificed to the general welfare and when should the reverse take place? Apart from the moral complexities these questions raise, there are also the concomitant, technical and quantitative questions which they also raise with respect to the measurement of welfare. These latter are, in a sense, measureable, as one can see from the work of Rothenberg.[12] These questions are also often logically decidable, as one can see from the work of Arrow.[13] But we are still lost, in a way, because we have no available philosophy of moral decision and no metaphysic governing moral choices, which will enable us to *feel* (and "feel" is the right word here) that there are contingencies when some general welfare must be sacrificed to the welfare of the individual. Nor are we sufficiently well educated in the emotional and humanistic sense to know when we are staring such an occasion in the face.

12 Jerome Rothenberg. *The Measurement of Social Welfare.* Englewood Cliffs, New Jersey: Prentice-Hall, 1961. 357 pp.
13 Kenneth J. Arrow. *Social Choice and Individual Values.* New York: Wiley, 1951. 99 pp.

If we then return to the problem of creating a flexible bureaucrat, we note that he must be well-informed, compassionate and humane, and concerned with the individual's plight rather than alienated from it by abstractions. In addition, he must be willing to devote adequate amounts of time to the individual case and the community must be willing to bear the costs which the provision of such time, entails. All this becomes an increasingly impossible expectation as centralization proceeds apace in a complex and technological society. Large-scale society generates new *individual* problems (as well as community problems) faster than it can deal with those which have been around for some time. In this sense we will not only never have enough time to permit the continued operation of a *flexible,* large-scale bureaucracy but we shall always be "running out of time." By contrast the small-scale community, functioning to human scale, generates fewer problems of this sort, gives rise to reasonable costs in connection with their solution, makes the task of being properly informed with respect to the issues involved, easier, and finally makes the human touch more natural because of the greater possibility of familiarity with the client and the greater frequency of face-to-face contacts which become institutionally possible. In this sense political and administrative decentralization offer opportunities for a more humane relationship between freedom and authority than the highly centralized governing or administrative unit.

In Chapters 22 and 23 we have been concerned with the political pathologies of metropolis, in the form of sometimes tragic, sometimes comic, but always frustrating expressions of overcentralization and bureaucracy in our lives. But overcentralization and bureaucracy have helped to create more than political pathology. The many forms of alienation which are the inevitable accompaniments of overcentralization, the decision-making incompetence so often associated with overcentralization and the blunders derived from it, have also produced other, more important types of urban pathology. I am referring here to the destruction of our physical environment—an environment which is the inescapable foundation for the establishment of community. I am also referring to the possibly irreparable destruction of the ecological balance between man and the environment which sustains him. This destruction is expressed in the physical pathologies of air and water pollution, water shortages in cities, waste of scarce water resources, and still other considerations closely related to these community tragedies of our time. These physical pathologies are deeply associated both with large-scale urbanization as well as urban bureaucracy and mismanagement. It is to these physical pathologies of overcentralization that we now turn.

# 24

# The Physical Pathologies
# of Overurbanization

## I. URBANIZATION AND HUMAN ECOLOGY

With the exception of man all living things are compelled to behave in accordance with natural laws and the population sizes which they reach are a function of a natural, ecological balance. This balance reflects the interdependence of many factors. Among these factors we find that we can include the following: soil, temperature and moisture, climate and weather, geography, the nature of the organisms living in the environment, flora indigenous to the same area, and the degree of protection from catastrophic, topographical changes which the environment of living things affords. The processes which maintain this ecological balance have been studied and are well understood. In some respects these processes can be reduced to a mathematical science and the reader can get the full sense of this statement by studying one classic monograph in this direction, namely, the work of Volterra and D'Ancona.[1] Under specific, favorable conditions certain species in certain areas reach a maximum and such a maximum is called by ecologists a "climax." Thus, for instance, before the westward migration of the white man occurred and before his predatory plundering and transformation of the ecology of the American Plains took place, the bison and the American Indian were "climax" crops in this region.

Man, however, due to mismanagement of his environment for economic gain, has upset the "natural ecological balance" between town and country in the form of large cities and the continuing processes of overurbanization. By a "natural ecological balance" we mean that the factors of interdependency in any given area establish the living or even the non-living things which will be the "climax" crops of that area. Even when the balance is upset for a spell, if time passes we find that there is a tendency for the climax species to again become dominant and for the

---

[1] M. Vito Volterra et M. Umberto D'Ancona. *Les Associations Biologiques au Point de Vue Mathématique*. Paris: Hermann et Cie, Editeurs, 1935. 96 pp.

old relationships of the region to reestablish themselves gradually. This tendency to return again and again to what we may call the "natural" condition or, as the ecologists put it, to a climax, is called "succession." Unfortunately, the growing size of man's cities forever prevents the phenomenon of succession within the areas which have been cleared for cities as well as in the surrounding areas.

What is worse, however, is that the imbalance between town and country, which man creates, destroys the basis of that natural wealth of raw material resources which satisfies his material needs. This, however, is only what we might call a "first-order," ecological pathology. For a period men living in metropolis ignore this destruction which they, themselves, have produced, because of the feeling that what they have done technologically has made them a climax crop in the area. But with the growth of urban centers and their close association with expanding industrialization, the metropolis begins to create conditions of a physio-logical and psychological nature which affect man's health, happiness, life-span, the quality of daily life and the social costs of maintaining even the facsimile of a genuine community. These conditions may be called the "second-order," ecological pathology. In this chapter some of the characteristics and conditions of both orders of ecological pathology are discussed, for it is these very characteristics and conditions which consti-tute *an ecological bill of particulars* against urban centralization.[2] Bearing these pathologies in mind, the decentralist pleads for the small commu-nity in which these pathologies are absent or, at least, negligible, and thereby for the reestablishment of a proper balance between town and country. Such reduction to scale—as we shall show in a subsequent chapter —is now feasible because of new developments in science and technology.

Let us first consider the ecological pathology that results from increas-ing real estate development and urban, industrial location, on the one hand, and a growing city population, on the other. The former is the inevitable accompaniment of unchecked urbanism. The latter is the result of many factors which will not be discussed here. Every day bull-dozers and steam shovels wipe out of existence a vast number of acres of land, most of which once served as useful cropland and pasture. Accord-ing to Donald A. Williams,[3] administrator of the Department of Agricul-ture's Soil Conservation Service, more than a million acres of cropland a year are destroyed this way. In 1957 [4] this same administrator stated that more than 17 million acres of the nation's best farmlands had been gobbled up in the previous 15 years for nonagricultural purposes, mostly,

[2] For some of the material in this chapter, illustrative of ecological pathology, the author has drawn upon the following volume: Lewis Herber. *Crisis in Our Cities.* Engle-wood Cliffs, New Jersey: Prentice-Hall, 1965. 239 pp.

[3] See *The New York Times,* August 6, 1961.

[4] See *The New York Times,* February 26, 1957.

of course, to accommodate urban sprawl. Williams also stated at that time that he expected another 27 million acres would be buried under concrete or its equivalent in another 10 years. All of this feverish urbanism results in the destruction of topsoil and does so at a time when the U.S. population is increasing.

A situation of this sort threatens the eventual food potential of the United States—a future threat which, perhaps, seems unreal in the light of our contemporary crop surpluses and the disposal problems faced by the Federal Surplus Commodity Corporation. Yet if nothing is done about such land mismanagement, Father Time will have the last laugh. To argue that our increasing agricultural productivity will more than compensate for the retirement of fertile land, is to ignore Vogt's [5] famous formula concerning the *biotic potential* of land, namely, $C = B : E$. In this formula C stands for the carrying capacity of any area of land, that is, its ability to produce food, drink and shelter for the creatures who live on it. B refers to the *biotic potential,* or the ability of the land to produce plants for sheltering, for clothing, and especially for feeding, since only plants can synthesize food from the raw materials of the earth and air in a form utilizable by animals. E stands for the resistance the environment places on the biotic potential, including, as part of that environment, *man's own urban artifacts.* In Vogt's formula the carrying capacity, C, is the resultant of the ratio between B and E. How does Vogt's formula relate directly to our present topic?

The removal of cropland because of overcentralizing urbanism is equivalent to reducing B in man's environment. The increase of urbanism and industrialization—with some of its resulting consequences, such as air and water pollution—is equivalent to raising E. This is the worst possible situation that can occur for man ecologically. We either want C to remain constant or, more realistically, to increase, so as to ensure an environment which will sustain our rising population. However, if B decreases and E increases, C decreases, and at quite a rapid rate. At the same time our population, P, is increasing. Thus C/P or the carrying capacity of the land per person is rapidly decreasing. It is this situation—seen in these abstract terms—which is under indictment by Williams. It is an example of a first-order, ecological pathology being created by rampant and irrational urbanization. Any decentralist, of course, throws up his hands in despair over this situation.

Many optimists believe that the worries of Vogt and other Neo-Malthusians, concerning the *declining availability of land* in man's ecology, are unwarranted. They will point to such an important and offsetting factor as the huge and potential, ecological resources of the seas and oceans of the world. At present, technologies for the exploitation of the

[5] William Vogt. *The Road to Survival.* New York: W. Sloane Associates, 1948. 335 pp.

marine resources of the world are only in their infancy, but there are justifiable grounds for optimism.[6] This optimism, however, misses the point, since the Neo-Malthusian argument takes the long-range point of view. This means that, even if advanced marine technologies were on hand tomorrow—capable of large-scale catches—nevertheless, Vogt's formula would *eventually* also apply to the world's seas and oceans just as readily as it applies to the earth's land areas. This must be true if world population continues to increase substantially, particularly at a rate which is more rapid than the rate of increase in the world's production of food from all sources. The coming age of ocean farming may *stave off* for quite some time the unhappy consequences of a decline in the ratio, $C/P$. But here too a day of reckoning must come, albeit in a much more remote future, since the ratio, $B: E$, is a relationship equally applicable to the coming oceanographic technologies of food production. In short, what we are saying here is that some form of Neo-Malthusianism is inescapable *in the long run.*

There are, however, other undesirable consequences of the excessive rate of retirement of land and forest. There are the aesthetic consequences to begin with, that is, the growing ugliness of a landscape sprawling with factories and with their detritus and sewage, with highways and their associated billboards and vending stands, with power lines, radio and television towers and storage bins and granaries, and with the clutter of buildings and objects created by the rampant commercialism attending tourism and recreation. There are such biological consequences as air and water pollution and the threat to our capacity to obtain a constant supply of fresh oxygen from the atmosphere as huge areas of woods and forests are forever removed. There are such economic consequences as a threatened shortage of wood and lumber as a result of the despoliation of our forests. Finally, there are the psychological consequences which will have to be faced up to, that is, the loss to man of a great and meaningful part of his heritage if the unchecked destruction of Nature were to result in the enormous reduction in the number of living creatures of forest, field and stream or even their complete extinction.

Let us, however, return to the subject of land mismanagement in the United States. A large, urban population tends to concentrate in coastal regions. As a result the drain on fresh ground water produced by such congested urban populations on the coastal plains, increasingly opens

---

[6] Some idea of the food potential of the world's oceans and seas can be obtained from the following, *untechnical* sources. F. G. Walton Smith and Henry Chapin. *The Sun, The Sea and Tomorrow. Potential Sources of Food, Energy and Minerals from the Sea.* New York: Charles Scribner's Sons, 1954. 210 pp. Marian Maury. *The Good War. The UN's world-wide fight against poverty, disease and ignorance.* New York: Macfadden Books, 1965. 191 pp. See particularly Chapter 9 "New Ways in Food Production," 97–110.

the way for the contamination of ground water by salt water. In these areas fresh ground water floats on, or is adjacent to, denser saline waters. These latter are remnants of ancient oceans which once flooded these areas. The top of the water-saturated zone below the earth's surface, is called the ground–water table. This table is substantially lowered when men pump wells, construct canals and drain land. If these operations are sufficiently near the coast, the lowering of the ground-water table—which is floating on or adjacent to the denser saline waters—gives the salt water an opportunity to invade the fresh ground water. Since fresh ground water is used to a great extent for irrigation in areas such as California, such an invasion is a threat to the continued usefulness of the ground-water for purposes of irrigation. As early as 1950 California reported that nearly 25 per cent of some 80 major ground-water reservoirs experienced salt-water intrusion. Much of California's agriculture is heavily dependent upon irrigation from *aquifers*. These are water-bearing formations consisting of beds of gravel, sand, loosely compacted sediments, porous sandstones, and thinly bedded or cavernous limestones. Contamination of ground-water reserves of the far West could destroy its agricultural potential for generations to come and even reduce a fertile region to desertlike terrain.

The point of all the preceding, however, is to note that this destruction of nature's bounty of water proceeds by all those activities of man *which can lower the water table*. These activities increase by leaps and bounds when huge conurbations, such as we have, for instance, in California, arise in coastal regions. They increase when industrial needs require wells or canals over the landscape. Above all, they multiply when land is drained for industrial purposes or reclaimed for purposes of new residential development.

## II. AIR POLLUTION AS URBAN PATHOLOGY

Air pollution as a problem is now nationally recognized. What is less recognized is that it is a distinct urban problem and one which bids fair to be aggravated as metropolises become larger and more centralized. Let us first note some of the sources of air pollution over our cities. These sources include the following: furnaces, incinerators, burning garbage dumps, motor vehicles, railroads, aircraft, factories, steel mills, chemical plants, power plants and oil refineries. Specific categories of pollutants are familiar to most of us. These are smoke, fumes, dusts, mists and a large variety of gases. About 100 air pollutants have been chemically identified by the experts thus far but we can expect that the number of agents which can be identified as air pollutants, will increase with further research.

Consider the industrial burning of a ton of coal. In the course of its combustion this fuel will release 150 pounds of solid pollutants in the form of soot and fly ash, 80 pounds of sulphur dioxide, 8 pounds of nitrogen dioxide, 30 pounds of acids and 20 pounds of mixed contaminants consisting largely of hydrocarbons. Some of the gases which are formed by the combustion of coal undergo subsequent chemical change and are transformed into more noxious substances than the original pollutants, themselves. Smoke, soot, and sulphur compounds form the more traditional type of air pollution—known as "London-type air pollution"—and prevails in the older cities of the U.S., like New York and Philadelphia. The type of chemical pollution prevailing over a city depends upon its industries. A city with aluminum, steel, phosphate, brick or pottery works is likely to contaminate the air with large amounts of hydrogen fluoride. Fluorides which accumulate in forage will cause poisoning of domestic animals. Some industrial communities may contaminate the air with other types of exotic pollutants—manganese compounds, radioactive isotopes and allergy-inducing dyes.

Another type of air-pollution is known as the Los-Angeles type. It is the product of a combination of petroleum wastes, sunlight, the automobile, and a number of meteorological conditions which exist in other urban centers in the United States. One of these meteorological conditions is "temperature inversion." Ordinarily the temperature of the air falls as we go upward until it can be rather cold a few thousand feet up. Occasions arise, however, when warm masses of air move over the upper-level, cooler masses. These warm masses act like a lid preventing the air nearer the ground from moving upward. This confined air becomes stagnant, hugging the earth until the warm mass disappears. In this stagnant layer air pollutants accumulate in high and harmful concentrations. It is this reversal of temperature layers which we call "temperature inversion." The warm masses of air which act as confining lids, sweep in over Los Angeles on the average about 260 days a year and produce from 30–50 days of irritating smog which causes tears, sneezing, and coughing. Many experts, at one time, believed that smog was a result of Los Angeles having become overindustrialized.

It was soon realized, however, that the *primary* source of Los Angeles air pollution lay elsewhere, since thousands continued to weep, sneeze and cough under conditions which could not clearly be traced to industrialization. Pinpointing this source did not take much time. It proved to be the exhaust fumes from America's most popular, family institution—the automobile. In the early 60's there were over three million automobiles in the Los Angeles area. This means that Los Angelenos are walking in an atmosphere which contains 9,000 tons of carbon monoxide a day, 1,180 tons of hydrocarbons, 330 tons of oxides of nitrogen, and many tons of aldehydes, sulphur compounds, acids, ammonia, lead and other poisons. To make matters worse sunlight produces changes in nitrogen dioxide yielding eventually such irritants as formaldehyde and acrolein, an ingredient of tear gas. The breakdown of the same nitrogen dioxide results in the formation of another irritant, ozone. Finally the incomplete combustion of gasoline in cars increases the amounts of formaldehyde and acrolein in the atmosphere.

What are some of the *suspected* physiological consequences of air-pollution? Although all the physiological consequences we are about to mention are still controversial, the grounds for suspecting that air pollution plays a heavy role in causing the conditions we are about to mention, are more than justified. The consequences, then, of air pollution include, but without limitation, air-pollution allergies, asthma, chronic bronchitis, lung cancer from air-borne carcinogens like the hydrocarbon, benzpyrene, carbon monoxide poisoning, increased susceptibility to common cold, emphysema (a breakdown of the architecture and physical materials of the lungs), a suspected linkage to some types of heart illness, pneumonia and various respiratory infections. In addition to the *possibility* that air pollution produces these menaces to public health, it definitely takes an economic toll of our national wealth, measured in billions of dollars. This is part of what we mean by "the social costs of private enterprise." Air pollutants cause damage to clothing, home furnishings, buildings, machinery and roads, animal and plant life, and to many other items of importance. Kapp [7] has furnished the figures for the social costs of these types of damages but inasmuch as his figures are now two decades old—sometimes more—the true and current figures would unquestionably be much higher.

Among the indictments made against the overurbanized, overindustrialized, and overcentralized metropolis, air pollution is a major one. Partisans of decentralization recognize that the small community is more than likely to minimize, if not eliminate, gross air pollution. One form or another of air pollution may prove to be inescapably associated with the industrialized metropolis. If this should prove to be so, then quite obviously the "nigger in the woodpile" would be excessive urbanization, itself.

The extent of the problem of air pollution has been indicated in a recent volume by Lewis.[8] This writer points out in his book the depressing fact that 60 percent of the American people live in areas which gov-

---

[7] K. William Kapp. *The Social Costs of Private Enterprise.* Cambridge, Massachusetts: Harvard University Press, 1950. 287 pp. See Chapter 5, "The Social Costs of Air Pollution," 67–79.

[8] Howard R. Lewis. *With Every Breath You Take.* New York: Crown Publishers, 1965. 322 pp. It is possible to reduce air pollution in our urban centers but new factors—such as more plants and factories and more automobiles—tend to offset the reductions we can make by means of certain practical devices and inventions, such as blowby devices, the direct vent tube system and the afterburner.

ernment experts classify as air-polluted. Other facts also bring home the extent of this problem. *Science Digest* reported in 1962 that United States physicians encountered 1,600,000 cases of illness associated with air pollution. These illnesses were among those we have already mentioned. What about the magnitude of the "social costs" of air pollution? America's *total* annual bill for the damage created by air pollution has been estimated at 14 billion dollars. The magnitude of this bill should not be surprising when we are told by New York City's Department of Air Pollution Control that more than 60 tons of soot—derived from air pollutants —are ground into a square mile of Manhattan every year.

All the preceding material on air pollution reflects part of the crisis existing in our overcentralized and overindustrialized cities. Air pollution is not, of course, brought about by centralization. It is, however, brought about by the conditions which a thoughtless centralization encourages— haphazard industrial location, indifference to the social costs created by the waste products of industry, indifference to the effects of the millions of automobiles in our cities and indifference to the poisoning of our atmosphere, created by urban traffic congestion. It is these factors—so heavily associated with the problem of air pollution—which justify the charge that thoughtless and cumbersome forms of urban centralization create much of the crisis in our cities.


## III. THE WATER CRISIS AS URBAN PATHOLOGY

The phrase, "water crisis," refers to two major phenomena in American life which have now come to public attention, namely, (1) water shortages or deficits in some of our big cities and (2) water pollution. The phrase, "water deficit" refers either to situations which have actually deprived urban populations of the full quota of water which they need or the phrase may refer to the threat of such a situation. The phrase, "water pollution," can mean a number of things but it *usually* refers to such matters as the undrinkability or lack of *potability* of water because of its taste, odor or appearance, its disease-carrying characteristics which therefore make it a menace to public health, its ability to destroy beneficial forms of marine life, and similar matters.

We propose in this section to discuss these matters as part of the indictment against excessive centralization in our lives. This excessive centralization—in connection with the water crises—may be reflected in several ways. (1) It may sometimes be reflected as haphazard, unplanned excessive industrialization associated with either of the two conditions constituting the water crises. (2) It may show up in the form of unchecked and irrational forms of urbanism. (3) Finally, it may reveal itself through some type of pathological bureaucratization associated with certain aspects of centralized mismanagement in our large cities. We shall discuss each of the two major aspects of the water crisis separately, although, in some respects, they are related.

## The Water Supply and Water Deficit

Water deficits—real or threatened—may be associated with either: (1) variations in the earth's hydrologic cycle, (2) waste disposal and water pollution, or (3) waste in relation to our standard of living. Let us discuss each of these in turn.

### Variations in the Earth's Hydrologic Cycle

The *hydrologic cycle* refers to the relationships which govern the presence of moisture and precipitation. Moisture and precipitation are the outcome of processes governed by the oceans and the earth's atmosphere working together to water the land.[9] One outcome of these processes is that the appearance of drought in some regions of the earth is almost always accompanied by heavy rainfall elsewhere. The water shortages in New York State during the early 60's were connected with *changes in the earth's hydrologic cycle*. Significantly, in the year 1963, changes in that same cycle were responsible for some of the floods suffered by areas in the Midwest, drought in Australia and heavy rains in central Europe.

The changes in the earth's hydrologic cycle, to which we have already referred, have acted to produce drought in New York City and its environs in the following fashion. Normally warm air heated by sunlight at the equator moves by convection towards the North Pole. Due to the rotation of the earth, this warm mass veers to the right as it moves northward. As a result this air stream breaks into an undulating planetary wave, writhing north and south. A single coil of this wave, stretching from west to east, spans 1000 to 1500 miles. Usually the moisture in one of the northbound loops of this wave is cooled as it passes over the Eastern sea coast of the United States and falls as rain. Unfortunately— and this is what we mean by a change in the earth's hydrologic cycle—the traditional, planetary wave pattern has shifted eastward in recent years. The reasons for this, unfortunately, are not well understood. One result of this shift, however, is that what would have been normal *sea coast rain* has been precipitated over the Atlantic rather than on the land.

---

[9] For an extended technical discussion of the hydrologic cycle, see Chapter 4 "Atmospheric Moisture and Precipitation," 68–87, in the following volume: Vernon C. Finch, Glenn T. Trewartha, Arthur H. Robinson and Edwin H. Hammond. *Elements of Geography*. 4th ed. New York: McGraw-Hill, 1957. 693 pp. For a highly simplified description of the hydrologic cycle and its relation to drought in the Northeastern part of the U.S., particularly New York State, see the following article: John Lear. "What Brought It On?" *Saturday Review*, October 23, 1965. 24–8 and 78–80. John Lear is the Science Editor of *Saturday Review*.

It is the absence of this precipitation during the early 60's, which produced the "dry spell" suffered by New York City and its environs. The cause of the drought can, therefore, in no sense be blamed upon centralization, industrialization, urbanization or bureaucratization. The response to it, however, or rather the lack of response to it, can definitely be blamed on some bureaucratic mismanagement which has occurred both in New York State and in New York City. Let us try to make clear what we mean by this charge.

As long ago as 1950, reports Wolman,[10] during an earlier dry spell, New York City was advised to build a pumping station on the Hudson River at a spot about 65 miles north of that city. This advice was intended to guarantee an emergency supply of water amounting to 100 million gallons per day or more, if required. New York State gave its permission for this project but stipulated that the pumping station was to be dismantled when the drought was over. That earlier dry spell ended when the station had been completed. As a result it was torn down before it was ever used. The nature of the stipulation that was required by New York State, is a perfect example of bureaucratic mismanagement.

A second example of bureaucratic mismanagement in response to the water crisis, has been reported by Bennett.[11] In 1965 a conflict between Armand D'Angelo, the Water Commissioner for New York City, and some of his rank-and-file water engineers, came to light. At the beginning of the then, four-year drought the engineers in his department had advised D'Angelo to take the public into his confidence and urge intelligent restraint in water use. They had further advised him to intensify the effort to curb leaks in New York City's water mains, to curb waste and to begin to take steps to meet water emergencies. This advice was not only ignored but Mr. D'Angelo actually blamed his engineers for policies framed by City Hall years before and policies which, even at that time, were against the advice of the city's engineers. Mr. D'Angelo preferred, instead, to lull the public and say nothing. He even reported to Mayor Wagner in 1964 that he saw no danger of a water shortage.

Mayor Wagner during that same period rejected a call for universal water metering. This was intended to make the public conscious of the fact that in a technological and urban society like ours, water is no longer a free good. Public awareness of this fact can be intensified by charging the taxpayer for his water. Mayor Wagner's attitude was that water is a natural resource that should be available to all. This attitude prevailed in spite of the fact that—as a result of changes in the hydrologic cycle—rainfall over the city's watersheds at that time had declined from 47

10 Abel Wolman. "The Metabolism of Cities." 156–74. In *Cities. A Scientific American Book.* New York: Alfred A. Knopf, 1965. 211 pp.
11 Charles G. Bennett. "New York: Engineers *vs.* Politicians." *Saturday Review,* October 23, 1965. 43–4. Charles G. Bennett, on the staff of the *New York Times,* specializes on the water problems of New York City.

inches in 1960 to 32 in the ensuing years. In 1951 the Mayor's Committee on Management Survey had recommended tapping the Hudson River in order to increase New York City's water supply. They had also recommended universal metering to reduce consumption and pleaded for a more efficient setup to repair water leaks. Water leaks from broken water mains are an important source of water waste in New York City. Waste from this source is so great that Interior Secretary Udall once claimed that New York City has one of the leakiest and most loosely managed of city water systems. Needless to say bureaucratic habits won out in 1951 and the report of the Mayor's Committee on Management Survey was ignored.

The preceding facts constitute a few examples of the way in which ill-informed, highly centralized, urban mismanagement can ignore a fundamental change in potential water supply. New York City's dry spell —due to fundamental changes in the local expression of the earth's hydrologic cycle—should have been understood, taken seriously and adapted to intelligently. Instead it was ignored. New York City may succeed in meeting its water crisis. The greatest danger lies in the possibility that other cities may ignore natural changes and conditions for so long as to reach a point of no return. Few such points of no return need be feared in the near future, provided urban management adapts early and intelligently to all the signs and portents of potential water crises. Whether the typical, urban bureaucrat, like Mr. D'Angelo, can reflect the type of management needed, remains to be seen. There is always room for pessimism here.

## Waste Disposal and Water Pollution

Actual or threatened water shortages can also be associated with the unwillingness of cities to tap huge, prospective and easily accessible water supplies because these are polluted and because various excuses may be used to avoid cleaning up the pollution. The Hudson River is one example of a neglected, potential source of water. New York City in the past had a choice between abating the pollution in the Hudson and capturing a new and tremendous water supply or continuing to use the Hudson as a sewer for waste disposal largely of an industrial nature. The blight of a thoughtless industrialization won out here and New York City chose to use the Hudson as a free sewer, preferring to make up its water deficits, instead, by turning to reservoirs. This decision in retrospect appears to have been somewhat questionable, when changes in the hydrologic cycle began to empty the city's reservoirs.

One of the bureaucratic arguments leveled against the suggestion that the Hudson be cleaned up, was that the costs of so doing would be prohibitive. There are precedents, however, which make such an excuse a feeble one. One conspicuous precedent which makes the argument shallow is the operation of the German Ruhrverband. The Ruhrverband is an industrial cooperative consisting of 250 towns and cities and 2,200 industries, which uses Ruhr River water. It keeps that water potable—after industrial waste has been emptied into the Ruhr—by dividing the cost burden of treatment among its members. The levies have allowed the Ruhrverband to establish 102 water purification plants along the river. The cost is prorated according to both the amount and kind of waste emptied into the Ruhr by a member. Steel mills along the Ruhr which were interested in reducing the cost of their assessments, were allowed the option of devising internal recirculation systems. These allow a mill to use the same water repeatedly. This has resulted in reducing both water-consumption and water-pollution. As one result of recirculation, the amount of water required to produce a ton of steel has been lowered from 130 cubic yards to 2.6 cubic yards.

The Ruhrverband started its operations before pollution became too heavy. The costs to New York City of treating a given volume of water in the Hudson would, of course, be greater than treating the same volume of polluted Ruhr water, if the latter were to be treated here. This, however, is no argument against liquidating the heavy pollution, in order to make available a new and huge supply of potable water. The irrelevance of the argument that costs would be prohibitive has been established at other cities in the United States, which also have serious, water-pollution problems. Thus St. Louis citizens in 1962 voted a 95 million dollar bond issue to halt pollution in the Mississippi River. As a result of an interstate clean-up program for pollution in the Great Lakes, Detroit will be spending at least 100 million dollars just to bring its sewage system up to date. Remedial measures along the whole lakeshore of the Erie will probably run into the billions. Two hundred thousand Ohioans have petitioned for clean water and have supported the campaign to "Save Lake Erie Now." A $300,000 city study was instituted to devise a master plan for pollution control in Cleveland. In the mid-1960's Chicago put into operation a 100 million dollar filtration plant to serve more than 2 million persons. Los Angeles is studying the possibility of establishing the world's largest sea water desalinization plant. This would be a nuclear-powered operation and would cost 300 million dollars. It would supply 150 million gallons daily and might be able to meet the water needs of as many as 750,000 people. Seattle residents voted to bond themselves for nearly 200 million dollars in order to install an elaborate sewage collection and treatment system to curb pollution of lakes and salty Puget Sound. The citizens of Seattle have done this even though these waters have no connection with their domestic water sources.

Yet in spite of the civic-minded and socially responsible attitudes being shown by the citizens of the various communities we have just mentioned, New York City and New York State officials have stood fast against bearing the costs of liquidating pollution in the Hudson River. It would seem reasonable to believe that if communities served by the Great Lakes and inland river systems are willing to spend billions to curb pollution, communities along the Hudson could cooperate to do likewise.[12] To the extent that communities refuse to deal with waste disposal and water pollution—for reasons of alleged, prohibitive costs or out of bureaucratic inertia or for any other reasons—they may face local water deficits which are entirely unnecessary.

In the disposal of waste to prevent pollution huge amounts of water are required in order to dilute waste material for treatment. These amounts of water for waste dilution promise to be a drain on local water supplies as urbanization increases and additional factories arise to meet the needs of growing urban populations. This drain on water supply is inevitable because an increase in factories must lead to an increase in industrial waste. Theoretically—in relation to population density and waste outflow facilities—there may be an optimum figure for population size if waste disposal is to be maximally efficient and if pollution is to be minimized. According to *Resources in America's Future*,[13] by 1980 the East will need approximately 252 billion gallons per day of water to be used for waste dilution; the West will need approximately 60 billion gallons per day; and the Pacific Northwest will need 29 billion gallons per day. Thus once again we see the strain on water supply which results even when socially responsible measures are taken to *prevent pollution*. The measures to end *existing pollution*, however, will actually add to our water supply and more than compensate for the huge amounts of water needed to dilute waste and prevent pollution. For reasons such as these, it would be the height of mismanagement in connection with the water crisis, to be penny-wise but pound-foolish and balk at the necessary costs of liquidating pollution in our largest bodies of water.

### Water Waste in Relation to the Standard of Living

Water deficits in our highly centralized cities can, to some extent, be associated both with family and social life in the metropolis and with the industrialization on which that life is based. Let us first consider the extent to which water is wasted as a result of our American standard of living or—as some American critics might put it—as a result of our emphasis on "gracious living."

12 The facts and figures quoted in connection with the liquidation of water-pollution, in the text above, are from the October 23, 1965 issue of *Saturday Review*. That issue—a special number—is entitled *The Crisis in Water: Its Sources, Pollution and Depletion*.

13 Hans H. Landsberg, Leonard L. Fischman and Joseph L. Fisher. *Resources in America's Future*. Published for *Resources for the Future, Inc.* by The Johns Hopkins Press, Baltimore, 1963. 1017 pp. See p. 271, Table 14–5.

We could talk most sensibly about the waste of water in urban life if we had some firm studies telling us the amount of water which is *reasonably necessary* for comfortable, urban living in a technologically advanced society like ours. There are, unfortunately, no such studies. Lear tells us that, in terms of genuine physical need, an adult human requires only three quarts of water per day for normal functioning.[14] This may account, perhaps, for the amount needed to satisfy one's thirst. A higher figure would certainly be required if we added the amounts of water needed for personal hygiene. But when we consider the amounts of water we demand for various urban amenities, the figure becomes enormously inflated. An urban family, says Herber,[15] uses about six times as much water as a farm family, which draws its water from a well, yet there is no reason to believe that the farm family, with its smaller consumption use, is being deprived of any basic needs. There is, as we have already noted, no scientific research on the amount of water actually needed to provide the amenities so dear to the hearts of urban dwellers, although there is plenty of evidence to suggest that many of the amenities provided by life in the metropolis are unnecessary and wasteful. These amenities include such refined and elaborated comforts as daily baths, flush toilets, air-coolers, automatic clothes washers, dish-washing machines, etc. How much water per capita is, in fact, consumed by an urban dweller in enjoying these amenities?

The answer to this question varies somewhat with different authorities. This is probably due to different elements of use included in the estimates, to different statistics employed and to different methods of calculation. Lear tells us that the per capita consumption of water by an urban dweller is 720 quarts per day. Revelle [16] tells us in one place that this figure is 1,700 gallons per day. Elsewhere Revelle [17] tells us that a million gallons a day will take care of the needs of a community of 5,000 to 10,000 people. This averages out to 100 to 200 gallons per capita. Converted into quarts this gives us 400 to 800 quarts per capita, which is in line with Lear's figure. Other authorities [18] tell us that each urban resident is supplied with 60 gallons of water per day for domestic uses, including lawn watering, air cooling, and laundering. Another 26 gallons per person per day, we are told, is supplied to commercial establishments connected to public supply systems and still another 25 gallons goes for

14 *Op. cit.*, p. 24.
15 *Op. cit.*, p. 92.
16 Roger Revelle. "Water," 53–69. In *Technology and Economic Development*. A *Scientific American* Book. New York: Alfred A. Knopf, 1963, 205 pp. See p. 56. Revelle, an oceanographer, is University Dean of Research at the University of California and director of that university's Scripps Institution of Oceanography.
17 *Ibid.*, p. 54.
18 *Resources In America's Future. Op. cit.* See particularly Chapter 14 "Water," 258–76. The data given are from the section on *Municipal use*, p. 262.

purely municipal functions like street cleaning and fire fighting. These figures add up to 111 gallons per day, a total which is also in line with the statistics already given. Wolman [19] states that 150 gallons are needed per person per day which is exactly halfway within the range suggested by Revelle's second figure. Since only the first of Revelle's figures are out of line with the others, we will assume that a range of 100–200 gallons per person per day is a reasonably accurate figure.

The discrepancy between actual consumption use and Lear's stated, physical need figure of 3 quarts a day, can, perhaps, be brought into somewhat better focus by mentioning the actual gallonage which enters into the enjoyment of a few amenities. Herber [20] tells us that 3 gallons of water are used to flush a toilet, 30 gallons to fill a typical sunken bathtub 6 inches in depth, and even more than this to clean a batch of clothing in an automatic washing machine. Many urban residents eat in air-conditioned cafeterias. These cafeterias typically use a 1,000-ton air conditioning unit. Such a unit uses up enough water to meet the daily needs of more than 30,000 people. Home air-conditioning also clearly uses up unrecoverable amounts of water.

If the amenities demanded by the urban dweller increase, the drain on available local water supply will also increase. Such bids fair to be the case, particularly for the "bathroom culture" of middle-class America, which both surprises and amuses Europeans. Let me cite some of the newer, prospective, water-consuming amenities which appear to be just over the horizon. An advertisement from the American Bidet Company leads off with a headline which reads "A new facility for immaculate bathroom cleanliness" and is succeeded by the following description of a new *bidet* or toilet facility.

Brand-new this fall is an American version of the bidet. It provides constantly warmed water and warmed air (for drying) aimed at the proper parts of the posterior. It enables one to wash after every use of the toilet and eliminates the use of paper. One switch controls both water and air. Cost about $180 (f.o.b. Gardena, Cal.), plus installation. The American Bidet Co.

This ad in turn is followed by an illuminating diagram which shows the position of a small orifice which ejects a cleansing jet of warm water, a warm-air door which opens automatically and a handle which shifts forward for warm water and backward for warm air.[21]

[19] *Op. cit.*, p. 158.
[20] *Op. cit.*, p. 92.
[21] Clearly this new technology of the bathroom is economically ruthless. What is to become of our toilet-tissue tycoons and the employees associated with the production of that amenity?

But this is not all. *Life* [22] magazine has delighted its predominantly urban readers with an article listed in its contents as "Indictment of U.S. Bathrooms. A Cornell research group finds plenty that's wrong." The article calls attention to a coming revolution in the American bathroom and then describes the following new features of the rosy, bathroom future: (1) a contoured washbowl whose water spray doubles as a drinking fountain and makes shampooing hair simple; (2) a chairlike toilet, nine inches off the floor, with two water jets, a fold-out separate urinal and separate electric flushing controls for toilet and urinal; and (3) a lounge-like bathtub which features a reclining back, grab bars and a nonslip bottom for safety, an easily-reached faucet panel, a height-adjustable, overhead shower, a telephone-type, hand spray for rinsing the bather and cleaning the tub, a seat for foot-washing or shampoos and its own lighting and ventilating systems. Other new bathroom features are also described in the article.

Apart from the scatophilous humor to which the new bathroom technology will lend itself initially, it is sure to become standard operating procedure for home hygiene in the years which lie ahead. From the standpoint of water waste, however, we can expect that the "bathorama" of the future will waste considerably more water than do our present toilet facilities, doubly so since research unearthed the fact that the middle-class bathroom is used for many activities of a nonhygienic nature. Among these activities are the following: a site for finger-painting and for sailing boats by children; a universal disposal unit for flushing away unwanted items, so as to save a trip to the kitchen garbage-can; and an establishment for washing pets, steaming clothes, shining shoes, storing toys, stacking wet umbrellas or as a photographic darkroom. It seems safe to conclude that the bathroom facilities of the future will encourage greater indifference to the proper use and waste of water.

In the years ahead it also seems reasonable to expect a per capita increase in the consumption of water as our anti-poverty programs bring the 77 million [23] people who were living in either *poverty* or *deprivation* in 1960, to enjoy our current and future middle-class standard of living. In the near future, then, it seems reasonable to conclude that per capita consumption of water may be represented by a range which shifts above 100–200 gallons per person.

[22] Michael Mok. "Modern Living. Scientists find hygiene-happy Americans are not as clean as they think they are. Blame the outmoded U.S. Bathroom." *Life,* Vol. 60, No. 20, May 20, 1965. 84C, 84D, 85–6.

[23] This is the figure supplied in the following publication: *Poverty and Deprivation in the United States. The Plight of Two-Fifths of a Nation.* Washington, D.C.: Conference On Economic Progress, April, 1962. 97 pp. In this study, *poverty* is defined as an annual income under $4,000 for a multiple-person family, while *deprivation* is defined as an annual income of $4,000–$6,000 for a multiple-person family. According to this report, as of 1960, there were 38 million persons living in poverty in the U.S. and 39 million living in deprivation.

## Water in Industrial Use

Closely related to the waste in personal use is the waste which occurs in industrial use. Before we talk about the waste of water in industrial use, we should take a look at the amounts of water needed to manufacture some of our industrial commodities. Lear [24] mentions the following data on industrial water requirements: to generate a kilowatt-hour of electricity by steam turbine, 1.32–170 gallons of water; to refine a gallon of crude petroleum, 1.73–44.5 gallons; to finish a ton of steel, 1,400–65,000 gallons; to make a pound of soap, 1.57–7.5 gallons; to make a pound of carbon black, .25–14 gallons; to make a pound of natural rubber, 2.54–6 gallons; to make a pound of artificial rubber, 13–305 gallons; to make a pound of aluminum, 1.24–36.33 gallons; to make a ton of glass bottles, 118–667 gallons; to make an automobile, 12,000–16,000 gallons; and to make a truck or bus, 15,000–20,000 gallons.

Revelle [25] states that one or two tons of water is needed per ton of product in the manufacture of brick; 250 tons of water per ton of paper and 600 tons of water per ton of nitrate fertilizer. Herber [26] supplies the following industrial use ratios: to produce a ton of paper, 50,000 gallons; a ton of copper, 100,000 gallons; a ton of rayon, 200,000 gallons; a ton of aluminum, 320,000 gallons; and a ton of synthetic rubber, 600,000 gallons. A large, steel mill, says Herber, can use enough water to satisfy all the normal needs of a city of several million. This latter fact should give us much food for thought with respect to the water costs of industrialization and urbanization. One wonders whether—in terms of social costs, human needs and any reputable hierarchy of values for a modern community—it would be possible in the face of a limited water supply, to justify diverting water from the needs of a million people to keep a large, steel mill going. Under the pressures of producing foodstuffs for a mass market through farming by irrigation, the drain on water supply is also enormous. Herber furnishes the following water usage: to grow a ton of barley, 350,000 gallons; a ton of corn, 400,000 gallons; and a ton of wheat, 450,000 gallons. Revelle [27] tells us that wheat, rice and cotton fiber, respectively, require, 1,500, 4,000 and 10,000 tons of water per ton of crop. To grow a ton of sugar or corn about 1,000 tons of water will be consumed in various ways.

From the requirement ratios supplied by Lear, Herber and Revelle, one can see that enormous amounts of water are needed for industrial production and urbanization. Where this water is reused little or no waste occurs. Where it is not reused and recirculated industrially, the

24 *Op. cit.*, p. 24.
25 *Op. cit.*, p. 54.
26 *Op. cit.*, pp. 92–3.
27 *Op. cit.*, p. 54.

waste is enormous and an unconscionable and immoral use of what should be regarded as a public resource, occurs. One obtains some idea of what an unprogressive and socially irresponsible type of industrialization can do to waste our water resources, particularly within the framework of a highly centralized, industrial-technological complex, if one notes the reduction in water use which comes as a benefit from the industrial recirculation of water. Lear tells us that when steel mills in the Ruhrverband devised industrial recirculation systems, the water requirement for a ton of steel went from 130 cubic yards to 2.6 cubic yards. If we assume that similar substantial savings of fresh water can be effected in the manufacture of other commodities, then clearly any failure to do so, will be, in most cases, a waste of and a drain upon our water supply. Fortunately, according to Wolman,[28] 80 to 98 percent of the water withdrawn by municipalities, industry and electric utilities, is available for reuse. For this reason there can be said to be little excuse for industry to avoid water reuse in manufacturing.

Above all, it must not be forgotten that greater savings can be effected in the reuse of water *by industry* than in the reuse of water by *municipalities*. This is because industry uses about half of the available water in the U.S. while municipalities use only about 10 percent of the nation's dependable water supply. As industry increases, if the fraction of industrial users refusing to use recirculated water were to increase, the waste of water resources would also increase. It remains to be seen how extensively and effectively the democratic processes of a highly centralized society can bring pressure to bear upon industrial users in the future, so that threatened water shortages can be averted.

It is now time to wind up the question of a possible future, shortage in the water supply of the U.S., particularly in relation to our increasing population and increasing industrialization. Here again we are faced with a difference of opinion. Authorities differ as to the imminence of a threatened, water shortage and their differences reside in the considerations to which they have given attention. Among these considerations are such technological guesses as to the extent to which industry will use recirculation systems or the speed with which desalinization will become both technically and economically feasible. Other differences center about projections of future population, estimates of resource supplies and forecasts of resource use. Again experts will differ on the speed and extent to which large bodies of polluted water can be cleaned up. Frequently differences in forecasts will center about the question of how large the future rates of industrial growth will be, or guesses as to how rapidly the unexploited water domains of the United States will be encroached upon. One thing

28 *Op. cit.,* p. 164.

is certain. Nature has fixed the biotic potential of our water supply—a statement which will continue to be true until such time as water desalinization is universal. Until that time it is conceivable that the population can grow more rapidly than the accessibility of as yet untouched water supplies. Should this happen—and given the American standard of living, together with its growing technological and industrial need for water—the time could, indeed, come when national demand for water proves to be greater than our national supply.

Wolf [29] tells us that by 1975 the population is expected to rise to 230 million and the water consumption to about 450 billion gallons a day. This would bring us to within 10 percent of using up all the normal water supply available. By 1980–85 the forecast is that the demand for water will exceed the available, natural supply. According to Wolf we are in a race with time. If by 1980–85 we are not reusing water heavily or not converting it from the oceans on a large scale, then, indeed, we are in for a national water shortage. Should this happen the tragedy would properly be attributable to overcentralized urbanism and industrialization. According to Herber,[30] by 1980 the national water deficit would be about 100 billion gallons a day. Such an eventuality, he believes, can be forestalled only by reusing water on a much larger scale than we do today.

Wolman,[31] on the other hand, is an optimist. He notes that almost half of our available water which is surface runoff from total annual precipitation, can be captured. This runoff amounts to 1,200 b.g.d. (billion gallons per day) and it has been estimated by some experts that 560 b.g.d. will be available for some time. Wolman, himself, feels this latter figure is too conservative and should be raised to 700 b.g.d. It has also been estimated that by the year A.D. 2000 we will probably need 900 b.g.d. At first glance Wolman's supply figure of 700 b.g.d. would then appear to be insufficient to meet the demand of 900 b.g.d. projected for A.D. 2000. Since, however, 80 to 98 percent of the water withdrawn by municipalities, industry and electric utilities is available for *reuse,* no shortage should develop. Wolman estimates that approximately 740 b.g.d. of water should be available for reuse in A.D. 2000. Thus the projected withdrawal rate for the year, 2000, of 900 b.g.d. should not prove difficult to meet whether the economically available supply is 560 b.g.d. or 700 b.g.d.

[29] Karl W. Wolf. "Can New Space and Scientific Technology be Applied to Basic Community Problems of Water Supply, Air Pollution, Public Health and Safety, and Sanitation?" 129–42. In *Conference on Space, Science, and Urban Life.* The Dunsmuir House Conference. Washington, D.C.: National Aeronautics and Space Administration, NASA SP-37, 1963. 254 pp.

[30] *Op. cit.,* p. 94.

[31] *Op. cit.,* pp. 161–4.

The authors of *Resources in America's Future* take a position which is intermediate between a pessimistic and an optimistic outlook. They argue that the water supply-demand outlook in the United States should cause neither alarm nor complacency. They argue that our natural endowment in fresh water is more than adequate to support projections of economic growth to A.D. 2000. Their projections assume a prospective quadrupling of gross national product and a near doubling of population. This will make the potential demand for streams and water courses for waste disposal enormous. They argue, however, that a large, affluent, urbanized population will exert great pressure to preserve the quality of the human environment. This may result in more water courses and streams for recreation and fewer for water supply. If this should happen, argue these authors, a water shortage could occur. Once again we observe an argument which is an open admission that *unchecked urbanism* and *bureaucratic decision-making* with respect to water supply, water consumption and the problems of waste disposal, create a water deficit.

We have tried in this section to indicate the extent to which water shortages, real or threatened, are associated with urban mismanagement, lack of bureaucratic foresight and the high rate of industrialization encouraged by population growth in our highly centralized conurbations. To this extent the threat to so basic a human need as water supply, the inability to ensure so staple a commodity in sufficient amounts to meet the standard of living of the populations of our cities, and the errors made by urban functionaries both in failing to understand and to deal with the problems of either municipal or industrial waste disposal, can all be regarded as part of the cost of excessive and, to some extent, unenlightened centralization. Once again we must caution the reader that the burden of our argument is not that excessive and unenlightened centralization *brings about* actual or threatened water shortages. Our point is rather that centralization of the type we have been describing *facilitates* errors and behavior leading to real or threatened shortages. It does this not only by encouraging men who lack foresight and imagination, to take the reins of government but also creates complex interdependencies which even the most enlightened and intelligent administrator cannot grasp—particularly a busy one. In this sense the water shortages of the modern community are *part* of the crisis of our cities and *part* of the indictment against centralization.

## IV. WATER POLLUTION AS URBAN PATHOLOGY

In recent years public consciousness has been focused upon the risk involved in allowing water bodies from which we draw our drinking water, to be contaminated by either municipal or industrial waste. The threat to public health which water pollution creates, has worried both some intelligent, civic-minded persons as well as some public health authorities. The situation has become so bad in some areas that there is some justification for Tom Lehrer [32] having quipped, while entertaining in San Francisco, that

> The breakfast garbage that you throw into the bay,
> They drink at lunch in San Jose.

As Lehrer's friends have pointed out, parallels to this quip could be constructed for other cities, such as

> The breakfast garbage they throw out in Troy,
> They drink at lunch in Perth Amboy.

These quips are not always exaggeration. The St. Louis *Globe Democrat* has remarked "Every time you take a glass of water in St. Louis you are drinking water from every flush toilet from here to Minnesota."

However, because industrial waste more severely aggravates the water-pollution problem than does the waste from urban households, the problems it creates should receive maximum emphasis.

A modern, urban water treatment plant makes use of sedimentation tanks, coagulators, filters, aerators and chlorinators. When municipal sewage is discharged into a waterway it passes through screens that catch large objects and the waste effluent then moves through a series of tanks which collect sand, gravel, and organic solids. The sludge from this material settles at the bottom. In the final stages of purification the waste-water is sprayed on a bed of rocks to remove impurities produced by bacteria and it is then chlorinated. A similar procedure is employed when water is drawn from polluted sources of supply and is to be used for municipal, household purposes. It is these water-treatment plants which must take care of both municipal and industrial sewage. Where urbanization and industrialization have been rapid and excessive in a given area, the on-site water-treatment plants may be insufficient to deal with the increased load of sewage requiring treatment. Furthermore, the mechanical and chemical processes which are being employed in water-treatment, may be entirely inappropriate for catching certain types of pollutants. Either of the two conditions we have just mentioned will result in polluting the water-supply but the second will mean that the water treated for municipal use may still be unfit for drinking purposes, for personal hygiene

---

[32] These lines are from a ditty sung by Tom Lehrer at *The Hungry i* (the original Beat center) in San Francisco. The song is entitled "Pollution." The words and music appear in the album: *That Was The Year That Was*. Reprise Records: r. R-6179. Recorded July, 1965. Lehrer is a mathematician and statistician who has also had a successful career as an entertainer in night clubs and concert halls. His forte is the humorous song.

and for other uses, largely because of the new types of pollutants which the water-treatment plant cannot trap.

Among these new and, to some extent, uncaptureable pollutants are industrial chemicals of relatively recent vintage. They include detergents, insecticides, herbicides, plastics, abrasives, food and fuel additives, pharmaceuticals, petroleum derivatives, and radioactive materials. As a result, in some cities which withdraw water from a polluted source, the water so withdrawn may not only be clearly offensive in odor and taste but may, at some future date, also prove to be a menace to public health. Often the particular waste treatment processes and water purification processes which are currently standard, fail to remove many of the contaminants from municipal and industrial waste. Although there is no incontrovertible evidence as yet that anyone has died or become seriously ill from water pollutants which reach the kitchen tap, some medical authorities point out that we have no knowledge at present concerning the effects that these pollutants may have on the human body and on human health, when they are ingested steadily and in small doses over long periods of time.

But although we have no incontrovertible evidence on these matters, we do have some evidence which points in directions which suggest that water pollution *may be* a menace to public health. One example of this, for instance, is a medical study by Diehl and Tromp,[33] two Dutch scientists, who found evidence pointing to a very strong possibility that cancer rates may be increased by polluted water. Perhaps, however, the clearest evidence that polluted water may be a menace to public health comes from the many fish kills which we read about in our papers. When a fish kill occurs we are referring to a situation in which thousands of fish die as a result of the pollution of the water which is their native habitat. A fish kill is sobering testimony to the fact that we have a water-pollution problem. Fish which are dying as a result of water pollution are hyperactive and have convulsions. They are often unable to maintain an upright position. Their abdomens are distended and their stomachs and intestines are filled with gases and liquids. Hemorrhages frequently occur on the skin and internal organs.

In 1963 it was estimated that 5 million fresh- and salt-water fish were killed in the Mississippi River alone, due to the presence of insecticides. Tremendous decreases in the supply of desirable fish in Lake Erie—which is, perhaps, one of the most heavily polluted water bodies in the country— has been reported by scientists. Further evidence of the possible menace to human beings, which may result from a polluted water supply, comes

---

[33] J. C. Diehl and S. W. Tromp. "First Report on the Geographical and Geological Distribution of Carcinoma in the Netherlands." *Stechting Ter Bevordering Van De Psychische Physica* (Leiden, 1953), p. 1200. This reference is given by Lewis Herber, *op. cit.*, pp. 118 and 215.

from the destruction of economically valuable marine life. The shellfish industries have been eliminated in some of our major cities because of the destruction of shellfish beds in estuaries near these cities. The oyster beds of Raritan Bay, near New York City, once a thriving marine resource, are no more. The New Jersey Board of Shell Fisheries traced this loss *in part* to industrial waste. Other areas still furnishing shellfish from polluted waters are supplying marine food to our cities—food which may be a source of disease both from bacterial and chemical causes.

The extent to which water pollution can go can, perhaps, best be suggested by noting the amounts of sewage which some areas and cities have to dispose of annually. The Philadelphia–Wilmington complex empties an amount of waste into the Delaware River, equivalent to the waste output of $4\frac{1}{2}$ million people. In the 1950's Los Angeles dumped 300 million gallons of sewage every day into Santa Monica Bay. Memphis empties 60 million gallons of raw sewage into the Mississippi River daily. Many more such urban statistics could be cited. They can all be summed up, however, by noting what they imply for the future. It has been estimated that if the rate of construction of municipal water-treatment plants does not increase, in relation to our rates of population and industrial growth, the amount of pollution in natural waters by 1980 will be the equivalent of the untreated sewage of 114 million people.

Why does polluted water kill fish and other forms of marine life? In waters carrying a limited amount of waste, the bacteria in these waters destroy that waste (whether sewage or natural waste) or it is rendered harmless by settling to the bottom. If, however, waste or sewage in water becomes excessive, the number of bacteria in the water will increase. In the course of their life processes they will use up most of the oxygen which is dissolved in the water. The water, thus lacking oxygen, will become an unfit habitat for fish and other forms of life.

A measure of the organic pollution load is Biochemical Oxygen Demand (BOD)—a measure which indicates the rate at which dissolved oxygen is drawn upon in waste-receiving water. The rate at which a given quantity and type of organic waste consumes oxygen depends chiefly upon the temperature of the water and the type of chemicals dissolved in it. Clearly the level of dissolved oxygen is a function both of the rate at which oxygen is restored to water and the BOD, itself. The BOD is, of course, affected by oxygen-consuming bacteria. Even if there were no oxygen-consuming bacteria, however, waste could still be broken down by anaerobic bacteria. But the amount of organic solids from urban municipal and industrial waste, may be too great for even the anaerobic bacteria to break down. What is not broken down therefore becomes a water pollutant or contaminant. These pollutants in turn not only affect the BOD but they also affect the metabolism of marine life.

The extent to which BOD can create water pollution is most cogently and deplorably illustrated in Lake Erie. Gladwin Hill [34] has reported that the accumulation over the years of new pollutants in this Great Lake has profoundly interfered with its ecology. Oxygen-absorbing chemicals have sapped its supply of free oxygen. One result of this is that there is a 2,600-square-mile area in the middle of the lake—somewhat more than 25 percent of its total area—where there is no oxygen in that portion of the water which stretches from the surface to ten feet from the bottom. The deficiency of oxygen in Lake Erie has reversed the usual evolution of marine forms. Marine life in Lake Erie is moving backwards, biologically speaking, from fish which are commercially valuable to primeval, anaerobic sludgeworms and fingernail clams.

Algae, particularly the type called *cladaphora,* and which are very malodorous, show a runaway growth. Millions of pounds of detergents are emptied into Lake Erie every year. Each pound of detergent, heavy in phosphate, will propagate 700 pounds of algae. When the oxygen-absorbing algae die, they sink to the bottom and release more phosphate which will propagate more algae, thereby increasing the BOD on Lake Erie. Scientists are not too sanguine about current efforts to end pollution in Lake Erie. That pollution is now so extensive that they feel a favorable outcome to current pollution-elimination programs could not be guaranteed even if all fresh pollution of the lake were to cease immediately.

As a result of all the preceding, fish and other forms of life die from both the causes we have mentioned—oxygen deprivation and metabolic poisoning. This would not happen if man built enough water-treatment plants which could both take care of the *volume* of organic contaminants in sewage and industrial waste and could remove the many new types of organic pollutants from industry. Many of our cities, however, lack both the necessary number of plants and many of the plants we already possess lack procedures for trapping some of the new types of pollutants and contaminants. This results in the water pollution crisis in many cities. What some authorities fear is that pollutants and contaminants noxious to marine life may yet prove to be noxious to human beings, when they enter man's water supply and are ingested slowly over long periods of time.

Other methods have been proposed for treating waste other than the use of water-treatment plants. They involve methods of removing dead algae from polluted waters or holding wastes in lagoons. The latter is appropriate where small cities are involved. Some methods envisage discharge of wastes into oceans rather than streams. It may even be possible to use methods for *extending* waste water treatment. These would be processes which are added to the mechanical and chemical processes now used in water-treatment plants. Distillation, for instance, might be one of

---

[34] Gladwin Hill. "The Great and Dirty Lakes." *Saturday Review. Op. cit.,* pp. 32–4.

these. Most of these extensions appear at present to be uneconomical. Whatever methods are used to reduce water pollution, it is generally agreed that the amount of oxygen in water must be about 4 parts per million to maintain fish life in most streams.

There are certain methods for the disposing of waste which would not only make a contribution to the *prevention* of pollution but would also result in some economic benefits. One of these methods has a bearing on agricultural activity; the other on the conservation of water supply. Higbee [35] reports that two Wisconsin agricultural specialists have demonstrated that sewage effluent has certain agricultural advantages. By irrigating pastures with stream water carrying sewage effluent from the disposal works of Madison, Wisconsin, they increased the dry matter forage yield of a pasture by 400 pounds per acre. Chemical tests indicated that the sewage waste contained valuable plant nutrients. These specialists suggested that where sewage effluent has been proven to be of value, it would be a simple matter to conduct it to crop lands and thereby obtain improved yields. A proposal of this sort could be meritorious only under one of two possible conditions. Either a way would have to be found of recovering the plant nutrients from sewage so as to reduce the health hazards which might stem from applying raw sewage to crops or we would have to find some way of determining which urban effluents intended to be utilized for agricultural purposes, would be safe from a public health standpoint and which would not.

Lear [36] tells us of a similar experiment launched by Pennsylvania State University. The results reported for that experiment were the following: (1) yields of corn and hay were three times the yields of fields not treated by the waste effluent; (2) the protein content of wheat treated by the effluent was greater than that for normally grown wheat; (3) Northern pine trees grew as rapidly as Southern pines normally do; (4) birds and animals thrived; and (5) microbes living in the top layer of the test plots digested all but a few percent of a detergent that had frothed the waste water. Impressed by these results St. Charles City in Maryland adopted the techniques used at Penn State for a new municipal waste disposal system.

Higbee [37] also reports an interesting industrial disposal of waste effluent. Seabrook Farms of southern New Jersey used a million gallons of water daily to wash fruits and vegetables before packing and freezing them. One can get some idea of the amounts of water used by noting that an average of 40 gallons of water was used to wash each pound of strawberries. Before trying its experiment Seabrook Farms found that its wash-

[35] Edward Higbee. *The Squeeze. Cities Without Space.* New York: William Morrow & Company, 1960. 348 pp. See particularly Chapter 10 "Covering the Water Front."
[36] John Lear. *Op. cit.*, p. 80.
[37] Edward Higbee. *Op cit.*, pp. 272-3.

water after use, which was flushed out onto open land, formed a marsh with offensive odors. Seabrook Farms experimented with a technique of conducting the wash-water through giant overhead sprays and having it fall like rain into a nearby forest. The litter of forest duff acted as a blotter to retain waste pollutants. The soil beneath the litter acted as a filter. As a result the water returned pure to the groundwater sources from which it had come in the first place. One of the conclusions drawn by Higbee is that wherever a ground water table can be recharged by this method, a city would be able to conserve part of its water supply if it maintained municipal forests nearby and used effluent disposal as Seabrook Farms did. Clearly, however, this proposal would be practical only for small communities with wooded, greenbelt areas nearby.

The central point, however, underlying all the data presented in the present section, is this. More water-treatment plants are needed to reduce urban water pollution, since urban pollution will increase as industrialization and urban congestion increase. Urban mismanagement, however, tends to be laggard in recognizing this fact. The extent of this urban mismanagement—often largely a result of political and bureaucratic considerations—can be gleaned by reading the record of urban pollution in some of our major cities, as given by *Saturday Review*. The failure of the politicians to deal adequately with the problem of water pollution, has been described for such cities as Chicago, Cleveland, Los Angeles, Miami, New York, Phoenix, Seattle and St. Louis. This mismanagement, then, is also part of the indictment against excessive urbanization and unenlightened centralization. The most recent and concise accounts of the incredible public apathy, misunderstanding and ignorance concerning the problems of water pollution and the even greater immorality, political mismanagement and political shenanigans in connection with those problems, has been given by Carr.[38] If the reader wishes to see the legacy of blight in terms of water pollution, that irresponsible industrialization and large-scale urbanization have bequeathed to tomorrow's generations, he has only to read this author. The situation couldn't be worse.

There are many other serious pathologies of overurbanization which limitations of space make it impossible to discuss here. Among these we would include the transportation problems of the big city, the problem of providing adequate housing, the maintenance of public health and adequate preventive medicine and hygiene, the clearance of our slums and a more progressive type of urban renewal, the reduction of crime, socially learned, juvenile delinquency and deviant behavior and the ob-

---

[38] Donald E. Carr. "Death of the Sweet Waters: The Politics of Pollution." *The Atlantic*. Vol. 27, No. 5, May 1966. 93–106. *The Atlantic* reported that Carr would be dealing with the problems of water pollution more fully in a volume to be published in 1966 under the title *Death of the Sweet Waters*.

jective of obtaining clean government and effective public education. In addition, we have the problem of preventing the destruction of wild life in fields, forests and streams which are adjacent to urban cities, the provision of proper food and nutrition to the huge masses in our urban centers,[39] the reduction of urban noise and congestion, the elimination of race prejudice and segregation, the prevention of family disintegration, the maintenance of steady employment, the solution of our problems of poverty and dependency, and proper care for the aged. Finally, there is a host of conditions which require treatment but which usually seem to be more remote to the average voter than those already mentioned. These would include the establishment of equitable taxation and financing for government,[40] the task of slowing up the degradation of popular culture, the reduction of alienation and anomie, the elimination of irrational, neighborhood differentiation, and the curtailment of political apathy.

# SUMMARY OF PART IV

In this section we have discussed the attributes of a genuine human community as contrasted with the notion of a physical settlement embracing a human collective. We have then dealt extensively with some of the major inadequacies and social pathologies which appear to be deeply related to the daily life of the heavily congested, ugly and sprawling metropolis. We have chosen to single out for discussion certain of these inadequacies and pathologies. The pathologies which have been selected for treatment are the following: (1) the psychological stresses and strains of the large, urban community and the psychological warping that it seems to promote among its inhabitants; (2) the degradations of the cultural life of man which are clearly associated with the mass society of metropolis; (3) various forms of political and bureaucratic pathology which seem to be the inevitable concomitants of the highly overcentralized, governing institutions of megalopolis; and (4) the many ecological imbalances and physical pathologies which the spreading metropolis continues to produce.

39 We are referring to the kinds of problems associated with the production of agricultural foodstuffs for our major cities, as these have been touched upon directly or indirectly in the following volumes. Rachel Carson. *Silent Spring*. Boston: Houghton Mifflin, 1962. 368 pp. Lewis Herber. *Our Synthetic Environment*. New York: Alfred A. Knopf, 1962. 285 pp.

40 In this connection the reader will find that he can gain some valuable insights from the following volume: Gabriel Kolko. *Wealth and Power in America. An Analysis of Social Class and Income Distribution*. New York: Frederick A. Praeger, 1964. 178 pp.

It may very well prove to be the case that excessive urbanization and its accompaniments of excessive industrialization, political overcentralization, and mounting bureaucratization, can only be ended through the decentralization of our cities, together with supporting forms of political, social, cultural, industrial and economic decentralization. It is therefore basic that we become familiar with up-to-date social philosophies of decentralization, with community planning and design which can give concrete expression to a philosophy of physical decentralization, and with some of the newer developments in science and technology which may make feasible several modern and future forms of community decentralization. These considerations constitute the themes of Part V.[41]

[41] Additional papers dealing with the themes of Part IV will be found in the following source: "Bibliography Of Publications By Henry Winthrop, 1932–1966." 181–203. In *Sociologia Religiosa. Rivista Di Storia E Sociologia Delle Religioni* (Padova, Italia), Anno X,º 15–16, 1967, Edizioni C.S.S.R., 208 pp.

# V

# Technology, Decentralization and the Restoration of Community

## ORIENTATION TO PART V

It is the purpose of this section to demonstrate the relevance of a philosophy of decentralization to the problems of our time. Traditional concepts like freedom, justice, and opportunity, are in danger of being reduced to negligible proportions as a result of our increasing centralization along political, social, cultural, industrial and economic lines. A considerable diminution of the many pathologies created by centralization and urbanization can be effected if the community of the future can be decentralized. The achievement of the physical decentralization of community is *necessary* if we are to take the first steps towards the reduction of the intensity of some of the social pathologies associated with the excessive urbanization of megalopolis, but, of course, it is not *sufficient*. New anticentralist institutional inventions will also be necessary. Such social inventions, however, can be effective only when they have a nurturing base in the *physically decentralized* community. For this reason, Part V will deal *chiefly* with new possibilities for *physical decentralization* made available by new developments in science and technology. The discussion of these possibilities will be sandwiched between explorations of the decentralist philosophy, undertaken in the opening and closing chapters of Part V. The faith which undergirds this section is the conviction that the achievement of genuine, physical decentralization can be expected to liquidate, to a considerable degree, the urban, social pathologies of our time.

# 25

# The Meaning of
# Decentralization for
# Twentieth-Century Man*

The contemporary reader, interested in such topics as problems of community, social philosophy for an age of science and technology and changing forms of political philosophy, is often unaware that there are ongoing currents of decentralist thinking which are quite relevant to concerns of this sort. There is a current tendency to devalue decentralist thought because most contemporary trends of social change are giving increasing expression to modern forms of centralization. The intelligent layman is indifferent to decentralist philosophy because he mistakenly believes that such a philosophy is irrelevant to the social, political and community needs of the age. In this, of course, he is greatly mistaken. A philosophy of decentralization, adapted to the problems of our age and implemented by the advantages of certain forms of modern science and technology, will, in fact, probably be found to be highly appropriate to some of our emerging problems. In addition, the layman should be disabused of the idea that decentralist thought repudiates all centralist objectives. On the contrary. The modern decentralist recognizes that there has to be a balance between centralized and decentralized activities in the communities, nations and regions of the world. The social reconstruction he pleads for and the germane social philosophy he seeks to develop in order to justify such needed social reconstruction, ask only that we be clear about the separate provinces of human concern to which the application of these two broad tendencies will be most appropriate.

The modern decentralist, in addition, has some pretty strong convictions concerning those contexts of social activity to which he believes the application of the decentralist outlook and decentralist measures, will produce more social welfare than the centralizing habits of our time. Further-

* Chapter 25, with adaptations and modifications, has been taken from the following source: Henry Winthrop. "The Meaning of Decentralization for Twentieth-Century-Man." *The American Journal of Economics and Sociology.* Vol. 26, No. 4, October, 1967, 351–366.

more, he often provides plans and social inventions which will give concrete expression to the decentralist weltanschauung, for specific problems and in specific contexts. The decentralist passions are aroused even more by the huge amount of existing but unnecessary social pathology which can be largely traced to excessive centralization, whether in the form of rampant, large-scale industrialization, spreading and unmanageable urbanism or inefficient, cost-consuming and inhumane bureaucratization.

Finally the contemporary reader is unacquainted with the fact that there are ongoing experiments in small-scale community life and small-scale industry which are direct expressions of the decentralist outlook. Self-conscious forms of modern decentralist thought and community developments which have appeared as expressions of that thought, will be found, for instance, in the life-work of Arthur E. Morgan [1] who was the first chairman and chief engineer of the Tennessee Valley Authority and a former President of Antioch College. Indirect expressions of the decentralist outlook are occurring in the extensive research work of the Stanford Research Institute [2] on small-scale industry in general and on modern small industry for developing countries, particularly in India. It will thus be seen that decentralist modes of social and economic expression are still alive and kicking, albeit completely overshadowed by the more numerous centralizing trends of our time—trends which clearly make an overwhelmingly far greater impact on our lives than the decentralist activities which they eclipse. It is contemporary, centralizing trends which determine the historic tone of the age.

The decentralist who is familiar with the emerging social and economic needs of both the present and the immediate future and who is concerned with the preservation of democracy and freedom, feels that

[1] In this connection see the following volumes by this author. *Industries for Small Communities. With Cases from Yellow Springs.* Yellow Springs, Ohio: Community Service, Inc., 1953, 107 pp. *The Small Community. Foundation Of Democratic Life. What It Is and How to Achieve It.* New York: Harper & Brothers, 1942, 312 pp. *A Business of My Own. Possibilities in Small Community Occupations and Industries.* Yellow Springs, Ohio: Community Service, Inc., 1946, 184 pp. *Bottom-Up Democracy. The Affiliation of Small Democratic Units for Common Service.* Yellow Springs, Ohio: Community Service, Inc., December, 1954, 64 pp. *The Heritage of Community. A critique of community living based on great ways of life practiced by small communities over the world.* (Arthur E. Morgan and Griscom Morgan, editors). Yellow Springs, Ohio: Community Service, Inc., March, 1956, 64 pp. See also the journal, *Community Comments,* published by Community Service, Inc. The items cited here constitute but a small sample of the writings of Arthur E. Morgan and his associates on decentralist thinking. The reader can obtain a complete bibliography of Morgan's work by writing to *Community Service, Inc.*

[2] See the publications of the International Industrial Development Center of the Stanford Research Institute on Small Industry. In particular read the following: S. Nanjundian, H. E. Robison and Eugene Staley. *Economic Research for Small Industry Development. Illustrated by India's Experience.* Bombay, India: Asia Publishing House, 1962, 316 pp. Eugene Staley and Richard Morse. *Modern Small Industry for Developing Countries.* New York: McGraw-Hill, 1965, 600 pp. The reader is advised to read or consult the McGraw-Hill Series in International Development.

there is a good chance that a better balance can be achieved between centralizing and decentralizing activities, both now and in the immediate future. Where the decentralist is aware of developments in modern science and technology which can make decentralized social, political, industrial and economic structures more viable in the future, provided there is an increase in the general familiarity with these possibilities and a public willingness to adapt them to democratic ways of life, the decentralist is fairly confident that the worm will turn and that a better balance will be struck between centralizing and decentralizing activities in human life. Because there is a real likelihood that such a better balance may be realized in the future, it becomes of paramount importance to acquaint ourselves with some aspects of modern decentralist thought. The present chapter is an effort to present the new decentralism as one of the many philosophies of our age which are competing for the right to structure the nature of our coming social order.

If we are going to talk about "decentralization" we had best be clear as to what the term means. We should try to obtain a general notion of its significance as well as some of the specialized meanings it possesses in different contexts. An excellent way to bring out the broad values sought by a decentralist outlook is to contrast that outlook in certain ways with that of partisans of a centralist position. Wilhelm Röpke,[3] one of the worlds most distinguished advocates of decentrism, polarizes much of modern thinking (though not all, of course) into "centrist" and "decentrist" outlooks. We can gain a good deal of insight into decentrist thinking by dwelling on the polarizing tendencies teased out of much of modern thought, by this distinguished figure. Röpke points out that centrists are attracted towards collectivity, that is, towards ideas for dealing with human beings in the aggregate, while decentrists are preoccupied with the fate of individuals, with their needs and their concerns. We can do no better than to let Röpke speak for himself.

. . . The former look at the structure of society from the top downwards, the latter from the bottom upwards. The first seek security, happiness, and fulfillment in the subordination of the individual and the small group to a delib-

---

3 Wilhelm Röpke. *A Humane Economy. The Social Framework of the Free Market.* Chicago: Henry Regnery Company, 1960. 312 pp.

Röpke uses the terms, "centrism" and "decentrism" in the same way that other writers use the terms, "centralization" and "decentralization." The parallel, of course, holds between "centrist" and "decentrist," on the one hand, and "centralist" and "decentralist," on the other.

Dr. Röpke has been called the architect of the economic policy of the West German government and in 1953 he received from President Heuss of the Federal Republic of Germany the Grand Cross of Merit for his services in the reconstruction of the West German economy. He is a co-editor of two distinguished, international scholarly journals, *Kyklos* and *Studium Generale*. I have been informed that at least one economic advisor in recent Presidential administrations, has been greatly influenced by Röpke, although I have been unable to check on this information.

erately and strictly organized community, which, from this point of view, is all the more attractive the larger it is; the others seek these benefits in the independence and autonomy of the individual and the small group. The difference in social outlook closely resembles another difference between two modes of thought: one which has a strange predilection for everything contrived, man made, manufactured, organized, and intricately constructed, for the drawing board, blueprint, and ruler; and another which prefers what is natural, organic, time tested, spontaneous, and self-regulating, and which endures through long eras. Still another difference in the outlook is connected with this. On the one side are those who believe that society and economy can be reconstructed from above and without considering the fine web of the past. They believe in radical new beginnings; they are reformers inspired by an optimism that is apparently proof against any failure. On the other side are those who possess a sense of history and are convinced that the social fabric is highly sensitive to any interference. They deeply distrust every kind of optimistic reforming spirit and do not believe in crusades to conquer some new Jerusalem; they hold, with Burke, that the true statesman must combine capacity for reform with the will to prudent preservation. (pp. 227-8)

It must be remembered that the two contrasting outlooks of centralization and decentralization are reflected in various contexts—not only in politics but also in administration, economy, culture, housing, technology, social and industrial organization, community formation, etc. Thus the decentralist is likely to be a friend of the small farmer, of craft production in contrast to machine production, and of those members of the middle class who are content with modest incomes and limited influence. He is likely to favor the small business enterprise and a wide distribution of private property and he is also likely to be an advocate of a free market and consumer sovereignty. He will often be found to be a lover of nature and a champion of all things adapted to human scale. The centralist, by contrast, is a champion of large-scale industry, of the rationalization of technology and corporate activity, of huge associations, organizations, pressure groups, of political parties and political machines, of giant cities which we have come to call conurbations and of economic and social planning from above.

From the standpoint of the decentralist, the advocate of centralization is a social rationalist—a person who believes that all of the ills of the human condition can be solved solely by the application of reason to human affairs. This social rationalism is then seen in the following terms by the decentralist. The centralist is regarded as a man who is convinced that if we obey the injunction "Come now and let us reason together," the reign of peace and justice will begin. The individual is likely to be lost sight of in the centralist's plans and calculations, since the social rationalist prefers to think about men in the aggregate. The decentralist notes that the centralist is most comfortable when he guides himself by means of mouth-filling moralistic phrases and by big abstractions, such as freedom, justice, law and order, human rights, the four freedoms, the great society, constitutional needs, the extended benefits of material prosperity and by many other similar phrases.

Such verbal legerdemain the decentralist regards as empty, serving chiefly as a focus for pep-talks. Behind these terms and phrases the decentralist claims that he observes a moralism which is strictly abstract and excessively intellectual. These terms and phrases involve high-level abstractions which have no roots either in human history or the current condition of man. These glittering generalities pay little attention to the unhappy consequences which are often seen to flow from the fulfillment of centralist demands. Furthermore, they often are used to support conditions which are exactly opposite to their apparently intended meanings. By contrast the decentralist feels that he, himself, thinks in terms of human beings, that he knows and respects history, that he is aware of the limits upon man which history reveals and that he recognizes the all-pervasive presence of Original Sin. He tends to be a political realist who recognizes the presence of evil in man, as does Reinhold Niebuhr.

The decentralist therefore does not expect men to function like angels socially and he does not set social goals for them which are contrary to human nature. He does not accept a false egalitarianism and he does not try to homogenize individual differences among men. Instead, he cherishes the preservation of these differences and the social consequences to which they lead, because he passionately believes in the necessity of social pluralism and the latter is best promoted by preserving and fostering individuality. The decentralist most often tends to be a conservative. But even if he is not a full-fledged conservative, he will show a conservative strain which, as Richard Weaver [4] has put it, grants that some persons are more entitled to convictions on some subjects than other persons, through superior natural insight, through hard study, or through seriousness which comes with responsibility. The same conservative strain will resent standardization in affairs of the mind and spirit and oppose the modern tendency to question apartness, to be suspicious of differences, to distrust distinctions and to be jealous about allowing privacy.

The decentralist notes that the moralism of the centralist often degenerates into its dialectical opposite. Thus the centralizing moralist may plead for the secular expression of Christian charity but be an intolerant hater and envier. He may speak out on behalf of pacificism and then wave the flag in situations of international conflict, stress and crisis. He may write papers and books about social justice and yet, in the context of his own work situation, he may be a status-seeker who unhesitatingly knifes those who stand in his way. In the context of civic concern he will often ally himself with the largest forces in order to be on the winning side.

[4] Richard Weaver. *Life Without Prejudice and Other Essays.* Chicago: Henry Regnery Company, 1965. 167 pp.

The decentralist finds himself fighting a rear-guard action against centralization because he notes that it is easier to widen the powers of the state than to curtail them and this widening almost invariably fosters totalitarianism.

Another way of defining decentralization has been well expressed by Borsodi.[5] He says

. . . Decentralization is that method of implementing ideas and organizing human operations in which individuals are enabled to satisfy their wants and to realize their aspirations as far as possible through personal action (depending as little as possible upon collective and mass-action), in which power is therefore diffused and distributed multilaterally among people generally. (p. 202, Vol. I)

From Borsodi's standpoint the moving spirit behind the decentralist impulse is the preservation of personal freedom. The decentralist is interested in all methods which will provide the greatest possible freedom and responsibility for individual human beings.[6] His reason for clinging to this ideal is to encourage independence of thought and action among men and women, as well as ethical conduct by example, while discouraging both subordination and domination in human relationships. At the same time the universalization of such a community ideal will minimize the tendency for political structures to become coercive. This means, hopefully, as little use as possible of the law, police power, and political control, since, presumably, ethical responsibility will have been inculcated in most people. Where collective, corporate or government operation is necessary and unavoidable, Borsodi points out, the decentralist prefers those forms of social organization which encourage and permit voluntary individual participation in community decision-making. Where collective, corporate or government operation must be more or less permanent, the decentralist pleads for *associations* of the type which minimize the control they can exercise over their memberships, which maximize personal freedom for their members and which maximize autonomy for their participating groups.

[5] Ralph Borsodi. *Education and Living*. Melbourne, Florida: Melbourne University Press, 1948. 2 volumes. 719 pp.

[6] Working against this decentralist objective is the fact that in the modern world —and particularly in technologically advanced societies—the average person feels little need for exercising his personal influence in community decisions. This shedding of social responsibility is, of course, what Fromm calls the desire to "escape from freedom." However, the decentralist frequently argues that this *political abulia*, that is, loss of the desire to participate in community, decision-making processes, is, itself, a product of excessive centralization in government, excessive geographical size of cities and excessive urban population. Consequently, he feels that a sense of community responsibility among individuals will be recovered when communities are much smaller than they are now and possess more local autonomy. This ideal, of course, is the decentralist thesis, applied to the *quest for community*.

Paul Goodman,[7] an ardent advocate of the need for and the practicality of more decentralization in the modern world, describes the contrast between centralist and decentralist attitudes in still another way—one which differs in emphasis from those of Röpke or Borsodi. As Goodman sees it, the processes of centralization in our society have become so widespread and so intense that they often prove to be socially disadvantageous. Centralizing processes often succeed in undermining the very objectives for which they were intended. They frequently involve costs which are wasteful and, probably, in many cases, offset the financial value of the benefits involved. They make a mockery on occasion of the meaning of democracy and create a vast amount of unnecessary frustration for individuals. Aspects of over-centralization in our society can be found in all sorts of institutions and sectors: in agriculture, industry, the church, our mass media of communication, government, public education, and culture and the arts, to take some limited examples. Our overcentralized institutions and sectors of the economy form functional interdependencies in the sense of systems analysis. Any effort to deal with any social pathology they may create has become very difficult, since the independent action involved tends to be resisted by the nature of the interlocking, social system involved. For Goodman, the only remedy is a modification of our social system so as to infuse it with community decentralist functions and activities, where this infusion is needed and is possible.

Goodman goes on to furnish some examples of the ill effects of overcentralization in American life. He points out that in large, industrial enterprises the function is taken to be the goal of the organization rather than that of any group of persons, except, of course, those persons who identify with the enterprise. In an industrial organization persons become personnel, with all the attendant alienation that such an abstract translation involves. Authority proceeds from the top down through the hierarchical layers of management. Data are gathered by rank and file for decision-making in headquarters. Such decisions involve the creation of policy, scheduling and standard operating procedures. The organizational system of an industrial enterprise is divided into departments and personnel with distinct roles. The bureaucratic partitioning of function that is thereby created can be found, says Goodman, in department stores, various levels of government, General Motors and the United Automobile Workers, our municipal school systems and our universities, in hospitals, neighborhood renewal, network broadcasting, the Associated Press, and in various types of market-control arrangements made between producers

---

[7] Paul Goodman. *People or Personnel. Decentralizing and the Mixed System.* New York: Random House, 1965. 247 pp. Dr. Goodman is at present a Fellow of the Institute for Policy Studies in Washington, D.C. In 1964 Dr. Goodman was the Knapp Distinguished Scholar (in Urban Affairs) at the University of Wisconsin.

and distributors. Centralizing systems are devised to discipline and control armies and constabularies, to keep records, collect taxes, and perform a wide variety of bureaucratic functions, and, in industry, itself, for the managerial shaping and control of certain types of mass production.

The preceding suggests the atmosphere and flavor of excessive centralization. Goodman gives us his notion of the contrasting spirit of *decentralization.* Here people share functions and a joint set of aims. The organization they form is simply *their* means of working together. Top-down authority is avoided as much as possible. A preference is demonstrated for several centers of policy-formation and decision-making and these centers can cooperate on the basis of the principle of voluntary association, whenever necessary. Information in a decentralized milieu is conveyed and jointly processed in face-to-face association between field and headquarters. Headquarters becomes the servant, rather than the creator, of the decisions and wishes of the community. Each person involved is helped to obtain a total picture of the system within which he has his being and he is expected to contribute voluntarily to its successful functioning, in terms of his capacities and talents. Scheduling is arranged by the functioning groups of the community. This kind of operation, imbued with the spirit of voluntary association, Goodman feels, has yielded most of the values of civilization but, he points out, our unquestioning acceptance of the increasing trend towards centralization makes decentralist proposals, thinking and suggested institutions seem alien to most citizens—and, of course, also impractical.

Decentralization, Goodman points out, is a type of coordination of social activity that eschews as motives for social cooperation, integration and cohesiveness, the current emphasis on top-down direction, standard rules and extrinsic rewards like salary and status. Goodman supplies examples of situations in which a centralizing emphasis is more conducive to human welfare and other situations in which a decentralizing emphasis has greater social advantages. Let us mention some of these at this point.

Modern large-scale scientific research has to be centralized for the best selection of personnel, the proper allocation of funds and, perhaps, the most efficient use of time and talent. Thus, population surveys, the building of atom smashers and manned spaceships, the control of space orbiting and the design of certain types of computer technology, must have lots of capital and central organization. Is it certain, however, that the centralization of scientific activity makes for better scientific progress? Goodman quotes Ben Seligman [8] to the effect that since 1900 about half of the important inventions affecting consumer goods have come from

---

[8] Ben B. Seligman was active for a decade in education and research activities conducted by the Retail Clerks International Association of the AFL–CIO. He is presently Professor of Economics and Director of the Labor Relations and Research Center at the University of Massachusetts.

independent researchers. It is hard to tell which style in scientific research —the centralist or the personal—would prove superior in making great and basic discoveries, since the best brains today are working in the centralist style, attracted both by the dramatic nature of the novel problems involved and the attractive salaries.

The centralist style, however, seems clearly necessary in such situations as the following: epidemic control or smog control; emerging situations bearing the potential for regional or national disaster, if unchecked; the carrying out of "routine," administrative functions; situations, as in ticket collecting or tax collecting, in which people do not have to be responded to as individuals but only in terms of one or two characteristics; situations in which a central authority is required for regulation and control so as to prevent the abuse of public rights, as in the operation of monopolies; the standardization of many materials entering into public works and public construction as well as into machine parts; and the growing public effects of automation, cybernation, and computer technology.

On the other hand Goodman notes that there are many aspects of urban administration which would lend themselves to decentralist control better than to centralist administration. Thus organization on a neighborhood basis would provide better results where housing, schooling, shopping, policing, social services and politics are integrally related. This could be done most efficiently, says Goodman, if each neighborhood had a local City Hall. Cultural activities like art exhibits, the provision of concerts, and the production of off-Broadway plays—carried on by *autonomous* groups—seem to give excellent results and allow for greater experimentation and originality than would commercial sponsorship. Decentralization of decision-making within giant industrial enterprises— such as General Motors—results in cost savings.

Industrial psychologists have found that a decentralist, psychological emphasis at work results in greater productivity and greater satisfaction. Decentralist work practises, themselves, are often found to have advantages for workers, apart from the greater productivity they often create for the firm. Thus, what is called the Coventry system in a certain area of England, is one example which substantiates this claim. The British capitalist in this area provides machinery and materials to his men. But everything else—such as work rules, schedule, and hiring—is left to the workgroup's decision. A group of this sort may vary from a few men to a thousand men. Among the advantages it creates for the workers are the following: men exchange jobs and acquire new skills; they adjust work schedules to their convenience or pleasure; they bring in and train apprentices; they invent labor-saving devices which are to their own advantage and they cover one another when sick or for special vacations. Such a system is clearly antithetical to the highly centralized and bureaucratic industrial atmosphere in America, where the industrial atmosphere emphasizes top-down regulation, time-clock discipline, labor-union details and the competitive spirit. Goodman also presents many examples of the extent to which costs of the same service, performed in both centralized and decentralized contexts, are almost invariably lower for the latter.

What does Goodman hope to gain if we have more decentralization of management in industry, government and urban affairs like housing and schooling? His *general* answer to this question is best given by indicating what he thinks are those *broad* lacks in our present highly centralized culture, which he feels will be reduced or eliminated under decentralized milieus which have proven to be practical. What then are these broad lacks in our culture, which Goodman [9] emphasizes? Apart from his insistence that a radical revolution in sexual attitudes is needed, there are other general requirements which he would emphasize. He believes that it is urgent that we restore a sense of individual worth and self-respect to work, by making it possible for people to contribute to the community services that are genuinely useful. This would, of course, be in contrast to our current tendency to approve of economically needed featherbedding on jobs in the public sector, in order to keep down the volume of unemployment among the unskilled and the semi-skilled. It would also be in contrast to our current tendency to lean upon Parkinson's law in the provision of clerical services, both in private industry and in government employment. We are increasingly providing mickey-mouse work in clerical and white-collar occupations, in order to provide bread-and-butter arrangements for a great deal of clerical help that would otherwise be redundant. Often this is being done as an expression of social responsibility on the part of employers but, unfortunately, it is a wasteful expression of such social responsibility. For employees with any pride of craftsmanship or employees who seek a feeling of social usefulness, mickey-mouse types of work fail to provide it.

It is also important, thinks Goodman, to provide an education which will enable the average man to understand the nature of his culture and, in a broad sense, its technological character. An education which conveys the nature of our technologically based society, will enable people to feel comfortable in the increasingly complex milieu brought about by technology. Such an education may even generate some technological inventiveness and creativity. Goodman also insists that we need more of an authentic, folk-culture to further a sense of community and a set of self-transcending community purposes which will gnerate more of an I–Thou atmosphere among our citizens. He particularly derides conformity and

---

[9] Paul Goodman. *Drawing the Line*. New York: Random House, 1962. 111 pp.

*uncritical* loyalty. He believes that if there were less false politeness and less desire to avoid civil rights protests and similar matters, and if there were more mature tendenciousness and an encouragement of significant political differences and profound differences in basic values, there would be less irrational hostility, explosiveness and bitter factionalism. The encouragement of alternatives to a monolithic, national attitude on fundamental community aims, would represent, in Goodman's opinion, a moral equivalent for war. Such considerations, he feels, are eminently practical, whether or not we label them utopian.

These brave words of a decentralist credo have been spelled out elsewhere in more detail by this same author, in order to provide some of the explicit aims of a decentralist philosophy, in relation to certain specific human contexts and concerns. Goodman's thinking is always in terms of the needed improvement of the human community—a pivot of thought which is both natural and centrally germane to decentralist thinking—and in terms of the quest for such improvement, Goodman feels that revolutionary social changes are usually required. We are clearly using the term "revolutionary" here in its figurative sense, not in its literal sense, although, of course, *some* social revolutions have been accomplished by force and violence. The needed types of revolutionary movement for improving the human condition and creating a more perfect and a more just social order, have occurred from time to time in human history. Social revolutions are not aimless; their social objectives are usually crystal clear. Goodman, however, classifies all such revolutions into three types. (1) *Successful social revolutions.* These are revolutions which succeed in establishing new communities. (2) *Missed social revolutions.* These are revolutions which are compromised, that is to say, revolutions which achieve some objectives that result in significant social changes but give up on others. As a result the total new society contains disparate, ambiguous and conflicting values that would not have occurred if the social change had been more thoroughgoing. A profound social revolution *in any field* is moved by the vision of a new workable kind of behavior, a new definition of the nature of man, or the projection of an entirely new possibility for social order. Frequently all three of these futurity-directed ideals move the self-conscious proponents of drastic social change. But when a social revolution is missed or compromised the prevailing traditions are disrupted and the new social balance which was striven for is never achieved. The new *status quo* takes on, in effect, a split personality in that it strives for a number of objectives which are mutually antagonistic. (3) *Compromised social revolutions.* These are revolutions which shatter the old community entirely but fail to substitute another in its place.

In terms of this tripartite classification Goodman [10] provides us with twenty-seven missed or compromised revolutions which have occurred in human history, particularly recent history. Each is described in some detail. The point in the present context, however, is that *most* (though not all, of course) of these missed revolutions could be brought to fulfillment if the strains of decentralist philosophy in Goodman's thought were more widely adopted by Western democracies, particularly our own. More concretely, the missed objectives of these compromised social revolutions could be brought into being if modern science, technology, industry and invention were married to a decentralist social philosophy. We can sum these missed objectives—all too briefly—in the following fashion.

For Goodman, American society has a variety of social pathologies and deficiencies which an unquestioning citizenry all too often either overlook or deemphasize. By mentioning what these are we produce an exaggerated and biased picture but one which is clear and, thinks Goodman, not unjust. Americans have allowed certain social pathologies and deficiencies to continue, when they could have eliminated them if they had a mind to do so. It is American willingness to allow these pathologies to continue which Goodman has in mind when he speaks of missed objectives and *compromised social revolutions*. What are the social pathologies and deficiencies that Goodman thinks ought to be brought into focus? They include the following: boondoggling industrial production, urban congestion which creates a variety of disorders, numerous middlemen who can be shown to be redundant to the process of distribution, and apathy towards cities which neglect or even eliminate the satisfaction of some of our basic human needs. Other social pathologies that should be stressed are these: too many garden cities for children, workmen who are indifferent to standards of craftsmanship and often socially irresponsible, too many underprivileged who are subject to niggardly welfare handouts, too much "joining" with little genuine relatedness, and too little genuine patriotism accompanied by too much flag-waving.

In our international relationships, Goodman thinks, we suffer too many front politicians and put up with a strong nationalism without a clear, positive, foreign policy—a nationalism which is moving towards a disastrous finish. In the councils of the nation, he feels, wise and forward-looking opinion gets swamped by the excitement of contemporary events. Free enterprise becomes a "fiction" and is sabotaged by monopoly, prejudice rather than tolerance seems able to galvanize large blocs of the citizenry, religion ignores or supports social evils and mass culture becomes increasingly jejune and debased. A new note in social pathology is the rise of specialized science whose practitioners are indifferent to the

[10] Paul Goodman. *Growing Up Absurd. Problems of Youth in the Organized System* New York: Random House, 1960. 296 pp. See, especially, Chapter XI, "The Missing Community," 216–36.

relationship of their work to issues of public philosophy, social value and personal morality. More and more, many of the results of scientific research are regarded as classified and the international exchange of the results of scientific research are aborted in the name of security. This occurs in many cases where scientists, themselves, can see no justification for regarding the problem or its results as involving our national security in any real sense.

Finally, Goodman indicts American society for producing average men who are inept in relation to the social responsibilities and knowledgeability required for maintaining a workable democracy which will preserve the spirit and ideals of an authentic, democratic ethos. At the same time it produces a younger generation who are ill-balanced sexually and who are obsessed with sex in many ways, a generation too many of whose members live purposelessly, unsure of what the gift of life is for, and whose aimlessness is aided and abetted by schools that provide an alienated and dysfunctional type of education.

Goodman recognizes that his indictment omits the positive side of the ledger, that is, the assets of American society. He is aware that there are some very important and praiseworthy accomplishments of our society. He states what he thinks these are. They include a persisting grand culture, continued progress in science, technology, scholarship and the arts, and steady advances in medicine, population health and public hygiene. We have the world's most affluent society with a figure for national income per capita that is the envy and benchmark of all nations. We have many examples of genuine civil peace, a reverence for, and a mature sense of, law and order. We have a grass-roots political wisdom and moral sense which often rise to affirm the democratic way of life, on those occasions when the average voter is properly informed. And best of all, Americans are a remarkably resilient and courageous people, given to a functional optimism that makes it easy for them to make a comeback following periods of national adversity or disaster. Finally, in spite of national conformity and intolerance of dissent, they can often spot the demagogue and are impatient with various forms of public hypocrisy.

In spite of these assets and virtues, the roster of social pathologies should make us stop short. Even that roster does not tell the whole story of our drift, according to Goodman. It omits our increasing tendency to surrender to the plans and arrangements of those in power and to the emerging semimonopolies of our time. This surrender is largely due to the fact that the average citizen in an overcentralized society does not have a true picture of the system of which he is a part and even less does he have a picture of the manner in which some of its more important component agencies and institutions function. Goodman furnishes examples of the types of surrender that augur ill for the American future. He declares, for instance, that IBM and the organized profession of psychological testers, determine the manner in which examinations will be conducted in our schools and their personnel will be chosen.

Civic developers like Webb and Knapp and Metropolitan Life, determine many of our day-to-day living habits, household practises and at-home, family activities. They plan communities on which they look forward to a modest return on investment but, from the standpoint of what genuine, communal living can be like under the dispensation of new and available science and technology, the people who live in these developments are poorly housed. Nor can these developments be said to be authentic communities in the sense of *gemeinschaft*. Charles Wilson tells the country that what is good for General Motors is good for the nation. With respect, however, to the cars being producd by General Motors, we find there is sufficient sociological data to demonstrate the ill effects that the 1960 ratio of one car for every 3 persons, is having on our cities and on the younger generation. The advertising profession and the dream-factory of Hollywood brainwash and manipulate the American audience and there is little one can do to oppose the debasement of communication for which they are responsible, since the means of communication are in their hands. No contravening mass medium is emerging to constitute some sort of spiritual opposition. Goodman also thinks that Americans are increasingly cowed by the interlocking of the FBI and local constabularies. If there was a will to do so, says Goodman, Americans could abolish these abuses. If there were some understanding of the dangers to which they seem to be leading, the will to end them might, in fact, be generated. But the fact that we now exhibit a national, social psychology which is pleased to tolerate all these social pathologies, is, for Goodman, the psychology of missed revolutions.

Once again we see some of the meanings which are wrapped up in a philosophy of decentralism. No matter how that philosophy is expressed and no matter in what contextual terms it is defined, certain major threads run through almost all the expressions of a decentralist credo. Let us mention some of these major threads. (1) A hatred of all the *unnecessary* forms of social pathology of technologically advanced civilizations and the conviction that these forms of social pathology are, in no sense, to be regarded as the inescapable, social costs of human progress. (2) An emphasis on the need to establish a sense of community on the human scale—one in which face-to-face relationships will occur more frequently but, even more importantly, one in which the direction of the human community will be from the bottom-up. (3) An emphasis on a social order which will encourage—not merely tolerate—individual diversity and social and cultural pluralism. The ideal social order from a decentralist standpoint is one which abhors all *unnecessary* forms of standardization and certainly does everything it can to prevent the appearance of socially pathological forms of standardization. Briefly, these latter forms of standardization are those which impinge on mind and spirit, that is, on the quality and free expression of ideas and ideals and on the right to translate these into action whenever such concrete translations do not impinge on the ability of others to give concrete expression to alternative notions of the good life.

These threads are in a sense the major ones and those which are common to most decentralist plans. There are, however, other threads that weave wished-for patterns of the good life and which would be held by many decentralists to be even more important than the three already mentioned. They are, however, somewhat less universal in their acceptability among decentralist thinkers than the three major ones. These "secondary"threads of decentralist thinking—if "secondary" is, indeed, the proper word—are aimed at reducing or eliminating specific forms of social pathology. In order to do them justice I propose merely to enumerate them in the paragraphs which follow, without entering into any discussion of them at all. Some of these "secondary" threads, then, of decentralist ideals, aimed at reducing or eliminating certain unbearable forms of social pathology, are the following.

Self-development and the achievement of a sense of personal identity; elimination or reduction of existing and unnecessary forms of alienation; the achievement of a balance between freedom and authority; the inauguration of social, cultural and community pluralism, particularly in economically advanced, technologically-based societies; an increase in organic, face-to-face personal and community relationships; the encouragement of individuality and intellectual independence; the fostering of an increase in the variety of human interests and concerns; and the achievement of a High Culture as opposed to a Mass Culture.

The establishment of small communities which can eliminate the social pathology traceable in whole or in part to excessive urbanization; the achievement of small communities without sacrificing the cultural, educational, scientific, technological, social and material gains which are mistakenly thought to be functionally dependent upon rampant industrialization and urbanization; the reduction of bureaucratization in human life; more direct participation by the non-governing voter in democratic decision-making; less brain-washing, manipulation and propaganda from our mass media; and the reduction of excessive organization in industry and politics.

A greater fostering of the virtues of a religious existentialism in interpersonal relationships, such as authenticity, less role-playing, more genuine encounters, more frequent commitment to worthy causes and needed social programs, more actual involvement following commitment, more concern for and social responsibility towards adversity experienced by others and less bad faith in personal relationships.

Less legal coercion in our lives and an end to the proliferation of legislation which tends to become deadwood rather early, on the statute books; less standardization of social life and cultural diffusion; less central dictation and determination of social and economic values; less ugly urbanization, less water and air pollution and healthier civic surroundings; and less waste of all sorts, whether through the unnecessary destruction of life in field, forest and stream, through the overuse of industrial raw materials whose finished products find no market, or other equally, important forms of waste, discussed by the present writer,[11] but which are too infrequently emphasized in social criticism.

More fellow-feeling or *gemeinschaftsgefuhl* in the human community; an increased use of the principle of voluntary association in community relationships; an effort by educators to reduce the amount of suggestibility in human life; more and clearer personal direction in peoples lives and a more self-conscious and consistent pattern of values; the reinstitution into modern education of the great, Greek ideals of paideia; [12] a reduction of social prejudice, an increase of good-will and more community effort to increase the amount of international understanding in our lives; less fostering of local and regional provincialism by industry and the mass media; more economic planning to cushion the impacts of automation and cybernation and preserve the individual's capacity to maintain himself and family economically; and a genuine effort to get at the causes of war, eliminate them and inaugurate a continued, public education on the subject of war and peace through information in depth rather than through headlines, editorials and glib analyses over the mass media.

All the preceding, then, provides a broad picture of the decentralist philosophy and of some of its contextual implications. Through a series of historical accidents, beginning with the Industrial Revolution, large-scale urbanization became the answer to the then-prevailing, large-scale technology. Today, however, there are technological developments—such as miniaturization but, of course, not confined merely to this one development—which make it potentially possible to have the small community, without any sacrifice of all the advantages which have been gained materially, scientifically and technologically, industrially, culturally and educationally. These newer technological developments can give practical and concrete expression to the decentralist outlook. That outlook infiltrates itself to some extent in the work and ideas of such distinguished scientists as Coon,[13] Glikson,[14] and Bronowski.[15]

[11] Henry Winthrop. "Waste as an Index of Social Pathology." *The American Behavioral Scientist,* 1961. Vol. 5, 18–21.

[12] *Paideia,* in the present context, refers to education which fosters self-development and a sense of social responsibility towards the community. It is to be contrasted with our current educational emphasis on vocation. The latter, of course, is to be preserved. What we have to ensure is that it does not monopolize educational philosophy.

[13] Carleton S. Coon. "Growth and Development of Social Groups." 120–31. In *Man and His Future* (Gordon Wolstenholme, editor). A Ciba Foundation Volume. Boston: Little, Brown and Company, 1963. 410 pp.

[14] Artur Glikson. "Man's Relationship to His Environment." 132–52. In *Man and His Future. Op. cit.*

[15] J. Bronowski. See this author's remarks in the discussion entitled "Sociological Aspects." 168–87. In *Man and His Future. Op. cit.*

It is not that communal decentralism has been tried and found wanting. Rather it has not been tried at all. What is now needed is a systematic, public program of education in the decentralist philosophy and systematic research to give concrete form and substance to that philosophy by community planning and design—if only on paper—which will make use of those forms of science and technology which lend themselves to community planning on a small scale. Such research should also block out the relationships between inescapable types of centralization needed in the modern world and the projected forms of decentralized communities and institutions. Only in this way can decentralists give substance to Goodman's notion of decentralizing and the mixed system.

One cannot predict whether decentralization will get a second chance. What one can be sure of, however, is that with the help of science and technology, it can be shown to furnish feasible solutions to *some* of our problems. Whether mankind will listen or whether the inertia of traditional thought and social habit will forever eclipse the possibilities for decentralization, is something that only time will settle. If we miss the boat with respect to the possibilities of decentralization, this will be the greatest "missed revolution" of them all.

# 26

# Megalopolis Enthroned:
# Technology and Urbanization

## I. CONTINUOUS URBANISM TO RELIEVE CONGESTION

A number of city planners and specialists in related areas *welcome* the *extension* of urbanism rather than its elimination. Overurbanization is welcomed either because it is felt to be a means of reducing population congestion or because it is thought to be inevitable in our highly industrialized and technologically advanced society. Therefore, it is argued, we must make our peace with urbanization but future urbanization should be guided and rationalized. Still other reasons are sometimes given for sponsoring further urbanization in the immediate future. Let us furnish a few examples of the proposals which have been made on behalf of further urbanization.

Jellicoe [1] has proposed a city to be called *Motopia* in which urban living and human functions have been subordinated to the automobile and the highway. The pattern of this utopian city consists of multi-level highways and their circular intersections, which are to be so constructed as to form the roofs of buildings located beneath them. Even this inversion of imagination and the hierarchy of human values—in which the automobile-and-the-highway tail wags the urban dog, instead of genuine human needs determining the proper place of human mobility in the scheme of things—is made to pale into insignificance by the proposals of Dr. C. A. Doxiadis. The latter has proposed a city—to be called *Dynapolis* —which reflects what has been called *ribbon* or *continuous urbanism*. For Doxiadis, urban growth per se is good and lineal urban growth is best. He proposes to start a city with a short stretch of high-rise buildings for office and merchandising purposes. These high-rise buildings are to be erected on both sides of a traffic artery and they, in turn, are to be backed up on either side by residential buildings and other types of construction, used for cultural and other purposes.

[1] Geoffrey A. Jellicoe. *Motopia*. New York: Praeger, 1961. 165 pp.

433

The growth of *Dynapolis* would be preplanned. Every few years an urban increment would be added to the initial short-stretch of community with which one had begun. The successive, urban increments would be longer and wider but all would be serviced by a central artery which would run continuously through them all as a permanent and uninterrupted ribbon. Theoretically *Dynapolis* could stretch from coast to coast or the full length of any continent. Overpopulation in any increment could be relieved by an overflow into a subsequent increment with the passage of time. The price in social, cultural and aesthetic considerations, to be paid for this way of relieving urban congestion, is not apparently regarded as a deterrent.

Actual plans have been executed or are in the offing, in certain parts of the world, to relieve urban, population congestion or density, by extending an existing urbanism which has already created community headaches. Thus The Greater London Plan of 1944 has aimed at relieving congestion by moving out more than a million people to new towns, housing developments and other types of community beyond the green belt. In addition, The Greater London Plan of 1944 aimed to redevelop the central district of London. The Plan was only partly successful. The number of residents decreased by approximately one million and factory jobs in metropolitan London decreased by half a million. However, office and service jobs increased and canceled out gains which had been made elsewhere, so that more people than ever before *work in London* and commute to it from greater distances. In this sense, metropolitan decongestion during working hours not only proved a fizzle but is, perhaps, greater than ever before.

In Paris a group of architects has proposed to relieve population congestion there by building a second Paris, to be called *Paris Parallele,* which would be separated from historical Paris by a green belt. The government, in contrast, wishes to build satellite towns around Paris. *Paris Parallele* would eventually be afflicted with all the headaches of historical Paris. The government proposal, if enacted, would probably give results similar to those of The Greater London Plan of 1944.

The city of Tokyo is likewise faced with two proposals for relieving the density created by a population of 10-to-11 million which increases at the rate of two to three hundred thousand per year. One proposal aims at using the Kanto Plain, establishing a green belt around Tokyo and building satellite towns outside this green belt, connected with Tokyo by high-speed transportation. The second proposal would build a second Tokyo in the Bay of Tokyo after a reclamation project had made the Bay available for city building and construction. The reclamation work would take 15–20 years and provide an area greater than the Tokyo of today.

Here again the results of these two proposals would be likely to be the same as the two proposals made for Paris.

All of the proposals which would build a twin city adjacent to an already overcongested metropolis, clearly welcome the extension of urbanism. They look upon the urban problem solely in terms of mainland ratios, ignoring the many pathologies associated with urbanization. In terms of the limited objective with which they begin—the relief of present and anticipated population densities—these plans may fail in some or all respects. Even if they should succeed wholly, in terms of their limited objective, the day of reckoning would merely be staved off. *Paris Parallele* and *Neo-Tokyo* would, one day, be beset with the same problems now faced by Paris and Tokyo. In any event, in no sense can these large-scale plans be said to be moving towards a quest for community.

## II. URBAN GIGANTISM WITHOUT DECONGESTION

Perhaps the most knowledgeable anticipation that the future will be one of extended urbanism, is that put forward by Meier.[2] Although the future urbanism with which this writer deals, is that which he anticipates will occur in the next few decades in the underdeveloped countries of The Third World, nevertheless, the picture which he foresees may also prove to hold true in the future for the existing metropolises in the West. The picture Meier foresees may also hold true for any *new* metropolises which may yet be built in developed countries from scratch or which may yet develop from Western communities which, at least, *currently* exist in manageable proportions. Meier sees continuous urbanism as the inescapable pattern of the city's future—although, of course, he is stressing the expected densities of the coming metropolises in underdeveloped countries—and he anticipates that the populations of the largest metropolises of the future would be in the *tens of millions* with densities of 50,000 persons per square mile.[3]

These anticipations should first of all be compared with such metropolitan densities in 1957 as the following: New York, 24,000; Tokyo, 33,500; Moscow, 51,000; Berlin, 9,800; and Chicago, 14,200.[4] Some more recent densities which might serve as a basis for comparison are the fol-

[2] Richard L. Meier. *Science and Economic Development: New Patterns of Living.* New York: The Technology Press Of M.I.T. and John Wiley, 1956. 266 pp. See particularly Chapter IV, Section 3 "Characteristics of the New Urbanization" and Section 4 "The New Industries," pp. 170–97.

[3] This anticipated density figure is given on p. 396 of the following volume: Richard L. Meier. *Developmental Planning.* McGraw-Hill, 1965. 420 pp.

[4] These figures were obtained from the following source. Paul and Percival Goodman. *Communitas. Means of Livelihood and Ways of Life.* New York: Vintage Books (Random House), 1960. 248 pp. See p. 133.

lowing. For the five boroughs of New York City we had in 1960: Bronx, 33,135; Brooklyn, 34,570; Manhattan, 77,195; Queens, 16,014; and Richmond (Staten Island), 3,700. For the same year the density for Chicago is given as 15,836; for Los Angeles, 5,451; and for Philadelphia, 15,743.[5] We are also told that in 1960 the density for Paris was 73,000 and for Rome, 1,300.[6]

Meier's anticipations should also be compared with those of some independent communities and some countries. The Woytinskys [7] in 1950 reported the following unusual population densities for some physical entities which were larger than cities. In 1950 population densities per square mile for such entities were: 5,750 for Hong Kong and 3,333 for Singapore. In Western Europe the highest population density reported was for Belgium, 716.7, while in the Western Hemisphere, Puerto Rico had the highest density, namely, 737.0. Finally one ought also to bear in mind the population densities of the following large cities and a few special communities scattered throughout the world: Tokyo (1958), 11,506; London (1956), 29,974; Shanghai (1957), 8,938; Hong Kong Islands (1955), 34,483; Kowloon Peninsula (1955), 285,714; Berlin (1960), 11,871; Rio de Janeiro (1960), 206; Copenhagen Commune (1960), 22,543 and Prague (1958), 567.[8]

Meier does not, of course, stand alone in his vision of the urban "Sardinopolis" of the future. Fleisher [9] anticipates that by 1985 a city of 25 million can exist and by A.D. 2010 a metropolis may hold 50 million.[10] Clearly, the implicit assumption here is that continuous urbanism is likely to be the pattern of the future metropolis.

[5] *County and City Data Book, 1962.* Washington, D.C. U.S. Department of Commerce, Bureau of the Census, June, 1962. 669 pp. The figure for the five boroughs of New York City and for the other U.S. cities shown, are from 1960 census data.

[6] *Collier's Encyclopaedia.* New York: Crowell-Collier Publishing Co., 1964.

[7] W. S. Woytinsky and E. S. Woytinsky. *World Population and Production. Trends and Outlook.* New York: The Twentieth Century Fund, 1953. 1268 pp. See Table 19, pp. 48–9.

[8] These urban density figures, as well as those for the special communities shown, were obtained from the following source. *Encyclopaedia Britannica. World Atlas.* Published by the *Encyclopaedia Britannica, Inc.,* 1963. 518 pp. Where Britannica figures differ from those given by the Goodmans, this is probably due to a different area basis for calculation. One example of different area bases, for instance, will occur when a city area is defined in terms of its boundaries proper, by one source, and then defined by another source in terms of its greater metropolitan area. There are, of course, other differences in area or population chosen, which may account for such differences.

[9] Aaron Fleisher. "The Influence of Technology on Urban Forms," 48–60. *Daedalus,* Vol. 90, No. 1, Winter 1961, Proceedings of the American Academy of Arts and Sciences, 216 pp. This issue is entitled *The Future Metropolis.*

[10] According to the *Population Bulletin* (Sept. 1960), published by the Population Reference Bureau, Inc., Calcutta then had 5.7 million people. An estimate of its population for A.D. 2000, based on present trends, would be 35–66 million in an area the size of Rhode Island. Thus one can see that the giant megalopolises envisioned by Meier and Fleisher may prove not to have been mere guesses.

For Meier the population densities which he envisages will be made possible by some of the new technologies available to modern man. The metropolis of the future will have to employ within its own boundaries such food technologies as algal culture, hydroponics, fish farming and very intensive gardening. Berkner,[11] using a similar line of reasoning, envisages a metropolitan agriculture *which is wholly industrialized,* employing advanced concepts of mechanics, hydraulics, biology, genetics, chemistry and biochemistry. The new technologies and their associated industries, which, according to Meier, will make possible the giant metropolises of the future, include the following: microbiological food technology, atomic power installations, the manufacture of steel by hydrogen reduction, the preparation of fresh water from sea water, cheaper communication systems and fully rationalized methods of construction.

Thousands of acres can be set aside, devoted to algal culture, and the production processes involved in algal culture can become almost fully automatic. Furthermore, certain industries would be associated with this algal culture. Thus, intensive gardening would take place in the vicinity. Also associated with algal culture would be container manufacture, antibiotics manufacturing plants, ponds for intensive pisciculture,[12, 13] spice and preservative distributors and food machinery fabrication. Atomic power will be associated with industrial complexes in which chemical and metallurgical processes will be dominant. Such industries, feeding symbiotically on each other's services and wastes, will be able to produce such items as iron, aluminum, magnesium, chlorine, caustic soda, nitrogen, phosphate and acetylene. Four different technical processes are available for the industrial desalination of inland brackish waters or from sea water, in order to manufacture fresh water. Communications

[11] L. V. Berkner. "The Rise of the Metropolis," 144–9. In *The World in 1984.* (Nigel Calder, editor). Vol. 2. Baltimore: Penguin Books, 1965. 205 pp.

[12] Inland fish farming has already been successfully tried in the El Ghab valley of northwestern Syria. From 22 experimental ponds built in 1958, the take in 1961 was 1,760 pounds of carp per acre. As a result of the success of this experiment—known as the Kalaat el Moudik experiment—the Syrian government is extending inland fish farming. See the following volume: Marian Maury. *The Good War. The UN's world-wide fight against poverty, disease and ignorance.* New York: Macfadden Books, 1965. 191 pp. See Chapter 9 "New Ways in Food Production," 97–110, particularly pp. 106–7.

[13] Inland fish farming has also been successfully undertaken by J. E. Shelbourne, of the Fisheries Laboratory of the British Ministry of Agriculture, Fisheries, and Food. Plaice (that is, flounders) have been reared at Port Erin in the Isle of Man at the rate of one million per year. Before long Shelbourne expects his fish factories to produce 10 million per year and by 1984 he expects many fish factories to be spread along the English coasts. See Sir Alister Hardy. "New and Richer Marine Harvests Forecast," 100–3. In *The World in 1984* (Nigel Calder, editor). Vol. 1. Baltimore: Penguin Books, 1965. 215 pp.

networks, capable of being fully automated, can be devised which will integrate radio, television, telephone and films.[14] Prefabrication of different types of construction will depend on a greater industrial effort aimed at the standardization of designs and parts.

In addition Meier foresees that industry in the giant megalopolises of the future will make use chiefly of only a few modes of production. These are likely to be integrated "assembly lines," continuous-flow processes and the "automatic factory." In the development of underdeveloped countries, the government planners have to make a choice between three industrial patterns for industrial development. These are (1) the stimulation of small-scale industry using makeshift equipment and methods, (2) a decision to decentralize government sponsored factories with local participation and some centralized regulation or (3) the construction of large-scale industrial units and complexes, initially pushed along by the government, itself. A mixed approach is expected to prove advantageous, one in which 20 to 40 percent of all capital investment goes into the third alternative, and remaining investment goes into primitive-type factories and ordinary, assembly line methods of production.

Meier sees urban gigantism as inescapable and skirts the issue of whether a sense of community will be achieved in the superurban conglomerations of the future. Furthermore, the continuous urbanization which he welcomes does not even pretend to alleviate urban congestion. In fact it will increase it. All the preceding plans, then, adapt to the population pressures of metropolis by a kind of urban homeopathy—that is to say, the disease is to be cured by an intensification of a fresh urban infection of the same sort. This may be said to be an adaptation, but if men seek a restoration of the sense of community, such an adaptation is fated to make the achievement of community recede ever more rapidly over the horizon. The urban, homeopathic treatment simply cannot cater to the community ideal at all.

As for the prospects which Meier envisages, there is no pretense at all at a quest for community. In fact, Meier points out that in order to achieve efficiency in urban life, group and communal living may have to go by the board, including the nuclear family and the extended family. In justice to him, he states that primary groups different from those we have known historically may have to be invented. Presumably the sense of community would then have to be redefined for these new groups of the giant

---

14 One example of the establishment of cheaper communications systems, not touched upon by Meier, is the integration of book publishing with computer technology. This gives rise to the new technology of *copying machines* which promises to make the cost of obtaining a book much smaller than it is today and, in addition, promises to make copying possible anywhere, using one printed volume in a central location. Even home-copiers are in the offing. See in this connection the following: Herbert S. Bailey. "Book Publishing and the New Technologies," 41–3. *Saturday Review,* June 11, 1966.

metropolises of the future. Since we are here concerned with the restoration of a sense of community which has traditionally been inherent in small aggregations of people, and since we believe that human nature is built to dispose attention, feeling and identification only for small numbers of other people, we part company with Meier's belief that the sense of community can be redefined, presumably for large aggregates. Because we believe that, just as there is a limit on perceptual span, which psychologists call "subitizing," so too do we believe there is a communal subitizing which places limits on the size of the human aggregate which can be meaningful to individuals. If such meaningful but small aggregates should be unrealizable in the giant metropolises of the future, then we would have to see metropolises as experiments in anti-community. In this sense they are not genuine alternatives on the road to community.

If the preceding picture seems to be a somewhat gloomy one to the reader who feels that the technological changes being forecast are not worth the social and psychological costs which they may bring in their wake, then he may feel even more depressed by the plans presently being pushed for *new types* of cities for the immediate future. These innovations in city planning—stemming largely from the efforts of town planners and architects—represent attempts to conduct city life efficiently and economically and, at the same time, preserve the landscape and stop wasting vital, natural resources. They do not, of course, come to grips with the problem of community but they do come to grips with the problem of avoiding the "anti-city." A discussion of some of the advanced designs for putting metropolis on a paying basis is in order at this point. These designs have been described in an extremely interesting article by Young [15] and suggest all too clearly how much the effort to avoid urban sprawl physically is often taken to be the equivalent of the achievement of a sense of community.

The first of the plans to give the metropolis a face-lifting has been christened a *Megastructure*. A Megastructure will consist of immense buildings which, in effect, will be linear, self-contained, autonomous cities. One such plan—for metropolitan New Jersey—will be a linear city, stretching anywhere from 8 to 10 miles in length (perhaps, even for 20 miles) and will be approximately one mile wide. All traffic flow will occur and be regulated within the compass of a topographically, three-dimensional ribbon, with numerous exits to highways that cross the flowing landscape and plain, both of which will be outside of Megastructure. As a result, traffic jams are never expected to occur. Industries will be disposed on one side of Megastructure, a side which will be relatively low-lying. Another

---

[15] Warren R. Young. "What's to Come. Satellites, Megastructures, Platforms—Marvels to Choose From." *Life*. Vol. 59, No. 26, December 24, 1965, 143–56. Also *Life*, same issue, pp. 158–167.

side, essentially a collection of high-rise units stretching for many miles, will be a nearly endless "downtown," containing residential quarters, shops, services, and so on. A cross-ring structure, connecting the relatively high-level and low-level components of Megastructure, will lie above an area between the two, and this area will contain schools, churches, hospitals and municipal, administrative units.

At one side of Megastructure will be built highways for small electric cars. These will run the length of the city. At the very bottom of Megastructure will be traffic arteries which run directly under walkways intended entirely for pedestrians. Above these pedestrian paths will be arteries carrying intraurban, motor traffic and these arteries will be reached by ramps. Above the city's vehicular trafficways will be built parking tiers and freight-handling areas which run right through the city. People who have to leave Megastructure will never have to travel more than a mile to reach open highway.

Some of the tiers in the "downtown" unit—tiers which will be six stories above ground-level—will provide open-air cafes, shops, pedestrians walks and vantage points for viewing the entire surrounding landscape. Above these establishments will be built apartments and at the very top of the high-rise component of Megastructure will be found restaurants, pools and penthouses.

A business center adjacent to the industrial areas, will contain two or three levels of department stores and specialty establishments. Above these will be placed neighborhood shops and professional offices. The demand for central, large retail establishments will not arise because the planners of Megastructure are designing automated channels running the length of the city—channels which will distribute goods.

Except for some internal park and garden areas, Megastructure mutually quarantines the physical community and the landscape from each other. Decentralist city planning would insist upon the necessity of *interweaving* town and country, human settlements and wooded areas. The restoration of such an ecological relationship is precisely what many planners feel to be fundamental. Alienation from Nature, it is felt, brings too many social pathologies in its wake. Apart, however, from these sheer physical considerations is the fact that Megastructure is not very likely to restore the authentic atmosphere of community or *gemeinschaft*. But this is precisely the point at issue when dealing with the social pathologies so heavily associated with metropolis. Megastructure then becomes simply a three-dimensional, technologically advanced, urban complex, a sort of technological commune, in which the conditions of overurbanization that come in so heavily for social criticism, are, if anything, aggravated. It does not seem likely that a city which puts urban stress and strain on a technologically advanced basis, will be the answer to the charges regularly made by many social critics, that megalopolis is mentally unhealthy.

A second, major design for cities, intended to preserve the spirit of megalopolis, is the Platform City. In the Platform City the object is, *in part,* to keep traffic moving beneath the open city, itself, and to control the effect of the automobile on the human environment. Most buildings would therefore be erected on platforms or stilts. All or most streets would run under these modern, "lake-dwelling" land forms. Ground-levels in the Platform City—or, at least, of the business districts in the Platform City—would feature green landscapes and gardens. In the Platform City automobiles wishing to leave the city would reach ground level by ramp or escalator and then be able to travel through the city proper. The latter will presumably be a healthier and visually more appealing entity. A fringe benefit for the Platform City is the fact that municipal facilities like sewer works, power cables, phone lines, and water mains and pipes could extend along concealed roadways, thus facilitating the problem of physical maintenance and repair.

Cities like Hartford have applied the Platform City idea to the rebuilding of its center. The Urbana Design Studio of the University of Illinois is planning a series of Platform Cities to be built not too far from Chicago, to be called "Chicago West." Chicago West will consist of a series of two mile-long "urban spines" whose buildings will stand on platforms. Each of these spines will accommodate a community of 100,000 people. Like the Megastructure, the Platform City will have a high population density. Both the Megastructure and the Platform City will have some park areas and copses within them, but these will not be fully as organically related to the landscape as they would be in some of the many plans which have been proposed for the decentralization of our urban-industrial complexes. The Platform City concept can, of course, be combined with that of Megastructure for some types of city design.

The shortcomings of the Platform City are likely to be the same as those of the Megastructure, namely, the absence of an authentic sense of community and an exacerbation of the social pathologies of metropolis.

Proposed solutions for traffic management in the new technological urbanism, whether in the form of Motopia, Dynapolis, Megastructure, The Platform City or any other plan which still retains high levels of human density, while neglecting the community sense of *gemeinschaft,* are both novel and ingenious. The new inventions for transportation are both intraurban and interurban in nature. I mention only a few of them here.

Plans are in the works for moving sidewalks and for escalators and elevators which need not be restricted to vertical ascent or descent. With respect to transportation vehicles, plans are afoot for Ground Effect Machines (GEM's) of various sorts. These are vehicles which support themselves by downward blasts of air. The public has been familiarized with them by Sunday supplement articles on Hovercraft and Aircars. In effect they emancipate traffic from roads and highways since they have no physical contact with the surface beneath them. As a result they can travel easily over ice, snow, plowed fields, swamps, water bodies, etc. If a future metropolis should ever be built upon an island, a GEM "hovership" is very likely to be able to revolutionize life in such a metropolitan island community. Clarke [16] has given us a rather succinct description of the performance capabilities of GEM's and it seems quite clear that traffic problems, as we know them, may be solved by means of these machines. Whether they will produce traffic problems of their own remains to be seen. The wide-scale use of GEM's, however, does not bring us any nearer to the establishment of an authentic sense of community.

A revolution in design for track-hugging or road-hugging vehicles is also being projected. Monorail transportation is being tried here and there. Vehicles with aircraft design are being considered for rapid ground transportation. Overground pipelines are being proposed for cross-country traffic as well as unusually long, underground tunnels. Engineers are thinking seriously of high-speed, interurban trains. Some types would be powered by conventional electric motors. Others would be blown along by propellers. Some are designed to be sucked pneumatically through tubes. Still others are to be driven by "linear induction motors." The design for this last-mentioned type of interurban train would, in fact, contain no moving parts. Movement is effected as follows. Electrically charged coils are buried along the route of travel. These coils are energized in sequence. This energizing process produces an electromagnetic wave. This wave travels down the line. The magnetism it produces operates metal parts underneath the trains, themselves, in such a way as to move them forward at high speed.

In order to help the average American continue his love bout with the automobile, a new type passenger car—the Urbmobile—may make its appearance in the near future. These will move from suburb to city and back again on special type rails which supply the power for the car. Destination, via special highways, is selected by push-button. When the Urbmobile leaves the special highway it can travel along conventional highways and traffic arteries by means of installed battery power. Thus the Urbmobile becomes a source of both public and private transportation and commutation. Superspeed cars for special highways—other than the Urbmobile—are also being developed. They would require special qualifications and tests, however, for would-be drivers.

A group of applied scientists and technicians at Cornell University have been designing another innovation to relieve urban traffic problems. This is called the Master Modemixer. It is a round building—essentially

16 Arthur C. Clarke. *Profiles of the Future. An Inquiry into the Limits of the Possible.* New York and Evanston: Harper & Row, 1963. 234 pp. See, particularly, Chapter 4 "Riding on Air," 37–45.

a downtown transfer center—which accommodates efficiently Urbmobiles and Century Cruisers (self-propelled vehicles traveling on special expressways at 100 mph), Vertical Take-off and Landing Aircraft (VTOLs), amphibious air cushion vehicles, and luxurious, auto-carrying Aquamotels. Special parking devices and parking lifts are built into the Master Modemixer. The latter is to be located in a busy, downtown area.

In general the future of road-hugging and rail-hugging transportation will be laying much stress on automatic controls and special types of highways as well as on new types of vehicular traffic. A revealing picture of the potentialities in the offing is supplied by Calder.[17]

[17] Nigel Calder (editor). *The World in 1984.* Vol. 1, Baltimore: Penguin Books, 1965. 215 pp. See the section, *Surface Transport,* containing the following contributions. 1. C. S. Cockerell. "The Prospects for Hover Transports," 179–82; 2. Camille Martin. "The Railways of Tomorrow," 183–6; and Sir William Glanville. "Roads and Traffic in 1984," 187–9.

# Modern Proposals for
# the Physical Decentralization
# of Community*

## I. DECENTRALIZATION AND DISPERSAL

In E. A. Gutkind [1] we have, perhaps, one of the most radical proponents
for creating genuine communities which shall be free of the social pathology of megalopolis and yet shall possess all the social and cultural advantages of an advanced, technological civilization. Gutkind firmly
believes that the modern city—built around a trading, commercial or
industrial center—is doomed to extinction sometime in the future. He
believes that if plans were made currently to facilitate the death-throes
of megalopolis then the genuine, small and decentralized community of
the future—aided and abetted by science and technology—would be
brought that much closer in time. The radical innovations which Gutkind proposes in order to create genuine communities for an advanced
scientific and technological civilization, would clearly involve staggering
costs. However, these costs would probably be less than the combined
sums the world now allocates for such items as the following: (1) the
costs of all past and present wars and the costs of defense against future
aggression; (2) the costs of space exploration and the development of the
technologies associated with it; (3) the costs of producing commercial
"illth" and the costs involved in supplying the immature distractions of
mass culture; (4) the outlays involved in unnecessary extensions of the
standard of living in the West in order to achieve status and prestige; and

---

* Chapter 27, with adaptations and modifications has been taken from the
following source: Henry Winthrop. "Modern Proposals for the Physical Decentralization
of Community." *Land Economics.* Vol. XLIII, No. 1, February 1967, 10–24.
[1] E. A. Gutkind. *The Twilight of Cities.* New York: The Free Press of Glencoe,
1962. 201 pp.

(5) a thousand and one forms of waste [2] which can be stopped by large blocs of responsible and enlightened citizens everywhere, provided they are willing to strip for action. In any event, the radical innovations which Gutkind proposes involve the judgment that the *social costs* of *failing* to reconstruct the physical community will, in the end, be greater than the material costs which would be incurred in doing so—material costs the expenditure of which most planners would be unwilling to recommend.

Gutkind believes that the genuine community can only be created through *social, cultural* and *physical* decentralization and dispersal. However, his book stresses the problem of *physical decentralization and dispersal*. Because he believes that the *cultural and social advantages* of megalopolis can be duplicated in small-scale communities which can be physically dispersed throughout a region—if we make effective and imaginative use of new and available science and technology—his own professional concern is with the new types of physical communities that can be created and dispersed geographically.

Like many other decentralists, Gutkind recognizes that the genuine expression of the communal spirit requires *social, political, industrial* and *cultural* decentralization, in addition to the *physical* decentralization of the gigantic urban center. However, like most decentralists, he believes that social, political, industrial and cultural decentralization will either be obtainable with great difficulty or, perhaps, *not obtainable at all, unless physical decentralization has already occurred*. Physical decentralization is, therefore, seen as a *necessary* although not a *sufficient* condition for authentic community. Once physical decentralization has occurred, then an enlightened and responsible citizenry would have to bend its efforts towards the development of institutional innovations which would create social, political, industrial and cultural decentralization. Many thinkers, of course, feel that it is perfectly possible to have all the forms of decentralization which we have mentioned, occurring at the same time, although, of course, not at the same pace. Even these thinkers, however, would recognize that if a system of priorities were to be established for various forms of decentralization, physical decentralization would still have top priority. Nearly all decentralist thinkers, however, recognize that only if social, political, industrial and cultural types of institutional decentralization are married to physical decentralization, can we expect the restoration in the future of the authentic community of *gemeinschaft*. It is for this reason that so many decentralists, Gutkind among them, begin with what they take to be the basic or primary task, namely, the physical decentralization of the modern metropolis and the

2 For a discussion of the range of matters which can be subsumed under the problem of waste and the probable costs of these wastes for modern man, see the following: Henry Winthrop. "Waste as an Index of Social Pathology." *The American Behavioral Scientist*. Vol. V, No. 2, October, 1961. 18–21 pp.

establishment of an organic relationship between town and country. We shall therefore limit ourselves here to Gutkind's ideas concerning physical decentralization and dispersal.

Gutkind recognizes that modern science and technology are now in a position to create a revolution in the human environment. If this revolution is haphazard, we get the excessive urbanization, centralization, industrialization, and bureaucratization, which are part of the social pathology of our time. If guided, directed and planned for, however, we can obtain cities of breathtaking beauty and efficiency, cities which will provide the opportunity for the most ideal of relations among men and a flowering of culture hitherto undreamt of. Above all, these will be cities which enter into a partnership with nature instead of excluding her, as do our modern conurbations. They will be cities which restore man's sense of community as a partnership with the life around him and create a balanced, human and natural ecology which is becoming harder and harder to preserve.

In passing, let us note one instance of the way in which excessive urbanization may destroy the balance of nature. The rise of settlements everywhere, as a result of growing populations, is resulting in extensive and rapid deforestation and devegetation. These latter processes in turn are pushing animals from their natural habitats. Thus a balanced natural ecology and a balanced human ecology in partnership, will become increasingly impossible as more and more land is used up either to extend metropolis or to start fresh communities which are satellites to metropolis. If nothing is done to halt present trends, believes Chandrasekhar,[3] the world by 1984 may be bereft of all animals. Since animals are a proper part of a natural ecology, we would then be living in a world which this writer calls "empty and unbeautiful." This is *one* of the tragedies which Gutkind's proposals are aimed at halting, although, of course, his major concern is with the *elimination of the social pathologies of metropolis.*

Gutkind proposes to create a revolution in environment, which will make possible a humane exploitation of science and technology, by the twin processes of *organic decentralization and dispersal.* The conventional meaning of *decentralization* refers to all forms of urban planning which aim to relieve the congestion and pressures upon our urban centers by developing suburbs on the fringes of the central city. All such forms of urban planning are based on the notion that the most important part of megalopolis is its center—that area of concentration for trade, commerce, banking and industry. Conventional forms of urban planning assume that the most important parts of our cities are these centers and that they must be made more functional through less overcrowding. The

3 S. Chandrasekhar. "A Prosperous but Unbeautiful World?" 189–90. In *The World In 1984* (Nigel Calder, editor) Vol. 2. Baltimore: Penguin Books, 1965. 205 pp.

meaning of *organic decentralization* will be discussed in the paragraphs which follow.

By *dispersal* Gutkind means the abandonment of the idolatry which seeks to preserve a central city for metropolis, at any cost, and, instead, invokes measures which are aimed at creating equally effective, socially and culturally advantageous, small and genuine communities, which are quasi-autonomous and scattered throughout a natural environment. Each such community is to be a healthy, beautiful, culturally progressive and socially inspiring unit—a small facsimile of the best which the metropolis has to offer, while being free of the many liabilities which seem to be inescapably associated with overurbanization.

## II. THE ACHIEVEMENT OF ORGANIC DECENTRALIZATION AND DISPERSAL

Gutkind defines *organic decentralization* [4] operationally as follows. When cities are to be decentralized, three points are to be observed. (1) Slums which are cleared are not to be rebuilt but, instead, the cleared areas are to be retained as open spaces. (2) The core of the urban area is to be converted gradually into an open space by disengaging from it commercial enterprises, entertainment and cultural institutions, and small industries. These are to be located elsewhere. (3) All open spaces are eventually to be interrelated as a continuous park system. This continuous park system will cover what were the central open spaces of our giant cities, their former slums, their industrial districts and their thinned-out, residential neighborhoods. The final effect of such decentralization would be to break up our ugly, giant cities, creating in the process a series of small communities which are penetrated by green belts or green islands, and which would restore a balanced ecology to the urban areas which now reflect only the "conquest of nature." These decentralized cities would still contain *Desk Cities* for the ordinary conduct of community business, but these would be located at the fringes of the central park. They would be empty at night and used only in the daytime. Gutkind realizes, of course, that a process of decentralization of this sort might take half a century or more. However, he feels that a start should be made in our time, before we reach a point of no return in the quest for community.

The *advantage* that would be created by a decentralizing process of this sort, as Gutkind sees it, is that it would constitute a marriage of architecture with Nature. Such a marriage would bring other *advantages*

---

[4] The usual use of the term decentralization in social and political thought—not community planning—is identical with the meaning which Gutkind attaches to the term "dispersal." Outside of the more constricted meaning which we attach to the term, "decentralization," *when referring to Gutkind's writing,* this term will otherwise be used throughout our work in the sense of "dispersal."

in its wake. It would create a unifying element for every community, it would act to dramatize social life and stimulate each citizen to examine afresh that portion of the Greek ideal of *paideia,* which stresses personal development. It would foster the transfer of excess population into surrounding regions so as to form new communities, would create direct interaction between the region and its community sites as well as an intimate communion with Nature in all her forms and expressions. Decentralization would change the physical form of community by loosening up the block system, would split up the block front and spell the death knell to real estate speculation. Physically decentralization would guarantee fresh air, sunlight and natural modes of recreation. Finally, it would foster diversity of layout and construction, a healthier and more aesthetic relation of architecture to space and a real solution to the problem of traffic control. Traffic problems would fail to appear because of the existence of a continuous grid of parks, parkways, and highways for superspeed travel, covering the whole country.

Certain *disadvantages* of overurbanization would be liquidated by the type of decentralization which Gutkind proposes. Such decentralization, he feels, would reject piecemeal incoherence and self-centered insensibility. It would end once and for all overcrowding and high densities, disfiguration of the countryside by urban sprawl and a conflict of interest between town and country. In terms of architecture and neighborhood characteristics decentralization would end rigidity, uniformity, and houses which all look alike. The balance between green area and community artifact would prevent stagnation and pollution of the air, the construction or utilization of sunless, drab rooms and indoor rustiness. Finally, says Gutkind, decentralization would avoid repetition, traditional humbug, and those types of stopgap modifications now so common in urban renewal and planning.

Gutkind's notion of *dispersal* looks forward to the end of continued metropolitan agglomeration. He envisages small, organic settlements throughout a region—to be restricted in size—which specialize in some function or service: theatre and opera, communities which specialize in museums and art galleries, towns which specialize in the conduct of festivals and special entertainments, college and university towns, etc. Since new developments in transportation are increasing our mobility all the time, such specialized communities can remain functionally *interdependent,* servicing one another. The people in any region would then find that if they desired any one of these specialized services, they could visit almost any community in less than an hour, by car, on electrically controlled highways, or by train. Occasionally these services could, themselves, be made mobile for the region, such as, for instance, an art exhibit, a library, a traveling theatre troupe, etc.

In such a region loosely grouped *industrial units* would be located at larger distances both from one another and from the specialized communities, themselves. They would be dispersed at suitable intervals between the residential communities. A region of dispersed communities would consist of settlements which would have no central city and the region, itself, would have no dominant big cities. No conurbations would ever appear because, from many points of view, all the satisfactions which the metropolis now provides, could be obtained in the region of functionally specialized communities and in a total atmosphere infinitely superior to the noise and crowded conditions of the metropolis, its closed-in entertainment facilities, its dirt, grime and polluted air, etc. Each such settlement in some functional or cultural sense would be a *primus inter pares* and for the holistically inclined, educated and sensitive citizens of an organic civilization, all services would be likely to have approximately equal social status.

Gutkind attempts to sharpen the sense of the values inherent in *dispersal* by contrasting the virtues of a region of dispersed small communities with the defects and sins of the present metropolitan agglomerations. The faults of excessive urbanization, as he sees them, are the following: (1) an antagonism arises between town and country, (2) the landscape is tolerated until the need arises to remove it for more urbanization, (3) the urban community is imperfectly decentralized under the type of contemporary planning now employed, (4) different cities tend to possess unequal status and prestige and the same is true for different neighborhoods within the same urban center, (5) social stratification and cultural concentration are the inevitable concomitants of modern urbanism, (6) both industrial disorder and rural isolation increase as the metropolitan area is extended, and (7) farm units tend to become archaic while the productive functions of the community become the commanding leitmotifs of daily life.

There are other criticisms Gutkind makes of megalopolis. In physical appearance it lacks a visually unified and aesthetic pattern. It comes to consist of large fragments or sectors unrelated to each other. The greenbelt environment contracts with the passing of time. Rigidity and regimentation of both urban artifacts and urban processes are the rule. Pedestrian traffic specialization is common and Main Street becomes its expression. Commercialized dawdling and social monotony appear to be unavoidable. The community concentrates chiefly on matters connected either with industry or with agriculture—rarely both. Finally, says Gutkind, the cinema becomes the symbol of urban civilization.

By contrast, according to Gutkind, a region of dispersed communities would exhibit the following virtues. Such a region (1) would really constitute a single living area, (2) the landscape would be present everywhere, (3) an approximate type of equality in status would prevail among the small communities which compose it, (4) the dispersal would be rational and planned, (5) communities would possess social affinities for one another, (6) all forms of culture would be widespread and—in spite of cultural specialization—easily accessible to all, (7) industrial units and processes would be isolated from human settlements, (8) rural areas would be integrated with dispersed small communities by means of superior highways and our modern forms of mobility, and (9) farming units would be planned, rational, flexible, adaptive to change and up-to-date. In such a region human needs in their widest sense and human consumption—both material, social and cultural—would determine the expressions of daily life.

In physical appearance, too, a region of dispersed communities, would differ from urban sprawl. Living units would be small. The environment would be expanding all the time. The whole region would exhibit an air of vitality and openness. The region would have a patterned unity and yet allow diversity of appearance both in dwellings as well as in cultural and social artifacts. Park areas would be continuous over the region. Social centers would be prominent and recreation well nigh universal. Social awareness would be the rule rather than the exception. Every dispersed community would show an increased measure of social responsibility by devoting time, thought and energy to *both* industry *and* agriculture. The symbol of civilization suggested by such a region, says Gutkind, would be its *total environment*.

Dispersal will result in face-to-face, small-scale community life in which man enters into partnership with Nature. The subsequent environment of a region of dispersed, small communities will possess such characteristics as (1) compactness and openness of settlement, (2) order and flexibility, (3) differentiation and homogeneity, and (4) privacy [5] and social intercourse. Dispersal will also encourage the opening up of new regions within a country, while leaving Nature largely dominant within the region.

## III. SOME DETAILS OF DECENTRALIZATION

If Gutkind is the philosopher of a radical urban decentralization and dispersal, Hilberseimer [6] is a designer of a type of city planning which

[5] It is difficult to imagine that the invasion of the privacy of personal and family life which is now becoming so widespread a feature of metropolitan and industrial life, could get much of a foothold, if any, in the small, organic community—whether of the type envisaged by Gutkind or any other type. For an account of how extensive this invasion of privacy has become, the reader is referred to the following items. Vance Packard. *The Naked Society.* New York: David McKay, 1964. 369 pp. Myron Brenton. *The Privacy Invaders.* New York: Fawcett World Library (Crest Books), 1964. 176 pp. "The Big Snoop." *Life.* Vol. 60, No. 20, May 20, 1966, 38–47.

[6] L. Hilberseimer. *The Nature of Cities. Origin, Growth, and Decline. Pattern and Form. Planning Problems.* Chicago: Paul Theobald & Co., 1955. 286 pp.

will give expression in concrete detail to the ideas elaborated upon so fully by Gutkind. Hilberseimer has expressed a social philosophy of decentralization and dispersal which is very similar to that expressed in the theses of Gutkind. Hilberseimer, however, has worked out in great detail the physical and community planning necessary to make effective a translation of a social philosophy of decentralization and dispersal. Some of his plans are identical with those of Gutkind and some are conspicuously different. It is to a description of some of Hilberseimer's ideas that we shall now turn.

Hilberseimer feels that all community design must provide essentially for the three main elements of community life: residential living, working arrangements, and recreational expression. The latter, of course, would include cultural facilities. Each of the three main expressions of community life should be physically related both to each other and to the total design of the community. If these relations are properly fulfilled, the related areas will be within walking distance of each other and the need for local transportation can be reduced or eliminated. Thus *intraurban* traffic problems do not put in an appearance.

Hilberseimer would construct a modern community so that it would consist of either a *self-contained, settlement unit* or some *aggregation* of such units. These aggregates would be limited in number, the limitation to be determined by the fact that any collection of *settlement units* must be small enough to preserve an organic community life of group relatedness and make it possible for a *genuine democracy* to prevail—in which every individual who so wishes can participate in community activities. Let us first deal with this author's ideas concerning *dispersal*.

Most settlement units would have a main transportation line or artery running through them somewhere. On one side of this line would be placed first an industrial area consisting of buildings for commerce and administration. Beyond these would be placed the residential areas. The industrial area would be located within a green belt. The residential area would be surrounded by park and wooded areas. These would be accessible without having to cross streets. Schools, public buildings and cultural edifices would be located in the surrounding park area. The settlement unit is intended to blend town and country. Its size would be determined by walking distances which would never exceed 15–20 minutes in going from one point on its periphery to another. Other factors—apart from the planning features, themselves—which would affect the settlement unit's size, would be the social and personal requirements of its population, the need to offer variety in work and daily living, and yet be large enough to support communal, cultural and hygienic institutions.

Each settlement unit would be so constructed as to reduce the amount of street area to a minimum. There would be residential lanes for pedestrians only and main highways restricted to automobiles. Lanes in residential areas would connect with central streets which, in turn, would lead to local highways and working areas. Local highways would constitute arteries that bound together different settlement units and, at certain points, would intersect the main highway. Within a unit there would be closed-end streets. All through traffic within residential areas would be eliminated.[7] By a proper disposition of working and residential areas within a unit, people could walk to work and back. If a person living in one unit chose to work in another, this would be made easy by transport facilities which functioned most efficiently due to the improved layouts of *community design.*

Nowhere does Hilberseimer spell out the nature of the transportation facilities between communities consisting of aggregates of settlement units. Clearly there are many possibilities for achieving desirable modes of interurban (interaggregate) transport. One possibility, however, might be something closely resembling San Francisco's Bay Area Rapid Transit District (BARTD). Trains of this rapid-transit system—expected to be functioning by 1968—will consist of fast, quiet, air-conditioned, computer-controlled cars, 70 feet long, possessing woven-vinyl seats, gray-tinted windows and low-level lighting. It is planned to be a 75-mile network with cars traveling at 90 second intervals.[8] San Francisco's BARTD is only one of the many new urban transport systems contemplated under the Urban Mass Transportation Act, passed by Congress in 1964.

Hilberseimer's designs for settlement units provide great variety in choice of dwelling unit, from single family homes to apartment houses. The units, themselves, are adaptable to a wide variety of terrain and environments. The details of the layout of the total unit suggest a perfect solution for the problems of motorists and a safe solution for pedestrians. Industrial areas are, in a sense, quarantined, that is, set off by themselves, away from the settlement units. Full-time workers are encouraged to grow some produce in gardens, contiguous to their homes, while part-time workers are encouraged to work on farms nearby. Everywhere the emphasis is on a balance between town and country. Component features of Hilberseimer's planning are aimed to abate air pollution by techno-

[7] Although not identical with Hilberseimer's designs, the new community of Reston, 18 miles from Washington, possesses features which Hilberseimer has proposed. See the following: (1) Wolf Von Eckard. "The Community: Could This be our Town?," 17–24. In *The New Republic.* Anniversary Issue. *America Tomorrow. Creating the Great Society.* Vol. 151, No. 19, Issue 2607, November 7, 1964; and (2) *Life,* Vol. 59, No. 26, December 24, 1965, 145. In addition, *some* of Hilberseimer's ideas and *some* of Gutkind's will be incorporated in the designs for Germantown, a satellite city which is also to be located near Washington, approximately 20 miles from the national capital. However, whereas Gutkind thinks in terms of *specialized communities,* Germantown, by contrast, will exhibit *specialized complexes.* These will be complexes or areas for the following purposes: a major shopping center; a high school campus and stadium; a municipal government and finance center; an art and entertainment district; a "clean factory" area; a college, and a research and development center.

[8] *Look,* Vol. 29, No. 19, September 21, 1965, 62–5.

chemical devices or the replacement of coal by electricity for power and for heating. An attack on air pollution is facilitated by studying the different wind conditions and wind patterns of an area. A technology of construction and housing pattern maximizes the sunlight available for dwelling units. The results of a scientific approach to dwelling construction and dwelling location within settlement units, are exhibited in great detail by Hilberseimer. The total community of settlement aggregates can be designed so as to work towards either fixed or flexible patterns of community development. Community shapes or layouts can be made highly variable. All, however, have one purpose in mind. The city is to be ruralized and the country is to be industrialized but the industrialization of the country is aimed at preserving the balance between town and country and escaping forever the giant conurbations of our time. The beauty of the many visual layouts presented by this author are breathtaking but—what is more important—the physical ecology of settlement units and aggregates of such units end once and for all the physical pathologies of metropolis and—to a great extent—can also be expected to end some of the social pathologies of metropolis. The leitmotif everywhere is decentralization. So much for Hilberseimer's ideas on dispersal.

When it comes to decentralization of our major cities, Hilberseimer would make use of approaches very similar to those of Gutkind. He illustrates in great detail first the replanning of *parts* of our cities and then the replanning of *entire* cities. Like Gutkind, some of his plans would introduce park areas to what were once slum areas or commercially congested areas. Unlike Gutkind, however, Hilberseimer would introduce specialized, parking spaces into big cities, in order to deal with traffic problems. Hilberseimer shows how *parts* of such cities as Chicago and St. Paul could be replanned. This is followed up by the *total* replanning of such cities as a small community—Elkhorn, Wisconsin, a medium sized city—Rockford, Illinois, and a large metropolis—Chicago. The transformations to be effected would leave each of these cities closely resembling the *aggregates* of settlement units involved in Hilberseimer's plans for dispersal, achieving the desired balance between, and integration of, human settlements, on the one hand, and park and wooded areas, on the other. In the replanning of a giant metropolis like Chicago, Hilberseimer would locate some of its present industrial areas outside of the city, in order to reduce air pollution.

If Chicago were replanned in line with Hilberseimer's ideas, he believes certain ends would be accomplished. Urban disorder would give way to order. Neither slums nor suburbanization could take root. Traffic congestion and hazards would be eliminated. A solution to the city's parking problems would become feasible. Finally, Chicago would become a city in a garden. In all of the total replanning of cities envisaged by this author, firebreaks would be used. These consist of parks and wooded areas between *rows* of settlement units, and wooded areas between *individual* settlement units, all united. Firebreaks for a replanned Chicago would be at least one mile wide.

Hilberseimer has also shown how regional decentralization can be effected in different belts of the Eastern United States and how different types of decentralized settlements can be adapted to a great variety of topography. In further illustration of the concrete details of regional decentralization, he has replanned one of the Hawaiian islands, Maui, and a few selected communities elsewhere, such as many of the villages in India.

Hilberseimer's philosophy of decentralization parallels the outlook of that most practical of men, Henry Ford. The great industrialist was convinced that the overhead costs of doing business in our large cities was becoming too burdensome to be bearable. Ford felt that these costs placed so great a tax upon us as to cut deeply into what otherwise might be enjoyed as a more satisfying standard of living. The great industrialist felt that most of our social ailments stemmed from metropolis. He was convinced that the notion that an industrial country has to concentrate its industries, is unsound. Above all, Ford was convinced that industries would have to decentralize and that the modern urban-industrial complex was doomed to disappear. He regarded it merely as a transient stage in the evolution of the city of man.

The whole subject of the design of community is bound up with the Western tradition of thought which is concerned with the establishment of the Ideal Community or the construction of a Utopia. Many of the Utopias which have been described in Western literature actually contain some excellent ideas for community planning and decentralization—often in embryo, to be sure—but, nevertheless, ideas which can frequently prove useful when elaborated. The utility of descriptions of an Ideal Community resides in the fact that, if some of these were to be made technologically and administratively concrete, they would result in types of community which would severely restrict the appearance of—if not entirely liquidate—the social pathologies of modern urbanization. In dealing therefore with the topic of community decentralization and innovation, the reader will find it invaluable to have some idea of the potential possessed by various Ideal Communities for reversing the pathological trends which have been created by the modern, urban-industrial complex. An attempt at such an evaluation has been made by Reiner.[9]

Reiner's studies extend our notions of the transformations required in reshaping the physical community. They enrich the ideas of Gutkind and Hilberseimer. They make clear what the problems of deurbanization

---

[9] Thomas A. Reiner. *The Place of the Ideal Community in Urban Planning*. Philadelphia: University of Pennsylvania Press, 1963. 194 pp.

are when seen from the viewpoint of the architect and city planner.[10] Reiner, himself, points out the advantages which the analysis of an Ideal Community can provide the community planner. In the first place such an analysis may provide the germ of a model, one which, from our standpoint, may furnish one expression of physical decentralization. Such models can become the basis for a science and history of community planning. They also may serve to indicate areas of agreement among varied proposals. From our standpoint this last advantage may also serve to point up the common core of convictions concerning the notions of how physical decentralization may be achieved—convictions which may be held by critics of our urban civilization. The analysis of Ideal Communities may also help considerably to indicate some of the practical consequences which could characterize certain types of decentralized community. It is important to foresee such consequences in relation to the fact that social, cultural and political decentralization have to be married to them or, at least, successfully juxtaposed with them. Finally, if decentralized communities, themselves, are to be improved over the course of time, continued research is required. Much of such research can be guided by the analysis of one or another type of Ideal Community—an analysis which projects the ideals involved into a modern socioeconomic and technological context.

The success of Gutkind's or Hilberseimer's radical proposals for decentralization and dispersal depend upon various advances in science and technology, without which their ideas could not be made viable either in the 20th or the 21st century. It would be impossible to discuss all those developments in science and technology which could make decentralization and dispersal feasible. The most important of all these developments, however, would be the new sources of power—other than the fossil fuels, coal and oil—available to modern man. These, together with the technologies available for converting new potential sources of energy into mechanical or electrical power, may prove to be the required energy resource pool of the future. Such new sources of "clean energy" supply, for use by small communities seeking to escape the worst features of large-scale industrialization and excessive urbanization, may carry the promise of providing the technological support for patterns of decentralization. It is to these possibilities, then, which could give meaning to Gutkind's and Hilberseimer's ideas, that we shall now turn.

[10] The reader may be interested in noting how notions of ideal types of community can affect city planners and reinforce the decentralist style of planning. Thus concepts of Ideal Community have resulted in the building of Cumbernauld New Town, near Glasgow, Scotland. This community—planned for a *maximum* population of 70,000—has been selected by a jury from The American Institute of Architects as the "Western world's highest achievement in new urban design for modern human needs." A description of its key features is furnished in *The Tampa Tribune,* May 14, 1967 (Section 7-c) but special stories on this community can probably be found in other American newspapers of the same date.

# 28

# New Energy Sources and
# Technology for Community

## I. TECHNOLOGY AND THE URBAN REVOLUTION

Megalopolis depends upon coal and oil—the "fossil fuels"—as energy sources, and such devices as the internal combustion engine as a principal source of transportation. The fossil fuels are used most economically in immense power plants, high-rise multiple dwellings, and in large industrial and commercial enterprises. An economy which uses fossil fuels tends to require gigantic industrial enterprises for their sound, economic use. Such gigantic enterprises, in turn, tend to gather human, residential settlements around them which are really parasitic upon the industrial enterprise for survival. Later these settlements agglomerate and begin to form the excessively industrialized conurbations of our time. This agglomeration has been hastened by the invention of the automobile and the railroad, both of which make it possible to commute from large distances to our urban, industrial centers. The successful defiance of time and space, produced by the modern automobile, creates both a larger area dependent upon large-scale industry, a larger population nurtured by it, and eventually a greater need to agglomerate and centralize the satellite towns and suburbias surrounding the original urban-industrial center.

In the next few decades, however, new technologies may become available to support industrial operations—technologies which are utterly different from the historical coal and oil technologies of our time.[1] Most of these technologies, however, with the exception of nuclear power technology, are unsuited to the economic support of megalopolis with its large population. For the time being and for the foreseeable future the technologies which can release modern man from the traditional coal and oil technologies, would be better suited to small-scale, human settlements.

[1] For a discussion of the importance of energy to human ecologies and a review of traditional and new sources available to man, see the following: John McHale. *The Ecological Context: Energy and Materials*. Carbondale, Illinois: Southern Illinois University, 1967. 136 pp. This is a publication of the *World Resources Inventory* and is Document 6 of the series entitled *World Design Science Decade 1965–1975*.

Thus these technologies may prove to be just the answer to the question as to what energy sources would be appropriate for the industrial units which can be expected to provide the economies of the functionally specialized communities which Gutkind's and Hilberseimer's programs for *dispersal* envisage. In short—if we may now be allowed to use the term, "decentralization," with the meaning that Gutkind attaches to the term, "dispersal"—the quasi-autonomous, decentralized, organic communities which Gutkind and Hilberseimer envisage, must, in a sense, use "clean sources of power" for support, and reject the use of coal and oil technologies, primarily because they lead inevitably to urban gigantism.

There are other important reasons, of course, for rejecting coal and oil technologies—such as the question of air-pollution and the value of fossil fuels as raw material starting points for certain types of manufacturing—but the primary reason in the present context is the need to end our current tendencies towards excessive urbanization. We wish to avoid this excessive urbanization because of the various pathologies to which such excessive urbanization leads. We can think about this matter two ways. We can think of the decentralized community—and the decentralized industrial units which are to serve its needs—as seeking a marriage with the technologies which can appropriately serve them or we can think of the new technologies which can provide clean sources of power as seeking an inspired outlet in a type of community which is appropriate to their ebb and flow patterns and other characteristics. In this sense a future region of decentralized communities—whether in the United States, Europe or elsewhere—will be one in which the small scale of human settlement goes hand in hand with the kinds of technologies and energy sources that may prove appropriate to settlements of that type. The new technologies may, then, prove to be appropriate for small scale communities of the semi-autonomous type, envisaged by Gutkind and Hilberseimer. They may also prove to be appropriate for autarchic communities, that is, for decentralized, organic, small-scale communities which hope to preserve all the social and cultural advantages of metropolis within their own boundaries, thus avoiding functional interdependence with other communities. Autarchic communities could also make use of small-scale, industrial units, employing clean energy sources— industrial units which are located, perhaps, around the external periphery of such a community or in one small area of it, rather than in an adjacent greenbelt area. The decentralized communities which we have been describing may succeed in sloughing off, perhaps, for all time, the urban pathologies which are so deplorable today. Thus, in a sense, the small but technologically advanced community may be able to eat its cake and have it too.

But whether or not we have semi-autonomous or autarchic communities in mind, the important consideration at this point is to discuss the new technologies available for decentralization, the technologies which can provide power without the use of coal or oil. Let us, therefore, turn at this point to a discussion of a small sample of some of these newer technologies.[2] Before doing so, however, we wish to remind the reader once again, that the process of decentralization which we are envisaging, de-emphasizes monetary costs and plays up, instead, the question of social costs. Consequently, if it were to cost a small-scale community more to employ a new energy source than to use coal or oil, this would not be a deterrent. We are assuming that the men and women who prefer de-centralization are willing to pay a higher price for it than for urban living, whether this high price is measured in money or energy costs. In such a context the most important consideration will be the social cost of failing to avail oneself of the new technologies and the new sources of energy.[3]

## II. SOLAR ENERGY

The heat energy which falls on a single acre of the earth's middle lati-tudes is equivalent to the combustion of approximately three tons of coal. The solar energy that falls on the continental United States would be the equivalent of the power that could be supplied in 1,900 billion tons of bituminous coal. We call solar energy a clean source of energy because its utilization would not result in soot, fly ash, noxious gases or other air-pollutants. Solar energy can be captured by trapping the heat from the sun. This can be done in several ways. One common way of doing this is to permit sunlight to impinge upon a blackened metallic surface after passing through a pane of specially treated glass. Parabolic collectors, no bigger than an open umbrella, can be built which are lined with alumi-num foil. Focused mirrors can also be used to concentrate the sun's rays. These mirrors will produce a temperature high enough to operate a steam boiler.

Trombe [4] discusses in some detail the following significant and experimentally established uses of solar energy: to run engines, drive water pumps for irrigation, for space heating and cooling in dwelling

2 For a brief but interesting examination of some of the lesser known technologies for energy supply, see the following material. "Economics and Future Energy Sources." 119–30. This is Chapter 11 of the following volume. Robert W. Prehoda. *Designing the Future. The Role of Technological Forecasting.* Philadelphia: Chilton Book Company, 1967. 310 pp.

3 An examination of new sources of energy which *may* be exploitable by small-scale communities, as well as a discussion of new types of equipment which can be utilized in the exploitation of such new energy sources, will be found in the: *Conference on New Technology.* Washington, D.C.: National Aeronautics and Space Administration, 1964. 156 pp.

4 F. Trombe. "Some Aspects of the Utilization of Natural Radiation, Especially in the Developing Countries." *Impact of Science on Society.* Vol. 15, No. 4, 1965, 247–60.

houses, for high-temperature furnaces, for refrigeration, and as a means of water heating and distillation. Solar energy can, in principle, be exploited for motive power, in the preparation of food by solar cookers, and in photopiles and thermopiles to feed transistor equipment used for public and private telecommunication purposes. Brown [5] points out that in many regions of the world it would be possible to substitute solar heat for that now obtained from coal, oil, natural gas, hydroelectricity, wood, and other organic substances. To do so, however, would involve special housing designs which call for new techniques in the manufacture of glass and new advances in architecture. These would, of course, be exactly the type of innovation with which the small, decentralized community can afford to experiment. A study prepared for government use by the Stanford Research Institute [6] points out that a breakthrough in the applied sciences of solar energy utilization could provide energy for sunny areas where the demand is not heavy (the small community in a sunny clime, would, of course, be one such area); in villages and residential areas for household uses, for lighting streets or roads, and for small industries where simplicity and low technological complexity can be important. In principle, in many parts of the world, more solar energy could be captured from the roof tops of individual homes than is provided annually from conventional sources. Even the Western world may yet see an extended use of solar-heated houses. As early as 1952 it was predicted that by 1975 there may be a market in the United States for 13 million solar-heated houses, mostly in the southern part of the nation.[7] If this prediction should have any cogency this could mean that any isolated attempts at decentralization in that part of the country in the future, could certainly solve the problem of energy for housing and shelter without too much difficulty. Small power plants, supplying one to ten kilowatts, were, at one time, being explored developmentally. It is expected that once designs for such small type, power plants have successfully proven themselves, an effort will be made to develop power plants which can furnish 10,000-kilowatts. A generator of this size would require an area of only 46 acres and might be quite suitable for a small, decentralized community.

[5] Harrison Brown. *The Challenge of Man's Future. An Inquiry Concerning the Condition of Man During the Years that Lie Ahead.* New York: The Viking Press, 1954. 290 pp.

[6] *United States Foreign Policy. Possible Nonmilitary Scientific Developments and Their Potential Impact on Foreign Policy Problems of the United States.* A Study Prepared at the Request of the Committee on Foreign Relations United States Senate by Stanford Research Institute. September 1959. Washington: United States Government Printing Office, 1959. 100 pp.

[7] President's Materials Policy Commission, *Resources for Freedom* (Washington, D.C., 1952).

Solar heat, Guéron [8] tells us, could substantially improve the lot of up to one billion human beings, provided technical and political action is steadily sustained. He further states that solar energy may make a widespread dent in the West just as soon as a cheap compact accumulator emerges. Here again we should note that decentralized communities—not seeking the *cheapest* source of energy nor the cheapest available devices for obtaining energy—could afford to experiment with the use of solar energy even before it becomes competitive with conventional forms of energy. In order to contrast the costs for the reader who prefers to think in economic terms, let us note here that it has been estimated that electricity could be produced directly from solar energy in Arizona at a cost of about 2 cents per kilowatt-hour. Electricity supplied by coal-operated generators can be supplied at about half a cent per kilowatt-hour. Meier [9] has pointed out that solar energy can also be used for air-conditioning, climate control and the generation of electrical energy by means of semiconductors, such as highly purified silicon crystals and cadmium sulfide.

In general, we can sum up the established or anticipated uses of solar energy by saying that it can be applied in the following ways: solar cooking, water heating, house heating, refrigeration, housecooling, in heat pumps, distillation of salt water, the pumping of water, in high temperature furnaces, for power plants, in solar energy collectors, in radiation concentrators for producing high temperatures, with special surfaces for producing high temperatures, for heat engines, heat storage, power storage, for direct conversion into electricity, in photosynthesis for the production of fuels and power, in which we make use at times of algae and other plant organisms, in photochemical reactions and photoelectric conversions, and for electric lighting.[10]

The technical details in the applications of solar energy, the devices which have been developed for exploiting it, the costs which have been incurred and the various efficiencies which it can provide, have all been supplied extensively by Thirring.[11] This same author has also furnished a fairly full description of the famous Dover House which has solved the problem of solar house-heating and Trombe has provided a fairly full description of the designs for prototype solar houses which have been developed by the National Center for Scientific Research in France. Some

---

8 J. Guéron. "The Uses of Energy," 75-9. In *The World in 1984.* (Nigel Calder, editor). Vol. 1. Baltimore: Penguin Books, 1965. 215 pp.

9 Richard L. Meier. *Science and Economic Development: New Patterns of Living.* New York: Wiley, 1956. 266 pp.

10 *New Sources of Energy and Economic Development. Solar Energy, Wind Energy, Tidal Energy, Geothermic Energy and Thermal Energy of the Seas.* New York: United Nations, Department of Economic and Social Affairs, 1957. 150 pp.

11 Hans Thirring. *Energy For Man. From Windmills to Nuclear Power.* New York: Harper & Row, 1962. 409 pp. The reader will find Chapter 13 "Solar Energy and Other Sources," 261-88, most informative.

unusually significant research aimed at making appropriate use of solar energy, has been going on in Israel, and has been described by Tabor.[12] This same author has stressed the fact that Israeli scientists are making encouraging progress in the use of *solar ponds* for energy. These are manufactured. Tabor estimates that such a pond one square kilometer in size would yield, in a sunny clime like Israel's, 30 million kilowatt-hours of electricity. Since the annual, domestic consumption of electricity in the United States in 1950 was 1,825 kilowatt-hours, if a decentralized community were to make a demand for domestic energy equivalent to the average per capita household demand of 1950, this would mean that one solar pond alone could satisfy the domestic needs of a community of more than 16,000 people. Depending upon how extensive their industrial units would be and how high the standard of living which was demanded by such a community, and assuming further that solar energy could be captured for industrial use, a few more solar ponds scattered on the periphery of a decentralized community might be able to service all of its industrial demands for electricity. The power of a solar pond would be obtainable without any fuel costs. The pond merely has to lie in the sun.

The list of uses of solar energy is important and promises to grow. What is more important, however, is the number of these technological possibilities that can be used by decentralized, small communities to supply basic human needs and to supply some of the amenities which usually only the metropolis can supply. These possibilities can be accelerated when decentralization plays down competitive costs and is predominantly concerned with the quest for community—using available technology only as a means to this human end.

### III. ENERGY FROM THE WINDS

In machinery which is now being developed to produce electric power from the energy provided by wind, we find that such electric power can be produced at costs that are competitive with those created by the burning of fossil fuels. Modern turbines can be designed and built by engineers to utilize the energy potential of wind power. Research undertaken in several Western countries indicates that electricity can be generated by these turbines for about $\frac{1}{2}$ cent per kilowatt hour, which is less than the cost of generating the same power in New York City. Wind turbines can only be used where the wind velocity reaches a critical figure. Below 18 miles per hour there is very little energy. To be *economically* attractive in the United States, this critical figure would have to be an average annual velocity of about 28 miles an hour at hub height—that is, the height of

[12] Henry Tabor. "Solar Energy," 102–12. In *Science and the New Nations* (Ruth Gruber, editor). The Proceedings of the International Conference on Science in the advancement of New States at Rehovoth, Israel. New York: Basic Books, 1961. 314 pp.

the hub of the wind-wheel of the modern windmill. If, however, we ignore the economic aspects of power generation from modern windmills and concentrate only on the potentialities of these devices for supplying the energy needs of a small community, then it should be emphasized that all the major mechanical problems of wind-generated electric power have now been solved.

Where can wind-power be used? A study made in Great Britain indicated that there are literally hundreds of sites which could be used in that country for wind plants and it is quite safe to say that there are many natural sites for the use of wind regimes in other countries as well as Great Britain. More interest, however, in wind power can be expected to occur in Great Britain because of her poor hydroelectric potentialities. If all the potential British sites were developed, that country could obtain several million kilowatts of electric power, an amount equivalent to a British annual consumption of 2 to 4 million tons of coal. Small, power-generating windmills have been built in Scotland, Germany and Russia, which were in the 100-kilowatt range. In the United States engineers working for the Federal Power Commission have designed wind generators approaching the 8,000 kilowatt range. This range would be sufficient to provide electricity for a small community of 50,000 people. An *experimental unit* was built in Vermont in 1940 which was in the 1,250 kilowatt range and which operated efficiently for several years, feeding alternate current into the lines of the Central Vermont Public Service Company.

Of central importance in connection with the prospect of achieving community decentralization is the fact that the combined use of one or more wind power and solar power plants, together with one fuel-burning plant, might allow a widespread use of electricity in small communities. The load demands on such a small energy-complex would, however, have to be carefully regulated. Not only could such an energy-complex assure an evening supply of power for small communities but the daytime maximum output can be used for rural industrial and handicraft purposes, for some agricultural purposes or for fans and air-conditioning.[13]

So great is the potential of wind power in some places that the Soviet Union is planning the production of 600,000 turbine units. Thirring[14] tells us that the contribution of these units, once installed, would add to the Soviet Union's sources of power, an amount of electricity which is 30 to 40 percent more than the present annual production of electricity from all sources in the United Kingdom. The same author points out that it has been estimated that the ultimate installed capacity of large, wind turbines in several countries near good wind regimes, can be ex-

---

[13] The possibilities of such an energy-complex are mentioned in the United Nations publication, *New Sources of Energy and Economic Development. Op. cit.*, p. 281.
[14] *Op. cit.*

pected to provide an amount of electricity twice as great as the world's present hydro-electric production. Thirring believes that eventually wind power may rank second to water power as a recurrent source of energy.

Wind-power plants either *commercially available* or *under development,* intended for the exploitation of wind power, are proceeding chiefly in such countries as Denmark, France, Germany, the USSR, the United Kingdom, Australia, Canada, the United States and, to some extent, a few other countries. The purposes for which such wind power is being exploited, include the following: battery charging, electric lighting and small domestic power, pumping water, feeding power into alternating and direct current networks, and supplying electricity or pumping water in remote areas, farms and isolated communities. The plant capacities generally involved vary from one-quarter kilowatt to 200 kilowatts, although in France and Germany some units are being planned with a capacity of 600 kilowatts. These are all described in the research publication of the United Nations [15] to which we have already referred.

What must be stressed here, however, is that wind-power technology is eminently suited for the decentralized small community and that the number of places throughout the world which have appropriate wind regimes is quite numerous. There is no reason why the initial attempts to achieve community decentralization might not occur in Western Europe or elsewhere, rather than in the United States. At the same time the generation of power from wind can be made fully competitive with the costs of conventional power from coal, oil, or water. The exploitation of windpower, like that of solar power, eliminates many of the unhealthy byproducts from the burning of coal and oil, which act as air-pollutants. Above all, the *size* of the modern wind turbine does not dominate the landscape. The heights of the towers involved in the construction of the modern windmill *usually* vary from as little as 33 feet to no more than 100 feet. Thus even the aesthetic aspects so essential to good small community formation, are assured.

## IV. THE ENERGY OF THE TIDES

Tidal energies are an important source of power when they can be harnessed. Only small communities which hope to establish themselves on the littoral, that is, on seacoasts adjacent to the oceans of the world, can think of using tidal power as a source of clean energy. Decentralized, coastal communities, however, would have certain advantages. Among these would be the following. (1) Such communities would have the seas and oceans of the world as a rich, direct and easily accessible source of protein from marine life, particularly in the light of new technologies

[15] *Op. cit.*

now available for a small-scale, fishing industry.[16] (2) Decentralized communities would also have sea water as a source of chemical, raw materials for certain types of manufacturing. (3) Finally, such small-scale communities would have sea water as an inexhaustible source for creating a supply of fresh water, through one or more different methods for desalination and the energy costs of such desalination would, themselves, be low, since these energy costs would presumably be supplied by tidal power, itself.

Thus far, France and England have reported more useful sites for tidal power installations than other countries. The Rance tidal-power project in Rance, France—perhaps, the best known of all tidal power projects—is based upon a very simple principle. Sea water is trapped behind a dam as the tide rises. This captured water is used as head and released when needed into generating turbines. In short, the tides create huge reservoirs of water behind a retaining wall and are then used to generate electricity in much the same fashion as a conventional, hydroelectric, power plant. The Rance Power Plant, adopted by the French Parliament in 1956 and which was planned for completion in less than 10 years, is expected to produce 820 million kilowatt-hours per year. Its guaranteed capacity will be 150 megawatts, its peak capacity, 320 megawatts, and it will produce the energy equivalent of one billion kilowatt-hours of coal. The Rance Power Plant was expected to be fairly large. However, if competitive costs and economic considerations are played down, while the value of the semi-autonomous, decentralized community is played up, then *small* tidal installations—suitable for small communities with moderate populations—may become feasible. These can easily furnish 10 megawatts and 25 to 30 million kilowatt-hours per square kilometer. Where this is still too large, techniques exist for obtaining one megawatt and a few million kilowatt-hours per year. Such small, tidal power plants can be operated during the day for such activities as paper pulping, ground-nut crushing, flour milling, or—in conjunction with one or more Diesels—pumping activities can be carried out at night.[17]

[16] Some of the new technologies available for farming the oceans have been discussed in the following volume: Marian Maury. *The Good War. The UN's World-Wide Fight Against Poverty, Disease and Ignorance.* New York: Macfadden Books, 1965. 191 pp. See particularly Chapter 9 "New Ways in Food Production." 97–100. The fisheries industry now has sensitive echo-sounding equipment that guides fishing vessels and enables them to spot fish under and around their ships. With new electronic equipment fishermen are able to drop their trawling nets to just the right depth. Using electrotaxis the Russians have reported being able to catch 7 tons of sprat in 9 minutes. With the use of new types of large seines the Russians and Japanese can engage in fishing operations 5,000 or more miles from their home shores. The catch can now be frozen and canned on board fishing vessels, and new irradiation methods can preserve fish at a cost of less than 1¢ a pound. One or two small vessels carrying small models of all these new devices can ensure a decentralized community a supply of fish-protein for a year, after going out but once or twice.

[17] See the chapter on "Tidal Energy," 62–75, in *New Sources of Energy and Economic Development. Op. cit.*

Most projected, tidal power plants, however, will have to be large—
by virtue of economic, geophysical, scientific and technological considerations—so that the hydroelectric energy from such plants may have to be
shared by a group of decentralized communities scattered along a seacoast
or scattered throughout a region. This will have to be a region in which
facilities can be constructed for pro-rating the large volumes of electrical
energy which could be applied by the artificial basins engineers can create
to capture the energy of the tides. If a region is to be supplied, provi-
sions have to be made for the storage of water and one such technology
for storage has been described by Thirring.[18] It depends essentially on the
alternate use of two adjacent basins both of which are connected through
large gates with the open sea.

Areas exist throughout the world for the favorable location of tidal
power plants. The most favorable locations are those which have a great
tidal amplitude—defined as the difference of level between consecutive
high and low water. Most sites with known great amplitudes are in England, Wales and France. In the United States a good site for a tidal power
station is known to exist at Passamaquoddy Bay on the United States–
Canadian frontier. In general, the degree to which tidal power can be
practically exploited will depend upon advances made in science with
respect to a theory of tides. Many problems in this area of human
knowledge still remain to be solved.

Decentralized communities which can take advantage of tidal power
would be those likely to be located elsewhere than in the United States.
There is no suitable place along the Atlantic Coast south of Maine and
none at all on the Pacific Coast except in Alaska. Ley [19] points out that
the reason no large-scale, tidal power plant (whose output, of course,
could be shared by a region of decentralized communities) has been built
in the past, is due to the fact that they are expensive both in construction
and upkeep. They therefore cannot compete with other types of power
plants. In terms of conventional, economic emphases, large-scale tidal
power plants are not likely to come into their own until the easy accessibility to fossil fuels disappears and their prices go up. However, if a
regional group of decentralized communities in Western Europe or elsewhere should be willing to incur the costs of a large, tidal-power plant
installation, while putting the emphasis on the social and community
advantages such an energy source may provide, rather than on the prime
monetary costs, then the burden might not at all be considered too great.
If a planned regionalism of the type Gutkind and Hilberseimer envisage
is ever encouraged in the future, in Western Europe, the tidal power
plant may yet come into its own as a source of clean energy.

18 Hans Thirring. *Op. cit.*
19 Willi Ley. *Engineers' Dreams.* New York: The Viking Press, 1954. 239 pp. See
the chapter "Waves and Warm Water," 189–218.

The best geographic possibilities, of course, for experimenting with a tidal-power, energy base for a decentralized community, exist in sites both along the coasts of England and Wales and those of France. Most of these areas have sites with great tidal amplitudes, a prime prerequisite for the exploitation of tidal energies. Considering the French penchant for individualism in public life and British consciousness of the ugly effects of overurbanization—already demonstrated by its "new town" projects—it would appear that any self-conscious attempts at community decentralization in the future, hoping to rest on an unconventional, clean-energy source such as tidal power, are more likely to be initiated in France or England than anywhere else.

## V. THERMAL ENERGY OF THE SEAS

The basic fact that lies behind the technology for thermal energy from the seas is the existence of a temperature difference or gradient between the surface of a body of water—usually heated by the sun—and a layer of water somewhat below the surface. Such a difference is found, for instance, in tropical or equatorial seas, where the temperature of the water at the surface is maintained by the heat of the sun while deep below the surface is to be found cold water of great density which has come from the polar regions. There are, of course, many other places in the seas and oceans of the world in which a temperature gradient exists. The natural causes for the existence of these gradients likewise vary. The capture and conversion to useful energy of heat stored in sea water represents an ingenious application of the scientific principle that heat can be converted to mechanical work when two heat reservoirs of different temperatures are available. In order to produce electricity the temperature difference between surface and subsurface water should be about 20° C.

Power stations can be built to take advantage of these thermal gradients. They may be large or small. They may be land-based or sea-based. Land-based stations may depend on pipelines from shore to sea depths or on tunnels bored under the shore and opening into the required depths. Sea-based stations may be based on floating foundations (hydrodromes), they may be submerged a little below the surface, they may be sited on sea beds at great depth or they may be built on artificial islands—for example, an island built on an underwater peak. A successful, experimental model which exploits the thermal energies of the seas, was tested at Abidjan, in Africa's Ivory Coast. This model was only about two meters in diameter. A model was tested off the coast of Cuba which succeeded in getting a small demonstration turbine of some tens of kilowatts to run for a few days. A thermal-energy, pilot plant to produce fresh water, has been tested in California.

Most of the favorable sites for thermal-energy, power-plants are in Central and South America, the Caribbean, Africa, Asia, Oceania and the Pacific. In general the favorable sites are contained within the isotherms of 25° C at the surface, which virtually means that they never go outside the lines of the tropics.

Surprisingly, the technology which has proved successful at Abidjan, involving plant on the industrial scale but of relatively small size, indicates that, under some circumstances, thermal energy from the seas would be cheaper than power from the most modern conventional thermal units. Large thermal-energy, power-plants might actually have a competitive advantage over conventional thermal stations.

In the production of mechanical or electrical energy from the thermal energies of the seas, there is almost a 40-year background of theoretical and laboratory research. Experiments have been conducted on a semi-industrial scale and systematic, scientific explorations concerning the possibilities for exploiting thermal energy on the industrial scale, have likewise been made. The certainty now exists that the conversion of thermal energy is technically feasible and viable over an enormous field. There are also some by-products associated with the conversion of thermal energies. These include fringe benefits in the form of low-priced fresh water, salt, and easy fish catches which can be landed during the process of thermal energy conversion. The latter can be used for human food, cattle feed, or the manufacture of oils and fertilizers. Similarly, benefits to health in the form of air-conditioning for homes and other contexts, may be a by-product of the technical processes involved in çonverting the thermal energy of the seas to human use.

The point to stress here, however, is that if some types of new but small communities were feasible for tropical areas, then the energy needs of such communities could be well taken care of. Since Bates [20] has shown the extent to which a scientific and technologically based civilization could be successfully exported to the tropics, the notion of founding rational and humane, small communities in the tropics in the future, is not a wild one. One of the problems which such communities would probably be able to tackle successfully is the acquisition of an assured source of clean energy through the thermal energy of the seas and an assured freshwater supply based on desalination. This would be half the battle won in the effort to avoid the mistakes of excessive industrialization which have occurred in the metropolises of the temperate zone. In general, the designs for thermal, power-plant installations involve units of relatively moderate size, so that they would be appropriate for small community development.

[20] Marston Bates. *Where Winter Never Comes. A Study of Man and Nature in the Tropics.* New York: Charles Scribner's Sons, 1952. 310 pp. See particularly Chapter 16 "The Planetary Neighborhood," 261–75.

## VI. NUCLEAR ENERGY

In nuclear fuels we may have the primary source of energy in the future. According to Thirring [21] atomic power plants are on the march and will be the source of a considerable percentage of the value of electricity produced in 20 to 30 years. This writer feels that atomic power plants may even make obsolete some of the projects now being worked on for obtaining power from recurring sources like solar, wind and tidal plants. It should be obvious that where we have succeeded in building nuclear-powered ships and submarines and where it may also be feasible to design nuclear-powered engines for large-aircraft propulsion, then it would seem to be feasible, *a fortiori*, to design small, nuclear-powered plants for small communities, taken singly or in combination, and whether decentralized or not. Britain today is working on a long-range plan for nuclear powered plants and, of course, already has some in existence. One of the better known, nuclear, power plants is that at Shippingport, Pennsylvania. The Euratom countries have similar plans. Both the Soviet Union and the United States have stepped up plans for nuclear powered plants. Japan and India have also made small but modest starts in the same direction. The U.S. Atomic Energy Commission has encouraged five distinct technological approaches with experimental reactor power plants. These are (1) pressurized water reactors; (2) boiling-water reactors; (3) sodium-graphite reactors; (4) homogeneous reactors, and (5) fast breeder reactors. The advantage of nuclear plants over power stations using wind, water or solar energy, is that they can operate with greater load factors and can avoid costs and losses caused by energy storage and long-distance transmission.

New and revolutionary technologies may still take place to hasten the day when nuclear power plants will be extensively used. One such possibility is the development of an economical and efficient thermocouple or some other device to convert nuclear energy directly into electricity. A second such possibility is related to Operation Plowshare, that is, to the feasibility of using underground nuclear explosions to generate power. Nuclear explosions in underground liquid reservoirs may provide steam to operate turbines and generators. Guéron [22] believes that as we learn to manage underground nuclear explosions the road will be open to "geographical engineering" which, on a large scale, could lead to increased access to conventional fuel and ore reserves and to climate modification.

Not all those who are giving thought to the possible exploitation of atomic energy exhibit an optimistic outlook with respect to its future.

[21] Hans Thirring. *Op. cit.*
[22] J. Guéron. *Op. cit.*

Baade's [23] evaluation of the prospect for atomic energy is quite opposite to that of Thirring's. Baade believes that those who hold that the future will be ushering in an impending exhaustion of conventional energy sources and a relatively advanced stage of atomic energy—are wrong on both counts. He believes that conventional energy sources will last not for decades but for centuries. In terms of conventional fuels, he believes that the world has energy resources in excess of its needs and that there will be no reason for the remainder of this century to exploit atomic energy. The world now suffers, says Baade, from a *surplus* of coal, not a deficit, and—as Baade sees it—if the fear that the world may run out of conventional fuels is what has given rise to projects devoted to practical applications of nuclear energy, then that fear has been mistaken. Similar pessimism about extensive industrial use of atomic energy before the 21st century, but on technological grounds, has been expressed by some very well-known scientists—by L. A. Artsimovich of the USSR, by Edward Teller of the USA, and by Sir John Cockroft of Great Britain.[24]

However, even if there should be universal consensus on the prematurity with which scientists and engineers envisaged a rapid depletion of fossil fuels, a depletion which, presumably, would be compensated by the successful and economic exploitation of atomic energy—nevertheless, research aimed at establishing nuclear power plants is likely to continue. It is likely to continue through sheer inertia, scientific curiosity and the fact that atomic energy could conceivably become cheaper than conventional energy or because nations might want atomic energy to *supplement* conventional sources of energy. The real problem, however, with respect to nuclear energy is the safe disposal of radioactive wastes. The more extensive the public use of nuclear energy, the more difficult would the solution of this problem be and the greater the subsequent threat to man's environment.

However, the waste disposal problem may not have to be faced if scientists succeed in making a breakthrough to the creation of power production through controlled thermonuclear fusion. Thermonuclear power holds the promise of free, *nonradioactive*, unlimited power for 15 billion years, according to Thirring.[25] Thermonuclear reactions occur in the hydrogen bomb but in an uncontrolled fashion. If these reactions can be controlled, they will provide unlimited sources of energy. Dr. Richard F. Post of the Lawrence Radiation Laboratory has called the search for controlled thermonuclear power, the toughest scientific problem which

---

[23] Fritz Baade. *The Race to the Year 2000. Our Future: A Paradise or the Suicide of Mankind.* New York: Doubleday, 1962. 246 pp. See particularly the discussion "Conventional Energy Sources or Atomic Energy?," pp. 141-3.

[24] *Possible Nonmilitary Scientific Developments and Their Potential Impact on Foreign Policy Problems of the United States. Op. cit.,* p. 52.

[25] Hans Thirring. *Op. cit.,* p. 379.

man has ever tried to deal with. The program for research on controlled thermonuclear reactions, under the auspices of the U.S. Atomic Energy Commission (U.S.A.E.C.), is Project Sherwood. An account of the technologies involved in this program has been given by Bishop.[26] Scientists in other countries are also working at this project, and some are extremely optimistic. The Indian physicist, Homi L. Babha, Chairman of the Atoms for Peace Conference held in Geneva in August 1955, expressed *at that time* the hope that some method of controlling thermonuclear reactions would be found within the two decades following.

From the standpoint of technologies available for satisfying the energy needs of small, decentralized communities *in the future,* it is clear that controlled thermonuclear energy offers one of the best hopes in this direction. There are many different models or types of devices, related to different types of thermonuclear technology, which have been developed. If one of these—or some device which will be used in the future —succeeds in controlling thermonuclear reactions, we can only hope that small, efficient and safe models of the device will become practical and be capable of supplying the energy needs of a decentralized community anywhere. Many of the models developed until recently under Project Sherwood are given in Appendix X of Bishop's volume. Thus, if one takes a sufficiently forward view, combines Gutkind's and Hilberseimer's ideas of community dispersal with the Indian physicist, Babha's optimism that success at controlling thermonuclear reactions will be only a matter of decades, then, indeed, the energy resources of the future would seem to complement the possibility of large-scale, regional decentralization. Not only would the continuation of the traditional fossil fuel technology seem absurd at such a time but it would also be wasteful. Fossil fuels will then have greater value as raw materials for starting points in manufacturing rather than as sources of energy. On the positive side, it would seem pointless to preserve megalopolises or create new ones in a world of unlimited energy resources. Certainly we have to do more thinking about the possibility that unlimited energy resources and the small-scale community may be natural complements.

The reader should note the following points about the few energy technologies to which we have referred so briefly in this chapter.

1. The time-scale for possible adaptation is uncertain. Some small-scale communities may not try any of them for decades. Some of these clean energy sources—or others which we now know of but which we have

26 Amasa S. Bishop. *Project Sherwood. The U.S. Program in Controlled Fusion.* New York: Doubleday, 1960. 227 pp. Bishop was the European Scientific Representative and Former Chief of the Controlled Thermonuclear Branch Division of Research, U.S.A.E.C. This volume was prepared for the U.S.A.E.C.

omitted from our discussion—may never be tried by any communities at all but, instead, may always remain in an experimental or developmental stage.

2. Other technologies and sources of energy may be adapted to general urban use or even be found superior to those we have described, for purposes of small-community formation.

3. Devices may be invented which will burn fossil fuels in such a way that the ordinary air-pollutants which they produce may be completely eradicated. Furthermore, such devices may be technically modified into small-scale, conventional-type, power plants that are capable of effecting clean-combustion operations, so that these, instead of clean-energy converters, may prove to be appropriate for supplying the needs of small, decentralized communities.

4. Future designs for converters of clean energy will, no doubt, require several units in order to deal with the energy needs of the small, decentralized community. The number of units required will clearly be a function of the size of the population to be served. The manner in which they will be spread around a community which is still on the planner's drawing board will unquestionably be such as to preserve continuous greenbelt areas and other aesthetic features of the planned community.

5. It is quite likely that the *small* community of the future may find it feasible to use *combinations* of these various new energy sources, together with the clean burning of fossil fuels, themselves. Although one of these many energy sources may be primarily emphasized in a given future, decentralized community, nevertheless many such communities will probably avail themselves of different types of technology, depending upon the resources of the region, the time of the year, its climate, and other factors. The willingness to shift from one energy source to another, within the same community, as circumstances require, involves the concept of *energy pattern* in which one tries to *optimize* the use of an *energy load* over time, in relation to the factors we have already mentioned, namely, resources, season, weather and climate. A willingness to shift from one energy source to another will automatically create a regional consciousness for dwellers in small communities and make them ever aware of the importance of striking a balance between town and country.

6. Even if we cannot guess the types of energy converters which will be adapted to small-scale community-formation, this *would not* affect the nature of the arguments put forward by Gutkind and Hilberseimer. That is to say, both the need for, and the requirements of, regional decentralization (dispersal) may be found feasible in the long-run—whatever that should prove to be in terms of time.

For all of the preceding reasons the quality of Gutkind's and Hilberseimer's proposals are unaffected by whether or not we have guessed correctly what sources of energy and types of converters will be best adapted to small-scale, community decentralization. In the end, engineers, scientists and technologists, with an understanding and appreciation of the need for and values of decentralization, will be in a position to give the most practical advice on which technologies—both those related to energy-conversion and those concerned with ensuring *all the other essentials of community formation*—will put the task of small-scale, community construction on a firm, practical, and, perhaps, permanent basis. These experts, assisted by architects, forward-looking city planners, and transportation specialists who can design for any type of mobility required for regional decentralization, can surely place the task of decentralization on a firm basis.

They can do so, however, only if citizens wish to liquidate excessive urbanization and the various social pathologies which are clearly heavily associated with it. If the will is widespread to refuse any longer to put up with the many undesirable social costs of overurbanization—regardless of the monetary or energy costs such a decision would entail—then decentralization may become a recognized means of community life and formation. Only time will tell whether men will come to feel the need for so drastic a change in community style or continue to drift, instead, into various types of continuous metropolitan urbanism and the formation of increasing numbers of conurbations, with all their deplorable, pathological effects.

# 29

# Some Unconventional Forms
## of Decentralization

## I. THE REVOLUTION IN CONSTRUCTION

Buckminster Fuller, a highly original, American thinker and inventor, who has made significant and major contributions to the sphere of engineering, architecture, and city planning, has come up with a number of inventions which could revolutionize human settlements in the future. The impact his inventions and ideas are likely to have upon the human community will be determined largely by the degree to which modern man can free himself from traditional ecological habits and the extent to which mass production will be applied to the fabrication of the types of structure Fuller has proposed for a variety of human residential, cultural and industrial needs. The depth of this thinker's originality was shown rather early in a famous volume entitled *Nine Chains to the Moon* which will be more than an eye-opener for those who care to read this volume.[1] Fuller's mind works strictly in terms of man's current, technological potential for reshaping the human landscape and the nature of the city and much of his thinking is geared to the benefits that can be derived from modern aircraft and aircraft technology.

The *Dymaxion House*—which is meant to be an isolated shelter for the individual or the family—is one of Fuller's more famous inventions. Traditionally man has satisfied his needs by exploiting Nature or entering into partnership with her. He has done this by borrowing much that she has, like power, water, and other resources, by going outside of his home to get these things. The Dymaxion House proposes to bring man's external environment indoors. It is to be a mass-produced home, light in weight, without foundations, and transportable by helicopter or other types of familiar aircraft or by aircraft still to be designed in the future. The transportation problems connected with this type of structure were

[1] Buckminster Fuller. *Nine Chains to the Moon*. Carbondale, Illinois: Southern Illinois University Press, 1963. 375 pp. This volume was published in 1938.

studied by Fuller [2] in the Twenties and are discussed in his autobiography. The Dymaxion House is meant to meet the internal needs of its occupants by building into it some of the best labor-saving equipment, communication devices and the entire spectrum of household gadgets to which Western man has become accustomed. In addition, machines proposed or designed by Fuller, but not yet built, would also go into it.

The Dymaxion House is, in a sense, to be like a ship at sea, but landlocked. Like a ship at sea, it will be free from the necessity of having to depend upon a land-based, power technology and power lines for its supply of electrical power. It will likewise be independent of an urban sewer system, by virtue of internal but advanced, septic-tank design. It is likewise to be relatively free of urban, water-supply systems by means of devices which have been studied by engineers closely associated with Fuller. Although, during the years when Fuller was devoting thought to the Dymaxion technology, there was no extensive talk of water desalination, there is no particular reason why a technology of small-scale, water desalination cannot be one of the complements of Dymaxion technology. Perhaps more than one of the four different processes by which present efforts to achieve desalinization economically, are being tried, will lend themselves to the construction of small units for location either within or outside the Dymaxion House. Then, if such a house is sited near inland brackish waters or near a salt-water body, a fresh-water supply may be permanently assured. Many other devices have been proposed or designed by Fuller, to make the Dymaxion house as technologically a self-sufficient unit as a battleship at sea. In short, the Dymaxion House is to be a minuscule but autarchic dwelling unit which, because it is mobile in the sense that its component units can be assembled or disassembled easily, can be airlifted anywhere.[3]

The Dymaxion House, itself, is suspended on a central mast. This mast makes use of the superior tensile strength of steel. The house is hexagonal in shape so that its component parts can be triangulated and easily assembled or easily disassembled for change of site. This assembling can take place in 24 hours or less. The total package represented by the Dymaxion House is light enough to be airlifted by one or two aircraft. The Dymaxion can be made to rotate so as to follow the sun, while turning on its axis, thereby providing *part* of the healthy commitment to Nature, demanded by our modern sun-worshippers. The central mast houses some of the Dymaxion's central machinery such as, for instance, its sun-finder machine, its Diesel engine and its septic tank. As Buck-

[2] Robert W. Mark (editor). Buckminster Fuller. *Ideas and Integrities. A Spontaneous Autobiographical Disclosure.* Englewood Cliffs, New Jersey: Prentice-Hall, 1963. 318 pp.
[3] Ground types of transportation for Dymaxion units may also be found to be economical, depending upon such future factors as weight reduction, lowered fuel costs, and so on.

minster Fuller puts it, the good life—at least in its material aspects—is to be planned from the inside out. By virtue of all these technical developments and the devices which have been built into the Dymaxion to provide many of the amenities which have now become essential for Western man, the Dymaxion House has been made independent of site and tradition.

In his autobiography Fuller has included pictures of his Dymaxion 4-D House in Chicago (1927) and a Dymaxion House, weighing 6,000 pounds, which was built in Wichita, Kansas. It is interesting to note that the Fuller house which was built in 1945 did not contain a single part which weighed more than 10 pounds. Fuller has also designed a Dymaxion 4-D Automobile, a Dymaxion Bathroom, and a Dymaxion Deployment Unit (DDU). The latter was planned as a major housing facility in the United States in 1940–41. The DDU was actually used on the Persian Gulf as radar shacks and desert dormitories for American personnel.

An even more distinguished contribution and invention than the Dymaxion House is Fuller's famous Geodesic Dome. This is an all-purpose shelter or rooftop, based upon a system of tetrahedrons. Like the Dymaxion the Geodesic Dome is easily transportable. It can be used for a variety of specialized edifices such as, for instance, a theatre, a civic center, bank, or tank-car repair area. Fuller's Geodesic Dome has certain structural advantages over the architectural exteriors of conventional dwelling units. One of these is that it provides optimal resistance to both internal and external pressures. Another is that one pound of the structural material in a geodesic dome can embrace as much space as one ton of conventional, structural materials. Still a third advantage is the fact that the geodesic dome is stable under such extreme stresses as those created by earthquakes, typhoons, Arctic cold, and tropic heat. The contemporary and conventional city dwelling is hardly likely to be able to adapt to such a variety of conditions. Fuller has built geodesic structures for the U.S. Marine Corps, which were found to be easily deliverable by air. In the opinion of Marine Corps engineers, the geodesic dome is the first basic improvement in the mobile control of the environment which man has produced in the last 2600 years.

Fuller has shown that a geodesic dome, weighing 600 pounds and which is a hemisphere 50 feet in diameter, could be designed to replace the uneconomical and clumsy shell of the conventional dwelling. Into such a geodesic dome can be packed many modern appurtenances: furniture, electrical appliances, radios, cameras, sporting goods, garden club machinery, home machine and woodworking shop supplies, and pretty nearly every other gadget that one can think of, for supplying conventional amenities. A unit of this kind for a family of six would have a volume of 1600 cubic feet, would weigh 2,000 pounds and—if mass produced—would have cost at the time it was designed, $7,000. All the amenity-producing gadgets desired could be fixed to the surfaces of such a geodesic dome, using assembly line methods. The dome will cover an 864 foot platform. In addition to the advantages of the geodesic dome, which we have already mentioned, it possesses many other advantages which are related to the heating and cooling of its interior, and to the provision of a fresh-water supply.

The transportation advantages of geodesic domes have also been demonstrated. In 1954 the U.S. Marine Corps airlifted a geodesic dome which had a 30-foot diameter and which was capable of meeting the minimum requirements of a one-family, U.S. dwelling unit. It was delivered at 60 knots. Two years later a geodesic dome was airlifted at the same speed but this time had a 55-foot diameter and was an item that had been used as a three-helicopter hangar by an aircraft carrier. One helicopter can airlift one dome. Fuller envisages technological improvements in weight reduction which will enable one airship to deliver a dome by 1970, intended as the covering shell for a stadium, and do so at 60 knots. In June 1956 a geodesic dome 100 feet in diameter and which covered a floor space of 9,000 square feet, was delivered by one airplane to Kabul, Afghanistan, from Raleigh, North Carolina. This was for the International Trade Fair Geodesic Pavilion. This dome was made of aluminum tubing and outwardly stretched, nylon–neoprene skin. It was subsequently unhinged again and delivered elsewhere.

Geodesic domes are so easy to assemble that unskilled labor can complete the setting up of one unit in less than 48 hours. The assembly is made easy by color-coding, so that no directions have to be printed in the native language. Many of the DEW (Distant Early Warning) sites have *radome* installations which were assembled by Eskimos in 14 hours, at their chosen Arctic sites. The assembly is so easy and the possibilities of end-use so novel that, at one time, Fuller proposed an air-conditioned, geodesic dome, two miles in diameter, that would have covered midtown Manhattan. Geodesic domes have been made of metal, paperboard and bamboo. Domes have existed or still do exist for such purposes as the following: the Ford Motor Company Rotunda Building at Dearborn; to shelter a radio telescope; to cover a swimming pool at Aspen, Colorado; for use as hangars by aircraft carriers; for an indoor auditorium; for a chapel for the Columbian Fathers in Korea; as a repair site for the Union Tank Car Company in Baton Rouge, Louisiana; to enclose the Anheuser–Busch Aviary in Tampa, Florida; for the Miami Seaquarium; for the gymnasium at Palomar College in San Marcos, California; as a hot weather pavilion; for Buckminster Fuller's own residence in Carbondale, Illinois; for a Lutheran church in Florida; for military housing; and for a variety of other purposes at colleges and universities both in the United States and throughout the world.

What is the importance of the revolution in construction which Fuller has helped to bring about? Simply this. Whenever either governments or voluntary associations of individuals wish to finance an experiment involving one or more decentralized, small communities, all of which are to be capable of being mobile, the types of construction unit for which we are indebted to Fuller, would be peculiarly appropriate. Not only would the Dymaxion House assure the most modern and convenient type of household dwelling but, because of its mobility, it can be sited anywhere. The family which uses it is free of both the physical and psychological pathologies of metropolis. At the same time such a family does not have to sacrifice any of the amenities provided by the urban-industrial civilization whose liabilities it seeks to escape. A group of such families can, at will, form an independent community.

Such a physically decentralized community would, at the same time, be able to achieve social and cultural decentralization. This can be done by exploiting the mobile, all-purpose geodesic dome for such architectural structures as churches, markets, schools, libraries, research laboratories, hospital units, theatres, auditoria, stadia, playing fields, swimming pools, sites for light industry, and many other types of structures too numerous to mention here. Because such a Dymaxion-Geodesic Community is not restricted to any area, any time it wished—if the purpose to be achieved warranted footing the bill—it could pick up and move elsewhere. Such a contingency is wholly beyond the present capabilities of either small or large cities. A mobile, *modern* community has never, as yet, appeared in history and even a *traditional–type* army equipped with tents would not have been its precise equivalent, because such armies could not have carried the volume of domestic technology which a mobile Dymaxion-Geodesic Community would be able to carry.[4]

A decentralized community of the type we are envisaging here could have its own transportation vehicles and hangars, both for travel and contact with the conventional communities of the surrounding areas and for the task of community relocation. The interiors of Dymaxion Homes can be made just as beautiful—if not more so—than some of our luxurious middle-class dwellings and, at the same time, they can probably provide on the outside as many or more of the conveniences which the urban housewife demands. The exterior, visual designs and coloring of the geodesic dome lend themselves to a certain amount of variety. The shape is fixed but this is equally true of most of our residential structures. More family privacy can be assured than many of our modern construction practices and building codes will allow. The most important point of all, however, is to recognize that the purpose of a Dymaxion-Geodesic Com-

---

4 This, of course, would not be true for a modern-type army which depends on the most advanced types of technology.

munity would be to escape the physical and social pathologies of mega-lopolis, while retaining almost all of its cultural, social, educational and economic advantages. This, we think, it could do.

It is interesting to note that Fuller, himself, is reported as envisag-ing entire cities in the future—as contrasted with entire buildings and edifices—which will be enclosed within geodesic domes that are climate-controlled. This is reported in an article entitled "R. Buckminster Fuller: Dean of the Dome" (*Look*, Vol. 30, No. 17, August 23, 1966, pp. 56-8). The same article describes Fuller's 20-story, transparent dome for Canada's world's fair (The U.S. Exhibition Building at Canada's Expo 67) as a revolution in new building technology. *Look* describes it as follows:

The lightweight steel frame now being erected on Montreal's island of St. Helene in the St. Lawrence River will enclose 6.7 million cubic feet of space. This sky frame will support a transparent Plexiglas skin self-protected from the sun by means of a computer programmed to trigger into action some 260 motors. These in turn will open and close 5,000 silvery plastic shades to shield the interior. On a sunny day, areas of the dome will change from shining trans-parency to glistening glow. On escalator-linked platforms, exhibits will range from space exploration to a history of the movies. Devised by the Cambridge Seven—a team of young architects and designers—they will dramatize the theme "Creative America." (p. 56)

## II. THE CLIMATICALLY IMMUNE CITY

Calder [5] has painted a word picture of the opening up of cities in the Arctic, consisting of as many as 50,000 people. This word picture is important to partisans of decentralization and the small community for the following reasons. (1) In spite of their relatively good-sized popula-tions, the Arctic cities envisaged by Calder can avoid the worst of the social and physical pathologies of megalopolis first, because they are pre-planned, and second, because their sources of power would be atomic energy. (2) They make use of Fuller's principle of the *dome*, a dome which can render any new city immune from the rigors and disadvan-tages of any particular climate. (3) Calder's entire picture is reasonable and sober—rather than an interesting piece of science fiction—precisely because it is based upon present scientific knowledge, technology and experience. We say something about that technology and experience later. Because the Arctic city described by Calder represents another way in which man may achieve physical decentralization in the future, it is of real importance to discuss it here.

[5] Ritchie Calder. *After the Seventh Day. The World Man Created.* New York: Simon & Schuster, 1961. 448 pp. See particularly the section entitled "Summit Con-ference, A.D. 2061," pp. 363-71.

Calder envisages an Arctic City, called Alert, which is only 400 miles from the North Pole. A bay adjacent to the city is kept unfrozen all the time by the heat from Alert's nuclear reactors. This accommodates the bay to submarine shipping of various sorts. The long night of the Arctic has been turned into perpetual day. This has been accomplished by man-made "sunlight." Man-made sunlight is produced by firing rockets into space in the vacuum just beyond the earth's atmosphere. There the rockets release sodium. The ionizing radiations of the atmospheric layer which is just beyond that of the earth, passes through the suspended and finely dispersed sodium gas. This fills the sky with a bright yellow glow which lights up the Arctic darkness. The effectiveness of this type of lighting is increased because the white snows of the Arctic reflect it. A second purpose of the artificially ionized layer is to act as a man-made mirror in the skies to reflect television waves so that programs emanating from the Arctic may be seen round the world.

Alert is a city of high-rise massive buildings which can be heated without melting the permanently frozen subsoil. This is accomplished by new types of effective insulation which guarantees sound foundations. The city plan for Alert is interesting. Alert is in the form of a great circle. From above, the circumference of the city's design looks like the rim of a wheel. This rim is a circular runway which receives vertical-lift aircraft. These aircraft are lowered by elevators into garages in the interior of the rim. Inside the circular corridor of the rim, 200 feet above the ground, we find a moving roadway which takes people from one group of buildings to another. These buildings are both linked to one another at various levels and joined to a *City Center*. The streets of the corridor radiate to that City Center or hub like the spokes of a wheel. The City Center, itself, is half a mile in diameter enclosed in a high *dome* which rises far above the ground. The dome functions like an enormous vacuum flask. It possesses both an inner and an outer shell with an insulated space between the two. The dome, made of transparent plastic, is *immune* to heat or cold. Calder's general treatment of the dome reminds us of some of the technical and environmental advantages of Fuller's Geodesic Dome.

Within this Center we find a closed type of agriculture. The Center contains gardens which produce a variety of crops. The Center also houses every type of municipal architecture and a central market which supplements neighborhood markets on the perimeter. The City Center is suffused with ultraviolet radiation which provides the population with a healthy tan just as visually flattering as that which can be obtained from warmer climes. On the outskirts of Alert are rocket airports where remotely controlled rocket liners can land safely under any type of weather condition, through advanced application of information-processing devices. The wealth of the Arctic is being unlocked through the power supplied by atomic energy stations which do not need continuous supply by pipeline or rail, since the coal and oil technology has been left behind long ago. The reactor fuels require replenishing by air very infrequently. The abundant heat and power from atomic power stations have created "industrial oases" in the north as well as communities which have all the amenities of cities elsewhere.

Industries concerned with the mining of ores were easily established. Farming was made a familiar affair by the creation of plants adapted to the conditions of the far north. This was done by speeding up plant variations through intensive selection, using atomic radiation and chemical mutagens to obtain desirable types of grains, root crops and vegetables. These were also fast-growing crops adapted to the short season of the far north. Soil conditioning was also used to help produce a northern agriculture and northern forestry industries. Through animal genetics hardy cows were produced, adapted to the farm areas of the domed Arctic cities and yet which were excellent milk producers. Sea farming was created on a vast scale. Power from atomic reactors supplied the heat needed for the fish nurseries. These fish were fenced within cold, natural waters by means of electric currents and therefore heat was required to help keep fish nurseries healthy. Air prospecting uncovered amazing deposits of natural wealth in northern Canada and the Arctic—oil, ores, and coal. Lakes or seas were permanently frozen by the surplus energy provided by northern installations. This allowed all year round aircraft shipping.

Calder mentions the technological realities of the late Fifties which make his projection a sober one. Each of these technologies is discussed by him in quite some detail.[6] Atomic submarines by the late Fifties had already made traffic under polar ice feasible. In 1959 plans were on the drawing board for nuclear-powered submarine tankers and freighters. Ice-free ports were already practical, using compressed air to keep ice from forming. Plans for constructing the domed city of Frobisher in Baffin Land had been created. Because of the magnitude of transportation costs in getting conventional fuels to the far North, it had been demonstrated that atomic energy stations might be economically feasible under certain circumstances. The possibility of an "industrial oasis" was illustrated by the construction of the El Dorado Mine for uranium, situated on Lake Athabaska. The ability to build communities was illustrated by the success at flying in equipment for the DEW Line. The extent of Polar oil fields was verified by Operation Franklin which was conducted to reconnoiter the polar islands north of the Canadian mainland. The success of the polar submarines *Nautilus* and *Skate* demonstrated indirectly the feasibility of a submarine freight transport industry.

[6] *Op. cit.* See "Top of the World, A.D. 1961," pp. 372–90.

The possibilities for crops in the far north were impressively illustrated by those grown experimentally at the Dominion Agricultural Research Station at Fort Simpson. These crops included spring wheat, barley, oats, Indian corn, potatoes, alfalfa, clover, timothy grass, asparagus, rhubarb, bush beans, broad beans, pole beans, beets, broccoli, brussels sprouts, cabbage, carrots, cauliflower, celery, chard, cucumbers, lettuce, melons, parsnips, peas, spinach, raspberries, currants, and strawberries. Likewise some of the world's most beautiful flowers were successfully grown there. The possibilities of creating all sorts of new plants—adaptable to the far north—has also been demonstrated by scientists in Sweden. Finally, the Arctic is known to be growing warmer which clearly increases the feasibility of human settlement.

The great value of scientific projections of the sort described by Calder, does not lie primarily in this author's emphasis upon the fact that the world's unsettled regions could give men in the future a chance to start cities all over again, unencumbered by the "errors" of industrialization which were generated by the traditional coal and oil technologies. Nor does it reside primarily in the ability to achieve immunity against unfavorable climates. Both these factors, it is true, are quite important. The major value of a projection of this sort, however, lies in its demonstration of how city planning can be combined with modern science and technology to make a fresh start. In this lies one of the major hopes of the small community of the future. It offers a second chance to avoid the pathologies of overurbanization, overcentralization and bureaucratization in our lives. We have the intelligence and creativity needed for a fresh start, among many of our architects and city planners. We also have a plethora of science and technology to make almost any spot on the earth's surface blossom like the rose. All that the men and women of tomorrow will need is imagination, will and the desire to control their own destinies, together with a renascence of the ideals of freedom, creativity and self-development to an intensity never seen before.

## III. MARINE ENVIRONMENTS AS A BASIS FOR DECENTRALIZATION

A large, naval vessel at sea is essentially a mobile, small community which, for limited periods, is a self-sufficient, maritime community. However, its naval and ship's stores and its producers' goods are not self-made. If one can envision a large maritime vessel that could manufacture its own producers' goods, obtain all of its raw material supplies from sea water, and make its own consumer perishables and consumer durable goods, this would increase the degree of its self-sufficiency. If, in addition, such a vessel could provide food for its human cargo through such techniques as hydroponic cultivation, algae production and processing, and even soil plots and banks on board ship, and if it could obtain its water supplies by economically feasible desalination, the self-sufficiency of this fictitious maritime community would be additionally enhanced. If it could produce its sources of power from sun, wind, and sea, as described so well by Smith and Chapin,[7] its autarchy would be further increased. If it did not have to renew anything it needed from shore-based supplies for long stretches of time, it would, in effect, be a scientific intentional microcommunity of a maritime type. In fact, it would be a *cruising hydropolis* that, if large enough, could provide all the amenities and advantages of landlocked living for a considerable period.

A naval vessel's functions are essentially military. If we had a large vessel that could add to the efficiencies we have just mentioned, the amenities and cultural activities of a luxurious passenger liner, and radio, television, movies, ship-to-shore communication, etc., then we would really have an autonomous, decentralized maritime community or, at least, a small mobile maritime community which had succeeded in freeing itself from the worst physical and psychological pathologies of metropolis.

The large, seagoing vessel today depends on oil. Not so long ago it burned coal. The hydropolis which we are describing could be designed today. It is technologically feasible. Several things, however, stand in the way. First, there is no community demand for a *hydropolis*. Second, the cost would be beyond the financial resources of most individuals or groups of individuals. Only a wealthy, Western government or the United Nations could finance the building of such a project which would cost only an insignificant fraction of the sums now spent for space research, the development of military technology and hardware or any one of several major projects that now receive government support. Since the building of a hydropolis will serve neither military ends, scientific research nor national grandeur, no one is going to press for its construction. Nevertheless, if we forget costs and involve a time-scale which looks ahead several decades or, perhaps, even a century, such a scheme—let us christen it Project Hydropolis—would represent another method for achieving decentralization and freedom from megalopolis.

Fuller,[8] as a naval man and technician, learned to admire the almost complete functional autonomy of a naval vessel. He realized early that this marine quasi-autarchy could be introduced into landlocked structures. Even more important than this is the reverse of this situation, namely, that the amenities and advantages of stable, landlocked commu-

---

[7] F. G. Walton Smith and Henry Chapin. *The Sun, The Sea, and Tomorrow.* New York: Charles Scribner's Sons, 1954. 210 pp.

[8] *Ideas and Integrities. Op. cit.*

nities could be adapted to the technical possibilities of cruising, semi-independent ships at sea.

Where large-scale financial support cannot be obtained for Project Hydropolis in the future, practical designers interested in the decentralized community, might have to try to interest industry and/or investors in designing small maritime vessels which would offer as much living space as the average dwelling unit and as many, if not more, of the amenities of the small private home or high-rise apartment. These smaller vessels would have to be powered by devices of limited size, which could make free use of the energies of the sun, wind and tides. This change of scale might bring the costs down to a point where a good many citizens with accumulated savings could, perhaps, purchase such a small, mobile, semi-autarchic unit. The purpose, here again, would be to provide a family escape from the worst features of metropolis.

Meier [9] has recognized that another way of life will have to be found in the future for living on and with the sea. He notes that the physical equipment for life at sea has been developed only for vessels with seagoing purposes and not for prolonged residence and a maritime way of life. He recognizes that a whole new technology is needed for houseboats, marine apartment units and floating platforms. We say more about the latter later. An amphibious style of life has been developing for years along almost every continental shore line. The introduction of new materials of construction and advanced communication technologies has made it safe and rewarding to occupy protected water surfaces which are near large cities. The areas of the seas on which people can live a semi-independent, maritime existence, thinks Meier, will be near subtropical and tropical regions. According to this writer the seas and oceans of the world provide the last, huge promising area of new settlement for individuals and families in the society of the future. He believes that specialized communities will launch themselves from coastal metropolises, each such community intent on creating a common lifestyle for a group of like-minded people. Such communities—the first of their kind—will be the *marinopolises* of the future. It is almost certain that they will be small and politically decentralized, owing few duties and obligations to shore authorities. It is equally certain that they will be free of the social pathologies of large-scale urbanism. According to Meier the number of styles of life available to marinopolises will be very great.

The problem of transportation for *select* individuals on *emergency* trips, over large distances from ship to shore, can easily be solved by big seagoing vessels, using helicopters which rest in deck hangars of the geodesic dome variety. Mass transportation over *short* distances can prob-

[9] Richard L. Meier. *Developmental Planning.* New York: McGraw-Hill, 1965. 420 pp. See pp. 396–7.

ably be solved by devices which will be essentially inflatable two-or-three passenger, special-rubber rafts plied by oar, and for somewhat longer distances, auxiliary, power-drawn boats, capable of accommodating over a dozen people at once. For a small fleet of vessels forming a marinopolis, a jointly owned, modernized type of hangar-covered scow with high enough sides, could be used to tow small hydroplanes for emergency use. Failing this, perhaps new and *small, lightweight* types of helicopter, with retractable, sliding parts, could be stored aboard each hydropolis—helicopters which do not interfere with the small vessel's stability or center of gravity, consume little space, are hooked to the top of a specially built, strong platform when not in use and which are capable of easy vertical ascent when they are made ready for service. Better still, perhaps, such small aircraft can combine features of both a hydroplane and a helicopter.

The large hydropolis is an efficient facsimile of a modern community and can therefore offer the social and cultural advantages of such a community. The small, family-type, hydropolis would, unfortunately, lack these advantages, as would the aggregated marinopolis, itself. The problem of supplying church services, educational facilities, sports stadia, theatres and musical auditoria, would somehow have to be solved, otherwise such unity would have to depend on coastal facilities for most of these. The *seadrome* (discussed below) whose location is fixed at sea may represent one device through which such services may be provided for a marine community. Programmed instruction and teaching machines could probably provide *some* on-board, educational services for the family-type hydropolis.

One of the new aquatic technologies available for ocean-going life—which Meier does not mention—is the *seadrome*. Designs for these have been described by Ley.[10] The seadrome would be a floating platform in the middle of the ocean. It is an artificial island. Originally, when seadromes were first proposed, they were intended to be floating islands for use as airports, in order to make transatlantic crossings by plane easier. The first design for a seadrome took care of every possible, practical contingency, and would have secured the structure in position by so-called sea anchors. It would have had runways, a repair shop, a few hangars, a radio station and hotel and, in addition, two ocean-going tugs to tow in flying boats that might have had to make an emergency landing. It also had resting or anchorage spots for flying boats and pontoon planes. A later design, meant for land-based aircraft only—the "Armstrong seadrome"—aroused the strong interest of Franklin Delano Roosevelt. The Armstrong seadrome would have been 1,370 feet long, over 350 feet wide and 100 feet above the ocean's surface. Underneath the flight deck there would have been storage rooms and machine shops, kitchen and laun-

[10] Willi Ley. *Engineers' Dreams*. New York: The Viking Press, 1954. 239 pp. See Chapter 2, "Islands Afloat," 46–65.

dries, dining and recreation rooms, crew quarters and staterooms, a laboratory for use by marine biologists and a weather station. Many other models of newer types of seadromes have been developed since Armstrong first made his design. A later Armstrong design would have provided a seadrome 3,550 feet long, with a maximum width of 400 feet and a runway in the center of the flight deck, 150 feet wide. It was estimated that this later model would have cost $10 million. Due to advances in aircraft technology, seadromes proved not to be essential.

From the standpoint, however, of developing autonomous, small aquatic communities, the principles underlying the seadrome could still be applied to the problem of marine settlements. These would then be true communities, offering everything which a land-based megalopolis could offer except, hopefully, its pathologies. The seadrome or "floating island" community, because it is so practical, may, in fact, turn out to be the prototype of aquatic settlement in the future. Thousands of them—true decentralized, marine communities—may dot the future seascapes of the world. This would then prove to be a major opportunity for human beings to have all the major advantages of civilization with none of the liabilities which have been associated with the urban-industrial complex of the last 200 years.

A large hydropolis, a marinopolis or a seadrome could all use the technology of underwater exploration developed by Cousteau.[11, 12] Using the Conshelf Three, a two-storied, undersea station in the form of a sphere 18 feet in diameter, Cousteau and his aides have not only explored the ocean bottom at certain limited depths, but have also managed to come close to obtaining oil from ocean-bottom, oil-bearing beds. If, therefore, as a result of small-scale, modern machinery carried on a seadrome for manufacturing purposes, oil was needed as a chemical starting material for the manufacture of various commodities, it apparently can be obtained, where the seadrome is not too far above the continental shelf. Future Conshelf designs may enable the recovery of all sorts of valuable marine resources—other than oil—for use by the population of a seadrome community, all of which would tend to increase the autonomy of the latter and reduce the number of items for which it would have to depend on landlocked settlements.

Small-scale manufacturing, whether beginning with oil or any other material, could probably be conducted at a small "industrial site" on the seadrome, probably designed to be ancillary to the residential portion, itself. Wind, solar and ocean thermal power would be available to a seadrome community, using appropriately designed units for capture. Small-scale desalinators will, by then, most likely have become available so as

11 Captain J. Y. Cousteau. *The Silent World.* New York: Pocket Books, 1955. 225 pp.
12 Captain J. Y. Cousteau. "Working for Weeks on the Sea Floor." 498–537. *National Geographic,* Vol. 129, No. 4, April, 1966.

to ensure a fresh-water supply. Modern fishing seines and trawlers can be used for the capture of marine foods. Gardens and hydroponic culture can probably be introduced on board seadrome communities. All these advantages would be unavailable to a small hydropolis, or a marinopolis consisting of such small hydropolises. They would be available only to a large hydropolis or a seadrome community.

One must not rule out the possibility of achieving decentralization in the future, by means of aquatic settlements. After all, not less than 65 percent of the earth's surface is water, the figure varying with what is included as a body of water. "Ocean consciousness," says Allegato,[13] is emerging in our time. The growth of marine communities, semi-autonomous in nature, is sure to be encouraged by the need to acquire the vast wealth of the ocean's bottom and to explore its natural advantages. Among the ends to be gained by a command of the ocean's bottom, are the following: the development of a mining technology for the ocean's bottom; defense bases under the sea; the possibility of subsurface, marine "homesteading" on the continental shelf, chiefly for scientific exploration for short periods; the securing of fresh water supplies from seawater wells or artesian (fresh water) wells in the briny deep; control of the world's climates to some extent as a result of the control of the ocean's currents; the establishment of recreational facilities on the continental shelves; and, most important of all, the desire to harvest minerals (magnesium, bromine, sulfur, coal, tin, platinum, copper, gold, and diamonds), foods, and other riches of the sea, including oil and gases.

Oceanographic research, pioneered by the U.S. Navy's Sealab II, has been encouraging with respect to the objectives mentioned. By 1970 the Navy expects to put the *Habitat,* a home in the sea, 600 feet below the surface, for aquanauts who will be using a small sub stored in the *Habitat,* for purposes of exploration. Much exploration, prospecting, surveying and research, undertaken by both private and public bodies, will soon be taking place. A substantial amount of this underwater research may find it convenient, in the future, to be located near an aquatic settlement on the surface. The desire for such convenience will undoubtedly result in the rapid advance of technologies for comfortable, marine living, on fixed surface communities. These advanced technologies will then, no doubt, later be exploited for entirely different purposes. They may be exploited by groups of people intent on establishing decentralized, aquatic settlements for a more democratic type of community life, unencumbered by contemporary types of urban pathology. Clearly aquatic communities can be established for purposes of social and political experimentation just as readily as for industrial and commercial advantages.

[13] Rose Allegato. "Ocean Consciousness." A feature story of the Chicago Daily News Service, appearing in *The Tampa Times,* Monday, June 27, 1966, p. 6.

Once again the vision of such future aquatic settlements represents a technique of cutting loose from the disadvantages of metropolis. It suggests how science and technology could develop a healthier type of human community. In these matters the principle to bear in mind is "nothing ventured, nothing gained."

The unconventional form of decentralized community most likely to get a hearing—from the average citizen, the government and the professions and industries concerned with urban problems and city planning —is one whose landscape will have some familiar features, even if its mode of performing essential functions and providing essential services, should represent a radical, community innovation and even, to some extent, a break with the past. One proposal for community planning which is likely to meet the requirement of being familiar and which will, at the same time, be a fresh and radical break with the city as we know it, has been put forward by Athelstan Spilhaus,[14] Dean of the Institute of Technology, of the University of Minnesota. Spilhaus has proposed a new type of decentralized community which he calls the *Experimental City*. This will be a city which, it is hoped, will eliminate or reduce *chiefly* the physical pathologies of the large, urban center but, at the same time, also the social and psychological pathologies of the modern metropolis. The Experimental City will be a city without slums, traffic jams, noise, smog, water shortage, pollution, industrial blight, junk yards and several other undesirable features of contemporary urban life. It is designed to function like a machine, under computer control, and not to grow organically, dysgenically, haphazardly and disharmoniously, as a result of historical accident. These are the ways, of course, in which megalopolis has traditionally grown.

Every Experimental City will have an optimum population and symbiotically related industries, that is, industries whose outputs and wastes are inputs to one another. Such a city will endeavor to be a "closed system" in the scientific sense of this phrase, that is to say, it will try to be as self-sufficient as possible and one in which industrial production will pass through a cycle of use-return-change-reuse. Ideally the Experimental City will also be self-sufficient in food production, growing its own food in a vast municipal greenhouse for which the fertilizer will be its own waste products and for which water will come from recycling water recovered from evaporation. The "closed-loop" concept will also apply to all of the Experimental City's utilities. Central heating will presumably be from atomic power and excess or waste heat from industry will be used to supplement this source. Traffic out of the city—which today is often deadhead traffic, that is, traffic carrying no load—will carry products that result from the processing of intra-municipal waste. New

[14] Athelstan Spilhaus: "Experimental City. Keys to Future: Total Planning." *The St. Petersburg Times*, January 22, 1967. Section D, *Perspective*, pp. 1, 4.

technologies for water, sewer systems would be developed, to avoid flushing away economically valuable wastes. In addition, there would be an air, sewer system, to collect chemically valuable industrial fumes and stack gases, and at the same time, reduce the pathology of air pollution. Both industrial and residential construction will turn to a technology and design in which easily disassembled and reusable parts and modules will be built. Such a technology of building construction will eliminate slums and, to some extent, urban sprawl and zoning problems. This is because a technology of this sort does away with obsolescence and allows a building—whether industrial or residential—to be put together in a new way by virtue of the many architectural possibilities that prefabricated construction parts will allow. An Experimental City would be so designed that the traffic problems of the urban center, as we know them now, could be almost completely eliminated.

By virtue of the many technologies upon which the design of an Experimental City would depend, such a city could be located anywhere, even in the middle of a desert. Its self-sufficiency would free it from dependency upon those ecological advantages which are the basis of most of our historically located metropolises. An Experimental City would not have to be near a river, lake or ocean. It would not require fertile soil, rainfall, *locally available* fuel, power and energy sources, or even *locally available* natural resources as starting raw materials for industrial production. In the latter eventuality it will, of course, depend upon most of its needed materials from the outside for its "nutrition." Thus an Experimental City dependent upon imports for its supply base will be less self-sufficient than one which contains all it needs both within its limits and, to some extent, outside its limits but close to its periphery. Finally, it is to be remembered, that such a city would be completely prefabricated before anyone even moved into it.

On the socio-psychological side an Experimental City would also provide all the cultural and educational amenities of contemporary life, together with all the services we have in mind when we speak of "gracious living." An Experimental City would also provide peace and quiet, wooded natural areas within its borders, little noise, a marked reduction of the "rat race" of the enervating urban center, and, hopefully, the elimination or reduction of the socioeconomic stresses produced by our present demand schedules for professional and nonprofessional services within the urban community. These are stresses which Herber [15] has re-

---

[15] Lewis Herber. *Crisis in Our Cities*. Englewood Cliffs, New Jersey: Prentice-Hall, 1965. 239 pp. See chapter 7, "Living on Nervous Energy," particularly the account of the effects of *socioeconomic stress* in accountants who practise their profession in large, urban centers, pp. 128–30. Herber is reporting on the Mount Zion Hospital experiment in San Francisco, in January 1957, conducted by medical researchers who studied the tensions created in urban professionals whose way of life makes such tensions inescapable. These professional tensions, reinforced by the conditions of urban living, were called "socioeconomic" stress by the medical researchers who conducted the experiment.

ported upon. Everyone who came to live in an Experimental City would do so freely, on the basis of the principal of voluntary association. Volunteers would be screened in many ways but chiefly on a vocational basis, aimed at locating the skills the community required and not skills that were useless to its way of life. Because of the radically new ways an Experimental City would supply essential services, the municipal per capita tax burden would be considerably diminished. Because cybernation and the willingness to exploit the abilities of the modern computer, would both be features of an Experimental City, shopping, banking, the supplying of news, the furnishing of entertainment via our mass media, the arrangements for voting and other civic functions in which the average citizen is free to participate, and dozens of other personal services the city dweller now takes for granted, would be rendered more efficiently and at less cost. Many such services could be supplied without the city dweller even stepping outside of his own home.

On another level the cybernated community and its widespread computer technology could serve every business, industry and utility in the city. Based upon suitable market research and the newer methodologies of planning, from operations research to simulation theory, an Experimental City could do many things more efficiently than they are now done by rule-of-thumb methods. It could program daily production schedules in each factory, control inventories, keep books and records for any business, register vital statistics, legal records, academic or medical histories, run the public library or sell you tickets to a play or a concert. The utilization of building structures would also be more efficient, since —unlike the patterns established by traditional architectural and city planning—the prefabricated construction used by an Experimental City would encourage the use of buildings for multi-purpose objectives. This would result both in less waste and a more conservative and efficient use of both space and land. The entire atmosphere of an Experimental City is intended to reduce the cost of community living, improve the quality of life, reduce urban stress, improve productivity and, above all, *eliminate the various pathologies now associated with urban life.*

In this chapter we were concerned with *unconventional* forms of decentralization.[16] There is, however, one type of unconventional form of decentralization which deserves entirely separate treatment. This form of decentralization would occur whenever a community chose to achieve *almost complete self-sufficiency,* depending on the host milieu for almost nothing. This would be a community, consisting of like-minded people, all of whom hoped to organize a community which would express their notions of the good life and do so with little or no interference from the

---

16 For an interesting compilation of considerations that *may* be relevant to unconventional forms of decentralization, see the following item: *Perspecta 11. The Yale Architectural Journal,* 1967. 227 pp.

outside world. In short, such a community would try to achieve a status as close as possible to political, social, cultural, economic, industrial and physical *autarchy* or *autonomy*. Such a community would not, of course, cut itself off from the world of increasing centralization, bureaucratization and urbanization. On the contrary, it would relate to such a world in many matters, but always on the basis of the principle of voluntary association. However, it would try hard *not to have to depend* on any part of its civilized environment for goods or services on which its continued survival was based. Such a community would, of course, be open to attack and misunderstanding. From this there is no escape. If left in peace, however, and if its communal enterprise was successful, such an autarchic or quasi-autarchic, decentralized community might serve as a model to illustrate another way in which personal and social freedom could be enhanced and the pathologies of the modern metropolis avoided.

Self-sufficient communities of this sort are sometimes called "intentional" communities. The type of intentional community, however, which we are envisaging here, would have to exploit fully many of the recent advances in science, technology and invention (and also, perhaps, some innovations in social invention) in order to remove its communal objectives from the status of visionary and utopian ideals to the status of a practical and workable community, albeit an *unconventional* one. *Small* communities of this kind, which would deliberately set out to exploit modern science, technology and invention, in order to recover a satisfying form of *gemeinschaft* and communal authenticity, would be communities which should be properly christened. Let us call them *scientific intentional microcommunities or* SIMC, if we designate their baptismal name in terms of the initial letters of our italicized phrase. Chapter 30 therefore, is devoted to a further discussion of unconventional forms of decentralization, by examining the purposes, problems and the nature of SIMC, some of which may conceivably be attempted in the decades which lie ahead. In doing so we shall also be able to derive some idea of the social gains to be made if SIMC cease to become a rarity even if they never become commonplace.

In the chapter that follows whenever we use the abbreviation, SIMC, we are referring to "scientific, intentional microcommunities."

# The Scientific
# Intentional Microcommunity[*]

## I. MIXED POLITY

The present discussion concerns the degree to which rational and organic relatedness among men and the degree to which the termination of war as an instrument of national policy, are both inherent in a scientifically and humanistically focused intentional community—a type of community which history has not as yet produced. I do not regard this objective as the *only way out* but I do regard it as one of the waves of the future in the next development of man. A metaphysics for practical decentralization is now a vital necessity, if industrial and scientific research and development are not to degenerate into a comic opera for the gods. It is with this hope in mind that I enter upon the discussion which follows. The basic presupposition needed for this new type of intentional community will have to be the acceptance of the idea of mixed polity. By mixed polity, we are referring to a civilization which consists of a mixture of large scale industrialization and urbanization, on the one hand, and a social pluralism in the form of numerous intentional communities, on the other. These latter will express a variety of ways of living and of achieving organic relatedness, culturally, socially and politically, while avoiding the characteristic alienation and sickness of soul to which modern bureaucracy, sprawling industrialism and conurbation have contributed so heavily. Even more importantly, in a society of mixed polity there will be important relationships between intentional communities and standard corporate ones—relationships of an economic and social nature which will be psychologically and materially beneficial to both. It is in this way, as we have already mentioned, that intentional communities will serve as models for the standard type of community, so that whenever dissatisfaction is widespread, citizens of such standard commu-

* Chapter 30, with adaptations and modifications, has been taken from the following source: Henry Winthrop. "Some Proposals Towards Experiments in Peaceful and Non-Competitive Living." *Darshana International*. Vol. IV, No. 2, April 1964, Issue 14, 74–97.

nities will have a choice of models or designs for living to adopt and copy, and efforts at large scale, social reconversion from megalopolis to intentional community, will have technical and social benchmarks for guiding such reconversion.

The concept of "mixed polity" is the social and political analogue of the *mixed* or *compensatory economy* in economics. The latter is, of course, accepted both intellectually and institutionally. The former is almost wholly alien to public thinking, with the exception of the thinking of a small number of city planners, decentralists, social scientists and technicians in whose works this idea has received some expression, although its systematic elaboration in new designs for living which shall constitute the next development of man, still remains to be done. A move to expand the sense and meaning of the concept of "community" in this direction is entirely feasible. The leading difficulties are certainly not technical, and where they are, they are far from insuperable. What is needed is, of course, public education and dedicated bands of individuals and families, who have determination, energy, imagination, time, money and patience. Know-how is already sufficiently widespread, ideologically and technologically, to provide more than the needed amount of leadership. It is followership which is needed, patience which will prompt us to engage in lobbying and education for years, and even more patience in waiting for desired results as experiments in scientific, intentional microcommunities are running their course.

As for the long-term feasibility of widespread changeover on the part of that larger fraction of society which will remain outside the pale of such social experiments for decades and perhaps for centuries, the difficulties, once that larger fraction becomes sufficiently impressed, are far fewer than popular imagination would suggest. It has been estimated that, at the present time, about 33 percent of GNP has its source in methods of mass production, that is to say, 33 percent of the dollar value of GNP must be produced at present by large-scale methods of production. If the majority of individuals in modern society did not wish to forego the consumption of most of the types of items in this fraction of GNP, it would then seem that societies and communities in the near future would have to live permanently with some form of large-scale production and the social pathology it brings in its wake. This will be true, of course, if current technology remains the same or is superseded by other forms of large-scale producers' goods.

Against this eventuality, however, are the following considerations. (1) Education in the future may turn people away more and more from Rostow's [1] terminal socioeconomic stage of high mass consumption to the

[1] For a discussion of Rostow's by now well-known theory concerning the stages of economic development, see the following work. W. W. Rostow. *The Stages of Economic Growth. A Non-Communist Manifesto.* Cambridge: Cambridge University Press, 1960. 179 pp.

stage which Rostow forgot, namely, highly personalized and autonomous consumption, in which human thought concerning valid consumption needs and appropriate standards and patterns of living, dictate the nature and level of needed technology, rather than the other way around. (2) As a result of current war preparations and the ability to establish *industrial defense complexes* anywhere at the present time, we are learning lessons in social, industrial, economic, and community decentralization, which will probably reduce the extent of mass-produced GNP well below the figure of 33 percent. This would make large-scale conversion and changeover, if it ever comes, that much less formidable. (3) Finally, with the advent of new technologies, such as prefabricated housing or a modified form of Buckminster Fuller's Dymaxion, with miniaturization and microminiaturization, with the possibilities of atomic power plants and above all, automation, it will become possible to produce many, possibly all, of those items which now require mass production methods for their fabrication. All that is needed are new types of technology which will economize on space and personnel, which can be rendered almost completely automatic and which therefore dispense with the urban concentration of industry and personnel as we now know it. Deconcentration, for instance, may be aided and abetted by *mobile residential living,* that is, the section trailer house used during the construction of the TVA. If pathological forms of urbanization can be made to disappear as a result of these technological possibilities, then again large-scale, social changeover to forms of small community, would clearly become much easier in the future.

During the very extended transition period, possibly lasting several hundred years, between the formation of the first scientific, intentional microcommunity and the liquidation of the last standard, highly industrialized, bureaucratized and urbanized community, all individuals would face a choice in their way of life—a choice between living in mass society or living in an intentional community. Such a transition period is, of course, a period of mixed polity. Even under mixed polity, however, the type of community we envisage will be able to free itself to a certain extent from dependency upon megalopolis, with respect to the product lines now included in the 33 percent fraction of mass produced GNP.

This may occur in one of two ways. (1) Such intentional communities may find acceptable substitutes for certain mass-product lines. Suppose such a community restricts itself industrially, for instance, to the establishment and location of light industry only—industry which is located on the periphery of such a community (which is, of course, only one type of possible balance between industrial and residential location). Will it still not need mass produced transportation vehicles for both work and pleasure—vehicles which will mean dependency on large-scale production of such items outside the community? It may be possible to dispense with passenger cars, trucks, and rail and plane *passenger* facilities (not in-freight facilities, of course). This might be done by exploiting its existing light industry and manufacturing small, collapsible vehicles somewhat like the modern helicopter or autogyro, whose parts can be manufactured locally as *sub-assemblies* in small plants and can subsequently be easily linked to each other through standard coupling devices, before flight. Such vehicles may possess both speed and safety factors and, of course, give economies of space in housing when disassembled. Different models could carry with comfort from one to four persons. The U.S. Navy was in fact exploring the reconnaissance possibilities of items of this sort in the early Fifties and the predicted cost of manufacture when mass produced was low enough to suggest that the cost of production of similar items in scientific, intentional microcommunities would not at all be prohibitive. These considerations then illustrate one way in which a population could free itself from dependency on large-scale industry for items which are now clearly necessities. (2) A second way in which intentional communities might make themselves independent of large-scale transport facilities (we use the example of the same commodity only for convenience of exposition) involving mass-produced items, would occur if members of such communities were willing to forego comfort, and travel anywhere intracontinentally by locally produced, small-type vehicles similar to motorcycles or small motorboats which could be produced in relatively small sub-assemblies for subsequent assembly and use. For intercontinental travel, of course, dependency upon passenger plane or ship would be unavoidable.

## II. INDEPENDENCE AND DEPENDENCE UNDER MIXED POLITY

SIMC can, at best, be semi-autarchic. They will achieve independence from host states more easily in some matters than in others. Let us therefore try to set forth some of the likely dependencies and interdependencies to be expected within SIMC which operate under the principle of mixed polity.

1. Such a community can establish *part* of its total economy and some of the techniques of allocation to its members, of that portion of its total GNP which it, itself, produces.

2. A community of this sort will be in a position to establish its own type of education. If its schools are unaccredited, this presents no problem because of the increasing number of educational devices which are appearing in possible host communities in the West, which enable young adults who can pass certain tests, to be admitted into standard, academic institutions. Considering that such terminal barriers are being increas-

ingly removed, the potentialities for experimenting with a socially significant and unalienated type of education—and pretty nearly all of our
standard forms of education are now highly alienated—are unlimited. If
a host community insists on laying down some educational constraints, it
should still be possible to devise a compromise through addition to the
host community's curriculum—additions which are desired by the intentional community even at the cost of extra instructional time furnished
voluntarily by its members. It may also be able to evade restraints
through the use of private schools.

3. Certain types of social experimentation are open to intentional
communities of the type we are considering—experimentation which is
free of permanent, institutional commitment. By not committing itself
to a rigid adherence to any single social practise or social institution, any
community gains precisely the flexibility which is needed in a world
which is changing as rapidly as ours. Thus it simultaneously avoids the
blockages and inertia of megalopolis—blockages and inertia which come
from vested interests, human laziness and the economic prospect of having to face a costly obsolescence which may wipe out years of accumulated profits, with no opportunity to pass on the loss to the consumer.
Since, in an intentional community, no bookkeeping is done on the quality of life, and no economic cost is regarded as too great to be borne on
behalf of achieving desirable social relations—the reversal of the typical
attitude under private enterprise—the *adaptability* of the intentional community to human needs should be infinitely greater than it is in the
standard, urban center as we now have it.

As a result of this institutional flexibility and the high degree of
social autarchy it confers, the intentional community should be able to
experiment with matters such as the following: methods of social cooperation, new forms of cultural expression which would ordinarily die a-born-
ing if they required commercial mid-wives, new forms of, and materials
for, architecture, new types of community structure and self-government,
new types of light industry and new forms of technology which would
not be feasible for large-scale adoption, novel uses of automation, social
uses for data-processing, computers and electronic controls and the development of amenities precisely adapted to small-scale living through the
use of novel products fabricated by technologies of miniaturization and
microminiaturization. These advantages, exercised during a period of
mixed polity, should be able to move the scientific, intentional microcommunity closer to that state of economic and political autarchy which
spells almost complete independence.

4. Because intentional communities of this type can have their own
press, theatre, radio and TV, and their own publishing facilities and
microfilm storage capacity, they will be in a position to encourage a
whole spectrum of opinion on all extra-local issues, an asset which is

being lost more and more in the bureaucratic, rigidly institutionalized conurbations of our time. As Mills has put it, we no longer have mass media of communication but only mass media of distraction. In intentional communities the mass media can provide information honestly and without *homogenizing* it, in Dwight Macdonald's sense of this term, so that different news items will also be presented humanely and with the perspectives and the varying emphases which they properly deserve. They will thus add another dimension of understanding to that achieved by free and open discussion on local issues. Thus through their dispassionate knowledgeability, such communities may be able to assume leadership roles in times of world crisis.

Undoubtedly some technical communications device will have to be employed to keep radio and television broadcasts from falling on the ears of possibly hostile elements outside such communities—elements which would be enraged at honest and open unmasking of the activities of vested interests and their selfish motivations. Corporate groups under fire might seek to retaliate against such intentional communities by arousing public sentiment against their continuation. Such risks, of course, should be minimized wherever possible. It would undoubtedly be fairly easy to develop devices which maintain rigid geographical boundaries for broadcasts, so that such a problem would, I think, present minimum difficulties.

5. Intentional communities will be free to experiment with new forms of marriage and the sexual relationship, provided that wisdom, maturity and self-control accompany the existing liberal outlook. This can be done if such communities can provide so great a variety of significant self-expression, that sexuality can be taken in stride, without becoming obsessive, as it does now in hypocritical, puritanical atmospheres, or compulsive, as it does today in the authority-rebellion of youth. Furthermore, if honesty in the sexual relationship is encouraged as an expression of honesty in community living, then we can expect that such communities will be willing to regard the support of children who were born, perhaps unexpectedly, out of wedlock, as a *community responsibility*—particularly where restraint and birth-control information makes the unplanned for birth an infrequent event. Bastardy, of course, will be unknown, as it is in Sweden. The possibilities for wise guidance of, and experimentation with, sexuality in the enlightened and humane intentional community, are unlimited, and this most important of human impulses will, perhaps, for the first time in history, be treated properly. A pluralism of choice in the sexual relationship can, perhaps, be encouraged institutionally, somewhat in the manner described by Aldous Huxley in his introduction to a very famous volume by Unwin.[2]

2 Joseph D. Unwin. *Hopousia or the Sexual and Economic Foundations of a New Society*. New York: Oskar Piest, 1940. 475 pp.

6. The scientific, intentional microcommunity will be the first modern community in a position to undertake research and development from the standpoint of its value to the consumer rather than its prospective profitability for a producer. This shift of attention from the profits standpoint to considerations of social welfare, will result in large measure in the pursuit of a different type of research problem. Such communities will be free of what we have now, where the first question regarding a new development is to ascertain the possible market for it, its possible competition and what it will cost to awaken consumer demand for it. Only years later do we recognize and admit the undesirable social consequences that a given development produced and worry about what can be done.

A reversal of this attitude is sure to follow in the intentional community. This reversal will take the form of first asking what effect a certain proposed development would have on the community *in the long run,* before time, energy, thought, money and skill are expended upon trying to achieve it. The reversal of attitude will also more likely take the form of asking what are the still as yet unfulfilled community needs and the still as yet unsolved community problems, and then focusing research energies on these. Such considerations are bound to shift the direction of research considerably, since we should be going from haphazard development and scientific serendipity to planned development. As a corollary to these considerations, we can expect that knowledgeable members of scientifically focused, intentional communities will spend a good deal of time, during the period of mixed polity, ransacking patent office literature and files for inventions which continue to accumulate the dust of time. These are inventions which, under a fierce type of industrial competitiveness, would not have been profitable, if commercially exploited. Sometimes, in contrast, they will have been unused due to interferences from patent pools, where they would have been *too profitable,* if commercially exploited by entrepreneurial newcomers, but which would have wiped out existing producers laboring under an antiquated technology. It would be of considerable value socially if the rights to such inventions could be purchased outright by an intentional community and if they could be exploited for communal purposes only. Thus the social significance of science, technology, invention, research and development are likely to be substantially different in the intentional community from what they are in megalopolis and cosmopolis whose faces are turned solely to free enterprise.

7. The social sciences are likely to come into their own in an intentional community in a way hardly envisaged by Zetterberg [3] in considering their applications to the modern, bureaucratic or industrial community.

[3] Hans L. Zetterberg. *Social Theory and Social Practice.* New York: The Bedminster Press, 1962. 190 pp.

The intentional community whose members are, by and large, suffused with the scientific attitude, is very likely to encourage research on questions which would be tabu in the standard community. It is also likely to encourage the use of types of data from within or without the intentional community, whose use would be forbidden by the modern, alienated, bureaucratic community which cannot afford to be honest about its own social pathology. The effects of such research, if they do not succeed in undermining the intentional communities, themselves, should succeed in undermining some of the horrible conditions in modern, corporate society which lead to social suffering and war. In fact, one of the best services which the intentional community can provide a suffering world, is to take the lead in basic social research and disseminate the results wherever they will do the most good socially, taking full advantage of freedom of the press, while it lasts. If such communities wish to escape the effects of outside wrath, they can eat their cake and have it too, by disseminating the results through individual and institutional contacts which are extra-local, and concealing its sources, thereby living to investigate again another day.

8. Although intentional communities are initially formed by individuals of more than average intellectual endowments, they will be among the first of our future communities to discharge properly our social obligations to those of average or less than average intellectual endowments. This they may do in several ways. First, they may conscientiously seek to develop improved techniques of programmed instruction for the average and less than average range in the distribution of human intelligence. Second, they may find improved ways, via pharmacological or surgical techniques, for offsetting tragic, intellectual statuses which have been produced by nature, herself. Third, they may solve the problem in a sense by avoiding it, through an advanced outlook which will permit genetic experiments on as yet unborn human beings, through exploitation of some of the many techniques suggested by the great biologist, Rostand.[4] Lessened public misunderstanding and a wider and more comprehensive social ethics, should result in a greater social toleration of experimentation in human genetics and a recognition of the desirability of man's controlling his own evolution.

Regardless of which techniques are adopted, the important point in this connection is that we can expect a more humane, fraternal and socially responsible attitude towards the less gifted, who are born into the intentional community. Research will, I feel certain, be conducted so as to find a satisfying place for them and, hopefully, an improvement of their intellectual status. In the dog-eat-dog world of the present this possibility does not exist and with the increasing social and industrial

---

[4] Jean Rostand. *Can Man be Modified?* New York: Basic Books, 1959. 105 pp.

complexity of our time, more and more of the ungifted are being disfranchised from any satisfactory place in our scheme of things and are being forced, as Goodman puts it, to grow up absurd. This disfranchisement is sure to blow up in our faces in the next decade or two, with ungifted youth finding that they have little that is worth anyone's money to buy—a point emphasized originally by Norbert Wiener. These are the young men and women who normally would have entered the work-force but who, under the impact of automation, other types of technology and the economic demands of an industrial management which is facing severe competition, find themselves at the end of the road before they have even begun their journey.

9. Where the intentional community has become an accepted world institution, the newer methodologies which are now ancillary to planning, can be used not only for industrial and national planning but for the special type of planning which will be needed by the scientific, intentional microcommunity. I am referring to the use of operations research, linear programming, activity analysis, general systems theory, simulation and computer technologies, administration and organization theory, game and information theory, etc. Because all modern communities are nodes in the corporate society, the application of these methods is largely confined to problems of scheduling, cost minimization, optimum distribution of inventory flows, best mixes of commodities, time and effort from a profits standpoint, and similar considerations. When, however, planning is total for a community which is fairly independent of the conditions of the corporate, host community, and when its expression is in terms of welfare functions, such as those so brilliantly treated by Rothenberg,[5] particularly in relation to what has come to be called the "condition of nondictatorship," then these methodologies will be working for a change towards the improvement of the quality of life.

At the present time these methodologies are devoted chiefly to the objectives of industrial, regional, and national planning, to helping underdeveloped countries find their economic places in the corporate sun, and to tightening the bureaucratic controls of modern organization men —controls which in the end often produce a good deal of the social pathology against whose excesses the intentional community is one answer. The planning required for the scientifically focused intentional community which seeks to improve the quality of life and the fund of personal choice and freedom, will surely involve types of problems to which these methods have not as yet been applied. When this occurs, however, I would guess that the social fruits of their applications will unquestionably be greater than they are now. At this time any one seeking to squeeze out of their applicability the social welfare type of objec-

[5] Jerome Rothenberg. *The Measurement of Social Welfare.* Englewood Cliffs, New Jersey: Prentice-Hall, 1961. 357 pp.

tive which these methods could help to achieve, is not likely to find a buyer. No seller of this "misdirected use" will currently find much enthusiasm for it. No one now has the independence for this sort of thing. However, that very independence in use and social profitability will, I believe, be guaranteed by the intentional community which puts human welfare above entrepreneural returns. The worst features of planning—when it is used for power and production rather than used for consumption and social welfare and runs the risk of turning into the diseased variety made explicit by Jewkes [6]—are likely to be avoided by a goal which sees to it that these new methodologies serve that improvement of the quality of life which is the basic concern of the intentional community.

10. Finally we come to a major value of the intentional community, namely, certain roles which it can play in staving off war. Where successful, intentional communities have a membership composition which is international in nature, as is the case currently with Philia,* they can serve as mediators in international legal and political conflicts short of war. Where their members have made themselves highly knowledgeable with respect to the issues involved, where they can furnish mediating committees containing no members who were originally from the countries in conflict, and where such communities, giving instructions to such mediating committees, represent about the most disinterested bodies one might find anywhere—no better source of adjudication can possibly be found. Such communities offering mediation, conciliation and arbitration services on a voluntary basis to the United Nations and other international bodies, can help considerably to lessen the threat of aggression and war, not only through these types of services but also through their ability to function as *disinterested* "peace agents" whose fairness and wisdom have gradually won for them an international fund of good will. The more such international, intentional communities exist and have been successfully able to settle international conflicts over important issues in a way which has been satisfying to all parties, the more likely will it be that they will be taken as models for emulation internationally. This would, of course, be all to the good.

In addition, one can encourage the formation of intentional communities of international composition by international exchange. By this I am referring to exchanges between such communities, whose membership is homogeneous with respect to national composition, in which they reciprocally take in contingents for substantial periods. This would, of course, have the effect of producing cross-fertilization with respect to the variety of meaning inherent in the phrase, "quality of life." Even more

---

[6] John Jewkes. *Ordeal by Planning.* New York: Macmillan, 1948. 248 pp.

* Philia was an intentional community that welcomed members from all countries. It was located on an island near New Zealand in the early Sixties.

importantly, such exchanges would probably result in permanent trans-fers, either because of a more appealing design for living or because of international marriage and family formation in which the individuals involved are already highly selected for their sensitivity, sense of com-munity, intelligence and social cooperativeness. Thus, apart from the use of the intentional community of international composition, as a source for adjudication in international conflict and apart from its use as a model to emulate and duplicate in social change-over during times of historical stress and crisis, it would provide one more advantage. It would increase the amount and quality in this world of what Allport calls ego-extension, that is, the capacity of the individual to identify with the values, interests, ideas, ideals, sentiments, attitudes and levels of aspira-tion, of other persons and other places. The importance of this lies in the fact that as the fund of ego-extension increases internationally, the psychological atmospheres conducive to aggression and war diminish accordingly.

During a period of mixed polity, there will also be many types of *interdependency* between corporate society and intentional community. Some of these interdependencies will be mentioned very briefly at this point.

1. In their *initial* stages scientific, intentional microcommunities will probably try to cushion their financial risks by selling surpluses of what-ever commodities they produce, to the larger corporate society. This will not basically involve a market dependency but rather a source of cash accumulation for the purchase of those types of producer goods with which their plans must continue, since such communities, by definition, *initially* possess no capital accumulation. By the same token, of course, members of such communities will initially be working part of the time in their host communities. In general, the foundation stage of the inland community will be quite different from its later stages and even more different from the foundation stage of a community which chooses an outlying island as a site.

2. Members of inland intentional communities will have two choices with respect to war and peace. They will either have to serve the host community militarily in time of war or assume the status of conscientious objectors and, if the experience of World War II can serve as a model, they will be forced to leave their experimental communities. In either case, for practical purposes, the social experimentation is at an end, since the intentional community requires both sustained peace and approxi-mately a 1:1 sex ratio. The result we have described is far less likely to happen to far-away island communities settled by citizens of a nation currently in conflict, if thermonuclear war has broken out. Inland com-munity members may also decide that the evil of military service up to the cessation of the anticipated short-term hostilities of the atomic age, is

worth the suspension of social experimentation, if there is a community to come back to.

3. While mixed polity continues to be the rule, members of intentional communities can avail themselves of the right to vote on issues affecting the host community or they can abstain if they see fit. Participation in voting, however, may subject them to subsequent retaliation in the form of political interference, if their vote is predominantly on the losing side. On the other hand, they may also lose some rights and equities via indifference on the part of the host community to some of their basic needs, like public services, perhaps. This can result even while they continue to pay taxes. It might occur, for instance, because such communities failed to exercise the franchise at all.

4. Intentional communities will initially have to use the currency of their host communities. This will, of course, subject them to the risk of inflation whose fundamental effect will be to raise the costs of initial financing.

5. Intentional communities seeking to buy patent rights will arouse more suspicion than any other group, be seen as more of a threat to the industrial sector of the host community (which, indeed, they will be) and can expect to be refused in some cases and forced to pay exorbitant costs or royalties in others. Difficulties with patent rights would, however, cause no basic hardship, for the role of machinery will, in any event, be limited in the intentional community. This limitation, together with the enlightened practise of birth control, will result in maintaining a better relation between man and nature, that is, between town and country, than might otherwise be obtained.

6. All necessary purchases from the existing corporate structure, during the period of mixed polity, is really exogenous demand on the host community. Such exogenous demand morally continues to support those activities and institutions against which the intentional community is rebelling in the first place. By the same token such economic transactions will also continue to support all the types of waste which are inherent in the structure of the host community. Moral secession, however, demands as its price, initial contradiction, and the intentional community gambles that such economic interdependencies can eventually be reduced to zero.

7. Intentional communities may find it hard to escape certain types of institutional service like those furnished by the post office, phone service, waste disposal, flood control, etc. Almost all such interdependencies can be eliminated in the later stages of their existence, however, if intentional communities take advantage of unusual uses of new forms of technology and bend them to these needs.

8. As we move toward one world in the senses of communication and distribution, we shall continue to have the larger relationships of nations, regions and, perhaps, continents, as well as, of course, world gov-

ernment. Certain interdependencies will therefore be unavoidable and scientific, intentional microcommunities will have to work out relationships of integration into each of these. In the distant future, however, if some of the larger geographical entities we have mentioned, can be made to consist of loose regional federations of intentional communities, based upon the principle of voluntary association, this would, perhaps, constitute an ideal change. The real difficulties in talking about geographical and political integration, based upon the principle of voluntary association, in a world consisting largely, if not wholly, of scientifically focused communities, is this. We cannot now foresee all those social needs which will be universal and whose satisfaction will be a mandatory task for a world of such communities. We must assume, however, that there will be a roster of such needs, even if that roster should consist only of curiosity and information desired about one another's activities. Certainly there will have to be pooling of effort, skill and responsibility with respect to such activities as space research, oceanography, the need to pool scientific and technical knowledge internationally, various indispensable commodities which require jointly supported sites of large-scale production, international travel, etc. In a world of such communities many of whose members will be truly enlightened, it will be recognized that activities requiring pooled effort may be defined as the areas of coercive participation in the work and responsibilities of the larger geographical units. Activity which involves coercive participation cannot be subject to the principle of voluntary association but the activities which can be defined as areas requiring coercive participation, cannot currently be laid down for future generations. Interdependencies of this sort, that is, interdependencies due to coercive participation, will, of course, remain permanent and must be accepted. Interdependencies of the dysgenic sort, however, as mentioned in point six, will hopefully vanish to zero.

## III. OVERVIEW

It should be noticed that I have felt this discussion should center about only one possibility for dealing with the fearful imbalances which have gripped the modern world. I have been concerned with a broad-gauge description of only one form of possible solution. The consideration which underlies the approach I have suggested here was best conveyed by Mills [7] who emphasized that it was our task continually to make new beginnings. In fact the spirit in which such new beginnings should be made is best expressed in his own words.

---

[7] C. Wright Mills. *The Causes of World War Three.* New York: Simon & Schuster, 1958. 172 pp.

We must release the human imagination, in order to open up a new exploration of the alternatives now possible for the human community; we must set forth general and detailed plans, ideas, visions; in brief, programs. We must transcend the mere exhortation of general principle and opportunist reactions. What are needed are commanding views of the future, and it is our opportunity and our task to provide them . . . (pp. 139–40).

Mills is but one of a small band of thinkers, like Riesman,[8] who recognize the social value of keeping alive a tradition of utopian thinking.

Because the alternative described here exists essentially in outline form, some very important details which would properly be of great interest to the intelligent reader and which would require extended discussion in a series of separate papers, have not been dealt with. This omission, of course, is perfectly proper in the present context. It should be appropriate, however, to list seriatim some of these concerns which would be of major significance in making a fresh start. This we shall now do.

The scientific, intentional microcommunity (SIMC) will have to solve the following problems sooner or later, and preferably before making its beginnings.

1. Some research will have to be undertaken on the *optimum size of population* appropriate to different designs for living and different types of technology which it is planned to employ, if the objective is to achieve democratic polity, self-actualization, organic relatedness, and freedom from the ills to which we now, ourselves, are heir.

2. Some thought will have to be expended on a definition of an "appropriate standard of living" in relation to the technology to be employed and institutions to be developed. This standard of living, however, *is not to be defined* either in terms of Goodman's [9] *minimum subsistence* or Rowntree's [10] *minimum adequate standard of living.*

3. A whole new science, in effect, will have to be developed, which will be concerned with both the varieties of plans and the varieties of planning methods, which are appropriate for SIMC.

4. Problems will have to be solved which center about the renewal of resources in the later stages of SIMC and, if it should be necessary to purchase some of these, the manner of providing accumulated funds which can be drawn upon to do so.

[8] See the following: David Riesman. "Some Observations on Community Plans and Utopia." 70–98. This is Chapter 5 of *Individualism Reconsidered and Other Essays.* Glencoe, Illinois: The Free Press, 1954. 529 pp. Although this chapter is wholly devoted to a review and criticism of the volume, *Communitas,* by the Goodmans, Riesman makes clear in section iv of this chapter, his stand on utopian thinking.

[9] Percival and Paul Goodman. *Communitas. Means of Livelihood and Ways of Life.* New York: Vintage Books, 1960. 248 pp.

[10] Seebohm B. Rowntree. *The Human Needs of Labour.* London: Nelson and Sons, 1918. 168 pp.

5. Ideas will have to be developed for determining the different types of *agrindustry* appropriate both to the design for living which has been chosen, the technologies which are to be employed and the scale of production and consumption which will be relevant to SIMC. Originality of thought will be needed for planning a variety of balanced ecologies between man, natural community resources and available and relevant technologies.[11]

6. The possible use of technologies for exploiting the resources in sea-water piped into SIMC, where these are located not too far from the littoral, will have to be explored.

7. Some advance decisions will have to be made by SIMC on the proper uses of leisure, in terms which will be as penetrating as those of de Grazia.[12] Goodman [13] has very roughly estimated that if the standard of living is a subsistence one, an individual would have to spend anywhere from one year in 4 or 5 to one year in 10, in working on behalf of the community. Since SIMC will assume a high but unexcessive standard of living, these ratios will probably become larger but, perhaps, not too much so. SIMC will, in fact, be the pilot models of the future, in which the perils with which leisure is fraught in mass society, may be overcome by discovery of mature and humane uses to which it should be put. The dangers in the misuse of leisure have recently been emphasized by Gabor [14] according to newspaper report, and the uses to which he feels it should be put, apply to the corporate society. The uses to which it must be put in the SIMC of the future, remain to be worked out, in much the same imaginative vein that was exercised by Morris.[15]

11 An illuminating and nontechnical orientation to possibilities in this direction and in relation to many other items which should be of proper concern to SIMC, has already aroused widespread general interest. I am referring to the following work: Harrison Brown's *The Challenge of Man's Future*. New York: The Viking Press, 1954. 290 pp.

12 Sebastian de Grazia. *Of Time, Work & Leisure*. New York: The Twentieth Century Fund, 1962. 559 pp.

13 Percival and Paul Goodman. *Op. Cit.*

14 I am referring here to an AP dispatch of March 18, 1963, quoting Denis Gabor, 63-year-old professor of applied electronic physics at London University. In his book, *Inventing the Future* (London: Secker & Warburg, 1963, 231 pp.), according to the dispatch story, Gabor discusses the perils which await mankind at the prospect of unbounded human leisure, as a result of the taking over of almost all labor, by advanced forms of technology. Without going into all the points mentioned in the AP story, I feel that what must be emphasized here is that probably a global institution in the form of SIMC has the best chance of working out successful and rational adjustments to the problems surrounding unbounded leisure. For a suggestive picture of how an island SIMC will probably have to deal *in part* with this problem, see the following work. Frederick J. Grew's *Wealth and the Common Man*. New York: Wisdom Library, 1959. 184 pp.

15 William Morris. *News From Nowhere*. New York: Longmans, Green & Co., 1901. 278 pp.

8. SIMC will have to solve problems connected with the utilization of energy and power sources *on a small scale,* e. g., the possible use of solar energy.

9. Some methods will have to be worked out in SIMC for the proper evaluation of personal services in relation to individual consumption schedules. Corollary to this will be the task of working out a judicious and propitious division of *political and cultural responsibility* among members of SIMC and equitable methods of rotating these responsibilities.

10. SIMC will continually have to devote time to changing, and usually expanding, the meaning of the phrase "quality of life," as its members take advantage of ever-new and appropriate changes in science, technology, invention, culture and education, which can be favorably adapted to their ways of life. This may mean occasional community redesign, in a physical sense as well as in an economic one.

11. For all SIMC, agreement upon the areas of social relations within the community which are properly coercive or noncoercive, will be subject to constant modification.

12. All SIMC will have to work out in detail proper relations between themselves and their host communities. For densely populated host communities, SIMC may have to reconcile themselves initially to bringing the public services provided by the host community into the intentional community, paying for these, and gambling that they will not be an open door to interference with their social experimentation.

13. SIMC will usually be able to develop surplus production. Since, by definition, they will be producing primarily for use (consumption) and not for profit, all surpluses can be sold and the revenues used for expanding the quality of life in various ways. However, to continue to do this results in simulating the marketing activities of host communities, an activity to be avoided in the *later stages* of development of SIMC. The principle of an "ever normal granary" will also make little sense in the socioeconomic atmosphere of a technologically efficient, intentional community. Thus decisions will have to be made with regard to the dispositions of such surpluses in the later stages of the community's development. One such socially intelligent decision would be to provide other struggling SIMC with these surpluses, in the initial stages of *their* development. The principle of *mutual aid* should be a *sine que non* for all SIMC.

14. SIMC will have to develop plans for avoiding the horrible, social (this word should, properly speaking, be "unsocial") costs of private enterprise as these have been described, for instance, by Kapp,[16] Carson [17]

---

[16] William S. Kapp. *The Social Costs of Private Enterprise.* Cambridge, Massachusetts: Harvard University Press, 1950. 287 pp.

[17] Rachel Carson. *Silent Spring.* Boston: Houghton Mifflin, 1962. 368 pp.

and Herber,[18] to name a few representative critics. They will also, as a corollary to this, have to strike socially reasonable attitudes towards idle plant capacity.

15. Educational goals in all SIMC will have to move in directions aimed at avoiding the worst features of *mass society*, as these have now been aptly described in a voluminous literature on the subject.

16. Some groups of individuals, interested in SIMC, may wish to devote energy, educational effort and years of lobbying, in trying to get moral support for and interest in their ventures, from the general public. Many such groups, with clear-cut community plans and designs for living, may wish to lobby for financial support from the United Nations and other international bodies, from philanthropical foundations and other public-spirited agencies, from financially able religious groups, etc. In general, I believe it would be best for groups interested in founding SIMC, to stand on their own resources only, regardless of how difficult their subsequent struggles may be.

17. All SIMC will have to make use of a variety of educational and psychological techniques, such as operant learning and conditioning procedures, for ensuring a type of altruistic character-structure in the developing young. Such a character-structure will be a necessity if we wish to realize the ideals of community and undo the unsocial impulses and egocentric, behavior patterns which are rewarded by corporate society. In addition, SIMC will have to recognize that different temperaments correspond to different ways of life, in the sense described by Charles Morris,[19] so that the quality of life offered by a community will, to some degree, have to cater to these broad differences in temperament. This will mean, of course, an internal pluralism. Community specialization along these lines would be impossible, since no one can predict the modes of living which will be congenial to the as-yet unborn children of the community.

The focus of attention for most SIMC will be once again—in contrast with modern corporate society—to put the emphasis on the quality of life, on a plurality of modes of social existence, on organic personal relatedness, personal development and rationality, on limited but mature consumption patterns, economic and political decentralization and last, but certainly not least, the possibility of eventual reduction of aggression and the winning of a lasting peace. On the negative side—and this is almost of equal importance—all SIMC will seek to avoid the social pathology of the corporate West, which is perhaps most pithily described in the words of C. Wright Mills.[20]

18 Lewis Herber. *Our Synthetic Environment*. New York: Knopf, 1962. 285 pp.
19 Charles Morris. *Varieties of Human Value*. Chicago: University of Chicago Press, 1956. 209 pp.
20 C. Wright Mills. *Op. Cit.*

Were we to welcome the extension of our current industrialization to the world as a whole, we would simply be allowing the social and psychological evils which have thus far accompanied it, to be reflected on a grander scale. It is about time that the rich plethora of scientific findings which have accumulated for centuries, be put to work for us. Such a change is long overdue. The sociotechnical mistakes of humanity's pre-scientific past and the social and personal tragedy and suffering they have caused when science has been used in a haphazard fashion, are no longer necessary. With a more enlightened concept of community, in which we strive to exploit the findings of science primarily for human and humane ends, there need be no limit to the possibilities for human and social improvement. We need more widespread recognition of the correctness of C. Wright Mills' conviction that the utopian way

. . . is now the only adequate way to think about world politics and the human condition . . . and the only realistic way to work seriously as intellectuals for the conditions of peace. (p. 94).

# SUMMARY OF PART V

Clearly if men are going to depend increasingly in the future on bending science and technology to aid them in the achievement of authentic forms of communal expression, then it behooves us to formulate a social philosophy for an age of technology. This we have tried to do in the *Epilogue*. A social philosophy for an age of technology may then serve as a guidepost for turning human ingenuity, in the form of science, technology and invention, to the service of the best qualities of the human spirit and the facilitation of community life which is morally, socially, and culturally appealing. In this way we can prevent technology from dictating its own imperatives so that men live for the artifacts they have created instead of bending these to the human spirit. It is only through a social philosophy for an age of technology that we can prevent the sorcerer's broom from getting out of hand. It is only through such a social philosophy that our apprenticeship to social mismanagement can be terminated.

# 31

*Epilogue:*
## Social Philosophy for an
## Age of Technology*

### I. THE TRUE TASKS OF SOCIAL PHILOSOPHY

There are six archetypal relationships which give an almost complete description of the human condition, that is to say, it is within these six archetypes that the goals of men must be formulated, that social structures and processes must be striven for and that regulative, social principles must be recommended. These six basic archetypal relationships are: (1) man's relationship to himself, (2) the relationship of the sexes to each other, (3) man's relationship to his fellow-man, (4) man's relationship to society, (5) man's relationship to work or leisure, and (6) man's relationship to Nature. The true task of social philosophy, in an age in which science and technology set the framework for human action, is to posit a social order which will try to guarantee a satisfying quality to each of these relationships for most and, hopefully, all men. But inasmuch as both the promises and the frustrations of science and technology are changing all the time, we should really speak of the true task of social philosophy as that of postulating *those alternative social orders* which can potentially provide a satisfying quality to these relationships.

The task of a technologically based social philosophy, whose practitioners are familiar with the technological promise of the age, is then, in a general sense, twofold. First, such a social philosophy must set forth the many alternative designs for living, that is, the various ways of life which can be expected to fulfil each of these archetypal relationships. These designs for living, however, must be achievable within the framework of our existing technology. Second, such a social philosophy must suggest an over-all structure of social existence, that is, an over-all

* Chapter 31, with adaptations and modifications, has been taken from the following source: Henry Winthrop. "The Archetypes of Human Concern." *Systematics* (Great Britain). Vol. 3, 1966, 334–360.

philosophy of community, which will juxtapose these archetypal themes into a consistent and mutually reinforcing pattern. The quest for community in an age in which science and technology are the piper and call the tune, can no longer be separated from the landscape of human discovery which stretches from the files of the patent office to the latest "brainstorm" of an excited team of scientific workers in some research and development laboratory.

In order, however, for a scientific and a technological base to serve the archetypal relationships we have already mentioned, two considerations are of major importance. The first of these is that we must possess some general understanding of each of the basic archetypal relations which normatively define the human condition. The second is that we have to achieve an understanding of the *technologies of coordination* by which the social institutions and modalities attempting to fulfill the basic, archetypal relationships, are knit into a consistent and mutually reinforcing pattern. The second of these considerations involves some understanding of the strategems of social and economic planning and, although I am not going to invoke the science of planning in any form in this chapter, it should not be overlooked that a social philosophy in modern dress *must understand* to some extent the art of knitting together the institutional modes by which men try to achieve satisfactory expression and fulfilment of the six archetypal relationships already mentioned. A wrong weave can abort the best laid plans of mice and men. Having taken due notice then of these two considerations, let us return to the heart of the present chapter—namely, the task of providing an understanding of each of the archetypal relationships—an understanding which should be regarded as the proper underpinning of a modern social philosophy.

## II. THE ARCHETYPAL RELATIONSHIPS
## OF SOCIAL PHILOSOPHY

### Man's Relationship to Himself

If men are at war with themselves, if they cannot govern themselves and if they do not really know what are their true identities, then the quest for community is purposeless. This is because the quest for community is predicated upon the ideal assumption that we can have an organically related collection of men each of whom knows who he is and what constitutes his proper direction and each of whom strives for a determinate budget of meaning in that flicker between eternities which we call "our lives." This is the reason why self-knowledge takes on importance for a social philosophy. In order for men to achieve an appropriate "I–Thou" relationship— about which we shall have something to say shortly—each man must be a clear-cut "I" and a clear-cut "Thou" to his neighbour. A modern social philosophy, then, must plump for a social order which makes clear self-knowledge and firm self-direction possible.

From the psychologist's standpoint such a social order must guarantee what Maslow [1] calls "self-actualization," that is, must guarantee the fulfilment of all the native potentialities of each man or woman—potentialities which can be seen early enough in most people to be nurtured and promoted by others. From a sociologist's standpoint such a social order must provide institutions which furnish the individual a maximum of personal freedom and, in the present context, I am employing the word "freedom" to mean the largest possible number of choices that can be made available to achieve individual goals. From both a psychological and a sociological standpoint, a social order which makes it its business to provide a satisfying quality to man's relationship to himself, is a social order which will minimize the degree of self-alienation which can threaten to overwhelm the individual. Self-alienation has been a major concern of a stream of writing characteristic of the twentieth century—a stream of writing which has given rise to a tradition emphasizing the nightmarish effects on the human soul of uncritical industrialization, rampant urbanization and overidolized bureaucratization. Mills,[2] in sociology, Fromm [3] in psychology, Ortega y Gasset [4] in philosophy and the humanities, and the Josephsons [5] on a somewhat more interdisciplinary canvas, are just a few of the critics who have recognized the disastrous and degrading effects which alienation can have upon the quest for community.

Thus, from the standpoint of the concepts of "self-actualization," "freedom" and "self-alienation," a social philosophy in modern dress must suggest a social order which will help man and woman to achieve satisfying content to this archetypal relationship. Realism demands that such a social philosophy be properly acquainted with those areas in psychology which pursue inquiries concerning those factors—particularly social ones—which promote and maintain the self-concept. Without such knowledge no social philosophy can suggest a social fabric which will not threaten to come apart at the seams. If, in the words of Bacon [6] but in a sense he never intended, the function of social philosophy is "to give out a dream of our own imagination for a pattern of the world," then that pattern must contain the promise of fulfilment for the ancient, Socratic injunction "Know thyself."

1 Abraham H. Maslow. *Motivation and Personality*. New York: Harper, 1964. 411 pp.

2 C. Wright Mills. *The Sociological Imagination*. New York: Oxford University Press, 1959. 234 pp.

3 Erich Fromm. *The Sane Society*. New York: Rinehart, 1955. 370 pp.

4 José Ortega y Gasset. *Man and People*. New York: W. W. Norton, 1957. 272 pp.

5 Eric and Mary Josephson (editors). *Man Alone. Alienation in Modern Society*. New York: Dell, 1962. 592 pp.

6 Francis Bacon. *The Great Instauration: The Plan of the Work*, 1620. Reprinted in *Selected Writings of Francis Bacon* (with an introduction and notes by Hugh G. Dick). New York: Modern Library, 1955. See pages 439–451.

### One's Relationship to the Opposite Sex

Historically in most cultures, woman has been both exploited and mis-understood—exploited not only because she is weaker but even more as a result of the shackles of time, and misunderstood because man tends to expect the same reactional biographies from women as he does from members of his own sex. If he allows for differences he often superciliously assumes these to be only native elements of irrationality in woman that the male must put up with in return for the pleasures, blessings and benefits woman can give. These irrationalities, however, have histor-ically been the only way in which woman as an institutionally helpless slave, could show displeasure. They need not be a proper part of the psychosexual persona of the female. In spite of a tendency among un-critical and extreme behaviourists to assume that men and women are psychosexual blank tablets upon which sexual differences in a psycho-logical sense are impressed as roles, there is abundant evidence of sexual differences which are rooted in nature rather than nurture. Such evidence has been impressively collated by Scheinfeld.[7] These differences should be understood and when it comes to comprehending them, the question of whether one assumes that psychosexual differences are wholly a result of nature, wholly a result of social conditioning or the result of some mixture of both of these, is not important in the present context. It also makes little difference that by any conventional, Western definition of femininity, some men are psychologically more feminine than the average woman and some women are psychologically more masculine than the average man. The really important consideration in the present con-nection is that a social philosophy realistically rooted in a knowledge of biology and psychology, must champion a social order in which the rela-tionship of man and woman must be mutually satisfying and eminently fair. This will not occur unless we understand the nature of woman, and if we give her situation priority over that of the male, when discussing the relationship of the sexes, this is because historically she has been the more injured of the two.

To achieve a satisfying relationship between the sexes, *personhood* must be emphasized in both sexes and given precedence over achieved masculinity and achieved femininity. *Personhood* is so totally different a concept from *manhood* or *womanhood* that few people understand this and fewer still are prepared to face up to its implications. To do the concept of "personhood" justice would require a volume in itself. Here let us adumbrate what we intend by noting ever so briefly that "person-hood" refers to qualities of mind, heart, and spirit, to the effective moral

[7] Avram Scheinfeld. *Men and Women.* New York: Harcourt, Brace and World, 1944. 453 pp.

calibre and the degree of fellow-feeling of a subject. Personhood is concerned with that kind of individuality which springs from authenticity and an honest conception of the self, in contrast with a self defined in terms of role and social expectation. Traditionally the need for *personhood* in both sexes has rarely risen to the level of consciousness.

The so-called "wiles of woman" constitute the behavioural repertoire by which an institutionally imprisoned subject gets her way from a master and captor. Historically this master and captor has tended to look upon her as mistress, wife, mother and, hopefully, as suffering silent partner in adversity and as blissful and not so silent partner when fortune smiles on him.

The so-called selfishness and impetuosity of the overbearing male is really the reaction we get when the insecure lord of the manor discovers to his chagrin that his junior partner has all the time been leading him around by the nose. The male asserts his prerogative over woman as mistress and wife in return for his role of caretaker of the ménage. The female asserts her right to be taken care of for her sexual and morale-building favours—the payoff function, as it were. With such traditional attitudes both sexes tend to exploit one another and being a person means only being a "good man" or a "good woman." When men and women can look upon one another as persons and when personhood is either more important than or, at least, coequal with manhood and womanhood, then and only then, will we begin to move towards a more satisfying and more just relationship between the sexes. The achievement of such a desired relationship in this most fundamental archetype should be the first order of business for a social philosophy which takes its responsibilities seriously.

Women who resent rather than think through the historical basis of their unjust position, attack the archetypal male image when the male is as much a psychological victim of historical accident as is woman. It would be pointless, however, for a mature social philosophy to encourage this. For a social philosopher to insist on woman being treated as the equal of man—and to mean by this only the achievement of the right to the same selfish privileges man now enjoys—would be absurd. Yet this is the type of blunder which runs as an obsession throughout the work of such a protestant as Betty Friedan.[8] To seek to wipe out differences which may be native, as Simone de Beauvoir [9] often seems on the verge of doing, would be equally irrelevant to the task at hand. To cultivate the mordant quip, the squelch which deflates and the castrating sally which disarms, as does Mary McCarthy,[10] is to act as though "getting even" psychosexually will improve the relationship of the sexes—which is an

8 Betty Friedan. *The Feminine Mystique*. New York: Dell, 1963. 384 pp.
9 Simone de Beauvoir. *The Second Sex*. New York: Bantam Books, 1961. 705 pp.
10 Mary McCarthy. *A Charmed Life*. New York: Dell, 1958. 288 pp.

assumption even more absurd than the others. All that such an approach is likely to result in, is an increase in spinsters.

Woman, of course, is more tempted to strike off along irrational and rampaging paths to redress the historical imbalance between male and female rights, precisely because she is the more exploited of the two. There is a vast literature which attests to this fact of which the work of Wylie,[11] Farnham and Lundberg,[12] and Dingwall [13] are examples in point. The real answer, of course, to the problem of how to redress the historical imbalance between the sexes and how to create the conditions for personhood for both men and women, is the formulation of a social philosophy appropriate to the age. Such a social philosophy must suggest in detail the attributes of a social order that will produce conditions which conspire towards this end. This must be a social philosophy which can formulate both formal and informal educational ideals, plans, curricula and methods which make personhood rewarding, without detracting from those ideals of manhood and womanhood which a society is disposed to hold in high esteem. This is a task to which any serious social philosophy worthy of the name, must devote itself. The effort involved will be Sisyphean in nature but the result—an archetypal relationship between the sexes which is conducive to the happiness and effectiveness of both—will be of immeasurable social value over the course of time.

## Man's Relationship to Man

Of all the fundamental, archetypal relationships, this is the one which, above all the others, must be satisfactorily fulfilled in order to achieve a sense of community. In fact the achievement of community may be operationally defined as ideally the creation of a reported, mutually satisfactory relationship among men for every pair of subjects who have occasion to relate to one another in more than a casual fashion. Many things can be said about the relationship of man to man but this relationship can come, so to speak, in the large-size package or the small-size package. These picturesque phrases refer to the fact that there are two generic forms which characterize this archetype—forms which the philosopher Buber [14] describes as the "I–Thou" relationship and the "I–It" relationship, or which the psychologist Maslow [15] describes as "B-Love" and "D-Love." Discriminations of this sort refer to the fact that men may either treat each other as persons and behave so as to reinforce that

---

[11] Philip Wylie. *Generation of Vipers*. New York: Pocket Books, 1955. 312 pp.

[12] Marynia Farnham and Ferdinand Lundberg. *Modern Woman: The Lost Sex.* New York: Harper, 1947. 497 pp.

[13] Eric John Dingwall. *The American Woman*. New York: Rinehart, 1956. 309 pp.

[14] Martin Buber. *I and Thou*. New York: Charles Scribner's Sons, 1958. 137 pp.

[15] Abraham H. Maslow. *Towards a Psychology of Being*. Princeton, New Jersey: Van Nostrand, 1962. 214 pp.

personhood, or they may treat each other as objects and behave so as to use each other to satisfy unrequited needs. When the former attitude is present in ourselves, the process of self-actualization is promoted and reinforced in those to whom we relate. When the latter attitude character- izes our posture, every form of spiritual atrophy by which men disengage themselves from one another psychologically, sets in. These forms of disengagement include many types of alienation, anomie, depersonaliza- tion and dehumanization. Alienation and anomie do not require defini- tion but, perhaps, the concepts of depersonalization and dehumanization need some slight expression here. In depersonalization, people glory in making themselves interchangeable with one another as a result of culti- vating the same roles, postures, habits, attitudes, sentiments, rituals, and religious mimesis. By dehumanization we refer to the effects on ourselves of egocentric impulses such as overweening ambition, pride, material cupidity, lust, the pursuit of power, etc. Dehumanization sets in when we conspire to obtain these by wounding others, depriving them of their rights as human beings, ruthlessly destroying their reputations, frustrat- ing their needs, and preventing them from realizing their potentialities. Dehumanization is also reflected when individuals try to manipulate others as objects to serve their own ends, when they chronically fail to assess the consequences of their imperious behaviour for others, when they remain indifferent to suffering which does not touch them immedi- ately, etc.

Above all, however, the archetypal relationship of man to man is concerned with the meaning of human love, with *agape,* and with all that it takes to support the being and potentialities of others. This, of course, has been the objective on this side of Paradise, of all the great religions. It has been that part of their content which is not preoccupied with other- worldliness, salvation and an after-life. In an effort both to understand and to produce love between man and man we have, perhaps, the most central concern of community. Where this concern focuses upon both the cognitive and the emotional modes of relating to others—and by the emo- tional modes of relationship we refer to socially desirable forms of empa- thy and sympathy—we find men preoccupied with the true meaning of the religious impulse. In fact the term "religion" comes from the Latin "religare"—"to bind together"—and refers to all those sentiments and feelings which will either promote a unity between man and his Maker, that is, the powers of Nature, or promote unity and understanding among men, themselves. Where the concern with human love focuses only or chiefly upon the *cognitive element* in the relationship of man to man, either we obtain the legalistic approach as contrasted with the prophetic approach—the legalistic approach which is so characteristic of Judaic learning and the tradition of the rabbinical commentary—or we obtain the *traditional enterprise* known as social philosophy.

The weakness of the philosophical enterprise known as social philosophy, lies precisely in this defect. An alleged concern with the relationship of man to man is meaningless without the presence of the necessary existentialist biases in terms of "Sorge" or care, commitment, involvement, and engagement. The achievement of a satisfying quality in the relationship of man to man is impossible unless individuals act authentically rather than in terms of role-expectations. We cannot, in fact, speak of a relationship unless two people seek a genuine encounter, that is, seek really to know one another at their respective, vital centres. The phrase, "a genuine encounter" is to be contrasted with the existentially absurd activity of signalling to each other in the form of social gamesmanship, as this has been described by the psychiatrist, Berne.[16]

The traditional forms of speculation in social philosophy lack this needed existentialist bias and therefore, when social philosophers have talked about the need for brotherhood and the need of love for one's fellow-man, their exhortations have tended to have a hollow ring, not because of any error in analysis but rather because fellow-feeling cannot be aroused merely by what Morris [17] calls *designative-informative* and *formative–informative* discourse. Fellow-feeling may be aroused by hortatory types of discourse, by personal example which is a symbolic form of hortatory discourse and by the moving power of great works in the arts and in letters, which are examples of hortatory metaphor and simile in the service of man. Above all, fellow-feeling is aroused by forms of religious discourse, which are not merely the empty, verbal shells of social altruism but which, instead, carry that ring of existentialist sincerity and emotional resonance which will bring out the best in others. The tuning-up of sympathy and emotional understanding is essential precisely because it promotes *identification* with the plight and the needs of others.

This is why I feel safe in saying that a social philosophy which has been updated for an age of science and technology, will not only stress the need to be informed of the means man has at hand for achieving his social ends, but even more, will recognize the need to move men in other dimensions than the strictly cognitive. These other dimensions must include—in addition to an effective analysis of the human condition and the construction of interpretive fictions for a philosophy of community—those types of moving and concrete personal appeal and those types of persuasion which move men to achieve the finest fruits of social altruism. The arousal of fellow-feeling must be achieved through hortatory discourse of every sort, from art to religion, from allegory to symbol, and

---

[16] Eric Berne. *Games People Play. The Psychology of Human Relationships.* New York: Grove Press, 1964. 192 pp.

[17] Charles Morris. *Signs, Language and Behaviour.* New York: George Braziller, 1955. 365 pp.

from mild concern to flaming passion, if need be—but a passion which is always well-tempered by intelligence and good will.

All of the preceding become vital necessities in achieving a satisfying quality in the relationship of man to man because without this satisfactory archetype it is meaningless to talk about the quest for community. Saint Augustine's City of God, the dreams of a Utopian and even the average American's more prosaic vision of good government—all depend upon an improvement in the relationship of man to man. Even more they depend upon implementing this relationship by means of every institutional, psychological, educational, technological and cultural device which will encourage men to be their brothers' keepers or, in more mundane and actuarial terms, will prompt men to underwrite the guaranteed fulfilment of one another's potentialities. The quest for community must be the central task of a reborn and renovated social philosophy. *Gemeinschaft* or true community rests almost solely on the quality of the relationship of man to man. This is why, although the dreams of reason are important in social philosophy, a millenial vision of fellow-feeling and a grasp of what the emotional quality of brotherhood should truly be like, are even more important. When the millenial vision is sound, a social philosophy can be developed which will be such a union of heart and mind as to exceed in appeal the most rationally designed of human communities—where these reflect insufficiently other dimensions of man's being. And so in the quest for social order, social justice and social concern and in the effort to achieve a balance between freedom and authority, a responsible social philosophy must make the perfecting of the relationship of man to man, one of its most central concerns.

## Man's Relationship to Society

I now wish to concern myself with the negative side of the human community—that aspect of human trial and tribulation which results when a true sense of community has been frustrated. This sense of social frustration is the concern of a literature of social protest and social criticism which rejects those haphazard forms of achieved community in the world today, which are the result of the historical accidents of a rampant industrialization, an unchecked urbanization and an increasing bureaucratization of modern life. In our time this literature has emphasized—often passionately—the blighting effects upon individuality which have been produced by megalopolis and by the alienating characteristics which go with megalopolis. Voices of dissent have been raised against the unnecessary suffering and frustration caused by institutional and corporate bigness, and various forms of reaction against these forms of social pathology have been suggested. The conventional type of protest takes the form of advocating remedial measures within the social framework already achieved, usually in terms of new legislation and the development of new institutions to meet unfulfilled needs, or the liquidation of certain institutions to get rid of unwanted evils.

Less popular forms of protest bid for the allegiance of the individual to ideologies which seemingly make a complete break with the democratic *status quo.* These forms generally reflect either a reliance on some philosophical justification of Fascist totalitarianism, an eschatological plea for the support of some version of Marxism-Leninism, or a not too militant advocacy of some form of democratic socialism, as in India. Still other forms of philosophic protest envision salvation from the corporate pathology of the West in terms of some decentralist vision, such as those which move Röpke,[18] Mumford [19] or Borsodi,[20] or in terms of the construction of intentional communities, such as those sketched by the Goodmans,[21] Bishop [22] or Winthrop.[23] In contrast with the decentralist dreams of our age we have many who look forward to a variety of types of world government, such as those described by Wagar.[24] There are still other dreams of social salvation, such as those of technocracy, the plans for Demintry, or the democratic integration of industry, as described by Hills,[25] the description of an economy in which human labour is no longer necessary, now being explored by Theobald,[26] and many other dreams and plans too numerous to mention here. It matters not what vision one regards as the road to social and political salvation. The important point is that those who are discontent with the *status quo,* with society as they currently find it spread before them, must take some posture *now* towards a world they never made. Such people will always be marginal to their societies. What shall that posture be?

Historically, marginality has been frequently expressed in terms of socialism, anarchism and nihilism, such as was characteristic of Russian intellectuals under the Czar. Sometimes it is expressed in the form of

[18] Wilhelm A. Röpke. *A Humane Economy. The Social Framework of the Free Market.* Chicago: Henry Regnery, 1960. 312 pp.

[19] Lewis Mumford. *Technics and Civilization.* New York: Harcourt, Brace and World, 1963. 495 pp.

[20] Ralph Borsodi. *Education and Living.* Melbourne, Florida: Melbourne University Press, 1948. 2 vols. 719 pp.

[21] Percival and Paul Goodman. *Communitas. Means of Livelihood and Ways of Life.* New York: Vintage Books, 1960. 248 pp.

[22] Claire Huchet Bishop. *All Things Common.* New York: Harper, 1950. 274 pp.

[23] Henry Winthrop. "Some Proposals Towards Experiments in Peaceful and Non-Competitive Living." *Darshana International.* Vol. IV, No. 2, April, 1964. 74–97.

[24] W. Warren Wagar. *The City of Man. Prophecies of a World Civilization in Twentieth-Century Thought.* Boston: Houghton Mifflin, 1963. 310 pp.

[25] Christopher B. Hills. *Demintry. The Democratic Co-Ownership of Industry.* Mimeographed separate. 9 pp. (Obtainable from the author by writing to 101 Harbour Street, Kingston, Jamaica, W.I.).

[26] Robert Theobald. *Free Men and Free Markets.* New York: Clarkson N. Potter, 1963. 203 pp.

social withdrawal, such as that which characterized the flight of the painter Gauguin to Tahiti. A safer posture has been that of *youthful Bohemianism* which allowed the protestant to enjoy whatever benefits he could safely capture without effort from the bourgeois society of his time, while sniping at that sane society from the sidelines. The most recent form of marginality of this type has been the philosophy of the Beats, that nondescript group which Lipton [27] has called "The Holy Barbarians." In contrast to these two forms of Bohemianism—which is regarded only as a harmless eccentricity—we have the more unpopular posture of *youthful radicalism* in which a certain amount of Bohemian unconventionality is permitted as an accompaniment, however, to the *more central pursuit of* social justice, an open rejection of social hypocrisy and often a passionate parroting of ill-digested, intellectual credos.

In the 30's—when a non-affluent society provided a social justification for the existence of youthful radicals—there was a distinct difference between Bohemianism and radicalism. The Bohemians then were satisfied if they had a basement for a pad. The radicals, however, could satisfy their enormous appetites only by trying to take over the whole world for their pad. The most respectable form of marginality, however, has always been intellectual and consists of a systematic indictment of the current social fabric. In these indictments a social philosophy is sometimes explicitly formulated or implicitly invoked. More often the *status quo* is criticized but no constructive social and institutional forms are suggested as substitutes. So numerous are the forms of these indictments and so varied are their scope, that it would be impossible even to begin to do them justice by the mere mention of them here. Suffice to say, for illustrative purposes only, we would include such critiques as those of Fromm,[28] Seidenberg,[29, 30] Ortega y Gasset,[31] Mumford [32] and Northrop.[33]

The point of all the preceding is that the social philosopher has to recommend a social stance which is to be regarded as an alternative to the existing forms of society which he rejects. Such a recommendation

27 Lawrence Lipton. *The Holy Barbarians.* New York: Grove Press, 1959. 318 pp. This is one of the better studies of the *Beat Generation.*

28 Erich Fromm. *Beyond the Chains of Illusion. My Encounter with Marx and Freud.* New York: Simon & Schuster, 1962. 182 pp.

29 Roderick Seidenberg. *Post-Historic Man. An Inquiry.* Boston: Beacon Press, 1957. 246 pp.

30 Roderick Seidenberg. *Anatomy of the Future.* Chapel Hill, North Carolina: The University of North Carolina Press, 1961. 173 pp.

31 José Ortega y Gasset. *The Modern Theme.* New York: Harper, 1961. 152 pp.

32 Lewis Mumford. *The Transformations of Man.* New York: Collier Books, 1962. 188 pp.

33 F. S. C. Northrop. *Philosophical Anthropology and Practical Politics. A Prelude to War or to Just Law.* New York: Macmillan, 1960. 384 pp.

then becomes, willy-nilly, the proposed optimum relationship of man to society. The social philosopher may, of course, advocate one of the existing ideologies we have already mentioned or one of the more limited forms of social protest to which I have already referred. He may, on the contrary, prefer the path of reform from within—which he takes to be practical—or he may feel duty-bound to limit himself intellectually to certain forms of social criticism. Nor should we overlook the fact that he may be an activist and plead for commitment to smaller gains than the complete reconstruction of the social fabric—such as, for instance, the fight for civil rights, the effort to improve the human situation for some of his fellow-men through Peace Corps activity, or he may advocate joining one of the many peace movements to prevent a third world war. There are innumerable ways today in which the individual can express his ethical good-will and his social altruism. He must, however, in some concrete fashion, give form to his discontent with the fabric of society, and the particular, social activities through which he hopes to express this discontent are implicitly his answers to the question of what man's relationship to society should be.

The only avenue from which social philosophy is excluded is the advocacy of a do-nothing attitude. The only social values it must eschew are those which give rise to the social fabric it detests. The only attitudes it must abhor are those which encourage conformity to, and acceptance of, existing social pathology. The major sins which it must extricate root and branch is any tendency to justify existing evil by forms of social hypocrisy, and any tendency to rationalize moral cowardice in the face of evil by hiding behind the excuse that the individual is powerless. Fundamentally there are only three attitudes which can be expressed in man's relationship to the achieved forms of community, that is, to society. Either you love them, you lash them, or you live with them. "You pays yer money an you takes yer choice."

The task of a committed social philosophy with respect, then, to the improvement of man's relationship to society is to remind us that no man is an island unto himself. In fulfilling that task a committed social philosophy must suggest ways of living with the social Caliban, while trying to pacify and tame him. Those recommendations which insist that social marginality is the only expression of intellectual and spiritual honesty are social philosophies of repudiation, and these are almost invariably underwritten by some form of millennial dream. These are the philosophies which are disreputable—with which Philistines have no patience precisely because Philistines lack extended feeling and social vision. In order, however, to improve man's relationship to society, one has to recognize that the many social hells which are becoming more of a reality with the passage of time cannot be dissipated by "gracious living." Their threat can be liquidated only by a social philosophy which recognizes the truth of the famous hit-song in the musical *South Pacific*—that song which bore the title, "You Gotta Have a Dream."

## Man's Relationship to Work and Leisure

It is not given to the healthy human to be inactive. Man is a focus of energy which cannot be bottled up without risking psychological disorder or social trouble. That energy is either spent on toil, directed towards play and recreation, or spent in leisure which will, hopefully, be used fruitfully and creatively. Thus man has to relate himself both to a system of production which returns him his physical needs and to a period of free time which must be deployed in some fashion which will be optimal for his creative energies. When man is in an organic relationship both to his labour, when it is self-directing, and to the products of that labour, he generally derives a quiet satisfaction from his work. When man is forced into an undignified and taxing form of labour by circumstances which might have been otherwise, and when his labour contributes to the creation of only part of a product whose consumer is not in an I–Thou relationship with its producer, then work is an affliction. When a man's labour seems repetitive and meaningless, instead of creative, and when the product of that labour meets no real human need as contrasted with human fancy—then work only succeeds in crushing the human spirit. When conditions such as these truly describe human work, we speak of such work as alienated.

There is a vast literature today which is deeply concerned with the degree to which alienation from work is on the increase. Arendt,[34] Fromm,[35] Friedmann,[36] Ellul,[37] Juenger,[38] Mumford,[39] Wiener,[40] and many others too numerous to mention, have been concerned with the devastating effects upon the human psyche of alienation from work and the robotizing effects on human potentialities which the misuse and abuse of science and technology have created in modern civilization. All of these writers feel that if work is to continue to play a role in the life of mankind such alienation must be eliminated. All of them feel strongly that social philosophy must be enriched by an understanding of the role

[34] Hannah Arendt. *The Human Condition. A Study of the Central Dilemmas Facing Modern Man.* New York: Doubleday, 1959. 385 pp.

[35] Erich Fromm. *Op. cit.,* see footnote 3.

[36] Georges Friedmann. *The Anatomy of Work. Labor, Leisure and the Implications of Automation.* New York: The Free Press of Glencoe, Inc., 1961. 203 pp.

[37] Jacques Ellul. *The Technological Society.* New York: Alfred A. Knopf, 1964. 449 pp.

[38] Friedrich G. Juenger. *The Failure of Technology.* Chicago: Henry Regnery, 1956. 189 pp.

[39] Lewis Mumford. *Op. cit.,* see footnote 19.

[40] Norbert Wiener. *The Human Use of Human Beings. Cybernetics and Society.* New York: Doubleday, 1956. 199 pp.

which science and technology plays in determining the nature of human work. All of them are committed to the conviction that social philosophy must now be rooted in an understanding of the place of science and technology in modern civilization. They reject that type of social philosophy which is an *apologetics* for a series of abstract regulative principles to guide the conduct of men, once men have foolishly accepted uncritically modern industrialism and the social damage it has wrought. All of these social critics insist that a social philosophy is not worthy of the name which fails to give central consideration to the place of work in human life, and fails to design and promote a social order which shall guarantee that work—so long as it shall prove necessary for man—bear a psychologically satisfying quality and provide meaningful, social experience. Under such a dispensation man's relationship to work would not be the horror and the absurdity it tends to be for most human labour as we know that labour today.

In short, a mature social philosophy demands that the archetypal relationship of man to work and leisure be changed drastically and freed from the degradation and direction forced upon it. This degradation and direction are largely the consequences of a modern industrialization, urbanization and bureaucratization preoccupied only with the expansion of markets and profits, the promotion of human greed and avarice, the infantile arousal of desires which serve almost exclusively status needs and the waste of natural resources. All this is social *disorder* rather than social order.

Any social philosophy which has come of age does not fail to notice that one of the positive benefits of modern industrialism has been an increase in leisure time. It also does not fail to notice the betrayal which has occurred to the promise originally implicit in that increase. The sad and absurd uses to which men and women put their leisure are daily being catalogued by sociologists and humanists who are trying to account for the follies now being perpetrated in the name of leisure. The average man's uses of leisure are also being widely lampooned. Back in the mainstream of history, leisure was linked to the Greek ideal of *paideia*—self-development and the perfecting of social responsibility. Today this has become an impossible ideal under the onslaughts of mass society. Instead, leisure today is being frittered away in a spectrum of intellectual, spiritual and cultural waste, the many forms of which are being ably reported by Rosenberg and White,[41] Larrabee and Meyersohn,[42] Hoggart,[43] Loe-

[41] Bernard Rosenberg and David M. White (editors). *Mass Culture. The Popular Arts in America*. Glencoe, Illinois: The Free Press and The Falcon's Wing Press, 1957. 561 pp.

[42] Eric Larrabee and Rolf Meyersohn. *Mass Leisure*. Glencoe, Illinois: The Free Press, 1958. 429 pp.

[43] Richard Hoggart. *The Uses of Literacy. Changing Patterns in English Mass Culture*. Boston: Beacon Press, 1957. 319 pp.

wenthal,[44] and many others. A dialogue has now arisen among educators and social philosophers, concerned with what is worth borrowing from the past and what is worth preserving from industrial society. Among those engaging in this dialogue are Phenix,[45] Ayres,[46] Whyte,[47] Diesing,[48] Frank,[49] and many others. From this dialogue may yet arise an informed judgment concerning the most opportune uses of available leisure time and some idea as to how the Greek ideal of *paideia* may yet be restored in modern dress. Thus far the battles are being won by the worst forms of mass culture but—in the light of an event I should now like to deal with—the war itself, for a mature, fruitful and humane use of leisure may yet be won for all of mankind.

The event to which I refer is the increasing recognition by many competent thinkers in our time that we are moving towards a period— apparently not too far away—which can only be called an Age of Leisure. This period will be characterized by the fact that many people will not have to work at all, and that most people who will be working will be putting in token labour time. That in modern science and technology lies the possibility of such an age is presaged by Donald Michael [50] and expected by Friedmann.[51] It is being planned for by the conservative economist Robert Theobald,[52] and is seen as inevitable by many other serious students of the possible and future social effects of science and modern computer technology. The conviction that it is now *technically feasible* (not psychologically, of course) to move towards a workless world, is the thesis of the members of the new *Institute For Cybercultural Research* and of the individuals who have become known as the signers of the *Manifesto of the Ad Hoc Committee on The Triple Revolution.* The radical new technology which now makes this possible is "cybernation," a term coined by Michael, and which may be defined as production by automated machinery controlled by master computers, with few or no people in the production process. The *period* which a cybernated society

44 Leo Lowenthal. *Literature, Popular Culture, and Society.* Englewood Cliffs, New Jersey: Prentice-Hall, 1961. 169 pp.

45 Philip Phenix. *Realms of Meaning. A Philosophy of the Curriculum for General Education.* New York: McGraw-Hill, 1964. 391 pp.

46 C. E. Ayres. *Toward a Reasonable Society. The Values of Industrial Civilization.* Austin: The University of Texas Press, 1961. 301 pp.

47 Lancelot L. Whyte. *The Next Development in Man.* New York: Mentor Books, 1962. 254 pp.

48 Paul Diesing. *Reason in Society. Five Types of Decisions and Their Social Conditions.* Urbana: University of Illinois Press, 1962. 262 pp.

49 Waldo Frank. *The Rediscovery of Man. A Memoir and a Methodology of Modern Life.* New York: George Braziller, 1958. 491 pp.

50 Donald N. Michael. *Cybernation: The Silent Conquest.* Santa Barbara, California: Center For The Study Of Democratic Institutions, 1962. 48 pp.

51 Georges Friedmann. *Op. cit.*

52 Robert Theobald. *Op. cit.*

would usher in has been christened the *Age of Cyberculture.* The group of thinkers who have come to be known as cyberculturists are definitely optimistic about the huge amounts of free time which the computer technology of tomorrow must automatically and inevitably bring about.

The big problem in this connection, which is thrown down as a gauntlet for a reborn and refashioned social philosophy, is the following. In a rational and humane social order, based upon science and technology, and which a social philosophy must plead for and help to design, what shall be regarded as a satisfying, archetypal relationship between man and the potentialities for leisure which are foreseen for him? Two camps of social philosophers have arisen in connection with the answer to this question. In the first camp we find the optimists—all those we have already mentioned and many others besides—who believe that we can be led to a fruitful rather than a dysgenic use of leisure. The optimists believe that the spiritually and intellectually stultifying horrors of mass culture can be made to disappear eventually, so that the cultural absurdities created by industrialization, urbanization and bureaucratization will be seen historically in the future to have been only a transient, social nightmare.

Against this camp is ranged that of the pessimists who do not believe that science and technology can restore the Greek ideals of personal cultivation and social responsibility to a mass civilization. These are the people who feel that the nature of a high civilization, such as that described by Bell,[53] is made impossible by the continued existence of *The Puritan Ethic,* originally applied to work, but which carries over into mass-man's free time. The Puritan Ethic, they feel, aborts the millenial dream of optimists in the West. At the same time, unfortunately, the analogues of *The Puritan Ethic* also exist in the Communist world. They exist in the form of such concepts as *ideiinost*—the identification of personal and social goals and the love of toil for its own sake—and *grazhdanstvennost,* a sort of Soviet humanism whose function it is to arouse the enthusiasm of each citizen for all the goals of Soviet society, particularly its emphasis on work and the Herculean labours involved in building up the classless society. The pessimists feel that the average individual, faced with the prospect of extended leisure, tends to feel guilty at the suggestion that such leisure ought to be used for the cultivation of the mind and spirit as well as the enhancing of sensitivity towards aesthetic experience.

Our current types of organization men, the pessimists claim, react uneasily to the suggestion that leisure may be used to heighten the religious impulse, establish an appreciation for the thoughtways and activities of modern science, promote the cultivation of the social graces and, most particularly, resuscitate the lost art of fruitful and stimulating

[53] Clive Bell. *Civilization. An Essay.* West Drayton, Middlesex, England: Penguin Books, 1947. 157 pp.

conversation. Among the pessimists are some of the world's most distinguished scientists and scholars, men of the stamp of Gabor,[54] Ellul,[55] Riesman,[56] de Grazia,[57] Sir George Thompson,[58] and Sir Charles Galton Darwin.[59] In short and in summary the pessimists assert that the heritage of our work ethic from our Puritan forbears and its reinforcement in modern, industrialized mass society, will make it impossible for man to improve the quality of the archetypal relationship between man and the promise and prospects of his coming leisure. Our sense of guilt, which has been created by the *activist* credo of industrialism, unfits modern man for the Greek ideal of *paideia* and this unfitness will be dynastically transmitted to his descendants for some time to come.

This issue—whether the optimists or the pessimists are right—will not, of course, be settled by vain disputation and argument. Nor will it be settled by scholars who write on the subject. It will be settled in the limbo of time, by the degree to which we gain control over the end-uses to which science and technology are put in the immediate future and by the vision and the technical erudition that social philosophers will exhibit in designing communities and institutions which provide for a fruitful use of man's leisure. The termination of the dialogue between the optimists and the pessimists will, *in part,* be brought about by the degree to which inventive social philosophers can so influence the reconstruction of the educational curriculum and so employ the arts of persuasion, that we may hopefully look forward to a generation most of whose members will have proven fertile ground for the dreams of the optimists. In any event social philosophy cannot evade the task of indicating those patterns of social value and social process which can lead to the desired fruitful use of leisure. Only in this way can social philosophy meet responsibly the burden of improving the quality of the archetypal relationship of man to the conditions of both work and leisure.

## Man's Relationship to Nature

Men have lost their relatedness to Nature in *at least* three ways each of which is directly or indirectly a product of the use, abuse and misuse of

---

[54] Dennis Gabor. *Inventing the Future*. London: Secker & Warburg, 1963. 231 pp.

[55] Jacques Ellul. *Op. cit.*

[56] David Riesman. *Abundance For What? And Other Essays*. New York: Doubleday, 1964. 610 pp. This book deserves special attention with respect to the problem of leisure. Riesman is pessimistic about some groups and optimistic about others, when discussing the possibility of a fruitful use of leisure. He is thus essentially a middle-of-the-roader.

[57] Sebastian de Grazia. *Of Time, Work, and Leisure*. New York: The Twentieth Century Fund, 1962. 558 pp.

[58] Sir George Thompson. *The Foreseeable Future*. Cambridge: The Cambridge University Press, 1955. 166 pp.

[59] Sir Charles G. Darwin. *The Next Million Years*. Soho Square, London: Rupert Hart-Davis, 1952. 210 pp.

science and technology. The correction of these aberrations must now be a task of grave and major concern for a technologically sophisticated, social philosophy.

The first form of alienation from Nature, to which I have just referred, is Western man's loss of a sense of kinship with his environment and with his growing inability to enjoy his natural surroundings and be psychologically refreshed by communion with them. The promotion of what Fromm calls *biophilia*, that is, life-affirmation, and which Schweitzer has called "reverence for life," occurs most easily when men understand their dependence upon other forms of life, when they can enjoy the beauty and the characteristics of the flora and the fauna of the natural woodland and when they can react both aesthetically and empathically to Nature's sights and sounds and to her varied topography of mountain, field and stream. Renewal and recovery of perspective have been traditionally accomplished by human retreat in solitude into the natural landscape. That natural landscape's varied expressions serve to remind us of our kinship with other living forms and enable us occasionally to beat our way back to the rediscovery of the "natural man"—that figure of spontaneity and perceptiveness concerning life's true bounties, who has usually lost himself amidst the trammels of his social roles.

The first form of alienation is an inevitable accompaniment of urbanization and the pathology it spawns. The youngster who has known chiefly skyscrapers, tenements, automobiles, trains and factories, and who has never known the countryside directly, has been deprived of a birthright the loss of which is going to show up as some sort of an imbalance or insensitivity in his later adulthood. He will be the individual who can neither see nor enjoy the rolling hills and fields of grass visible from the highway, because he is engrossed in reading, instead, the Burma Shave sign. He is the highway engineer who looks at a beautiful tract of untouched woods and wonders when this blight will be removed so that he can improve the traffic arteries of his rapidly growing community. A love for and a feeling of protectiveness towards God's creatures—both wild and domestic—is not likely to be engendered in the bosom of a child whose only contact with living things has been the sick and mangy cur haunting some sidewalk refuse cans or a yowling tomcat on a backyard fence.

Men like Frank Lloyd Wright [60, 61] and architects and town planners like Ebenezer Howard,[62] have sought to redress this form of alienation by proposing to restore various balances between town and country. They

---

[60] Frank Lloyd Wright. *The Living City*. New York: Mentor Books, 1963. 255 pp.
[61] Frank Lloyd Wright. *The Future of Architecture*. New York: Mentor Books, 1953. 351 pp.
[62] Ebenezer Howard. *Garden Cities of Tomorrow*. New York: Transatlantic Publishers, 1946. 168 pp.

have grasped the potentialities of science and technology for doing this and have tried to develop embryo social philosophies in justification of the necessity to achieve a balance between Nature and man's communal artefacts. Their hands, their hearts and their minds have been turned against the alienation produced by modern urbanization and industrialization. Their social philosophies, however, have been no match for human insensitivity and greed. These are expressed in the form of haphazard real-estate development aimed at meeting the flight from the city, insane highway building aimed at urban traffic management, and chamber of commerce boosting aimed at interurban accommodation of weekend pleasant trips and summer accommodation of vacationers. The unsystematic social philosophies of men of vision, like Frank Lloyd Wright and Ebenezer Howard, are also no match for a spreading industrialization aimed at meeting the fantasies of a rising and excessive standard of living and the cry for necessities coming from the hearts of men and women in underdeveloped economies experiencing unchecked population explosions.

A social philosophy which makes no provision for reducing and eliminating this first form of alienation from Nature is one not rooted in twentieth century sociotechnological realities. The abstractions of our traditional social philosophies are, themselves, alienated. The cloud-cuckoo-land in which they have their being will meet modern social necessities about as well as a medicine man's incantations will meet the need for rain.

This neglect of the problem of striking a balance between town and country in human life brings us to our second form of alienation from Nature—the destruction of the countryside. This alienation is expressed in man's growing indifference to his own ecology and his failure to recognize his inescapable interdependence with Nature. Man's thoughtlessness, ruthlessness and lack of foresight are now showing up in the destruction of the countryside, the excessive rate of exploitation of natural resources, the pollution of field and stream by chemicals and industrial wastes, the wanton hunting and unnecessary killing of millions of living creatures in "open seasons" and the failure to preserve those birds and other creatures who are his natural symbiotic partners in agricultural productivity. The horrors and consequences of this callousness have been catalogued by Rachel Carson [63] and have brought this form of alienation from Nature to the attention of millions of Americans. Miss Carson was one of a long list of protestants over the last four or five decades who have been calling our sins in this respect to national attention, but she has been the most effective one so far. This same tragedy—the threat of turning a once beautiful nation into an "ugly" America—has been occupying the minds and hearts of a long procession of conservationists.

[63] Rachel Carson. *Silent Spring.* Boston: Houghton Mifflin, 1962. 368 pp.

Among some of the more emphatic critics of our dangerous destruction of natural resources have been Osborn,[64] Lyons [65] and, quite recently, our own Secretary of the Interior, Udall.[66] Destruction of America's natural beauty by real-estate developers and investors seeking the "fast buck" has also been succinctly and feelingly brought to the attention of Americans by Cubbedge.[67] Here again one notes the need for a social philosophy, preoccupied with the quest for community, which will take stock of the systematic abuses of science and technology and which will propose designs for living which will end such abuses and the alienation they produce.

The third and last form of man's alienation from Nature is only just beginning to be emphasized for public scrutiny. It is a form of alienation which was recognized earlier but, unfortunately, in a most diffuse fashion. This is that form of alienation which may properly be described as man's indifference to the social pathology and risk to life and health, created by industrial ventures undertaken without thought of their effects and of what the morrow will bring. Lewis Herber's [68] *Our Synthetic Environment* and K. William Kapp's [69] *The Social Costs of Private Enterprise* are two distinguished works which take note of this form of alienation from the natural environment. This form of alienation from Nature recognizes that man has begun to lose sight of the factors which make for a sound mind in a sound body. In short, man—facing some of the ill-understood consequences of a rampant industrialism which is lacking in social responsibility—is unaware of how much individual and racial health is dependent upon a pre-industrial "normal" environment. Among some of the factors working against that "normal" environment and man's maintenance of his own health are the following: certain dangerous chemicals in food production and food processing; the effects of radiation on human germ plasm; the effects of fallout, such as that of strontium 90, in the world's food supply, a matter which has been done full justice by Hoopes; [70] the dangerous effects of air and water pollution; the effects of industrial poisons on worker's health and the rise of illness due to stress,

---

[64] Fairfield Osborn. *The Limits of the Earth.* Boston: Little, Brown and Company, 1953. 238 pp.

[65] Barrow Lyons. *Tomorrow's Birthright: A Political and Economic Interpretation of Our Natural Resources.* New York: Funk & Wagnalls, 1955. 424 pp.

[66] Stewart Udall. *The Quiet Crisis.* With an introduction by John F. Kennedy. New York: Avon Books, 1963. 224 pp.

[67] Robert E. Cubbedge. *The Destroyers of America.* New York: Macfadden Books, 1964. 128 pp.

[68] Lewis Herber. *Our Synthetic Environment.* New York: Alfred A. Knopf, 1962. 285 pp.

[69] William K. Kapp. *The Social Costs of Private Enterprise.* Cambridge, Massachusetts: Harvard University Press, 1950. 287 pp.

[70] Roy Hoopes. *A Report on Fallout in Your Food.* New York: Signet Books, 1962. 128 pp.

a theme which has been the lifelong concern of Selye.[71] Dysgenic factors such as these, and many others we have failed to mention here, are making man a prisoner of a physically pathological environment which is blinding him to the conditions of "normal" individual and racial health.

Unless we develop a systematic and sophisticated social philosophy for an age of science and technology—a social philosophy which will help to usher out all of the evils we have described above, and one which is willing to act as midwife to a proper social application of man's scientific and technical ingenuity—all these types of alienation from Nature can be expected to increase by leaps and bounds. Traditionally and currently social philosophers have neglected so mundane a task. They prefer to dwell in a never-never land of elliptically formulated abstractions which rarely take stock of the realities and necessities of the human condition. An enlightened social philosophy in an age of science and technology must, however, make a fairly complete break with its past—at least in respect to taking stock of the impact of science and technology in producing the undesirable forms of alienation from Nature, which we have already described. Such a social philosophy must take partial responsibility for the design of communities which will avoid these forms of alienation from Nature. This will demand a restatement of the proper concerns and values of men and of the manner in which these concerns and values must be fulfilled by newer and less pathological forms of urbanization and industrialization.

## CONCLUSION

A social philosophy which intends to make new beginnings, must concern itself with the unquestionable relevance of planning for satisfying the archetypal relationships which we have discussed. Such a social philosophy will have to develop a body of concepts, theoretical frameworks and those ideological justifications within which an efficient technology of planning can be shown to be capable of thoroughly reinforcing *the democratic ethos*. The planning, however, which such a social philosophy must encourage will have to be far wider than economic planning. A social philosophy, rooted in the Greek ideals of *paideia* and deeply aware of the current promise of science and technology, must be prepared to justify the development of *social planning* rather than restrict itself solely to economic planning.

The appropriate social planning for a scientifically and technologically based social philosophy will be one which recognizes that all human effort moves towards the satisfactory expression of our six, fundamental, archetypal relationships. For this reason a social philosophy

71 Hans Selye. *The Stress of Life.* New York: McGraw-Hill, 1956. 324 pp.

which acts as a metapolitics for the widest sort of planning and guidance for the human community and the human condition must be prepared to state and examine those values and think through those justifications for social, institutional and cultural change which meet the needs of men. This will call for a metapolitics which can truly be said to promote the human fulfilment of the six basic and archetypal relationships. Such a descriptive metapolitics is philosophy's way of spelling out the nature and requirements of human existence. A social philosophy of this sort must, in addition, be prepared to *knit together into a consistent and complementary weave,* those designs which are proposed for the fulfilment of the six basic archetypes. In this way a technologically based social philosophy succeeds, at the same time, in developing the expanding meaning of the concept of coordination in social planning.

This, then, is the vision of a social philosophy for an age of technology. This, then, is the millennial dream. This is the *ultima ratio* which must move men who have learned to distinguish between means and ends in social life. When, and only when, social philosophy abandons the pale and academic abstractions of its own past and begins again, can it be said to be looking towards the future. When, and only when, social philosophy starts taking its cues from the social realities of modern civilization and the still unfulfilled needs of mankind, shall we be able to say that we are pursuing a social philosophy fit for an age of science and technology.

# Author Index*

* The letter, n, accompanying a name refers to an author for whom a book or paper has been cited in a footnote. Such names, therefore, provide an *unalphabetized* bibliography. All other names are either unaccompanied by footnotes or—where they do occur in footnotes—make no reference to published material.

# Subject Index